Reader in

Public

Opinion

and

Communication

Second Edition

READER IN

Public

and

Edited by
BERNARD BERELSON
and MORRIS JANOWITZ

Opinion Communication

Second Edition

THE FREE PRESS, New York City
Collier-Macmillan Limited, London

Contents

v

2

Formation of Public Opinion

3

Impact of Public Opinion on Public Policy

4

Theory of Communication

5

Communication Media: Structure and Control

6

Communication Content

Analysis of Media Content

Popular Culture

7

Communication Audiences

CONTENTS

11
Research Methods

Introduction

CONDITIONS of modern life call increasing attention to the importance of public opinion and communication. Growing secularization has meant that more and more areas of life are open to opinion rather than divine law, and to communication rather than revelation. Advanced industrialization has not only extended literacy, it has also provided the technical facilities for mass communication. Urbanization has not only brought large audiences together, it has also created the need for communication within and between audiences, and among many diverse social groups. The development of democratic processes has widened the publics whose opinions count, and has increased the social and political responsibilities of the communication media.

The importance of public opinion and communication is clear. It is especially clear since the hope is no longer prevalent that democratic institutions are automatically strengthened with the growth of the mass media, the development of literacy, and the extension of the popular franchise. Nor is there widespread belief that the dynamics of public opinion without concerted leadership are likely to guarantee a world community in which either the risks of self-destructive nuclear war or the disruptive effects of a delicate balance of terror are adequately controlled.

It is clear that study of the field has been increasing over the last four decades. The events of World War I and the subsequent concern over the pervasive effects of "propaganda" mark the initial acceleration of interest. Basic changes in public opinion during the depression, and the monopoly market in opinion and communication under totalitarian governments helped to stimulate research in the field. Commercial interest in audience research and in opinion polls contributed certain techniques which could be applied to other problems. Research in the field was accelerated during World War II by demands for studies on the effect of

1

communications upon military personnel, adjustment to army life and attitudes toward military leaders, enemy propaganda, and civilian morale. After the war this growing interest led to the establishment of university centers for the study of public opinion and communication by the methods of social science. These centers, together with the continuing activities of industry and government, and the efforts of individual scholars, came to represent large-scale research enterprises.

After World War II, the introduction of television provided a strong stimulus for research. The transformation of a modern society, with an ever-growing emphasis on formal and higher education had similar effects, as the potentialities and the limitations of new media were explored for educational objectives. In the broadest sense, under advanced industrialism and economic prosperity, the social consequences of "popular culture" became a subject of debate and systematic research.

But the affluent society produced new social problems and continued to be taunted by old ones, especially as the demands for social justice increased. As a result, topics such as racial integration, mental health, and poverty have come to be seen in the light of the dynamics of public opinion and mass communication. At the same time, presidential polling came to be part of the national culture. It was the emergence of a radical right, however, that will be seen in retrospect as a very important factor in influencing these research trends, because the new forms of extremism sharpened the focus of public opinion research on more political issues.

On the international scene, the cold war and the problems of international security posed new questions about the public opinion process and the role of the mass media. One of the results was a sharper effort to study elites and opinion leaders. In a similar fashion the rise of the so-called new nations called for a more comparative perspective. Even the study of totalitarian nations included opinion and communication topics, especially as the lessening of controls in the Soviet bloc presented one of the most striking events in modern history.

All of this activity has produced volumes of theoretical speculation and formulation, as well as other volumes of empirical research. The raw materials of public opinion and communication research are so extensive that only the most modern electronic-data retrieval schemes suffice as central storage bins. Throughout these materials runs the central problematic issue of the power and influence of the mass media. The older formulations that were presented after World War I emphasized the powerful impact of propaganda and of advertising. The first results of empirical research, particularly because they dealt with short term media consequences, was to challenge such a perspective and to debunk popular notions. It was understandable, as specific empirical findings accumulated, that there was an over emphasis on the noneffects of the mass media. This emphasis reached a high point in the early 1950's. As more comprehensive

2

research has been developed, particularly as more meaningful theoretical constructs were applied, an enlarged view emerged which sought to isolate the conditions under which the mass media have, and do not have, effects.

Similarly, a more balanced view about the direct and the indirect effect of the media is coming into perspective. Initially, the scientific approach was to point to the mass aspects of the mass media, to its ability to influence attitudes and behavior directly because it reached the large audiences under conditions of relative suggestibility. As empirical research evidence accumulated, the emphasis shifted to the role of primary groups and opinion leaders as mediators in the communications process. The result was also to downgrade the impact of the media and overlook the direct mass character of the media which has its effects mainly over the long run. Contemporary theory is developing a more subtle and differentiated approach in which both direct and indirect (via opinion leaders) effects are seen as possible, depending on the message and the context.

When the original edition of the *Reader in Public Opinion and Communication* was prepared in 1950, it was precisely because there were no volumes which adequately synthesized and collated the available concepts and propositions in the field. In the absence of such a volume, the editors attempted to prepare the next best thing—a collection of readings representative of the best work in the field. Since the publication of the original *Reader*, there have been attempts at synthesizing. Some of these are most noteworthy, and their results are included in this volume. However, it did appear that it would still be useful to update the original selections.

The scope of the volume is best defined by its table of contents. Throughout the volume we have attempted to respresent the distinctive contributions made by students of various schools of thought within the field. The major criterion of selection was the quality of the contribution. The contribution could be made as a theoretical or conceptual analysis (Cooley or Lasswell), as an addition to substantive knowledge (Nixon or Schein), or as an application of research methods to substantive problems (Wilensky or Hovland). Again, contributions were selected which dealt mainly with evaluative issues (Shils) or with methodological questions (Hyman or Osgood). Special consideration was given to comparative and cross national analysis, mainly because of the growing importance of these topics. Since it would be impossible to "cover" the field of public opinion and communications within the limits of this volume, no attempt was made to do so. We do hope, however, that despite the difficulty of selection, we have succeeded in representing the major streams of interests and modes of thought now active in the field.

This volume is designed primarily for the advanced students in the field and in the neighboring social sciences. We hope it will also be useful

3

to practitioners in the field, to teachers, and to research workers in public opinion and communications. The brief introductions to each section of the *Reader* are intended primarily to explain the bases of selection operating in particular instances. We have also included a selected bibliography of additional readings for each section of the outline.

Our grateful thanks go to the authors of the items for their permission to reprint. Formal acknowledgements and citations are presented in connection with each selection.

University of Chicago
January, 1965

1
Theory of Public Opinion

In the first edition of the *Reader in Public Opinion and Communication* it was stated, "There is no generally accepted theory of public opinion, nor even a generally recognized attempt at the formulation of such a theory, in the sense of a body of inter-related propositions of high generality and explanatory power. But there are a series of writings from various standpoints within the social sciences—political science, psychology, sociology—which provide not only clarifying definitions and classifications, but also invaluable portrayals of the functioning of public opinion in modern society." Fifteen years later it is still true that there is no generally accepted theory of public opinion, nor does it appear likely that one will emerge in the immediate future. However, in the intervening years significant progress has been made, especially in more explicit and systematic formulation of the central issues.

Contrary to popular notions and even to the ideas of some practitioners in the field, the study of public opinion did not spring full-panoplied from the brow of George Gallup in the 1930's. Political theorists had always

5

given consideration to the problems of public opinion, even though they did not always call it by that term. A series of writings by political theorists of the 19th and early 20th centuries began to give the field its modern definition (represented here by Thompson, Bryce, and Lowell). They were concerned with such themes as the relationship between the development of public opinion and population trends; the influence of industrialization, urbanization, and democratization upon the growth and character of public opinion; the moral implications of broadening the opinion base through education and suffrage; the relationship of public opinion to the procedures of democratic government; the role of opinion in theories of political power. In them, we find not only conceptualization and problem-statement, but also a growing emphasis upon the empirical analysis of opinion phenomena.

This trend, carried forward after World War I by American students of public opinion, led into the advances of the 1930's and 1940's which, often, served to shift attention from theoretical problems by overattention to methodological concerns. Indicative of one central theoretical approach is the selection from Lasswell which applies principles of dynamic psychology to the area of politics, in an analysis of broad symbols of identification. Another approach, based upon the social psychology of Mead, is represented by the selection from Blumer. Finally, the article by Daniel Katz illustrates contemporary attempts to formulate theoretical concerns about attitudes in such a fashion as to be relevant for guiding empirical research operations, thus typifying efforts to bring research and theory into a relationship of mutual enrichment instead of the antagonisms which previously characterized much of the literature of the field. The tendency to use theory in the statement of researchable problems and to build theory on the foundation of empirical results is now becoming characteristic of the best work in the field.

GEORGE CARSLAKE THOMPSON

The Evaluation of Public Opinion

IN CONSIDERING ITS PLACE in our Constitution we have been speaking of public opinion as if it were one and indivisible. But in fact when one course from among several possible courses has to be chosen in reference to a matter which concerns a number of people, it often happens that a controversy ensues. People may disagree about the facts; or, agreeing about the facts, they may differ in their calculations; or agreeing in the calculation that a certain course will attain one object at the sacrifice of another, they may differ in their estimation of the relative worth of these objects; and this last element of difference may spring from any one of an infinite series of sources, ranging from mere differences of personal sentiment or interest up to the most general and fundamental differences of thought and principle. Consultation may do much to bring about an agreement as to what is practicable in many instances, but in others the conflict of opinions will remain irreconcilable, and then the course finally adopted will be adopted without the consent and against the will of some of the persons concerned. This is true of any body of people associated together, but if they form a *State* then the power of determining upon the course to be adopted and of constraining the acquiescence even of those who dislike or disapprove it must reside somewhere, and it is this power which writers on jurisprudence call sovereignty.

It must be remembered that "public opinion," "the will of the nation," and phrases of that kind are really nothing but metaphors, for thought and will are attributes of a single mind, and "the public" or "the nation" are aggregates of many minds.

One of Mr. Galton's typical portraits, formed by super-imposing the portraits of a number of individuals, in which the individual peculiarities are eliminated and the features which are common to the type come out,

7

is in some respects an analogue of "public opinion." But this method assumes a general conformity of type among the individuals who are grouped together, and if we attempt too wide a generalization, or if we have to deal with diverse, still more with conflicting, types, the method breaks down. To get at any satisfactory result we must group burglars with burglars and philanthropists with philanthropists. Under circumstances such as those with which we have to deal, where the discrepancies are great and numerous, we cannot reduce public opinion to one type, but we can reduce it to a limited number of types.

With regard to the expression "the national will" the case is somewhat different. The national will must always be one, however fierce may be the internal dissensions. The psychological analogy seems to hold good, for will is the expression of the final impulse after all the motives have had play. The national will, then, is that which would be the will of the sovereign if sovereignty were vested in a single man. Apart from the occasional use of the phrase as applied to the people in distinction from, or in opposition to, their government, the phrase always has an implied reference to this hypothetical autocrat, with his mind made up and acting accordingly. And though he may vacillate, at any one moment he must will one thing. How he makes up his mind is the question to which an account of the constitution of any country is the answer, and how the imaginary being who stands for the will of England made up his mind in the particular case we are considering is the question which we must try to solve. We shall see him torn, as it were, by conflicting motives, and if we can gauge the strength of each legitimate motive, we may be able to judge by the course actually pursued whether there were any bye motives operating.

The opinion which is politically predominant, or in other words sovereign, is a matter which can be definitely ascertained by reference to the course which the State actually follows. But that is not what we mean when we speak of the "predominant" or "preponderating" opinion. By such phrases as these, we mean the same thing which men have in their minds when they talk of the true, or the real opinion of the country, and it is another question whether this is actually sovereign or not. If the constitution of a state insures that power shall be exercised according to the preponderating public opinion, we say shortly that in such a state public opinion is sovereign. We conceive of the persons who contribute to the predominating public opinion as forming a quasicorporate body, and we need not stop to consider the metaphysical problem, whether sovereignty is vested for the time being in these shifting and indeterminate individuals, or in the officials who are intrusted with the actual exercise of power.

The question now arises, "What criterion have we which will enable us, amid conflicting counsels, to say where the weight of opinion lies?" Public opinion being manifold, we want some calculus by which to distinguish that particular opinion which preponderates.

So far as public opinion is organized on some such form as Parliament, the preponderating opinion can of course be easily ascertained. But all organization or machinery is imperfect, and though Parliament professedly exists as the reflex of the country's opinion, and derives its authority from that fact, yet there are occasions when it is felt that the true opinion of the country is something distinct from that of Parliament. How then is this true opinion to be ascertained?

But it may be questioned whether the problem suggested is one which, in the nature of things, admits of a complete and satisfactory solution even in theory, irrespective of imperfections in the machinery through which, as a matter of practical politics, the attempt must be made to give effect to the best approximation attainable. May not some of the factors of the weight of public opinion be ultimately incommensurate? For instance, a small number of great philosophers and statesmen might be opposed to a large number of ignorant persons. In such a case could anything be said more than some such account of the matter as this?—"Here is so much opinion of such a kind on one side, and so much more opinion of such another kind on the other side." On the other hand if the numbers on each side were even approximately equal, there would be no difficulty in pronouncing that the opinion of the philosophers preponderated. Thus, although cases may occur where we must confess ourselves baffled, there are others—and these are practically the most numerous and important—where the difficulty does not appear to be insuperable.

We want to know then, what the considerations are which we should consciously or unconsciously apply, if, as unprejudiced observers, with the facts fully before us, we were pronouncing on the relative weight of competing opinions.

In the first place we should find that we need not bring into the competition every minute variety of opinion which could possibly be discovered. As has already been observed, opinion though manifold may be practically treated as grouped according to certain types. Therefore we need not go the full length of the maxim, "*Quot homines tot sententiæ.*" Again, as it is not every singular or obscure crotchet, neither is it every passing flash of like or dislike, which must be taken into the account; an opinion must have a certain *persistence* as well as a certain *volume*, to entitle it to rank as "public opinion" at all. Volume (or the number of persons among whom the opinion is *diffused*), and persistence in duration, are quantitative elements of opinion. These go some way to measuring its importance; but not the whole way, for there are qualitative elements which must be regarded too. We recognize that a few men who hold a definite opinion *earnestly* and on *rational grounds* will outweigh a greater number who merely entertain a slight preference which they cannot explain for something vague and general.

The words "on rational grounds" suggest a difficulty. It may be said the phrase is merely a veil for the meaning "on grounds with which the person who used it agrees." Are we entitled to pronounce that to be the most reasonable opinion which seems to us to be so? A man could only answer "yes" on the assumption that he was possessed of a perfectly normal mind. After all, it seems to be the same difficulty which presents itself when an ultimate objective standard is sought in any department of inquiry into human conduct, from ethics down to taste;—the difficulty which Aristotle sought to get over by the introduction of the "wise man." The desideratum seems to be to eliminate everything of the nature of "personal equation."

There are, as we said above, three main causes which may lead to a difference of opinion between men in politics; firstly, differences in the views of facts; secondly, differences in the estimation of the best means for attaining desired ends; and thirdly, differences in the appraisement of various ends. The phrase "on rational grounds" then means, with regard to differences about facts, an opinion which rests on some basis of evidence; as to the estimate of the best means for securing desired ends, it means a carefully reasoned view which has the support of appropriate analogies; and with regard to the appraisement of ends, the phrase indicates that the end on which political action is based is one which reasonable men recognize as affording an appropriate motive.

For the purpose of weighing individual opinions we should take into account the opportunities the individuals have had of informing themselves of the facts, and the manner in which they have drawn their conclusions. And so before the principle of majority or diffusion can be accepted in estimating the weight of public opinion, there are two scrutinies that must be applied to it. First, it must be considered whether the majority is determined by any question of class interest. Next, we must endeavor to distinguish between cases where the volume of an opinion consists in the unanimity of a number of uninstructed people, who all take their political creed on trust from a similar source; and cases where there is a real consensus of many minds of differing types who have reasoned their way to the same conclusion. Where we have a consensus which shows itself, when tried by either of these scrutinies, *independent,* it carries an authority of a far higher degree than that which is due to its mere numbers. We should expect to find the *best* public opinion in the verdict of such a consensus, when confirmed by the weight of numbers, and when held with such intensity and persistence as to preclude the notion that the reasons which led men to it were frivolous or transient.

Thus there are four principal characteristics which, it seems, should be taken into account in the evaluation of public opinion:—diffusion, persistence, intensity, and reasonableness. One very important element of reasonableness is *elaboration,* which term may be used to denote either on the one hand *definiteness with regard to practical action,* or on the other the degree to which the opinion in question results from a thought-out political theory; let us say *theoretical completeness*.

If we classify opinions according to their definiteness with regard to practical action we can distinguish these three ascending stages:

1st. A general preference.

2nd. A wish for a particular end or course of action.

3rd. A belief as to the best practical means for achieving those particular ends which are desired.

Or, to put the same thing in another light, when we enumerate the different factors of public opinion which appeared during the discussion on the Eastern question, we find that they group themselves as answers to the three following questions:

1. What is the kind of political action which I like generally to see England engaged in?

2. What are the considerations in connection with the Eastern question which strike me as important?

3. What do I think the English government had better do, looking at matters all round?

If we denote the answers to these questions respectively as biases, notions, and policies, we get three words, answering to the three ascending stages of definiteness, by which we can class such opinions as had volume and persistence enough to rank as public. In terms of this nomenclature, then, a policy is the most definite form which anything diffused enough to count as public opinion assumes. It is not merely an approval of a certain sort of conduct, or a desire for a particular end. It is all this, together with a conception of certain means as the best practicable for attaining that particular end which is regarded as most important, having regard to all the surrounding circumstances. Out-of-door public opinion can hardly strike out a policy for itself. It must have the assurance that the means are practicable from some one whose position implies that he has the opportunity of knowing the facts. A policy implies a notion, or in most cases a group of notions, which may be regarded as its factors, and also a belief that all the material circumstances have been taken into account. Policies, at least for the most part, are mutually exclusive.

It is otherwise when we descend a stage in the order of definiteness, and come to notions; for several ends can be desired at the same time, and in fact one man will probably hold several allied notions, nay, one man may consistently hold notions which are factors of different policies, and two men who have adopted different policies may entertain a notion in common—they may both recognize the end as desirable, but one may give it the first place, and the other think it should give way to something which he considers of greater importance. Thus, though a policy implies a notion, the converse is not the case; for a notion may have existed in a man's mind without leading him to adopt a policy at all; it may be be-

11

cause he has not advanced from the conception of ends to that of means, or perhaps, because he considers he has not all the factors of the problem before him, or again, because he may fail to decide which notion should weigh for most among several which commend themselves to him, but which point to different policies.

If we turn for a moment to the consideration of the specific factors of English public opinion about the Eastern question of 1876, and make a list of the "notions" which can be distinguished, arranged in such a way as to exhibit what may be called the continuity of public opinion, we shall be struck with the fact that the transition from any one notion to the next on the list is not violent. If a man holds one he will be very likely to hold the next too; and yet when we pass over several steps, a divergence becomes apparent, and presently perhaps we come to a notion which is the direct negation of that with which we began. Thus some of these notions are mutually exclusive, while others of them can exist simultaneously in the same mind, and many of them are so nearly allied that they most probably will be held together. Arranged in this way the notions fall naturally into groups which we may call "views," for they seem to answer to the views one or other of which actual men would entertain; actual men, that is to say, as distinguished from the ideal politician whom it is convenient to imagine for purposes of analysis, whose mind takes in one notion, and one notion only. The views seem to occupy an intermediate position between the policies and the notions.

We notice that subjectively the notions are of two kinds. In the first place there are those which positively lead men to approve policies and to adopt views, and in the second place there are apologetic notions which are called in argumentatively to reinforce and defend a foregone conclusion.

The conviction of the importance of a particular end, or the desire for a particular course of action, while they are confined to small knots or individual thinkers, lack that volume which entitles them to rank as public opinion at all. But such ideas industriously preached with favoring circumstances often gather volume (if losing something of their elaboration), till they fairly rank as notions or as policies in the sense we have given to these terms. They are the germs which falling on fruitful soil will grow to something which may move the world, or falling on stony ground may perish. Mr. Freeman long looked upon himself, as he said, as one preaching in the wilderness, but his anti-Turkish doctrine became a view of mighty power. Mr. Grant Duff's nostrum for solving the Eastern question by enthroning the Duke and Duchess of Edinburgh at Constantinople never became a policy.

JAMES BRYCE

The Nature of Public Opinion

IN NO COUNTRY is public opinion so powerful as in the United States: in no country can it be so well studied. Before I proceed to describe how it works upon the government of the nation and the States, it may be proper to consider briefly how it is formed, and what is the nature of the influence which it everywhere exercises upon government.

What do we mean by public opinion? The difficulties which occur in discussing its action mostly arise from confounding opinion itself with the organs whence people try to gather it, and from using the term to denote, sometimes everybody's views,—that is, the aggregate of all that is thought and said on a subject,—sometimes merely the views of the majority, the particular type of thought and speech which prevails over other types.

The simplest form in which public opinion presents itself is when a sentiment spontaneously rises in the mind and flows from the lips of the average man upon his seeing or hearing something done or said. Homer presents this with his usual vivid directness in the line which frequently recurs in the Iliad when the effect produced by a speech or event is to be conveyed: "And thus any one was saying as he looked at his neighbour." This phrase describes what may be called the rudimentary stage of opinion. It is the prevalent impression of the moment. It is what any man (not every man) says, *i.e.* it is the natural and the general thought or wish which an occurrence evokes. But before opinion begins to tell upon government, it has to go through several other stages. These stages are various in different ages and countries. Let us try to note what they are in England or America at the present time, and how each stage grows out of the other.

A business man reads in his newspaper at breakfast the events of the

Reprinted from *The American Commonwealth* Vol. II (1900) pp. 247–254 by permission of the publisher. (Copyright, 1900, by Macmillan.)

preceding day. He reads that Prince Bismarck has announced a policy of protection for German industry, or that Mr. Henry George has been nominated for the mayoralty of New York. These statements arouse in his mind sentiments of approval or disapproval, which may be strong or weak according to his previous predilection for or against protection or Mr. Henry George, and of course according to his personal interest in the matter. They rouse also an expectation of certain consequences likely to follow. Neither the sentiment nor the expectation is based on processes of conscious reasoning—our business man has not time to reason at breakfast—they are merely impressions formed on the spur of the moment. He turns to the leading article in the newspaper, and his sentiments and expectations are confirmed or weakened according as he finds that they are or are not shared by the newspaper writer. He goes down to his office in the train, talks there to two or three acquaintances, and perceives that they agree or do not agree with his own still faint impressions. In his counting-house he finds his partner and a bundle of other newspapers which he glances at; their words further affect him, and thus by the afternoon his mind is beginning to settle down into a definite view, which approves or condemns Prince Bismarck's declaration or the nomination of Mr. George. Meanwhile a similar process has been going on in the minds of others, and particularly of the journalists, whose business it is to discover what people are thinking. The evening paper has collected the opinions of the morning papers, and is rather more positive in its forecast of results. Next day the leading journals have articles still more definite and positive in approval or condemnation and in prediction of consequences to follow; and the opinion of ordinary minds, hitherto fluid and undetermined, has begun to crystallize into a solid mass. This is the second stage. Then debate and controversy begin. The men and the newspapers who approve Mr. George's nomination argue with those who do not; they find out who are friends and who opponents. The effect of controversy is to drive the partisans on either side from some of their arguments, which are shown to be weak; to confirm them in others, which they think strong; and to make them take up a definite position on one side. This is the third stage. The fourth is reached when action becomes necessary. When a citizen has to give a vote, he votes as a member of a party; his party prepossessions and party allegiance lay hold on him, and generally stifle any doubts or repulsions he may feel. Bringing men up to the polls is like passing a steam roller over stones newly laid on a road: the angularities are pressed down, and an appearance of smooth and even uniformity is given which did not exist before. When a man has voted, he is committed: he has thereafter an interest in backing the view which he has sought to make prevail. Moreover, opinion, which may have been manifold till the polling, is thereafter generally twofold only. There is a view which has triumphed and a view which has been vanquished.

14

In examining the process by which opinion is formed, we cannot fail to note how small a part of the view which the average man entertains when he goes to vote is really of his own making. His original impression was faint and perhaps shapeless: its present definiteness and strength are mainly due to what he has heard and read. He has been told what to think, and why to think it. Arguments have been supplied to him from without, and controversy has imbedded them in his mind. Although he supposes his view to be his own, he holds it rather because his acquaintances, his newspapers, his party leaders all hold it. His acquaintances do the like. Each man believes and repeats certain phrases, because he thinks that everybody else on his own side believes them, and of what each believes only a small part is his own original impression, the far larger part being the result of the commingling and mutual action and reaction of the impressions of a multitude of individuals, in which the element of pure personal conviction, based on individual thinking, is but small.

Every one is of course predisposed to see things in some one particular light by his previous education, habits of mind, accepted dogmas, religious or social affinities, notions of his own personal interest. No event, no speech or article, ever falls upon a perfectly virgin soil: the reader or listener is always more or less biassed already. When some important event happens, which calls for the formation of a view, these pre-existing habits, dogmas, affinities, help to determine the impression which each man experiences, and so far are factors in the view he forms. But they operate chiefly in determining the first impression, and they operate over many minds at once. They do not produce variety and independence: they are soon overlaid by the influences which each man derives from his fellows, from his leaders, from the press.

Orthodox democratic theory assumes that every citizen has, or ought to have, thought out for himself certain opinions, *i.e.* ought to have a definite view, defensible by arguments, of what the country needs, of what principles ought to be applied in governing it, of the men to whose hands the government ought to be entrusted. There are persons who talk, though certainly very few who act, as if they believed this theory, which may be compared to the theory of some ultra-Protestants that every good Christian has or ought to have, by the strength of his own reason, worked out for himself from the Bible a system of theology. But one need only try the experiment of talking to that representative of public opinion whom the Americans call "the man in the cars," to realize how uniform opinion is among all classes of people, how little there is in the ideas of each individual of that individuality which they would have if he had formed them for himself, how little solidity and substance there is in the political or social beliefs of nineteen persons out of every twenty. These beliefs, when examined, mostly resolve themselves into two or three prejudices and aversions, two or three prepossessions for a particular leader or party or

15

section of a party, two or three phases or catchwords suggesting or em-
bodying arguments which the man who repeats them has not analyzed. It
is not that these nineteen persons are incapable of appreciating good arguments, or are unwilling to receive them. On the contrary, and this is
especially true of the working classes, an audience is pleased when solid
arguments are addressed to it, and men read with most relish the articles
or leaflets, supposing them to be smartly written, which contain the most
carefully sifted facts and the most exact thought. But to the great mass of
mankind in all places, public questions come in the third or fourth rank
among the interests of life, and obtain less than a third or a fourth of the
leisure available for thinking. It is therefore rather sentiment than thought
that the mass can contribute, a sentiment grounded on a few broad considerations and simple trains of reasoning; and the soundness and elevation
of their sentiment will have more to do with their taking their stand on the
side of justice, honour, and peace, than any reasoning they can apply to
the sifting of the multifarious facts thrown before them, and to the drawing of the legitimate inferences therefrom.

It may be suggested that this analysis, if true of the uneducated, is not
true of the educated clesses. It is less true of that small class which in
Europe specially occupies itself with politics; which, whether it reasons
well or ill, does no doubt reason. But it is substantially no less applicable
to the commercial and professional classes than to the working classes;
for in the former, as well as in the latter, one finds few persons who take
the pains, or have the leisure, or indeed possess the knowledge, to enable
them to form an independent judgment. The chief difference between the
so-called upper, or wealthier, and the humbler strata of society is, that
the former are less influenced by sentiment and possibly more influenced
by notions, often erroneous, of their own interest. Having something to
lose, they imagine dangers to their property or their class ascendency.
Moving in a more artificial society, their sympathies are less readily excited, and they more frequently indulge the tendency to cynicism natural
to those who lead a life full of unreality and conventionalisms.

The apparent paradox that where the humbler classes have differed in
opinion from the higher, they have often been proved by the event to have
been right and their so-called betters wrong (a fact sufficiently illustrated
by the experience of many European countries during the last half-
century[1]), may perhaps be explained by considering that the historical
and scientific data on which the solution of a difficult political problem
depends are really just as little known to the wealthy as to the poor.
Ordinary education, even the sort of education which is represented by a
university degree, does not fit a man to handle these questions, and it
sometimes fills him with a vain conceit of his own competence which
closes his mind to argument and to the accumulating evidence of facts.
Education ought, no doubt, to enlighten a man; but the educated classes,

speaking generally, are the property-holding classes, and the possession of property does more to make a man timid than education does to make him hopeful. He is apt to underrate the power as well as the worth of sentiment; he overvalues the restraints which existing institutions impose, he has a faint appreciation of the curative power of freedom, and of the tendency which brings things right when men have been left to their own devices, and have learnt from failure how to attain success. In the less-educated man a certain simplicity and openness of mind go some way to compensate for the lack of knowledge. He is more apt to be influenced by the authority of leaders; but as, at least in England and America, he is generally shrewd enough to discern between a great man and a demagogue, this is more a gain than a loss.

While suggesting these as explanations of the paradox, I admit that it remains a paradox. The paradox is not in the statement, however, but in the facts themselves. Nearly all great political and social causes have made their way first among the middle or humbler classes. The original impulse which has set the cause in motion, the inspiring ideas that have drawn men to it, have come from lofty and piercing minds, and minds generally belonging to the cultivated class. But the principles and precepts these minds have delivered have waxed strong because the common people received them gladly, while the wealthy and educated classes have frowned on or persecuted them. The most striking instance of all is to be found in the early history of Christianity.

The analysis, however, which I have sought to give of opinion applies only to the nineteen men out of twenty, and not to the twentieth. It applies to what may be called passive opinion—the opinion of those who have no special interest in politics, or concern with them beyond that of voting, of those who receive or propagate, but do not originate, views on public matters. Or, to put the same thing in different words, we have been considering how public opinion grows and spreads, as it were, spontaneously and naturally. But opinion does not merely grow; it is also made. There is not merely the passive class of persons; there is the active class, who occupy themselves primarily with public affairs, who aspire to create and lead opinion. The processes which these guides follow are too well known to need description. There are, however, one or two points which must be noted, in order to appreciate the reflex action of the passive upon the active class.

The man who tries to lead public opinion, be he statesman, journalist, or lecturer, finds in himself, when he has to form a judgment upon any current event, a larger measure of individual prepossession, and of what may be called political theory and doctrine, than belongs to the average citizen. His view is therefore likely to have more individuality, as well as more intellectual value. On the other hand, he has also a stronger motive than the average citizen for keeping in agreement with his friends and his party, because if he stands aloof and advances a view of his own, he may lose his influence and his position. He has a past, and is prevented, by the fear of seeming inconsistent, from departing from what he has previously said. He has a future, and dreads to injure it by severing himself ever so little from his party. He is accordingly driven to make the same sort of compromise between his individual tendencies and the general tendency which the average citizen makes. But he makes it more consciously, realizing far more distinctly the difference between what he would think, say, and do, if left to himself, and what he says and does as a politician, who can be useful and prosperous only as a member of a body of persons acting together and professing to think alike.

Accordingly, though the largest part of the work of forming opinion is done by these men,—whom I do not call professional politicians, because in Europe many of them are not solely occupied with politics, while in America the name of professionals must be reserved for another class,— we must not forget the reaction constantly exercised upon them by the passive majority. Sometimes a leading statesman or journalist takes a line to which he finds that the mass of those who usually agree with him are not responsive. He perceives that they will not follow him, and that he must choose between isolation and a modification of his own views. A statesman may sometimes venture on the former course, and in very rare cases succeed in imposing his own will and judgment on his party. A journalist, however, is obliged to hark back if he has inadvertently taken up a position disagreeable to his *clientèle*, because the proprietors of the paper have their circulation to consider. To avoid so disagreeable a choice a statesman or a journalist is usually on the alert to sound the general opinion before he commits himself on a new issue. He tries to feel the pulse of the mass of average citizens; and as the mass, on the other hand, look to him for initiative, this is a delicate process. In European countries it is generally the view of the leaders which prevails, but it is modified by the reception which the mass give it; it becomes accentuated in the points which they appreciate; while those parts of it, or those ways of stating it, which have failed to find popular favour, fall back into the shade.

This mutual action and reaction of the makers or leaders of opinion upon the mass, and of the mass upon them, is the most curious part of the whole process by which opinion is produced. It is also that part in which there is the greatest difference between one free country and another. In some countries, the leaders count for, say, three-fourths of the product, and the mass for one-fourth only. In others these proportions are reversed. In some countries the mass of the voters are not only markedly inferior in education to the few who lead, but also diffident, more disposed to look up to their betters. In others the difference of intellectual level between those who busy themselves with politics and the average voter is far smaller. Perhaps the leader is not so well instructed a man as in the countries first

18

referred to; perhaps the average voter is better instructed and more self-confident. Where both of these phenomena coincide, so that the difference of level is inconsiderable, public opinion will evidently be a different thing from what it is in countries where, though the Constitution has become democratic, the habits of the nation are still aristocratic. This is the difference between America and the countries of Western Europe.

NOTES

1. It may be said that this has been so because the movements of the last half-century have been mostly movements in a democratic direction, which obtained the sympathy of the humbler classes because tending to break down the power and privilege which the upper classes previously enjoyed. This observation, however, does not meet all the cases, among which may be mentioned the attitude of the English working classes towards Italy from 1848 onwards, as well as their attitude in the American Civil War from 1861 to 1865, and in the Eastern Question from 1876 onwards, for in none of these instances had they any personal interest.

A. LAWRENCE LOWELL

Public Opinion

"VOX POPULI may be Vox Dei, but very little attention shows that there has never been any agreement as to what Vox means or as to what Populus means." In spite of endless discussions about democracy, this remark of Sir Henry Maine is still so far true that no other excuse is needed for studying the conceptions which lie at the very base of popular government. In doing so one must distinguish the form from the substance; for the world of politics is full of forms in which the spirit is dead—mere shams, but sometimes not recognized as such even by the chief actors, sometimes deceiving the outside multitude, sometimes no longer misleading anyone. Shams are, indeed, not without value. Political shams have done for English government what fictions have done for English law. They have promoted growth without revolutionary change. But while shams play an important part in political evolution, they are snares for the political philosopher who fails to see through them, who ascribes to the forms a meaning that they do not really possess. Popular government may in substance exist under the form of a monarchy, and an autocratic despotism can be set up without destroying the forms of democracy. If we look through the forms to observe the vital forces behind them; if we fix our attention, not on the procedure, the extent of the franchise, the machinery of elections, and such outward things, but on the essence of the matter, popular government, in one important aspect at least, may be said to consist of the control of political affairs by public opinion. In this book, therefore, an attempt is made to analyze public opinion in order to determine its nature, the conditions under which it can exist, the subjects to which it can apply, the methods by which it can be faithfully expressed, and the regulation under a popular government of affairs to which it is not directly applicable.

Reprinted from *Public Opinion and Popular Government* (1913), pp. 3–15, by permission of the publisher. (Copyright, 1913, by Longmans, Green and Co.)

Each of the two words that make up the expression "public opinion" is significant, and each of them may be examined by itself. To fulfil the requirement an opinion must be public, and it must be really an opinion. Let us begin with the first of these qualities.

If two highwaymen meet a belated traveller on a dark road and propose to relieve him of his watch and wallet, it would clearly be an abuse of terms to say that in the assemblage on that lonely spot there was a public opinon in favor of a redistribution of property. Nor would it make any difference, for this purpose, whether there were two highwaymen and one traveller, or one robber and two victims. The absurdity in such a case of speaking about the duty of the minority to submit to the verdict of public opinion is self-evident; and it is not due to the fact that the three men on the road form part of a larger community, or that they are subject to the jurisdiction of a common government. The expression would be quite as inappropriate if no organized state existed; on a savage island, for example, where two cannibals were greedy to devour one shipwrecked mariner. In short the three men in each of the cases supposed do not form a community that is capable of a public opinion on the question involved. May this not be equally true under an organized government, among people that are for certain purposes a community?

To take an illustration nearer home. At the time of the Reconstruction that followed the American Civil War the question whether public opinion in a southern state was, or was not, in favor of extending the suffrage to the negroes could not in any true sense be said to depend on which of the two races had a slight numerical majority. One opinion may have been public or general in regard to the whites, the other public or general in regard to the negroes, but neither opinion was public or general in regard to the whole population. Examples of this kind could be multiplied indefinitely. They can be found in Ireland, in Austria-Hungary, in Turkey, in India, in any country where the cleavage of race, religion, or politics is sharp and deep enough to cut the community into fragments too far apart for an accord on fundamental matters. When the Mohammedans spread the faith of Islam by the sword, could the question whether public opinion in a conquered country favored Christianity or Mohammedanism be said to depend on a small preponderance in numbers of the Christians or the followers of the Prophet; and were the minority under any obligation to surrender their creed? The government was entirely in the hands of the Mussulmans, but would it be rational to assert that if they numbered ninety-nine thousand against one hundred thousand Christians public opinion in the country was against them, whereas if they were to massacre two thousand of the Christians public opinion would then be on their side? Likewise in Bohemia at the present day, where the Germans and the Czechs are struggling for supremacy, would there not be an obvious fallacy in claiming that whichever race could show a

21

bare majority would have the support of public opinion in requiring its own language to be taught to all the children in the schools.

In all these instances an opinion cannot be public or general with respect to both elements in the state. For that purpose they are as distinct as if they belonged to different commonwealths. You may count heads, you may break heads, you may impose uniformity by force; but on the matters at stake the two elements do not form a community capable of an opinion that is in any rational sense public or general. As Mr. Bryce points out, a great deal of confusion arises from using the term sometimes to mean everybody's views, that is, the aggregate of all that is thought, and sometimes the views of the majority. If we are to employ the term in a sense that is significant for government, that imports any obligation moral or political on the part of the minority, surely enough has been said to show that the opinion of a mere majority does not by itself always suffice. Something more is clearly needed.

But if the opinion of a majority does not of itself constitute a public opinion, it is equally certain that unanimity is not required. To confine the term to cases where there is no dissent would deprive it of all value and would be equivalent to saying that it rarely, if ever, exists. Moreover, unanimous opinion is of no importance for our purpose, because it is perfectly sure to be effective in any form of government, however despotic, and it is, therefore, of no particular interest in the study of democracy. Legislation by unanimity was actually tried in the kingdom of Poland, where each member of the assembly had the right of *liberum veto* on any measure, and it prevented progress, fostered violence, and spelled failure. The Polish system has been lauded as the acme of liberty, but in fact it was directly opposed to the fundamental principle of modern popular government; that is, the conduct of public affairs in accord with a public opinion which is general, although not universal, and which implies under certain conditions a duty on the part of the minority to submit.

If then unanimity is not necessary to public opinion and a majority is not enough, where shall we seek the essential elements of its existence? A suggestion much in point may be found in the speculations of the most ingenious political philosopher of the eighteenth century. In his *Contrat Social* Rousseau attempts to prove that in becoming a member of a state the natural man may remain perfectly free and continue to obey only his own will. He tells us that in forming a state men desire to enforce the common will of all the members; and he takes as the basis of all political action this common will, which is nearly akin to our idea of public opinion. Now, in order to reconcile the absolute freedom of every citizen to obey only his own volition, with the passing of laws in every civilized state against opposition, he says that when the assembled people are consulted on any measure, their votes express, not their personal wishes upon the subject, but their opinions in regard to the common will, and thus the defeated minority have not had their desires thwarted, but have simply been mistaken in their views about the common will. All men, he insists, want to give effect to this common will, which becomes, therefore, the universal will of everyone and is always carried out.

Though stated in a somewhat fanciful way, the theory contains a highly important truth, which may be clothed in a more modern dress. A body of men are politically capable of a public opinion only so far as they are agreed upon the ends and aims of government and upon the principles by which those ends shall be attained. They must be united, also, about the means whereby the action of the government is to be determined, in a conviction, for example, that the views of a majority—or it may be some other portion of their numbers—ought to prevail; and a political community as a whole is capable of public opinion only when this is true of the great bulk of the citizens. Such an assumption was implied, though usually not expressed in all theories of the Social Compact; and, indeed, it is involved in all theories that base rightful government upon the consent of the governed, for the consent required is not a universal approval by all the people of every measure enacted, but a consensus in regard to the legitimate character of the ruling authority and its right to decide the questions that arise.

The power of the courts in America to hold statutes unconstitutional furnishes an illustration of this doctrine. It rests upon a distinction between those things that may be done by ordinary legislative procedure and those that may not; the theory being that in the case of the former the people have consented to abide by the decision of the majority as expressed by their representatives, whereas in the case of matters not placed by the constitution within the competence of the legislature, the people as a whole have given no such consent. With regard to these they have agreed to abide only by a decree uttered in more solemn forms, or by the determination of something greater than a mere majority. The court, therefore, in holding a statute unconstitutional, is in effect deciding that it is not within the range of acts to which the whole people have given their consent; so that while the opinion in favor of the act may be an opinion of the majority of the voters, it is not a public opinion of the community, because it is not one where the people as a whole are united in a conviction that the views of the majority, at least as expressed through the ordinary channels, ought to prevail.

We have seen that in some countries the population has contained, and for that matter still contains, distinct elements which are sharply at odds upon the vital political questions of the day. In such a case the discordant forces may be violent enough to preclude a general consent that the opinion of the majority ought to prevail; but this is not always true. If they are not, the assumption which lies at the foundation of popular government remains unimpaired. If they are, the forms of democracy may still be in operation, although their meaning is essentially altered. It may be worth while to dwell on this contrast a moment because it makes clear the difference between true public opinion and the opinion of a majority.

Leaving out of account those doctrines whereby political authority is traced to a direct supernatural origin, government among men is commonly based in theory either on consent or on force, and in fact each of these factors plays a larger or smaller part in every civilized country. So far as the preponderating opinion is one which the minority does not share, but which it feels ought, as the opinion of the majority, to be carried out, the government is conducted by a true public opinion or by consent. So far as the preponderating opinion is one the execution of which the minority would resist by force if it could do so successfully, the government is based upon force. At times it may be necessary to give effect to an opinion of the majority against the violent resistance, or through the reluctant submission, of the minority. A violent resistance may involve the suppression of an armed insurrection or civil war. But even when there is no resort to actual force it remains true that in any case where the minority does not concede the right of the majority to decide, submission is yielded only to obviously superior strength; and obedience is the result of compulsion, not of public opinion. The power to carry out its will under such conditions must to some extent be inherent in every government. Habitual criminals are held in check by force everywhere. But in many nations at the present day there are great masses of well-intentioned citizens who do not admit the right of the majority to rule. These persons and the political parties in which they group themselves are termed irreconcilable, and when we speak of public opinion in that country we cannot include them. So far as they are concerned there can be no general or public opinion.

Let us be perfectly clear upon this point. The presence of irreconcilables does not mean that the government is illegitimate, or that it is not justified in enforcing its will upon the reluctant minority. That will depend upon other considerations. The use of force may be unavoidable if any settled government is to be upheld, if civic order is to be maintained. But it does meant that the fundamental assumption of popular government, the control of political affairs by an opinion which is truly public, is set aside. Florence may, or may not, have been justified in disfranchising her noble families, but Freeman was certainly right in his opinion that by so doing she lost her right to be called a democracy,—that is, a government by all the people,—and it makes little difference for this purpose whether a part of the body politic is formally excluded from any share in public affairs or overawed by force into submission.

One more remark must be made before quitting the subject of the relation of public opinion to the opinion of the majority. The late Gabriel Tarde, with his habitual keen insight, insisted on the importance of the intensity of belief as a factor in the spread of opinions. There is a common impression that public opinion depends upon and is measured by the mere number of persons to be found on each side of a question; but this is far from accurate. If forty-nine per cent of a community feel very strongly on one side, and fifty-one per cent are lukewarmly on the other, the former opinion has the greater public force behind it and is certain to prevail ultimately if it does not at once. The ideas of people who possess the greatest knowledge of a subject are also of more weight than those of an equal number of ignorant persons. If, for example, all the physicians, backed by all other educated men, are confident that an impure water supply causes typhoid fever, while the rest of the people are mildly incredulous, it can hardly be said that public opinion is opposed to that notion. One man who holds his belief tenaciously counts for as much as several men who hold theirs weakly, because he is more aggressive, and thereby compels and overawes others into apparent agreement with him, or at least into silence and inaction. This is, perhaps, especially true of moral questions. It is not improbable that a large part of the accepted moral code is maintained by the earnestness of a minority, while more than half of the community is indifferent or unconvinced. In short, public opinion is not strictly the opinion of the numerical majority, and no form of its expression measures the mere majority, for individual views are always to some extent weighed as well as counted. Without attempting to consider how the weight attaching to intensity and intelligence can be accurately gauged, it is enough for our purpose to point out that when we speak of the opinion of a majority we mean, not the numerical, but the effective majority.

No doubt differences in the intensity of belief explain some sudden transformations in politics and in ethical standards, many people holding their views with so little conviction that they are ready to follow in the wake of any strong leader in thought or action. On the other hand they explain in part also cases where a law is enacted readily but enforced with difficulty; for the law may be carried through by a comparatively small body of very earnest men, who produce a disproportionate effect by the heat of their conviction; while the bulk of the people are apathetic and unwilling to support the effort required to overcome a steady passive resistance to the enforcement of the law.

The problem of intensity of belief is connected, moreover, with the fact that different ways of ascertaining the popular will may give different results, in accordance with the larger or smaller proportion of the indifferent who are gathered in to vote. But this is a matter that belongs properly to a later discussion of the methods of expressing public opinion. We are dealing here only with its essential nature.

To sum up what has been said in this chapter: public opinion to be worthy of the name, to be the proper motive force in a democracy, must be really public; and popular government is based upon the assumption of a public opinion of that kind. In order that it may be public a majority is not enough, and unanimity is not required, but the opinion must be such that while the minority may not share it, they feel bound, by conviction not by fear, to accept it; and if democracy is complete the submission of the minority must be given ungrudgingly. An essential difference between government by public opinion as thus defined and by the bare will of a selfish majority has been well expressed by President Hadley. After saying that laws imposed by a majority on a reluctant minority are commonly inoperative, he adds, "It cannot be too often repeated that those opinions which a man is prepared to maintain at another's cost, but not at his own, count for little in forming the general sentiment of a community, or in producing any effective public movement."

HAROLD D. LASSWELL

Nations and Classes:
The Symbols of Identification

WHEN Ernst Werner Techow, Erwin Kern, and Hermann Fischer assassinated Walther Rathenau in 1922, they invoked the name of the Fatherland, the monarchy, the spirit of Potsdam. When Friedrich Adler shot the Austrian Prime Minister in 1916, he said it was not because he desired publicity, or because he enjoyed the pleasure of murdering his fellow man, but because the working classes required it. When Pilsudski and Stalin robbed banks in the years before 1917, they said it was not because they needed money and adventure for themselves, but because the overthrow of czarism and the liberation of the oppressed working masses of the world demanded it. When the Paris commune was drowned in blood, it was because the interests of "patriotism" and of "civilization" required it. The millions who struggled from 1914 to 1918 in the thin zones which surrounded the Central Powers were fighting for "God," "country," "civilization," "humanity," "international law," "a war to end war," and a "lasting peace."

The role of these justifying symbols in politics is one of the principal topics of analytic inquiry. With which acts are particular symbols connected? How are the justifying symbols grouped geographically throughout the world? How are they related to one another and to the whole context of political change? The embittered paranoiac who slays the first passer-by whom he suspects of turning destructive rays upon him is of mediocre interest to the student of politics, though a paranoiac like Gorgulov who kills the President of France as the "enemy" of his people becomes relevant on account of the target of his act and the accompanying

Reprinted from *World Politics and Personal Insecurity: A Contribution to Political Psychiatry* (1935), pp. 29–51 by permission of the author. (Copyright, 1935.)

verbalizations. The person who views himself as representative of a larger unity has widened the configuration against which his act is to be construed. To be of greatest interest to us, the act of demolishing another must be enshrined in justifications. The muscle movements must occur in a context of verbal legitimacy. There must be evidence of the process of self-justification by referring to entities larger than the self, another contribution to the voluminous chapter of human history entitled "The Story of Man and His Justifications."

A satisfactory geography of politics would chart the symbols which men invoke to justify their pretensions, and disclose the nature of the acts with which each symbol is affiliated.[1] Our usual maps show the world of "states," but the world of politics is richer, including acts justified in the name of churches, races, nationalities, tribes, classes, and dynasties. From the study of psychological areas we can often surmise the nature of coming changes in the activity and organization areas. Particularistic expressions in the old Dual Monarchy presaged the approaching end of the state and no doubt the spread of class symbols in the contemporary world is the precursor of drastic changes of boundary lines.

If we look with fresh naïveté at the distribution of persons who use common identifying symbols, many anomalies appear. How does it happen that a man living by Lake Michigan identifies himself with a name that includes the population of New York, a thousand miles east, and of San Diego, several thousand miles west, and yet excludes the population of Winnipeg and Toronto? How does he come to associate himself with the "poor white trash" of the South, and not with the farmers of Alberta; or with the blacks of Georgia, and not with the whites of Quebec?

The relationship between geographical features and symbols seems fast and loose. Australians occupy a continent and the whites, at least, have a unifying term, but the Europeans, Asiatics, Africans, North and South Americans, who occupy continents, are split into parochial groups. Those who live in the Mississippi River Valley call themselves by one inclusive name, but those who are settled in the valley of the Danube use many names. Most of the inhabitants of the principal Japanese islands have a common term, but the North Irelanders are distinct from the South Irelanders.

Symbols do not unite all those who live on the great highlands or in the great lowlands of the earth. If the Italian peninsula is, in a fashion, unified, the Scandinavian peninsula is disunited. Geographical zones which are defined by deciduous or coniferous forests, or by characteristic temperature, rainfall, or barometric ranges, do not neatly coincide with areas of identification.

The relations are discrepant even between such highly organized areas as states and the zones of common national sentiment. The German organization area does not now include Alsace and Lorraine, Eupen and

28

Malmédy, Upper Silesia and the corridor, or Austria; Magyars are to be found in the organization area of Roumania, Yugoslavia, and Czechoslovakia; Bulgarians live in Macedonia, Thrace, and the Dobruja; Ukrainians are in Polish Galicia, Roumanian Bukovina, and Bessarabia; Arabs are in French Syria, British Palestine, and elsewhere; Greeks appear in Cyprus, the Dodecanese, and Constantinople. Self-assertive minorities are found within the empires of Great Britain, France, the Netherlands, Japan, Portugal, and the United States.

If we examine the relation between areas of sentiment and of organization, on the one hand, and areas of special activity on the other, instances of noncongruence multiply. The iron and steel manufacturing districts of South Chicago, northern Ohio, and Alabama, together with the Lake Superior ore deposits and various coal and limestone areas, are all included within the United States; but the industrial region of the Rhineland is split between two antagonistic states and nationalities.

The symbols referred to thus far have historically been connected with geographical locations. Another powerful body of symbols has fixed upon some nonspatial characteristic. Most portentous of these is the "proletariat," in whose name various working-class districts of the world are being mobilized to reject the authority of those who use the symbols of "nationalism" or "individualism," and to accept the authority of those who invoke the new verbalism. Even here curious discrepancies reveal themselves, since many of the active proletarians turn out to be lawyers, university graduates, publicists, sons of middle-class or upper-class families, and many of the inactive proletarians prove to be serfs or wage earners in the Southern black belt, in South African mines, or on Caribbean fruit plantations.

No doubt our hypothetically naïve observer would innocently ask why so much stress is put on "place" words or "economic" words as unifying symbols. The wonder grows if one remembers that the number of words which can be used to distinguish one person from another is unlimited. All the curly-haired people might be united in curly-haired consciousness versus all the straight-haired people; all the dry-skinned people might be united against the oily-skinned people; but words about propinquity and tradition and economic standing have thus far outcompeted physical words in the rivalry for human loyalty.

If one took seriously the task of guiding the sentimentalization of likenesses and differences, it would doubtless be essential to sift out very complex types and to christen them appropriately. The world might with some justification be united into those who are thin, leptosomic in physique, schizoid in temperament, and disposed to schizophrenia, and into those who are plumpish, pyknic in physique, manic-depressive in temperament, and disposed to manic depressive psychoses. Dr. Ernst Kretschmer, since he invented this modern synthesis, could be the George Washington of this division[2] and wars could be fought over whether the leptosomes are right in calling him leptosomic, or whether the pyknics are right in calling him pyknic. Dr. Carl Jung has done much to create an "introvert" and "extravert" consciousness in mankind, yet the introverts and extraverts are not yet demanding self-determination.[3]

Now this purely schematic consideration of potentialities in human relations may emancipate some of us personally from automatic loyalty to the particular symbolisms which we have incorporated into our personality. Such formalism, however, is far removed from the state of the circumambient world, where specific national and class differences are taken with so much seriousness. For better or worse we are embedded in historical configurations which are characterized by the existence of a large number of comprehensive symbols in the name of which people die or kill. In examining these phenomena, we may in some respects be guided by the results of intensive personality studies which have disclosed so much about the dynamics of the process of identification itself.

We know that the components of behavior which are prominent in the early history of the organism, but which are modified as unacceptable to the environment, persist within the adult structure. They display themselves in crassest form during the regressive manifestations of severe mental disease, when the later integrations break up and the earlier coordinations are freed. Such adults may be unable to control their elementary excretions, or to masticate food, or to utter more than primitive cries and sounds. Training does not abolish the earlier action formations of the biopsychic structure but stylizes them in various conventional ways. However, this stylization in the form of appropriate language, gesture, and dress never entirely succeeds; the elementary components secure partial expression as socially irrelevant physiological tensions, as peculiar mannerisms and stereotyped movements, as verbal slips, as forgetting, as embarrassment, as tones of elation or depression. We know that the personality in relation to another personality is reacting with an organism which has been modified in consequence of its whole history in human relations, and that these modifications are comparatively unstable. What we call being civilized consists in using the "appropriate" patterns for the gratification of the elementary and the complicated impulse structures which are activated in particular situations. Only the special student of personality can hope to discern much of the meaning of slight deviations from the conventional, and he can be reasonably sure of his interpretations only when he has an opportunity to examine the personality under specialized conditions.

To say that the organism reacts as an organism means specifically what it says: the organism performs complicated acts of integration whose elementary components are sucking and spitting, biting, swallowing, striking, scratching, tearing, shoving, touching and rubbing, injecting or rejecting genital organs, looking, presenting for inspection, holding, expelling from the mouth, from intestinal, urethral, and genital tracts, running away, covering and throwing the body. Behavior consists of inordinately complex ways of disposing of such activations. With developed personalities, activity components are stylized in relation to the immediate situations in such ways that the simple acts which are initiated in any situation create tensions which are disposed of smoothly and for the most part indirectly.

We may grasp the hand of the person next to us according to the accepted forms of the social situation, smiling genially; yet repressed hostilities may be expressed in moods of slight depression or constraint, in some speech blocking as one repeats the conventional verbal forms, or in such bodily symptoms as localized skin irritations. The significance of these various formations as compromises between impulses to attack the other person and impulses to inhibit overt hostility can only become manifest when the individual learns how to employ the free-fantasy technique of exposing his reactive structure.[4]

Now what is it that happens when one person becomes emotionally bound to the symbol of another, or to the symbol of the collectivity? An emotional attachment occurs when the symbol of the other is taken as one means of gratifying the affectionate (the libidinal) impulses which are not permitted to exhaust themselves in direct and primitive ways upon the object. Strictly speaking, the symbol of the aspect of the self which is taken by the self to be characterized by an "external" reference secures the libidinal charge.

The emotional relations which are directly relevant to our field of discourse arise in the perception of similarities between an object and ourselves (by partial identification[5]). The necessary prerequisite is the presence of aim-inhibited impulses which are available for redirection toward substitute symbols. We identify with others (a process which is not necessarily accompanied by acute self-awareness) by perceiving that they are from the same college, the same town, the same country; that they admire the same politicians, scientists, or teachers; that they exercise the same skills; that they resemble our past attachments, and so on through an incalculably vast list of possibilities.

The emotional relation to the other is not necessarily positive; we do not invariably remodel ourselves by taking over some feature of his personality pattern. We may react negatively by identifying him with some aspect of our own personality which we deplore as weak or disreputable. In this case we reject the proffered pattern and release profoundly destructive impulses.

Quite often persons are related to the same object (as viewed by a specified observer) without a common externalized symbol of the object, and without a common symbol of all those who are identified with the

31

object. I may be impressed by a stranger whom I see walking alone in the Bois de Boulogne, but my subjective symbol of the stranger may not be related to a name which I could use as an external symbol of the man, or to a symbol of the other people who, unknown to me, have also partially identified with him. This relationship of the man and the several people who have no externalized symbols of him or of one another is one which we shall call *multiple identification*. This condition is highly potential for the more complex identification relationships. The transition to *counteridentification* may be very quickly managed when the multiply identified discover one another and develop external symbols of one another and of the person to whom they occupy a common relation. We may learn that the lone stranger in the Bois de Boulogne is Dr. X, who has new theories of stopping disease through irradiation, and we may be disposed to accept and propagate his methods. The disciples of a political sage or the associates of an active agitator may be bound by the ties of counteridentification.[6]

Of great political relevance is *mutual identification*, whose distinguishing mark is the inclusion of persons within the field of reference of the symbol who are beyond the face-to-face experience of any one person. The term "American" includes persons who are dead and gone and those who are geographically remote, and thus beyond the primary experience of those identified with the word. Interlapping identifications among persons in relation to this symbol make such mutual identifications possible.

Some politically significant reference symbols have comparatively circumscribed fields of allusion, like "Gandhi," but others are extremely difficult to characterize. No very circumscribed aspect of the world can be chosen as the reference frame for the "United States"; historically it is by no means certain when sufficient identifications had arisen to constitute a relationship for which a separate name was relevant. "Americans" is a word that does not apply to all who fall within the organization area called the United States of America, for one excludes those who reside within the legal jurisdiction without becoming psychologically organized toward the unifying symbol.

The early subjective life of the infant appears without sharp references to the surrounding objects in the environment. There is no evidence that ego references are clearly separated from environmental references. This imprecise relationship between the ego and its surroundings is recaptured in the sense of cosmic participation so characteristic of states of deep psychic regression. Those who emerge from them can often recount that they felt at one with the sun, the moon, and the stars, that they seemed to occupy the heavens and the earth, being indistinguishable from them, and aware of no boundary between the "I" and the "cosmos." Such mental states can be temporarily achieved by means of drugs, brain concussions, and spiritual exercises.

The environment of the infant and child is teeming with words of ambiguous reference, which take on positive or negative significance long before there is enough contact with reality either to define their frames of reference, or to distinguish those whose frames of reference are wholly indeterminate. As an "adult" the individual continues to respond to these articulations in many childish and juvenile ways, very often imputing some special and even awesome significance to them. Such words are "law and order," "patriotism," "a gentleman and a soldier," "truth," "justice," "honor," "good," "bad," "loyalty," "duty," "Germans," "French," "Negroes," "national hero," "good citizens," "national interest," "king," "constitution"; but these words do not stand alone in primitive concentrations of irrelevant affect. The whole of our vocabulary, plus our non-verbal symbols, is caught in the mesh of early structuralizations of this kind, so that the inner meaning of our symbols is never revealed except through the technique of free fantasy.

Identification with any particular symbol by any person at any phase of his career line initiates a complex process of symbol elaboration. All the earlier loves tend to be reactivated in relation to the new symbol. The individual who late in life experiences "conversion" and becomes an "American" or a "Czech" or a "Lithuanian" or a "Communist" or a "Socialist" or a "Catholic" reads into this symbol the loves and hopes of his entire personality. His elaborations of the symbol will depend upon the forms of expression with which his personality has been equipped through aptitude and training. If he belongs to those who require large emotional responses from the environment, and if he has a facile technique for the oral or written production of language, he may fill the auditoriums of his vicinity with rhetoric and the printing presses with poetry and prose. When the Dreyfus affair in France awakened the Jewish self-consciousness of Theodor Herzl, he quickly expressed himself in lectures, plays, essays, and programs for the recovery of a national home. These symbol elaborations were also determined by the patterns formed for the glorification of a collective symbol of identification within the culture to which he had been exposed. Hence a "Jewish nation" at such a time and place seemed to Herzl to demand immediate statehood.

The displacement of the infantile, childish, and juvenile affects upon symbols of ambiguous reference has led to the creation of remarkable monuments to human vanity. Nations, classes, tribes, and churches have been treated as collective symbols in the name of which the individual may indulge his elementary urges for supreme power, for omniscience, for amorality, for security.[7]

The examination of such symbol structures became one of the interesting exercises of the eighteenth century intellectuals as the clashes among organization areas broadened into clashes among "nations." One of the studies of the day was an *Essay on National Pride*, by Dr. J. G. Zimmerman, physician to His Britannic Majesty at Hanover, and a minor literary light.[8] His book appeared two years after the beginning of the Seven Years War, and he commented shrewdly that "Newton will often be called an almanac maker, and Montesquieu a blockhead, while the French and English struggle with all their power for the mastery of the American trade." The principal part of his essay classifies illustrations of national and tribal symbolism, taken from the history and ethnology of the period. He comments upon "the Greenlander, who laps with his dog in the same platter" and holds himself superior to the Danish invader. "Ask the Carribee Indians who live at the mouth of the Orinoque, from what nation they derive their origin; they answer 'Why, we only are men.' " He repeats the Indian fable of the nation of hunchbacks who derided and scorned the straight backs. "The inhabitants of the Ladrones believe that their language is the only one in the world, and therefore that all the other nations on the earth are dumb." He notes that "the vanity of mankind has ever filled the immense vacuity beyond the authentic memorials of the origin of every nation with fabulous history, at pleasing removing their antiquity to the remotest ages, in order to proportionally increase its luster." He cites "the yet uncivilized inhabitants of Paraguay" who "give to the moon the endearing appellation of mother; and when their parent is eclipsed, they run out of their huts with the greatest activity, and making the most hideous lamentations, they shoot a vast number of arrows into the air in order to defend the moon from the dogs who attack her." Observing that men prefer the diet to which they are accustomed, the Doctor pungently adds, "The love of our country is little more, in many cases, than the love of an ass for his manger."

The prominence of physical features has prompted innumerable attempts to elaborate the superior claims of collective symbols by imputing special significance to bodily characteristics. It was formerly held that the "inferior races" had "ugly" features, such as slant eyes, large noses, flat noses, thick lips. The Japanese soon presented a special problem here, because they showed as much industrial and fighting ability as many Europeans; but they thought the large eyes and aquiline noses of the West were ugly. The growing recognition of the influence of suggestion on forms of aesthetic taste renders such comparisons of relative "beauty" rather ludicrous. Pigmentation of the skin has also been a focus of "superiority-inferiority" claims, but investigation has revealed that pigmentation scarcely correlates with any agreed index of "capacity."

At the First Universal Congress of Races inventories were made of the bodily details which had been chosen by various people to rationalize their superiority claims. These covered a wide gamut, including pigmentation of the hair, pigmentation of the iris, the pattern of the hair sectioned transversely, the nasal index, the cephalic index, the geometric variations in the form of the cranium or the face, the amount of hemoglobin in the blood, the rapidity of the pulse, "vital capacity," muscular strength, quantity of urine, weight, height, variation in the respiration of civilized and noncivilized women, shape of the female sex organs, shape of the breasts, distribution of fat on women's hips, protrusion of the lower jaw, convolution of the ears, depth and carrying power of the voice, resistance to disease, quantity of water in the tissues, and weight of the brain.[9] Much skepticism prevails among scientists on all efforts to relate somatic differences to general ideas about supremacy.[10]   1364016

Each symbol of identification is elaborated according to the patterns already existing in the culture for symbols of that class. There are thus preformed praise patterns of symbol and practice available for application to the new symbol. Since our Western European culture was so long dominated by the symbolism of Christianity, the rising national and proletarian movements, quite without premeditation, look over the Christian patterns. A classical instance of this is the famous procession at the first session of the Legislative Assembly in France in the autumn of 1791, when twelve elderly patriarchs went in search of the Book of the Constitution.

> They came back, having at their head the archivist Camus, who, holding up the Book with his two hands and resting it on his breast, carried with slow and measured tread the new Blessed Sacrament of the French. All the deputies arose and bared their heads. Camus, with meditative mien, kept his eyes lowered.[11]

Writters on many of our contemporary symbols of identification have recently become acutely aware of these connections. It is frequently noted how the principal symbol is endowed with godlike attributes, the collective mission is idealized, an elaborate ritualism is evolved about a banner, pledges of unswerving fidelity are taken ("I pledge allegiance to my flag . . ."), holidays (holy days) are observed, the veneration of statues, pictures, and shrines increases, a body of official doctrines is reverently reiterated and stoutly defended, learned commentators elaborate the subtleties of the official ideology, and devices of popularization are exploited to reach every stratum of the supporting community and to proselytle among the unconverted.[12]

The modern phenomenon of nationalism represents a complicated synthesis of religious, cultural, state, democratic, and allied patterns. Once partly integrated around a particular symbol each new configurtion diffused as a culture complex, eliciting fresh acts of identification from some, and provoking decisive acts of rejection from others. Affirmation aroused counteraffirmation, and the outcome of the dialectic was to insure the propagation of the general pattern, subject to profound differentiations in detail.

Since the possession of a distinctive language came to be regarded as one of the details essential to the status of the fully developed national symbol, language revivals became inseparable from the early history of most nationalistic movements. Restrictions of any kind upon the use of the vernacular in schools, universities, law courts, legislatures, forums, churches, or markets were bitterly resented. Intellectuals expanded the national vocabulary as well as the national literature. In Finland the vernacular was fashioned into a literary vehicle on a par with Swedish; in Bohemia the Czech language supplanted the foreign literary speech, which was German; in Albania the nationalists remodeled the crude vernacular into a literary medium. In Greece the artificial "pure" Greek was launched, but failed, the popular "demotike" winning out. Among the Vlachs in Macedonia a national movement got under way with the revival of the vernacular, Roumanian, which the Greeks failed to suppress. In Roumania the spread of nationalism went hand in hand with the expansion of the national tongue. In Hungary the vernacular was modified into a phonetic language that supplanted German as the polite medium. In Norway the Norse dialects were modified into Landsmaal, which has been recognized as co-official with Riksmaal or Dano-Norwegian. Similar processes occurred in Iceland, Ireland, Lithuania, Poland, Ukrainia, Armenia, Wales, Scotland, Flemish Belgium, French Canada, Palestine, and some other communities.[13]

The general objects of collective effort on behalf of the collective symbol are thus profoundly affected by the patterns conceived to be appropriate in the culture to symbols of this class. Identification with the collective symbol likewise involves identification with many, if not all, of these status symbols, and the discrepancy between the existing position of the collective symbol and the patterns deemed appropriate to the class defines the objectives of concerted effort.

The remodeling of the personality through identification varies from minor changes in vocabulary to profound redefinitions of career, in which individuals devote themselves to the performance of specialized functions in the collective enterprise. They may become devoted missionaries of the cause, exhorting in public and private, or they may carry on the detailed work of administering central office routine, collecting information, soliciting funds, distributing material. The professional revolutionary is one of the most prominent examples of full-time devotion to the expression of the claims of a collective symbol.

The adaptive processes which are initiated in identification modify the relation of the symbol to other symbols in the lives of the persons affected; these other symbols are both "public" and "private" and their interconnections may be infinitely complex. The symbol of the local merchants' association may be reenforced to strengthen the symbol of the nation; but this process of redefinition may involve the inclusion of certain commercial policy demands into the national symbol. This latter process, by means of which special and private demands are legitimized in terms of the more inclusive symbol, adds greatly to the acceptability of the latter. A central core of allusion is sustained and redefined in terms of "tactical" or "strategical" considerations. Personalities display prodigious skill in justifying private goals in terms of master symbols; insofar as this process is unconscious, it is rationalization; insofar as it is conscious, it is justification.

The relation between symbols of identification and of demand, which have just been indicated, may be amplified by noticing the relations between symbols of identification and of expectation. Identification with collective symbols usually modifies the outlook of the person on the future of the world. Expectations are generated about the benevolent implications of future history for cherished aspirations. The result is over-optimism about the future status of the master symbol. Over-optimism about the future may lead to direct action under very unfavorable circumstances. The tragic consequences of the March action in the year 1921 in Germany were partly ascribable to the unduly sanguine expectations of recent converts to the left proletarian cause. Recent converts to a master symbol are notoriously prone to overestimate the future. Conversion experiences come as solutions of acute conflicts between strong tendency systems within the personality, and the convert is not infrequently driven to impulsive acts of expiation for the hostilities which were so long directed against the newly introjected symbol. The redefinition of future expectations is in part due to the relatively exclusive preoccupation of the individual with the fate of the master symbol. The whole meaning of history is sharpened into some simplified struggle between Good and Evil, bourgeois and proletarian, oppressor and oppressed. The future derives its portentous quality from the fact that it alone can disclose the fate of the contending symbols.

Symbols of identification, demand, and expectation reciprocally influence one another, and interplay with changes in the division of labor. Optimism and devotion may affect the work rate and the birth rate, modifying the value hierarchy. The development of power machinery may cheapen production and lead to the expansion of the market. Demands which are serviceable in extending the market may be redefined in terms of the master symbols of nation or state. Such dynamic interrelations between "material" and "ideological" continue to redefine areas of activity, sentiment, and organization.

From the foregoing it is evident that the spread of any master identifying symbol depends upon the connections among details of great apparent diversity. The success of any symbol in competition with other symbols depends upon frequency of exposure in forms capable of eliciting favorable response, and upon presentation at times when the readjustive possibilities of the population are high. The level of general reactivity is itself modified by many changes in the material and symbolic configuration of specific persons, and any process of diffusion, once under way, reacts with each new aspect of the continually shifting context in which it operates. The study of the historical spread of symbols and practices has clarified many conditions which facilitate the process,[14] and the use of psychoanalysis has disclosed significant intrapsychic connections of which we were formerly unaware. In particular, psychoanalysis provides an infinitely enriched conception of all that is implied in those unconscious receptivities which, spontaneously aligned in the direction of dominating personalities, constitute the interlapping matrices through which symbols radiate with special rapidity and intensity throughout society.

All research confirms the importance of exposing the specific sequence through which symbol clusters pass. When did a national symbol of identification become associated with demands to oust foreigners from jobs in the army and the bureaucracy? When did sensitiveness to being ruled by executives of foreign origin develop? When did it cease to be good form to speak a foreign tongue? When did it become socially necessary to patronize native art? When did it become imperative to "buy Chinese" or "sell Chinese?" When did it become socially advisable to name children after political heroes? When did it become disloyal to accept favors in return for exercising an official duty?[15]

Recent social science has undertaken to follow and to explain the speedy diffusion of nationalism since the later years of the eighteenth century.[16] In the foreground appears the rapid application of modern technology to production, profoundly altering the life situation of many members of the community. Perceiving new possibilities of profit, self-selected enterprisers took the initiative in demanding many modifications in traditional ways of life, clashing with the symbols and practices favorable to the landed property group. Finding themselves in organization areas where decision-making was a restricted privilege, needing ways and means of rendering themselves effective at the centers of dominance, they responded positively to symbols of protest and plan which were circulated by specialized verbalizers. Gradually the ideology of the ruling élite was called into question in the name of mankind as a whole. Democratic language assisted in mobilizing the animosities of the "underprivileged" in mass action which finally altered the methods of élite recruitment and the language of justification. Where members of the bourgeoisie got control of the government, as in France, they transformed their earlier antistate orientation into a pro-state and pro-governmental ideology. Nationalism became henceforth a means of nullifying proletarian challenges from within, and of fostering the power of the state in the world balance. Where the bourgeoisie was particularly weak, and an older social formation needed military support from the masses to defend itself from invasion, the older élite exploited as much as possible of the place-, time-, and tradition-bound symbolism at hand. In Prussia the bourgeoisie never succeeded in capturing the language of nationalism from the monarchy and the feudality that rallied to repulse the French.

In the competition of merely local enterprises with one another, merely local differences are emphasized; hence effective nationalism could not appear until the expansion of the market made possible the concentrating of strong initiative in the hands of enterprisers who were situated at the principal metropoles.

The upper bourgeoisie at the chief marketing centers were receptive to the elaborated symbols of nationalism as they were developed by orators, journalists, poets, novelists, essayists, and systematists. The ideological incorporation of the lesser centers and the back country into the policy of the bourgeois state spread from the centers of dominance by means of the propagation of literacy and by the expansion of such secondary means of incessant stimulation as the press. The expansion of capitalist enterprise tended to promote the active widening of the marketing area for certain goods, like textiles, and, later, iron and steel products. The result was to facilitate the growth of a world-marketing area, which in turn set up many dialectical processes in the form of local opposition to foreign competition. These acute localistic reactions created groups which were favorably disposed toward new local nationalistic expressions. We notice the discovery of local identities throughout Europe, and beyond, as the nineteenth century wore on. The multiplication of state organization areas at the end of the World War is one of the residues of this process.

The emergence in an old organization area of a new élite which speaks in the name of the proletariat challenges the official symbolism of the ruling élites elsewhere. Unity of action would seem to be advantageous among these various élites in the face of the new threat, but intercapitalistic conflicts are still fostered by the importance of safeguarding foreign economic outlets and of uniting the community around nationalistic symbols; there is also a general tendency to doubt the immediate acuteness of the crisis.[17]

The calculation of pecuniary advantage is a highly "rational" process; yet the social patterns which permit this rational process to go on must be sustained by an irrational consensus. Hence the tension between the rational and the traditional is peculiarly high under capitalism, which requires consensus, yet fosters the rational analysis of every acquired symbol and practice. The rationalism of capitalism has rendered it peculiarly dependent for positive values, ethical imperatives, and unifying goal symbols upon its legacies from previous cultures. The vestiges of primitive folk culture (Gemeinschaft) have been drags upon the completely ruthless application of the principle of calculated pecuniary advantage in The Great Society.[18] The insecurities arising from the changes in the material environment have been augmented by the stresses arising from the decline in potency of the older religious symbols and practices. Nationalism and

39

proletarianism are secularized alternatives to the surviving religious patterns, answering to the need of personalities to restabilize themselves in a mobile world.

The emergence of the last world-revolutionary pattern has intensified appeals to parochialism in the postwar world.[19] The older middle-class formulations have revivified the national symbols at the expense of class or world symbols, and supplied blood, money, and applause to programs which have been designed to curb the "alien" and "radical" elements in the community. German Nationalism Socialism relies on the older middle classes. If proletarian strategists can devise ways and means of disintegrating the loyalties of the middle classes, proletarian struggles might in time of advancing economic distress eventuate successfully, short of the demoralization involved in prolonged or unsuccessful war.

NOTES

1. Concerning the theory of the symbol in the logical, psychological, and socio-political sense, see E. Cassirer, *Philosophie der symbolischen Formen*, 2 vols., Berlin, 1923–1925; C. I. Lewis, *The Mind and World Order*, New York, 1929; A. N. Whitehead, *Symbolism, Its Meaning and Effect*, Cambridge, Mass., 1928; Charles W. Morris, *Six Theories of Mind*, Chicago, 1932; C. K. Ogden and I. A. Richards, *The Meaning of Meaning*, New York, 1925; the forthcoming posthumous publications of George Herbert Mead; Charles E. Merriam, *The Making of Citizens*, Chicago, 1931; Isidor Ginsburg, "National Symbolism," Chap. 17 in Paul Kosok, *Modern Germany*, Chicago, 1933; John F. Markey, *The Symbolic Process and Its Integration in Children*, New York, 1928.

2. See *Physique and Character*, New York, 1925.

3. *Psychological Types*, New York, 1924. For the growth of the identification symbolism, reference might be made to Dow Thompson, *A Mind That Was Different*, Harlow Publishing Co., Oklahoma City, 1931.

4. See my *Psychopathology and Politics*, Chaps. 2 and 3, Chicago, 1930.

5. The identification dynamisms are summarized in S. Freud, *Group Psychology and the Analysis of the Ego*, Chap. 7, London, 1922.

6. *Identification* is to be distinguished from *affiliation*, in which the conscious components are preponderant.

7. The developmental formula of the political personality has been stated as follows:

$$p\} \; d\} \; r = P$$

The symbol p represents private motives, d displacement on to public objects, r rationalization in terms of public interest; P signifies the political man. The d and the r are mainly derived from the contact of the personality with secondary group symbols. See my *Psychopathology and Politics*, pp. 261–263, Chicago, 1930.

8. First Edition, Zurich, 1758. English by Samuel H. Wilcocke, New York. Printed by M. L. and W. A. Davis for H. Caritat, Bookseller and Librarian,

1799. See my "Two Forgotten Studies in Political Psychology," *American Political Science Review*, 19 (1925):707–717.

9. Gustav Spiller edited the *Papers on Inter-racial Problems* of the *Universal Races Congress*, London, 1911.

10. See Jean Finot, *Le préjugé des races*, Paris, 1905; F. H. Hankins, *The Racial Basis of Civilization*, New York, 1926; Franz Boas, *Anthropology and Modern Life*, New York, 1928; Friedrich Hertz, *Race and Civilization*, New York, 1928. The principal result of the general intelligence-testing movement has been to expose subtle cultural differences. See T. R. Garth, *Race Psychology: A Study of Racial Mental Differences*, New York, 1931.

11. A. Mathiez, *Les origines des cultes révolutionnaires*, Paris, 1904, p. 27.

12. Religion and nationalism is extensively discussed in the works of Carlton J. H. Hayes, Hans Kohn, and Charles E. Merriam previously referred to. For religion and proletarianism, see Werner Sombart, and also Waldemar Gurian, *Bolshevism; Theory and Practice*, New York, 1932.

13. See Carl D. Buck, "Language and the Sentiment of Nationality," *American Political Science Review*, 10 (1916):44–69. G. S. H. Rossouw traced the rise of Afrikander in South Africa in *Nationalism and Language*, University of Chicago, 1922, Ph. D. dissertation, and reviewed the literature.

14. Cultural anthropologists have contributed to our knowledge of the dynamics of diffusion. See Edward Sapir, *Time Perspective in Aboriginal American Culture*, Memoir 90, pp. 30ff., Canada, Geological Survey, 1916; Edward Sapir, "Custom," *Encyclopedia of the Social Sciences*; Roland B. Dixon, *Building of Cultures*, pp. 59ff., New York, 1928; Leslie Spier, "The Sun Dance of the Plains Indians: Its Development and Diffusion," *Anthropological Papers of the American Museum of Natural History*, Vol. 16, Part 7, especially pp. 501 ff., New York, 1921; Paul Radin, "A Sketch of the Peyote Cult of the Winnebago: A Study in Borrowing," *Journal of Religious Psychology*, 7 (1914): 1–22.

15. See the studies in the history of patriotism by Roberto Michels and Carlton J. H. Hayes; the Civic Training Series edited by Charles E. Merriam; Charles A. Beard and G. H. E. Smith, *The Idea of National Interest; An Analytical Study in American Foreign Policy*, New York, 1934.

16. In addition to the literature previously cited, see Friedrich Hertz, "Wesen und Werden der Nation," *Nation und Nationalität*, Erg.- Bd., *Jahrbuch für Soziologie*, Karlsrühe, 1927; H. O. Ziegler, *Die Modern Nation, Ein Beitrag zur politischen Soziologie*, Tübingen, 1931; R. Johannet, *Le principe des nationalités*, Paris, 1923; *Verhandlungen des zweiten deutschen Soziologentages vom 20. bis 22. Oktober, 1912, in Berlin*, Tübingen, 1913; Otto Bauer, *Die Nationalitätenfrage und die Sozialdemokratie*, Vienna, 1924; Karl Renner, *Der Kampf der österreichischen Nationen um den Staat*, 2 vols., Vienna, 1902; Karl Renner, *Der nationale Streit um die Aemter und die Sozialdemokratie*, Vienna, 1908; Koppel S. Pinson, *Bibliographical Introduction to Nationalism* (announced); and various books of Harry Elmer Barnes.

17. Many of the economic aspects of nationalism are well handled in Waldemar Mitscherlich, *Nationalismus: Die Geschichte einer Idee*, Leipzig, 1929; R. G. Hawtrey, *Economic Aspects of Sovereignty*, London, 1930; Walter Sulzbach, *Nationales Gemeinschaftsgefühl und wirtschaftliches Interesse*, Leipzig, 1929; József Eötvös, *Der Einfluss der herrschenden Ideen des 19 Jahrhunderts auf den staat* (from Hungarian), Leipzig, 1854; and in the writings of Bukharin, Lenin, and other historical materialists.

41

18. The relations between *Gemeinschaft* and *Gesellschaft*, first extensively deveolped by Ferdinand Tönnies, are carefully restated in Hans Freyer, *Soziologie als Wirklichkeitswissenschaft*, pp. 230–252, Leipzig and Berlin, 1930.

19. See Helen Martin, *Nationalism and Children's Books* (University of Chicago Ph. D. dissertation, 1934), which applies a rigorous technique to the study of the factors affecting the diffusion of children's books throughout the world.

HERBERT BLUMER

The Mass, the Public, and Public Opinion

WE ARE SELECTING the term *mass* to denote an elementary and spontaneous collective grouping which, in many respects, is like the crowd but fundamentally different from it in other ways. *The mass is represented by people who participate in mass behavior*, such as those who are excited by some national event, those who share in a land boom, those who are interested in a murder trial which is reported in the press, or those who participate in some large migration.

DISTINGUISHABLE FEATURES OF THE MASS

So conceived, the mass has a number of distinguishable features. *First,* its membership may come from all walks of life, and from all distinguishable social strata; it may include people of different class position, of different vocation, of different cultural attainment, and of different wealth. One can recognize this in the case of the mass of people who follow a murder trial. *Secondly,* the mass is an anonymous group, or more exactly, is composed of anonymous individuals. *Third,* there exists little interaction or change of experience between the members of the mass. They are usually physically separated from one another, and, being anonymous, do not have the opportunity to mill as do the members of the crowd. *Fourth,* the mass is very loosely organized and is not able to act with the concertedness or unity that marks the crowd.

Reprinted from *New Outline of the Principles of Sociology* (1946), edited by Alfred McClung Lee, pp. 185–93, by permission of the author and the publisher. (Copyright, 1946, by Barnes and Noble.)

The Rôle of Individuals in the Mass

The fact that the mass consists of individuals belonging to a wide variety of local groups and cultures is important. For it signifies that the object of interest which gains the attention of those who form the mass is something which lies on the outside of the local cultures and groups; and therefore, that this object of interest is not defined or explained in terms of the understandings or rules of these local groups. The object of mass interest can be thought of as attracting the attention of people away from their local cultures and spheres of life and turning it toward a wider universe, toward areas which are not defined or covered by rules, regulations, or expectations. In this sense the mass can be viewed as constituted by detached and alienated individuals who face objects or areas of life which are interesting, but which are also puzzling and not easy to understand and order. Consequently, before such objects, the members of the mass are likely to be confused and uncertain in their actions. Further, in not being able to communicate with each other, except in limited and imperfect ways, the members of the mass are forced to act separately, as individuals.

Society and the Mass

From this brief characterization it can be seen that the mass is devoid of the features of a society or a community. It has no social organization, no body of custom and tradition, no established set of rules or rituals, no organized group of sentiments, no structure of status rôles, and no established leadership. It merely consists of an aggregation of individuals who are separate, detached, anonymous, and thus, homogeneous as far as mass behavior is concerned. It can be seen, further, that the behavior of the mass, just because it is not made by preëstablished rule or expectation, is spontaneous, indigenous, and elementary. In these respects, the mass is a great deal like the crowd.

In other repects, there is an important difference. It has already been noted that the mass does not mill or interact as the crowd does. Instead, the individuals are separated from one another and unknown to one another. This fact means that the individual in the mass, instead of being stripped of his self awareness is, on the other hand apt to be rather acutely self-conscious. Instead of acting in response to the suggestions and excited stimulation of those with whom he is in rapport, he acts in response to the object that has gained his attention and on the basis of the impulses that are aroused by it.

Nature of Mass Behavior

This raises the question as to how the mass behaves. The answer is in terms of each individual's seeking to answer his own needs. The form of mass behavior, paradoxically, is laid down by individual lines of activity and not by concerted action. These individual activities are primarily in the form of selections—such as the selection of a new dentifrice, a book, a play, a party platform, a new fashion, a philosophy, or a gospel—selections which are made in response to the vague impulses and feelings which are awakened by the object of mass interest. Mass behavior, even though a congeries of individual lines of action, may become of momentous significance. If these lines converge, the influence of the mass may be enormous, as is shown by the far-reaching effects on institutions ensuing from shifts in the selective interest of the mass. A political party may be disorganized or a commercial institution wrecked by such shifts in interest or taste.

When mass behavior becomes organized as into a movement, it ceases to be mass behavior, but becomes societal in nature. Its whole nature changes in acquiring a structure, a program, a defining culture, traditions, prescribed rules, an in-group attitude, and a we-consciousness. It is for this reason that we have appropriately limited it to the forms of behavior which have been described.

Increasing Importance of Mass Behavior

Under conditions of modern urban and industrial life, mass behavior has emerged in increasing magnitude and importance. This is due primarily to the operation of factors which have detached people from their local cultures and local group settings. Migration, changes of residence, newspapers, motion pictures, the radio, education—all have operated to detach individuals from customary moorings and thrust them into a new and wider world. In the face of this world, individuals have had to make adjustments on the basis of largely unaided selections. The convergence of their selections has made the mass a potent influence. At times, its behavior comes to approximate that of a crowd, especially under conditions of excitement. At such times it is likely to be influenced by excited appeals as these appear in the press or over the radio—appeals that play upon primitive impulses, antipathies, and traditional hatreds. This should not obscure the fact that the mass may behave without such crowd-like frenzy. It may be much more influenced by an artist or a writer who happens to sense the vague feelings of the mass and to give expression and articulation to them.

Instances of Mass Behavior

In order to make clearer the nature of the mass and of mass behavior, a brief consideration can be given to a few instances. Gold rushes and land rushes illustrate many of the features of mass behavior. The people who participate in them usually come from a wide variety of backgrounds; together they constitute a heterogeneous assemblage. Thus, those who engaged in the Klondike Rush or the Oklahoma Land Boom came from different localities and areas. In the rush, each individual (or at best, family) had his own goal or objective, so that between the participants there was a minimum of coöperation and very little feeling of allegiance or loyalty. Each was trying to get ahead of the other, and each had to take care of himself. Once the rush is under way, there is little discipline, and no organization to enforce order. Under such conditions it is easy to see how a rush turns into a stampede or a panic.

MASS ADVERTISING

Some further appreciation of the nature of mass behavior is yielded by a brief treatment of mass advertising. In such advertising, the appeal has to be addressed to the anonymous individual. The relation between the advertisement and the prospective purchaser is a direct one—there is no organization or leadership which can deliver, so to speak, the body of purchasers to the seller. Instead, each individual acts upon the basis of his own selection. The purchasers are a heterogeneous group coming from many communities and walks of life; as members of the mass, however, because of their anonymity, they are homogeneous or essentially alike.

PROLETARIAN MASSES

What are sometimes spoken of as the proletarian masses illustrate other features of the mass. They represent a large population with little organization or effective communication. Such people usually have been wrested loose from a stable group life. They are usually disturbed, even though it be only in the form of vague hopes or new tastes and interests. Consequently, there is a lot of groping in their behavior—an uncertain process of selection among objects and ideas that come to their attention.

NATURE OF THE PUBLIC

We shall consider the public as the remaining elementary collective grouping. The term *public* is used to refer to a group of people (*a*) who are confronted by an issue, (*b*) who are divided in their ideas as to how to meet the issue, and (*c*) who engage in discussion over the issue. As such, it is to be distinguished from a public in the sense of a national people, as when one speaks of the public of the United States, and also from a *following*, as in the instance of the "public" of a motion picture star. The presence of an issue, of discussion, and of a collective opinion is the mark of the public.

THE PUBLIC AS A GROUP

We refer to the public as an elementary and spontaneous collective grouping because it comes into existence not as a result of design, but as a natural response to a certain kind of situation. That the public does not exist as an established group and that its behavior is not prescribed by traditions or cultural patterns is indicated by the very fact that its existence centers on the presence of an issue. As issues vary, so do the corresponding publics. And the fact that an issue exists signifies the presence of a situation which cannot be met on the basis of a cultural rule but which must be met by a collective decision arrived at through a process of discussion. In this sense, the public is a grouping that is natural and not conventional, one that is spontaneous and not preëstablished.

CHARACTERISTIC FEATURES OF THE PUBLIC

This elementary and natural character of the public can be better appreciated by noticing that the public, like the crowd and the mass, is lacking in the characteristic features of a society. The existence of an issue means that the group has to act; yet there are no understandings, definitions, or rules prescribing what that action should be. If there were, there would be, of course, no issue. It is in this sense that we can speak of the public as having no culture—no traditions to dictate what its action shall be. Further, since a public comes into existence only with an issue it does not have the form or organization of a society. In it, people do not have fixed status rôles. Nor does the public have any we-feeling or consciousness of its identity. Instead, the public is a kind of amorphous group whose size and membership varies with the issue; instead of having its activity prescribed, it is engaged in an effort to arrive at an act, and therefore forced to *create* its action.

The peculiarity of the public is that it is marked by disagreement and hence by *discussion* as to what should be done. This fact has a number of implications. For one thing, it indicates that the interaction that occurs in the public is markedly different from that which takes place in the crowd. A crowd mills, develops rapport, and reaches a unanimity unmarred by disagreement. The public interacts on the basis of interpretation, enters into dispute, and consequently is characterized by conflict relations. Correspondingly, individuals in he public are likely to have their self-consciousness intensified and their critical powers heightened instead of losing self-awareness and critical ability as occurs in the crowd. In the public, arguments are advanced, are criticized, and are met by counter-arguments. The interaction, therefore, makes for opposition instead of the mutual support and unanimity that mark the crowd.

Another point of interest is that this discussion, which is based on difference, places some premium on facts and makes for rational consideration. While, as we shall see, the interaction may fall short by far of realizing these characteristics, the tendency is in their direction. The crowd means that rumor and spectacular suggestion predominate; but the presence of opposition and disagreement in the public mean that contentions are challenged and become subject to criticism. In the face of attack that threatens to undermine their character, such contentions have to be bolstered or revised in the face of criticisms that cannot be ignored. Since facts can maintain their validity, they come to be valued; and since the discussion is argumentative, rational considerations come to occupy a rôle of some importance.

Behavior Patterns of the Public

Now we can consider the question as to how a public acts. This question is interesting, particularly because the public does not act like a society, a crowd, or the mass. A society manages to act by following a prescribed rule or consensus; a crowd, by developing rapport; and the mass, by the convergence of individual selections. But the public faces, in a sense, the dilemma of how to become a unit when it is actually divided, of how to act concertedly when there is a disagreement as to what the action should be. The public acquires its particular type of unity and manages to act by arriving at a collective decision or by developing a collective opinion. It becomes necessary to consider now the nature of public opinion and the manner of its formation.

Public Opinion

Public opinion should be viewed as a collective product. As such, it is not a unanimous opinion with which everyone in the public agrees, nor is it necessarily the opinion of a majority. Being a collective opinion it may be (and usually is) different from the opinion of any of the groups in the public. It can be thought of, perhaps, as a composite opinion formed out of the several opinions that are held in the public; or better, as the central tendency set by the striving among these separate opinions and, consequently, as being shaped by the relative strength and play of opposition among them. In this process, the opinion of some minority group may exert a much greater influence in the shaping of the collective opinion than does the view of a majority group. Being a collective product, public opinion does represent the entire public as it is being mobilized to act on the issue, and as such, does enable concerted action which is not necessarily based on consensus, rapport, or chance alignment of individual choices. Public opinion is always moving toward a decision even though it never is unanimous.

The Universe of Discourse

The formation of public opinion occurs through the give and take of discussion. Argument and counter-argument become the means by which it is shaped. For this process of discussion to go on, it is essential for the public to have what has been called a "universe of discourse"—the possession of a common language or the ability to agree on the meaning of fundamental terms. Unless they can understand one another, discussion and argumentation are not only fruitless, but impossible. Public discussion today, particularly on certain national issues, is likely to be hampered by the absence of a universe of discourse. Further, if the groups or parties in the public adopt dogmatic and sectarian positions, public discussion comes to a standstill; for such sectarian attitudes are tantamount to a refusal to adopt the point of view of one another and to alter one's own position in the face of attack or criticism. The formation of public opinion implies that people share one another's experience and are willing to make compromises and concessions. It is only in this way that the public, divided as it is, can come to act as a unit.

INTEREST GROUPS

The public, ordinarily, is made up of interest groups and a more detached and disinterested spectator-like body. The issue which creates the public is usually set by contesting interest groups. These interest groups have an immediate private concern in the way the issue is met and, therefore, they endeavor to win to their position the support and allegiance of the outside disinterested groups. This puts the disinterested group, as Lippmann has pointed out, in the position of arbiter and judge. It is their alignment which determines, usually, which of the competing schemes is likely to enter most freely into the final action. This strategic and decisive place held by those not identified with the immediate interest groups means that public discussion is carried on primarily among them. The interest groups endeavor to shape and set the opinions of these relatively disinterested people.

Viewed in this way, one can understand the varying quality of public opinion, and also the use of means of influence such as propaganda, which subvert intelligent public discussion. A given public opinion is likely to be anywhere between a highly emotional and prejudiced point of view and a highly intelligent and thoughtful opinion. In other words, public discussion may be carried on different levels, with different degrees of thoroughness and limitation. The efforts made by interest groups to shape public opinion may be primarily attempts to arouse or set emotional attitudes and to provide misinformation. It is this feature which has led many students of public opinion to deny its rational character and to emphasize instead, its emotional and unreasoned nature. One must recognize, however, that the very process of controversial discussion forces a certain amount of rational consideration and that, consequently, the resulting collective opinion has a certain rational character. The fact that contentions have to be defended and justified and opposing contentions criticized and shown to be untenable, involves evaluation, weighing, and judgment. Perhaps it would be accurate to say that public opinion is rational, but need not be intelligent.

The Rôle of Public Discussion

It is clear that the quality of public opinion depends to a large extent on the effectiveness of public discussion. In turn, this effectiveness depends on the availability and flexibility of the agencies of public communication, such as the press, the radio, and public meetings. Basic to their effective use is the possibility of free discussion. If certain of the contending views are barred from gaining presentation to the disinterested public or suffer some discrimination as to the possibility of being argued before them, then, correspondingly, there is interference with effective public discussion.

As mentioned above, the concerns of interest groups readily lead them to efforts to manipulate public opinion. This is particularly true today, when public issues are many and the opportunities for thorough discussion are limited. This setting has been conducive to the employment, in increasing degree, of "propaganda"; today most students of public opinion find that their chief concern is the study of propaganda.

DANIEL KATZ

The Functional Approach
to the Study of Attitudes

THE STUDY of opinion formation and attitude change is basic to an understanding of the public opinion process even though it should not be equated with this process. The public opinion process is one phase of the influencing of collective decisions, and its investigation involves knowledge of channels of communication, of the power structures of a society, of the character of mass media, of the relation between elites, factions and masses, of the role of formal and informal leaders, of the institutionalized access to officials. But the raw material out of which public opinion develops is to be found in the attitudes of individuals, whether they be followers or leaders and whether these attitudes be at the general level of tendencies to conform to legitimate authority or majority opinion or at the specific level of favoring or opposing the particular aspects of the issue under consideration. The nature of the organization of attitudes within the personality and the processes which account for attitude change are thus critical areas for the understanding of the collective product known as public opinion.

Early Approaches to the Study
of Attitude and Opinion

There have been two main streams of thinking with respect to the determination of man's attitudes. The one tradition assumes an irrational model of man: specifically it holds that men have very limited powers of

Reprinted from *Public Opinion Quarterly*, Vol. XXIV (Summer 1960), pp. 163–176, by permission of the author and the publisher. (Copyright, 1960, by Princeton University Press.)

51

reason and reflection, weak capacity to discriminate, only the most primitive self-insight, and very short memories. Whatever mental capacities
people do possess are easily overwhelmed by emotional forces and appeals
to self-interest and vanity. The early books on the psychology of advertising, with their emphasis on the doctrine of suggestion, exemplify this
approach. One expression of this philosophy is in the propagandist's concern with tricks and traps to manipulate the public. A modern form of it
appears in *The Hidden Persuaders,* or the use of subliminal and marginal
suggestion, or the devices supposedly employed by "the Madison Avenue
boys." Experiments to support this line of thinking started with laboratory
demonstrations of the power of hypnotic suggestion and were soon extended to show that people would change their attitudes in an uncritical
manner under the influence of the prestige of authority and numbers. For
example, individuals would accept or reject the same idea depending upon
whether it came from a positive or a negative prestige source.[1]

The second approach is that of the ideologist who invokes a rational
model of man. It assumes that the human being has a cerebral cortex, that
he seeks understanding, that he consistently attempts to make sense of the
world about him, that he possesses discriminating and reasoning powers
which will assert themselves over time, and that he is capable of self-
criticism and self-insight. It relies heavily upon getting adequate information to people. Our educational system is based upon this rational model.
The present emphasis upon the improvement of communication, upon developing more adequate channels of two-way communication, of conferences and institutes, upon bringing people together to interchange ideas,
are all indications of the belief in the importance of intelligence and comprehension in the formation and change of men's opinions.

Now either school of thought can point to evidence which supports
its assumptions, and can make fairly damaging criticisms of its opponent.
Solomon Asch and his colleagues, in attacking the irrational model, have
called attention to the biased character of the old experiments on prestige
suggestion which gave the subject little opportunity to demonstrate critical thinking.[2] And further exploration of subjects in these stupid situations
does indicate that they try to make sense of a nonsensical matter as far as
possible. Though the same statement is presented by the experimenter to
two groups, the first time as coming from a positive source and the second
time as coming from a negative source, it is given a different meaning dependent upon the context in which it appears.[3] Thus the experimental
subject does his best to give some rational meaning to the problem. On the
other hand, a large body of experimental work indicates that there are
many limitations in the rational approach in that people see their world in
terms of their own needs, remember what they want to remember, and
interpret information on the basis of wishful thinking. H. H. Hyman and
P. Sheatsley have demonstrated that these experimental results have direct

relevance to information campaigns directed at influencing public opinion.[4] These authors assembled facts about such campaigns and showed conclusively that increasing the flow of information to people does not necessarily increase the knowledge absorbed or produce the attitude changes desired.

The major difficulty with these conflicting approaches is their lack of specification of the conditions under which men do act as the theory would predict. For the facts are that people do act at times as if they had been decorticated and at times with intelligence and comprehension. And people themselves do recognize that on occasion they have behaved blindly, impulsively, and thoughtlessly. A second major difficulty is that the rationality-irrationality dimension is not clearly defined. At the extremes it is easy to point to examples, as in the case of the acceptance of stupid suggestions under emotional stress on the one hand, or brilliant problem solving on the other; but this does not provide adequate guidance for the many cases in the middle of the scale where one attempts to discriminate between rationalization and reason.

Reconciliation of the Conflict in a Functional Approach

The conflict between the rationality and irrationality models was saved from becoming a worthless debate because of the experimentation and research suggested by these models. The findings of this research pointed toward the elements of truth in each approach and gave some indication of the conditions under which each model could make fairly accurate predictions. In general the irrational approach was at its best where the situation imposed heavy restrictions upon search behavior and response alternatives. Where individuals must give quick responses without adequate opportunities to explore the nature of the problem, where there are very few response alternatives available to them, where their own deep emotional needs are aroused, they will in general react much as does the unthinking subject under hypnosis. On the other hand, where the individual can have more adequate commerce with the relevant environmental setting, where he has time to obtain more feedback from his reality testing, and where he has a number of realistic choices, his behavior will reflect the use of his rational faculties.[5] The child will often respond to the directive of the parent not by implicit obedience but by testing out whether or not the parent really meant what he said.

Many of the papers in this issue, which describe research and theory concerning consistency and consonance, represent one outcome of the rationality model. The theory of psychological consonance, or cognitive balance, assumes that man attempts to reduce discrepancies in his beliefs, attitudes, and behavior by appropriate changes in these processes. While the emphasis here is upon consistency or logicality, the theory deals with all dissonances, no matter how produced. Thus they could result from irrational factors of distorted perception and wishful thinking as well as from rational factors of realistic appraisal of a problem and an accurate estimate of its consequences. Moreover, the theory would predict only that the individual will move to reduce dissonance, whether such movement is a good adjustment to the world or leads to the delusional systems of the paranoiac. In a sense, then, this theory would avoid the conflict between the old approaches of the rational and the irrational man by not dealing with the specific antecedent causes of behavior or with the particular ways in which the individual solves his problems.

In addition to the present preoccupation with the development of formal models concerned with cognitive balance and consonance, there is a growing interest in a more comprehensive framework for dealing with the complex variables and for bringing order within the field. The thoughtful system of Ulf Himmelstrand, presented in the following pages, is one such attempt. Another point of departure is represented by two groups of workers who have organized their theories around the functions which attitudes perform for the personality. Sarnoff, Katz, and McClintock, in taking this functional approach, have given primary attention to the motivational bases of attitudes and the processes of attitude change.[6] The basic assumption of this group is that both attitude formation and attitude change must be understood in terms of the needs they serve and that, as these motivational processes differ, so too will the conditions and techniques for attitude change. Smith, Bruner, and White have also analyzed the different functions which attitudes perform for the personality.[7] Both groups present essentially the same functions, but Smith, Bruner, and White give more attention to perceptual and cognitive processes and Sarnoff, Katz, and McClintock to the specific conditions of atttitude change.

The importance of the functional approach is threefold.

1. Many previous studies of attitude change have dealt with factors which are not genuine psychological variables, for example, the effect on group prejudice of contact between two groups, or the exposure of a group of subjects to a communication in the mass media. Now contact serves different psychological functions for the individual and merely knowing that people have seen a movie or watched a television program tells us nothing about the personal values engaged or not engaged by such a presentation. If, however, we can gear our research to the functions attitudes perform, we can develop some generalizations about human behavior. Dealing with nonfunctional variables makes such generalization difficult, if not impossible.

2. By concerning ourselves with the different functions attitudes can perform we can avoid the great error of oversimplification—the error of attributing a single cause to given types of attitude. It was once popular to ascribe radicalism in economic and political matters to the psychopathology of the insecure and to attribute conservatism to the rigidity of the mentally aged. At the present time it is common practice to see in attitudes of group prejudice the repressed hostilities stemming from childhood frustrations, though Hyman and Sheatsley have pointed out that prejudiced attitudes can serve a normative function of gaining acceptance in one's own group as readily as releasing unconscious hatred.[8] In short, not only are there a number of motivational forces to take into account in considering attitudes and behavior, but the same attitude can have a different motivational basis in different people.

3. Finally, recognition of the complex motivational sources of behavior can help to remedy the neglect in general theories which lack specification of conditions under which given types of attitude will change. Gestalt theory tells us, for example, that attitudes will change to give better cognitive organization to the psychological field. This theoretical generalization is suggestive, but to carry out significant research we need some middle-level concepts to bridge the gap between a high level of abstraction and particularistic or phenotypical events. We need concepts that will point toward the types of motive and methods of motive satisfaction which are operative in bringing about cognitive reorganization.

Before we attempt a detailed analysis of the four major functions which attitudes can serve, it is appropriate to consider the nature of attitudes, their dimensions, and their relations to other psychological structures and processes.

Nature of Attitudes: Their Dimensions

Attitude is the predisposition of the individual to evaluate some symbol or object or aspect of his world in a favorable or unfavorable manner. Opinion is the verbal expression of an attitude, but attitudes can also be expressed in nonverbal behavior. Attitudes include both the affective, or feeling core of liking or disliking, and the cognitive, or belief, elements which describe the object of the attitude, its characteristics, and its relations to other objects. All attitudes thus include beliefs, but not all beliefs are attitudes. When specific attitudes are organized into a hierarchical structure, they comprise *value systems*. Thus a person may not only hold specific attitudes against deficit spending and unbalanced budgets but may also have a systematic organization of such beliefs and attitudes in the form of a value system of economic conservatism.

The dimensions of attitudes can be stated more precisely if the above distinctions between beliefs and feelings and attitudes and value systems are kept in mind. The *intensity* of an attitude refers to the strength of the *affective* component. In fact, rating scales and even Thurstone scales deal primarily with the intensity of feeling of the individual for or against some social object. The cognitive, or belief, component suggests two additional dimensions, the *specificity* or *generality* of the attitude and the *degree of differentiation* of the beliefs. Differentiation refers to the number of beliefs or cognitive items contained in the attitude, and the general assumption is that the simpler the attitude in cognitive structure the easier it is to change.[9] For simple structures there is no defense in depth, and once a single item of belief has been changed the attitude will change. A rather different dimension of attitude is the *number and strength of its linkages to a related value system.* If an attitude favoring budget balancing by the Federal government is tied in strongly with a value system of economic conservatism, it will be more difficult to change than if it were a fairly isolated attitude of the person. Finally, the relation of the value system to the personality is a consideration of first importance. If an attitude is tied to a value system which is closely related to, or which consists of, the individual's conception of himself, then the appropriate change procedures become more complex. The *centrality* of an attitude refers to its role as part of a value system which is closely related to the individual's self-concept.

An additional aspect of attitudes is not clearly described in most theories, namely, their relation to action or overt behavior. Though behavior related to the attitude has other determinants than the attitude itself, it is also true that some attitudes in themselves have more of what Cartwright calls an action structure than do others.[10] Brewster Smith refers to this dimension as policy orientation[11] and Katz and Stotland speak of it as the action component.[12] For example, while many people have attitudes of approval toward one or the other of the two political parties, these attitudes will differ in their structure with respect to relevant action. One man may be prepared to vote on election day and will know where and when he should vote and will go to the polls no matter what the weather or how great the inconvenience. Another man will only vote if a party worker calls for him in a car. Himmelstrand's work is concerned with all aspects of the relationship between attitude and behavior, but he deals with the action structure of the attitude itself by distinguishing between attitudes where the affect is tied to verbal expression and attitudes where the affect is tied to behavior concerned with more objective referents of the attitude.[13] In the first case an individual derives satisfaction from talking about a problem; in the second case he derives satisfaction from taking some form of concrete action.

Attempts to change attitudes can be directed primarily at the belief component or at the feeling, or affective, component. Rosenberg theorizes that an effective change in one component will result in changes in the other component and presents experimental evidence to confirm this hypothesis.[14] For example, a political candidate will often attempt to win people by making them like him and dislike his opponent, and thus communicate affect rather than ideas. If he is successful, people will not only like him but entertain favorable beliefs about him. Another candidate may deal primarily with ideas and hope that, if he can change people's beliefs about an assue, their feelings will also change.

Four Functions Which Attitudes Perform for the Individual

The major functions which attitudes perform for the personality can be grouped according to their motivational basis as follows:

1. *The instrumental, adjustive, or utilitarian function* upon which Jeremy Bentham and the utilitarians constructed their model of man. A modern expression of this approach can be found in behavioristic learning theory.

2. *The ego-defensive function* in which the person protects himself from acknowledging the basic truths about himself or the harsh realities in his external world. Freudian psychology and neo-Freudian thinking have been preoccupied with this type of motivation and its outcomes.

3. *The value-expressive function* in which the individual derives satisfactions from expressing attitudes appropriate to his personal values and to his concept of himself. This function is central to doctrines of ego psychology which stress the importance of self-expression, self-development, and self-realization.

4. *The knowledge function* based upon the individual's need to give adequate structure to his universe. The search for meaning, the need to understand, the trend toward better organization of perceptions and beliefs to provide clarity and consistency for the individual, are other descriptions of this function. The development of principles about perceptual and cognitive structure have been the contributions of Gestalt psychology.

Stated simply, the functional approach is the attempt to understand the reasons people hold the attitudes they do. The reasons, however, are at the level of psychological motivations and not of the accidents of external events and circumstances. Unless we know the psychological need which is met by the holding of an attitude we are in a poor position to predict when and how it will change. Moreover, the same attitude expressed toward a political candidate may not perform the same function for all the people who express it. And while many attitudes are predominantly in the service of a single type of motivational process, as described above, other attitudes may serve more than one purpose for the individual. A fuller discussion of how attitudes serve the above four functions is in order.

1. The Adjustment Function

Essentially this function is a recognition of the fact that people strive to maximize the rewards in their external environment and to minimize the penalties. The child develops favorable attitudes toward the objects in his world which are associated with the satisfactions of his needs and unfavorable attitudes toward objects which thwart him or punish him. Attitudes acquired in the service of the adjustment function are either the means for reaching the desired goal or avoiding the undesirable one, or are affective associations based upon experiences in attaining motive satisfactions.[15] The attitudes of the worker favoring a political party which will advance his economic lot are an example of the first type of utilitarian attitude. The pleasant image one has of one's favorite food is an example of the second type of utilitarian attitude.

In general, then, the dynamics of attitude formation with respect to the adjustment function are dependent upon present or past perceptions of the utility of the attitudinal object for the individual. The clarity, consistency, and nearness of rewards and punishments, as they relate to the individual's activities and goals, are important factors in the acquisition of such attitudes. Both attitudes and habits are formed toward specific objects, people, and symbols as they satisfy specific needs. The closer these objects are to actual need satisfaction and the more they are clearly perceived as relevant to need satisfaction, the greater are the probabilities of positive attitude formation. These principles of attitude formation are often observed in the breach rather than the compliance. In industry, management frequently expects to create favorable attitudes toward job performance through programs for making the company more attractive to the worker, such as providing recreational facilities and fringe benefits. Such programs, however, are much more likely to produce favorable attitudes toward the company as a desirable place to work than toward performance on the job. The company benefits and advantages are applied across the board to all employees and are not specifically relevant to increased effort in task performance by the individual worker.

Consistency of reward and punishment also contributes to the clarity of the instrumental object for goal attainment. If a political party bestows recognition and favors on party workers in an unpredictable and inconsistent fashion, it will destroy the favorable evaluation of the importance of working hard for the party among those whose motivation is of the utilitarian sort. But, curiously, while consistency of reward needs to be observed, 100 per cent consistency is not as effective as a pattern which is usually consistent but in which there are some lapses. When animal or human subjects are invariably rewarded for a correct performance, they do not retain their learned responses as well as when the reward is sometimes skipped.[16]

2. THE EGO-DEFENSIVE FUNCTION

People not only seek to make the most of their external world and what it offers, but they also expend a great deal of their energy on living with themselves. The mechanisms by which the individual protects his ego from his own unacceptable impulses and from the knowledge of threatening forces from without, and the methods by which he reduces his anxieties created by such problems, are known as mechanisms of ego defense. A more complete account of their origin and nature will be found in Sarnoff's article in this issue.[17] They include the devices by which the individual avoids facing either the inner reality of the kind of person he is, or the outer reality of the dangers the world holds for him. They stem basically from internal conflict with its resulting insecurities. In one sense the mechanisms of defense are adaptive in temporarily removing the sharp edges of conflict and in saving the individual from complete disaster. In another sense they are not adaptive in that they handicap the individual in his social adjustments and in obtaining the maximum satisfactions available to him from the world in which he lives. The worker who persistently quarrels with his boss and his fellow workers, because he is acting out some of his own internal conflicts, may in this manner relieve himself of some of the emotional tensions which beset him. He is not, however, solving his problem of adjusting to his work situation and thus may deprive himself of advancement or even of steady employment.

Defense mechanisms, Miller and Swanson point out, may be classified into two families on the basis of the more or less primitive nature of the devices employed.[18] The first family, more primitive in nature, are more socially handicapping and consist of denial and complete avoidance. The individual in such cases obliterates through withdrawal and denial the realities which confront him. The exaggerated case of such primitive mechanisms is the fantasy world of the paranoiac. The second type of defense is less handicapping and makes for distortion rather than denial. It includes rationalization, projection, and displacement.

Many of our attitudes have the function of defending our self-image. When we cannot admit to ourselves that we have deep feelings of inferiority we may project those feelings onto some convenient minority group and bolster our egos by attitudes of superiority toward this underprivileged group. The formation of such defensive attitudes differs in essential ways from the formation of attitudes which serve the adjustment function. They proceed from within the person, and the objects and situation to which they are attached are merely convenient outlets for their expression. Not all targets are equally satisfactory for a given defense mechanism, but the point is that the attitude is not created by the target but by the individual's emotional conflicts. And when no convenient target exists the individual will create one. Utilitarian attitudes, on the other hand, are formed with specific reference to the nature of the attitudinal object. They are thus appropriate to the nature of the social world to which they are geared. The high school student who values high grades because he wants to be admitted to a good college has a utilitarian attitude appropriate to the situation to which it is related.

All people employ defense mechanisms, but they differ with respect to the extent that they use them and some of their attitudes may be more defensive in function than others. It follows that the techniques and conditions for attitude change will not be the same for ego-defensive as for utilitarian attitudes.

Moreover, though people are ordinarily unaware of their defense mechanisms, especially at the time of employing them, they differ with respect to the amount of insight they may show at some later time about their use of defenses. In some cases they recognize that they have been protecting their egos without knowing the reason why. In other cases they may not even be aware of the devices they have been using to delude themselves.

3. The Value-Expressive Function

While many attitudes have the function of preventing the individual from revealing to himself and others his true nature, other attitudes have the function of giving positive expression to his central values and to the type of person he conceives himself to be. A man may consider himself to be an enlightened conservative or an internationalist or a liberal, and will hold attitudes which are the appropriate indication of his central values. Thus we need to take account of the fact that not all behavior has the negative function of reducing the tensions of biological drives or of internal conflicts. Satisfactions also accrue to the person from the expression of attitudes which reflect his cherished beliefs and his self-image. The reward to the person in these instances is not so much a matter of gaining social recognition or monetary rewards as of establishing his self-identity and confirming his notion of the sort of person he sees himself to be. The gratifications obtained from value expression may go beyond the confirmation of self-identity. Just as we find satisfaction in the exercise of our talents and abilities, so we find reward in the expression of any attributes associated with our egos.

Value-expressive attitudes not only give clarity to the self-image but also mold that self-image closer to the heart's desire. The teenager who by dress and speech establishes his identity as similar to his own peer group may appear to the outsider a weakling and a craven conformer. To himself he is asserting his independence of the adult world to which he has rendered childlike subservience and conformity all his life. Very early in the development of the personality the need for clarity of self-image is important—the need to know "who I am." Later it may be even more important to know that in some measure I am the type of person I want to be. Even as adults, however, the clarity and stability of the self-image is of primary significance. Just as the kind, considerate person will cover over his acts of selfishness, so too will the ruthless individualist become confused and embarrassed by his acts of sympathetic compassion. One reason it is difficult to change the character of the adult is that he is not comfortable with the new "me." Group support for such personality change is almost a necessity, as in Alcoholics Anonymous, so that the individual is aware of approval of his new self by people who are like him.

The socialization process during the formative years sets the basic outlines for the individual's self-concept. Parents constantly hold up before the child the model of the good character they want him to be. A good boy eats his spinach, does not hit girls, etc. The candy and the stick are less in evidence in training the child than the constant appeal to his notion of his own character. It is small wonder, then, that children reflect the acceptance of this model by inquiring about the characters of the actors in every drama, whether it be a television play, a political contest, or a war, wanting to know who are the "good guys" and who are the "bad guys." Even as adults we persist in labeling others in the terms of such character images. Joe McCarthy and his cause collapsed in fantastic fashion when the telecast of the Army hearings showed him in the role of the villain attacking the gentle, good man represented by Joseph Welch.

A related but somewhat different process from childhood socialization takes place when individuals enter a new group or organization. The individual will often take over and internalize the values of the group. What accounts, however, for the fact that sometimes this occurs and sometimes it does not? Four factors are probably operative, and some combination of them may be necessary for internalization.

1. The values of the new group may be highly consistent with existing values central to the personality. The girl who enters the nursing profession finds it congenial to consider herself a good nurse because of previous values of the importance of contributing to the welfare of others.

2. The new group may in its ideology have a clear model of what the good group member should be like and may persistently indoctrinate group members in these terms. One of the reasons for the code of conduct for members of the armed forces, devised after the revelations about the conduct of American prisoners in the Korean War, was to attempt to establish a model for what a good soldier does and does not do.

61

3. The activities of the group in moving toward its goal permit the individual genuine opportunity for participation. To become ego-involved so that he can internalize group values, the new member must find one of two conditions. The group activity open to him must tap his talents and abilities so that his chance to show what he is worth can be tied into the group effort. Or else the activities of the group must give him an active voice in group decisions. His particular talents and abilities may not be tapped but he does have the opportunity to enter into group decisions, and thus his need for self-determination is satisfied. He then identifies with the group in which such opportunities for ego-involvement are available. It is not necessary that opportunities for self-expression and self-determination be of great magnitude in an objective sense, so long as they are important for the psychological economy of the individuals themselves.

4. Finally, the individual may come to see himself as a group member if he can share in the rewards of group activity which includes his own efforts. The worker may not play much of a part in building a ship or make any decisions in the process of building it. Nevertheless, if he and his fellow workers are given a share in every boat they build and a return on the proceeds from the earnings of the ship, they may soon come to identify with the ship-building company and see themselves as builders of ships.

4. The Knowledge Function

Individuals not only acquire beliefs in the interest of satisfying various specific needs, they also seek knowledge to give meaning to what would otherwise be an unorganized chaotic universe. People need standards or frames of reference for understanding their world, and attitudes help to supply such standards. The problem of understanding, as John Dewey made clear years ago, is one "of introducing (1) *definiteness* and *distinction* and (2) *consistency* and *stability* of meaning into what is otherwise vague and wavering."[19] The definiteness and stability are provided in good measure by the norms of our culture, which give the otherwise perplexed individual ready-made attitudes for comprehending his universe. Walter Lippmann's classical contribution to the study of opinions and attitudes was his description of stereotypes and the way they provided order and clarity for a bewildering set of complexities.[20] The most interesting finding in Herzog's familiar study of the gratifications obtained by housewives in listening to daytime serials was the unsuspected role of information and advice.[21] The stories were liked "because they explained things to the inarticulate listener."

The need to know does not of course imply that people are driven by a thirst for universal knowledge. The American public's appalling lack of political information has been documented many times. In 1956, for example, only 13 per cent of the people in Detroit could correctly name the two United States Senators from the state of Michigan and only 18 per cent knew the name of their own Congressman.[22] People are not avid seekers after knowledge as judged by what the educator or social reformer would desire. But they do want to understand the events which impinge directly on their own life. Moreover, many of the attitudes they have already acquired give them sufficient basis for interpreting much of what they perceive to be important for them. Our already existing stereotypes, in Lippmann's language, "are an ordered, more or less consistent picture of the world, to which our habits, our tastes, our capacities, our comforts and our hopes have adjusted themselves. They may not be a complete picture of the world, but they are a picture of a possible world to which we are adapted."[23] It follows that new information will not modify old attitudes unless there is some inadequacy or incompleteness or inconsistency in the existing attitudinal structure as it relates to the perceptions of new situations.

NOTES

1. Muzafer Sherif, *The Psychology of Social Norms*, New York, Harper, 1936.
2. Solomon E. Asch, *Social Psychology*, New York, Prentice-Hall, 1952.
3. *Ibid.*, pp. 426–427. The following statement was attributed to its rightful author, John Adams, for some subjects and to Karl Marx for others: "those who hold and those who are without property have ever formed distinct interests in society." When the statement was attributed to Marx, this type of comment appeared: "Marx is stressing the need for a redistribution of wealth." When it was attributed to Adams, this comment appeared: "This social division is innate in mankind."
4. Herbert H. Hyman and Paul B. Sheatsley, "Some Reasons Why Information Campaigns Fail," *Public Opinion Quarterly*, Vol. 11, 1947, pp. 413–423.
5. William A. Scott points out that in the area of international relations the incompleteness and remoteness of the information and the lack of pressures on the individual to defend his views result in inconsistencies. Inconsistent elements with respect to a system of international beliefs may, however, be consistent with the larger system of the personality. "Rationality and Non-rationality of International Attitudes," *Journal of Conflict Resolution*, Vol. 2, 1958, pp. 9–16.
6. Irving Sarnoff and Daniel Katz, "The Motivational Bases of Attitude Change," *Journal of Abnormal and Social Psychology*, Vol. 49, 1954, pp. 115–124.
7. M. Brewster Smith, Jerome S. Bruner, and Robert W. White, *Opinions and Personality*, New York, Wiley, 1956.
8. Herbert H. Hyman and Paul B. Sheatsley, "The Authoritarian Personality: A Methodological Critique," in Richard Christie and Marie Jahoda, editors, *Studies in the Scope and Method of the Authoritarian Personality*, Glencoe, Ill., Free Press, 1954, pp. 50–122.

9. David Krech and Richard S. Crutchfield, *Theory and Problems of Social Psychology*, New York, McGraw-Hill, 1948, pp. 160–163.

10. Dorwin Cartwright, "Some Principles of Mass Persuasion," *Human Relations*, Vol. 2, 1949, pp. 253–267.

11. M. Brewster Smith, "The Personal Setting of Public Opinions: A Study of Attitudes toward Russia," *Public Opinion Quarterly*, Vol. 11, 1947, pp. 507–523.

12. Daniel Katz and Ezra Stotland, "A Preliminary Statement to a Theory of Attitude Structure and Change," in Sigmund Koch, editor, *Psychology: A Study of a Science*, Vol. 3, New York, McGraw-Hill, 1959, pp. 423–475.

13. Ulf Himmelstrand, "Verbal Attitudes and Behavior: A Paradigm for the study of Message Transmission and Transformation," *Public Opinion Quarterly*, Vol. XXIV (1960), pp. 224–250.

14. Milton J. Rosenberg, "A Structural Theory of Attitude Dynamics," *Public Opinion Quarterly*, Vol. XXIV (1960), pp. 319–340.

15. Katz and Stotland, *op. cit.*, pp. 434–443.

16. William O. Jenkins and Julian C. Stanley, "Partial Reinforcement: A Review and Critique," *Psychological Bulletin*, Vol. 47, 1950, pp. 193–234.

17. Irving Sarnoff, "Psychoanalytic Theory and Social Attitudes," *Public Opinion Quarterly*, Vol. XXIV (1960), p. 251–279.

18. Daniel R. Miller and Guy E. Swanson, *Inner Conflict and Defense*, New York, Holt, 1960, pp. 194–288.

19. John Dewey, *How We Think*, New York, Macmillan, 1910.

20. Walter Lippmann, *Public Opinion*, New York, Macmillan, 1922.

21. Herta Herzog, "What Do We Really Know about Daytime Serial Listeners?" in Paul F. Lazarsfeld and Frank N. Stanton, editors, *Radio Research 1942–1943*, New York, Duell, Sloan & Pearce, 1944, pp. 3–33.

22. From a study of the impact of party organization on political behavior in the Detroit area, by Daniel Katz and Samuel Eldersveld, in manuscript.

23. Lippmann, *op. cit.*, p. 95.

2

Formation of Public Opinion

Because of technical and practical considerations, more research attention has been paid to descriptions of opinions than to analyses of the formation and development of opinion. Accordingly, there is now available a whole inventory of opinions toward a wide range of topics held by various social and political groups in the United States and other countries. The findings of such studies have their value for the instruction of scholars, the decisions of policy makers, and the enlightenment of the general public. No simple descriptive studies have been included here because of specific usefulness. Of course, descriptive studies which extend over long periods of time and record trends are of great value.

Beyond descriptive studies, the literature does contain certain examples of substantive and methodological contributions to the basic question of why people hold the opinions they do. First, there is the speculation of the insightful observer mentally exploring the psychological processes of opinion formation, represented here in the selection from Lippmann. The accumulation of a body of opinion data makes it possible to carry out analyses of some of the personal and social determinants of opinion. Typical of this variety of reanalysis is S. M. Lipset's description of the characteristics of the supporters of the John Birch Society. But the main contribution of opinion polling to the understanding of opinion formation is through the accumulation of trend data over time. After public opinion polling had provided a body of answers to standardized opinion questions, it became possible to chart the trends in the gross development of opinions and relate them to external political and military events. Unfortunately, the number of such long-term bodies of data is limited because survey organizations have generally not accepted responsibility for this task. In addition, trend data must be analyzed and evaluated in an analytic framework. Bettelheim and Janowitz present such a longer term study for prejudice, a subject on which relevant data have been collected for over a period of twenty-five yers. The problems of opinion formation have also been attacked by means of repeated interviewing and observation of the same people; the selection from *The People's Choice,* by Paul F. Lazarsfeld, illustrates the application of this procedure to the temporal development of opinion. Criticism of these approaches as "superficial" has led to attempts to conduct research on opinion formation with the concepts and techniques of dynamic psychology. While no examples of this approach are included, case studies, intensive interviews, and projection tests have become standard devices of public opinion research, and the bibliography contains numerous references to these.

WALTER LIPPMANN

Stereotypes

EACH OF US lives and works on a small part of the earth's surface, moves in a small circle, and of these acquaintances knows only a few intimately. Of any public event that has wide effects we see at best only a phase and an aspect. This is as true of the eminent insiders who draft treaties, make laws, and issue orders, as it is of those who have treaties framed for them, laws promulgated to them, orders given at them. Inevitably our opinions cover a bigger space, a longer reach of time, a greater number of things, than we can directly observe. They have, therefore, to be pieced together out of what others have reported and what we can imagine.

Yet even the eyewitness does not bring back a naïve picture of the scene.[1] For experience seems to show that he himself brings something to the scene which later he takes away from it, that oftener than not what he imagines to be the account of an event is really a transfiguration of it. Few facts in consciousness seem to be merely given. Most facts in consciousness seem to be partly made. A report is the joint product of the knower and known, in which the rôle of the observer is always selective and usually creative. The facts we see depend on where we are placed, and the habits of our eyes.

An unfamiliar scene is like the baby's world, "one great, blooming, buzzing confusion."[2] This is the way, says Mr. John Dewey,[3] that any new thing strikes an adult, so far as the thing is really new and strange. "Foreign languages that we do not understand always seem jibberings, babblings, in which it is impossible to fix a definite, clearcut, individualized group of sounds. The countryman in the crowded street, the landlubber at sea, the ignoramus in sport at a contest between experts in a complicated game, are further instances. Put an inexperienced man in a factory, and at first the work seems to him a meaningless medley. All strangers of another

Reprinted from *Public Opinion* (1922), pp. 59–70, by permission of the author and the publisher. (Copyright, 1922, by Macmillan Co.)

race proverbially look alike to the visiting stranger. Only gross differences of size or color are perceived by an outsider in a flock of sheep, each of which is perfectly individualized to the shepherd. A diffusive blur and an indiscriminately shifting suction characterize what we do not understand. The problem of the acquisition of meaning by things, or (stated in another way) of forming habits of simple apprehension, is thus the problem of introducing (1) *definiteness* and *distinction* and (2) *consistency* or *stability* of meaning into what is otherwise vague and wavering."

But the kind of definiteness and consistency introduced depends upon who introduces them. In a later passage[4] Dewey gives an example of how differently an experienced layman and a chemist might define the word metal. "Smoothness, hardness, glossiness, and brilliancy, heavy weight for its size . . . the serviceable properties of capacity for being hammered and pulled without breaking, of being softened by heat and hardened by cold, of retaining the shape and form given, of resistance to pressure and decay, would probably be included" in the layman's definition. But the chemist would likely as not ignore these esthetic and utilitarian qualities, and define a metal as "any chemical element that enters into combination with oxygen so as to form a base."

For the most part we do not first see, and then define, we define first and then see. In the great blooming, buzzing confusion of the outer world we pick out what our culture has already defined for us, and we tend to perceive that which we have picked out in the form stereotyped for us by our culture. Of the great men who assembled at Paris to settle the affairs of mankind, how many were there who were able to see much of the Europe about them, rather than their commitments about Europe? Could anyone have penetrated the mind of M. Clemenceau, would he have found there images of the Europe of 1919, or a great sediment of stereotyped ideas accumulated and hardened in a long and pugnacious existence? Did he see the Germans of 1919, or the German type as he had learned to see it since 1871? He saw the type, and among the reports that came to him from Germany, he took to heart those reports, and, it seems, those only, which fitted the type that was in his mind. If a junker blustered, that was an authentic German; if a labor leader confessed the guilt of the empire, he was not an authentic German.

At a Congress of Psychology in Göttingen an interesting experiment was made with a crowd of presumably trained observers.[5]

Not far from the hall in which the Congress was sitting there was a public fête with a masked ball. Suddenly the door of the hall was thrown open and a clown rushed in madly pursued by a negro, revolver in hand. They stopped in the middle of the room fighting; the clown fell, the negro leapt upon him, fired, and then both rushed out of the hall. The whole incident hardly lasted twenty seconds.

The President asked those present to write immediately a report since there was sure to be a judicial inquiry. Forty reports were sent in. Only one had less than 20% of mistakes in regard to the principal facts; fourteen had 20% to 40% of mistakes; twelve from 40% to 50%; thirteen more than 50%. Moreover in twenty-four accounts 10% of the details were pure inventions and this proportion was exceeded in ten accounts and diminished in six. Briefly a quarter of the accounts were false.

It goes without saying that the whole scene had been arranged and even photographed in advance. The ten false reports may then be relegated to the category of tales and legends; twenty-four accounts are half legendary, and six have a value approximating to exact evidence.

Thus out of forty trained observers writing a responsible account of a scene that had just happened before their eyes, more than a majority saw a scene that had not taken place. What then did they see? One would suppose it was easier to tell what had occurred, than to invent something which had not occurred. They saw their stereotype of such a brawl. All of them had in the course of their lives acquired a series of images of brawls, and these images flickered before their eyes. In one man these images displaced less than 20% of the actual scene, in thirteen men more than half. In thirty-four out of the forty observers the stereotypes preëmpted at least one-tenth of the scene.

A distinguished art critic said[6] that "what with the almost numberless shapes assumed by an object. . . . What with our insensitiveness and inattention, things scarcely would have for us features and outlines so determined and clear that we could recall them at will, but for the stereotyped shapes art has lent them." The truth is even broader than that, for the stereotyped shapes lent to the world come not merely from art, in the sense of painting and sculpture and literature, but from our moral codes and our social philosophies and our political agitations as well. Substitute in the following passage of Mr. Berenson's the words "politics," "business," and "society," for the word "art" and the sentences will be no less true: ". . . unless years devoted to the study of all schools of art have taught us also to see with our own eyes, we soon fall into the habit of moulding whatever we look at into the forms borrowed from the one art with which we are acquainted. There is our standard of artistic reality. Let anyone give us shapes and colors which we cannot instantly match in our paltry stock of hackneyed forms and tints, and we shake our heads at his failure to reproduce things as we know they certainly are, or we accuse him of insincerity."

Mr. Berenson speaks of our displeasure when a painter "does not visualize objects exactly as we do," and of the difficulty of appreciating the art of the Middle Ages because since then "our manner of visualizing forms has changed in a thousand ways."[7] He goes on to show how in regard to the human figure we have been taught to see what we do see. "Created by Donatello and Masaccio, and sanctioned by the Humanists, the new canon of the human figure, the new cast of features . . . presented to the ruling classes of that time the type of human being most likely to

69

win the day in the combat of human forces. . . . Who had the power to break through this new standard of vision and, out of the chaos of things, to select shapes more definitely expressive of reality than those fixed by men of genius? No one had such power. People had perforce to see things in that way and in no other, and to see only the shapes depicted, to love only the ideals presented. . . ."[8]

If we cannot fully understand the acts of other people, until we know what they think they know, then in order to do justice we have to appraise not only the information which has been at their disposal, but the minds through which they have filtered it. For the accepted types, the current patterns, the standard versions, intercept information on its way to consciousness. Americanization, for example, is superficially at least the substitution of American for European stereotypes. Thus the peasant who might see his landlord as if he were the lord of the manor, his employer as he saw the local magnate, is taught by Americanization to see the landlord and employer according to American standards. This constitutes a change of mind, which is, in effect, when the inoculation succeeds, a change of vision. His eyes see differently. One kindly gentlewoman has confessed that the stereotypes are of such overwhelming importance, that when hers are not indulged, she at least is unable to accept the brotherhood of man and the fatherhood of God: "we are strangely affected by the clothes we wear. Garments create a mental and social atmosphere. What can be hoped for the Americanism of a man who insists on employing a London tailor? One's very food affects his Americanism. What kind of American consciousness can grow in the atmosphere of sauerkraut and Limburger cheese? Or what can you expect of the Americanism of the man whose breath always reeks of garlic?"[9]

This lady might well have been the patron of a pageant which a friend of mine once attended. It was called "The Melting Pot," and it was given on the Fourth of July in an automobile town where many foreign-born workers are employed. In the center of the baseball park at second base stood a huge wooden and canvas pot. There were flights of steps up to the rim on two sides. After the audience had settled itself, and the band had played, a procession came through an opening at one side of the field. It was made up of men of all the foreign nationalities employed in the factories. They wore their native costumes, they were singing their national songs; they danced their folk dances, and carried the banners of all Europe. The master of ceremonies was the principal of the grade school dressed as Uncle Sam. He led them to the pot. He directed them up the steps to the rim, and inside. He called them out again on the other side. They came, dressed in derby hats, coats, pants, vest, stiff collar and polka-dot tie, undoubtedly, said my friend, each with an Eversharp pencil in his pocket, and all singing the Star-Spangled Banner.

To the promoters of this pageant, and probably to most of the actors, it seemed as if they had managed to express the most intimate difficulty to friendly association between the older peoples of America and the newer. The contradiction of their stereotypes interfered with the full recognition of their common humanity. The people who change their names know this. They mean to change themselves, and the attitude of strangers toward them.

There is, of course, some connection between the scene outside and the mind through which we watch it, just as there are some long-haired men and short-haired women in radical gatherings. But to the hurried observer a slight connection is enough. If there are two bobbed heads and four beards in the audience, it will be a bobbed and bearded audience to the reporter who knows beforehand that such gatherings are composed of people with these tastes in the management of their hair. There is a connection between our vision and the facts, but it is often a strange connection. A man has rarely looked at a landscape, let us say, except to examine its possibilities for division into building lots, but he has seen a number of landscapes hanging in the parlor. And from them he has learned to think of a landscape as a rosy sunset, or as a country road with a church steeple and a silver moon. One day he goes to the country, and for hours he does not see a single landscape. Then the sun goes down looking rosy. At once he recognizes a landscape and exclaims that it is beautiful. But two days later, when he tries to recall what he saw, the odds are that he will remember chiefly some landscape in a parlor.

Unless he has been drunk or dreaming or insane he did see a sunset, but he saw in it, and above all remembers from it, more of what the oil painting taught him to observe, than what an impressionist painter, for example, or a cultivated Japanese would have seen and taken away with him. And the Japanese and the painter in turn will have seen and remembered more of the form they had learned, unless they happen to be the very rare people who find fresh sight for mankind. In untrained observation we pick recognizable signs out of the environment. The signs stand for ideas, and these ideas we fill out with our stock of images. We do not so much see this man and that subject; rather we notice that the thing is man or sunset, and then see chiefly what our mind is already full of on those subjects.

There is economy in this. For the attempt to see all things freshly and in detail, rather than as types and generalities, is exhausting, and among busy affairs practically out of the question. In a circle of friends, and in relation to close associates or competitors, there is no shortcut through, and no substitute for, an individualized understanding. Those whom we love and admire most are the men and women whose consciousness is peopled thickly with persons rather than with types, who know us rather than the classification into which we might fit. For even without phrasing it to ourselves, we feel intuitively that all classification is in relation to

71

some purpose not necessarily our own; that between two human beings no association has final dignity in which each does not take the other as an end in himself. There is a taint on any contact between two people which does not affirm as an axiom the personal inviolability of both.

But modern life is hurried and multifarious, above all physical distance separates men who are often in vital contact with each other, such as employer and employee, official and voter. There is neither time nor opportunity for intimate acquaintance. Instead we notice a trait which marks a well known type, and fill in the rest of the picture by means of the stereotypes we carry about in our heads. He is an agitator. That much we notice, or are told. Well, an agitator is this sort of person, and so *he* is this sort of person. He is an intellectual. He is a plutocrat. He is a foreigner. He is a "South European." He is from Back Bay. He is a Harvard Man. How different from the statement: he is a Yale Man. He is a regular fellow. He is a West Pointer. He is an old army sergeant. He is a Greenwich Villager: what don't we know about him then, and about her? He is an international banker. He is from Main Street.

The subtlest and most pervasive of all influences are those which create and maintain the repertory of stereotypes. We are told about the world before we see it. We imagine most things before we experience them. And those preconceptions, unless education has made us acutely aware, govern deeply the whole process of perception. They mark out certain objects as familiar or strange, emphasizing the difference, so that the slightly familiar is seen as very familiar, and the somewhat strange as sharply alien. They are aroused by small signs, which may vary from a true index to a vague analogy. Aroused, they flood fresh vision with older images, and project into the world what has been resurrected in memory. Were there no practical uniformities in the environment, there would be no economy and only error in the human habit of accepting foresight for sight. But there are uniformities sufficiently accurate, and the need of economizing attention is so inevitable, that the abandonment of all stereotypes for a whole innocent approach to experience would impoverish human life.

What matters is the character of the stereotypes, and the gullibility with which we employ them. And these in the end depend upon those inclusive patterns which constitute our philosophy of life. If in that philosophy we assume that the world is codified according to a code which we possess, we are likely to make our reports of what is going on describe a world run by our code. But if our philosophy tells us that each man is only a small part of the world, that his intelligence catches at best only phases and aspects in a coarse net of ideas, then, when we use our stereotypes, we tend to know that they are only stereotypes, to hold them lightly, to modify them gladly. We tend, also, to realize more and more clearly when our ideas started, where they started, how they came to us, why we accepted them. All useful history is antiseptic in this fashion. It enables us to know what fairy tale, what school book, what tradition, what novel, play, picture, phrase, planted one preconception in this mind, another in that mind.

Those who wish to censor art do not at least underestimate this influence. They generally misunderstand it, and almost always they are absurdly bent on preventing other people from discovering anything not sanctioned by them. But at any rate, like Plato in his argument about the poets, they feel vaguely that the types acquired through fiction tend to be imposed on reality. Thus there can be little doubt that the moving picture is steadily building up imagery which is then evoked by the words people read in their newspapers. In the whole experience of the race there has been no aid to visualization comparable to the cinema. If a Florentine wished to visualize the saints, he could go to the frescoes in his church, where he might see a vision of saints standardized for his time by Giotto. If an Athenian wished to visualize the gods he went to the temples. But the number of objects which were pictured was not great. And in the East, where the spirit of the second commandment was widely accepted, the portraiture of concrete things was even more meager, and for that reason perhaps the faculty of practical decision was by so much reduced. In the western world, however, during the last few centuries there has been an enormous increase in the volume and scope of secular description, the word picture, the narrative, the illustrated narrative, and finally the moving picture and, perhaps, the talking picture.

Photographs have the kind of authority over imagination to-day, which the printed word had yesterday, and the spoken word before that. They seem utterly real. They come, we imagine, directly to us without human meddling, and they are the most effortless food for the mind conceivable. Any description in words, or even any inert picture, requires an effort of memory before a picture exists in the mind. But on the screen the whole process of observing, describing, reporting, and then imagining, has been accomplished for you. Without more trouble than is needed to stay awake the result which your imagination is always aiming at is reeled off on the screen. The shadowy idea becomes vivid; your hazy notion, let us say, of the Ku Klux Klan, thanks to Mr. Griffiths, takes vivid shape when you see *The Birth of a Nation*. Historically it may be the wrong shape, morally it may be a pernicious shape, but it is a shape, and I doubt whether anyone who has seen the film and does not know more about the Ku Klux Klan than Mr. Griffiths, will ever hear the name again without seeing those white horsemen.

And so when we speak of the mind of a group of people, of the French mind, the militarist mind, the bolshevik mind, we are liable to serious confusion unless we agree to separate the instinctive equipment from the stereotypes, and the formulae which play so decisive a part in building

73

up the mental world to which the native character is adapted and responds. Failure to make this distinction accounts for oceans of loose talk about collective minds, national souls, and race psychology. To be sure a stereotype may be so consistently and authoritatively transmitted in each generation from parent to child that it seems almost like a biological fact. In some respects, we may indeed have become, as Mr. Wallas says,[10] biologically parasitic upon our social heritage. But certainly there is not the least scientific evidence which would enable anyone to argue that men are born with the political habits of the country in which they are born. In so far as political habits are alike in a nation, the first places to look for an explanation are the nursery, the school, the church, not in that limbo inhabited by Group Minds and National Souls. Until you have thoroughly failed to see tradition being handed on from parents, teachers, priests, and uncles, it is a solecism of the worst order to ascribe political differences to the germ plasm.

It is possible to generalize tentatively and with a decent humility about comparative differences within the same category of education and experience. Yet even this is a tricky enterprise. For almost no two experiences are exactly alike, not even of two children in the same household. The older son never does have the experience of being the younger. And therefore, until we are able to discount the difference in nurture, we must withhold judgment about differences of nature. As well judge the productivity of two soils by comparing their yield before you know which is in Labrador and which is in Iowa, whether they have been cultivated and enriched, exhausted, or allowed to run wild.

NOTES

1. *E.g. cf.* Edmond Locard, *L'Enquête Criminelle et les Méthodes Scientifiques.* A great deal of interesting material has been gathered in late years on the credibility of the witness, which shows, as an able reviewer of Dr. Locard's book says in *The Times* (London) Literary Supplement (August 18, 1921), that credibility varies as to classes of witnesses and classes of events, and also as to type of perception. Thus, perception of touch, odor, and taste have low evidential value. Our hearing is defective and arbitrary when it judges the sources and direction of sound, and in listening to the talk of other people "words which are not heard will be supplied by the witness in all good faith. He will have a theory of the purport of the conversation, and will arrange the sounds he heard to fit it." Even visual perceptions are liable to great error, as in identification, recognition, judgment of distance, estimates of numbers, for example, the size of a crowd. In the untrained observer the sense of time is highly variable. All these original weaknesses are complicated by tricks of memory, and the incessant creative quality of the imagination. Cf. also Sherrington, *The Integrative Action of the Nervous System,* pp. 318–327.

The late Professor Hugo Münsterberg wrote a popular book on this subject called *On the Witness Stand.*

2. Wm. James, *Principles of Psychology*, Vol. I, p. 488.

3. John Dewey, *How We Think*, p. 121.

4. *Op. cit.*, p. 133.

5. A von Gennep, *La formation des légendes*, pp. 158–159. Cited F. van Langenhove, *The Growth of a Legend*, pp. 120–122.

6. Bernard Berenson, *The Central Italian Painters of the Renaissance*, pp. 60, *et seq.*

7. *Cf.* also his comment on *Dante's Visual Images, and his Early Illustrators* in *The Study and Criticism of Italian Art* (First Series), p. 13. "We cannot help dressing Virgil as a Roman, and giving him a 'Classical profile' and 'statuesque carriage,' but Dante's visual image of Virgil was probably no less mediaeval, no more based on a critical reconstruction of antiquity, than his entire conception of the Roman poet. Fourteenth Century illustrators make Virgil look like a mediaeval scholar, dressed in cap and gown, and there is no reason why Dante's visual image of him should have been other than this."

8. *The Central Italian Painters*, pp. 66–67.

9. Cited by Mr. Edward Hale Bierstadt, *New Republic*, June 1, 1921, p. 21.

10. Graham Wallas, *Our Social Heritage*, p. 17.

SEYMOUR M. LIPSET

The Supporters of the John Birch Society

THE ANALYSIS of the supporters of the John Birch Society presents some special problems. Because it lacks a nationally known leader, espouses a virulent and extremist ideology which gives rise to attacks on the moderate leaders of both major parties as Communists, and upholds an economic program promoting the interests and values of the small stratum of moderately well-to-do businessmen and professionals, it has appealed to a much smaller segment of the general public than did Coughlin or McCarthy. Further, the Society is only dimly known to many people. For example, a Gallup Survey that inquired into attitudes toward the John Birch Society in the beginning of 1962 found that over two-thirds of those interviewed had not heard of it, or else had no opinion of it (Table 1). Among

Table 1—Opinion of a National Sample on the Birch Society—
February, 1962 (Gallup)

Opinion	Per Cent
Favorable to the Society	5
Unfavorable	26
No Opinion	27
Have Not Heard of the Society	42
	100%
	(1616)

those who did express opinions, negative judgments outnumbered positive ones by five to one: 5 per cent favored the Society and 26 per cent opposed it.

Reprinted from *The Radical Right*, Daniel Bell, editor, (1963), pp. 349–363, by permission of the author and the publisher. (Copyright, 1963, S. G. Phillips.)

76

These results were obtained four years after the Society was first organized, and over a year after it began to receive widespread attention in the general press, as well as sharp criticism from liberal political leaders and journals.

Because the bulk of the national sample had no opinion on the Birchers, certain limitations are imposed in drawing conclusions from the data. Comparisons between population subgroups, as presented for the Coughlin and McCarthy data, must be interpreted with extreme caution, since they may at times be quite misleading. In analyzing support for the Birchers in terms of such categories, it is necessary to compare such small percentages as three per cent pro-Birch among Democrats and seven per cent among Republicans. Such comparisons are made all the more difficult because the proportion of respondents without opinions varies widely from sub-group to sub-group, following the pattern typically associated with political knowledge, opinion, and participation.

As Table 2 shows, the proportion without an opinion is 44 per cent among those who went to college, but 85 per cent among the grammar-school-educated. Further examination of the table discloses that the college-trained have a higher proportion of Birch supporters—and also Birch opponents—than do the grade-school-educated. To take another example, professionals appear much more pro-Birch than farmers, if one looks only at the percentage of the two occupations that is favorable to the Society; however, 60 per cent of the professionals expressed an opinion, as contrasted with 15 per cent of the farmers. (To emphasize the differing contributions of various population subgroups to opinion, both pro and con, on the Birch Society, Table 3 is included, based on the same data as Table 2, but showing the relative contribution of subgroups to the pro-Birch and anti-Birch groups, rather than the opinion distribution of the subgroups on the Birch issue.)

The low level of opinion on the Society has additional implications for an analysis of Birch support. These concern the extent of possible latent support. One cannot assume that, because the low-income element (family income under $4000) of the population divided 4 to 1 against the Birchers in 1962, the same division of opinion would obtain at a time when, perhaps, a majority of these persons will know of, and have views regarding, the Birchers. At the time of the Gallup Survey, only 20 per cent of low-income respondents had an opinion on the organization. One cannot guess whether the balance of judgment would remain the same if 50 per cent—or 80 per cent—of this group had opinions to offer. In short, under different conditions arising either within the country or outside it, and with different policies and techniques pursued by the Society itself, the Birchers may come to the attention of segments of the population they are not presently reaching, and the relative distribution of supporters and opponents within different analytic categories may become quite different.

Table 2—Attitudes Toward Birch Society by Selected Characteristics in Per Cent—February, 1962 (Gallup)

Characteristics	Pro	Con	Don't Know, Haven't Heard	N
Party				
Democrat	3%	21	76	(787)
Independent	5%	34	61	(368)
Republican	7%	28	65	(444)
Religion				
Protestant	4%	24	72	(1108)
Catholic	5%	27	68	(390)
Jewish	6%	48	46	(54)
Region				
Northeast	4%	34	62	(460)
Midwest	4%	20	76	(538)
South	4%	19	77	(359)
West	7%	35	58	(259)
Education				
Grade	2%	13	85	(428)
High	5%	25	70	(889)
College	8%	48	44	(294)
Income				
Low	4%	16	80	(509)
Medium	5%	24	71	(605)
High	6%	39	55	(483)
Sex				
Men	5%	30	65	(784)
Women	4%	22	74	(820)
Occupation				
Professional	9%	51	40	(166)
Business, executive	6%	33	61	(176)
Clerical, sales	7%	34	57	(193)
Skilled labor	5%	19	76	(258)
Unskilled, serv.	3%	18	79	(381)
Farmer	1%	14	85	(173)
Non-labor force	5%	22	73	(235)
Nonmanual	7%	39	54	(535)
Manual	4%	19	77	(639)
Age				
21–29	5%	23	72	(232)
30–49	3%	29	68	(700)
50 and over	6%	23	71	(623)
Total Sample	5%	26	69	(1616)

Table 3—Characteristics of Birch Supporters and Opponents in Per Cent—February, 1962 (Gallup)

| | | ATTITUDE GROUPS | | |
Characteristics	Total Sample	Pro-Birch	Anti-Birch	Don't Know Haven't Heard
Party				
Democrat	49%	33%	40%	54%
Independent	23	24	30	20
Republican	28	43	30	26
Religion				
Protestant	72	66	66	74
Catholic	25	30	27	24
Jewish	3	4	7	2
Region				
Northeast	28	25	37	25
Midwest	34	32	25	36
South	22	21	16	26
West	16	22	22	13
Education				
Grade	27	13	13	33
High	55	57	53	57
College	18	30	34	12
Income				
Low	32	24	20	37
Medium	38	38	35	39
High	30	38	45	24
Sex				
Men	49	57	57	45
Women	51	43	43	55
Occupation				
Professional	11	20	21	6
Business, executive	11	13	15	10
Clerical, sales	12	17	16	10
Skilled labor	16	16	12	18
Farmer	11	1	6	13
Non-labor force	15	17	13	16
Unskilled, serv.	24	16	17	27
Nonmanual	34	50	52	26
Manual	40	32	29	45
Age				
21–29	15	15	13	15
30–49	45	33	51	44
50 and over	40	52	36	41
	100%	100%	100%	100%
N	(1616)	(76)	(416)	(1124)

Given these difficulties in interpreting the results of the national survey, I shall not discuss them in great detail. It is possible, however, to specify some of the factors that are associated with opinion toward the Society by concentrating on an analysis of attitudes within the one state in the Union in which the Society has become an important election issue and source of controversy—California. The California Poll, a state-wide survey organization, reports that in January, 1962, 82 per cent of a sample of 1100 Californians had heard of the Society. The national Gallup Survey, cited earlier, which was taken at about the same time, indicates that among respondents in the three Pacific Coast states, 79 per cent had heard of the Society as contrasted with 58 per cent in the nation as a whole.[1] The salience of the Birch issue in California in 1962 can hardly be disputed: at the time, two California congressmen were avowed members of the organization; the Attorney General of the State issued a detailed report on the Society that was extensively reported and discussed in the newspapers; the Republican Assembly, meeting to endorse candidates for the 1962 primaries, spent considerable time debating the Party's position with respect to the Society; and both gubernatorial candidates, Governor Edmund Brown and former Vice-President Nixon, vied in attacking the Birchites.[2]

Given the salience of the Birch issue in California politics, and the high degree of public knowledge of the organization, findings for the state of California may be interpreted with somewhat greater confidence than the national data. The January, 1962, California Poll permitted the construction of a measure of Birch support and opposition similar to that used for McCarthy in the I.N.R.A. Survey. The Poll inquired first whether respondents would be more or less likely to vote for a gubernatorial candidate who welcomed Birch Society support, and second whether they would be more or less likely to vote for a candidate who rejected the Society's endorsement. From responses on these two questions, respondents were divided into three groups: those who were sympathetic to the Birch Society on at least one question; those who said that the Birch issue would not affect their vote; and those who were unsympathetic to the Birch Society on one or both questions. A fourth group contained those who did not have an opinion on either question, together with persons who had never heard of the Society. Table 4 gives the distribution among California respondents in these four categories.

It is clear that in California, as in the nation as a whole, the bulk of those with opinions about the Birchers were hostile. Among the national sample, as we have seen, unfavorable replies outnumbered favorable by a magnitude of five to one (26 per cent to 5 per cent); in California, the negative exceeded the positive by seven to one (41 per cent to 6 per cent). Exact comparisons are, of course, impossible since the questions posed

**Table 4—Attitudes Toward the Birch Society Among Californians—
January, 1962 (California Poll)**

Attitude	Per Cent
Favorable	6
Neutral	15
Unfavorable	41
No Opinion[a]	
Never Heard	38
	100%
N	(1186)

a. No Opinion includes 2 per cent who gave contradictory responses.

were so different. Moreover, it might be argued that the neutral category in California, those who reported that it made no difference whether a candidate was pro-Birch Society or not—the anti-anti-Birchers, so to speak—were "soft on Birchism." In spite of the propaganda emphasizing the anti-democratic propensities of the Birch Society and its attacks on Eisenhower and other major figures as Communists or dupes, these persons were still willing to say that a candidate's involvement in the Birch Society would not prejudice them against him.

An examination of the data reported in Tables 5 and 6 point up a number of factors associated with Birch support in California. A supporter of the Society is more likely to be a Republican than a Democrat, to live in Southern California, to be better educated, and to be in a higher economic category. Occupational variations as such do not seem to be significantly related to attitudes toward the Birchers, with the exception of the fact that the small group of farmers in the sample seem to be the most strongly pro-Birch among the vocational categories. Differences between religious groups are small, although Catholics are somewhat less likely to back the Birch Society than are Protestants.

Since party identification appears so crucial in determining attitude toward the Birch Society, it is possible that some of the above-mentioned relationships are indirectly a consequence of political affiliation. For example, the political commitment of Protestants and Catholics varies greatly. In California, Protestants divide 50–50 in allegiance to the major parties, whereas among Catholics, Democrats outnumber Republicans 4 to 1. These results suggest that the Democratic commitment of Catholics may account for their slightly greater opposition to the Birch Society. And in fact we find that when religious groups are compared *within* party categories Catholics are slightly more likely to favor the Birch Society than are Protestants[3] (Table 7).

When the effect of education on attitudes toward the Birch Society is analyzed within party groups, the data suggest little difference among

**Table 5—Attitudes Toward Birch Society by Selected Characteristics
in Per Cent—January, 1962 (California Poll)**

Characteristics	Pro	Neutral	Con	Don't Know Haven't Heard	Total	N
			ATTITUDES ON BIRCH SOCIETY			
Party						
Democratic	3%	11	45	41	100%	(673)
Republican	10	21	36	33	100	(468)
Religion						
Protestant	6	17	39	38	100	(769)
Catholic	6	11	42	41	100	(273)
Jewish	4	6	63	27	100	(67)
Region						
No. California	3	13	37	47	100	(499)
So. California	8	17	44	31	100	(687)
Education						
Grade School	2	15	25	58	100	(127)
High School	4	13	36	47	100	(594)
1–2 Coll./Trade	8	16	50	26	100	(230)
3+ College	11	17	55	17	100	(235)
Econ. Level						
Low	5	11	36	48	100	(306)
Medium	5	17	42	36	100	(639)
High	10	14	47	29	100	(240)
Sex						
Men	7	17	42	34	100	(590)
Women	5	13	40	42	100	(595)
Occupation						
Professional	6	15	53	25	100	(162)
Exec/Mgr	7	18	47	28	100	(71)
Self-empl business	4	20	39	37	100	(67)
Cler/Sales	6	13	47	34	100	(191)
Skilled	4	12	42	42	100	(203)
Unskilled & service	5	12	34	49	100	(258)
Farm	17	29	20	34	100	(35)
Ret'd, etc.	8	17	37	38	100	(174)
Nonmanual	6	15	48	31	100	(492)
Manual	5	12	37	46	100	(461)
Age						
21–29	6	15	39	40	100	(226)
30–49	6	13	47	34	100	(538)
50 and over	6	17	35	42	100	(421)
Total Sample	6	15	41	38	100%	(1186)

Table 6—Characteristics of Birch Supporters Contrasted with Birch Opponents in Per Cent—January, 1962 (California Poll)

		ATTITUDE GROUPS			
Characteristics	Total Sample	Pro-Birch	Neutral	Anti-Birch	Don't Know Haven't Heard
Party					
Democrat	59%	28%	45%	64%	64%
Republican	41	72	55	36	36
Religion					
Protestant	69%	71%	79%	66%	70%
Catholic	25	25	19	25	26
Jewish	6	5	2	9	4
Region					
No. California	42%	22%	36%	38%	53%
So. California	58	78	64	62	47
Education					
Grade School	11%	4%	11%	7%	16%
High School	50	34	46	43	62
1–2 Coll. or Trade	19	26	20	23	14
3+ College	20	36	23	27	8
Econ. Level					
Low	20%	21%	20%	22%	33%
Medium	54	44	61	55	52
High	26	35	19	23	15
Sex					
Men	50%	57%	57%	51%	45%
Women	50	43	43	49	55
Occupation					
Professional	14%	14%	15%	18%	9%
Business	12	11	15	13	10
Cler/sales	17	15	15	19	15
Skilled	17	12	15	17	19
Unskilled & service	22	20	18	18	28
Farm	3	8	6	1	5
Ret'd, etc.	15	20	17	14	15
Nonmanual	43%	40%	45%	50%	34%
Manual	39	32	33	35	47
Age					
21–29	19%	19%	19%	18%	20%
30–49	45	47	39	52	41
50 and over	36	34	42	30	39
	100%	100%	100%	100%	100%
	N (1186)	N (73)	N (176)	N (488)	N (449)

**Table 7—Relationship of Party Affiliation and Religion to Attitude Toward
John Birch Society in California in Per Cent—January, 1962
(California Poll)**

Party and Religion	ATTITUDE TOWARD BIRCH SOCIETY					
	Pro	Neutral	Against	Don't Know or Never Heard	Total	N
Democrats						
Protestants	2%	14	41	43	100%	(387)
Catholics	4%	8	44	44	100%	(206)
Republicans						
Protestants	10%	21	37	32	100%	(380)
Catholics	14%	21	32	33	100%	(57)

Democrats according to education. If anything, better-educated Democrats are more likely to be more anti-Birch. Among Republicans, however, greater education is associated with being pro-Birch. To a considerable extent these variations would seem to be a product of socio-economic status. That is, with increasing economic level, Republicans are more disposed to support the Birch Society, while Democrats at higher-status levels are somewhat more inclined to oppose the organization that their less-privileged party brethren (Table 8).

The data clearly reflect the strong connection between attitudes toward the Birch Society and basic party commitment—a relationship that is hardly surprising, given the tenor of the organization. Basically, the Birch Society appeals most to well-to-do Republicans, and somewhat

**Table 8—Relationship of Party Affiliation and Economic Level to Attitudes
Toward the Birch Society in California, in Per Cent—January, 1962
(California Poll)**

Party and SES	ATTITUDE ON BIRCH SOCIETY					
	Pro	Neutral	Against	Don't Know or Never Heard	Total	N
Democrats						
High	3%	12	50	35	100%	(109)
Medium	3%	11	49	37	100%	(358)
Low	3%	11	36	50	100%	(218)
Republicans						
High	18%	14	45	23	100%	(126)
Medium	8%	25	33	34	100%	(274)
Low	6%	15	32	47	100%	(68)

more to the Catholics among them than to the Protestants. These findings suggest that the Society's appeal is most effective among those to whom economic conservatism and fear of Communism are crucial issues.

SEYMOUR M. LIPSET: The Supporters of the John Birch Society

Evidence for this interpretation may be drawn from an analysis of attitudes toward the Birch Society as related to preferences among likely contenders for the G.O.P. Presidential nomination in 1964, and as related to opinions on the importance of the threat of internal Communism. (The first comparison is made only for Republicans.) Among Republicans who supported the Birch Society, almost three-fifths (59 per cent) favored Senator Goldwater for President in 1964 (Table 9). Conversely, while former Vice-President Nixon was the leading candidate among the other categories, Republicans who opposed the Birch Society contained a larger proportion of Rockefeller backers than did any other opinion groups. Examined in terms of the attitudes of the supporters of the different candidates, the data show that 71 per cent of the Rockefeller partisans were anti-Birch, as contrasted with 56 per cent of the Nixon supporters, and 45 per cent of the Goldwater advocates. Clearly, Birchism and general political conservatism were strongly related among California Republicans in 1962.

Table 9—Opinion Toward the Birch Society According to Preferred Republican
Presidential Choice in 1964 Among California Republicans
(California Poll)—January, 1962

Preferred Candidate	OPINION OF BIRCH SOCIETY				
	Favorable	Neutral	Against	Don't Know or Never Heard	Total Sample
Rockefeller	4%	15%	23%	21%	19%
Nixon	25	38	38	33	35
Romney	8	11	4	7	7
Goldwater	59	22	23	18	25
Don't Know	4	14	12	21	14
	100%	100%	100%	100%	100%
N	(48)	(96)	(170)	(154)	(468)

Among followers of both parties, attitudes toward the Birchers are influenced by views on the importance of internal Communism as a threat to the nation. Three-fourths of Birch supporters see the danger of domestic Communism as great, as contrasted with slightly more than half of the neutral group and a little less than half of the anti-Birch element. Those perceiving minimal threat from internal Communism constituted 4 per cent of the pro-Birchers, 14 per cent of the neutrals, and 20 per cent of the anti-Birchers (Table 10). (The same relationship between Birch opinion and perceived threat holds when Republicans and Democrats are taken separately, although Republicans more often than Democrats perceive the threat as high.)

There is also a difference between supporters and opponents of the

Society who agree that the internal Communist threat is great in their opinion of the adequacy of existing agencies dealing with the problem. Approximately three-fifths of the Society's opponents who agree that domestic Communism is a major problem feel that it is not being adequately dealt with, as compared with four-fifths of the Society's supporters. Thus, those who like the Society differ sharply from those who dislike it in their evaluation of the extent of the threat and the way it is being handled. Considering both opinions together, we find that twice the proportion of the former group (60 per cent) feels that the threat is great and that it is being inadequately handled, compared to the latter (30 per cent).

Table 10—Birch Opinion Related to Perception of Domestic Communist Threat Among Californians—January, 1962 (California Poll)

Percepton of Communist Threat	OPINION ON BIRCH SOCIETY				
	Pro	Neutral	Con	Don't Know or Haven't Heard	Total Sample
High	75%	53%	48%	50%	51%
Medium	21	33	32	37	33
Low	4	14	20	13	16
	100%	100%	100%	100%	100%
N	(67)	(173)	(471)	(407)	(1118)

Neither the national Gallup Survey nor the California Poll included questions concerning attitudes on issues other than those reported above. However, a questionnaire study conducted in the San Francisco Bay Area in the spring of 1962, primarily for the purpose of studying opinions on peace issues, included a question on the John Birch Society and other attitudes relevant to this investigation. Though designed to secure a representative sample of the Bay Area population, the survey suffered from defects not uncommon in surveys utilizing self-administered questionnaires as opposed to interviews—that is, a heavy bias in the direction of responses by the better educated.[4] Forty-seven per cent of those who answered the questionnaire had at least some college education and two-thirds were engaged in nonmanual occupations. It is impossible, therefore, to draw any reliable conclusions from this survey as to the social characteristics of Birch supporters in the San Francisco region. But since the study did contain a number of attitude items on a variety of issues, and because the social characteristics of Birch supporters and opponents corresponded on the whole with the findings of the California Poll, a brief report on its results seems warranted.[5]

Of particular interest in this survey were a number of questions dealing with attitudes toward minority ethnic and religious groups. Respondents were asked, "In choosing your friends and associates, how do you feel about the following types of people?" Response categories were, "Would rather not deal with," "Feel some reservations about dealing with," and "Feel the same about them as others." It was found that those approving the Birch Society (9 per cent) tended to be more prejudiced against Negroes and Mexicans than those who opposed the organization.[6] The pro-Birch group was also somewhat more hostile to Orientals and Jews than the opposing element, but the differences were relatively minor. The findings held when respondents of differing educational attainment were treated separately, indicating that, despite the greater prejudice of the less educated generally, Birch supporters tended to show more prejudice than Birch opponents.

Table 11—Prejudice Toward Ethnic and Religious Minorities According to Opinion on Birch Society (White Christians Only)[a]

Prejudiced Toward:	Proportion Expressing Pro-Birch Group	Prejudice Among: Anti-Birch Group
Negroes	53%	37%
Mexicans	38	27
Orientals	22	17
Jews	15	11
Jehovah's Witnesses	44	40
N	(42)	(303)
Catholics[b]	7	8
	(26)	(193)

a. Data presented through the courtesy of Robert Schutz of the Northern California Lobby for Peace and Thomas Tissue, graduate assistant in sociology.
b. Only responses by Protestants are presented—N = 26 Pro-Birch, N = 193 Anti-Birch.

Supporters of the Birch Society were less willing to grant civil liberties to Communists, atheists, and pacifists than those unfavorable to the organization; they were also less likely to feel that search warrants should be required of police entering a house, more likely to favor censorship of "crime comic books," and more likely to deny the right of public meetings to those opposing "our form of government." However, it is important to note that degree of education tended to have a much greater effect on attitude than did opinion of the Birch Society. For example, college-educated Birch *supporters* were more inclined to allow Communists to speak in their community than were Birch *opponents* who had not attended college (38 per cent versus 28 per cent). Supporters of the Society also exhibit more prejudice toward Negroes and Mexicans, although they do not register a significantly higher degree of anti-Semitism than the population at large. In all likelihood, more refined and comprehensive analysis of various sorts of ethnic and religious prejudice will be necessary before definitive conclusions may be reached regarding the relationship, or relationships, of these phenomena to current forms of right-wing extremism.

Thus far, I have omitted any discussion of the fact that the Birch Society is much stronger in Southern than in Northern California. In fact, the data from the California Poll survey discussed here and a later one completed in May, 1962 (too late to be analyzed and reported in detail here) indicate that California support for the Society is largely a phenomenon of the south. It has even less backing in Northern California than in most other sections of the country.

The explanation for the variations between the two sections would seem to lie largely in certain differences in their community structure. Northern California, centered around San Francisco, is the old, established part of the State. It was the original dominant center of population. Los Angeles and Southern California have emerged as major population centers only since World War I, and their really rapid mass growth occurred after 1940. Although Northern California has continued to increase in population, its major center, San Francisco, has grown little for many decades. There are many old families in the Bay Area who represent four and five generations of wealth, the descendants of those who made their money in mining, commerce, or railroads in the first decades after statehood, from 1850–80. Wealth in Los Angeles, on the other hand, is almost exclusively *nouveaux riches*, and the well-to-do there possess the attitudes toward politics and economics characteristic of this stratum. They are more likely to back the rightist groups that oppose the welfare state, the income tax, and trade unions, and, lacking political and cultural sophistication, are more prone to accept conspiracy interpretations of the strength behind liberal or welfare measures. There is little that is stabilized or institutionalized in Southern California. New, rapidly expanding centers of population lack a traditional leadership structure accustomed to the responsibilities of running community institutions and supportive of the rights of various groups to share in community decisions and authority. Ethnic and racial tensions are high in the south, and whereas in the north community leaders co-operate to repress any potential conflict, in the south there is little co-operation to ease such tensions.

Some evidence for the hypothesis that the strength of the Birch Society in Southern California (and in Arizona, Texas, and Florida, as well) is related to the tensions of population growth and community integration may be found in the second (May) California Poll. This survey inquired among those not native to the state as to when they moved to California. When respondents are divided between those who have been in the state more, or less, than 15 years, the data indicate that a larger proportion of the supporters of the Society (39 per cent) are among those who migrated to the state since World War II than is true among opponents (29 per cent). Unfortunately, there are no available data that bear directly on the political effects of social mobility; that is, the extent to which the experience of a change in socio-economic position, up or down the social hierarchy, is related to these political issues. The California Poll data do clearly suggest, however, that respondents whose educational and occupational attainments are not congruent—e.g., manual workers who went to college, or those in high-status positions with little education—are more likely to be pro-Birch than others within their strata whose statuses on these two stratification dimensions are roughly similar. These findings (based unfortunately on far too few cases of Birch supporters to be significant) are in line with the assumption that social mobility and/or status discrepancies predispose those involved in such experiences to accept extremist forms of politics.

The support the John Birch Society has received is seemingly somewhat different from the radical-rightist movement discussed earlier. As compared to them, it has drawn more heavily from ideological conservatives, those committed to the Republican Party, and, within the ranks of the Republicans, from among the more well-to-do and better educated.[7] Twenty-two per cent of high economic level, college-educated Republicans in the California Poll were favorable to the Birchers, as compared with 6 per cent in the sample as a whole.[8] As a group advocating economic conservatism, the Society naturally has little appeal for the economically deprived. It is difficult to see a movement with so little popular appeal— and with so conspiratorial a view of the American political process— making headway among the general population. But the considerable progress it has made among well-to-do Republicans who can afford to support their political convictions financially may mean that the Birch Society will be able to maintain the impression of a powerful mass-supported group for some time to come.[9]

NOTES

1. The wording of the question in the two surveys was similar but not identical, since the California Poll item read: "Have you heard anything about a political group called the John Birch Society?" And the Gallup query did not include the word "political."

2. It should be noted, however, that this does not mean that Californians are more in favor of the Birch Society than those in other parts of the country. Actually, among those with opinions, there are proportionately more pro-Birchers in the Midwest and in the South than in the Far West.

3. The same pattern occurs in the national Gallup data.

4. The questionnaires were left at the homes of those chosen in the sample, to be filled out by the respondent and picked up the following day.

5. The survey indicated that Bay Area Birch supporters are more likely to be Republicans than Democrats, college-educated rather than less schooled,

and white Christians rather than members of racial or religious minorities. Thus, of the white, Christian, college-trained Republicans in the sample, 16 per cent reported themselves generally favorable to the Birchers. No Jews or Orientals and only 4 per cent of the Negroes queried were pro-Birch.

6. Only white Christians were included in these comparisons, since the findings would presumably have been distorted by the inclusion of the minorities in ratings of their own groups.

7. Stories reported in the California press concerning internal conflicts within the Republican Party and the attitudes of wealthy Republicans toward contributing to Nixon's campaign suggest that the Party is troubled by the fact that support for the Birch Society is much greater among Party activists and wealthy contributors than among the Republican electorate. Recent evidence from analysis of national data indicates that local Republican leaders around the country tend to be considerably more conservative than the rank and file of the G.O.P. See Herbert McClosky, Paul J. Hoffman, and Rosemary O'Hara, "Issue Conflict and Consensus Among Party Leaders and Followers," *American Political Science Review*, 54 (1960), pp. 406–27; see, especially, pp. 422–24.

8. Similar conclusions concerning differences between the support of McCarthy and of the Birch Society drawn from survey data have recently been suggested in a report of a comparative study of mail attacking Senatorial critics of the radical right (Senator Fulbright for his opposition to McCarthy and Senator Kuchel for his attacks on the Birch Society). The report states that "only 15 per cent of the McCarthyite mail could—charitably, at best—be described as reasonable in tone, substance, or literacy." However, the "Birch mail is much more moderate in tone than McCarthy mail, even though it may be as extremist in objective. It is better written and better reasoned. . . . The great bulk of the mail came from people who acknowledge membership in the Birch Society or from sympathizers. . . . Many of the writers seem genuinely concerned over the rise of Communism. . . . But many of them seem more aroused over social-welfare legislation, income taxes, and foreign aid than they are over Communism." (See Herman Edelsberg, "Birchites Make Polite Pen Pals," *The A. D. L. Bulletin*, April, 1962, pp. 7–8.)

Presumably, the differences in style and tone of the letters reflected the variation in the class and educational levels of the supporters of both tendencies.

9. Various journalistic accounts indicate that the Birch Society includes among its members the heads of a number of medium-size corporations, such as independent oil companies, and manufacturing concerns. such men also supported McCarthy, and they are often willing to back up their antagonism to "creeping Socialism" with heavy contributions.

BRUNO BETTELHEIM AND MORRIS JANOWITZ

Trends in Prejudice

SOCIAL SCIENTISTS are hard pressed when they are called upon to describe and analyze, on the basis of their objective research data, how social change fashions and refashions human attitudes. In the past 15 years, the United States has developed further as an advanced industrial society. The trends of advanced industrialization are generally considered to imply social change in the direction of less prejudice because of three sets of variables: higher levels of education, growth of middle-income occupations and professions, and increased urbanization. Even if prejudice was found to have declined during this period, one must raise the question whether the trend was the consequence of these three factors or other ones. For example, it is not easy to separate internal social change from developments in the world arena.

We assumed in our original study that "progress" in industrial development does not automatically carry with it "progress" toward tolerance. We question, therefore, the frame of reference implicit in Samuel Stouffer's comprehensive study of *Communism, Conformity, and Civil Liberties*.[1] He found young age, more education, higher socioeconomic position, and urban residence positively associated with a tolerance of political nonconformity. Thus, he saw contemporary trends in social change as resulting in higher levels of tolerant attitudes. He emphasized that "great social, economic and technological forces are working on the side of exposing even larger proportions of our population to the idea that 'people are different from me, with different systems of values, and they can be good people.' "[2] Clearly, people's attitudes toward political nonconformity are different from their attitudes toward minority groups. Yet his analysis included both, and he saw these social trends as also weakening ethnic prejudice.

Reprinted from *Social Change and Prejudice* (1964), pp. 3–24, by permission of the authors and the publisher. (Copyright, 1964, by Free Press, New York.)

By contrast, we see two aspects of the problem: one of tracing the consequences of those social trends that work to reduce ethnic hostility, and the other of probing their actual and potential countereffects. Thus, our basic orientation is that in an advanced industrial society where individualistic values predominate, those sociological variables that tend to weaken ethnic hostility have some limits and may even generate countertrends.[3] These same advances in industrialization may also create new societal stresses and personal disruptions. For example, even during a period of high prosperity and relative economic growth, some persons experience downward social mobility—the status of sons becomes lower than their fathers'. And such downward social mobility seems to affect as much as 20 per cent of the male population.[4] Yet downward mobility is but one of the characteristics of an advanced industrialized society which we assume to be a source of ethnic intolerance, as against those sociological trends toward greater tolerance.

Decline in Prejudice

THE JEWS

What, then, during these 15 years have been the long-term national shifts in attitude toward Jews and Negroes? Despite the proliferation of national attitude surveys, no comprehensive and systematic body of trend data has been collected over these years. Investigations have been episodic and specialized. With the notable exception of survey findings by the Division of Scientific Research of the American Jewish Committee and the more limited efforts of the National Opinion Research Center, there has been too little emphasis on the repeated use of standardized questions over time to chart contemporary social history.[5] Social scientists engaged in survey research have not assumed the responsibility for writing current social history by means of systematic trend reporting. Nevertheless, there are convincing data to support the proposition that since 1945, for the nation as a whole, there has been a decline in the "average" or over-all level of anti-Jewish and anti-Negro attitudes. But it cannot be asserted there has been a similar marked decline in the percentage of persons with "hard-core" extremist attitudes toward these minorities. The available data from national samples are by far more adequate for charting shifts in the more "normal" levels of mild intolerance toward Jews than for measuring the concentration of intense anti-Semitic attitudes.

While the 15-year period has seen a long-term decline in prejudice toward Jews, much of the change occurred as a sharp shift after World War II, namely, during 1946–1950. Evidence of this shift appears in

Table 1. It shows responses collected for the Division of Scientific Research of the American Jewish Committee from comparable national samples between 1940 and 1959 to the question: "Have you heard any criticism or talk against the Jews in the last six months?" Although the question has defects as a probe of anti-Semitic attitudes, it is useful because it was repeated in standardized fashion since 1940. Apparently it was designed as a projective question. But even if it reflects an objective shift in public and private discussion about Jews rather than a change in personal feelings of hostility, the two are probably manifestly linked. Despite limitations of the measure, the shift from roughly 50 per cent to 12 per cent "yes" is still very pronounced and striking.

If it is argued that this downward trend is related to basic changes in the social structure of an advanced industrial nation state, it is still necessary to observe and explain the short-term shifts. The body of data underlines that anti-Semitic attitudes have a volatility that is touched off by political and economic events. First, the period of 1940 to 1946 revealed a definite increase in anti-Semitic attitudes that might be ascribed to the tensions of the war and to dislocations after the war. Despite the fact that we were at war with a nation that persecuted Jews, there is reason to believe that anti-Semitic attitudes were strengthened among those elements which believed that the Jews were a major cause of World War II. Second, the most dramatic short-term shift came during the years 1946–1950. The marked decline in "yes" responses during those years cannot be ascribed to changes in technical research methods, although these were at work, since a different field agency collected the data. The same sharp drop around 1950 is also documented by national sample responses to a question designed to measure more extremist attitudes, namely, what groups in this country were considered a "threat to America?" (Table 2.) The frequency of the response "yes, the Jews," was 19 per cent in 1945, 18 per cent in 1946, and 5 per cent in 1950. This

Table 1—"Have You Heard Any Criticism or Talk Against the Jews in the Last Six Months?"[a]

NATIONAL SAMPLES: 1940–1959[b]
(Percentage)

	1940	1942	1944	1946	1950	1953	1955	1956	1957	1959
Yes	46	52	60	64	24	20	13	11	16	12
No	52	44	37	34	75	80	87	89	84	88
No opinion	2	4	3	2	1	—	—	—	—	—
Total	100	100	100	100	100	100	100	100	100	100
Number	(3,101)	(2,637)	(2,296)	(1,337)	(1,203)	(1,291)	(1,270)	(1,286)	(1,279)	(1,470)

a. Based on samples of total white Christian population plus Negroes. Data supplied by Dr. Marshall Sklare, Division of Scientific Research, American Jewish Committee, New York City.

b. Studies for the 1940–1946 period were conducted by Opinion Research Corporation, Princeton, New Jersey; for the 1950–1957 period, by National Opinion Research Center, University of Chicago; the 1959 study was by Gallup Organization, Inc.

short-term shift may well have been influenced by the exposure of Nazi genocide practices. Another possible explanation was the consequences of the "cold war" and the rise of the Soviet Union as an object that drained off hostility. On the domestic front, the Jews dropped out of a

Table 2—Jews as a "Threat to America"[a]

NATIONAL SAMPLES: 1945–1950[b]
(Percentage)

	1945	1946	1950
Yes	19	18	5
Number	(2,500)	(1,300)	(1,250)

[a] "In your opinion are there any religious, nationality, or racial groups in this country that are a threat to America?"

[b] 1945 and 1946 data collected by Opinion Research Corporation; 1950 data by National Opinion Research Center.

public prominence associated with World War II. This was also the period of the establishment of Israel, and the image of the fighting Israeli Army may well have weakened anti-Semitic attitudes in the United States. Third, the downward trend continues after 1950, with a short-term rise in 1957, which might be linked to the economic recession.

Long-term data on the decline in prejudice toward Jews are also found in three time samplings of college students by Emory S. Bogardus. Using his social distance scale, he found no difference in attitudes during the 20-year period 1926–1946. But in 1956, he found a decline in feelings of social distance from the Jews, similar to the postwar decline of prejudice shown in the data above.[6]

Data on shifts in the percentage of "hard-core" anti-Semites during this period are not fully adequate. In the *Dynamics of Prejudice,* four attitude patterns were identified for anti-Jewish and anti-Negro attitudes: tolerant, stereotyped, outspoken, and intensely prejudiced.[7] "Intensely anti-Semitic" were those persons holding an elaborate range of negative stereotypes and spontaneously recommending strong restrictive action against Jews. As of 1945, the conclusion drawn from 20 national and specialized polls was that not more than 10 per cent of the adult population could be classified as intensely anti-Semitic. More specifically, the well-known *Fortune Survey* of 1946 revealed that 9 per cent of the nation's population had strongly anti-Semitic attitudes. The conclusion was based on the percentage who spontaneously named the Jews either as "a group harmful to the country unless curbed" or who designated Jews as "people trying to get ahead at the expense of people like yourself." (There was no mention of Jews in the questions by the interviewer.)

Unfortunately the type of question used in Table 2 has not been

94

used in national polls in recent years. However, in the 1950's the spontaneous remarks that Communists are most likely to be Jews became a useful measure of intense anti-Semitism, though with an element of ambiguity. One cannot overlook the fact that among a very small group of sophisticated persons, the high incidence of Jews among the Communist party would be taken for granted as a political and social fact. But this group is probably too small to influence national opinion poll results. Therefore, the general question of which groups are likely to be Communists appears to tap intense prejudice among the population at large. In 1950, a national sample was asked the direct question: "In this country do you think any of the people listed here are more likely to be Communist than others?" Eleven per cent named "the Jews" from the designated list.[8] In 1954, when the question was put in indirect form without specific reference to the Jews, "What kind of people in America are most likely to be Communists?" only 5 per cent of a national cross section said that Jews were most likely to be Communists.[9] But the difference between the two sets of responses could in large measure be attributed to the different form of the question and thus it is impossible to infer any actual decline of extremist anti-Semitic attitudes.

Have there been any significant changes in the stereotypes held about Jews, as well as in the level of hostility? Among the original sample, the four most frequent groups of stereotypes were: (a) they are clannish, they help one another; (b) they have the money; (c) they control everything, they are trying to get power; and (d) they use underhanded business methods.[10] More contemporary patterns of stereotypes were revealed in the 1957 and 1959 national surveys by those who volunteered what criticism they had heard of the Jews within the last six months. The striking change was that the "clannish" stereotype had become very infrequent, while the other three stereotypes persisted with the same order of frequency. A comparison of stereotypes among Princeton undergraduates of 1932 and 1949 reveals that there was a "fading of highly negative group stereotypes."[11]

Additional evidence of changing stereotypes comes from direct questions in the 1957 and 1959 national samplings. No pronounced shifts were expected in a two-year period, yet these data show that stereotypes fluctuate. Direct questions probed the stereotypes that Jews spoil neighborhoods and that Jewish businessmen are so shrewd and "tricky" that other people do not have a fair chance in competition. (Table 3.) In 1959, there was much more belief that Jewish businessmen are shrewd and "tricky" than that Jews spoil neighborhoods (30 per cent agreed strongly about business, in contrast to only 11 per cent about neighborhoods). But while both stereotypes weakened to a statistically significant degree in the short two-year period, the pattern of change differed. In the case of Jews spoiling neighborhoods, the shift was in the more tolerant direction among all attitude groups. There was an increase among those who disagreed with the stereotype and a decrease among those who agreed with it. In the case of the stereotypes about Jewish businessmen, there was a drop in the percentage of those who agreed, but no corresponding rise among those who disagreed. The shift away from acceptance of the stereotype merely produced more uncertain responses. In other words, the decline in the stereotype about neighborhoods was more pronounced than the one about Jewish businessmen.

Stereotypes about the behavior of the Jews—namely, in spoiling neighborhoods—seem much more likely to weaken under the impact of direct contact than do those involving group characteristics that are illusive and hard to disprove—namely, that Jewish businessmen are shrewd and "tricky." Another plausible explanation of these shifts (if in fact the shifts are significant) is that Jews have become more integrated into residential communities and voluntary associations. And during the same period, the Negro was becoming more of a "threat" to many prejudiced

Table 3—Stereotypes About Jews: Housing and Business

NATIONAL SAMPLES: 1957–1959[a]

(Percentage)

	1957	1959
Jews Spoil Neighborhoods[b]		
Strongly agree	7	2
Agree	12	9
Uncertain	25	26
Disagree	44	46
Strongly disagree	12	17
Total	100	100
Number	(1,058)	(1,294)
Jewish Businessmen Are Shrewd and Tricky[c]		
Strongly agree	12	6
Agree	25	24
Uncertain	15	22
Disagree	38	38
Strongly disagree	10	10
Total	100	100
Number	(1,058)	(1,294)

a. Sample of Christian white persons. Data collected by Gallup Organization, Inc.
b. "The trouble with letting Jews into a nice neighborhood is that sooner or later they spoil it for other people."
c. "The trouble with Jewish businessmen is that they are so shrewd and tricky that other people do not have a fair chance in competition."

persons by pressing for residential movement into white areas. This pressure may well have been felt as more of a threat, so that resentment toward Jews moving into non-Jewish neighborhoods weakened. Jewish neighbors, previously shunned, may now appear as relatively acceptable as compared with Negro neighbors. Since stereotypes are to some degree based on social reality, there has also been a parallel corroding of the stereotyped symbol of the "clannish Jews" living in a private world of high social solidarity—enforced though it may be by the non-Jewish world. Such an explanation flows from the assumption that those stereotypes which are easiest to check against direct experience are also most likely to change as the intensity of prejudice declines. Conversely, the more remote stereotypes, such as "they control everything" and "they are trying to get power," would be expected to, and in fact do, persist most strongly.

THE NEGROES

The pattern of change in "typical" attitudes toward the American Negro can be inferred from data collected by the National Opinion Research Center of the University of Chicago in its periodic national samplings since 1942. At four intervals, comparable national samples, excluding Negroes, were asked, "In general, do you think Negroes are as intelligent as white people—that is, can they learn things just as well if they are given the same education and training?" The results summarize a basic transformation in attitudes toward the Negro.[12] (Table 4). For the total white population in the United States, attitudes have risen from 42 per cent who answered "yes" in 1942 to 77 per cent in 1956. A change of attitude among Southern whites on this question is equally marked during the same period, shifting from 21 per cent to 59 per cent answering "yes."

Residential and school integration became focal points for measuring changing attitudes about discrimination. In 1942, two-thirds of the popu-

Table 4—Changing Attitudes Toward Negroes
NATIONAL SAMPLES: 1942–1956

	NORTHERN WHITE POPULATION	SOUTHERN WHITE POPULATION	TOTAL U.S. WHITE POPULATION
	(Percentage) "Yes, Negroes Are as Intelligent as Whites"[a]		
1942	48	20	42
1944	47	28	44
1946	60	33	53
1956	82	59	77

a. "In general, do you think Negroes are as intelligent as white people—that is, can they learn things just as well if they are given the same education and training?" Data collected by the National Opinion Research Center.

lation, as measured by national sampling, objected to the idea of living in the same block with a Negro; but by 1956, a majority declared that they would not object.[13] In 1942, fewer than one-third of the respondents in the nation favored school integration; by 1956 almost half endorsed the idea. This shift took place in both the North and the South. In the North, support for school integration had risen among white people from 41 per cent in 1942 to 61 per cent in 1956. In the South in 1942, only 2 per cent of the white people favored school integration; by 1956, the figure had increased to 14 per cent.

Even after 1956, as "massive" resistance to school integration temporarily developed, the national trend toward tolerant responses on this item continued, though perhaps at a slower pace. By 1959 the over-all national level expressing support for integration stood at 56 per cent as compared with just under half in 1956.[14] This slight upward trend was at work in both the North and the South. But what changes took place in the South were in the "Border States" as compared with the "Deep South." Breakdowns within the South reveal 4 per cent of the Deep South approving school integration and 23 per cent in the Border South.

Although adequate data are lacking, it is necessary to raise the question whether attitude change concerning school integration is connected with the growth of suburban, private, and parochial schools. With the growth of these school systems it may well be that more white parents are willing to express approval of integrated schools because there is little or no likelihood that their children would attend such schools.

Trends in response to "social distance" questions from national samples highlight the intensity and persistence of prejudice toward the Negro even during this period of social change. From 1948 to 1958, whatever the changes that took place in attitudes toward racial intermarriage, they hardly produced extensive tolerance. In answer to the blunt question, "Do you approve or disapprove of marriage between white and colored people," 4 per cent approved as of 1958 and most of the approval was among college graduates. By contrast, there was the marked decline in prejudice against Negroes as neighbors as measured by attitudes expressed in surveys. In 1942, two-thirds of the population objected to the idea of living in the same block with a Negro. But by 1956 a majority did not object, and in 1958, 56 per cent answered "no" to the question, "If colored people came to live next door would you move?"[15] In his study of college students, Bogardus found that between 1946 and 1956 "social distance" between these students and Negroes declined somewhat, as measured by his questionnaire tests.[16]

What, then, has changed and what remains stable in American attitudes toward the Negro during the last 15 years? Gunnar Myrdal coined the phrase the "American Dilemma" to emphasize the white man's involvement in race relations. In his comprehensive study of the position of the Negro in the United States before World War II, Myrdal stated that the majority's sense of conscience—its commitment to the creed of equality and dignity—created a powerful dilemma that was a constant source of pressure for social change. He believed that the "American Dilemma" operates with greater force among community and political leaders, but exists also as a moral norm for society at large. The greater the sense of a "dilemma," the more likely the person seems to be saying that the Negro is being treated unfairly.

How strong is this awareness of an "American Dilemma?" What changes have reshaped these attitudes since World War II? The question, "Do you think most Negroes in the United States are being treated fairly or unfairly?" supplies a crude but revealing index. (Table 5.)

Table 5—Changing Attitudes Toward Negroes
NATIONAL SAMPLES: 1944–1956[a]

	NORTHERN WHITE POPULATION	SOUTHERN WHITE POPULATION	TOTAL U.S. WHITE POPULATION
	(Percentage)		
	"Yes, most U.S. Negroes are treated fairly"[b]		
1944	62	77	66
1946	63	76	66
1956	63	79	69

a. Data collected by National Opinion Research Corporation.
b. "Do you think most Negroes in the United States are being treated fairly or unfairly?"

It is crude because it mobilizes defensive sentiments; it is revealing because on this score, United States attitudes have changed little over the years. As of 1944, 66 per cent of a national sample thought that the Negro was being treated fairly (or the "American Dilemma" was being felt by much less than a majority).[17] And as expected, the percentage answering "fairly" was greater in the South than in the North (77 per cent in the South, 62 per cent in the North).

Moreover, neither the greater transformation in attitudes toward Negroes nor the actual change in practices of the last 15 years has brought any measurable changes in this response pattern. In 1946, the national percentage remained at 66; by 1956, it had risen only to 69. The greater tendency of Southerners to say "fairly" persisted. In short, there was no increase of popular sensitivity to the "American Dilemma" even during this period of greater agitation for equality within the United States, and of a greater salience of race in international affairs. One plausible explanation is that the social, economic, and political progress of the Negro during this period has served to prevent any increase in a sense of moral dilemma.

Attitude patterns toward the United States Supreme Court decision that "racial segregation in the public schools is illegal" also indicate the extent to which there has been a resistance to attitude change, particularly in the South, in the face of legal and administrative changes. In 1954, 24 per cent of the Southern population approved of the decision, and by 1961, the percentage remained at the same level. The highest it had reached was 27 per cent in 1957. During the same period for the nation as a whole, the per cent rise was from 54 per cent in 1954 to 62 per cent in 1961.

Age, Education, and Socioeconomic Status

To what extent are these recent trends in prejudice, as revealed in national opinion surveys, related to basic changes in the social structure during the last 15 years? To explore this question, the social changes produced by advanced industrialism can be crudely highlighted by the key variables of age, education, and socioeconomic status. If the data were adequate, we could assess how important these variables, singly and in combination, may have been in accounting for the trend toward less prejudice. Unfortunately, the available data are hardly adequate for this purpose, but they do offer some revealing findings.

In the original study we assumed—and the data supported the conclusion—that particular sociological variables such as age, education and socioeconomic status *per se* would not be very powerful in accounting for patterns of ethnic hostility; a more dynamic and interactive analysis would. Fifteen years later Melvin Tumin, in his review study of empirical work on American anti-Semitism, comes to the same conclusion.[18] "We are led first to the realization that no single sociological characteristic will suffice to give adequate understanding or prediction of where we will encounter the greatest amount and intensity of anti-Semitism. Not age, nor income, nor education, nor region, nor any other (sociological factor) by itself, is adequate. Nor can valid statements be made about the impact of various combinations of these characteristics, unless we specify the situational context."

Nevertheless, while the impact of the variables is likely to be complex and interactive, each of the key variables permits a general trend hypothesis about its effect on prejudice. First, younger persons are likely to be less prejudiced than older persons; second, better educated persons are likely to be less prejudiced than less well-educated persons; and third, higher socioeconomic status is likely to be associated with less prejudice than is lower status.[19] To what extent does new research evidence support or throw doubt on these general hypothesis? Moreover, to what extent have changes in the age, education, and socioeconomic structure of American society contributed to shifts in prejudice patterns during the last 15 years? We have already seen that an important amount of the shift in attitude toward Jews took place in a short time span after the close of the war, and must therefore be linked to specific events—both domestic and international. On the other hand, the struggle for desegregation in the South after 1956 seems to have slowed but not stopped the trend toward greater tolerance toward Negroes. Despite these short-term shifts, we still need to explore the underlying shifts in social structure that might account for the longer-term trends.

AGE

A fundamental rationale for the hypothesis that younger persons are less prejudiced than older persons lies in the conflict between the generations.[20] The older generation is the carrier of basic values and norms in society, while the younger generation is being socialized into accepting these values. Invariably there is tension and struggle between the generations and this is greater in an advanced industrialized society as the standards of the older generation are more quickly made obsolete by the tempo of social change. Attitudes toward minority groups become one aspect of this tension, just as do styles of clothing and standards of morality. In the search for identity, the younger age groups tend to assert their independence from the older groups, and greater tolerance toward ethnic groups is a frequent expression of this assertion. Thus, where the general trend in society is toward tolerance, the younger age groups are apt to be even more tolerant. In this sense, age is an index to the broader processes of social change. That is, the hypothesis that younger persons are less prejudiced than older persons is more than just a symptom of the conflict of generations. All of the changes of a more advanced industrialized society, such as in the United States, that might result in a decline in prejudice are likely to affect younger persons most. Numerous studies of specialized samples have found this relation between age and attitudes toward minority groups. There are historical and political conditions that have produced a reversal of this trend, however, as for example, in Germany where younger age groups were more Nazi than older groups.

This pattern of tolerance is also at work for political attitudes as well. Thus, Samuel Stouffer in his extensive national sample study of tolerance for political nonconformity found that young people were clearly more tolerant than older people. The concentration of "more tolerant" responses in the age group twenty-one to twenty-nine was 47 per cent, and it dropped systematically with age. Those persons sixty years and over revealed only 18 per cent in the tolerant category.[21]

In contrast to the findings on age grading, there is no adequate body of empirical data dealing with the life cycle of the individual and his attitudes toward minority groups. Is there any basis for speculating that as a person grows older his attitudes toward minority groups become less tolerant? It seems very plausible that they do. Impressionistic accounts of the political behavior of older people emphasize a rigidity of outlook and more extremistic demands. However, older people tend to focus on concrete economic issues and to show less concern with minority groups and the social order in general.

Given a link between age grading and prejudice, the basic question remains: To what extent can the decline in ethnic hostility during the last 15 years be explained by shifts in age composition among the population at large? Examination of the changes in gross age composition during this period, marked though they were compared with other periods in history, shows them to be unimportant factors in the trends in prejudice. The age structure is still relatively stable, decade by decade, and those changes that have occurred were in the age groupings under seventeen and over sixty-five. Neither one would explain the trend toward greater tolerance.[22]

The analysis of age structure and prejudice requires a more refined approach involving cohort analysis. Are the new cohorts of young people entering the adult population reducing the over-all level of prejudice because they are replacing the old cohorts above sixty years of age, who are dying off and who are more prejudiced than the middle and younger cohorts? We have no adequate cohort data but we presume that they are. Although such a cohort analysis would be important, it would not explain the process of attitude change. In particular, it remains to be shown whether growing older tends to produce a rigidity of attitudes toward minority groups, even during a period of greater tolerance.

The relationship between age and tolerance is complicated by the results of education. Young persons are more likely to be better educated and to have an education compatible with ethnic tolerance. In fact, one could argue that the general hypothesis of younger persons being more tolerant rests to some degree on the fact that the younger are better educated. That makes education the second basic variable in assessing trends toward greater tolerance.

EDUCATION

Education correlates with a wide variety of social behavior, from consumer behavior to political attitudes. But in analyzing the consequences of education and an ever rising level of attainment, we must distinguish between education in its "intellectual" and moral value content, and education as a precondition for occupational mobility. However, the rationale for the hypothesis that better educated persons are likely to be less prejudiced does not rest solely on the argument that education is an index to socioeconomic position. Education should be

102

positively correlated with tolerance both because of what is socially experienced during the educational process and because of the selective processes that determine who will receive advanced schooling. It can be assumed that the effects of education will be different for different social groups. For example, the higher the socioeconomic position a person starts from, the less effect education will have on intolerant attitudes, because for such persons family and social background have already operated to influence the extent of their tolerant attitudes. But education in a political democracy is designed *per se* to strengthen one's personal controls and to broaden one's understanding of social reality (in Karl Mannheim's term "substantive rationality"). And both of these social processes are assumed to weaken ethnic prejudice.

The very fact that a significant portion of college graduates still hold stereotypes and support discrimination reflects the limits of the educational system in modifying attitudes. Yet on the basis of some 25 national sample surveys since 1945, the positive effect seems to be real, not spurious. The lower levels of prejudice among the better educated seem to involve the social experience of education specifically and not merely the sociological origins of the educated. Throughout most of the United States outside of the South, the content of education involves some indoctrination in a tolerant outlook toward minorities. Thus, to speak of the impact of education involves more than the effort to increase intellectual skills and aptitudes; it involves also exposure to a specific liberal content. In parts of the South where the education system does not contain such a content, the effects of education would be different.

However, the impact of education is not a simple process. The available data underscore areas in which education operates to reduce prejudice. But the same body of data highlight the persistence of prejudice among the educated, as well as some instability of attitudes. These data are relevant in accounting for the persistence of a "hard core" of very prejudiced persons.

In his careful review of the effects of schooling on prejudice, Charles H. Stember concludes that the better educated are: (*a*) less likely to hold traditional stereotypes about Jews and Negroes, (*b*) less likely to favor discriminatory policies, and (*c*) less apt to reject casual contacts with minority group members.[23] Education seems to reduce a provincial outlook and to weaken primitive misconceptions. On the other hand, the more educated, according to Stember, are also: (*a*) more likely to hold highly charged and derogatory stereotypes, (*b*) more likely to favor informal discrimination in some areas of behavior, and (*c*) more apt to reject intimate contacts with minority groups.

Thus, for example, the better educated are more prone to accept the stereotypes that Jews (*a*) are loud, arrogant and have bad manners, (*b*) are shady and unscrupulous, and (*c*) have too much business power.

Moreover, the question administered in 1952: "In this country do you think any of the people listed here are more likely to be Communists than others?" revealed that a higher concentration among the college graduates than among those with only grammar school education answered "Jews" (17 per cent for college education; 10 per cent for grammar school). Evidence that this is not merely a politically sophisticated response comes from the findings that the better educated are also more likely to perceive Jews as a "threat to the country" and as unwilling to serve in the armed forces.

The limits of social acceptance often are sharply drawn by better educated people. Covert discrimination continues to be acceptable and the desire to keep minorities at some social distance remains. These findings need to be interpreted in the light of available data which reveal that college-educated persons (and thus persons of higher socioeconomic status) have more actual contact with Jews than do less educated persons. Moreover, the better educated show no greater concern with the problem of discrimination than others, on the basis of national sample studies. In particular, better educated persons show marked concern about sending their children to school with Negroes, presumably because the educational standards are assumed to be lower in such schools. There is an important regional difference in this finding. In the South, Melvin Tumin found that among his sample in Guilford County, North Carolina, the best educated were the most prone to accept integration in the public schools.[24]

The data on education and stereotypes confirm the theory and findings of the *Dynamics of Prejudice*. Since stereotypes are rooted in social and psychological needs, schooling alone does not consistently bring a rejection of stereotypes. The better educated are more likely to reject certain kinds of stereotypes, but new ones emerge and old images persist. Apparently, the attitudes of the educated are more liable to change under the impact of particular events. The less educated seem more stable in their attitudes. Clearly, these data indicate the persistence of prejudice despite the rising United States level of education.

In recent years, there has been, of course, swift progress in raising the educational level of the United States. During the period 1940–1957, the proportion of the population classified as functional illiterates (less than five years of elementary school) decreased by one-third. Shortly before 1940, the average citizen was a graduate of elementary school. By about 1965, the average citizen will be a high school graduate. These dramatic changes are important ingredients in the over-all decline in prejudice, although the pattern of decline is different toward Jews than toward Negroes. Each increase in education seems to be linked to less prejudice; but in the case of anti-Negro attitudes there seems to be a threshold: College-level education is necessary before attitudes toward Negroes change significantly.

Findings on education must be assessed in the light of a crucial observation based on repeated surveys: Education as a separate factor has less consequences at the upper social levels. Within the upper socio-economic groups, educational differences make less of a difference in prejudice (toward both Negroes and Jews) than at the lower levels. Again education seems to have built-in limitations as an agent of social change for reducing prejudice; those who get the most education have been and are the least likely to be influenced by it *per se*. If the trend toward a "middle class" society continues, it may be that the future effects of expanding education will not be as powerful as in the recent past. Or, to put it differently, the specific content of education and its personal impact as opposed to amount of it will grow in importance.

We have spoken here of the consequences of education. However, both access to education and the effects of education depend on a person's socioeconomic status.

SOCIOECONOMIC STATUS

A number of sociological arguments would lead one to anticipate that persons of middle and upper socioeconomic status would be less prejudiced than those of lower status. It can be argued that higher social position may make for greater personal security and therefore the person may feel less threatened by out-groups. Higher social position, like education, also serves to broaden personal perspectives and in turn to reduce prejudice. In the same vein, upper status groups have a greater stake in the existing social arrangements and are less likely to hold extremist attitudes, including those toward minority groups. The same reasoning can be extended to portions of the middle class, especially those in the new bureaucratic occupations. But it can be argued that there are other portions of the middle class vulnerable to economic competition and social change and therefore likely to be more exposed to factors increasing ethnic intolerance.

As a result, it is not possible to postulate simple and direct relations between social class and prejudice. Likewise, to explain the trends of the last 15 years, these differences make it necessary to reject a simple economic conflict model of prejudice, although economic pressures are clearly important. Specific ethnic and religious differences within the middle class, as well as within the lower class, strongly modify the class patterns of ethnic intolerance. Finally, it was originally assumed in the *Dynamics of Prejudice* that to locate a person in the over-all stratification system—as measured by his income or occupation—was only a first step.[25] We then had to investigate the dynamics of mobility by which a person reached his socioeconomic position.

National surveys reveal that for the population as a whole and for very broad socioeconomic groupings a limited association with very general forms of ethnic prejudice does emerge. The upper social groups are at least more inhibited in their expression of ethnic intolerance. But much more relevant is what can be learned by selecting a particular metropolitan community instead of a national sample. Within the metropolitan community the interplay of social stratification and ethnic prejudice can be seen more precisely. Important regional differences are ruled out—the South versus the other regions of the country. The differences between urban and rural areas are also controlled, for there is a gradual decrease in the level of ethnic intolerance as one goes from rural areas and small towns to cities under a million to cities over a million. The use of metropolitan community samples focuses more sharply on the realities of social stratification in what we now call the mass society.

Thus, it appears that within the metropolitan community, when occupation is the measure of socioeconomic status, the difference in levels of prejudice within the middle and working classes emerge. Data collected by the Detroit Area Study in 1957, for a representative sample of the adult population, allow for a breakdown of anti-Negro attitudes by heads of households. (Table 6.) In these data, the concentration

Table 6—Socioeconomic Status and Negro Prejudice

DETROIT METROPOLITAN AREA SAMPLE: 1957
(Percentage)

	Tolerant	Mildly Intolerant	Strongly Intolerant	Total Percentage	No.
Professional, managerial, and proprietors	32.6	53.3	14.1	100	(92)
Clerical, sales, and kindred	28.9	44.6	26.5	100	(83)
Craftsmen and foremen	31.7	50.0	18.3	100	(82)
Operatives, service, etc.	30.0	33.8	36.2	100	(80)
Number	(104)	(154)	(79)		(337)

of persons in the tolerant category remains relatively stable, and the shifts by socioeconomic status are in the strongly intolerant category. The top of the social structure—the professional and managerial group—displayed the lowest amount of strong intolerance, while the very bottom —the operatives and service, etc.—had the highest amount. There was, however, no straight line progression in the intolerant category as one moved down the hierarchy. While the professional and managerial category roughly represented the upper-middle stratum with less prejudice, the lower-middle stratum (clerical, sales, and kindred workers) revealed a markedly higher level. Crossing the white collar–blue collar line, the upper working class stratum (craftsmen and foremen) was more tolerant than the lower-middle class stratum and much like the top professional and managerial group. The lower working class group, the most intolerant, was more prejudiced than even the lower-middle class, which is often described impressionistically as being especially prone to extremist attitudes.[26] This pattern of ethnic prejudice in which the upper strata of both the middle and working classes are less prejudiced than the lower strata of the same classes runs parallel to the distribution of the authoritarian syndrome in representative national samples.[27]

In the metropolitan community, personal contacts between majority groups and minority groups are stratified. These contacts influence stereotypes and ethnic hostility. The Jewish minority is essentially a middle and upper class group, although a Jewish "proletariat" exists in the largest metropolitan centers. By contrast, Negroes in the urban centers are predominantly a lower and lower-middle class group. These patterns of contact help explain the higher incidence of certain stereotypes about the Jews among the better educated and upper socioeconomic status groups. Earlier, we pointed out an over-all decline in frequency of the stereotype that the Jews are "clannish" and stick together. This decline may well be linked to the greater social integration of the Jews into the metropolitan community, mainly through residence and membership in voluntary associations. Nevertheless, the "clannish" Jew is one of those select stereotypes more likely to be mentioned by upper status persons as compared with working class persons.[28] Middle class persons have most contact with Jews, and this is a case where contact does not necessarily result in weakening a stereotype. It is plausible that they are more observant of the ambiguities that result from the interplay of Jewish demands for social equality and the practice of social withdrawal into Jewish communal life. Therefore, while this stereotype decreases in the over-all measures, it reveals a greater incidence as one moves up the social structure.

A very similar reaction was found in the case of the "inferior intelligence" of Negroes. This again is one of the select stereotypes about Negroes that increases with higher socioeconomic status. Presumably, middle class persons have more chance to observe and judge the consequences of the Negro's lack of cultural preparation for higher education. For defensive reasons, middle class persons are then more prone than lower class persons to label the Negroes as inferior in intelligence. linked to changes in the social structure of an advanced industrial society; namely, changes in the age structure, higher levels of education, and a broadening of the middle strata. While the consequences of changes in the age structure are equivocal, the higher levels of education and the broadening of the middle strata have operated to weaken ethnic prejudice. But these variables, singly or in combination, cannot account for the modification of patterns of prejudice over the last 15 years. Changes in the structure of social controls, such as the law, political organization, and the mass media, must be brought into the analysis. More important for our analysis at this point is the conclusion that these basic sociological variables as they change under advanced industrialism do not automatically result in "progress," if by progress we mean the further reduction of ethnic prejudice. The consequences of these variables are complex, and we have observed limits on their impact, particularly in the case of education. Changes in the stratification system under advanced industrialism also reveal similar limitations, and even indicate countertrends when we examine—as we do in the next chapter—the consequences of social mobility.

NOTES

1. Samuel A. Stouffer, *Communism, Conformity, and Civil Liberties*, Garden City, N.Y., Doubleday and Co., 1955.
2. *Ibid.*, p. 220.
3. A similar position on "race relations" is argued by Everett C. Hughes and Helen M. Hughes, *Where People Meet*, New York, The Free Press of Glencoe, 1952.
4. Despite sociological interest in the question of social mobility in the United States, satisfactory data do not exist. The best estimates are derived from a study by the National Opinion Research Center, "Jobs and Occupations: A Popular Evaluation," *Opinion News*, September, 1947; and Richard Centers, "Occupational Mobility of Urban Occupational Strata," *American Sociological Review*, XIII, April, 1948, p. 198.
5. It must be recognized that standardized questions are only a partial approach to charting trends in ethnic prejudice. The meaning of standardized questions changes and new dimensions of prejudice emerge. On the basis of available evidence from a wide variety of studies, there is no reason to believe that these two limitations contributed in any significant degree to the over-all trend.
6. Emory S. Bogardus, "Racial Distance Changes in the United States During the Past 30 Years," *Sociology and Social Research*, XLIII, November, 1958, pp. 127–34. Similar findings on the relative stability of anti-Semitic attitudes until after World War II are contained in H. H. Remmers and W. F. Wood, "Changes in Attitudes Toward Germans, Japanese, Jews and Negroes," *School and Society*, LXV, June, 1947, pp. 484–87.
7. See *Dynamics of Prejudice*, New York, Harper and Bros., 1950, pp. 12–14.
8. Data collected by National Opinion Research Center, from a sample of 1,250 white Christians.
9. Data collected by American Institute of Public Opinion and National Opinion Research Center from a sample of 4,933 persons.
10. See *Dynamics of Prejudice, op. cit.*, pp. 32–47.

11. G. M. Gilbert, "Stereotype Persistence and Change Among College Students," *Journal of Abnormal and Social Psychology*, XLVI, April, 1951, pp. 245–54.

12. Herbert Hyman and Paul B. Sheatsley, "Attitudes Toward Desegregation," *Scientific American*, December, 1956, pp. 35–39.

13. *Ibid.*, p. 38.

14. American Jewish Committee Research Report, *The Nationwide Poll of 1959*, p. 5. Data collected by Gallup Organization, Inc., from 1,297 white Christians.

15. Data collected by American Institute of Public Opinion, from 1,650 whites.

16. Emory S. Bogardus, *op. cit.*, p. 131.

17. Hyman and Sheatsley, *op. cit.*, p. 39.

18. Melvin Tumin, *Inventory and Appraisal of Research on American Anti-Semitism*, New York, Freedom Books, 1961, p. 28.

19. Of course, in empirical studies of prejudice, more educated persons or those of high status may be more skillful in obscuring their prejudices.

20. The sample used in the *Dynamics of Prejudice* was not meant to be representative but rather to concentrate on the young age group. Nevertheless, it was possible to divide the sample into younger and older veterans; the general hypothesis held that the young were more tolerant.

21. Samuel A. Stouffer, *op. cit.*, p. 92.

22. During the 1950–1960 decade, the median age of the population declined for the first time since 1900; it dropped from 30.2 years in 1950 to 29.3 years in 1959. But the median is a poor measure of the changes in age composition. The important changes that have occurred are those in the age groupings under seventeen years and those over sixty-five years. While the total increase in population during the decade was 17.2 per cent, those under seventeen years and over sixty-five years grew at a much faster rate (fourteen to seventeen years, 30.7 per cent; sixty-five years and over, 26.1 per cent). Middle-age cohorts remained relatively stable or grew at a rate lower than the national rate.

23. Charles H. Stember, *Education and Attitude Change: The Effects of Schooling on Prejudice Against Minority Groups*, New York, Institute of Human Relations Press, 1961, pp. 168ff.

24. Melvin Tumin, *Desegregation: Resistance and Readiness*, Princeton, N.J., Princeton University Press, 1958, p. 193.

25. See *Dynamics of Prejudice, op. cit.*, pp. 57–61.

26. Stratification in the metropolitan community involves not only the occupational category but also differential risks of unemployment. The incidence of unemployment falls heaviest on the lower socioeconomic strata. The Detroit Metropolitan area during the 1950's was representative of the urban center where unemployment has persisted. The higher level of ethnic hostility expected among the unemployed, as compared with the employed labor force, was found present.

27. Morris Janowitz and Dwaine Marvick, "Authoritarianism and Political Behavior," *Public Opinion Quarterly*, XVII, September, 1953, pp. 185–201.

28. Based on data collected from 3,000 Christians by Ben Gaffin, *Catholic Digest Religious Study*, 1952.

PAUL F. LAZARSFELD, BERNARD BERELSON, AND HAZEL GAUDET

Time of Final Decision

ALL during an election campaign, people can make up their minds. Many traditional party voters, however, know far in advance of the campaign for whom they will vote. It might be possible now to forecast the party for which Southerners will vote in 1960, although the issue and candidates will not be known for fifteen years. Others decide during a particular term of office whether they will support the incumbent and his party at the next election. Many know in May, even before candidates are nominated, how they will vote in November.

Interviews with the panel permitted us to distinguish three kinds of voters classified according to the time when they made their *final vote decision*—the decision which they followed throughout the rest of the campaign and in the voting booth.

"MAY VOTERS"

These pre-campaign deciders knew in May, at our first interview, how they would vote, maintained their choice throughout the campaign, and actually voted for that choice in November. Their votes had been finally determined by May.

"JUNE-TO-AUGUST VOTERS"

These people settled upon a candidate during the convention period (our August interview was the first interview after both conventions), maintained their choice throughout the rest of the campaign, and actually voted for that choice in November. Their votes were finally determined in June, July or August.

Reprinted with minor editorial adaptations from *The People's Choice: How the Voter Makes Up His Mind in a Presidential Campaign* (1944), pp 52–61; 65–69, by permission of the authors and the publisher. (Copyright, 1948, by the Columbia University Press.)

These people did not definitely make up their minds until the last few months of the campaign, some of them not until Election Day itself. Their votes were finally determined only in September, October or November.

What were the significant differences among these groups of people? Why did some people make up their minds before the campaign began, others during the first months of the campaign, and still others not until the end of the campaign?

The analysis of this chapter develops two major factors influencing the time of final decision. First, the people whose decision was delayed had *less interest* in the election. Second, those who made their choice in the late days of the campaign were people subject to *more cross-pressures*. By "cross-pressures" we mean the conflicts and inconsistencies among the factors which influence vote decision. Some of these factors in the environment of the voter may influence him toward the Republicans while others may operate in favor of the Democrats. In other words, cross-pressures upon the voter drive him in opposite directions.

Interest and Time of Decision

The more interested people were in the election, the sooner they definitely decided how they would vote. Almost two-thirds of the voters with great interest had already made up their minds by May; but considerably less than half of the voters with less interest in the election had made up their minds by May. Only one-eighth of the greatly interested waited until the late period of the campaign before finally deciding how they would vote; twice as many of the less interested delayed their decision until that period.

The general tendency for late decision among the less interested held for both parties. But on each level of interest, the Democrats tended to decide later than the Republicans.

Certain other manifestations of interest also wane in the group whose decision is postponed until the later stages of a campaign. At one point respondents were asked whether they were "very anxious" to see their candidate elected, whether it was "not terribly important" although "I would like to see my candidate elected," or whether "it doesn't make much difference."

The particular persons who were "very anxious" to have their candidate win were those who decided on their vote early in the campaign. The same reasons which impelled them to choose a candidate early in the game and stick with him also served to make them quite concerned about his election. The people who were not particularly concerned about the outcome of the election were those who decided late in the campaign. They felt that nothing much was at stake and waited for happenstance or friends to make up their minds for them. As the campaign moved on, the respondents who answered "don't know" were also saying in effect "don't care."

The campaign managers were thus continuously faced with the task of propagandizing not only a steadily shrinking segment of the electorate but also a segment whose interest in and concern with the election also steadily shrank. By the end of the campaign, the managers were exerting their greatest efforts to catch the few votes of the least interested and least involved persons.

Cross-Pressures and Time of Decision

We have indicated that there were a number of factors differentiating Republican and Democratic voters. Each of these factors could be considered a "pressure" upon final vote decision. We found the Protestant vote allied to the Republicans and the Catholic vote more strongly Democratic. We found that individuals on the higher socio-economic status levels tended to vote Republican and their poorer neighbors to vote Democratic. In other words, a vote decision can be considered the net effect of a variety of pressures.

Now what if these individual factors work in opposite directions? Suppose an individual is *both* prosperous and Catholic? How will he make up his mind? Or suppose he belongs to the Protestant faith and lives in a poor section of the community? Which of the conflicting influences will win out? People who are subject to contradictory and opposing influences of this kind are said to be under cross-pressures.

The more evenly balanced these opposing pressures were, the longer the voter delayed in making up his mind. We shall use six instances of cross-pressures to show their effect in delaying the time of decision. The first three cases involve personal characteristics of the voter; the next two, relationships between the voter and other people around him; and the last, the voter's basic political attitudes.

1. RELIGION AND SOCIOECONOMIC STATUS LEVEL

The first cross-pressure we have already mentioned. Protestants on lower socio-economic status levels (C− & D) and Catholics on upper socio-economic status levels (A, B, & C+) were subject to this cross-pressure.

2. OCCUPATION AND IDENTIFICATION

In the November interview respondents were asked with what groups in the community they identified themselves—big business, small business, labor, etc. While most people identified themselves with the class to which they would have been assigned by occupation, some semi-skilled and un-skilled workers tended to think of themselves as belonging with the business class and a few white-collar people thought of themselves as belonging with labor. Since the business group ordinarily supported one party and the labor group the other, a cross-pressure was set up between the voter's objective occupation and his subjective identification.

3. 1936 Vote and 1940 Vote

Most of the people—but again not all of them—voted for the same party in both presidential elections. The voters who changed between the 1936 and 1940 elections—primarily made up of persons who had voted for Roosevelt in 1936 but were for Willkie in 1940—could be regarded as having something of a tradition to overcome. Their way was psychologically more obstructed than that of the people who voted consistently for the same party in all recent elections.

4. The Voter and His Family

As we shall see, the American family maintains considerable political solidarity, with all adult members voting the same way. But sometimes other members of the respondent's family disagreed with him and oftener other members of the family were undecided. In either case, the respondent was under a cross-pressure between the views of two members of the family or between his own ideas and those of at least one other member of his family.

5. The Voter and His Associates

Friends as well as family create a political environment which may be congenial or hostile. In the October interviews, respondents were asked whether they had noticed changes in vote intention on the part of people around them. Republicans who noted a trend toward Willkie and Democrats who were aware mainly of changes toward Roosevelt were in a congenial situation. What they saw going on around them coincided with their own preferences. But the few who noticed trends towards the opposition party were subjected thereby to conflicting pressures from their associates.

6. 1940 Vote Intention and Attitude Toward Business and Government

And, finally, cross-pressures may exist between a person's vote intention and his attitude on a basic issue of the election. In the October interview, respondents were questioned on their attitudes toward one such issue: they were asked whether they considered it more important for a president to have experience in business or in government. Most people with Republican vote intentions wanted a president with business experience and most people who intended to vote Democratic preferred government experience in their candidate. There were, however, some respondents whose attitude and vote intention were conflicting—Republicans who wanted government experience in their presidential candidate and Democrats who thought business experience was more important. These deviates, then, were subject to a certain amount of cross-pressure.

Whatever the source of the conflicting pressures, whether from social status or class identification, from voting traditions or the attitudes of associates, the consistent result was to delay the voter's final decision. The voters who were subject to cross-pressures on their vote decided later than the voters for whom the various factors reinforced one another. And of all the cross-pressures which we have identified the single most effective one in delaying vote decision was the lack of complete agreement within the family.

Why did people subject to cross-pressures delay their final decisions as to how they should vote? In the first place, it was difficult for them to make up their minds simply because they had good reasons for voting for both candidates. Sometimes such reasons were so completely balanced that the decision had to be referred to a third factor for settlement. The doubt as to which was the better course—to vote Republican or to vote Democratic—combined with the process of self-argument caused the delay in the final vote decision of such people.

In the second place, some of the people subject to cross-pressures delayed their final vote decisions because they were waiting for events to resolve the conflicting pressures. In the case of conflicting personal characteristics, such resolution was hardly possible but in other cases a reconciliation of conflicting interests might be anticipated. A person might hope that during the campaign he could convince other members of his family, or even more, he might give the family every chance to bring him around to their way of thinking. And the family often does just that. Or, again, he might wait for events in the campaign to provide him with a basis for making up his mind. Although there is a tendency toward consistency in attitudes, sometimes the contradiction was not resolved and the voter actually went to the polls with the cross-pressures still in operation.

Such conflicting pressures make voters "fair game" for the campaign managers of both parties, for they have a foot in each party. They are subject to factors which influence them to vote Republican and others, perhaps equally strong, which influence them to vote Democratic.

From this particular point of view, the heavy campaigning of both parties at the end of the campaign is a good investment for both sides— to the extent to which it can be effective at all. We will recall that the people who make up their minds last are those who think the election will affect them least. It may be, then, that explicit attempts by the candidates and their managers to prove to them that the election *will* make a difference to them would be more effective than any amount of continued argumentation of the issues as such. One hypothesis is that the person or the party that convinces the hesitant voter of the imporance of the election to him personally—in terms of what he concretely wants—can have his vote.

The Types of Changes

People delayed their final vote decisions either because they did not have enough interest in the election to push through to a definite choice or because the selection of a candidate put them in a difficult situation, containing elements favorable to both sides. But the process of delay did not work identically for all of them. Some people were "Don't Know's" until sometime during the campaign and then definitely decided on their vote. Others decided early in the campaign for one of the candidates, then had a period of doubt when they became undecided or even went over to the other side, and finally came back to the original choice. Still others changed from one particular party to the other. In short, the people who did not make up their minds until some time during the campaign proper differed in the ways in which they came to their final vote decision. In this sense, the three main kinds of changers were the following (the figures are percentages of the voters as a whole):

28% *Crystallizers:* They are people who had no vote intention in May but later acquired one; they went from "Don't Know" to Republican (14%) or from "Don't Know" to Democrat (14%).

15% *Waverers:* They are people who started out with a vote intention, then fell away from it (either to "Don't Know" or to the other party) and later returned to their original choice. Most of them went from a party to "Don't Know" and then back to the original party (11%: Republicans, 5.5%; Democrats, 5.5%), and others from a party to the other party and then back to the first party (4%: Republicans, 1%; Democrats, 3%).

8% *Party Changers:* They are people who started out with a vote intention and later changed to the other party, finally voting for it. They went from Republican to Democrat (2%) or from Democrat to Republican (6%).

We might note now, for use later, that all the changes of the crystallizers and most of the waverers involved only one of the parties; the other part of the change was a "Don't Know" opinion. On the other hand, all the party changers and some of the waverers were at one time or another in the camp of each party; their changes involved allegiance to both parties

115

at different times. In other words, 39% of the changes made by the voters involved only one party and only 12% of them involved both parties. Or, adding the constants from May to November, the vote intentions of 88% of all the voters were limited to one party and the vote intentions of only 12% of the voters took in both parties, at one time or another.

Of the waverers who left their original choice for indecision, fully 82% returned to it as the more congenial home. But those who wandered away to the other party did not return so readily; only 32% came back to the party of their first choice. If a person leaves his party for indecision he almost always returns to it later, but if he leaves it for the opposition, he seldom returns to it.

As the campaign wore on, what kinds of changers were still left to be convinced, once and for all?

The three kinds of changers—the crystallizers, the waverers, and the party changers—all came to their final decision sometime after May, but not all at the same time. Actually, the crystallizers decided much earlier than the others; 68% had settled their vote by August as against only 48% of the party changers and 46% of the waverers.

But the waverers—the people who left the party of their original choice but later came back and voted for it—comprise a special group because, as we noted above, there were two different kinds of waverers. There were those who wavered only to indecision and there were those who wavered all the way to the other party. The "distance" of the wavering is significant both for time of final decision and, as we shall see, for the roles of interest and cross-pressures. The indecision waverers definitely decided much earlier than the party waverers (57% by August as against 14%). If, then, we divide the changers into two groups—the one-party changers (crystallizers and indecision waverers) and the two-party changers (the straight party changers and the party waverers)—we find that the people who intended sometime during the campaign to vote for both parties took much longer to reach a final vote decision than those who varied only between one of the parties and indecision. Almost two-thirds of the two-party changers did not definitely decide until the last period of the campaign; almost two-thirds of the one-party changers definitely decided by August. As the campaign went into its last weeks, the people who were still to make up their minds, relatively speaking, were those who had been in the camp of the opposition earlier.

What were the roles of interest in the election and cross-pressures in voting background for these groups of voters who had arrived at their final vote decision in different ways? Did these two influential factors differentiate such voters?

The story is clear. There was a steady decrease of interest and a steady increase of cross-pressures from constants to one-party changers to two-party changers. The people who changed their position during the campaign but never enough to move into both parties stood between the constants and the two-party people. In other words, the more interest and the fewer conflicting pressures a person had, the more he tended to decide once and for all early in the game and never change his mind thereafter. If a person had somewhat less interest and somewhat more cross-pressures, then he tended to doubt longer and oftener than the constants but he slid back only to a tentative "don't know" and never far enough to get into the other camp. Only those people who had much less interest and many more conflicting pressures actually vacillated between the two parties.

That tells the story of the two-party changers: they were the people who were torn in both directions and who did not have enough interest in the election to cut through the conflicting pressures upon them and come to a deliberate and definite decision. Instead, they drifted along during the campaign, drifting into both parties. They not only delayed longer than any other group of voters in making their final vote decision but when they did make it, as we shall see, they were as likely as not to be swayed by someone in their immediate environment. These people, who in a sense were the only ones of the entire electorate to make a complete change during the campaign were: the least interested in the election; the least concerned about its outcome; the least attentive to political material in the formal media of communication; the last to settle upon a vote decision; and the most likely to be persuaded, finally, by a personal contact, not an "issue" of the election.

In short, the party changers—relatively, the people whose votes still remained to be definitely determined during the last stages of the campaign, the people who could swing an election during those last days— were, so to speak, available to the person who saw them last before Election Day. The notion that the people who switch parties during the campaign are mainly the reasoned, thoughtful, conscientious people who were convinced by the issues of the election is just plain wrong. Actually, they were mainly just the opposite.

3

Impact of Public Opinion on Public Policy

IN THE PRECEDING section we were concerned with problems in the formation of public opinion, i.e., how opinions come to be what they are. In
this section we are concerned not with the "causes" of opinion, but with
its consequences. Our central consideration here has to do with the ways
in which public opinion is, or should be, applied in the determination of
public policy. Does the legislative process follow the dictates of public
opinion, and should it? Under what conditions is public opinion more,
and less, appropriate as a guide for public action? In what sense does
public opinion form the basis of legislation, decree, or law?

A broad historical analysis of the inter-relations between law and public opinion is contained in the selection from Dicey's classical work in
that field. Key, the contemporary political scientist, seeks to set forth a
framework for understanding the impact of public opinion, in terms of
the orientation of the elites and the institutions through which they exercise political influence. The role of the mass media is of course crucial

119

both in forming public opinion and influencing its impact on public policy. This is especially the case in matters of foreign policy where the citizenry has limited direct sources of information and must rely on expert evaluations. Cohen presents a case study in which foreign policy formation is analyzed in terms of the interaction of the press and public opinion.

A. V. DICEY

The Relation Between Law and Public Opinion

MY AIM in these lectures is to exhibit the close dependence of legislation, and even of the absence of legislation, in England during the nineteenth century upon the varying currents of public opinion.

The fact of this dependence will be assumed by most students with even too great readiness. We are all of us so accustomed to endow public opinion with a mysterious or almost supernatural power, that we neglect to examine what it is that we mean by public opinion, to measure the true limits of its authority, and to ascertain the mode of its operation. Surprise may indeed be felt, not at the statement that law depends upon opinion, but at this assertion being limited to England, and to England during the last century. The limitation, however, is intentional, and admits of full justification.

True indeed it is that the existence and the alteration of human institutions must, in a sense, always and everywhere depend upon the beliefs or feelings, or, in other words, upon the opinion of the society in which such institutions flourish.

"As force," writes Hume, "is always on the side of the governed, the governors have nothing to support them but opinion. It is, therefore, on opinion only that government is founded; and this maxim extends to the most despotic and most military governments, as well as to the most free and most popular. The Soldan of Egypt, or the Emperor of Rome, might drive his harmless subjects, like brute beasts, against their sentiments and inclination; but he must, at least, have led his mamelukes, or praetorian bands, like men, by their opinion."

Reprinted from *Lectures on The Relation of Law and Public Opinion in England During the Nineteenth Century* (1914), pp. 1–7, by permission of the publisher. (Copyright, 1914, by Macmillan Co.)

And so true is this observation that the authority even of a Southern planter over his slaves rested at bottom upon the opinion of the Negroes whom he at his pleasure flogged or killed. Their combined physical force exceeded the planter's own personal strength, and the strength of the few whites who might be expected to stand by him. The blacks obeyed the slave-owner from the opinion, whether well or ill founded, that in the long run they would in a contest with their masters have the worst of the fight; and even more from that habit of submission which, though enforced by the occasional punishment of rebels, was grounded upon a number of complicated sentiments, such, for example, as admiration for superior ability and courage, or gratitude for kindness, which cannot by any fair analysis be reduced to a mere form of fear, but constitutes a kind of prevalent moral atmosphere. The whites, in short, ruled in virtue of the opinion, entertained by their slaves no less than themselves, that the slave-owners possessed qualities which gave them the might, and even the right, to be masters. With the rightness or wrongness of this conviction we are not here in any way concerned. Its existence is adduced only as a proof that, even in the most extreme case conceivable, Hume's doctrine holds good, and the opinion of the governed is the real foundation of all government.

But, though obedience to law must of necessity be enforced by opinion of some sort, and Hume's paradox thus turns out to be a truism, this statement does not involve the admission that the law of every country is itself the result of what we mean by "public opinion." This term, when used in reference to legislation, is merely a short way of describing the belief or conviction prevalent in a given society that particular laws are beneficial and therefore ought to be maintained, or repealed in accordance with the opinion or wishes of its inhabitants. Now this assertion, though it is, if properly understood, true with regard to England at the present day, is clearly not true of all countries, at all times, and indeed has not always been true even of England.

For, in the first place, there exist many communities in which public opinion—if by that term be meant speculative views held by the mass of the people as to the alteration or improvement of their institutions—can hardly be said to have any existence. The members of such societies are influenced by habit rather than by thought. Their mode of life is determined by customary rules, which may indeed have originated in the necessities of a given social condition, or even in speculative doctrines entertained by ancient law-givers, but which, whatever be their origin, assuredly owe their continuance to use and wont. It is, in truth, only under the peculiar conditions of an advanced civilisation that opinion dictates legislative change. In many Eastern countries, opinion—which is better described as traditional or instinctive feeling—has for ages been, in general, hostile to change and favourable to the maintenance of inherited habits. There, as in the West, opinion, in a very wide sense of that word, rules;

but such aversion to change as for ages keeps a society within the limits of traditional action, is a very different thing from the public opinion which in the England of the nineteenth and twentieth centuries has demanded constant improvements in the law of the land.

It is possible, in the second place, to point to realms where laws and institutions have been altered or revolutionised in deference to opinion, but where the beliefs which have guided legislative reform have not been what we mean in England by "public" opinion. They have been, not ideas entertained by the inhabitants of a country, or by the greater part thereof, but convictions held by a small number of men, or even by a single individual who happened to be placed in a position of commanding authority. We must, indeed, remember that no ruler, however powerful, can stand completely alone, and that the despots who have caused or guided revolutions have been influenced by the opinion, if not of their own country, yet of their generation. But it may be asserted with substantial truth that Peter the Great laid the foundation of Russian power without much deference to the opinion of Russia, and that modern Prussia was created by Frederick the Great, who certainly drew his ideas of good government from other than Prussian sources. It was not, then, the public opinion of the Russian people or the public opinion of the Prussians, but the convictions of a single man which in each case moulded the laws and institutions of a powerful country. At this moment legislation in British India is the work of a body of English specialists who follow to a great extent the current of English opinion. They are, indeed, it is to be hoped, guided far more by their own experience and by their practical knowledge of India, than by English sentiment; but Anglo-Indian officials though they may not always obey the transitory feelings of the English public, certainly do not represent Indian public opinion.

In the third place, the law of a country may fail, for a time, to represent public opinion owing to the lack of any legislative organ which adequately responds to the sentiment of the age. A portion, at least, of that accumulation of abuses, which was the cause of the occasion of the French Revolution, may fairly be ascribed to the want of any legislative body possessing both the power and the will to carry out reforms which had long been demanded by the intelligence of the French nation. Some critics may, it is true, deny that a legislative organ was lacking: a French king held in his hands under the *ancient régime* an authority nearly approaching to sovereign power, and an enlightened despot might, it has been suggested, have conferred upon the country all the benefits promised by the Revolution. But the power of the French Crown was practically more limited than modern critics always perceive, whilst the circumstances no less than the character of Louis XV and Louis XVI disqualified these monarchs for performing the part of enlightened despots. The "Parliaments," again, which assuredly possessed some legislative power, might, it

123

has been argued, have reformed the laws and institutions of the country. But the Parliaments were after all Courts, not legislatures, and represented the prejudices of lawyers, not the aspirations of reformers; Frenchmen, zealous for the removal of abuses, looked, as a matter of fact, with more hope to the action of the king than to the legislation of Parliaments which represented the antiquated conservatism of a past age. The want, then, of a legislative organ was in France a check upon the influence of public opinion. Nor can it be denied that even in England defective legislative machinery has at times lessened the immediate influence of opinion. The chief cause, no doubt, of the arrest of almost every kind of reform during the latest years of the eighteenth and the earlier part of the nineteenth century, was a state of feeling so hostile to revolution that it forbade the most salutary innovations. But "legislative stagnation," as it has been termed, lasted in England for at least ten or twenty years beyond the date when it ought naturally to have come to an end; and it can hardly be disputed that this delay in the improvement of English institutions was due in part to the defects of the unreformed Parliament—that is, to the non-existence of a satisfactory legislative organ.

V. O. KEY, JR.

Public Opinion and Democratic Politics

THE EXPLORATION of public attitudes is a pursuit of endless fascination—and frustration. Depiction of the distribution of opinions within the public, identification of the qualities of opinion, isolation of the odd and of the obvious correlates of opinion, and ascertainment of the modes of opinion formation are pursuits that excite human curiosity. Yet these endeavors are bootless unless the findings about the preferences, aspirations, and prejudices of the public can be connected with the workings of the governmental system. . . . Consideration of the role of public opinion drives the observer to the more fundamental question of how it is that democratic governments manage to operate at all. Despite endless speculation on that problem, perplexities still exist about what critical circumstances, beliefs, outlooks, faiths, and conditions are conducive to the maintenance of regimes under which public opinion is controlling, at least in principle, and is, in fact, highly influential.

A Missing Piece of the Puzzle

In an earlier day public opinion seemed to be pictured as a mysterious vapor that emanated from the undifferentiated citizenry and in some way or another enveloped the apparatus of government to bring it into conformity with the public will. These weird conceptions passed out of style as the technique of the sample survey permitted the determination, with some accuracy, of the distribution of opinions within the population. Vast areas of ignorance remain in our information about people's opinions and aspirations; nevertheless, a far more revealing map of the gross topog-

Reprinted from *Public Opinion and American Democracy*, (1961), pp. 535–543, by permission of the publisher. (Copyright, 1961, by Alfred A. Knopf).

125

raphy of public opinion can now be drawn than could have been a quarter of a century ago.

Despite their power as instruments for the observation of mass opinion, sampling procedures do not bring within their range elements of the political system basic for the understanding of the role of mass opinion within the system. Repeatedly, as we have sought to explain particular distributions, movements, and qualities of mass opinion, we have had to go beyond the survey data and make assumptions and estimates about the role and behavior of that thin stratum of persons referred to variously as the political elite, the political activists, the leadership echelons, or the influentials. In the normal operation of surveys designed to obtain tests of mass sentiment, so few persons from this activist stratum fall into the sample that they cannot well be differentiated, even in a static description, from those persons less involved politically. The data tell us almost nothing about the dynamic relations between the upper layer of activists and mass opinion. The missing piece of our puzzle is this elite element of the opinion system. That these political influentials both affect mass opinion and are conditioned in their behavior by it is obvious. Yet systematic knowledge of the composition, distribution in the social structure, and patterns of behavior of this sector of the political system remains far from satisfactory.

The longer one frets with the puzzle of how democratic regimes manage to function, the more plausible it appears that a substantial part of the explanation is to be found in the motives that actuate the leadership echelon, the values that it holds, in the rules of the political game to which it adheres, in the expectations which it entertains about its own status in society, and perhaps in some of the objective circumstances, both material and institutional, in which it functions. Focus of attention on this sector of the opinion system contrasts with the more usual quest for the qualities of the people that may be thought to make democratic practices feasible. That focus does not deny the importance of mass attitudes. It rather emphasizes that the pieces of the puzzle are different in form and function, and that for the existence of a democratic opinion-oriented system each piece must possess the characteristics necessary for it to fit together with the others in a working whole. The superimposition over a people habituated to tyranny of a leadership imbued with democratic ideals probably would not create a viable democratic order.

VALUES AND MOTIVES OF THE ACTIVIST SUBCULTURE

The traits and characteristics of political activists assume importance in the light of a theory about why the leadership and governing levels in any society behave as they do. That theory amounts to the proposition that these political actors constitute in effect a subculture with its own peculiar set of norms of behavior, motives, and approved standards. Processes of indoctrination internalize such norms among those who are born to or climb to positions of power and leadership; they serve as standards of action, which are reinforced by a social discipline among the political activists. In some regimes the standards of the ruling groups prescribe practices of firmness toward the governed who are regarded as menials with no rights; they deserve no more than the rough and arbitrary treatment they receive. The rules of the game may prescribe that the proper practice for rulers is to maximize their own advantage as well as the correlative deprivations of the ruled. The ignorant, the poor, and the incompetent may be seen as entitled to what they get, which is very little. Or the rules of the game of a regime may mitigate the harshness of these outlooks by a compassionate attitude toward the wretched masses who cannot help themselves. Hence, we may have little fathers of the people. The point is that the politically active classes may develop characteristic norms and practices that tend to guide their behavior. In a loose sense these may be the norms of a subculture, that of the specialists in politics and government. Beliefs generally accepted among these persons tend to establish habits and patterns of behavior with considerable power of self-maintenance or persistence through time.

While the ruling classes of a democratic order are in a way invisible because of the vagueness of the lines defining the influentials and the relative ease of entry to their ranks, it is plain that the modal norms and standards of a democratic elite have their peculiarities. Not all persons in leadership echelons have precisely the same basic beliefs; some may even regard the people as a beast. Yet a fairly high concentration prevails around the modal beliefs, even though the definition of those beliefs must be imprecise. Fundamental is a regard for public opinion, a belief that in some way or another it should prevail. Even those who cynically humbug the people make a great show of deference to the populace. The basic doctrine goes further to include a sense of trusteeship for the people generally and an adherence to the basic doctrine that collective efforts should be dedicated to the promotion of mass gains rather than of narrow class advantage; elite elements tethered to narrow group interest have no slack for maneuver to accommodate themselves to mass aspirations. Ultimate expression of these faiths comes in the willingness to abide by the outcome of popular elections. The growth of leadership structures with beliefs including these broad articles of faith is probably accomplished only over a considerable period of time, and then only under auspicious circumstances.

If an elite is not to monopolize power and thereby to bring an end to democratic practices, its rules of the game must include restraints in the exploitation of public opinion. Dimly perceptible are rules of etiquette that limit the kinds of appeals to public opinion that may be properly made. If it is assumed that the public is manipulable at the hands of unscrupulous leadership (as it is under some conditions), the maintenance of a democratic order requires the inculcation in leadership elements of a taboo against appeals that would endanger the existence of democratic practices. Inflammation of the sentiments of a sector of the public disposed to exert the tyranny of an intolerant majority (or minority) would be a means of destruction of a democratic order. Or by the exploitation of latent differences and conflicts within the citizenry it may at times be possible to paralyze a regime as intense hatreds among classes of people come to dominate public affairs. Or by encouraging unrealistic expectations among the people a clique of politicians may rise to power, a position to be kept by repression as disillusionment sets in.[1] In an experienced democracy such tactics may be "unfair" competition among members of the politically active class. In short, certain restraints on political competition help keep competition within tolerable limits. The observation of a few American political campaigns might lead one to the conclusion that there are no restraints on politicians as they attempt to humbug the people. Even so, admonitions ever recur against arousing class against class, against stirring the animosities of religious groups, and against demagoguery in its more extreme forms. American politicians manifest considerable restraint in this regard when they are tested against the standards of behavior of politicians of most of those regimes that have failed in the attempt to establish or maintain democratic practices.

The norms of the practice of politics in an order that has regard for public opinion include broad rules of etiquette governing relations among the activists, as well as rules governing the relations of activists with the public. Those rules, in their fundamental effect, assure the existence of a minority among the political activists; if those who control government can suppress opposition activists, an instrument essential for the formation and expression of public opinion is destroyed. A body of customs that amounts to a policy of "live and let live" must prevail. In constitutional democracies some of these rules are crystallized into fundamental law in guarantees such as those of freedom of speech, freedom of press, and the right to appeal to the electorate for power. Relevant also are procedures for the protection of property rights; a political opposition may be destroyed by expropriation as well as by execution.[2] While such rules extend in their application to the entire population, one of their major functions is to prevent politicians from putting each other into jail or from destroying each other in the ordinary course of their competitive endeavors. All these elements of the rules of the game gain strength, not from their statements in the statutes and codes, but from their incorporation into the norms that guide the behavior of the political activists.[3]

FORM AND STRUCTURE

Certain broad structural or organizational characteristics may need to be maintained among the activists of a democratic order if they are to perform their functions in the system. Fundamental is the absence of sufficient cohesion among the activists to unite them into a single group dedicated to the management of public affairs and public opinion. Solidification of the elite by definition forecloses opportunity for public choice among alternative governing groups and also destroys the mechanism for the unfettered expression of public opinion or of the opinions of the many subpublics. Maintenance of division and competition among political activists requires the kinds of etiquette that have been mentioned to govern their relations among themselves. Those rules, though, do not create the cleavages among the activists. Competitive segments of the leadership echelons normally have their roots in interests or opinion blocs within society. A degree of social diversity thus may be, if not a prerequisite, at least helpful in the construction of a leadership appropriate for a democratic regime. A series of independent social bases provide the foundations for a political elite difficult to bring to the state of unification that either prevents the rise of democratic processes or converts them into sham rituals.

At a more earthy level, maintenance of a multiplicity of centers of leadership and political activism requires arrangements by which men may gain a livelihood despite the fact that they are out of power. Consider the consequences for the structure of opinion leadership of a socio-economic system in which those skilled in the arts of governance have open to them no way of obtaining a livelihood save by the exercise of those skills. In the United States the high incidence of lawyers among the politically influential provides a base of economic independence; the defeated politician can always find a few clients. Extensive reliance on part-time, amateur politicians in representative bodies and in many governing commissions has assured an economic cushion for many political activists. The custom of making many such offices economically unattractive has, in effect, required that they be filled by persons with an economic base independent of the public treasury. Opinion leaders and managers often find economic independence in posts with business associations and other voluntary societies. Communications enterprises, important in the operation of democracies, gain independence from government by their commercial position. The structure of government itself, through its many independent units and agencies, assures havens of some security for spokesmen for a variety of viewpoints. All this may boil down to the contention that development and maintenance of the type of leadership essential for the operation of a democratic political order is facilitated by the existence of a social system of some complexity with many centers that have some au-

129

tonomy and economic independence. Perhaps a safer formulation would be that societies that do not meet these requisites may encounter difficult problems in the support of a fractionalized stratum of political activists; they need to construct functional equivalents of the means we have been describing to assure the maintenance of competing centers of leadership.[4]

When viewed from another angle, these comments about the utility of independent foundations for competing sectors of the political elite relate to the more general proposition that regimes deferential to public opinion may best flourish when the deprivations contingent upon the loss of an election are limited. The structure of government itself may also contribute to that loss limitation. In federal regimes and in regimes with extensive devolution to elective local governmental authorities the prospect of loss of a national election may be faced with some equanimity, for the national minority may retain its position in many subordinate units of the nation and remain in a measure undisturbed by the alternations of control within the nation as a whole. The same function of loss limitation may be served by constitutional and customary expectations that limit the permissible range of governmental action.

Another characteristic may be mentioned as one that, if not a prerequisite to government by public opinion, may profoundly affect the nature of a democratic order. This is the distribution through the social structure of those persons highly active in politics. By various analyses, none founded on completely satisfactory data, we have shown that in the United States the political activists—if we define the term broadly—are scattered through the socio-economic hierarchy. The upper-income and occupational groups, to be sure, contribute disproportionately; nevertheless, individuals of high political participation are sprinkled throughout the lesser occupational strata. Contrast the circumstances when the highly active political stratum coincides with the high socio-economic stratum. Conceivably the winning of consent and the creation of a sense of political participation and of sharing in public affairs may be far simpler when political activists of some degree are spread through all social strata. The alternative circumstance may induce an insensitivity to mass opinion, a special reliance on mass communications, and a sharpened sense of cleavage and separatism within the political order. The contention made here amounts to more than the axiom that democracies can exist only in societies that possess a well-developed middle class. In a modern industrial society with universal suffrage the chances are that a considerable sprinkling of political activists need to exist in groups below the "middle class," however that term of vague referent may be defined. The correct general proposition may be that the operation of democratic processes may be facilitated by the distribution of persons participating in the order through all strata of the electorate. When the belief that democracy depended upon the middle class flourished, a comparatively narrow suffrage prevailed.

Allied with these questions is the matter of access to the wider circles of political leadership and of the recruitment and indoctrination of these political activists. Relative ease of access to the arena of active politics may be a preventive of the rise of intransigent blocs of opinion managed by those denied participation in the regularized processes of politics. In a sense, ease of access is a necessary consequence of the existence of a somewhat fragmented stratum of political activists. Systems built on rigid class lines or on the dominance of clusters of families may be especially prone to the exclusion of those not to the proper status born—or married. Yet ease of access does not alone suffice. It must be accompanied by means, either deliberate or informal, for the indoctrination of those admitted in the special mores and customs of the activist elements of the polity. Otherwise, ease of access may only facilitate the depredations of those alienated from the values of the political order. By their nature democratic political systems have large opportunity—if there is the necessary will—to extend widely opportunities for political participation in lesser capacities and thereby to sift out those capable of achieving access to the more restricted circles of influentials. Whether the builders of political orders ever set about deliberately and systematically to tackle such problems of recruitment and indoctrination may be doubtful. Those problems may be solved, when they are solved, by the unconscious and unwilled processes of evolutionary adaptation of social systems.

This discussion in terms of leadership echelons, political activists, or elites falls painfully on the ears of democratic romantics. The mystique of democracy has in it no place for ruling classes. As perhaps with all powerful systems of faith, it is vague on the operating details. Yet by their nature governing systems, be they democratic or not, involve a division of social labor. Once that axiom is accepted, the comprehension of democratic practices requires a search for the peculiar characteristics of the political influentials in such an order, for the special conditions under which they work, and for the means by which the people keep them in check. The vagueness of the mystique of democracy is matched by the intricacy of its operating practices. If it is true that those who rule tend sooner or later to prove themselves enemies of the rights of man—and there is something to be said for the validity of this proposition—then any system that restrains that tendency however slightly can excite only awe.

NOTES

1. The politicians of some of the new democracies have installed new regimes as they took the unfortunate step of arousing popular expectations beyond hope of early fulfillment.

2. Rules against the use of public authority for the private advantage of officials also have their political bearing. Officials who build huge fortunes or enterprises by the abuse of official position can yield power only at enormous cost.

3. Probably a critical stage in the evolution toward democracy occurs at the moment when those in authority conclude that their acceptance of the unfavorable outcome of an election would not result in grievous harm to them. Genetic analyses of democracies with a focus of attention on this point would be instructive.

4. Consider the problem of a regime that seeks to carry out economic development in large measure through governmental enterprise.

BERNARD C. COHEN

The Press, the Public and Foreign Policy

THE BELIEF among newspapermen that the citizen's requirement for more and more information about public affairs must be met by wider and wider distribution of news and opinion[1] has its source as much in the historical development of the American newspaper as in the independent elaboration of a democratic political ideology. In the first half of the nineteenth century, the conditions of newspaper publishing favored journals of limited circulation, which were aimed at small and specialized communities of interest. It was only in the latter half of the century that a developing technology and an increasing urbanization made possible the larger journal that "synthesized the newspaper-reading audience by appealing in a single paper to a wide range of interests."[2] Once the process was under way, competitive pressures sustained it; the increasing investment that newspapers represented in plant and in news-gathering facilities necessitated increased advertising revenues, which in turn meant that newspapers had to appeal to larger and larger publics by including in one inexpensive paper all the subjects and features that separate audiences had hitherto found in specialized publications. The big city newspaper had acquired much of its present form by the last quarter of the nineteenth century, and set the model for the papers in the rest of the country.[3]

One result of this homogenization of the newspaper was the homogenization of the concept of the newspaper reader; the special interests of special readers were substantially lost in the adaptation of the newspaper to the interests, standards, and pastimes of a mass public that was lightly educated and in the market for diversion and amusement. Foreign affairs, a special subject that would have been easy to handle in the era of special-audience newspapers, came to public attention just at the time when the

Reprinted from *The Press and Foreign Policy*, (1963), pp. 248–263, by permission of the author and the publisher. (Copyright, 1963, by Princeton University Press).

133

newspaper had successfully absorbed all areas and all subjects. The means of giving it wide public distribution were thus at hand when the movement for more democratic control of foreign policy spread in the early twentieth century. The juncture of these two phenomena further strengthened the image held by journalists (and others) of an undifferentiated mass audience for foreign affairs who should be and could be reached by foreign affairs coverage in the newspapers and, once reached, would be an unparalleled force, by virtue of its informed opinions, for wisdom and peace in the conduct of foreign policy.

In its capacity to withstand the direct and indirect assaults that have been made on this image in the years since it took clear shape, the American press has demonstrated not only its resilience but also its insensitivity to insight and knowledge. One of the earliest and most enduring attacks came from a young journalist; Walter Lippmann brilliantly dissected the theoretical premises underlying the role of the press in the public life of the American democracy, arguing that "It is not possible to assume that a world carried on by division of labor and distribution of authority, can be governed by universal opinions in the whole population. . . . Acting upon everybody for thirty minutes in twenty-four hours, the press is asked to create a mystical force called Public Opinion that will take up the slack in public institutions."[4] The burden of Lippmann's criticism has been supported in recent years by the main lines of social science research in the field of mass communications, and also in the specific area of public opinion and foreign policy. This research has pointed to the differentiation in exposure and receptivity of individuals to communications on various subjects, and has stressed the connections between this communications behavior and political, social, and psychological variables.[5] This line of inquiry in the communications field, focusing also on the different political and social roles of various audiences, has invaded modern schools of journalism and their affiliated research institutions as well as their professional journals;[6] yet it has not made much of a dent in the public philosophy of practicing journalists in the foreign affairs field, who seem to possess only the vaguest and most fragmentary notions of whom they are writing for, and the uses that this audience makes of their work.[7] But what are the essential facts of the situation, and what do they suggest by way of alternative possibilities on the part of the press? How much is read, and by whom?

The volume of international news is a small proportion of total news space in most newspapers, and small in absolute terms as well. If little foreign affairs news is published, even less is read, on the average (a most important qualification). The extent of such readership is suggested in the American Institute of Public Opinion's readership survey of 51 newspapers, conducted for the International Press Institute; of the daily average of 106 column inches of international news from home and abroad that was published, the average number of column inches actually read by adult readers came to 12, or about a half a column. It was further estimated that only two and one-third minutes were devoted to reading this material.[8] Other studies suggest the same general pattern of over-all readership of foreign affairs news.[9]

These figures are likely to dismay anyone who is intensely interested in international affairs and who shares a philosophic concern for extensive public participation in foreign policymaking. They are also confusing to newspaper people, who often overlook the fact that these data represent an *average* of very different levels of interest in and exposure to foreign affairs news. The reactions of the press, in the face of this kind of evidence, are manifested in a continuing "debate" over who is to blame for the situation: the public, the newspapers, or both. One point of view claims that the reader sets the pace, that popular demand will not support greater coverage or more analytical content, and that the comparatively low volume of foreign affairs news in American newspapers represents the editors' normal response to lack of reader interest. A United Nations reporter, for example, said, ". . . I don't absolve reporters, editors and publishers and networks entirely of blame in this matter, but they cannot go beyond what the public demands."[10] And a columnist explained why foreign correspondents write material that does not get into the papers: "It goes back to exactly the same thing we've been talking about—the American people are too distracted, too busy, too indifferent. They don't want it."[11] This side of the debate has been able to introduce, as evidence to support its claim, the results of public opinion polls showing that the public is substantially satisfied with the existing amount of foreign affairs coverage in its newspapers, and is unwilling to see local or national news reduced in order to give more space to foreign news.[12]

In view of the strength of their conviction that the reader determines the character and amount of foreign affairs news that is published, it is interesting that so few newspaper people acknowledge the inconsistencies that it gives rise to: in particular, the common situation wherein the newspaper gives the reader only a minimal dose of foreign affairs news, on the ground that he is not interested in the subject and will not take any more of it, and then puts that small dose on the front page and in lead positions (in line with the recommendations of the wire service budgets), where it presumably responds to what editors refer to as "the public's news values."[13] This circumstance points to the role of the press in forcing foreign policy material to the forefront of policy attention even though the large majority of the population would be as happy to see it sink into oblivion—and indeed immediately consigns it there. It is in this sense that the press should be seen as a significant part of the public audience for foreign policy, a creator of a structure of policy attention that has a very limited additional public audience and may never even be recorded in the mind of the *average* newspaper reader.

The contrary position in this argument is that the state of foreign affairs coverage, and therefore of readership, reflects editorial choices, and hence that editors and publishers rather than readers are responsible for the current conditions of coverage. News from Latin America provides a current case study of a situation in which the blame for the lack of material in the press is assigned, explicitly or implicitly, to the editors. Barrett and Kimball quote a UPI general news manager, Earl J. Johnson, who said: "After more than 20 years of pushing Latin American news on the wires, I've concluded that very few editors are really interested. Much is said at inter-American press meetings about the importance of printing more news from Latin American countries. But not much is done about it when the North American delegates return to their desks."[14] An Associated Press house organ recently raised the question, "Is there a gap between what managing editors tell us they want and what their papers actually print? . . . Recently Max Harrelson spent two weeks in Canada, then wrote a five-part series on Canada-U.S. relations. William L. Ryan put in two months on a Latin American tour. . . . Harrelson's series was used in 11 of 40 AMs [morning papers] checked. Two articles by Ryan from Brazil showed in 14 of 50 AMs. . . ."[15] Leo Rosten candidly put the responsibility on the editors, with the argument that "giving the public what it wants" is another way of saying "what we [i.e., the editors] *say* the public wants."[16] Another important and familiar claim on this side of the debate is that the average reader is actually a lot more interested in foreign affairs than he is given credit for, and that his disinclintion to read foreign affairs material in the press is due to the complexity of the material that is presented to him. The burden of altering this situation is thus transferred to reporters and editors, who are challenged, in Lester Markel's words, to present foreign news "in terms that are correct, concise and, above all, clear."[17]

Finally, there are others who are frankly puzzled over the location of responsibility, or who regard it as a "vicious circle," with both parties equally at fault. Thus, "Newspapers do not emphasize foreign affairs because the people are not interested, and the people are not interested because they do not find much foreign news in their papers."[18] This position is no doubt closest to the truth in the sense that the pattern of coverage is a response to perceived interests and priorities at both ends of the line. When the editor fails to draw attention to a subject because the prevailing news judgments give priority to other topics, then the majority of readers who are only marginally interested are not persuaded that it is important enough to read; and the editor in turn looks at the readership figures and draws justifiable conclusions about what people are reading. But the vulnerable part of this chain of reasoning, and of the whole argu-

ment, is the failure of the vast majority of reporters and editors to differentiate among their readers—to understand that some of the public *will*
read more foreign affairs news if it is offered to them, even though there
may be no new recruits to the over-all readership ranks of foreign affairs
news. What patterns of readership are involved here?

Readership of foreign affairs news is a poorly understood subject
despite the attention that has been paid to the problem of audience analysis
in communications research. One reason for this is that efforts to delineate
the audience structure of the media of mass communication have rarely
focused explicitly on foreign affairs news as a classification of newspaper
content. Another reason for the uncertainties is that the available data are
apparently misleading, in the sense that they appear to overstate both the
extent and the depth of newspaper reading in the foreign affairs field. To
ask a sample of respondents where they get their information about foreign news events,[19] and to learn that between 44 and 50 per cent of the
respondents get most of their foreign affairs information from newspapers
and a similar proportion from the electronic media, implies a level of
exposure and information-seeking that exaggerates the true state of
affairs.[20] Similarly, to learn that "For their news on foreign affairs, more
than 90 per cent of the population depends principally on . . . the radio and
the daily newspaper,[21] or even that about 90 per cent of the population
reads a daily newspaper, is also suggestive of a much higher state of exposure to the news in it than is actually the case. Studies of communities
deprived of newspapers in the course of strikes make the point that newspapers fulfill social and psychological functions more often than intellectual or intelligence functions, even when readers express their loss in terms
of missing "what is going on in the world."[22] A more accurate impression
of the extent of readership of international news is suggested by data
from a survey in Albany, New York, in 1949.[23] Forty-seven per cent of
the respondents read "just the headlines" of the national and international
news, 4 per cent did not read even that much, and another 4 per cent read
"not much more than headlines." At the other end of the spectrum, 6 per
cent claimed to read both kinds of news "very carefully," and another 1
per cent read international news carefully, but not national news. In the
middle, 33 per cent picked and chose among items, and "sometimes read
carefully, sometimes not." V. O. Key's interpretation of these data is that
"Day in and day out the odds are that less than 10 per cent of the adult
population could be regarded as careful readers of the political news,"[24]
and one would have to knock a few percentage points off even that figure
for news of foreign affairs.

Who are these few careful readers? They seem to be the same few
people who show up as well-informed on repeated surveys of information
on international affairs, the people whom Gabriel Almond called the
"elites" and the "attentive public."[25] Readership of foreign affairs news

increases with age, education, and economic status; with an increase in these variables, the newspaper is used increasingly for information and decreasingly for entertainment; more men than women read such news; the larger the community (counting suburbs as part of metropolitan areas), the higher the interest in and readership of international events. Basically, however, it is educational level and socio-economic status that seem to be the best predictors of newspaper readership of foreign affairs.[26]

The significance of all this is generally missed by newspapermen, many of whom tend to think that the market for foreign affairs news can be—and should be—enlarged by techniques of simplifying the news and making it more attractive,[27] or even by providing more of it.[28] But an individual's exposure to foreign policy communication and his interest in international affairs that directs the exposure are concomitants of attitudes that have deep roots in his psychological orientations and his social setting.[29] And so long as this is the case, the important variables in determining interest and participation in foreign affairs and exposure to information on the subject will be found chiefly in the life patterns of individuals, in the things that are relevant to their perceptions of and orientations to the political universe, and only marginally in such ephemeral things as the way foreign affairs stories are written for the newspapers, the amount of pictorial or human-interest content in them, and so forth.[30] These relevant variables change slowly, and they are not readily amenable to modification by the stream of information the very exposure to which they in fact regulate. Consequently, the hope that the audience can be expanded significantly by a greatly simplified discussion of foreign affairs is illusory. It is no doubt true that most newspaper readers find foreign affairs news rather complicated and difficult to understand, but it does not necessarily follow that their interest would be stimulated if the material were presented in more simplified ways or more abundantly. It is equally likely that their basic disinterest in the material contributes to their impression of its difficulty. Furthermore, even if the hope were not illusory, even if one could succeed in attracting substantially larger numbers of readers to a discussion of foreign affairs that has been simplified by the use of pictures and one-syllable words, leavened with human interest, and related to everyday life on Main Street, the degree of simplification involved would be so great as to cause some doubt whether there would be any net increase in the capacity of the American people to understand and think through the undeniably complex issues of international relations. In other words, simplification might succeed in drawing a new audience, but to material that is so far from reflecting difficult international political realities as they confront responsible statesmen that it has no politically relevant public opinion uses.

Since the available evidence suggests that the chief market for foreign affairs coverage in the American press is a small policy and opinion elite, and a somewhat larger attentive public whose personal characteristics and interests are much the same as those of the policy and opinion elite, though their roles are not so specialized, it is important to think about foreign affairs coverage in terms of its relevance and usefulness for the professional and personal interests and needs of this audience. This argues for a quantitative and qualitative improvement, an up-grading, of foreign policy news and comment, rather than the down-grading that is implicit in the attempt to attract new people into audience. Two problems immediately arise in connection with such a suggestion: the philosophical problem wrapped up in "the people's right to know," and the practical problem of ensuring the survival of newspapers and even cultivating their prosperity through mass circulation.

Let us consider the latter first. The present endeavors of reporters and editors represent a compromise between the foreign policy interests of a few and the news values or tastes of a mass audience that "ought" to be interested in foreign affairs but presumably has to be seduced into reading about them. The practical effect is that the specialists and the attentive few are thus drawing and depending heavily on material written for a mass market that is relatively indifferent to the effort made on its behalf. This compromise is clearly not to the taste of any of the parties involved. Those who are steady consumers of foreign affairs news are dissatisfied with the daily fare they get in almost all American newspapers, to judge from the comments of foreign policy officials and of Congressmen, from the running criticism of the press in intellectual circles, and from the 8 per cent of the population who would like to see newspapers reduce the amount of local or national news in order to make more space for foreign news.[31] The large majority that rarely or never looks at foreign affairs news is most likely neutral towards its presence, in the sense that it is merely something these people walk around; but their non-readership is itself a good measure of their preference for other kinds of newspaper content.

It is possible to conceive of ways to satisfy the needs or preferences of a small audience for a higher order of foreign policy intelligence without raising the costs of publication, and without changing the character of a newspaper in ways that might alienate the larger numbers of non-readers —granting, however, that we do not even know what kind or proportions of material would give offense to people who do not read it.[32] The important obstacle, it would seem, has been thinking about this problem in the context of the customary shape and format of the daily newspaper. But there is no reason why larger amounts and different kinds of foreign affairs content, whatever its sources, need take up more frontpage space than at present, or be reflected more often in the dominant headlines. Since it would be meant to serve a specialized audience, it could be handled like other materials that have few customers, like financial news or shipping news (or even materials like comics and sports that have many customers!): whatever was not deemed important by conventional standards could be put in an unobtrusive place without much regard for format, headlines, and the other trappings of "news." It is possible in this way to think of substantially increasing the amount of foreign affairs information in the average newspaper without changing the over-all identity of the newspaper and with only a very marginal increase in the cost of production.

Since such an endeavor would take nothing away from the present exposure of the general public to foreign affairs news, there could be no complaint about it on philosophical grounds that cannot already be leveled at the mass media. Despite the low level of attentiveness to problems of foreign policy and the low priority given them by the public at large, one can justify the general order of importance that the press attaches to a few foreign policy questions on the ground that it is important to pretend that everybody is listening—that acting *as if* foreign affairs were of widespread public interest has important consequences in the realm of public confidence in the basic actions of government. This particular function, however, can no doubt continue to be served by the present (comparatively small) allocation of front-page foreign affairs news, thus permitting us to think about additional coverage more in terms of the particular needs of particular audiences. In any case, since there is considerable evidence that much of the information on world affairs currently at the disposal of the general public comes to it not directly from the media but at one remove or more, via people who have a greater interest in the subject and expose themselves to mass media discussions of it,[33] any alternative that increases the flow of information and analysis to these primary consumers should result in a subsequent larger flow to *their* secondary audience. Thus the broad political-philosophical purposes of press coverage of foreign affairs can be served by additional news that is directed primarily towards its few direct and heavy readers than to its many marginal scanners.

Further support for this argument stems from the point that the press is itself one of the most important components in the public audience for foreign affairs. From this point of view, greater press responsiveness to foreign policy developments and problems of foreign affairs, even in the form of specialized inside-page coverage of them, would inherently enlarge the scope of interaction between the government and its foreign policy public. Hence, increased coverage and more substantial analysis of more specialized problems as well as of issues already "in the news" would be an important contribution to democratic foreign policy-making even if this material were read only by foreign policy officials and a small group of attentive citizens. At its best, it might narrow the range within which major miscalculations in policy might be made as a consequence of insufficient exploration of alternatives and their implications within the confines of a bureaucratic structure, and as a consequence of insufficient interchange of value premises and preferences among policy officials and articulate people on the outside. The history of America's China policy after the Second World War should stand as a vivid reminder of the things that can happen when the political interests of outside publics have not been engaged in policy discussion and formulation.

But a problem still confronts us. There are also many historical examples of rigidities introduced into foreign policy when the political interests of outside publics *have* been engaged—for instance, America's China policy after the Korean War. This reminds us that wide public participation is not the only criterion of a good foreign policy, or the automatic guarantee of one.

NOTES

1. Expressed in different ways by reporters and editors, this view gets authoritative restatement in Theodore Peterson, "The Social Responsibility Theory of the Press," in Siebert, Peterson, and Schramm, *Four Theories of the Press.* See esp. p. 91, where Peterson associates "the press" with the viewpoint of the Commission on the Freedom of the Press, as expressed in *A Free and Responsible Press,* Chicago, University of Chicago Press, 1947.

2. Bernard A. Weisberger, *The American Newspaperman,* p. 89.

3. *Ibid.,* esp. chaps. 3 and 4.

4. Walter Lippmann, *Public Opinion,* p. 274.

5. Communications research has been so extensive in the last generation that its output fills two standard bibliographies: Bruce Lannes Smith, Harold D. Lasswell, and Ralph D. Casey, *Propaganda, Communication and Public Opinion,* Princeton, Princeton University Press, 1946; and Bruce Lannes Smith and Chitra M. Smith, *International Communication and Political Opinion: A Guide to the Literature,* Princeton, Princeton University Press, 1956. Representative collections of material on the mass media include Wilbur Schramm, ed., *The Process and Effects of Mass Communication,* Urbana, University of Illinois Press, 1955; and Wilbur Schramm, ed., *Mass Communications,* 2nd edn., Urbana, University of Illinois Press, 1960. The relation between communications behavior and foreign policy has been explored in Gabriel A. Almond, *The American People and Foreign Policy;* James N. Rosenau, *Public Opinion and Foreign Policy;* Lester Markel, ed., *Public Opinion and Foreign Policy;* Bernard C. Cohen, *Citizen Education in World Affairs;* and Alfred O. Hero, *Mass Media and World Affairs,* Boston, World Peace Foundation, 1959.

6. Cf., e.g., the work of such organizations as the Institute for Communications Research, Stanford University; the Institute of Communications Research, University of Illinois; the Mass Communications Research Center, University of Wisconsin; the Communication Research Center, Michigan State University. See also *Journalism Quarterly,* published by the Association for Education in Journalism, with editorial offices at the School of Journalism, University of Minnesota.

7. The practitioners are not alone in this respect, as is evident, e.g., in this argument by Theodore Kruglak: ". . . the owners of the American information

media have the duty and obligation toward their fellow Americans to re-examine their European news coverage on the basis of their answers to the following questions: . . . 3. Do you think that your present reports are giving the people in your community enough material upon which to base an informed opinion?" (*The Foreign Correspondents*, pp. 122–23.)

8. *The Flow of the News*, pp. 62–63.

9. Cf. Hero's canvass of the literature, *op. cit.*, pp. 80–81.

10. Pauline Frederick, NBC reporter, in UMBS series: "The United Nations Reporter."

11. Marquis Childs, in *ibid.*: "The Foreign Correspondent." Cf. also Alfred Zimmern, *Learning and Leadership*, p. 46, as quoted in Robert W. Desmond, *The Press and World Affairs*, New York, D. Appleton-Century Co., 1937, p. 169: ". . . the evils complained of [especially sensational coverage, in this case] are not of the newspapers' own creation. They are a response to a public demand." And Edward W. Barrett and Penn T. Kimball, "The Role of the Press and Communications," in American Assembly, *The United States and Latin America*, p. 88: "The pessimistic view of what North Americans will read about Latin Americans prevails, however, even in circles fervently hopeful of an opposite result."

12. See, e.g., results of AIPO polls conducted for the International Press Institute between February 16 and May 18, 1953, as reported in *The Flow of the News*, p. 58: "Would you like to have your newspaper reduce the amount of local or national news in order to give you more foreign news?" Would— 8 per cent; would not—78 per cent; no opinion—14 per cent. Thomas A. Bailey, in *The Man in the Street*, New York, Macmillan Co., 1948, p. 306, reports comparable results (but no figures) in a 1946 poll.

13. The only newspaperman I have discovered who seemed to be aware of this anomaly is Louis B. Selzer of the *Cleveland Press*. Selzer attributed the phenomenon to the influence of the *New York Times* on other editors around the country.

14. Barrett and Kimball, *op. cit.*, p. 96; Johnson's AP counterpart said much the same thing.

15. Associated Press, "AP Log," March 2–8, 1961.

16. Leo Rosten, *The Washington Correspondents*, p. 268.

17. Lester Markel, "The Flow of the News to Marilyn Monroe," *Problems of Journalism*, 1960, p. 77.

18. Martin Kriesberg, "Dark Areas of Ignorance," in Lester Markel, ed., *Public Opinion and Foreign Policy*, p. 62. Barrett and Kimball cite Herbert Matthews of the *New York Times* on "the vicious circle of Latin American coverage. . . . The failure to provide the news perpetuates the ignorance of the reader, and this ignorance leads to the lack of interest." (*Op. cit.*, p. 87.)

19. Cf. surveys by NORC and AIPO, the former quoted in Paul Lazarsfeld and Patricia Kendall, *Radio Listening in America*, New York, Prentice-Hall, 1948, p. 34, the latter in *The Flow of the News*, p. 58, both of which are cited in Theodore Kruglak, *The Foreign Correspondents*, p. 41n.

20. Cf., e.g., the data of this kind on p. 58 of *The Flow of the News*, and the data showing the low levels of information actually held by readers, on the pages immediately following.

21. Cf. Martin Kriesberg, "Dark Areas of Ignorance," in Markel, ed., *Public Opinion and Foreign Policy*, p. 60.

22. Bernard Berelson, "What 'Missing the Newspaper' Means," reprinted from Paul Lazarsfeld and Frank N. Stanton, eds., *Communications Research*,

1948–1949, in Wilbur Schramm, ed., *The Process and Effects of Mass Communications;* Charles F. Cannell and Harry Sharp, "The Impact of the 1955–56 Detroit Newspaper Strike," *Journalism Quarterly*, xxxv, No. 1, Winter 1958, pp. 26–35; Penn T. Kimball, "People Without Papers," *Public Opinion Quarterly*, xxiii, No. 2, Fall 1959, pp. 289–98.

23. Survey Research Center, *Interest, Information, and Attitudes in the Field of World Affairs*, Ann Arbor, Mich., 1949; these data are reproduced in V. O. Key, Jr., *Public Opinion and American Democracy*, as Table 14.5, p. 352.

24. Key, *op. cit.*, p. 353. He also suggests the importance that should be attached to headlines over national and international news stories, when that is all that half the people read; the suggestion is made via a reference to Percy H. Tannenbaum, "The Effect of Headlines on the Interpretation of News Stories," *Journalism Quarterly*, xxx, No. 2, Spring 1953, pp. 189–97.

25. *The American People and Foreign Policy*.

26. Cf. Wilbur Schramm and David M. White, "Age, Education, and Economic Status as Factors in Newspaper Reading," reprinted from *Journalism Quarterly*, xxvi, No. 2, June 1949, in Schramm, ed., *Mass Communications*, pp. 438–50; and Hero, *op. cit.*, esp. chap. 4, "Newspapers and World-Affairs Communications," which summarizes much of the literature on this subject. See also Key, *op. cit.*, and Kenneth P. Adler and Davis Bobrow, "Interest and Influence in Foreign Affairs," *Public Opinion Quarterly*, xx, No. 1. Spring 1956, pp. 89–101.

27. Cf. *The Flow of the News*, pp. 67–83; and Chapter IV, *supra*.

28. Cf. the remark of Herbert Matthews quoted above: "The failure to provide the news perpetuates the ignorance of the reader, and this ignorance leads to the lack of interest."

29. Cf. the extensive literature on attitudes and attitude change; esp. M. Brewster Smith, Jerome S. Bruner, and Robert W. White, *Opinions and Personality*, New York, John Wiley and Sons, 1956; and Carl I. Hovland, Irving L. Janis, and Harold H. Kelley, *Communication and Persuasion: Psychological Studies of Opinion Change*, New Haven, Yale University Press, 1953.

30. Cf. W. Phillips Davison, "On the Effects of Communication," *Public Opinion Quarterly*, xxiii, No. 3, Fall 1959, pp. 343–60.

31. See fn. 12, *supra*.

32. For the argument that "a publisher with the necessary resources and talents who wishes to run a paper with serious international content may make a go of it even in relatively 'unfavorable' communities," see Hero, *op. cit.*, p. 101.

33. See Key's summary of the literature on these propositions, *op. cit.*, pp. 359–66; in addition, see Elihu Katz, "The Two-Step Flow of Communication," *Public Opinion Quarterly*, xxi, No. 1, Spring 1957, pp. 61–78.

4

Theory of Communication

THEORETICAL analysis of the communication process emerges in some form whenever social scientists seek to describe society and social change. The crucial pervasiveness of communication activities, evident in the functioning of the simplest and most primitive social organizations, is particularly apparent in industrialized, urbanized, and secularized societies.

Contributions to a theory of communication have been made by workers in various fields—philosophy, sociology, anthropology, political science, psychology—and any unified theory (or theories) developing out of the current emphasis upon empirical work will have to take account of varied frames of reference. In the conceptualization of the communication process, one theoretical position (illustrated here in the selection from Cooley) sees the process as the binding force in organized society. This overall view of the social function of communication is followed by a selection from Mead dealing in detail with the specific psychological mechanisms at the basis of the individual's capacity to communicate with himself as with others. The articles by Sapir and Park are further examples of theoretical positions concerned with the interesting and disintegrating effects of communication upon organized group life.

145

Somewhat in contrast to these writers is the selection from Lasswell which typifies efforts to delimit and define the theoretical aspects of communication into formulations which are narrower in scope. Communications is seen as one aspect of social organization, and such a formulation is designed to be readily operationalized. In developing his theories of political influence, Lasswell has constructed a political formulation of the communication process which is abbreviated in his widely known formula, "Who says what to whom, with what effect?" His selection presents a set of categories for analyzing the communication process which has had wide influence on recent research.

CHARLES H. COOLEY

The Significance of Communication

BY COMMUNICATION is here meant the mechanism through which human relations exist and develop—all the symbols of the mind, together with the means of conveying them through space and preserving them in time. It includes the expression of the face, attitude and gesture, the tones of the voice, words, writing, printing, railways, telegraphs, telephones, and whatever else may be the latest achievement in the conquest of space and time. All these taken together, in the intricacy of their actual combination, make up an organic whole corresponding to the organic whole of human thought; and everything in the way of mental growth has an external existence therein. The more closely we consider this mechanism the more intimate will appear its relation to the inner life of mankind, and nothing will more help us to understand the latter than such consideration.

There is no sharp line between the means of communication and the rest of the external world. In a sense all objects and actions are symbols of the mind, and nearly anything may be used as a sign—as I may signify the moon or a squirrel to a child by merely pointing at it, or by imitating with the voice the chatter of the one or drawing an outline of the other. But there is also, almost from the first, a conventional development of communication, springing out of spontaneous signs but soon losing evident connection with them, a system of standard symbols existing for the mere purpose of conveying thought; and it is this we have chiefly to consider.

Without communication the mind does not develop a true human nature, but remains in an abnormal and nondescript state neither human nor properly brutal. This is movingly illustrated by the case of Helen Keller, who, as all the world knows, was cut off at *eighteen months* from the cheerful ways of men by the loss of sight and hearing; and did not re-

Reprinted from *Social Organization* (1909), pp. 61–65; 80–103, by permission of the publisher. (Copyright, 1909, by Charles Scribner's Sons; 1937, by Elsie Jones Cooley.)

147

new the connection until she was nearly *seven years* old. Although her mind was not wholly isolated during this period, since she retained the use of a considerable numbers of signs learned during infancy, yet her impulses were crude and uncontrolled, and her thought so unconnected that she afterward remembered almost nothing that occurred before the awakening which took place toward the close of her seventh year.

The story of that awakening, as told by her teacher, gives as vivid a picture as we need have of the significance to the individual mind of the general fact and idea of communication. For weeks Miss Sullivan had been spelling words into her hand which Helen had repeated and associated with objects; but she had not yet grasped the idea of language in general, the fact that everything had a name, and that through names she could share her own experiences with others, and learn theirs—the idea that there is *fellowship in thought*. This came quite suddenly.

This morning, writes her teacher, while she was washing, she wanted to know the name for water. . . . I spelled w-a-t-e-r and thought no more about it until after breakfast. Then it occurred to me that with the help of this new word I might succeed in straightening out the mug-milk difficulty [a confusion of ideas previously discussed]. We went out into the pump-house and I made Helen hold her mug under the pump while I pumped. As the cold water gushed forth filling the mug I spelled w-a-t-e-r in Helen's free hand. The word coming so close upon the sensation of cold water rushing over her hand seemed to startle her. She dropped the mug and stood as one transfixed. A new light came into her face. She spelled water several times. Then she dropped on the ground and asked for its name, and pointed to the pump and the trellis, and suddenly turning round she asked for my name. I spelled 'teacher.' Just then the nurse brought Helen's little sister into the pump-house, and Helen spelled 'baby' and pointed to the nurse. All the way back to the house she was highly excited, and learned the name of every object she touched, so that in a few hours she had added thirty new words to her vocabulary.

The following day Miss Sullivan writes, Helen got up this morning like a radiant fairy. She has flitted from object to object, asking the name of everything and kissing me for very gladness." And four days later, "Everything must have a name now. . . . She drops the signs and pantomime she used before, so soon as she has words to supply their place, and the acquirement of a new word affords her the liveliest pleasure. And we notice that her face grows more expressive each day.[1]

This experience is a type of what happens more gradually to all of us: it is through communication that we get our higher development. The faces and conversation of our associates; books, letters, travel, arts, and the like, by awakening thought and feeling and guiding them in certain channels, supply the stimulus and framework for all our growth.

In the same way, if we take a larger view and consider the life of a social group, we see that communication, including its organization into literature, art, and institutions, is truly the outside or visible structure of thought, as much cause as effect of the inside or conscious life of men.

All is one growth: the symbols, the traditions, the institutions are projected from the mind, to be sure, but in the very instant of their projection, and thereafter, they react upon it, and in a sense control it, stimulating, developing, and fixing certain thoughts at the expense of others to which no awakening suggestion comes. By the aid of this structure the individual is a member not only of a family, a class, and a state, but of a larger whole reaching back to prehistoric men whose thought has gone to build it up. In this whole he lives as in an element, drawing from it the materials of his growth and adding to it whatever constructive thought he may express.

Thus the system of communication is a tool, a progressive invention, whose improvements react upon mankind and alter the life of every individual and institution. A study of these improvements is one of the best ways by which to approach an understanding of the mental and social changes that are bound up with them; because it gives a tangible framework for our ideas—just as one who wished to grasp the organic character of industry and commerce might well begin with a study of the railway system and of the amount and kind of commodities it carries, proceeding thence to the more abstract transactions of finance.

And when we come to the modern era, especially, we can understand nothing rightly unless we perceive the manner in which the revolution in communication has made a new world for us. So in the pages that follow I shall aim to show what the growth of intercourse implies in the way of social development, inquiring particularly into the effect of recent changes.

Modern Communication: Enlargement and Animation

The changes that have taken place since the beginning of the nineteenth century are such as to constitute a new epoch in communication, and in the whole system of society. They deserve, therefore, careful consideration, not so much in their mechanical aspect, which is familiar to every one, as in their operation upon the larger mind.

If one were to analyze the mechanism of intercourse, he might, perhaps distinguish four factors that mainly contribute to its efficiency, namely:

Expressiveness, or the range of ideas and feelings it is competent to carry.

Permanence of record, or the overcoming of time.

Swiftness, or the overcoming of space.

Diffusion, or access to all classes of men.

Now while gains have no doubt been made in expressiveness, as in the enlargement of our vocabulary to embrace the ideas of modern science;

and even in permanence of record, for scientific and other special purposes; yet certainly the long steps of recent times have been made in the direction of swiftness and diffusion. For most purposes our speech is no better than in the age of Elizabeth, if so good; but what facility we have gained in the application of it! The cheapening of printing, permitting an inundation of popular books, magazines, and newspapers, has been supplemented by the rise of the modern postal system and the conquest of distance by railroads, telegraphs and telephones. And along with these extensions of the spoken or written word have come new arts of reproduction, such as photography, photo-engraving, phonography and the like —of greater social import than we realize—by which new kinds of impression from the visible or audible world may be fixed and disseminated.

It is not too much to say that these changes are the basis, from a mechanical standpoint, of nearly everything that is characteristic in the psychology of modern life. In a general way they mean the expansion of human nature, that is to say, of its power to express itself in social wholes. They make it possible for society to be organized more and more on the higher faculties of man, on intelligence and sympathy, rather than on authority, caste, and routine. They mean freedom, outlook, indefinite possibility. The public consciousness, instead of being confined as regards its more active phases to local groups, extends by even steps with that give-and-take of suggestions that the new intercourse makes possible, until wide nations, and finally the world itself, may be included in one lively mental whole.

The general character of this change is well expressed by the two words *enlargement* and *animation*. Social contacts are extended in space and quickened in time, and in the same degree the mental unity they imply becomes wider and more alert. The individual is broadened by coming into relation with a larger and more various life, and he is kept stirred up, sometimes to express, by the multitude of changing suggestions which this life brings to him.

From whatever point of view we study modern society to compare it with the past or to forecast the future, we ought to keep at least a sub-consciousness of this radical change in mechanism, without allowing for which nothing else can be understood.

In the United States, for instance, at the close of the eighteenth century, public consciousness of any active kind was confined to small localities. Travel was slow, uncomfortable and costly, and people undertaking a considerable journey often made their wills beforehand. The newspapers, appearing weekly in the larger towns, were entirely lacking in what we should call news; and the number of letters sent during a year in all the thirteen states was much less than that now handled by the New York office in a single day. People are far more alive to-day to what is going on in China, if it happens to interest them, than they were then to events a hundred miles away. The isolation of even large towns from the rest of the world, and the consequent introversion of men's minds upon local concerns, was something we can hardly conceive. In the country "the environment of the farm was the neighborhood; the environment of the village was the encircling farms and the local tradition; . . . few conventions assembled for discussion and common action; educational centres did not radiate the shock of a new intellectual life to every hamlet; federations and unions did not bind men, near and remote, into that fellowship that makes one composite type of many human sorts. It was an age of sects, intolerant from lack of acquaintance."[2]

The change to the present régime of railroads, telegraphs, daily papers, telephones and the rest has involved a revolution in every phase of life; in commerce, in politics, in education, even in mere sociability and gossip —this revolution always consisting in an enlargement and quickening of the kind of life in question.

Probably there is nothing in this new mechanism quite so pervasive and characteristic as the daily newspaper, which is as vehemently praised as it is abused, and in both cases with good reason. What a strange practice it is, when you think of it, that a man should sit down to his breakfast table and, instead of conversing with his wife, and children, hold before his face a sort of screen on which is inscribed a world-wide gossip!

The essential function of the newspaper is, of course, to serve as a bulletin of important news and a medium for the interchange of ideas, through the printing of interviews, letters, speeches and editorial comment. In this way it is indispensable to the organization of the public mind.

The bulk of its matter, however, is best described by the phase organized gossip. This sort of intercourse that people formerly carried on at cross-road stores or over the back fence, has now attained the dignity of print and an imposing system. That we absorb a flood of this does not necessarily mean that our minds are degenerate, but merely that we are gratifying an old appetite in a new way. Henry James speaks with a severity natural to literary sensibility of "the ubiquitous newspaper face, with its mere monstrosity and deformity of feature, and the vast open mouth, adjusted as to the chatter of Bedlam, that flings the flood-gates of vulgarity farther back [in America] than anywhere else on earth."[3] But after all is it any more vulgar than the older kind of gossip? No doubt it seems worse for venturing to share with literature the use of the printed word.

That the bulk of the contents of the newspaper is of the nature of gossip may be seen by noting three traits which together seem to make a fair definition of that word. It is copious, designed to occupy, without exerting, the mind. It consists mostly of personalities and appeals to superficial emotion. It is untrustworthy—except upon a few matters of moment which the public are likely to follow up and verify. These traits any one who is curious may substantiate by a study of his own morning journal.

There is a better and a worse side to this enlargement of gossip. On the former we may reckon the fact that it promotes a widespread sociability and sense of community; we know that people all over the country are laughing at the same jokes or thrilling with the same mild excitement over the foot-ball game, and we absorb a conviction that they are good fellows much like ourselves. It also tends powerfully, through the fear of publicity, to enforce a popular, somewhat vulgar, but sound and human standard of morality. On the other hand it fosters superficiality and commonplace in every sphere of thought and feeling, and is, of course, the antithesis of literature and of all high or fine spiritual achievement. It stands for diffusion as opposed to distinction.

In politics communication makes possible public opinion, which, when organized, is democracy. The whole growth of this, and of the popular education and enlightenment that go with it, is immediately dependent upon the telegraph, the newspaper and the fast mail, for there can be no popular mind upon questions of the day, over wide areas, except as the people are promptly informed of such questions and are enabled to exchange views regarding them.

Our government, under the Constitution, was not originally a democracy, and was not intended to be so by the men that framed it. It was expected to be a representative republic, the people choosing men of character and wisdom, who would proceed to the capital, inform themselves there upon current questions, and deliberate and decide regarding them. That the people might think and act more directly was not foreseen. The Constitution is not democratic in spirit, and, as Mr. Bryce has noted,[4] might under different conditions have become the basis of an aristocratic system.

That any system could have held even the original thirteen states in firm union without the advent of modern communication is very doubtful. Political philosophy, from Plato to Montesquieu, had taught that free states must be small, and Frederick the Great is said to have ridiculed the idea of one extending from Maine to Georgia. "A large empire," says Montesquieu, "supposes a despotic authority in the person who governs. It is necessary that the quickness of the prince's resolutions should supply the distance of the places they are sent to."[5]

Democracy has arisen here, as it seems to be arising everywhere in the civilized world, not, chiefly, because of changes in the formal constitution, but as the outcome of conditions which make it natural for the people to have and to express a consciousness regarding questions of the day. It is said by those who know China that while that country was at war with Japan the majority of the Chinese were unaware that a war was in progress. Such ignorance makes the sway of public opinion impossible; and, conversely, it seems likely that no state, having a vigorous people, can long escape that sway except by repressing the interchange of thought. When the people have information and discussion they will have a will, and this must sooner or later get hold of the institutions of society.

One is often impressed with the thought that there ought to be some wider name for the modern movement than democracy, some name which should more distinctly suggest the enlargement and quickening of the general mind, of which the formal rule of the people is only one among many manifestations. The current of new life that is sweeping with augmenting force through the older structures of society, now carrying them away, now leaving them outwardly undisturbed, has no adequate name.

Popular education is an inseparable part of all this: the individual must have at least those arts of reading and writing without which he can hardly be a vital member of the new organism. And that further development of education, rapidly becoming a conscious aim of modern society, which strives to give to every person a special training in preparation for whatever function he may have aptitude for, is also a phase of the freer and more flexible organization of mental energy. The same enlargement runs through all life, including fashion and other trivial or fugitive kinds of intercourse. And the widest phase of all, upon whose momentousness I need not dwell, is that rise of an international consciousness, in literature, in science and, finally, in politics, which holds out a trustworthy promise of the indefinite enlargement of justice and amity.

This unification of life by a freer course of thought is not only contemporaneous, overcoming space, but also historical, bringing the past into the present, and making every notable achievement of the race a possible factor in its current life—as when, by skilful reproduction the work of a mediæval painter is brought home to people dwelling five hundred years later on the other side of the globe. Our time is one of "large discourse, looking before and after."

There are remarkable possibilities in this diffusive vigor. Never, certainly, were great masses of men so rapidly rising to higher levels as now. There are the same facilities for disseminating improvement in mind and manners as in material devices; and the new communication has spread like morning light over the world, awakening, enlightening, enlarging, and filling with expectation. Human nature desires the good, when it once perceives it, and in all that is easily understood and imitated great headway is making.

Nor is there, as I shall try to show later, any good reason to think that the conditions are permanently unfavorable to the rise of special and select types of excellence. The same facility of communication which animates millions with the emulation of common models, also makes it easy for more discriminating minds to unite in small groups. The general fact is that human nature is set free; in time it will no doubt justify its freedom. The enlargement affects not only thought but feeling, favoring the growth of a sense of common humanity, of moral unity, between nations, races and classes. Among members of a communicating whole feeling may not always be friendly, but it must be, in a sense, sympathetic, involving some consciousness of the other's point of view. Even the animosities of modern nations are of a human and imaginative sort, not the blind animal hostility of a more primitive age. They are resentments, and resentment, as Charles Lamb says, is of the family of love.

The relations between persons or communities that are without mutual understanding are necessarily on a low plane. There may be indifference, or a blind anger due to interference or there may be a good-natured tolerance; but there is no consciousness of a common nature to warm up the kindly sentiments. A really human fellow-feeling was anciently confined within the tribe, men outside not being felt as members of a common whole. The alien was commonly treated as a more or less useful or dangerous animal—destroyed, despoiled or enslaved. Even in these days we care little about people whose life is not brought home to us by some kind of sympathetic contact. We may read statistics of the miserable life of the Italians and Jews in New York and Chicago; of bad housing, sweatshops and tuberculosis; but we care little more about them than we do about the sufferers from the Black Death, unless their life is realized to us in some human way, either by personal contact, or by pictures and imaginative description.

And we are getting this at the present time. The resources of modern communication are used in stimulating and gratifying our interest in every phase of human life. Russians, Japanese, Filipinos, fishermen, miners, millionaires, criminals, tramps and opium-eaters are brought home to us. The press well understands that nothing human is alien to us if it is only made comprehensible.

With a mind enlarged and supplied by such training, the man of to-day inclines to look for a common nature everywhere, and to demand that the whole world shall be brought under the sway of common principles of kindness and justice. He wants to see international strife allayed—in such a way, however, as not to prevent the expansion of capable races and the survival of better types; he wishes the friction of classes reduced and each interest fairly treated—but without checking individuality and enterprise. There was never so general an eagerness that righteousness should prevail; the chief matter of dispute is upon the principles under which it may be established.

The work of communication in enlarging human nature is partly immediate, through facilitating contact, but even more it is indirect, through favoring the increase of intelligence, the decline of mechanical and arbitrary forms of organization, and the rise of a more humane type of society. History may be regarded as a record of the struggle of man to realize his aspirations through organization; and the new communication is an efficient tool for this purpose. Assuming that the human heart and conscience, restricted only by the difficulties of organization, is the arbiter of what institutions are to become, we may expect the facility of intercourse to be the starting-point of an era of moral progress.

NOTES

1. *The Story of My Life,* pp. 316, 317.
2. W. L. Anderson, *The Country Town,* pp. 209, 210.
3. "The Manners of American Women," *Harper's Bazaar,* May, 1907.
4. *The American Commonwealth,* chap. 26.
5. *The Spirit of Laws,* book viii, chap. 19.

GEORGE HERBERT MEAD

Thought, Communication, and the Significant Symbol

WE HAVE CONTENDED that there is no particular faculty of imitation in the sense that the sound or the sight of another's response is itself a stimulus to carry out the same reaction, but rather that if there is already present in the individual an action like the action of another, then there is a situation which makes imitation possible. What is necessary now to carry through that imitation is that the conduct and the gesture of the individual which calls out a response in the other should also tend to call out the same response in himself. In the dog-fight this is not present: the attitude in the one dog does not tend to call out the same attitude in the other. In some respects that actually may occur in the case of two boxers. The man who makes a feint is calling out a certain blow from his opponent, and that act of his own does have that meaning to him, that is, he has in some sense initiated the same act in himself. It does not go clear through, but he has stirred up the centers in his central nervous system which would lead to his making the same blow that his opponent is led to make, so that he calls out in himself, or tends to call out, the same response which he calls out in the other. There you have the basis for so-called imitation. Such is the process which is so widely recognized at present in manners of speech, of dress, and of attitudes.

We are more or less unconsciously seeing ourselves as others see us. We are unconsciously addressing ourselves as others address us; in the same way as the sparrow takes up the note of the canary we pick up the dialects about us. Of course, there must be these particular responses in our own mechanism. We are calling out in the other person something we are calling out in ourselves, so that unconsciously we take over these attitudes. We are unconsciously putting ourselves in the place of others and acting as others act. I want simply to isolate the general mechanism here, because it is of very fundamental importance in the development of what

---

Reprinted from *Mind, Self, and Society* (1934), pp. 68–75, by permission of the editor, Charles Morris, and the publisher. (Copyright, 1934, by The University of Chicago Press.)

we call self-consciousness and the appearance of the self. We are, especially through the use of the vocal gestures, continually arousing in ourselves these responses which we call out in other persons, so that we are taking the attitudes of the other persons into our own conduct. The critical importance of language in the development of human experience lies in this fact that the stimulus is one that can react upon the speaking individual as it reacts upon the other.

A behaviorist, such as Watson, holds that all of our thinking is vocalization. In thinking we are simply starting to use certain words. That is in a sense true. However, Watson does not take into account all that is involved here, namely, that these stimuli are the essential elements in elaborate social processes and carry with them the value of those social processes. The vocal process as such has this great importance, and it is fair to assume that the vocal process, together with the intelligence and thought that go with it, is not simply a playing of particular vocal elements against each other. Such a view neglects the social context of language.[1]

The importance, then, of the vocal stimulus lies in this fact that the individual can hear what he says and in hearing what he says is tending to respond as the other person responds. When we speak now of this response on the part of the individual to the others we come back to the situation of asking some person to do something. We ordinarily express that by saying that one knows what he is asking you to do. Take the illustration of asking someone to do something, and then doing it one's self. Perhaps the person addressed does not hear you or acts slowly, and then you carry the action out yourself. You find in yourself, in this way, the same tendency which you are asking the other individual to carry out. Your request stirred up in you that same response which you stirred up in the other individual. How difficult it is to show someone else how to do something which you know how to do yourself! The slowness of the response makes it hard to restrain yourself from doing what you are teaching. You have aroused the same response in yourself as you arouse in the other individual.

In seeking for an explanation of this, we ordinarily assume a certain group of centers in the nervous system which are connected with each other, and which express themselves in the action. If we try to find in a central nervous system something that answers to our word "chair," what we should find would be presumably simply an organization of a whole group of possible reactions so connected that if one starts in one direction one will carry out one process, if in another direction one will carry out another process. The chair is primarily what one sits down in. It is a physical object at a distance. One may move toward an object at a distance and then enter upon the process of sitting down when one reaches it. There is a stimulus which excites certain paths which cause the individual to go toward that object and to sit down. Those centers are in some degree

157

physical. There is, it is to be noted, an influence of the later act on the earlier act. The later process which is to go on has already been initiated and that later process has its influence on the earlier process (the one that takes place before this process, already initiated, can be completed). Now, such an organization of a great group of nervous elements as will lead to conduct with reference to the objects about us is what one would find in the central nervous system answering to what we call an object. The complications are very great, but the central nervous system has an almost infinite number of elements in it, and they can be organized not only in spatial connection with each other, but also from a temporal stand-point. In virtue of this last fact, our conduct is made up of a series of steps which follow each other, and the later steps may be already started and influence the earlier ones. The thing we are going to do is playing back on what we are doing now. That organization in the neural elements in reference to what we call a physical object would be what we call a con-ceptual object stated in terms of the central nervous system.

In rough fashion it is the initiation of such a set of organized sets of responses that answers to what we call the idea or concept of a thing. If one asked what the idea of a dog is, and tried to find that idea in the central nervous system, one would find a whole group of responses which are more or less connected together by definite paths so that when one uses the term "dog" he does tend to call out this group of responses. A dog is a possible playmate, a possible enemy, one's own property or somebody else's. There is a whole series of possible responses. There are certain types of these responses which are in all of us, and there are others which vary with the individuals, but there is always an organization of the responses which can be called out by the term "dog." So if one is speaking of a dog to another person he is arousing in himself this set of responses which he is arousing in the other individual.

It is, of course, the relationship of this symbol, this vocal gesture, to such a set of responses in the individual himself as well as in the other that makes of that vocal gesture what I call a significant symbol. A symbol does tend to call out in the individual a group of reactions such as it calls out in the other, but there is something further that is involved in its being a significant symbol: this response within one's self to such a word as "chair," or "dog," is one which is a stimulus to the individual as well as a response. This is what, of course, is involved in what we term the meaning of a thing, or its significance.[2] We often act with reference to objects in what we call an intelligent fashion, although we can act without the mean-ing of the object being present in our experience. One can start to dress for dinner, as they tell of the absent-minded college professor, and find himself in his pajamas in bed. A certain process of undressing was started and car-ried out mechanically; he did not recognize the meaning of what he was doing. He intended to go to dinner and found he had gone to bed. The meaning involved in his action was not present. The steps in this case were all intelligent steps which controlled his conduct with reference to later action, but he did not think about what he was doing. The later action was not a stimulus to his response, but just carried itself out when it was once started.

When we speak of the meaning of what we are doing we are making the response itself that we are on the point of carrying out a stimulus to our action. It becomes a stimulus to a later stage of action which is to take place from the point of view of this particular response. In the case of the boxer the blow that he is starting to direct toward his opponent is to call out a certain response which will open up the guard of his opponent so that he can strike. The meaning is a stimulus for the preparation of the real blow he expects to deliver. The response which he calls out in himself (the guarding reaction) is the stimulus to him to strike where an opening is given. This action which he has initiated already in himself thus becomes a stimulus for his later response. He knows what his opponent is going to do, since the guarding movement is one which is already aroused, and becomes a stimulus to strike where the opening is given. The meaning would not have been present in his conduct unless it became a stimulus to strike where the favorable opening appears.

Such is the difference between intelligent conduct on the part of animals and what we call a reflective individual.[3] We say the animal does not think. He does not put himself in a position for which he is responsible; he does not put himself in the place of the other person and say, in effect, "He will act in such a way and I will act in this way. If the individual can act in this way, and the attitude which he calls out in himself can become a stimulus to him for another act, we have meaningful conduct. Where the response of the other person is called out and becomes a stimulus to control his action, then he has the meaning of the other person's act in his own experience. That is the general mechanism of what we term "thought," for in order that thought may exist there must be symbols, vocal gestures generally, which arouse in the individual himself the response which he is calling out in the other, and such that from the point of view of that response he is able to direct his later conduct. It involves not only communication in the sense in which birds and animals communicate with each other, but also an arousal in the individual himself of the response which he is calling out in the other individual, a taking of the rôle of the other, a tendency to act as the other person acts. One participates in the same process the other person is carrying out and controls his action with reference to that participation. It is that which constitutes the meaning of an object, namely, the common response in one's self as well as in the other person, which becomes, in turn, a stimulus to one's self.

If you conceive of the mind as just a sort of conscious substance in which there are certain impressions and states, and hold that one of those states is a universal, then a word becomes purely arbitrary—it is just a symbol.[4] You can then take words and pronounce them backwards, as children do; there seems to be absolute freedom of arrangement and language seems to be an entirely mechanical thing that lies outside of the process of intelligence. If you recognize that language is, however, just a part of a co-operative process, that part which does lead to an adjustment to the response of the other so that the whole activity can go on, then language has only a limited range of arbitrariness. If you are talking to another person you are, perhaps, able to scent the change in his attitude by something that would not strike a third person at all. You may know his mannerism, and that becomes a gesture to you, a part of the response of the individual. There is a certain range possible within the gesture as to what is to serve as the symbol. We may say that a whole set of separate symbols with one meaning are acceptable; but they always are gestures, that is, they are always parts of the act of the individual which reveal what he is going to do to the other person so that when the person utilizes the clue he calls out in himself the attitude of the other. Language is not ever arbitrary in the sense of simply denoting a bare state of consciousness by a word. What particular part of one's act will serve to direct co-operative activity is more or less arbitrary. Different phases of the act may do it. What seems unimportant in itself may be highly important in revealing what the attitude is. In that sense one can speak of the gesture itself as unimportant, but it is of great importance as to what the gesture is going to reveal. This is seen in the difference between the purely intellectual character of the symbol and its emotional character. A poet depends upon the latter; for him language is rich and full of values which we, perhaps, utterly ignore. In trying to express a message in something less than ten words, we merely want to convey a certain meaning, while the poet is dealing with what is really living tissue, the emotional throb in the expression itself. There is, then, a great range in our use of language; but whatever phase of this range is used is a part of a social process, and it is always that part by means of which we affect ourselves as we affect others and mediate the social situation through this understanding of what we are saying. That is fundamental for any language; if it is going to be language one has to understand what he is saying, has to affect himself as he affects others.

NOTES

1. Gestures, if carried back to the matrix from which they spring, are always found to inhere in or involve a larger social act of which they are phases. In dealing with communication we have first to recognize its earliest origins in the unconscious conversation of gestures. Conscious communication —conscious conversation of gestures—arises when gestures become signs, that

is, when they come to carry for the individuals making them and the individuals responding to them, definite meanings or significations in terms of the subsequent behavior of the individuals making them; so that, by serving as prior indications, to the individuals responding to them, of the subsequent behavior of the individuals making them, they make possible the mutual adjustment of the various individual components of the social act to one another, and also, by calling forth in the individuals making them the same responses implicitly that they call forth explicitly in the individuals to whom they are made, they render possible the rise of self-consciousness in connection with this mutual adjustment.

2. The inclusion of the matrix or complex of attitudes and responses constituting any given social situation or act, within the experience of any one of the individuals implicated in that situation or act (the inclusion within his experience of his attitudes toward other individuals, of their responses to his attitudes toward them, of their attitudes toward him, and of his responses to these attitudes) in all that an *idea* amounts to; or at any rate is the only basis for its occurrence or existence "in the mind" of the given individual.

In the case of the unconscious conversation of gestures, or in the case of the process of communication carried on by means of it, none of the individuals participating in it is conscious of the meaning of the conversation—that meaning does not appear in the experience of any one of the separate individuals involved in the conversation or carrying it on; whereas, in the case of the conscious conversation of gestures, or in the case of the process of communication carried on by means of it, each of the individuals participating in it is conscious of the meaning of the conversation, precisely because that meaning does appear in his experience, and because such appearance is what consciousness of that meaning implies.

3. For the nature of animal conduct see "Concerning Animal Perception," *Psychological Review*, XIV (1907), 383 ff.

4. Müller attempts to put the values of thought into language; but this attempt is fallacious, because language has those values only as the most effective mechanism of thought merely because it carries the conscious or significant conversation of gestures to its highest and most perfect development. There must be some sort of an implicit attitude (that is, a response which is initiated without being fully carried out) in the organism making the gesture—an attitude which answers to the overt response to the gesture on the part of another individual, and which corresponds to the attitude called forth or aroused in this other organism by the gesture—if thought is to develop in the organism making the gesture. And it is the central nervous system which provides the mechanism for such implicit attitudes or responses.

The identification of language with reason is in one sense an absurdity, but in another sense it is valid. It is valid, namely, in the sense that the process of language brings the total social act into the experience of the given individual as himself involved in the act, and thus makes the process of reason possible. But though the process of reason is and must be carried on in terms of the process of language—in terms, that is, of words—it is not simply constituted by the latter.

EDWARD SAPIR

Communication

IT IS OBVIOUS that for the building up of society, its units and subdivisions, and the understandings which prevail between its members some processes of communication are needed. While we often speak of society as though it were a static structure defined by tradition, it is, in the more intimate sense, nothing of the kind, but a highly intricate network of partial or complete understandings between the members of organizational units of every degree of size and complexity, ranging from a pair of lovers or a family to a league of nations or that ever increasing portion of humanity which can be reached by the press through all its transnational ramifications. It is only apparently a static sum of social institutions; actually it is being reanimated or creatively reaffirmed from day to day by particular acts of a communicative nature which obtain among individuals participating in it. Thus the Republican party cannot be said to exist as such, but only to the extent that its tradition is being constantly added to and upheld by such simple acts of communication as that John Doe votes the Republican ticket, thereby communicating a certain kind of message, or that a half dozen individuals meet at a certain time and place, formally or informally, in order to communicate ideas to one another and eventually to decide what points of national interest, real or supposed, are to be allowed to come up many months later for discussion in a gathering of members of the party. The Republican party as a historic entity is merely abstracted from thousands upon thousands of such single acts of communication, which have in common certain persistent features of reference. If we extend this example into every conceivable field in which communication has a place we soon realize that every cultural pattern and every single act of social behavior involve communication in either an explicit or an implicit sense.

Reprinted from *Encyclopedia of the Social Sciences*, edited by Edwin R. Seligman, Vol. IV (1931), pp. 78–80, by permission of the publisher. (Copyright, 1931, by the Macmillan Co.)

One may conveniently distinguish between certain fundamental techniques, or primary processes, which are communicative in character and certain secondary techniques which facilitate the process of communication. The distinction is perhaps of no great psychological importance but has a very real historical and sociological significance, inasmuch as the fundamental processes are common to all mankind, while the secondary techniques emerge only at relatively sophisticated levels of civilization. Among the primary communicative processes of society may be mentioned: language; gesture, in its widest sense; the imitation of overt behavior; and a large and ill defined group of implicit processes which grow out of overt behavior and which may be rather vaguely referred to as "social suggestion."

Language is the most explicit type of communicative behavior that we know of. It need not here be defined beyond pointing out that it consists in every case known to us of an absolutely complete referential apparatus of phonetic symbols which have the property of locating every known social referent, including all the recognized data of perception which the society that it serves carries in its tradition. Language is the communicative process par excellence in every known society, and it is exceedingly import to observe that whatever may be the shortcomings of a primitive society judged from the vantage point of civilization its language inevitably forms as sure, complete and potentially creative an apparatus of referential symbolism as the most sophisticated language that we know of. What this means for a theory of communication is that the mechanics of significant understanding between human beings are as sure and complex and rich in overtones in one society as in another, primitive or sophisticated.

Gesture includes much more than the manipulation of the hands and other visible and moveable parts of the organism. Intonations of the voice may register attitudes and feelings quite as significantly as the clenched fist, the wave of the hand, the shrugging of the shoulders or the lifting of the eyebrows. The field of gesture interplays constantly with that of language proper, but there are many facts of a psychological and historical order which show that there are subtle yet firm lines of demarcation between them. Thus, to give but one example, the consistent message delivered by language symbolism in the narrow sense, whether by speech or by writing, may flatly contradict the message communicated by the synchronous system of gestures, consisting of movements of the hands and head, intonations of the voice and breathing symbolisms. The former system may be entirely conscious, the latter entirely unconscious. Linguistic, as opposed to gesture, communication tends to be the official and socially accredited one; hence one may intuitively interpret the relatively unconscious symbolisms of gesture as psychologically more significant in a given context than the words actually used. In such cases as these we

163

have a conflict between explicit and implicit communications in the growth of the individual's social experience.

The primary condition for the consolidation of society is the imitation of overt behavior. Such imitation, while not communicative in intent, has always the retroactive value of a communication, for in the process of falling in with the ways of society one in effect acquiesces in the meanings that inhere in these ways. When one learns to go to church, for instance, because other members of the community set the pace for this kind of activity, it is as though a communication had been received and acted upon. It is the function of language to articulate and rationalize the full content of these informal communications in the growth of the individual's social experience.

Even less directly communicative in character than overt behavior and its imitation is "social suggestion" as the sum total of new acts and new meanings that are implicitly made possible by these types of social behavior. Thus, the particular method of revolting against the habit of church going in a given society, while contradictory, on the surface, of the conventional meanings of that society, may nevertheless receive all its social significance from hundreds of existing prior communications that belong to the culture of the group as a whole. The importance of the unformulated and unverbalized communications of society is so great that one who is not intuitively familiar with them is likely to be baffled by the significance of certain kinds of behavior, even if he is thoroughly aware of their external forms and of the verbal symbols that accompany them. It is largely the function of the artist to make articulate these more subtle intentions of society.

Communicative processes do not merely apply to society as such; they are indefinitely varied as to form and meaning for the various types of personal relationships into which society resolves itself. Thus, a fixed type of conduct or a linguistic symbol has not by any means necessarily the same communicative significance within the confines of the family, among the members of an economic group and in the nation at large. Generally speaking, the smaller the circle and the more complex the understandings already arrived at within it, the more economical can the act of communication afford to become. A single word passed between members of an intimate group, in spite of its apparent vagueness and ambiguity, may constitute a far more precise communication than volumes of carefully prepared correspondence interchanged between two governments.

There seem to be three main classes of techniques which have for their object the facilitation of the primary communicative processes of society. These may be referred to as: language transfers; symbolisms arising from special technical situations; and the creation of physical conditions favorable for the communicative act. Of language transfers the best known example is writing. The Morse telegraph code is another example. These and many other communicative techniques have this in common, that while they are overtly not at all like one another their organization is based on the primary symbolic organization which has arisen in the domain of speech. Psychologically, therefore, they extend the communicative character of speech to situations in which for one reason or another speech is not possible.

In the more special class of communicative symbolism one cannot make a word to word translation, as it were, back to speech but can only paraphrase in speech the intent of the communication. Here belong such symbolic systems as wigwagging, the use of railroad lights, bugle calls in the army and smoke signals. It is interesting to observe that while they are late in developing in the history of society they are very much less complex in structure than language itself. They are of value partly in helping out a situation where neither language nor any form of language transfer can be applied, partly where it is desired to encourage the automatic nature of the desired response. Thus, because language is extraordinarily rich in meaning it sometimes becomes a little annoying or even dangerous to rely upon it where only a simple this or that, or yes or no, is expected to be the response.

The importance of extending the physical conditions allowing for communication is obvious. The railroad, the telegraph, the telephone, the radio and the airplane are among the best examples. It is to be noted that such instruments as the railroad and the radio are not communicative in character as such; they become so only because they facilitate the presentation of types of stimuli which act as symbols of communication or which contain implications of communicative significance. Thus, a telephone is of no use unless the party at the other end understands the language of the person calling up. Again, the fact that a railroad runs me to a certain point is of no real communicative importance unless there are fixed bonds of interest which connect me with the inhabitants of the place. The failure to bear in mind these obvious points has tended to make some writers exaggerate the importance of the spread in modern times of such inventions as the railroad and the telephone.

The history of civilization has been marked by a progressive increase in the radius of communication. In a typically primitive society communication is reserved for the members of the tribe and at best a small number of surrounding tribes with whom relations are intermittent rather than continuous and who act as a kind of buffer between the significant psychological world—the world of one's own tribal culture—and the great unknown or unreal that lies beyond. Today, in our own civilization, the appearance of a new fashion in Paris is linked by a series of rapid and necessary events with the appearance of the same fashion in such distant places as Berlin, London, New York, San Francisco and Yokohama. The underlying reason for this remarkable change in the radius and rapidity of communication is the gradual diffusion of cultural traits or, in other words, of meaningful cultural reactions. Among the various types of cultural diffusion that of language itself is of paramount importance. Secondary technical devices making for ease of communication are also, of course, of great importance.

The multiplication of far-reaching techniques of communication has two important results. In the first place, it increases the sheer radius of communication, so that for certain purposes the whole civilized world is made the psychological equivalent of a primitive tribe. In the second place, it lessens the importance of mere geographical contiguity. Owing to the technical nature of these sophisticated communicative devices, parts of the world that are geographically remote may, in terms of behavior, be actually much closer to one another than adjoining regions, which, from the historical standpoint, are supposed to share a larger body of common understandings. This means, of course, a tendency to remap the world both sociologically and psychologically. Even now it is possible to say that the scattered "scientific world" is a social unity which has no clear cut geographical location. Further, the world of urban understanding in America contrasts rather sharply with the rural world. The weakening of the geographical factor in social organization must in the long run profoundly modify our attitude toward the meaning of personal relations and of social classes and even nationalities.

The increasing ease of communication is purchased at a price, for it is becoming increasingly difficult to keep an intended communication within the desired bounds. A humble example of this new problem is the inadvisability of making certain kinds of statement on the telephone. Another example is the insidious cheapening of literary and artistic values due to the foreseen and economically advantageous "widening of the appeal." All effects which demand a certain intimacy of understanding tend to become difficult and are therefore avoided. It is a question whether the obvious increase of overt communication is not constantly being corrected, as it were, by the creation of new obstacles to communication. The fear of being too easily understood may, in many cases, be more aptly defined as the fear of being understood by too many—so many, indeed, as to nedanger the psychological reality of the image of the enlarged self confronting the not-self.

On the whole, however, it is rather the obstacles to communication that are felt as annoying or ominous. The most important of these obstacles in the modern world is undoubtedly the great diversity of languages. The enormous amount of energy put into the task of translation implies a passionate desire to make as light of the language difficulty as possible. In the long run it seems almost unavoidable that the civilized world will adopt some one language of intercommunication, say English or Esperanto, which can be set aside for denotive purposes pure and simple.

ROBERT E. PARK

Reflections on Communication and Culture

WHAT does communication do and how does it function in the cultural process? It seems to do several different things. Communication creates, or makes possible at least, that consensus and understanding among the individual components of a social group which eventually gives it and them the character not merely of society but of a cultural unit. It spins a web of custom and mutual expectation which binds together social entities as diverse as the family group, a labor organization, or the haggling participants in a village market. Communication maintains the concert necessary to enable them to function, each in its several ways.

Family group or labor organization, every form of society except the most transient, has a life-history and a tradition. It is by communication that this tradition is transmitted. It is in this way that the continuity of common enterprises and social institutions is maintained, not merely from day to day, but from generation to generation. Thus, the function of communication seems to be to maintain the unity and integrity of the social group in its two dimensions—space and time. It is in recognition of this fact that John Dewey has said: "Society not only continues to exist by transmission, by communication, but may fairly be said to exist in transmission, in communication."

Implicit in Dewey's statement, however, is a conception of society that is not generally nor everywhere accepted, since it seems to identify the social with the moral order. By so doing it limits the term "social" to those relations of individuals that are personal, customary, and moral.

"When individuals use one another to get results, without reference

Reprinted from *The American Journal of Sociology*, Vol. XLIV (1939), pp. 191–205, by permission of the publisher. (Copyright, 1939, by *The American Journal of Sociology*.)

to their emotional or intellectual disposition and consent," says Dewey, they are involved in relations that are not social. To make the matter clear, he adds, "So far as the relations of parent and child, teacher and pupil, remain upon this level, they form no true social group, no matter how closely their respective activities touch one another."

It is obvious, however, that communication, if it is the typical social process, is not the only form of interaction that goes on among the individual units of a social group. "We are compelled to recognize," he admits, "that even within the most social group there are many relations which are not yet social"—not social, at any rate, in the sense in which he uses the term. Competition, for example, performs a social function of a somewhat different sort, but one that is at least comparable to that of communication. The economic order in society seems to be very largely a by-product of competition. In any case, competition is, as Cooley observes, "the very heart of the economic process." What we ordinarily designate as economic competition, however, is not competition in the Malthusian sense of that term in which it is identical with the struggle for existence. Economic competition is always competition that is controlled and regulated to some extent by convention, understanding, and law.

The investigations of plant and animal ecologists have discovered that even where competition is free and unrestricted, as it is in the so-called plant and animal communities, there exists among creatures living in the same habitat of kind of natural economy. What characterizes this economy is a division of labor and an unconscious co-operation of competing organisms. Wherever in nature competition or the struggle for existence brings about a stable organization among competing individuals, it is because they have achieved in some form or another a division of labor and some form of conscious or unconscious co-operation. In such case the competing species or individual, each occupying the particular niche in which it fits, will have created an environment in which all can live together under conditions where each could not live separately. This natural economy of plant and animals is called symbiosis.

Man's relation to other men is, to a very much larger extent than has hitherto been recognized, symbiotic rather than social, in the sense in which Dewey uses that term. Competition among plants and animals tends to bring about an orderly distribution as well as a mutual adaptation of the species living together in a common habitat. Competition among human beings has brought about, or at any rate helped to bring about, not merely a territorial, but an occupational distribution of races and peoples. Incidentally, it has brought about that inevitable division of labor which is fundamental to every permanent form of society from the family to the nation.

If the struggle for existence, as Darwin conceived it, was a determining factor in producing that diversity of living types described in the *Origin of the Species*, then economic competition, the struggle for a livelihood, seems to have been a decisive factor in bringing about among human beings a comparable occupational diversity. But this division of labor wherever it exists in human society is limited by custom; and custom is a product of communication.

As a matter of fact, competition and communication operate everywhere within the same local habitat and within the same community, but in relative independence of each other. The area of competition and of the symbiotic relationship is, however, invariably wider and more inclusive than the area of those intimate, personal, and moral relations initiated by communication. Commerce invariably expands more widely and rapidly than linguistic or cultural understanding. It is, it seems, this cultural lag that makes most of our political and cultural problems. But the main point is that communication, where it exists, invariably modifies and qualifies competition, and the cultural order imposes limitations on the symbiotic.

Most of you will perhaps recall Sumner's description of primitive society, a territory occupied by little scattered ethnocentric groups, each the focus and center of a little world in which all members are bound together in ties of mutual understanding and loyalty.

Outside of these little tribal and familial units, on the other hand, men live in relation with one another not unlike those in which they live with the plants and animals, that is to say, in a kind of symbiosis, very little modified by mutual understanding or agreements of any sort. Under these circumstances the fundamental social and economic order is enforced and maintained by competition, but competition modified and controlled to an ever increasing degree by custum, convention, and law.

As a matter of fact, society everywhere exhibits two fundamental forms of organization—the familial and the communal. Familial society seems to have had its source in the interest and in the urge of individuals, not merely to live as individuals but to perpetuate the race. Thus the family seems to rest, finally, on an instinctive basis. Communal society, on the other hand, has arisen out of the need of the individuals to survive as individuals. Under these conditions men have come together, not in response to some gregarious impulse comparable with the sexual instinct, but for the more pragmatic and intelligible reason that they are useful to one another.

In spite of the changes which time and civilization have wrought in the existing social order, man lives as he always has, in two worlds—the little world of family and the great world of commerce and politics. In the little world the order which predominates is intimate, personal, and moral. In the larger world man is free to pursue his individual interests in his own individual way, relatively uninhibited by the expectations and claims which, in a more intimate social order, the interests of others mght impose upon him. In the family it is communication and the personal influences which communication mediates that are the source and principle of order. In the world of commerce, and to a less degree in politics, it is competition in the more sublimated form of conflict and rivalry, which imposes such order as exists.

What all this suggests, though not perhaps so obviously as I should like, is that competition and communication, although they perform divergent and unco-ordinated social functions, nevertheless in the actual life of society they supplement and complete each other.

Competition seems to be the principle of individuation in the life of the person and of society. Under the influence of this principle the individual adapts and accommodates himself, not merely to the human habitat but to the occupational organization of the society of which he is a member. He follows the vocation and does the thing he can, rather than the thing he might like to do. Communication, on the other hand, operates primarily as an integrating and socializing principle.

It is true, of course, that when new forms of communication have brought about more intimate associations among individuals or peoples who have been culturally isolated, the first consequence may be to intensify competition. Furthermore, under the influence of communication, competition tends to assume a new character. It becomes conflict. In that case the struggle for existence is likely to be intensified by fears, animosities, and jealousies, which the presence of the competitor and the knowledge of his purposes arouse. Under such circumstances a competitor becomes an enemy.

On the other hand, it is always possible to come to terms with an enemy whom one knows and with whom one can communicate, and, in the long run, greater intimacy inevitably brings with it a more profound understanding, the result of which is to humanize social relations and to substitute a moral order for one that is fundamentally symbiotic rather than social, always in the restricted sense of that term.

DIFFUSION

Communication, whether it takes place through the medium of gesture, articulate speech, or conventional symbols of any sort whatever, always involves, it seems to me, an interpretation of the attitude or intent of the person whose word or gesture supplied the stimulus. What anything means to anyone at any time is substantially what it means, has meant, or will mean, to someone else. Communication is a process or form of interaction that is interpersonal, i.e., social in the narrower sense. The process is complete only when it results in some sort of understanding. In other words, communication is never merely a case of stimulus and response in the sense in which those terms are used in individual psychology. It is rather expression, interpretation, and response.

In some cases, in most cases perhaps, and particularly where the persons involved are *en rapport*, the response of individual A to an expressive action of individual B is likely to be immediate and well-nigh automatic. This is obviously so in the case of hypnotic suggestion, and particularly so under the condition of what is called "isolated rapport," where the subject responds to the suggestion of the hypnotizer and to that of no one else.

We must conceive individuals in society as living constantly enveloped in an atmosphere of subconscious suggestion. In this atmosphere they are constantly responsive, not merely to the overt acts but to the moods and the presence of other persons, in somewhat the same way that they are to the weather. What we call the fluctuations of public opinion, public sentiment, and fashion, are, in fact, a kind of social weather. These changes in the social weather evoke changes in internal tensions of persons who are *en rapport:* changes are so subtle that they amount to a kind of clairvoyance. It is only in moments of abstraction that this condition of clairvoyance is interrupted and then only partially. A suggestion is, of course, not a mere stimulus, but a stimulus that is interpreted as an expression of a wish or an attitude. The literature of hypnotism indicates how subtle suggestions may be and how responsive under certain conditions individuals may be to them.

Sometimes, to be sure, the sense and meaning of the behavior and language of those about us are obscure; this sets us thinking, and leaves us sometimes with a sense of frustration and confusion. At other times it arouses us, not to definite action, but to vague emotional protest or inarticulate opposition. This emotional expression of unrest, multiplied and intensified by the reflex influence of mind on mind, may take the form finally of a social brain storm like dancing mania of the Middle Ages or the commercial panic of 1929. Under more normal conditions unrest may express itself in social agitation or in the less violent form of discussion and debate.

These are some of the manifold ways in which communication operating within the limits of an existing culture group changes, directly and indirectly, the pattern of cultural life. If I merely refer to these manifestations here in passing it is because a fuller discussion of them would involve problems of collective behavior which are so diverse and manifold that they have become the subject of special discipline of the social sciences.

The cultural process ordinarily presents itself in two dimensions or aspects which are intimately bound up with and determined by the conditions under which communication inevitably takes place. They are: diffusion and acculturation.

As communication takes place between persons, it is necessarily involved in all the complexities incident to the transmission of a stimulus

171

from the source *a quo* to a terminus *ad quem*—I.e., from a person of whose mind it is an expression to the person in whose mind it finds a response. The obvious conditions which facilitate or obstruct these processes are mainly physical and in modern times they have been progressively overcome by means of technical devices like the alphabet, printing-press radio, etc.

The less obvious obstacles to effective communication are the difficulties that grow out of differences of language, tradition, experience, and interest. By interest in this instance I mean what Thomas refers to as the "run of attention." Everywhere and always, certain interests, persons, or events are in the focus of attention; certain things are in fashion. Whatever has importance and prestige at the moment has power to direct for a time the currents of public opinion, even if it does not change, in the long run, the trend of events. All these things are factors in communication and either facilitate or make difficult the transmission of news from one country to another. The manner in which news circulates is typical of one way in which cultural diffusion takes place.

Discussions of the deficiencies of the press often proceed on the implicit assumption that the communication of news from one cultural area to another—from the Orient to the Occident, for example, or from Berlin to New York—is an operation as simple as the transportation of a commodity like bricks. One can, of course, transport words across cultural marches, but the interpretations which they receive on two sides of a political or cultural boundary will depend upon the context which their different interpreters bring to them. That context, in turn, will depend rather more upon the past experience and present temper of the people to whom the words are addressed than upon either the art or the good will of the persons who report them.

Foreign correspondents know, as no one who has not had the experience, how difficult it is under ordinary circumstances to make the public read foreign news. They know, also, how much more difficult it is to make events happening beyond his horizon intelligible to the average man in the street. In general, news circulates widely in every direction in proportion as it is interesting and intelligible. In that respect it is not unlike any other cultural item, the oil cans of the Standard Oil Company or the Singer sewing-machine for example, which are now possibly the most widely dispersed of all our modern cultural artifacts.

Each and every artifact or item of news inevitably tends to reach the places where it will be appreciated and understood. Cultural traits are assimilated only as they are understood, and they are understood only as they are assimilated. This does not mean that a cultural artifact or an item of news will have everywhere the same meaning; quite the contrary. But the different meanings they do have in different places will tend to converge, as diffusion is succeeded by acculturation.

It is extraordinary to what extent and with what rapidity news tends to reach the minds of those to whom its message, if intelligible, is important. On the other hand, just as important, if less remarkable, is the difficulty of communicating a message that is neither important nor intelligible to the persons to whom it is addressed. This latter is a problem of the schools, particularly the problem of rote learning.

Thirty-three years ago the conclusion of the Russian-Japanese War made news that I suspect circulated farther and more rapidly than any other report of events had ever traveled before. One heard echoes of it in regions as far apart as the mountain fastnesses of Tibet and the forests of Central Africa. It was news that a nation of colored people had defeated and conquered a nation of white people. The same item of news might travel further and with greater speed today, but it would not have the same importance. The question of how and why and under what circumstances news circulates is an important one and deserves more attention than has yet been given to it.

It is a familiar observation of students of the cultural process that artifacts, the traits of a material culture, are more easily diffused and more rapidly assimilated than similar items of a nonmaterial culture—political institutions and religious practices, for example. That is no more than to say that trade expands, on the whole, more rapidly than religion. But that, too, depends upon circumstances. Consider, for example, the sudden rapid diffusion in the modern world of communism.

One reason the terms of a material culture are so widely diffused and assimilated is because their uses are obvious and their values, whatever they be, are rational and secular. One needs no rite or ceremony to initiate him into mysteries involved in the use of a wheelbarrow or rifle. When the first plow was introduced into South Africa, an old chief who was invited to be present and see the demonstration recognized its value at once. He said, "This is a great thing the white man has brought us." Then after some reflection he added: "It is worth as much as ten wives."

What we call civilization, as distinguished from culture, is largely composed of such artifacts and technical devices as can be diffused without undermining the existing social institutions and without impairing the ability of a people to act collectively, that is to say, consistently and in concert. Institutions seem to exist primarily to facilitate collective action, and anything that involves a society rather than the individuals of which that society is composed is hard to export. Diffusion takes place more easily when the social unity is relaxed.

It is no secret, I suppose, that there is invariably an intimate and indissoluble relation between commerce and the news. The centers of trade are invariably the centers of news; the centers to which the news inevitably comes and from whence it is diffused, first to the local community and then, according to its interests and importance, to the ends of the earth.

During this diffusion a process of selection necessarily takes place. Some news items travel further and more rapidly than others. This is true even when all or most of the physical obstacles to communication have been overcome. The reason of course is simple enough. It is bound up with the inevitably egocentric character of human beings and the ethnocentric character of human relations generally. An event is important only as we believe we can do something about it. It loses importance in proportion as the possibility of doing that something seems more remote. An earthquake in China assumes, in view of our incorrigible provincialism, less importance than a funeral in our village. This is an example of what is meant by social distance, which is the term in which sociologists seek to conceptualize and, in some sense, measure personal relations and personal intimacies. Importance is ultimately a personal matter; a matter of social distance.

The principle involved in the circulation of news is not different from that involved in the cultural process of diffusion, wherever it takes place. Individuals and societies assimilate most readily, as I have said, what is at once interesting and intelligible.

ACCULTURATION

If the market place is the center from which news is disseminated and cultural influences are diffused, it is, likewise, the center in which old ideas go into the crucible and new ideas emerge. The market place, where men gather to dicker and chaffer, is in the very nature of things a kind of forum where men of diverse interests and different minds are engaged in peaceful controversy, trying to come to terms about values and prices; trying, also, by a process that is fundamentally dialectical, to explore the different meanings things have for men of different interests; seeking to reach understandings based rather more on reason and rather less on tradition and the prejudices which custom has sanctioned, if not sanctified. It is for this reason that the great metropolitan cities—Rome, London, and Paris—cities to which peoples come and go from the four ends of the earth, are in a perpetual ferment of enlightenment; are continually involved—to use a German expression, in an *Aufklärung*. Under such conditions the historical process is quickened, and acculturation, the mutual interpenetration of minds and cultures, goes forward at a rapid pace.

When peoples of different races and divergent cultures seek to live together within the limits of the same local economy, they are likely to live for a time in relations which I have described as symbiotic rather than social, using that term in this connection as Dewey and others have used it, namely, as identical with cultural. They live, in short, in physical contiguity, but in more or less complete moral isolation, a situation which corresponds in effect if not in fact, to Sumner's description of primitive society.

This has been and still is the situation of some of those little religious sects like the Mennonites, which have from time to time sought refuge in the United States and elsewhere, settling on the frontiers of European civilization, where they might hope to live in something like tribal isolation—untrammeled and uncorrupted by intercourse with a Gentile world.

It was to preserve this isolation that some of Pennsylvania's "plain people," the Amish, protested against a gift of $112,000 of P.W.A. funds which the government was pressing upon them for new schoolhouses. New schools, in this case, involved the use of busses, to which the "plain people" were opposed. They believed, also, and no doubt quite correctly, that intimate association of Amish children with the mixed population of a consolidated school to whom Amish folkways would certainly seem quaint, would undermine the discipline and the sacred solidarity of Amish society.

This situation, in which peoples occupying the same territory live in a moral isolation more or less complete, was historically, so long as they lived in the seclusion of their religious community, the situation of a more sophisticated people than the Amish, namely, the Jews. It has been, to a less extent, the situation of every immigrant people which has for any reason sought to find a place in the economic order of an established society and at the same time maintain a cultural tradition that was alien to it.

Inevitably, however, in the natural course, under modern conditions of life, both the immigrant and the sectarian seek to escape from this isolation in order that they may participate more actively in the social life of the people about them. It is then, if not earlier, that they become aware of the social distance that sets them apart from the members of the dominant cultural group. Under these circumstances acculturation becomes involved in and part of the struggle of immigrants and sectarians alike for status. Everything that marks them as strangers—manners, accent, habits of speech and thought—makes this struggle difficult. The cultural conflict which then ensues—whether openly manifested or merely sensed—tends, as conflict invariably does, to heighten self-consciousness in members of both cultural groups, in those who are classed as aliens and in those who count themselves native.

However, anything that intensifies self-consciousness and stimulates introspection inevitably brings to the surface and into clear consciousness sentiments and attitudes that otherwise would escape rational criticism and interpretation. Otherwise they would probably, as the psychoanalysts tell us, continue active in the dark backgrounds of consciousness. They would still function as part of that "vital secret" to which William James refers in his essay *A Certain Blindness in Human Beings*—a secret of which each of us is profoundly conscious because it is the substance of one's own self-consciousness and of one's individual point of view—but for which we look in vain to others for sympathy and understanding. But conflict, and particularly cultural conflict, in so far as it brings into the light of understanding impulses and attitudes of which we would otherwise remain unconscious, inevitably increases our knowledge not merely of ourselves but of our fellows, since the attitudes and sentiments which we find in ourselves we are able to appreciate and understand, no matter how indirectly expressed, when we find them in the minds of others.

Acculturation, if we conceive it in radical fashion, may be said to begin with the intimate associations and understandings that grow up in the family between mother and child and somewhat later with other members of the family. But while mothers are necessarily, and under all ordinary circumstances, profoundly interested and responsive to their children, it is notorious that they do not always understand them.

The situation differs, but not greatly, with other members of the family —notably with the relations between husband and wife. Men are naturally and instinctively interested in and attracted by women, particularly strange women, but they often find them difficult to understand. In fact men have felt in the past and still feel in some obscure way, I suspect, that women, no matter how interesting, are not quite human in the sense and to the degree that this is true of themselves.

If this is not true to the same extent today that it once was, it is because men and women, in the family and outside of it, live in more intimate association with one another than they formerly did. They still have their separate worlds, but they get together as they formerly did not. They speak the same language. But this is true also of parents and children. Both understand each other better than they once did.

Men and women have learned a great deal about one another from experience, but they have learned more—in the sense of understanding one another and in the ability to communicate—from literature and the arts. In fact it is just the function of literature and the arts and of what are described in academic circles as the humanities to give us this intimate personal and inside knowledge of each other which makes social life more amiable and collective action possible.

I am, perhaps, wrong in describing the intimate associations which family life permits and enforces as if they were part and parcel of the cultural process. That may seem to be employing a term in a context which is so foreign to it as to destroy its original meaning. I am not sure, however, that this is quite true. At any rate, in the family in which husband and wife are of different racial stocks, with different cultural heritages, the process of acculturation—and acculturation in the sense in which it is familiar to students—takes place more obviously and more effectively than it does elsewhere. It is this fact and not its biological consequences which gives recent studies of race mixture and interracial marriage, like the studies of Romanzo Adams in Hawaii, a significance they would not otherwise have. It is in the life-histories of mixed bloods whose origin ordinarily imposes upon them the task of assimilating the heritages of two divergent cultures, that the process and consequences of acculturation are most obvious and open to investigation. The reason is that the man of mixed blood is a "marginal man," so called, that is, the man who lives in two worlds but is not quite at home in either.

Conclusion

In conclusion, I shall revert to the distinction with which I started—the distinction between language and forms of communication which are referential, as a scientific description, and language and forms of communication which are symbolic and expressive, as in literature and the fine arts. It seems clear that the function of news is definitely referential. If it does not have the status in science of a classified fact, it is at least indispensable to government and to business. On the other hand, the function of art and of the cinema is, on the whole, in spite of the use that has been made of it for educational purposes, definitely symbolic, and as such it profoundly influences sentiment and attitudes even when it does not make any real contribution to knowledge.

HAROLD D. LASSWELL

The Structure and Function
of Communication in Society

The Act of Communication

A CONVENIENT WAY to describe an act of communication is to answer the
following questions:

> Who
> Says What
> In Which Channel
> To Whom
> With What Effect?

The scientific study of the process of communication tends to concentrate
upon one or another of these questions. Scholars who study the "who,"
the communicator, look into the factors that initiate and guide the act of
communication. We call this subdivision of the field of research *control
analysis*. Specialists who focus upon the "says what" engage in *content
analysis*. Those who look primarily at the radio, press, film and other
channels of communication are doing *media analysis*. When the principal
concern is with the persons reached by the media, we speak of *audience
analysis*. If the question is the impact upon audiences, the problem is *effect
analysis*.[1]

Whether such distinctions are useful depends entirely upon the degree
of refinement which is regarded as appropriate to a given scientific and
managerial objective. Often it is simpler to combine audience and effect
analysis, for instance, than to keep them apart. On the other hand, we

Reprinted from *The Communication of Ideas*, Lyman Bryson, ed., (1948), pp.
37–51, by permission of the author and the publisher. (Copyright, 1948,
Harper and Row.)

may want to concentrate on the analysis of content, and for this purpose subdivide the field into the study of purport and style, the first referring to the message, and the second to the arrangement of the elements of which the message is composed.

Structure and Function

Enticing as it is to work out these categories in more detail, the present discussion has a different scope. We are less interested in dividing up the act of communication than in viewing the act as a whole in relation to the entire social process. Any process can be examined in two frames of reference, namely, structure and function; and our analysis of communication will deal with the specializations that carry on certain functions, of which the following may be clearly distinguished: (1) The surveillance of the environment; (2) the correlation of the parts of society in responding to the invironment; (3) the transmission of the social heritage from one generation to the next.

Biological Equivalencies

At the risk of calling up false analogies, we can gain perspective on human societies when we note the degree to which communication is a feature of life at every level. A vital entity, whether relatively isolated or in association, has specialized ways of receiving stimuli from the environment. The single-celled organism or the many-membered group tends to maintain an internal equilibrium and to respond to changes in the environment in a way that maintains this equilibrium. The responding process calls for specialized ways of bringing the parts of the whole into harmonious action. Multicelled animals specialize cells to the function of external contact and internal correlation. Thus, among the primates, specialization is exemplified by organs such as the ear and eye, and the nervous system itself. When the stimuli receiving and disseminating patterns operate smoothly, the several parts of the animal act in concert in reference to the environment ("feeding," "fleeing," "attacking").[2]

In some animal societies certain members perform specialized roles, and survey the environment. Individuals act as "sentinels," standing apart from the herd or flock and creating a disturbance whenever an alarming change occurs in the surroundings. The trumpeting, cackling or shrilling of the sentinel is enough to set the herd in motion. Among the activities engaged in by specialized "leaders" is the internal stimulation of "followers" to adapt in an orderly manner to the circumstances heralded by the sentinels.[3]

Within a single, highly differentiated organism, incoming nervous

179

impulses and outgoing impulses are transmitted along fibers that make synaptic junction with other fibers. The critical points in the process occur at the relay stations, where the arriving impulse may be too weak to reach the threshold which stirs the next link into action. At the higher centers, separate currents modify one another, producing results that differ in many ways from the outcome when each is allowed to continue a separate path. At any relay station there is no conductance, total conductance or intermediate conductance. The same categories apply to what goes on among members of an animal society. The sly fox may approach the barnyard in a way that supplies too meager stimuli for the sentinel to sound the alarm. Or the attacking animal may eliminate the sentinel before he makes more than a feeble outcry. Obviously there is every gradation possible between total conductance and no conductance.

Attention in World Society

When we examine the process of communication of any state in the world community, we note three categories of specialists. One group surveys the political environment of the state as a whole, another correlates the response of the whole state to the environment, and the third transmits certain patterns of response from the old to the young. Diplomats, attachés, and foreign correspondents are representative of those who specialize on the environment. Editors, journalists, and speakers are correlators of the internal response. Educators in family and school transmit the social inheritance.

Communications which originate abroad pass through sequences in which various senders and receivers are linked with one another. Subject to modification at each relay point in the chain, messages originating with a diplomat or foreign correspondent may pass through editorial desks and eventually reach large audiences.

If we think of the world attention process as a series of *attention frames,* it is possible to describe the rate at which comparable content is brought to the notice of individuals and groups. We can inquire into the point at which "conductance" no longer occurs; and we can look into the range between "total conductance" and "minimum conductance." The metropolitan and political centers of the world have much in common with the interdependence, differentiation, and activity of the cortical or subcortical centers of an individual organism. Hence the attention frames found in these spots are the most variable, refined, and interactive of all frames in the world community.

At the other extreme are the attention frames of primitive inhabitants of isolated areas. Not that folk cultures are wholly untouched by industrial civilization. Whether we parachute into the interior of New Guinea, or land on the slopes of the Himalayas, we find no tribe wholly out of contact with the world. The long threads of trade, of missionary zeal, of adventurous exploration and scientific field study, and of global war, reach the far distant places. No one is entirely out of this world.

Among primitives the final shape taken by communication is the ballad or tale. Remote happenings in the great world of affairs, happenings that come to the notice of metropolitan audiences, are reflected, however dimly, in the thematic material of ballad singers and reciters. In these creations far away political leaders may be shown supplying land to the peasants or restoring an abundance of game to the hills.[4]

When we push upstream of the flow of communication, we note that the immediate relay function for nomadic and remote tribesmen is sometimes performed by the inhabitants of settled villages with whom they come in occasional contact. The relayer can be the school teacher, doctor, judge, tax collector, policeman, soldier, peddler, salesman, missionary, student; in any case he is an assembly point of news and comment.

More Detailed Equivalencies

The communication processes of human society, when examined in detail, reveal many equivalencies to the specializations found in the physical organism, and in the lower animal societies. The diplomats, for instance, of a single state are stationed all over the world and send messages to a few focal points. Obviously, these incoming reports move from the many to the few, where they interact upon one another. Later on, the sequence spreads fanwise according to a few to many pattern, as when a foreign secretary gives a speech in public, an article is put out in the press, or a news film is distributed to the theaters. The lines leading from the outer environment of the state are functionally equivalent to the afferent channels that convey incoming nervous impulses to the central nervous system of a single animal, and to the means by which alarm is spread among a flock. Outgoing, or efferent impulses, display corresponding parallels.

The central nervous system of the body is only partly involved in the entire flow of afferent-efferent impulses. There are automatic systems that can act on one another without involving the "higher" centers at all. The stability of the internal environment is maintained principally through the mediation of the vegetive or autonomic specializations of the nervous system. Similarly, most of the messages within any state do not involve the central channels of communication. They take place within families, neighborhoods, shops, field gangs, and other local contexts. Most of the educational process is carried on the same way.

A further set of significant equivalencies is related to the circuits of communication, which are predominantly one-way or two-way, depending upon the degree of reciprocity between communicators and audience. Or, to express it differently, two-way communication occurs when the sending and receiving functions are performed with equal frequency by two or more persons. A conversation is usually assumed to be a pattern of two-way communication (although monologues are hardly unknown). The modern instruments of mass communication give an enormous advantage to the controllers of printing plants, broadcasting equipment, and other forms of fixed and specialized capital. But it should be noted that audiences do "talk back," after some delay; and many controllers of mass media use scientific methods of sampling in order to expedite this closing of the circuit.

Circuits of two-way contact are particularly in evidence among the great metropolitan, political and cultural centers in the world. New York, Moscow, London and Paris, for example, are in intense two-way contact, even when the flow is severely curtailed in volume (as between Moscow and New York). Even insignificant sites become world centers when they are transformed into capital cities (Canberra in Australia, Ankara in Turkey, the District of Columbia, U.S.A.). A cultural center like Vatican City is in intense two-way relationship with the dominant centers throughout the world. Even specialized production centers like Hollywood, despite their preponderance of outgoing material, receive an enormous volume of messages.

A further distinction can be made between message controlling and message handling centers and social formations. The message center in the vast Pentagon Building of the War Department in Washington, D.C., transmits with no more than accidental change incoming messages to addressees. This is the role of the printers and distributors of books; of dispatchers, linemen, and messengers connected with telegraphic communication; of radio engineers, and other technicians associated with broadcasting. Such message handlers may be contrasted with those who affect the content of what is said, which is the function of editors, censors, and propagandists. Speaking of the symbol specialists as a whole, therefore, we separate them into the manipulators (controllers) and the handlers; the first group typically modifies content, while the second does not.

Needs and Values

Though we have noted a number of functional and structural equivalencies between communication in human societies and other living entities, it is not implied that we can most fruitfully investigate the process of communication in America or the world by the methods most appropriate to research on the lower animals or on single physical organisms. In comparative psychology when we describe some part of the surroundings of a rat, cat, or monkey as a stimulus (that is, as part of the environment reaching the attention of the animal), we cannot ask the rat; we use other means of inferring perception. When human beings are our objects of investigation, we can interview the great "talking animal." (This is not that we take everything at face value. Sometimes we forecast the opposite of what the person says he intends to do. In this case, we depend on other indications, both verbal and non-verbal.)

In the study of living forms, it is rewarding, as we have said, to look at them as modifiers of the environment in the process of gratifying needs, and hence of maintaining a steady state of internal equilibrium. Food, sex, and other activities which involve the environment can be examined on a comparative basis. Since human beings exhibit speech reactions, we can investigate many more relationships than in the nonhuman species.[5] Allowing for the data furnished by speech (and other communicative acts), we can investigate human society in terms of values; that is, in reference to categories of relationships that are recognized objects of gratification. In America, for example, it requires no elaborate technique of study to discern that power and respect are values. We can demonstrate this by listening to testimony, and by watching what is done when opportunity is afforded.

It is possible to establish a list of values current in any group chosen for investigation. Further than this, we can discover the rank order in which these values are sought. We can rank the members of the group according to their position in relation to the values. So far as industrial civilization is concerned, we have no hesitation in saying that power, wealth, respect, well being, and enlightenment are among the values. If we stop with this list, which is not exhaustive, we can describe on the basis of available knowledge (fragmentary though it may often be), the social structure of most of the world. Since values are not equally distributed, the social structure reveals more or less concentration of relatively abundant shares of power, wealth and other values in a few hands. In some places this concentration is passed on from generation to generation, forming castes rather than a mobile society.

In every society the values are shaped and distributed according to more or less distinctive patterns (*institutions*). The institutions include communications which are invoked in support of the network as a whole. Such communications are the ideology; and in relation to power we can differentiate the political *doctrine*, the political *formula* and the *miranda*.[6] These are illustrated in the United States by the doctrine of individualism, the paragraphs of the Constitution, which are the formula, and the ceremonies and legends of public life, which comprise the miranda. The ideology is communicated to the rising generation through such specialized agencies as the home and school.

Ideology is only part of the myths of any given society. There may

183

be counter ideologies directed against the dominant doctrine, formula, and miranda. Today the power structure of world politics is deeply affected by ideological conflict, and by the role of two giant powers, the United States and Russia.[7] The ruling elites view one another as potential enemies, not only in the sense that interstate differences may be settled by war, but in the more urgent sense that the ideology of the other may appeal to disaffected elements at home and weaken the internal power position of each ruling class.

Social Conflict and Communication

Under the circumstances, one ruling element is especially alert to the other, and relies upon communication as a means of preserving power. One function of communication, therefore, is to provide intelligence about what the other elite is doing, and about its strength. Fearful that intelligence channels will be controlled by the other, in order to withhold and distort, there is a tendency to resort to secret surveillance. Hence international espionage is intensified above its usual level in peacetime. Moreover, efforts are made to "black out" the self in order to counteract the scrutiny of the potential enemy. In addition, communication is employed affirmatively for the purpose of establishing contact with audiences within the frontiers of the other power.

These varied activities are manifested in the use of open and secret agents to scrutinize the other, in counter intelligence work, in censorship and travel restriction, in broadcasting and other informational activities across frontiers.

Ruling elites are also sensitized to potential threats in the internal environment. Besides using open sources of information, secret measures are also adopted. Precautions are taken to impose "security" upon as many policy matters as possible. At the same time, the ideology of the elite is reaffirmed, and counter ideologies are suppressed.

The processes here sketched run parallel to phenomena to be observed throughout the animal kingdom. Specialized agencies are used to keep aware of threats and opportunities in the external environment. The parallels include the surveillance exercised over the internal environment, since among the lower animals some herd leaders sometimes give evidence of fearing attack on two fronts, internal and external; they keep an uneasy eye on both environments. As a means of preventing surveillance by an enemy, well known devices are at the disposal of certain species, e.g., the squid's use of a liquid fog screen, the protective coloration of the chameleon. However, there appears to be no correlate of the distinction between the "secret" and "open" channels of human society.

Inside a physical organism the closest parallel to social revolution would be the growth of new nervous connections with parts of the body that rival, and can take the place of, the existing structures of central integration. Can this be said to occur as the embryo develops in the mother's body? Or, if we take a destructive, as distinct from a reconstructive, process, can we properly say that internal surveillance occurs in regard to cancer, since cancers compete for the food supplies of the body?

Efficient Communication

The analysis up to the present implies certain criteria of efficiency or inefficiency in communication. In human society the process is efficient to the degree that rational judgments are facilitated. A rational judgment implements value-goals. In animal societies communication is efficient when it aids survival, or some other specified need of the aggregate. The same criteria can be applied to the single organism.

One task of a rationally organized society is to discover and control any factors that interfere with efficient communication. Some limiting factors are psychotechnical. Destructive radiation, for instance may be present in the environment, yet remain undetected owing to the limited range of the unaided organism.

But even technical insufficiencies can be overcome by knowledge. In recent years shortwave broadcasting has been interfered with by disturbances which will either be surmounted, or will eventually lead to the abandonment of this mode of broadcasting. During the past few years advances have been made toward providing satisfactory substitutes for defective hearing and seeing. A less dramatic, though no less important, development has been the discovery of how inadequate reading habits can be corrected.

There are, of course, deliberate obstacles put in the way of communication, like censorship and drastic curtailment of travel. To some extent obstacles can be surmounted by skillful evasion, but in the long run it will doubtless be more efficient to get rid of them by consent or coercion.

Sheer ignorance is a pervasive factor whose consequences have never been adequately assessed. Ignorance here means the absence, at a given point in the process of communication, of knowledge which is available elsewhere in society. Lacking proper training, the personnel engaged in gathering and disseminating intelligence is continually misconstruing or overlooking the facts, if we define the facts as what the objective, trained observer could find.

In accounting for inefficiency we must not overlook the low evaluations put upon skill in relevant communication. Too often irrelevant, or positively distorting, performances command prestige. In the interest of a "scoop," the reporter gives a sensational twist to a mild international

185

conference, and contributes to the popular image of international politics as chronic, intense conflict, and little else. Specialists in communication often fail to keep up with the expansion of knowledge about the process; note the reluctance with which many visual devices have been adopted. And despite research on vocabulary, many mass communicators select words that fail. This happens, for instance, when a foreign correspondent allows himself to become absorbed in the foreign scene and forgets that his home audience has no direct equivalents in experience for "left," "center," and other factional terms.

Besides skill factors, the level of efficiency is sometimes adversely influenced by personality structure. An optimistic, outgoing person may hunt "birds of a feather" and gain an uncorrected and hence exaggeratedly optimistic view of events. On the contrary, when pessimistic, brooding personalities mix, they choose quite different birds, who confirm their gloom. There are also important differences among people which spring from contrasts in intelligence and energy.

Some of the most serious threats to efficient communication for the community as a whole relate to the values of power, wealth and respect. Perhaps the most striking examples of power distortion occur when the content of communication is deliberately adjusted to fit an ideology or counter ideology. Distortions related to wealth not only arise from attempts to influence the market, for instance, but from rigid conceptions of economic interest. A typical instance of inefficiencies connected with respect (social class) occurs when an upper class person mixes only with persons of his own stratum and forgets to correct his perspective by being exposed to members of other classes.

Research on Communication

The foregoing reminders of some factors that interfere with efficient communication point to the kinds of research which can usefully be conducted on representative links in the chain of communication. Each agent is a vortex of interacting environmental and predispositional factors. Whoever performs a relay function can be examined in relation to input and output. What statements are brought to the attention of the relay link? What does he pass on verbatim? What does he drop out? What does he rework? What does he add? How do differences in input and output correlate with culture and personality? By answering such questions it is possible to weigh the various factors in conductance, no conductance and modified conductance.

Besides the relay link, we must consider the primary link in a communication sequence. In studying the focus of attention of the primary observer, we emphasize two sets of influences: Statements to which he is exposed; other features of his environment. An attaché or foreign correspondent exposes himself to mass media and private talk; also, he can count soldiers, measure gun emplacements, note hours of work in a factory, see butter and fat on the table.

Actually it is useful to consider the attention frame of the relay as well as the primary link in terms of media and non-media exposures. The role of non-media factors is very slight in the case of many relay operators, while it is certain to be significant in accounting for the primary observer.

Attention Aggregates and Publics

It should be pointed out that everyone is not a member of the world public, even though he belongs to some extent to the world attention aggregate. To belong to an attention aggregate it is only necessary to have common symbols of reference. Everyone who has a symbol of reference for New York, North America, the Western Hemisphere or the globe is a member respectively of the attention aggregate of New York, North America, the Western Hemisphere, the globe. To be a member of the New York public, however, it is essential to make demands for public action in New York, or expressly affecting New York.

The public of the United States, for instance, is not confined to residents or citizens, since non-citizens who live beyond the frontier may try to influence American politics. Conversely, everyone who lives in the United States is not a member of the American public, since something more than passive attention is necessary. An individual passes from an attention aggregate to the public when he begins to expect that what he wants can affect public policy.

Sentiment Groups and Publics

A further limitation must be taken into account before we can correctly classify a specific person or group as part of a public. The demands made regarding public policy must be debatable. The world public is relatively weak and undeveloped, partly because it is typically kept subordinate to sentiment areas in which no debate is permitted on policy matters. During a war or war crisis, for instance, the inhabitants of a region are overwhelmingly committed to impose certain policies on others. Since the outcome of the conflict depends on violence, and not debate, there is no public under such conditions. There is a network of sentiment groups that act as crowds, hence tolerate no dissent.[8]

From the foregoing analysis it is clear that there are attention, public and sentiment areas of many degrees of inclusiveness in world politics.

These areas are interrelated with the structural and functional features of world society, and especially of world power. It is evident, for instance, that *the strongest powers tend to be included in the same attention area,* since their ruling elites focus on one another as the source of great potential threat. The strongest powers usually pay proportionately less attention to the weaker powers than the weaker powers pay to them, since stronger powers are typically more important sources of threat, or of protection, for weaker powers than the weaker powers are for the stronger.[9]

The attention structure within a state is a valuable index of the degree of state integration. When the ruling classes fear the masses, the rulers do not share their picture of reality with the rank and file. When the reality picture of kings, presidents and cabinets is not permitted to circulate through the state as a whole, the degree of discrepancy shows the extent to which the ruling groups assume that their power depends on distortion.

Or, to express the matter another way: If the "truth" is not shared, the ruling elements expect internal conflict, rather than harmonious adjustment to the external environment of the state. Hence the channels of communication are controlled in the hope of organizing the attention of the community at large in such a way that only responses will be forthcoming which are deemed favorable to the power position of the ruling classes.

The Principle of Equivalent Enlightenment

It is often said in democratic theory that rational public opinion depends upon enlightenment. There is, however, much ambiguity about the nature of enlightenment, and the term is often made equivalent to perfect knowledge. A more modest and immediate conception is not perfect but equivalent enlightenment. The attention structure of the full time specialist on a given policy will be more elaborate and refined than that of the layman. That this difference will always exist, we must take for granted. Nevertheless, it is quite possible for the specialist and the layman to agree on the broad outlines of reality. A workable goal of democratic society is equivalent enlightenment as between expert, leader and layman.

Expert, leader and layman can have the same gross estimate of major population trends of the world. They can share the same general view of the likelihood of war. It is by no means fantastic to imagine that the controllers of mass media of communication will take the lead in bringing about a high degree of equivalence throughout society between the layman's picture of significant relationships, and the picture of the expert and the leader.

Summary

The communication process in society performs three functions: (a) *surveillance* of the environment, disclosing threats and opportunities affecting the value position of the community and of the component parts within it; (b) *correlation* of the components of society in making a response to the environment; (c) *transmission* of the social inheritance. In general, biological equivalents can be found in human and animal associations, and within the economy of a single organism.

In society, the communication process reveals special characteristics when the ruling element is afraid of the internal as well as the external environment. In gauging the efficiency of communication in any given context, it is necessary to take into account the values at stake, and the identity of the group whose position is being examined. In democratic societies, rational choices depend on enlightenment, which in turn depends upon communication; and especially upon the equivalence of attention among leaders, experts and rank and file.

NOTES

1. For more detail, consult the introductory matter in Bruce L. Smith, Harold D. Lasswell and Ralph D. Casey, *Propaganda, Communication, and Public Opinion: A Comprehensive Reference Guide*, Princeton University Press, Princeton, 1946.

2. To the extent that behavior patterns are transmitted in the structures inherited by the single animal, a function is performed parallel to the transmission of the "social heritage" by means of education.

3. On animal sociology see: Warder C. Allee, *Animal Aggregations*, University of Chicago Press, Chicago, 1931; *The Social Life of Animals*, Norton, New York, 1935.

4. Excellent examples are given in Robert Redfield's account of *Tepoztlan, A Mexican Village: A Study of Folk Life*, University of Chicago Press, Chicago, 1930.

5. Properly handled, the speech event can be described with as much reliability and validity as many non-speech events which are more conventionally used as data in scientific investigations.

6. These distinctions are derived and adapted from the writings of Charles E. Merriam, Gaetano Mosca, Karl Mannheim, and others.

7. See William T. R. Fox, *The Super-Powers*, Harcourt, Brace, New York, 1944, and Harold D. Lasswell, *World Politics Faces Economics*, McGraw-Hill, New York, 1945.

8. The distinction between the "crowd" and the "public" was worked out in the Italian, French and German literature of criticism that grew up around Le Bon's overgeneralized use of the crowd concept. For a summary of this literature by a scholar who later became one of the most productive social

scientists in the field, see Robert E. Park, *Masse und Publikum; Eine methologische und soziologische Untersuchung*, Lack and Grunau, Bern, 1904. (Heidelberg dissertation.)

9. The propositions in this paragraph are hypotheses capable of being subsumed under the general theory of power, referred to in footnote 6. See also Harold D. Lasswell and Joseph M. Goldsen, "Public Attention, Opinion and Action," *The International Journal of Opinion and Attitude Research*, Mexico City, I, 1947, pp. 3–11.

5

Communication Media:
Structure and Control

THE FACTS on the structure and control of the mass media of communication are many and varied. We have not represented them here because they are constantly changing, because they are readily available in standard sources, and because we have preferred to devote space to studies involving the correlation and interpretation of the facts. Thus the selections in this section were not chosen to present a simple description of the structure and control of the media, but were rather chosen as significant contributions to the method of control analysis or as significant attacks on special substantive problems.

Analysis of quantitative data on control structure is exemplified in Nixon's study of the concentration of newspaper ownership and the patterns of voter-media ownership, one of the central problems in this area. There are other important aspects of the structure and control of the mass media which are not represented here. Given space, we would have included selections dealing with the role of pressure groups, the impact of advertising, and the characteristics and functioning of media personnel.

Given appropriate material, we would have included studies of relatively neglected problems in this area, such as the relationship between control structure and communication content, and the remote yet powerful influence of the audience upon the determination of communication content.

The structure and control of the mass media involves, of course, the impact of government agencies and regulations. Because of the crucial problems of social and governmental control, there has developed a body of literature on the governmental relations of the mass media. Most of the studies deal with some particular aspect of the relationship and with special emphasis on the question of what the relationship should be. However, Schramm's study of differing concepts of mass media presents an overview of the problems from an historical and institutional point of view. Excerpts from Chafee's work on "Government and Mass Communication," deal with the relationship of government and the mass communication process from social, political, and legal perspectives. Finally, part of a famous report by the Federal Communications Commission is included as an example of a governmental agency's own statement of the evaluative factors to be taken into consideration in its regulatory activities.

RAYMOND B. NIXON
and JEAN WARD

Trends in Newspaper Ownership

THE LIVE BROADCASTS of presidential news conferences which began on January 25, 1961 have signalized the acceptance of radio and television as full and equal competitors of the daily newspaper in the servicing of news and opinion to the American public.

In fact, the last 16 years have brought us very close to the realization of a possibility mentioned by the senior author of this article in his earlier studies[1] of newspaper ownership trends: the possibility that competition from the broadcast media would increase to such an extent that fears as to the consequences of local newspaper "monopolies" would subside. For newspaper ownership in the United States now has stabilized according to a pattern of only one publisher to a community in all except the larger cities,[2] and the public obviously has accepted the situation with equanimity.

While this spectacular rise of the broadcast media has been taking place, daily newspapers as a whole have continued to prosper. Both the total number of U.S. cities with daily papers and the total circulation of all dailies are now at an all-time high, even though the total number of dailies has declined slightly since 1954. When radio and television also are brought into the picture, there can be no question that more Americans have daily access to a larger volume of news and comment than ever before.

Because of this sweeping change, the present article seeks not only to trace developments in daily newspaper ownership since the senior author's earlier studies, but also to determine the extent of the new competition.

Reprinted from *Journalism Quarterly*, Vol. XXXVIII, (Winter 1961), pp. 3–12, by permission of the author and the publisher. (Copyright, 1961, *Journalism Quarterly*).

Definitions of Terms

First, let us define our key terms. Some were used in the earlier studies, others are introduced here for the first time.

A "newspaper combination" or "local newspaper monopoly," as the terms are used here, refers to two or more newspapers (usually a morning-evening-Sunday combination) under one ownership in the same community.

"Joint printing" refers to the "agency" or "partial combination" arrangements whereby the business and mechanical operations of two newspapers are combined in the same plant, but separate control of editorial policies is maintained. Usually there is joint ownership of the printing plant, but not of the papers themselves.

An "inter-city daily" is "any non-metropolitan daily newspaper which, through consolidation or expansion, has become the dominant paper in two or more closely associated municipalities."[3]

A "newspaper group" (frequently called a "chain") refers to two or more newspapers in different cities under the same ultimate ownership or control.

The term "media voice" refers to an organization that owns or controls one or more media of news and opinion. In other words, each separate ownership of a newspaper, magazine or broadcasting station, or of a combination of these media, is one "media voice." The emphasis is on the number of owning or controlling organizations, rather than on the number of individual stations or newspapers.[4]

"Concentration of ownership" refers to the bringing of two or more newspapers or other media under the same ownership, either in a local combination or in a larger group. "Intensive concentration" is the term applied to jointly-owned units that are fairly close together geographically, while "extensive concentration" refers to ownership that extends over a wide area. For example, the Roy H. Thomson group, which has its headquarters in Canada and now includes some 85 newspapers in Canada, the United Kingdom, Ireland, Nigeria and the United States, is the most extensive concentration of newspaper ownership ever known.[5]

Trends in Daily Ownership

Concentration of ownership among American newspapers has been proceeding since the latter part of the 19th century, in the wake of even more far-reaching consolidations and mergers in business and industry at large. In the senior author's 1945 and 1954 studies, however, it was noted that concentration of ownership in the daily newspaper field has been becoming *more intensive* and *less extensive*. That is, local "monopolies," inter-city dailies and small regional groups have been increasing, while large national chains—in the United States, at least—have declined in size and circulation. At the same time, the long-term trend in total daily circulation has been steadily upward.[6]

Table 1 shows that these same trends have continued through 1960.

Table 1—Trends in Ownership of English-Language Dailies of General Circulation and Content in the United States, 1880–1960[a]

	1880	1909–10	1920	1930	1940	1944–5	1953–4	1960
Circulation (thousands)	3,093	22,426	27,791	39,589	41,132	45,955	54,472	58,881
Circulation (thousands), adjusted as noted below							54,140	58,080
Total Dailies	850	2,202	2,042	1,942	1,878	1,744	1,785	1,763
Total General Dailies, adjusted as noted below							1,760	1,733
Total Daily Cities	389	1,207	1,295	1,402	1,426	1,396	1,448	1,461
One-Daily Cities	149	509	716	1,002	1,092	1,107	1,188	1,222
% of Total	38.3	42.2	55.3	71.5	76.6	77.3	82.0	83.6
One Combination Cities	1	9	27	112	149	161	154	160
Joint Printing Cities	—	—	—	—	4	11	19	18
Total Noncompetitive	150	518	743	1,114	1,245	1,279	1,361	1,400
% of Total	38.6	42.9	57.4	79.4	87.3	91.6	94.0	95.8
Cities with Competing Dailies	239	689	552	288	181	117	87	61

	1910	1923	1930	1940	1945	1954	1960
Number of Newspaper groups	13	31	55	60	76	95	109
Number of group papers	62	153	311	319	368	485	560
Average number per group	4.7	4.9	5.6	5.3	4.8	5.1	5.1
Number of inter-city dailies					20	29	68

a. SOURCES: For 1960, figures are based upon records of American Newspaper Publishers Association as of December 31, 1960, with unadjusted figures for number of dailies and total daily circulation as of September 30, 1960 taken from "Ready Reckoner" in 1961 *Editor & Publisher International Year Book*. "Adjusted figures" for 1954 and 1960 represent these same totals less the figures for non-general dailies, duplicates of "all-day" papers (which *Editor & Publisher* counts twice) and papers which suspended or merged in 1960 after the *Editor & Publisher* list was compiled. For detailed sources of figures for earlier years, see Raymond B. Nixon, "Trends in Daily Newspaper Ownership since 1945," *Journalism Quarterly*, 31:7 (Winter 1954).

Daily circulation has made further gains, although at a slower rate than during the war and early postwar period. For example, the increase in circulation during the 1950's was 8.9%, or only about half the 18% population increase that took place between 1950 and 1960. This gain is not unimpressive, however, when it is considered that the increase in number of households and in number of adults over 20 years of age during these years was somewhat less than the increase in total population.[7]

On every other score, the record since 1945 has been one of remarkably stable growth. Because of further suspensions and mergers, the total number of English-language newspapers of general circulation and content (1,733) on January 1, 1961 was 27 less than in 1954 and 11 less than in 1945. The number would be approximately the same as in 1945 but for the mergers that have brought a number of papers in adjoining cities together into "inter-city" dailies.[8] Nevertheless, the total number of daily newspaper cities rose from 1,396 in 1945 to 1,461 in 1960. Cities with only one daily increased from 1,107 in 1945 and 1,188 in 1954 to 1,222, or 83.6% of the total, in 1960. When the 160 one-combination and 18 joint-printing cities are added to the one-daily places, the proportion of daily cities without local newspaper competition is 95.8%. Even if the joint-printing cities are regarded as competitive, as most of them are on the editorial side, the percentage of non-competitive cities is 94.5%.

On the basis of copies sold, 57.8% of the total daily newspaper circulation in 1960 was locally non-competitive, as compared with 46.2% in 1953 and 40.2% in 1945. Sunday circulation was 47.3% non-competitive in 1960, as against 34.9% in 1945.

As for ownerships involving two or more cities, the number of newspaper groups increased from 76 in 1945 and 95 in 1954 to 109 in 1960. However, the average size of these groups (5.1) is the same as in 1954 and still below the 1930 peak of 5.6 papers per group. This further supports the hypothesis advanced in the 1945 study: that in this country there is a point at which the economic advantages of group operation fail to compensate for the psychological disadvantages of absentee ownership. This may be one reason why absentee ownership of daily newspapers actually has declined: the proportion of group papers located in the same state as the home office or residence of the principal owner is now 62.5%, as compared with 60% in 1954 and 57.9% in 1945. While the growth of the Thomson chain[9] and the recent acquisition of the Odhams Press by the London *Daily Mirror*[10] seems to indicate that this principle does not apply in all countries, there is no evidence that a much larger degree of ownership concentration would be profitable, or even possible, in the United States. The proportion of total daily newspaper circulation controlled by groups in this country has changed very little during the last 30 years: it was 43.4% of the total in 1930 and 46.1% in 1960. Sunday papers in groups had 54.1% of the total Sunday circulation in 1930 and 54.2% in 1960.

The lines in Figure 1 clearly reveal the high degree of stabilization that has been attained by daily newspapers in the United States in recent years. During the 15 years from 1930 to 1945 there was a net loss of some 200 papers. Since 1945, however, the number of dailies merged or suspended has exceeded the number of new dailies established by only 17. Most of the "disappearing dailies" were "marginal" in the sense that they were located in cities too small to support them; some were former weeklies that went back to weekly publication. Where an old established daily in one of the larger cities has disappeared, it probably had been in competition with another paper for essentially the same readers and advertisers.

A comparison of the competitive situation by cities according to population in 1945 and 1960 (Table 2) brings out recent trends in an even more striking way. The number of one-daily cities with less than 10,000 population has dropped from 525 to 412 in 15 years, indicating that rising

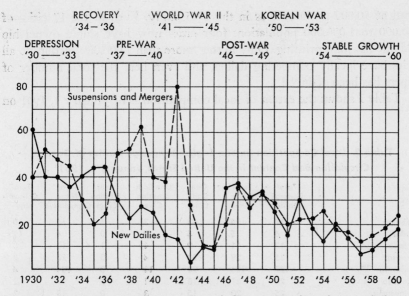

Figure 1—Daily newspapers suspended or merged and new dailies started in the United States, 1930–1960.

SOURCES: Bulletins of American Newspaper Publishers Association Special Standing Committee, Chicago, Ill., 1954–1960. The lists published by this Committee have been corrected to exclude Canadian dailies or specialized dailies not falling within the scope of this article.

costs have made it increasingly difficult to publish a daily in cities of this size. One daily is now the prevailing pattern in cities up to 100,000 population, whereas in 1945 it was the rule only in cities up to 50,000. Single ownership or joint printing of a morning-evening combination has become the customary arrangement in cities of 100,000 to 500,000 population, in-

Table 2—Population Analysis of All Daily Newspaper Cities in the
United States, March 1, 1945, and January 1, 1961[a]

Population Group	Total Daily Cities '45	'61	One-Daily Cities '45	'61	One Combination Cities '45	'61	Joint Printing Cities '45	'61	Total Non-Competitive '45	'61	Total Competitive '45	'61
Less than 10,000	548	417	525	412	9	2	—	—	534	414	14	3
10,001 to 25,000	475	539	409	517	45	12	—	—	454	529	21	10
25,001 to 50,000	183	230	118	182	45	40	2	1	166	223	17	7
50,001 to 100,000	93	148	33	88	40	50	5	1	78	139	15	9
100,001 to 200,000	51	66	15	20	12	29	4	9	31	58	20	8
200,001 to 300,000	17	19	5	2	6	11	—	4	11	17	6	2
300,001 to 400,000	12	11	1	1	3	7	—	1	4	9	8	2
400,001 to 500,000	3	9	—	—	1	5	—	1	1	6	2	3
500,001 to 1,000,000	9	17	—	—	—	4	—	1	—	5	9	12
More than 1,000,000	5	5	—	—	—	—	—	—	—	—	5	5
TOTALS	1,396	1,461	1,107	1,222	161	160	11	18	1,279	1,400	117	61

a. 1945 analysis taken from Raymond B. Nixon, "Concentration and Absenteeism in Daily Newspaper Ownership," Journalism Quarterly, 22:103 (June 1945); 1961 analysis based upon ANPA records of English-language dailies of general content being published on January 1, 1961, with cities classified by population according to 1960 Preliminary Census Report.

stead of 50,000 to 400,000 as in the 1945 study. Even in the 17 cities of 500,000 to 1,000,000 population, four cities now have single ownership and one has joint printing. Only in the "more than 1,000,000" group do all cities have locally competing dailies, and even here the total number of papers has been reduced.

Table 3 shows the extent of local competition as of January 1, 1961 on

Table 3—Local Competition among English-Language Dailies of General Circulation and Content in the United States, January 1, 1961[a]

	Total General Dailies	Total Daily Cities	One-Daily Cities	One Combination Cities	Joint Printing Cities	Total Non-Competitive	Total Competitive
Alabama	19	16	13	2	1	16	0
Alaska	6	5	4	0	0	4	1
Arizona	13	11	9	1	1	11	0
Arkansas	35	29	23	4	0	27	2
California	127	108	93	11	0	104	4
Colorado	24	21	18	1	0	19	2
Connecticut	25	20	15	3	0	18	2
Delaware	3	2	1	1	0	2	0
District of Columbia	3	1	0	0	0	0	1
Florida	46	34	23	7	0	30	4
Georgia	28	23	18	5	0	23	0
Hawaii	5	2	1	0	0	1	1
Idaho	15	13	11	2	0	13	0
Illinois	80	70	63	5	0	68	2
Indiana	86	72	59	7	2	68	4
Iowa	44	41	38	2	0	40	1
Kansas	51	48	45	3	0	48	0
Kentucky	26	23	20	2	0	22	1
Louisiana	18	14	10	3	1	14	0
Maine	9	7	5	2	0	7	0
Maryland	12	7	3	3	0	6	1
Massachusetts	51	41	36	3	0	39	2
Michigan	54	52	50	1	0	51	1
Minnesota	29	26	23	3	0	26	0
Mississippi	20	17	15	0	0	15	2
Missouri	54	44	34	6	1	41	3
Montana	18	14	10	4	0	14	0
Nebraska	20	18	16	1	1	18	0
Nevada	8	6	4	1	0	5	1
New Hampshire	9	9	9	0	0	9	0
New Jersey	27	24	21	0	0	21	3
New Mexico	19	18	17	0	1	18	0
New York	85	63	51	7	0	58	5
North Carolina	47	40	33	7	0	40	0
North Dakota	11	9	8	1	0	9	0
Ohio	95	87	79	5	1	85	2
Oklahoma	51	46	41	4	1	46	0
Oregon	20	18	16	1	0	17	1
Pennsylvania	118	103	88	10	0	98	5
Rhode Island	7	6	5	1	0	6	0
South Carolina	17	12	7	5	0	12	0
South Dakota	13	11	10	0	0	10	1

Table 3—(Continued)

	Total General Dailies	Total Daily Cities	One- Daily Cities	One Com- bination Cities	Joint Printing Cities	Total Non- Competitive	Total Competi- tive
Tennessee	28	21	14	3	3	20	1
Texas	108	89	72	12	1	85	4
Utah	5	4	3	0	1	4	0
Vermont	9	8	7	0	0	7	1
Virginia	31	24	17	6	1	24	0
Washington	26	21	16	3	0	19	2
West Virginia	30	21	12	8	1	21	0
Wisconsin	38	34	30	2	1	33	1
Wyoming	10	8	6	2	0	8	0
Totals	1,733	1,461	1,222	160	18	1,400	61
Less Alaska and Hawaii	1,722	1,454	1,217	160	18	1,395	59
Same 48 states in 1954	1,760	1,448	1,188	154	19	1,361	87
Same 48 states in 1945	1,744	1,396	1,107	161	11	1,279	117

a. SOURCES: Records of American Newspaper Publishers Association as of December 31, 1960.

a state-by-state basis. Twenty-eight states (out of 50) and the District of Columbia had one or more competitive cities, while 22 states had no locally competing dailies as compared with 11 (out of 48) in 1945.

Most of the new papers started since 1945 have been in the faster-growing small cities; in fact, there has been no successful new daily established in a city of more than 100,000 population during the last 15 years except the Jackson (Miss.) *State Times*. It is much less expensive to experiment with daily publication in a smaller city, and weekly papers frequently try it, sometimes in competition with an existing daily. After a few months, however, one of the two papers usually suspends publication, or merges with the other.

Causes of Consolidations

It is customary for publishers and trade publications to attribute suspensions and mergers to rising costs, or to the opposition of trade unions to new techniques or more efficient production methods. While these facts undoubtedly have accelerated the trends noted above, especially in the smaller cities, they probably have been no more than secondary causes. The primary causes of consolidation appear to go much deeper, and may be enumerated as follows:

1. *The decline in partisanship of the U.S. press.* Few newspapers are started or kept alive today for political reasons; the modern political party or pressure group hires a public relations director and makes use of all the available mass media.

2. *The growth in objective reporting among American newspapers.* As

newspapers have become more and more alike in their reporting of the news, and presenting both sides of controversial issues, there has come to be little more reason for two competing newspapers than there would be for two competing telephone companies.

3. *The desire of advertisers for larger circulations and less duplication of readership.* Once a newspaper is set into type and the plates put on the press, the cost of production per copy goes down as circulation goes up. Unless a city is large enough to support papers that appeal to distinctly different tyes of readers (as, for example, the New York *Times* and the New York *Daily News*), advertisers obviously prefer a single "omnibus" daily to competing papers.

4. *The growth of the suburbs.* For example, while the number of competing dailies in New York City proper has declined, the rise of successful new dailies in suburbs like Long Island has been phenomenal. A suburban dweller seems to prefer one downtown paper and one suburban paper to two or more papers from downtown, and for understandable reasons.

5. *The growing competition from the electronic media.* As one studies the trends of the last 30 years, this appears to be the single most important factor in the disappearance of locally competing daily newspapers. Certainly it is the circumstance that offers the most plausible explanation for the lack of any real agitation for more newspapers in most cities where there is now a single ownership. It also helps to explain why a previous study found no significant differences in the news and editorial content

Table 4—Radio and Television Stations with Newspaper Affiliations, 1931–1960

	AM Radio	News-paper-af-filiated	Pct.	FM Radio	News-paper-af-filiated	Pct.	Tele-vision	News-paper-af-filiated	Pct.
1931	612	68	11.1						
1936	632	159	25.2						
1940	814	250	30.8						
1945	943	260	27.6	53	17	32.0	9	1	11.1
1950	2086	472	22.6	743	273	36.8	97	41	42.0
1955	2669	465	17.4	552	170	30.8	439	149	34.0
1960	3506	429	12.2	753	145	19.2	553	175	31.1

Source: *Broadcasting Yearbooks.* All figures refer to stations actually on the air January 1. Earlier figures were compiled by Harvey J. Levin for *Broadcast Regulation and Joint Ownership of Media* (New York University Press, 1960), p. 5.

of non-competitive and competitive newspapers in cities of less than 400,000 population.[11]

One reason why some European journalists find it difficult to understand the acceptance of "monopoly" newspapers in American cities is that in most European countries radio and television are a government monopoly. In a situation of that kind the pattern of a single newspaper or publisher to a community might be much more of a threat to free discussion than it is in the United States. Here all the media are privately owned and are definitely in competition with each other for both advertising and news. Moreover, the policies of the Federal Communications Commission in recent years have encouraged diversification of ownership, even though they have not barred newspapers as a class from owning radio and television stations. But the proportion of radio and television stations affiliated with newspapers, as shown by Table 4, has been declining since 1945. During this same period, the total number of all broadcasting stations has increased fivefold.

EXTENT OF INTER-MEDIA COMPETITION

The extent of inter-media competition is illustrated dramatically by Figures 2 and 3. When newspapers alone are considered, only 155 out of 1,733 dailies still have local competition, and all but 61 of the 1,461 daily newspaper cities are non-competitive. But when all "media voices" in these same cities are included, it is found that there are 3,324 competing voices in 1,106 cities, and that only 355 single-voice cities remain. Most of these places are so close to a large city that the absence of any locally competing voices appears to be of little importance.

From our earlier definition of "media voice," it will be recalled that only *independent ownerships* are regarded as separate media voices. For example, if a newspaper or newspaper combination owns a radio or television station, then all the media under that ownership are treated as one voice. On this basis the proportion of American daily newspaper cities without locally competing voices in 1960 was only 24.2%. And in only 76 or 5.2% of these 1,461 cities did a "monopoly" newspaper publisher also have a monopoly over all the local broadcasting facilities.

Of even more significance, perhaps, is the fact that 1,014 other cities without a daily newspaper do have daily radio or television service, and that in only 29 of these cities does a local weekly own or control local broadcasting. It appears that the rise of local broadcasting stations may account for some of the shrinkage in the number of weekly newspaper towns, as reported by Wilbur Peterson.[12]

Certainly it seems to be more than a coincidence that the sharpest rise in the number of non-competitive daily cities occurred in the 1920s, immediately after the introduction of radio, and that the biggest increase in competition among all media voices took place after the lifting of the "freeze" on new television stations in 1953.

The extent to which radio and television actually compete with daily

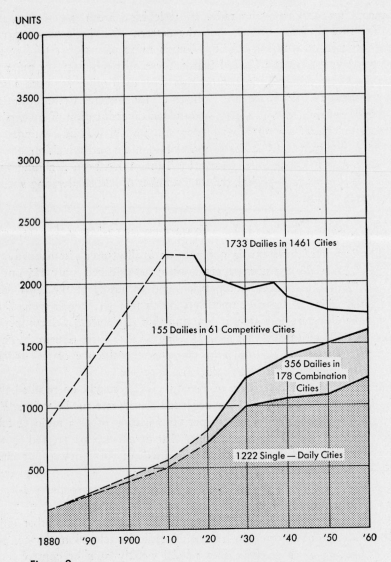

Figure 2.

sources: Same as for Table 1. The "178 combination cities" include the 160 one-combination cities and the 18 joint-printing
cities. Dotted lines indicate periods during which no intervening
checks were available between points of change noted.

newspapers in servicing news and opinion to the American public varies according to locality. Competition for readers' attention and for advertisers' revenue is, of course, well established. Moreover, nearly all radio and television stations subscribe to a wire service and read late bulletins

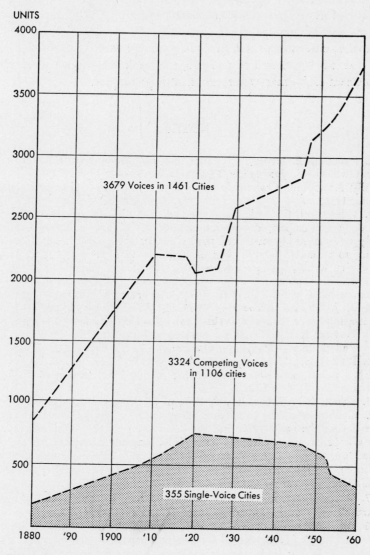

UNITS

3679 Voices in 1461 Cities

3324 Competing Voices
in 1106 cities

355 Single-Voice Cities

Figure 3.

SOURCES: Same as for Table 1, with addition of data on independent and newspaper-related radio-TV stations from Broadcasting Yearbooks. Dotted lines indicate that no intervening checks were available between points of change shown.

or summaries of news over the air. Even this much news serves as a sword of Damocles over the head of any "monopoly" publisher who might be tempted to grossly distort or to withhold news that he had received from the same wire service. The broadcasting of important political events and speeches undoubtedly provides the public with a far better check on the accuracy of newspapers than was possible even in a day of competing but violently partisan newspapers.

In those cities where each medium performs well the distinctive functions that it is best suited to perform, the media seem to supplement and complement each other even more than they compete.

NOTES

1. Raymond B. Nixon, "Concentration and Absenteeism in Daily Newspaper Ownership," *Journalism Quarterly*, 22:97–114 (June 1945); "Trends in Daily Newspaper Ownership since 1945," *Journalism Quarterly*, 31:2–14 (Winter 1954).

2. While both this article and the earlier studies are concerned primarily with daily newspapers, companion studies at Minnesota have shown that weekly newspaper ownership in towns of less than 8,000 has stabilized according to a similar pattern. For example, in 1955 the proportion of non-competitive weekly places (one weekly, one semi-weekly or tri-weekly, or "twin weeklies" under the same ownership) was found to be approximately the same as that in the daily field—94%. According to the study by Wilbur Peterson, *Journalism Quarterly*, 38:15–24 (Winter, 1961), the proportion of non-competitive "country weekly" towns in 1959 was 94.8%. See p. 23.

3. Howard Ray Rowland and Donald G. Hileman, "The Inter-City Daily in the United States," *Journalism Quarterly*, 37:373 (Summer 1960).

4. Ruth Inglis, "The Myth of Monopoly in Radio and the Press," unpublished paper based upon research for National Association of Radio and Television Broadcasters,1949.

5. *Editor & Publisher*, July 9, 1960, p. 15; August 20, 1960, p. 14.

6. Cyclical dips in circulation have occurred in periods such as the depression of the early 1930s and the "recession" of 1937–38, but subsequent gains always have exceeded the losses. The long-term trend seems to be explained up to now by population growth, and the cycles by economic conditions. See John Scott Davenport, "Trends and Cycles in Daily Newspaper Circulation," *Journalism Quarterly*, 27:282–7 (Summer 1950).

7. Wilbur Peterson, "Is Daily Circulation Keeping Pace with the Nation's Growth?" *Journalism Quarterly*, 36:12–22 (Winter 1959).

8. Rowland and Hileman, *op. cit.*, found that nine of the 68 inter-city dailies in 1960 had been formed by merging papers in two or more separate localities. Since any cluster of communities so served is regarded as one city in our tabulations, these mergers have reduced both the total number of papers and the total number of daily cities by nine or more.

9. *Supra,* p. 4.

10. *Editor & Publisher*, March 4, 1961, p. 9.

11. Raymond B. Nixon, "Changes in Reader Attitudes toward Daily

Newspapers," *Journalism Quarterly*, 31:421–33 (Fall 1954); Raymond B. Nixon and Robert L. Jones, "The Content of Non-Competitive vs. Competitive Newspapers," *Journalism Quarterly*, 33:299–314 (Summer 1956). While there have been no extensive studies of reader attitudes toward "monopolies" since the 1954 article, a study in Minneapolis indicates that readers there had an even higher regard for their local morning-evening combination in 1959 than they did in earlier years. For example, the percentage of those who thought that the Minneapolis papers "try to build up Minneapolis and the state of Minnesota" was 92% in 1959 as compared with 84% in 1949, and the proportion of those who said the newspapers "try to be fair in the news" went up from 71% in 1949 to 76% in 1953 and 77% in 1959.

    12. Peterson, *op. cit.*

WILBUR SCHRAMM

Two Concepts of Mass Communication

Authoritarianism

A SOCIAL SYSTEM like communication always reflects the social and political structures within which it operates. In trying to understand why mass communication develops as it does in different societies, then, we begin by looking at the societies. And we start with a look at certain basic assumptions which any society holds—assumptions concerning the nature of man, the nature of society and the state, the relation of man to the state, the nature of knowledge and truth and moral conduct.

Modern communication was born in 1450 into an authoritarian society. The essential characteristic of an authoritarian society is that the state ranks higher than the individual in the scale of social values. Only through subordinating himself to the state can the individual achieve his goals and develop his attributes as a civilized man. As an individual, he can do only a little; as a member of an organized community, his potential is enormously increased. This means not only that the state ranks the individual, but also that the state has a certain amount of caretaker function and the individual has a degree of dependent status.

Furthermore, individuals within the authoritarian state differ greatly in status. Authoritarian philosophers like Hegel ridicule the democratic belief that "all should participate in the business of the state."[1] In the authoritarian state there is a sharp distinction between leaders and followers. Only a few are cast in the role of leadership. Sometimes they are believed to be in their high positions because of divine selection, as, for example, were the Renaissance monarchs who claimed to rule by divine right. Sometimes they are leaders because of what is believed to be their superior intellect, wisdom, or experience. In any case, always in an

Reprinted from *Responsibility in Mass Communication* (1957), pp. 62–77, by permission of the author and the publisher. (Copyright, 1957, Harper and Row).

authoritarian state a man or a few men are in position to lead and be obeyed. These are rulers or advisers to rulers, and they stand at the locus of power.

What is the source of truth in an authoritarian society? It may be an accredited divine revelation, the wisdom of the race, or simply the superior ability of a leader or group to perceive dangers and opportunities. It may be, on the other hand, after a floundering reaction from disappointment with previously accepted truth, and emergent new promise—as sometimes happens when a country in desperation turns to a dictator. But whatever the source of truth it has two characteristics. It is restricted; not every man has access to it. And it becames the standard nevertheless for all members of the society. As Siebert says, it "acquires an absolutist aura which makes change undesirable, and stability or continuity a virtue in itself."[2] One of the functions of the authoritarian state, therefore, is to preserve unity of thought and action among its members, and to maintain continuity of leadership. To this end the authoritarian state employs such tools of persuasion and coercion as it commands.

Three powerful strands entered into the Renaissance authoritarianism which first played host to modern communication. One of these was the doctrine of divine right by which such monarchs as the Tudors and Stuarts claimed to rule, and which set apart a bevy of hereditary nobles from the rest of the population. The hereditary leaders, of course, protected their status in politics and war.

A second was the authoritarian tradition of the Roman Church, which had grown powerful in the Middle Ages. The Church considered itself the respository of divine revelation. Its responsibility, as shepherd of mankind, was to protect this revelation from being contaminated and to protect its sheep from impure doctrine. Where its authority reached it permitted debate, but not on basic assumptions, and not outside the qualified members of its own order. The Church enforced its dictates where it could by the use of imprimaturs, book proscriptions, and even excommunications. In many countries, for some centuries, it could command and usually receive the cooperation of the state in such control of opinion and expression.

A third strand was the long history of authoritarian political philosophy, stretching back to Plato. For all his idealism, Plato had argued that, once authority in a state is equally divided, degeneration sets in. Just as a man must govern his own baser instincts and appetites by intellectual control, so must the rulers of the state keep the material interests and selfish passions of the masses from dominating society. Plato's own theoretical "Republic" was governed by philosopher-kings. Plato's own master, Socrates, while vehemently arguing his freedom to deviate from the laws of Athens, just as readily admitted that the authorities were entitled to enforce those laws no matter how wrong. We sometimes forget how strict Plato was in the realm of art and thought. As MacIver writes, "Plato wanted to 'co-ordinate' the life of the citizens under a strict cultural code that banned all modes of art and even of opinion not in accord with his own gospel. Very politely, in the *Republic*, he would 'send to another city' all offenders against the rigid rules prescribed for the artist and the philosopher and the poet. With equal politeness, in the *Laws*, he would require poets first to submit their works to the magistrates, who should decide whether they were good for the spiritual health of the citizens"[3]

This tradition of authoritarian political philosophy was carried up to the early centuries of printing, though in quite different ways, by many other philosophers: Machiavelli, for example, who advocated that all else must be subordinated to the security of the state, and that nonmoral actions by the political leaders, as well as strict control of discussion and of dissemination of information are justified to that end; Thomas Hobbes, the naturalistic philosopher, whose theories of the state and its relation to the individual did much to justify the authoritarian policies of 17th-century governments; George Hegel, who has variously been called the father of both modern fascism and modern communism, and who gave to authoritarian philosophy its final idealistic touch by saying that the state is the "ethical spirit . . . Will . . . Mind . . . the state, being an end in itself, is provided with the maximum of rights over against the individual citizens, whose highest duty is to be members of the state."[4]

This was the tradition into which machine-duplicated communication was born. At first the tiny infant voice of printing was no threat to government, and there was no need to do anything about it. Before many decades, however, it became apparent that a new great voice was being heard in the land. This voice could be dangerous or helpful, according to who controlled it. The governments began making use of the regulative authority they possessed.

One of the first things they did was to control access to the new medium. By issuing patents or licenses to printers and publishers, they assumed the power of determining who could enter the business. Since each licensee had a monopoly, or at least a grant of great privilege, he was all the more likely to publish what the ruler wished.

But even this was not entirely satisfactory to the rulers. They instituted censorship, which required that all manuscripts or proof had to be examined and passed by a representative of government before being printed. Censorship, however, fell of its own weight, late in the 17th century. It was too cumbersome, too laborious. The coming of newspapers made too much to read. Clever journalists could get around it too easily. Even the censors disliked the job.

So censorship was largely replaced by the threat of punishment *after* printing—such as prosecution for treason (writing intended as a part of a plot to overthrow the government) or sedition (which is to treason as the flea-bite to the snakebite). And some governments went in for publishing their own papers, paying or bribing writers (Walpole's government was notorious for this), or subsidizing existing printers; but for the most part the media in this stage of authoritarianism were permitted to be privately owned.

The concept of public communication which developed in these first 250 years of printing was exactly what would be expected in an authoritarian setting. Printing was simply another tool to promote unity and continuity within the state. It was to carry wisdom and truth as wisdom and truth were identified by the rulers. Access to the medium was to be restricted to those individuals who would operate for "the good of the state" as judged by the rulers. The public at large were considered incapable of understanding political problems, and communication was therefore forbidden to "disturb the masses" or interest them in something they could not "understand." The media were not expected to criticize the rulers or political leaders, and above all they were not permitted to attempt to unseat the authorties. Discussion of political systems in broad principles was permitted (as is not the case with Communists); and it was all right to question the political machinery, but not the manipulators of that machinery.

The basis for communication ethics in such a system is easy to perceive. Negatively stated, there should be no publishing which, in the opinion of the authorities, would not be good for the state and (consequently) for its citizens. More positively, all publishing should contribute to the greatness of the beneficent state, which would as a consequence enable man to grow to his fullest usefulness and happiness within the state. But the important thing is that there is always an authority to serve as umpire. One need not decide himself. There is always revelation (if one can know it), the wisdom of the race or the past (if one can perceive it), or the guidance of the leader (the easiest to perceive and the commonest of all the guideposts).

Communication authoritarianism waned notably by the second half of the 18th century. By that time a line of liberal thinkers had thrown stones at the theory, and in several western countries a succession of democratic revolutions had knocked holes in the practice. The tide seemed to have turned away from authoritarianism. The new concept of public communication was that it should serve the individuals, not the state; that it should not offer unity, but rather diversity; that it should contribute to change as well as to continuity; and that it had every right to criticize the government in power. We shall have more to say about this later.

But let us not end this brief account of the older authoritarianism without pointing out that it did not die in 1750 or 1800. In many parts of the world it continues today, even though it may be disguised in democratic verbiage and in protestation of press freedom. Wherever a government operates in an authoritarian fashion, there you may expect to find some authoritarian controls over public communication. For example, the International Press Institute, which has its headquarters in Zurich, made an attempt in 1953 to assess the amount of press control and freedom throughout the world.[5] Altogether 248 editors in 48 countries answered the Institute's detailed questionnaire. On the basis of their replies, the Institute felt able to say: "Freedom of information is being especially threatened today." The report named specifically the following types of authoritarianism:

1. Countries where press control is complete—e.g., the Soviet Union and its satellites, also China, Yugoslavia, Portugal, Spain.

2. Countries where political criticism by the press is formally possible, but where censorship operates—e.g., Colombia, Egypt, Syria.

3. Countries where special laws or other discriminatory legislation expose editors to arrest and persecution—e.g., Union of South Africa, Persia, Pakistan, India, Iraq, Lebanon.

4. Countries where unofficial methods discourage press opposition—e.g., Turkey, Argentina, Indonesia.

These facts were for the year 1953. In some of the countries the situation may have changed by now. But the fact remains that authoritarianism has for more years in more countries been the dominant philosophy behind public communication than has any other pattern of thought.

Libertarianism

All through the 16th and 17th centuries a new theory of mass communication struggled to be born, drawing its prenatal strength from the great revolutions of the popular mind and the body politic which characterized western Europe in that period.

It was a time of great change, you will remember, succeeding apparent or relative changelessness. First there were the startling developments in geography and science, which challenged the traditional knowledge and seemed to vindicate the power of human reason as against inherited and revealed knowledge. There was the Reformation which challenged the authority of the Church of Rome, and resulted in a pattern of discussion and argument at variance with authoritarian patterns. There was the swift new growth of the middle class and of capitalism, challenging the old idea of fixed status, and ushering in a world of social mobility to replace one relatively fixed and permanent. There were political revolutions, like the one in England against the Stuarts, challenging the right to arbitrary rule.

But most importantly, the new theory put its roots down into the kind of intellectual change represented by the Enlightenment of the 17th and 18th centuries. This was one of the greatest revolutionary intellectual movements of all time. As Cassirer said, the basic idea of the Enlightenment was "the conviction that human understanding is capable of its own power and, without recourse to supernatural assistance, of comprehending the system of the world, and that this new way of understanding the world will lead to a new way of mastering it. Enlightenment sought to gain universal recognition for this principle in the natural and intellectual sciences, in physics and ethics, in the philosophies of religion, history, law, and politics." In other words, what was happening was that man who had already proved the world was round, who had looked at the planets through telescopes, who had discovered the circulation of the blood, and who had challenged the Church of Rome in argument, was now feeling his muscles and throwing down the gauntlet to all the old custodians of power and wisdom. He was declaring independence of all outside restrictions on his freedom to use his understanding for the solution of religious, political, and social problems.

In a sense, the intellectual revolution was chiefly a secular revolution, not only because it challenged the authority of the One Church, but also because it tended to transfer the rewards for good conduct nearer to the arena of worldly gains. It is hard for us now to realize the change in business and economics which was under way in the hundred years between the middle of the seventeenth and the middle of the eighteenth centuries. Heilbronner reminds us that in 1644 one Robert Keane of Boston was nearly excommunicated—not fined or imprisoned, *excommunicated*—for the crime of charging too much interest on a shilling loan, and the minister of Boston seized this opportunity to point out certain behavior which was unacceptable and well-nigh unforgivable.[7] This included:

That a man might sell as dear as he can, and buy as cheap as he can.
If a man lose by casualty of sea, etc., in some of his commodities, he may raise the price of the rest.
That he may sell as he bought, though he paid too dear.

"To seek riches for riches' sake," cried the minister, "is to fall into the sin of avarice." Yet, only a little over 100 years later, business was booming in America and England very much as it is now, and Adam Smith was preaching the laws of classical economics, including the commandment that government shall never (well, hardly ever) interfere with the market. Leave the market alone, he said, and it will regulate itself. Thus to Adam Smith, as to Jefferson, the best government is the one that governs least. In the eighteenth century, the central ethic was already coming to be the work-success ethic, in which man found his own level by the skill and hard work with which he seized opportunities in the free market.

To an even greater degree the intellectual revolution was a secular one for the reason that it succeeded in transferring the focus of interest from theology to science; that is, from theological controversy to scientific inquiry. Here again the rewards in the secular arena were great and enticing, both economically and intellectually. And the pattern that emerged from the scientific inquiry was rather well in phase with the new economics and politics. For here were Newton's idea of a universe which ran by itself like a time-machine and Lamarck's and Darwin's ideas of evolution in which the fittest survived in a free contest very much like Adam Smith's free market. If it were possible now to graph the focus of attention of men from the beginning of printing through the beginning of power printing—that is, from 1450 to a little after 1800—the result would certainly be a sharply rising line of secular interest, and a sharply falling line of sacred interest. And if we could guess where the lines crossed, we should probably place that point somewhere in the seventeenth century.

We are not implying that this change was all to the good. Indeed, a few paragraphs by Arnold Toynbee are worth pondering at this point.[8] He says:

The enlightened and well-intentioned authors of our seventeenth-century Western spiritual revolution did not succeed in achieving their two aims. They succeeded in establishing in the West a spirit of tolerance which lasted from the close of the seventeenth century until after the opening of the twentieth; and they accomplished this, as they had planned, by diverting Western Man's attention from theological controversy to scientific inquiry.

But this "transvaluation of values," which our seventeenth-century predecessors began, has gone, between their day and ours, to lengths which they would have deplored. The banishment of Christian fanaticism from Western souls has been followed by the eclipse of Christianity, while science and technology, after diverting Western Man's interest from theological controversy, have gone on to divert it from religion itself. Technology, instead of religion, is what our Western Civilization has come to stand for by our time, some three hundred years after the seventeenth century beginnings of our revolutionary Western "transvaluation of values." In making this diagnosis today, a non-Western observer of our twentieth century Western Civilization would be right. Yet we ourselves are speaking the truth when we declare that for us Western Civilization stands for not technology, but for the sacredness of the individual human personality.

We twentieth-century Westerners hold personal freedom just as sacred as our predecessors did: but here is the paradox in our present position. In becoming devotees of science and technology we have not ceased to be devotees of freedom. But, in relinquishing our hold on Christianity, we have deprived our belief in freedom of its religious foundations.

What has happened, therefore, is that the intellectual revolution, which formed the basis of the libertarian concept of mass communication, has run somewhat off the track on which it was started by the philosophers of the Enlightenment. And I think we shall see, later in this book, that the extent to which it has run off the track corresponds pretty closely with the extent to which we are today dissatisfied with the working of the theory of libertarian communication.

But let us return to some of those philosophers who have contributed doctrine and fighting phrases to what we call the libertarian theory of communication. Descartes was one of the first, and his great influence derived from his emphasis on reason as a road to truth. In England perhaps the most influential was John Locke. As we read back over him today, we can see how pivotal he was in the intellectual changes that we are considering. He argued, you will remember, that the center of power is the will of the people. The people delegate their authority to government and can at any time withdraw it. The people—each individual among them—has certain natural rights which cannot justifiably be abridged. In a rational act man has surrendered some of his personal rights to the state, but only in order that his natural rights may better be maintained and defended. The state, Locke argued, must be centered on the will and well-being of the people. It must maintain religious tolerance and freedom of individual enterprise. Many of Locke's phrases, as you can see, found their way into the American Declaration of Independence and the French Declaration of the Rights of Man.

John Milton's *Areopagitica*, a century before Locke, was one of the earliest of the great anti-authoritarian documents of this period. This is an eloquent argument for freedom of the press from governmental restriction. It was based on the premise that men have reason and wisdom to distinguish between right and wrong, good and bad. But they can exercise this ability to its full power only when they have a free choice. Given a "free and open encounter," Milton said, truth will demonstrate itself. Rational argument is a kind of "self-righting" process, by means of which the sound and true will survive. Therefore, government must not interfere with the argument. There must be no artificial restrictions on the free market place of ideas.[9] The relationship of the "free market place of ideas" to Smith's later self-running, self-controlling economic market and to Darwin's "survival of the fittest" in a kind of social market, will be clear.

Milton's argument had little effect in his own time, but in the eighteenth century it was revived and expanded by men like Thomas Paine, John Erskine, and Thomas Jefferson. Erskine, for example, defended Paine in a memorable court trial when Paine was accused of grievous error in publishing *The Rights of Man*. In the course of that defense Erskine stated a position which was instantly caught up by the defenders of the new theory of communication.[10]

The proposition which I mean to maintain as the basis of liberty of the press, and without which it is an empty sound, is this: that every man, not intending to mislead, but seeking to enlighten others with what his own reason and conscience, however erroneously, have dictated to him as truth, may address himself to the universal reason of the whole nation, either upon subjects of government in general, or upon that of our own particular country.

Notice carefully that phrase, *not intending to mislead*. Erskine would doubtless have said that a man who communicates in bad faith forfeits the moral right to defense of his freedom to communicate, even though the *legal* right may have to extend farther than the moral one.

Jefferson carried the point of view still farther. He contended that, just as the function of government was to establish and maintain a framework within which an individual can develop his own capabilities and pursue his own ends, so the chief function of the press is to inform the individual and to stand guard against deviation by government from its basic assignment. A constant victim of press vituperation during his own political career, Jefferson nevertheless maintained that a government which could not stand up under criticism deserved to fall. His general view of the press was stated in these words:

No experiment can be more interesting than what we are now trying, and which we trust will end in establishing the fact, that man may be governed by reason and truth. Our first object should therefore be, to leave open to him all the avenues of truth. The most effectual hitherto found, is the freedom of the press. It is therefore the first shut up by those who fear the investigation of their actions. The firmness with which the people have withstood the late abuses of the press, the discernment they have manifested between truth and falsehood, show that they may safely be trusted to hear everything true and false, and to form a correct judgment between them. I hold it, therefore, to be certain, that to open the doors of truth, and so fortify the habit of testing everything by reason, are the most effectual manacles we can rivet on the hands of our successors to prevent their manacling the people with their own consent.[11]

Here are most of the elements of the new theory—the reliance on reason to discriminate between truth and error; the need of a free market place of ideas in order that reason may work; and the function of the press as a check on government.

In the 19th century, John Stuart Mill defined the market place a bit more clearly. "If all mankind minus one," he wrote in a famous essay, *On Liberty*, "were of one opinion, and only one person were of the contrary opinion, mankind would be no more justified in silencing that one person, than he, if he had the power, would be justified in silencing mankind." Why? He answered that question with four propositions: First, if we silence an opinion, for all we know we may be silencing truth. Second, even a wrong opinion may contain the grain of truth that helps us find the whole truth. Third, even if the commonly held opinion is the whole truth, that opinion will not be held on rational grounds until it has been tested and defended. Fourth, unless a commonly held opinion is challenged from time to time, it loses its vitality and its effect.[12]

This was the philosophical tradition out of which the new theory of mass communication grew. It was foreshadowed in the sixteenth century, envisioned in the seventeenth, fought for in the eighteenth, and finally brought into widespread use in the nineteenth, when power was added to the printing press and machine-duplicated communication could be brought to a large part of the public. By that time the authoritarian system of communication was vanquished at least on the surface. Most countries had adopted at least the language of the new libertarianism, although many of the practices of authoritarianism still remained below the surface, and indeed still remain today.

To see what a revolutionary change this is from the authoritarian theory, let us ask of libertarian theory the same questions we asked of authoritarianism. The nature of man? According to authoritarianism, you will remember, he is a dependent animal, able to reach his highest level only under the guidance and care of the state. According to libertarian theory, he is an independent rational animal, able to choose between right and wrong, good and bad. In authoritarian theory, as you will remember, the state out-ranks man on the scale of values. In libertarian theory, on the other hand, the state exists only to provide a proper milieu in which man can develop his potentialities and enjoy the maximum of happiness. The state exists only because it has been given that assignment; if it fails in that task, it can be abolished or radically changed. As Siebert has remarked, the libertarian theory of knowledge and truth somewhat resembles early Christian theology, as opposed to the authoritarianism of the medieval church.[13] The power to reason was conceived in the 17th, 18th, and 19th centuries to be God-given, just as the knowledge of good and evil was God-given. Truth was therefore discernible by thinking men. Although that truth might be different from truth as previously perceived (as the Reformation contended), although the path to truth might lie through "a morass of argument and dispute" (as practice indicated), still as Emerson said, "The sun shines today also!" To every man is given this present power of discerning truth. Not the select few. Not the ruler alone. But potentially *every* man.

The task of society, then, is to provide a free market place of ideas, so that men may exercise this God-given gift of reason and choice. That is the essence of libertarian theory. The less control by government, the better. In place of more formal controls, libertarianism chose to trust the self-righting process of truth. That implies, of course, a truly free market place. Everyone must have access to the channels of communication. No viewpoints or opinions must be silenced, unless they are truly dangerous to the welfare of the whole group, and even that is hard to prove. Ideas must have an equal chance—and this has always been one of the hardest conditions for libertarianism to meet, because voices in the market place are not equal. Some viewpoints have a big paper, a big name behind them; others do not. Nevertheless, the goal is attractive, and the whole theory with its refreshing idealism and its complimentary view of man, is an extremely appealing one.

What kind of mass communication did libertarianism result in?

In theory, at least, it would be private enterprise, privately owned media competing in an open market. In theory, anyone with sufficient capital could start a paper or a magazine or a publishing house, and the capital demands should not be so severe that many viewpoints would be squeezed out of having their media spokesmen. The profit should be determined by the ability of the medium to satisfy customers. Thus the success of a communication enterprise, and hence its right to continue, would be measured by the final judges of its social usefulness—the public.

And it is true that in the United States and Great Britain, cradles of libertarianism, the printed media did develop very much as predicted. Notably in the 18th and early 19th centuries there were many small, privately owned papers, standing for every shade and variation of political viewpoint. For a long time in America and Britain, and even up to the present time in certain countries, the press was a "party press," representing and often supported by political groups. It was easy to enter publishing, and so practically every party found a voice. Unfortunately the party press was a severe strain on the vaunted ability of man's reason to discriminate between truth and falsehood, because its news was just as slanted as its editorial opinion.

After the middle of the 19th century, however, a change began to take place in the press. Its support began to come in larger measure from advertising rather than political subsidy. The cost of entering became greater. The attitude of some editors and reporters began to be that of observers, rather than participants in the politics of the day. It became a matter of pride, especially among American newsmen, to distinguish sharply between news and comment. A theory of what was called "objective news" began to be heard and followed. According to this theory, news should present only the raw facts of the day's events. News objectivity has become a favorite subject of argument in the last two or three decades, its opponents contending that it neglects to tell the whole truth or fill in the background for a news event. Many libertarian countries never adopted the idea of objective news at all. But it is perfectly true that the idea of news objectivity arose both from the new demands of wire services and from an honest desire to keep from contaminating the "free market place," and its development was one of the great accomplishments of western journalism.

When motion pictures came in they posed a special problem. Movies came in, strangely enough, under authoritarian, rather than libertarian, theory, though they became popular not long after 1900. This was because of their close relation to the theater. No one bothered to make a stirring plea for freedom of the theater, as Milton, Erskine, Paine, and Jefferson did for freedom of the press. The theater had been licensed and censored for centuries. Films, with their vast audiences and apparent potential for good or evil, naturally fell under the same kind of restrictions. But libertarian countries like the United States and Britain have become increasingly uneasy under this practice. Exactly how can film licensing and censorship be squared with libertarian theory? Exactly what differentiates films from newspapers and magazines, so far as censorship goes? The film also purveys opinions. It also has a news reel. It also watches the horizon, assists us in arriving at consensus, and tranmits our culture to the new members of our society. Why, then, should it not function in a free market place just as does the newspaper? The problem is a thorny one, which has only partly been solved by adoption of a "voluntary" code on the part of the producers, and by ameliorating decisions on the part of the courts.

Broadcasting also poses a problem. There are not enough channels for everyone who wants to broadcast. In order to avoid chaos on the air, and thus look after the public's interest, someone must distribute the channels. The obvious choice to represent the public in performing this task is the government. But on what basis will the channels be parceled out? The government must to this extent interfere in the free market place of ideas. The best standard we in the United States have developed is that of "public interest, convenience, and necessity"[14] a vague yardstick at best, and putting altogether more responsibility in the government's hands than Milton or Erskine or Jefferson might have approved. Actually, the American system of broadcasting, which is privately owned, comes closer to the principles of libertarianism than most other broadcasting systems throughout the world. In most countries, broadcasting is a government monopoly.

Thus survivals of authoritarian theory still exist, so far as films and broadcasting are concerned, even in the countries where libertarianism is strongest. And even in the case of the press, the libertarian theory was by no means adopted everywhere.

Many of the underdeveloped areas of the world have found it impossible to transplant the western ideas of a free press and support the resulting papers by private enterprise. In other countries, sometimes enthusiastic approval, sometimes lip service, was given the idea, but authoritarianism was too deeply grounded in the political system to be replaced. Dictators have in general found libertarianism too inefficient for their manipulative purposes. As a result the mass communication systems of Nazi Germany, Fascist Italy, and Communist Russia were built on authoritarian theory.

Even in democratic countries certain developments have in the twentieth century caused thoughtful people to question whether libertarianism is the ultimate in press theory. For one thing, to enter the mass communication industry is no longer easy; only a man with enormous capital can do it in any substantial way. That places a new responsibility on the mass communication media: to make a *restricted* market place truly a *free* market place of ideas and facts.

Furthermore, many of the fundamental philosophical bases of libertarianism have recently been challenged. As Carl Becker said:[15]

What confuses our purposes and defeats our hopes is that the simple concepts upon which the Age of Enlightenment relied with assurance have lost for us their universal and infallible quality. Natural Law turns out to be no more than a convenient and temporary hypothesis. Imprescriptible rights have such validity only as prescriptive law confers upon them. Liberty, once identified with emancipation of the individual from governmental restraint, is now seen to be inseparable from the complex pattern of social regulation. Even the sharp, definitive lines of reason and truth are blurred. Reason, we suspect, is a function of the animal organism, and truth no more than the perception of discordant experience pragmatically adjusted for a particular purpose and for the time being.

Even without adopting this pragmatic viewpoint, it is still possible to question some of the fundamental libertarian tenets. And increasingly that has been happening: men have been asking whether libertarianism is really the last stop on communication's road toward the ultimate wedding of freedom and responsibility.

Let us ask what are some of the implications of libertarian theory for communication ethics, and we have to answer, I think, that the chief implication is in regard to truth and the individual. With libertarianism, the well-spring of truth lies in reason, and with the individual's *own* reason. Therefore, it is assumed, he does not go to authority or custom for primary guidance as to moral conduct, but rather searches his own heart and mind.

Furthermore, it becomes a major matter of ethics for communicators to communicate the truth as they see it. Whether this is done by objective or subjective reporting will vary as between countries, even as between papers, but in either case it is of the greatest importance to extract and unveil. Especially it is important to reveal truth about government. And finally, the stimulating of controversy about politics, or attacks upon existing government, is in no way unethical, according to libertarianism, because of the God-given ability to reason and discriminate, and the right to know what one's government is doing so that the government's master, the public, can decide whether to change it.

The ethical responsibility of the publisher under libertarian theory might therefore be expressed by John Locke's phrase, "enlightened self-interest." The degree of "enlightenment" varies greatly with different individuals. At one extreme might be a Pulitzer, who wrote that "nothing less than the highest ideals, the most scrupulous anxiety to do right, the most accurate knowledge of the problems it has to meet, and a sincere sense of social responsibility will save journalism. . . ."[16] At the other extreme might be put the statement attributed to William Peter Hamilton, of the *Wall Street Journal:* "A newspaper is a private enterprise owing nothing whatever to the public, which grants it no franchise. It is therefore affected with no public interest. It is emphatically the property of the owner, who is selling a manufactured product at his own risk. . . ."[17] The second of these quotations is obviously an *abortion* of the theory. The first is a *development* of the theory, away from the abortions and toward some of the needs which have appeared in our own time.

NOTES

1. See Alfred Zimmern, editor, *Modern Political Doctrines.* New York: Oxford University Press, 1939, pp. 3 ff.
2. Fred S. Siebert, Theodore B. Peterson, and Wilbur Schramm. *Four Theories of the Press.* Urbana: University of Illinois Press, 1956, pp. 10 ff.
3. Robert MacIver. *The Web of Government.* New York: Macmillan, 1947.
4. Alfred Zimmern, *op. cit.,* p. 3.
5. This is in an appendix by the Secretariat of the International Press Institute to an ECOSOC report: Salvador P. Lopez, *Freedom of Information, 1953,* submitted to the Economic and Social Council of the United Nations, 16th session (Document E/2426).
6. Ernst Cassirer. "The Enlightenment," in *Encyclopedia of the Social Sciences.* New York: Macmillan, 1935, vol. 5, p. 547.
7. Robert L. Heilbronner. *The Worldly Philosophers.* New York: Simon and Schuster, 1953, pp. 13–14.
8. Arnold J. Toynbee. "Man Owes His Freedom to God," *Collier's,* vol. 137, pp. 7, 82.
9. John Milton. *Areopagitica.* George H. Sabine, editor. New York: Beacon Press, 1951.
10. Erskine's defense of Paine will be found in Thomas B. Howells, compiler, *A Complete Collection of State Trials.* London: 1704, vol. 22.
11. *The Writings of Thomas Jefferson.* A. A. Lipscomb, editor. Washington: Thomas Jefferson Memorial Association, 1904, vol. II, pp. 32–34.
12. John Stuart Mill. *On Liberty.* Alburey Castell, editor. New York: Crofts, 1947, p. 16.
13. Siebert, Peterson, and Schramm, *op. cit.,* p. 41.
14. The quotation is from the *Communications Act* of 1934.
15. Carl L. Becker. *New Liberties for Old.* New Haven: Yale University Press, 1941, p. 93.
16. Joseph Pulitzer. "The College of Journalism," *North American Review,* vol. 178, May 1904, pp. 641–680.
17. See Siebert, Peterson, and Schramm, *op. cit.,* p. 107.

ZECHARIAH CHAFEE

Government and Mass Communications

BESIDES THE RECENT LEGAL EVENTS to which I have just called attention, there are more deep-seated causes for grave anxiety about the future of the freedom of the press. Modern democratic society is in the greatest crisis of its history, because new conditions have been rapidly created by a technical civilization. The issue is whether the old ideal of a free society can be maintained against the hazards presented by these new conditions. Men are constantly called upon to learn over again how to live together. It is a hard task. When unprecedented disputes and difficulties confront them, they repeatedly turn for help to the government, as the recognized umpire. All the traditional liberties are subjected to novel strains, and freedom of the press cannot escape. Many problems of democracy extending far outside the range of this book are bound to influence mass communications. I propose to examine five general factors in the United States which have an indirect but strong tendency to increase governmental control over the distribution of news and opinions.

1. The Growth in Functions, Range of Activities, and Interventions of Government Generally

Technical instruments make for a more complete control of many social activities by the government, more particularly in order to redress disproportions and injustices created in the economic process. The same instruments make for a state control of public opinion. To put the point

Reprinted from *Government and Mass Communications* (1947), pp. 10–21; 773–81, by permission of the author and the publisher. (Copyright, 1947, by the University of Chicago Press.)

more broadly, the government has got into the habit of intervening in most other businesses, so why should it keep its hands off communications businesses? Why should the tendency toward collectivism stop when it is a question of regulating newspapers?

The physical facilities of communication are essential. Unless these are adequate, any program of free communication will fail. With the growing complexity of these facilities it is harder to keep them open. It did not matter how many packet ships or carrier pigeons brought news of Napoleon's battles—they did not interfere with each other. International radio circuits would. The government is not concerned if a new journal sets up its presses next door to an established organ. It steps in immediately when a new broadcasting station overlaps a used frequency.

It is true that what has just been said primarily concerns governmental encouragement of the flow of traffic rather than interference therewith. Yet it does have some tendency to increase restrictions as well. The three functions of government in relation to mass communications, described at the start of this chapter, are not separated by high barriers. Whatever makes the government more active in one respect about communications opens opportunities for further activity in other respects. Officials will think more and more about the press and other news agencies. For example, the Federal Communications Commission is mainly occupied with keeping the channels open, but, in so doing, it has been confronted with delicate problems of awarding frequencies to A or B with some attention to the content of their programs. "If A is happy, B is not," and B runs the risk of being put off the air for what he says. Thus far the Commission has suppressed virtually nothing, but the risk remains. Furthermore, if some action by the government happens to affect a newspaper or other communications enterprise adversely, people are likely to suspect that the officials are getting even with their critics, whether or not any such design exists. Admirers of Ralph Ingersoll firmly believed that he was drafted in the hope of wrecking *PM;* and the government's suit to open the channels of the Associated Press was supposed to be due to the hostility of the administration toward the editorial policies of the *Chicago Tribune.* Later I shall consider how the government can best promote communications or participate in them without penalizing persons of adverse views, but at the moment I wish to stress that all governmental activities in the field are in a sense interwoven.

In many subjects the complexity of the pertinent facts increases. Equal access to the facts becomes more and more difficult. The power of governments over the sources of information tends to grow. Hence the misuse of this power by governments becomes a more and more serious danger. Governments withhold one part of the facts and use the other for sales talk. This tendency is fostered by general worship of efficient salesmanship. Hence we observe an increasing amount of government activity in the field of what is called "propaganda," viz., the creation by government of various kinds of information and publicity, thus emphasizing and stimulating public interest and response in certain directions at the expense of other interests and ideas. Even when completely devoid of such intentions to falsify and propagandize, governments must make increasing use of communications. A modern government is an ever greater participant in social and economic affairs. This has created a necessity for more extensive and better intercommunication between it and the public in the interests of both. One gets a homely illustration of this by looking at the numerous kinds of placards on the walls of a post office today. How many subjects would not have been a government concern thirty years ago?

On the other hand, a modern government makes great demands for secrecy. Of course, state secrets are nothing new. Military information was always guarded from the enemy, and bureaucrats have often invoked public safety as a protection from criticism. What is significant is the enormous recent expansion of the subjects which officials are seeking to hide from publication until they give the signal. If persuasion fails to prevent leaks, they are tempted to use threats. The result may be a hush-hush attitude, likely to extend beyond the real public need for silence. This is illustrated by Burleson's postal censorship in the last war. A direct consequence of secrecy in the ordinary press may be great activity of the subsidiary press in disseminating the concealed material, and this is more dangerous than frank discussion in the general press. One may add that Drew Pearson's rumors are a poor substitute for frank official disclosures. Too often we get as gossip what ought to reach us as regular news.

No doubt there are many matters which ought not to be disclosed for a time, but the officials should not have a free hand to determine what those matters are or to lock them up forever. It may be human nature for them to want their mere say-so to be decisive on the need for secrecy, but the possession of such a power would allow them to hoist public safety as an umbrella to cover their own mistakes. Secrecy has other dangers. The controversy over atomic-bomb control shows how the claim of military security may possibly be used to hamper civilians in proper scientific activity, the progress of which depends on public communication in lectures and learned periodicals. In short, official encroachments on freedom of the press will be probable unless the boundary line between secrecy and publicity is very carefully demarcated. And officials must not do the demarcating. That is a job for the representatives of the people in Congress.

Having shown several reasons why the general tendency of government to expand in all directions is likely to reach the field of mass communications, I shall now go on to situations in the country at large which seem likely to encourage that result.

222

2. The Centralization of Economic Power Resulting from Technological Developments

A technical society makes for the centralization of economic power, and the drift toward monopoly aggravates the problem of obtaining justice. The same technical tendencies make for large-scale enterprises in the field of communications and present us with the problem as to how various sections of the community shall have adequate channels to make their appeal to the conscience and mind of the community. As the instrumentalities increase in quantity and variety, they tend to pass under the control of corporate wealth and like-minded individuals, so that they cease to express fully the diversified interests of the public. Big concentrations of economic power in other industries are also a danger to free speech because they do or can exert direct and indirect pressure upon newspapers and radio stations in various and subtle ways. Hence the government will be inclined to use compulsion on the press with the intent of promoting freedom. Examples of possible resulting government efforts to keep channels open are Sherman Act suits like that against the Associated Press and regulations by the Federal Communications Commission against the networks or against newspaper control of broadcasting stations.

The principle of freedom of the press was laid down when the press was a means of *individual* expression, comment, and criticism. Now it is an industry for profit, using techniques of mass suggestion and possessing great power. A government is always quicker to exercise control when organizations are involved rather than individuals. Is the old principle of the *Areopagitica* applicable to this new situation?

3. The Effect of Social Complexity in Splitting the Community into Groups

The American community is split into groups, with consequent feelings of ill-treatment and outbreaks of violence. Under such circumstances acrimonious controversy in the press may endanger unity. Hence the government may conceivably prohibit such controversy, or encourage people to pour oil on the troubled waters, or do its own pouring.

This split-up situation has further effects on the press. In a complex pluralistic and dynamic society we must pick one set of group standards; this inevitably increases tension with all the others. Concentration of newspapers and broadcasting stations in the hands of the wealthy group causes inadequate access to less fortunate groups, a peril to justice. The press then fails to satisfy the need for social health through adequate

223

communications in order to relieve the stresses and strains and class antagonisms caused by increasing industrialization. A widespread belief in the unfairness of the media arises. The challenge to the media as they are now operated, which lies behind all other challenges, is the left-wing challenge; that the means of production are owned and controlled by private groups who are not the servants of the people, not ultimately representative of their interests, and therefore do not fit into a coherent concept of public service. Stalin has compared the Soviet press with the American press and claimed the first is "free," the second "not free" because the people of the United States do not have access to paper, presses, etc. This is not only the classical Communist challenge. It is repeated in one form or another on every progressive level. Some social groups aspiring to recognition feel unrecognized, for instance, the Negroes. Other groups of rising economic importance feel that their new importance is not reflected by the media; this is true of organized workers in their various forms of self-articulation and representation. New workers' parties of every shade complain that capitalist control of the media is used to exclude their case from proportionate ("just") public attention. Even governmental bodies are inclined to regard the press as less progressive than the executive instrument of the constitutional authority. They tend to regard the media as not sufficiently tutored in the realities and responsibilities of public management and less co-operative in the business of government than they think they have reason to expect.

When a considerable number of people voice a grievance, they bring pressure on the government to do something on their behalf.

While many new groups have grown in power, one element in the community which possessed a great deal of influence at the time of the First Amendment has ceased to have any political importance—the intellectual élite of clergymen, scholars, lawyers, and plantation owners, which comprised not only Federalists but also Jefferson and numerous associates of his. The prolonged retention of preponderating political power by any aristocracy is objectionable, even by the aristocracy of the mind which Jefferson envisaged; but the absence of a recognized intellectual élite in America today does create dangers, which are the price we pay for free education and the largest electorate in the world. Until the middle of the nineteenth century, most writers wrote for a comparatively small group of well-educated men who formed a coherent body of opinion. The rulers and higher officials were members of this group and so followed its standards of literary freedom unless governmental interests were very seriously threatened. The rest of the community did not read much and did not care what was written. Now nearly everybody does read and care, but the standards are variegated. The lack of a strong united front among serious readers in the face of governmental restrictions on the free flow of ideas is illustrated whenever notable books are banned in Boston.

One other aspect of this division into groups has caused much trouble in recent years and is still a motive of governmental interference with the press. The emergence since 1917 of groups which propose to deny freedom if they succeed prompts the state to deny them freedom so that they will not succeed. The newspapers and pamphlets issued by these groups often attract attention from other special groups, who constantly demand restrictive measures. Farmers are arrayed against the Industrial Workers of the World, patriotic societies against Communists. The appeal of the "solid citizens" for governmental help is hard to resist.

4. The Effects of Large-scale Communication on Quality

A technical society tends to supplant additional and organic forms of cohesion with mechanistic and artificial forms of togetherness. When next-door neighbors do not even know each other, there is no formation of neighborhood opinion. The same technical tendencies replace the old process of talking it out with those around you, by mass instruments of communication in which the common interests of a community are reduced to the lowest common denominator. The Commission was greatly disturbed by the drift toward meaninglessness in the press.

This situation differs from those previously reviewed in that it does not directly impel the government to step in. For example, officials will get more excited about the power of radio networks than about the trivialities of soap opera. The point is that the low level of so much in mass communications will weaken resistance to the government whenever other reasons do lead it to interfere with newspapers or radio or films. When people have come to regard a publication as trash, they do not care much if it is kept from them. They readily forget the underlying issue of the importance of untrammeled discussion. What harm, they think, if something can no longer be published which was never worth publishing anyway. For example, if the Federal Communications Commission should limit the "commercial" element in each broadcast to ten seconds at the start, my first impulse would be to throw up my hat and cheer because I am so sick of the way toothpaste is mixed with toccatas and cosmetics with campaigns. Yet the implications of such a ruling for administrative dictation of contents would be very serious. Contrast the excitement over the banning of *Strange Fruit;* here was something known to be really good.

The maintenance and breadth of freedom depend ultimately on the toleration of private citizens. Hence it is alarming when a recent *Fortune*

225

survey shows that citizens do not place much value on free speech. One reason for this may be that they do not place much value on what would be suppressed.

5. The Growing Importance of Mass Media as Agencies for Maintaining Unity and Co-operative Understanding

The fact that the instrumentalities of communication reach many more people than formerly tends to make the government more solicitous about them. The Tory government around 1800 left the expensive newspapers to say what they pleased but tried to tax Cobbett's two-penny journal out of existence. Freedom of speech worked well when only five thousand people could hear what was being said and a few thousand more would read some book or pamphlet. Will this principle of laissez faire still be allowed to operate when audiences are now to be counted by the million? For example, suppose that television existed in December, 1941, and that an agency was about to send out a transmission of Pearl Harbor during the bombing. Would the government have permitted this? Did liberty of the press then cease to be desirable? The impulse to censor is obviously strengthened by the multiplied distribution of dubious material.

As the war went on, men came to realize that our technical civilization has created a potential world community. Obviously, a community with its citizens widely separated can be held together only by mass communications. This raises the problem as to how instruments of communication can be most responsibly used to further the cause of international comity. As the shrinking of world distances has changed the basis of international relations, it has become increasingly important to safeguard the channels of news for the sake of world-peace. This factor has its less idealistic side. A government sees its own interests in security, trade, etc., affected seriously by outward and inward communications and so has a strong reason for censoring or guiding them. Consequently, the United States government is bound to participate in the maintenance and management of cables and international radio circuits.

The value of domestic mass communications to the party in power is also becoming obvious. The totalitarians abroad made systematic use of newspapers, radio, and films. This may conceivably influence American politicians. Huey Long showed what can be done, with his sound trucks and his legislation to bludgeon opposition journals into line. Efforts will be needed to avoid this temptation.

Finally, the belief is growing that freedom of the press is so important to the state that it cannot be irresponsibly exercised. It is conceived to be so closely interwoven with the advance of society that it differs from other freedoms. Although this has been described as the Fascist point of view, it is not wholly remote from the position of many citizens who regard themselves as democratic, except that they want responsibility imposed without governmental compulsion. Indeed, insistence on the need of responsibility in the press is the leading theme of the Commission's general report. When men become very much aware of the importance of communications in modern life and are exploring the deficiencies which prevent their accomplishing what they might, the question is bound to arise: Why should not the governmental power, which is invoked to remove so many current evils, be asked to step in and straighten out this mess too? There are plenty of reasons for a negative answer, of course, but persons who overlook those reasons may easily make an affirmative reply because of the gloomy picture presented by the large amount of irresponsibility which is now exhibited by many agencies of communication.

The fact that active governmental participation in mass communications is sometimes advocated as a cure for the diseases of the commercial press naturally increases the resentment of newspapermen. This is not the only reason for a (government) information service, of course. Even if there were perfect private media, a government official still has to make his thoughts clear to the people. But the following position taken by a few rebellious Nieman Fellows, though presumably not typical of newspapermen, especially those toward the top, is shared by many outside critics of the press.

"I am less concerned by possible governmental restrictions than by the failure of the press to restrict itself. Press freedom is in danger because the press does not behave responsibly. Responsibility should go with power. Instead, a kind of Gresham's Law operates in the field of journalism. Just as bad money tends to drive out good, so newspapers with poor ethics tend to drive out papers with better standards. The government should act vigorously to make the newspaper press responsible. The existing libel laws fall short of the need. The best way to offset the misrepresentations of the mass-circulation media is to establish *one* government newspaper, *one* government radio station, and *one* government movie producer. This will enable the government to present its point of view to the public."

These advocates of a government-owned press and the newspaper leaders who are so terrified of its coming both seem to me completely off the road, although in different ditches. As to the first group, government ownership is not a satisfactory remedy for the present shortcomings of the communications industries. The evils of bigness will persist in a big government newspaper, unless indeed it is so unenterprising and dull as to be unread. And, on the other hand, the newspaper leaders who fight all efficient public information because it will give us something like *Pravda* and the British Broadcasting Corporation are either insincere or "fraidy-cats." Given the hostility of Congress toward mild experiments in the information field, the enormous funds required for a national newspaper will not be appropriated in any foreseeable future. It would be more sensible to expect the Federal Theater project of WPA to produce a replica of the Paris Opera House in Washington equipped with teachers of coloratura singing and the ballet. The nearest we ever came to a national domestic channel of mass communications was when President Roosevelt was offered a chance to buy the Blue Network and declined. Something can be said for a municipal radio station like WNYC or for broadcasting at a state university; but, so long as high federal officers find nation-wide hook-ups on all the networks available, any proposal for sending out much more than time signals and weather reports at the expense of the taxpayers is likely to fall on deaf ears in the Capitol. The notion that OWI would develop into a peacetime octopus seems to me ridiculous. If its Domestic Branch was open to blame, this was not because it was continually seeking new worlds to conquer but on the ground of undue caution for fear of what Congress might do. Its denunciators in high press circles have got so excited that they have mistaken Caspar Milquetoast for Boris Karloff.

There is much more basis for the fear that the government will work through the private press with propaganda and careful concealment of official weakness, although the demand for plate-glass objectivity comes with rather a bad grace from some newspapermen who are past masters at shaping facts to suit their own policies. An improvement in the accuracy and fairness of the regular press is likely to be paralleled in the performance of government publicity experts, who have often got their preliminary experience in work for newspapers, broadcasters, etc. As I said about the defects of the communications industries, it is mainly a question of raising professional standards. Not that we want to encourage devious practices in government just because the private media indulge in them, but the fact that some persons do wrong is not a conclusive reason for denying other persons the opportunity to do right in ways which the country badly needs. If Congress were more sympathetic to information services, as I have suggested, the past or potential publicity programs of specific agencies could be examined in relation to their honesty and abstention from objectionable propaganda. Bad actors could be denied funds and public-spirited performers encouraged. This is not a problem to be solved by sweeping formulas.

A final objection to further publicity is that it will add to what is now enormous in bulk. For example, the *New York Times* now gets twenty-one pounds of government handouts every day in Washington and ten pounds more at its home office. One is appalled by the prospect of more tonnage per annum—"of making many books there is no end; and much study is a weariness of the flesh." Certainly greater quantity can be justified only by distinctly higher quality. This was stressed by one member of our Commission, although he was strongly in favor of information services:

Some of the fear of the official mind on the part of members of the communications industries is unnatural. One point, however, we must allow them. They may not know how to use the influence of the press for all it is worth, but they will certainly be justified if they are preventing narrower or even more confused controls from affecting it. If their case is that their present system does tend to enrich, the case against them must be in the name of a system which will even more patently enrich as well as regulate. A merely negative approach, such as we have had too often from government information services, will only confirm these representatives of the press in their argument. It suggests for one thing a great improvement in the government's sense of the news media, which is capable of creating a greater trust in its advice and co-operation, particularly abroad. One of the keys to the freedom of the press may be, in fact, a re-examination of government information services, with the possibility of a 'free' public agency supplying an intelligence and information service to the press outside it, under an authority which is guaranteed to be free from political dictation.

The supporters of government information are between the devil and the deep sea. If the information is poorly contrived, we do not want it. If it is well contrived, it arouses the jealousy of Congress and the press. Still, as between the two alternatives, the choice is obvious.

In spite of all the objections, we are plainly going to have a good deal of government information of some sort or other. To say nothing more of press conferences and departmental handouts, the extent of its participation in mass communications is impressively evidenced by the following list (compiled in 1945), which shows twenty-eight federal agencies engaged in the production or use of motion pictures: Department of Agriculture; Alien Property Custodian (enemy-owned or controlled films in United States at outbreak of war); Bureau of the Budget (accounting of government film expenditures); Civil Service Commission (library of visual aids material for training officers in different agencies); Coast Guard; Department of Commerce; Office of Education (films for training war workers); Office of Inter-American Affairs; Department of the Interior; Department of Justice (films for federal penal institutions); Department of Labor; Library of Congress; Marine Corps; Maritime Commission; National Archives; Department of the Navy; Office of Price Administration; Public Health Service; Social Security Board; Department of State; Office of Strategic Services; Tennessee Valley Authority; Department of the Treasury (war-bond drives); Veterans Administration; Department of War; Office of War Information (Domestic and Overseas Branches); War Manpower Commission; War Production Board.

The list also gives six international or semigovernmental bodies which operate films in connection with our government; American Council on

Education; American Red Cross; Combined Production and Resources Board (allocation of film supplies among United States, United Kingdom, and Canada); Pan American Union (clearing-house and Sunday film shows); United Nations Central Training Film Library; United Nations Relief and Rehabilitation Administration.

Granted, then, that there is to be such a thing as governmental information service in peace, what are to be its nature and functions? This leads to at least two further questions, which I shall not attempt to answer, but which are so important that they ought to be stated.

First, should there be a centralized service something like OWI, although with more vision than its Domestic Branch possessed, or should we merely have several mutually independent services attached to different agencies as at present? Our Commission received conflicting views on this difficult problem. On one side was the experienced newspaperman whom I have already quoted as favoring only "consolidation up to the Cabinet level." His objection to an over-all service was: "It is skating on thin ice to depend on the standards of the men involved. If all information goes through one person, the situation is very dangerous." On the other hand, an equally experienced newspaperman, who had also worked for the government, said:

If the public is to get a clear, coherent, and comprehensive story of the operation of the bureaus, a centralized agency is necessary. There is assumed, of course, a reasonable degree of honesty in this agency. I disagree with [the preceding informant's] idea of governmental handouts at the department level. Without a centralized information agency, the reports given out by the various agencies that would come out in such reports are not altogether a fair representation of the facts. Often they are small parts of a big story, or are in fact personal feuds and rivalries rather than disagreements on policy. Reporters have often been used as instruments in personal rivalries, for example in the War Production Board. This practice is tempting to subordinate officials. The ordinary channels do not give a fair picture of how the government is operating, because peace, harmony, and brotherly love are not news as a rule; a fight is. Experience does not bear out the view that public airing of disputes expedites decisions. It serves the public interest to have the various departments reach agreements on the facts and the policy to be adopted before making them too public. Perhaps the revelation of the differences among officials serves as a check on bureaucracy, but the press will find out about these anyway without having them stressed by segregated information services of the agencies involved in a controversy. A related point is that a colorful figure in an agency may receive wide publicity, while his successor may do much better work in a quiet way and receive no attention from the reporters.

"The clearance function of a centralized agency is useful even in peace, but (unlike wartime) probably no great harm is done if there is no such agency. The result of its absence is not the withholding of the truth, but rather partial and incomplete information. An example of the way a centralized information agency would contribute to the clarification of the public mind is provided by the trouble that arose in connection with food stories during the war. Apart from such predictions of starvation as Louis Bromfield's, two or three government departments had adopted divergent views—on the basis of scattered data extrapolated in different directions. Eventually it was agreed that the Bureau of Agricultural Economics was more likely to be right than any other agency dealing with food, and the situation became much clearer."

This last point in favor of centralization has much weight. One can think of many nation-wide peacetime problems such as housing, inflation, unemployment, the attraction of venture capital to new businesses—to name only a few—which concern several different agencies. The segregated information bureau of a single agency does not see the problem as a whole. A pooling of knowledge and imagination is essential in order to make citizens understand the problem and the remedies which the government is undertaking.

On the other hand, there are objections to extreme centralization which have not yet been mentioned. An over-all information service lacks expertness in any one field, and yet this is indispensable if the law and the practical situation are to be satisfactorily explained. In this connection it is rather significant that Mr. Grierson spoke of the work of bureaucrats in the Canadian information service, whereas our Commission was told that the work of OFF and OWI did not affect the bureaus at all. "The information officers were not bureaucrats. The bureaucracy played a *nil* part in the information operations of the United States government." It may have been pleasant to avoid a hated word which would have increased the bombardment against OWI, and yet I surmise that the active participation of the officials of numerous permanent Canadian agencies in the projects of their unified information service had a good deal to do with its success as compared with the Domestic Branch of OWI.

Moreover, even if Congress should unexpectedly consent to a centralized information service, there would still have to be separate publicity groups in many federal agencies. This is proved by the fact that the existence of OWI during the war did not relieve the Office of Price Administration from issuing much explanatory matter about its regulations and aims. It is inconceivable that the establishment of a centralized service in peace would enable the Department of Agriculture to stop distributing bulletins to farmers. No doubt, more co-ordination of the separate information services is practicable and desirable, but I doubt whether they ought to be merged into any all-embracing office.

If a centralized information service of any sort is established, it will naturally be closely related to the President. It is interesting that Elmer Davis, in his final report to the President, recommended that if there is ever again a domestic OWI, it should be under the direction of the President's press secretary, who could blend White House publicity with all other publicity and guarantee that it really expressed the will of the head of the Administration.

My own feeling is that this question of many services versus one service does not need to be solved now. *Solvitur in ambulando.* If the separate services can be made increasingly fruitful and if they develop a desirable amount of co-ordination, questions of more unification or less will be worked out by the men participating and members of Congress, where (so I hope) the question will receive more light and less heat than in the past.

Second, should an information service merely distribute what is commonly known as news, or should it also deal with "pre-news," that is, questions of principle and decision—the considerations on which policy is based? The broader scope has much more effect on national morale. Accordingly, the Office of Facts and Figures charged itself with an obligation to provide the people of the country with whatever information it thought relevant to decisions on questions of principle. It felt no particular responsibility for getting out military communiqués with which it had had nothing to do. The American newspapers, being unfriendly, took the position that its only responsibility domestically was to get communiqués out promptly. This view was accepted by its successor, OWI, which evidently considered it had no duty to provide the people of this country with information relative to important decisions—questions of principle and policy. The problem in the war was whether the government was to perform the neuter and sterilized task of getting military communiqués out at 11:30 instead of 11:45, or whether its job was to enable a free people to govern themselves. Corresponding alternatives will be presented during peace. Of course, great masses of pure facts will always have to be distributed, for instance, crop reports. Whether more than this be practicable under present conditions is not for me to say, but much more than facts is needed by us citizens if we are to become conscious that we are partners and not just passengers in the difficult enterprise of government.

Public Service Responsibility of Broadcast Licensees: Some Aspects of "Public Interest" in Program Service

FEDERAL COMMUNICATIONS COMMISSION must determine, with respect to each application granted or denied or renewed, whether or not the program service proposed is "in the public interest, convenience, and necessity."

The Federal Radio Commission was faced with this problem from the very beginning, and in 1928 it laid down a broad definition which may still be cited in part:

> Broadcasting stations are licensed to serve the public and not for purpose of furthering the private or selfish interests of individuals or groups of individuals. The standard of public interest, convenience, or necessity means nothing if it does not mean this. . . . The emphasis should be on the *receiving* of service and the standard of public interest, convenience, or necessity should be construed accordingly. . . . The *entire* listening public within the service area of a station or of a group of stations in one community, is entitled to service from that station or stations. . . . In a sense a broadcasting station may be regarded as a sort of mouthpiece on the air for the community it serves, over which its public events of general interest, its political campaigns, its election results, its athletic contests, its orchestras and artists, and discussion of its public issues may be broadcast. *If . . . the station performs its duty in furnishing a well rounded program, the rights of the community* have been achieved. (In re Great Lakes Broadcasting Co., FRC. Docket No. 4900; cf. 3rd Annual Report of the F.R.C., pp. 32–36.)

Commission policy with respect to public interest determinations is for the most part set by opinion in particular cases. (See, for example,

Excerpted with minor editorial adaptations from the report of the Federal Communications Commission, *Public Service Responsibility of Broadcast Licensees*, March 7, 1946.

233

cases indexed under "Program Service" in Volumes 1 through 9 of the Commission's Decisions.) A useful purpose is served, however, by occasional overall reviews of Commission policy. This Part will discuss four major issues currently involved in the application of the "public interest" standard to program service policy; namely, (A) the carrying of sustaining programs, (B) the carrying of local live programs, (C) the carrying of programs devoted to public discussion, and (D) the elimination of commercial advertising excesses.

A. The Carrying of Sustaining Programs

The commercial program, paid for and in many instances also selected, written, casted, and produced by advertisers and advertising agencies, is the staple fare of American listening. More than half of all broadcast time is devoted to commercial programs; the most popular programs on the air are commercial. The evidence is overwhelming that the popularity of American broadcasting as we know it is based in no small part upon its commercial programs.

Nevertheless, since the early days of broadcasting, broadcasters and the Commission alike have recognized that sustaining programs also play an integral and irreplaceable part in the American system of broadcasting. The sustaining program has five distinctive and outstanding functions.

1. To secure for the station or network a means by which in the overall structure of its program service, it can achieve a *balanced* interpretation of public needs.

2. To provide programs which by their very nature may not be sponsored with propriety.

3. To provide programs for significant minority tastes and interests.

4. To provide programs devoted to the needs and purposes of non-profit organizations.

5. To provide a field for experiment in new types of programs, secure from the restrictions that obtain with reference to programs in which the advertiser's interest in selling goods predominates.

B. The Carrying of Local Live Programs

All or substantially all programs currently broadcast are of four kinds: (*1*) network programs, including programs furnished to a station by telephone circuit from another station; (*2*) recorded (including transcribed) programs; (*3*) wire programs (chiefly wire news, syndicated to many stations by telegraph or teletype and read off the wire by a local announcer); and (*4*) local live programs, including remote broadcasts.

Network Programs—The merit of network programs is universally recognized; indeed, the Commission's Chain Broadcasting Regulations

3.101 and 3.102 were designed in considerable part to insure a freer flow of network programs to the listener. In January, 1945, approximately 47.9% of all the time of standard broadcast stations was devoted to network programs.

Transcriptions—The transcribed or recorded program has not had similar recognition. As early as 1922, the Department of Commerce by regulation prohibited the playing of phonograph records by stations having the better (Class B) channel assignments except in emergencies or to fill in between program periods; and later in the year it amended the regulation to prohibit even such use of records by Class B stations. Through the years the phonograph record, and to a lesser extent the transcription, have been considered inferior program sources.

No good reason appears, however, for not recognizing today the significant role which the transcription and the record, like the network, can play in radio programming.

In January, 1945, approximately 32.3% of all the time of standard broadcast stations was devoted to transcriptions and recordings.

Wire Programs—The wire service, by which spot news and sometimes also other program texts are telegraphically distributed to stations, has in recent years assumed a role of increasing importance. By means of wire service for news and other texts of a timely nature, plus transcriptions for programs of less urgent timeliness, the unaffiliated station can very nearly achieve the breadth of service attained through network affiliation. No statistics are currently available concerning the proportion of time devoted to wire service programs.

Local Live Programs—There remains for discussion the local live program, for which also, no precise statistics are available. It is known, however, that in January, 1945, approximately 19.7% of all the time of standard broadcast stations was devoted to local live *and* wire service programs; and that during the best listening hours from 6 to 11 P.M., approximately 15.7% of all the time was devoted to these two classes of programs combined.

In granting and renewing licenses, the Commission has given repeated and explicit recognition to the need for adequate reflection in programs of local interests, activities and talent. Assurances by the applicant that "local talent will be available," that there will be "a reasonable portion of time for programs which include religious, educational, and civic matters"; that "time will be devoted to local news at frequent intervals, to market reports, agricultural topics and to various civic and political activities that occur in the city" have contributed to favorable decision on many applications. As the Commission noted in its *Supplemental Report on Chain Broadcasting* (1941):

It has been the consistent intention of the Commission to assure that an adequate amount of time *during the good listening hours* shall be made available to meet the needs of the community in terms of public expression and of local interest. If these regulations do not accomplish this objective, the subject will be given further consideration.

The networks themselves have recognized the importance of local live programs. Under date of October 9, 1944, the National Broadcasting Company, when requesting the Commission to amend Chain Broadcasting Regulation 3.104, stated:

Over the years our affiliated stations have been producing highly important local programs in these three open hours of the morning segment. From 8 a.m. to 10 a.m. N.Y.T., most of the stations have developed a variety of "morning clock" programs which have met popular acceptance. These periods are not only profitable to the individual station but are sought for use by civic, patriotic and religious groups for special appeals because of their local listening audience appeal. Likewise, from 12 noon to 1 p.m., they have developed highly important news farm programs or other local interest shows. *To interfere with local program schedules of many years' standing would deprive our stations of their full opportunity to render a desirable local public service.*

The Commission's reply, released December 20, 1944, as Mimeograph No. 79574, stated in part:

One purpose of Regulation 3.104 was to leave 14 of the 35 evening hours in each week free of network option, *in order to foster the development of local programs*[1] . . . The Commission . . . concurs fully in your statement that interference with local programs which have met with public acceptance and which are sought for use by local civic, patriotic and religious groups, local church services, and other highly important local program schedules of years' standing is to be avoided.

The courts have also supported the position taken by the Commission that the interests of the whole listening public require that provision be made for local program service. Where the record showed that of the two stations already functioning in an area, one carried 50 percent network programs and the other 85 percent, the court stated: "In view of this situation it is not difficult to see why the Commission decided that public interest would be served by the construction of a local non-network station."[2]

While parallels between broadcast stations and newspapers must be approached with caution, their common elements with respect to local interest may be significant. The local newspaper achieves world-wide news coverage through the great press associations, taps the country's foremost writers and cartoonists through the feature syndicates, and from the picture services procures photographs from everywhere in abundant quantity. But the local newspaper editor, faced with such abundant incoming material, does not therefore discharge his local reporters and photographers, nor does he seek to reproduce locally the New York *Times* or *Daily News*. He appreciates the keen interest in local material and makes the most of that material—especially on the front page. The hours from

6 to 11 P.M. are the "front page" of the broadcast station. The statistics of local programming during these hours, or generally, are not impressive.

C. DISCUSSION OF PUBLIC ISSUES

American broadcasters have always recognized that broadcasting is not merely a means of entertainment but also an unequaled medium for the dissemination of news, information, and opinion, and for the discussion of public issues. Radio's role in broadcasting the election returns of November 1920 is one of which broadcasters are justly proud; and during the quarter of a century which has since elapsed, broadcasting has continued to include news, information, opinion and public discussion in its regular budget of program material.

Especially in recent years, such information programs as news and news commentaries have achieved a popularity exceeding the popularity of any other single type of program. The war, of course, tremendously increased listener interest in such programs; but if broadcasters face the crucial problems of the post-war era with skill, fairness, and courage, there is no reason why broadcasting cannot play as important a role in our democracy hereafter as it has achieved during the war years.

The use of broadcasting as an instrument for the dissemination of news, ideas, and opinions raises a multitude of problems of a complex and sometimes delicate nature, which do not arise in connection with purely entertainment programs. A few such problems may be briefly noted, without any attempt to present an exhaustive list:

1. Shall time for the presentation of one point of view on a public issue be sold, or shall all such presentations of points of view be on sustaining time only?

2. If presentations of points of view are to be limited only to sustaining time, what measures can be taken to insure that adequate sustaining time during good listening hours is made available for such presentations, and that such time is equitably distributed?

3. If time is also on occasion to be sold for presentation of a point of view, what precautions are necessary to insure that the most time shall not gravitate to the side prepared to spend the most money?

4. Are forums, town meetings, and round-table type broadcasts, in which two or more points of view are aired together, intrinsically superior to the separate presentation of points of view at various times?

5. Should such programs be sponsored?

6. What measures will insure that such programs be indeed fair and well-ballanced among opposing points of view?

7. Should locally originated discussion programs in which residents of a community can themselves discuss issues of local, national, or international importance be encouraged, and if so how?

237

8. How can unbiased presentation of the news be achieved?

9. Should news be sponsored, and if so, to what extent should the advertiser influence or control the presentation of the news?

10. How and by whom should commentators be selected?

11. Should commentators be forbidden, permitted, or encouraged to express their own personal opinions?

12. Is a denial of free speech involved when a commentator is discharged or his program discontinued because something which he has said has offended (a) the advertiser, (b) the station, (c) a minority of his listeners, or (d) a majority of his listeners?

13. What provisions, over and above Section 315 of the Communications Acts of 1934,[3] are necessary or desirable in connection with the operation of broadcast stations during a political campaign?

14. Does a station operate in the public interest which charges a higher rate for political broadcasts than for commercial programs?

15. The Federal Communications Commission is forbidden by law to censor broadcasts. Should station licensees have the absolute right of censorship, or should their review of broadcasts be limited to protection against libel, dissemination of criminal matter, etc.?

16. Should broadcasters be relieved of responsibility for libel with respect to broadcasts over which they exercise no control?

17. Should the "right to reply" to broadcasts be afforded; and if so, to whom should the right be afforded, and under what circumstances?

18. When a station refuses time on the air requested for the discussion of public issues should it be required to state in writing its reasons for refusal? Should it be required to maintian a record of all such requests for time, and of the disposal made of them?

19. What measures can be taken to open broadcasting to types of informational programs which contravene the interests of large advertisers—for example, news of the reports and decisions of the Federal Trade Commission concerning unfair advertising; reports of the American Medical Association concerning the effects of cigarette-smoking; temperance broadcasts; etc.?

These are only a few of the many questions which are raised in complaints to the Commission from day to day. The future of American broadcasting as an instrument of democracy depends in no small part upon the establishment of sound solutions of such problems, and on the fair and impartial application of general solutions to particular cases.

Under the Communications Act, primary responsibility for solving these and similar issues rests upon the licensees of broadcast stations themselves. Probably no other type of problem in the entire broadcasting industry is as important, or requires of the broadcaster a greater sense of objectivity, responsibility, and fair play.

While primary responsibility in such matters rests with the individual broadcaster, the Commission is required by the statute to review periodically the station's operation, in order to determine whether the station has in fact been operated in the public interest. Certainly, the establishment of sound station policy with respect to news, information, and the discussion of public issues is a major factor in operation in the public interest.

The Commission has never laid down, and does not now propose to lay down, any categorical answers to such questions as those raised above. Rather than enunciating general policies, the Commission reaches decisions on such matters in the crucible of particular cases.[4]

One matter of primary concern, however, can be met by an over-all statement of policy, and must be met as part of the general problem of over-all program balance. This is the question of the *quantity* of time which should be made available for the discussion of public issues.

The problems involved in making time available for the discussion of public issues are admittedly complex. Any vigorous presentation of a point of view will of necessity annoy or offend at least some listeners. There may be a temptation, accordingly, for broadcasters to avoid as much as possible any discussion over their stations, and to limit their broadcasts to entertainment programs which offend no one.

To operate in this manner, obviously, is to thwart the effectiveness of broadcasting in a democracy.

The carrying of any particular public discussion, of course, is a problem for the individual broadcaster. But the public interest clearly requires that an adequate amount of time be made available for the discussion of public issues; and the Commission, in determining whether a station has served the public interest, will take into consideration the amount of time which has been or will be devoted to the discussion of public issues.

Summary and Conclusions—Proposals for Future Commission Policy

A. ROLE OF THE PUBLIC: Primary responsibility for the American system of broadcasting rests with the licensee of broadcast stations, including the network organizations. It is to the stations and networks rather than to federal regulation that listeners must primarily turn for improved standards of program service. The Commission, as the licensing agency established by Congress, has a responsibility to consider overall program service in its public interest determinations, but affirmative improvement of program service must be the result primarily of other forces.

One such force is self-regulation by the industry itself, through its trade associations.

Licensees acting individually can also do much to raise program service standards, and some progress has indeed been made. Here and there across the country, some stations have evidenced an increased awareness of the importance of sustaining programs, live programs, and discussion programs. Other stations have eliminated from their own program service the middle commercial, the transcribed commercial, the piling up of commercials, etc. This trend toward self-improvement, if continued, may further buttress the industry against the rising tide of informed and responsible criticism.

Forces outside the broadcasting industry similarly have a role in improved program service. There is need, for example, for professional radio critics, who will play in this field the role which literary and dramatic critics have long assumed in the older forms of artistic expression. It is, indeed, a curious instance of the time lag in our adjustment to changed circumstances that while plays and concerts performed to comparatively small audiences in the "legitimate" theater or concert hall are regularly reviewed in the press, radio's best productions performed before an audience of millions receive only occasional and limited critical consideration. *Publicity* for radio programs is useful, but limited in the function it performs. Responsible criticism can do much more than mere promotion; it can raise the standards of public appreciation and stimulate the free and unfettered development of radio as a new medium of artistic expression. The independent radio critic, assuming the same role long occupied by the dramatic critic and the literary critic, can bring to bear an objective judgment on questions of good taste and of artistic merit which lie outside the purview of this commission. The reviews and critiques published weekly in *Variety* afford an illustration of the role that independent criticism can play; newspapers and periodicals might well consider the institution of similar independent critiques for the general public.

Radio listener councils can do much to improve the quality of program service. Such councils, notably in Cleveland, Ohio, and Madison, Wisconsin, have already shown the possibilities of independent listener organization. First, they can provide a much needed channel through which listeners can convey to broadcasters the wishes of the vast but not generally articulate radio audience. Second, listener councils can engage in much needed research concerning public tastes and attitudes. Third, listener councils can check on the failure of network affiliates to carry outstanding network sustaining programs, and on the local programs substituted for outstanding network sustaining programs. Fourth, they can serve to publicize and to promote outstanding programs—especially sustaining programs which at present suffer a serious handicap for lack of the vast promotional enterprise which goes to publicize many commercial programs. Other useful functions would also no doubt result from an increase in the number and an extension of the range of activities of listener councils, cooperating with the broadcasting industry but speaking solely for the interest of listeners themselves.

Colleges and universities, some of them already active in the field, have a like distinctive role to play. Together with the public schools, they have it in their power to raise a new generation of listeners with higher standards and expectations of what radio can offer.

In radio workshops, knowledge may be acquired of the techniques of radio production. There are already many examples, of students graduating from such work who have found their way into the industry, carrying with them standards and conceptions of radio's role, as well as talents, by which radio service cannot fail to be enriched.

Even more important, however, is the role of colleges and universities in the field of radio research. There is room for a vast expansion of studies of the commercial, artistic and social aspects of radio. The cultural aspects of radio's influence provide in themselves a vast and fascinating field of research.

It is hoped that the facts emerging from this report and the recommendations which follow will be of interest to the groups mentioned. With them rather than with the Commission rests much of the hope for improved broadcasting quality.

B. ROLE OF THE COMMISSION

While much of the responsibility for improved program service lies with the broadcasting industry and with the public, the Commission has a statutory responsibility for the public interest, of which it cannot divest itself. The Commission's experience with the detailed review of broadcast renewal applications since April, 1945, together with the facts set forth in this report, indicate some current trends in broadcasting which, with reference to licensing procedure, require its particular attention.

In issuing and in renewing the licenses of broadcast stations the Commission proposes to give particular consideration to four program service factors relevant to the public interest. There are:

1. the carrying of sustaining programs, including network sustaining programs, with particular reference to the retention by licensees of a proper discretion and responsibility for maintaining a well-balanced program structure;

2. the carrying of local live programs;

3. the carrying of programs devoted to the discussion of public issues; and

4. the elimination of advertising excesses.

1. Sustaining Programs—The carrying of sustaining programs has always been deemed one aspect of broadcast operation in the public interest. Sustaining programs perform a five-fold function in (*a*) maintaining an overall program balance, (*b*) providing time for programs inappropriate for sponsorship, (*c*) providing time for programs serving particular minority tastes and interests, (*d*) providing time for non-profit organizations—religious, civic, agrcultural, labor, educaton, etc., and (*e*) providing time for experiment and for unfettered artistic self-expression.

Accordingly, the Commission concludes that one standard of operation in the public interest is a reasonable proportion of time devoted to sustaining programs.

Moreover, if sustaining programs are to perform their traditional functions in the American system of broadcasting, they must be broadcast at hours when the public is awake and listening. The time devoted to sustaining programs, accordingly, should be reasonably distributed among the various segments of the broadcast day.

For reasons set forth, the Commission in considering overall program balance, will also take note of network sustaining programs available to but not carried by a station, and of the programs which the station substitutes therefor.

2. *Local Live Programs*—The Commission has always placed a marked emphasis, and in some cases perhaps an undue emphasis, on the carrying of local live programs as a standard of public interest. The development of network, transcription, and wire news services is such that no sound public interest appears to be served by continuing to stress local live programs exclusively at the expense of these other categories. Nevertheless, reasonable provision for local self-expression still remains an essential function of a station's operation and will continue to be so regarded by the Commission. In particular, public interest requires that such programs should not be crowded out of the best listening hours.

3. *Programs devoted to the discussion of public issues*—The crucial need for discussion programs, at the local, national, and international levels alike is universally realized. Accordingly, the carrying of such programs in reasonable sufficiency, and during good listening hours, is a factor to be considered in any finding of public interest.

4. *Advertising excesses*—The evidence set forth above warrants the conclusion that some stations during some or many portions of the broadcast day have engaged in advertising excesses which are incompatible with their public responsibilities, and which threaten the good name of broadcasting itself.

As the broadcasting industry itself has insisted, the public interest clearly requires that the amount of time devoted to advertising matter shall bear a reasonable relationship to the amount of time devoted to programs. Accordingly, in its application forms the Commission will require the applicant to state how much time he proposes to devote to advertising matter in any one hour.

This by itself will not, of course, result in the elimination of some of the particular excesses described. This is a matter in which self-regulation by the industry may properly be sought and indeed expected. The Commission has no desire to concern itself with the particular length, content, or irritating qualities of particular commercial plugs.

NOTES

1. The failure of Regulation 3.104 to achieve this purpose is illustrated by the eight charts, presented elsewhere in the report, showing many stations which carried no non-network programs whatever during the evening hours on the two days analyzed.

2. *Great Western Broadcasting Association, Inc.* v. *F.C.C.*, 94 Fed. (2nd) 244,248. In the KHMO case, the court ordered the Commission to issue a license to an applicant for a local station in an area where three stations were already operating, none of which gave genuine local service. The court expressed approval of the Commission's findings in similar cases, that "under the direct provisions of the statute the *rights of the citizens to enjoy local broadcasting privileges were being denied.*" (*Courier Post Broadcasting Co.* v. *F.C.C.*, 104 [2] 213,218).

3. "Sec. 315. If any licensee shall permit any person who is a legally qualified candidate for any public office to use a broadcasting station, he shall afford equal opportunties to all other such candidates for that office in the use of such broadcasting station, and the Commission shall make rules and regulations to carry this provision into effect: *Provided,* That such licensee shall have no power of censorship over the material broadcast under the provisions of this section. No obligation is hereby imposed upon any licensee to allow the use of its station by any such candidate."

4. See, for example, the *Mayflower* case, 8 F.C.C. 333 and *United Broadcasting Company* (WHKC) case, decided June 26, 1945.

6

Communication Content

Analysis of Media Content

Many research problems in communications require description of the contents of the mass media in a rigorous fashion. For this purpose students in the field have developed the technique of qualitative and quantitative content analysis. Both approaches seek to be objective and systematic in analysis of symbol materials; the difference rests in the emphasis of quantitative concerns. The uses of content analysis in the study of the communication process are many and varied: they include the investigation of cultural patterns, the prediction of events, the identification of the communicator's intentions, the application of communication standards, and the description of responses to communications.

No attempt has been made to represent adequately the literature on the techniques of content analysis. However, the essay by Lasswell, a pioneer in this field, does deal with the central methodological question in the analysis of communication content. Lasswell addresses himself to the question, "Why Be Quantitative?", namely, what is the increment in knowledge when the content of the media are studied in numerical depth. The selection by Bernard Berelson draws on this perspective by seeking to set forth the various approaches and dimensions of different types of content analysis. Often the issues to which content analysis must be applied are most complex. For example, the article by Kris and Leites describes broad trends in political propaganda without the use of quantitative measurement.

Popular Culture

The extensive development of the mass media over the past half century has had important effects not only upon the social and political life of the country but upon its culture as well. The media have helped to create the largest and most varied audience that has ever existed. In doing so, every medium has developed a body of content with wide popular appeal and cultural influence—the TV serial and the radio disc jockey, the feature film, the short story in the popular magazine, the human interest story in the newspaper, best sellers and light fiction in the book field. The mass media have helped create what has come to be called "popular culture." Popular culture involves the creation of popular heroes and the recording of popular ceremonies.

The large amount of exposure to such materials both reflects the values of a modern society, and, in turn, contributes to molding its aspirations. In recent year, therefore, popular culture has become a subject of careful investigation by social scientists. Lang and Lang offer an account of the manner in which television modifies and distorts social reality—in this case a MacArthur Day celebration—in order to create the raw material of popular culture. The growth of popular culture also raises the basic issues of standards of taste. Have the mass media lowered standards of popular taste as they seek to reach the largest audiences? Or, does the content of popular culture reflect the entrance into society of new groups with lower standards who were formerly without a basis of participation in communications process? Wilensky presents a careful and detailed empirical investigation of patterns of exposure to popular culture in the mass media. His research is designed to probe the social and political consequences of such exposure. In the section of this volume on "Public Opinion, Communication, and Democratic Objectives," Shils analyzes from an historical and evaluative point of view the issues of popular culture as they relate to the institutions required for a democratic society.

HAROLD D. LASSWELL

Why Be Quantitative?

THE POINT OF VIEW of this book is that the study of politics can be advanced by the quantitative analysis of political discourse. Why be quantitative? In reply, it is perhaps appropriate to bring out the limitations of qualitative analysis in terms of the work of the present writer.

At the end of World War I, research on politically significant communication was almost entirely qualitative, consisting in the discovery and illustration of propaganda themes and their use. When the present writer described the propaganda of World War I in *Propaganda Technique in the World War* (1927)[1] he took note of certain common themes running through the propaganda of all belligerent powers. The themes were:

The enemy is a menace.
(German militarism threatens us all.)
We are protective.
(We protect ourselves and others.)
The enemy is obstructive.
(They block our future aims.)
We are helpful.
(We aid in the achievement of positive goals.)
The enemy is immoral and insolent.
(They violate legal and moral standards and they hold everyone else in contempt.)
We are moral and appreciative.
(We conform to moral and legal standards and we respect others.)
The enemy will be defeated.
We will win.

Reprinted from *Language of Politics* (1949), pp. 40–52, by permission of the author and the publisher. (Copyright, 1949, by The Policy Sciences Foundation.)

The book was organized to show the form taken by these themes when domestic, allied or enemy audiences were addressed. The chapter on "The Illusion of Victory" showed what was told the home audience on the themes, "The enemy will be defeated," "We will win." The chapter on "Satanism" described how the self was presented as "moral" and "appreciative" while the enemy was "immoral" and "insolent." The "menacing" and "obstructive" rôle of the enemy and our own "protective" and "helpful" activity were illustrated in the chapter on "War Guilt and War Aims." Special attention was paid to "preserving friendship" (of allies and neutrals) and "demoralizing the enemy." Each chapter was composed of excerpts selected chiefly from the propaganda of the United States, Great Britain, Germany and France.

Although none of the criteria which guided the choice of quotations is stated in the book, it is obvious that some selections were made because they clearly stated a theme or developed a theme in detail. No doubt these criteria justified the citation of the extended account of alleged Entente violations of international law which had been compiled by Dr. Ernst Müller-Meiningen (pp. 85–86). In some cases, the wide dissemination of the material was no doubt a selective factor, notably in the case of *J'accuse!*, an exposé of Germany by Richard Grelling (p. 54). Sometimes the eminence of the speaker appears to have been the deciding factor, as with the Bryce report on alleged atrocities perpetrated by the Germans in Belgium (p. 19). In certain instances, the excerpt was a sample of what was distributed by (or to) a professional, vocation, educational or other special group (pp. 70 ff.).

No evidence is given in the book that all the material studied by the author was examined with the same degree of care. We are not informed whether the author actually read or glanced through all the copies of the principal mass-circulation newspapers, periodicals, books and pamphlets of Germany and other countries; or whether he read British, French and American material as fully as German.

Of course, the study did not purport to be an exhaustive history of propaganda during the war. It was called an essay in technique, and the hope was expressed that it would have some influence in directing professional historians toward the study of propaganda, and that the scheme of classification would prove helpful in the organization of future research. The book was to some extent successful in both objectives. Research on war propaganda, as indeed on every phase of propaganda, went forward with vigor, many monographs growing out of the original essay or attributing some degree of influence to it.[2]

Among the most comprehensive books on the propaganda of World War II was those of Hans Thimme, *Weltkrieg ohne Waffen* (1932)[3], and George G. Bruntz, *Allied Propaganda and the Collapse of the German Empire in 1918* (1938)[4]. Both historians explored archives of newspaper, magazine and other source material, the first relying chiefly upon the Reich archives and the second utilizing the Hoover War Library at Stanford University.

Whenever the propaganda message was described, the method adopted by these writers was similar to that of *Propaganda Technique in the World War*. Excerpts were chosen to illustrate what was circulated to different publics and what themes were used. The authors left unspecified their criteria of choice, although these were obviously similar to those of the earlier work. In many respects these monographs are more satisfactory than the first book, since the authors made use of new source material, and employed to advantage the accumulated results of historical scholarship on the relative importance of persons, channels and symbols in the war.

The results, however, can not be accepted as in all respects satisfactory; many relevant questions remain unanswered. Can we assume that a scholar read his sources with the same degree of care throughout this research? Did he allow his eye to travel over the thousands upon thousands of pages of parliamentary debates, newspapers, magazines and other sources listed in his bibliography or notes? Or did he use a sampling system, scanning some pages superficially, though concentrating upon certain periods? Was the sampling system for the *Frankfurter Zeitung*, if one was employed, comparable with the one for the *Manchester Guardian*? Were the leaflets chosen simply because they were conveniently available to the scholar, or were they genuinely representative of the most widely circulated propaganda leaflets?

The very fact that such questions can be raised at all points to a certain lack of method in presenting and conducting research on the history of war propaganda. In all of the books to which reference has been made no explicit justification was given of most of the excerpts chosen to illustrate a specific theme, to characterize the content of any particular channel, or to describe the propaganda directed toward or reaching any given audience. It is impossible to determine from the final report whether the same number or a comparable number of mass circulation media were read for France as for England or Germany, or whether publications were explored with the same degree of intensity at all dates, or whether certain dates were singled out for intensive note-taking.

The limitations of these monographs are apparent when anyone undertakes to follow a particular theme through various periods, channels and audiences. We know that every belligerent used "war aim" propaganda. But suppose we want to find the degree of emphasis laid upon war aims from period to period. Or assume that we ask how they differed when presented to the upper, middle or lower classes of the home population, or to neutral, ally or enemy. Was the war aim propaganda more prominent in the magazines than in the pamphlets, or the reverse? The same questions apply to every theme.

To some extent, historians of war propaganda have sought to reduce ambiguity by multiplying the number of subperiods described within the whole period. Walter Zimmerman studied the English press from the time of Sarajevo to the entry of England into the war, selecting thirty daily newspapers, eight Sunday papers, nine weeklies, four monthlies and two quarterlies, intending to cover all the important regional and social groups in Great Britain.[5] Even in this period, however, we can not be certain of the criteria used in selecting quotations. It is obvious that Zimmerman does not summarize all thirty daily papers every day, but we are left in the dark about why he quotes one paper one day or week and omits it the next time. Even if we assume that his judgment is good, it is permissible to ask if such arbitrary selection procedures create a properly balanced picture, or whether they result in special pleading based, if not on deliberate deception, then on unconscious bias.

The same problem remains in the detailed monograph by Friederike Recktenwald, in which she restricts herself to a single set of themes having to do with British war aims.[6] Miss Recktenwald divides the course of the war into subperiods, and reproduces or summarizes material from the British press having to do with war aims. Although this procedure gives us a plausible indication of the relative amount of attention paid to war aims at different times, not all reasonable doubts are allayed. She follows no consistent scheme of reporting. During any given subperiod only a few quotations may be reproduced; yet this may not invariably mean that there was less war-aim news or diminished editorial prominence. It may signify no more than that what was said is less interesting to the historian because the style is less vivid and quotable. We can not rely upon Miss Recktenwald's excerpts to be true samples of the total stream of news and comment reaching the British public, or even of any particular newspaper, or group of newspapers. The moment we ask clear questions that call for reliable bases of comparison, the arbitrary and dubious character of the monograph is apparent.

It is possible, however, to find studies of great technical excellence. In matters of systematic definition and historic detail, we can go back half a century to *A Study of Public Opinion and Lord Beaconsfield, 1875–1880*, by George Carlake Thompson (1886).[7] At the beginning of that remarkable work, a series of terms for the analysis of public opinion is carefully defined. These terms are consistently applied throughout the two fact-stuffed volumes. One part of the analytical scheme names the standards applied by the British public on foreign policy questions. Among the standards were "international law," "interest," "morality," and "taste." Thompson pointed out that such standards were applied according to the public's conception of England's rôle in relation to other nations, and that these ranged all the way from "England as an island" to "England as a European or Asiatic great power."

In applying these standards and conceptions, Thompson distinguished certain broad motives—"sentimental" or "diplomatic"—that were operating among the members of the British public in their basic orientation toward foreign policy. At any given time—for instance, at the outbreak of war between Russia and Turkey—these standards, conceptions and motivations (public "notions") were fused into public "views." The views of the British public in 1876 were classified as "Anti-Turkism," "Anti-war," "Order," "Legalism," "Anti-Russianism and Philo-Turkism." Such views in turn were related to corresponding policies. In this way, "Anti-Turkism" was bracketed with "emancipation," "Anti-war" with "isolation." The book described each successive phase of England's reaction to the war between Russia and Turkey, and copiously illustrated every move by excerpts from a list of publications.

Thompson's treatise is noteworthy for the unification of carefully defined abstractions with exhaustive data from the sources. Nevertheless, the outcome of all the admirable intelligence and industry that went into this treatise does not yield maximum results, because of a basic failure: the problem of sampling, recording and summarizing sources was not resolved. Hence, the entire foundation of the work rests on shaky ground. Thompson divides the five years with which he deals into subperiods, according to some predominant characteristic. One such subperiod is the "incubation period, third phase," from the opening of the Parliamentary Session of 1876 to the Servian declaration of war. This is followed by the "atrocity period," which in turn is divided into several parts. For each subperiod, Thompson narrates the stream of events and selects from the sources the quotations that impress him as important not only because they are conspicuous, but because they bear some relationship to his systematic scheme of analysis (standards, conceptions, motivations, views and policies). However, the critical reader is still justified in remaining skeptical of the representativeness of the quotations. He can not be sure why they impressed the author when he was reading and making notes on the sources, or organizing his chapters. An excerpt may be the only one that appeared in a given newspaper or magazine on the same subject during the period; or, on the contrary, it may be only one among a tremendous gush of news and editorial items. Thompson does not tell us. The fundamental operation—of source handling—remained highly arbitrary.

If the excellence of the Thompson study lies in system and rich detail, a few recent publications rank above it in the sampling of sources. D. F. Willcox (1900)[8] classified the contents of a single issue of 240 newspapers according to topic (by column inches). Later A. A. Tenney, Jr., at Columbia University, interested a number of students in space measurement and initiated investigations of immediate value to world politics.

Julian L. Woodward examined the foreign news published in 40 American morning newspapers and improved the technical state of the subject by showing the effect of different sampling methods upon the result. In general, he found that a small number of issues distributed throughout the year were enough to give a reliable picture of the amount of attention usually given by an American morning newspaper to foreign news (at least during a non-crisis period).[9]

In general, these investigations were not expressly related to political science. They were made by statisticians interested in having something to count, or sciologists who were exploring the general social process. The senior author of the present work undertook to direct research toward the use of objective procedures in gathering the data pertinent to political hypotheses. Schuyler Foster, for example, examined the treatment given European war news in the New York *Times* during definite periods before our participation in the war of 1914–18. He summarized his results in tabular and graphical form, and showed that the crisis that led immediately to our entry into the war was the final one in a series of crises of ever-increasing intensity. He measured these fluctuations by recording the frequency with which different kinds of news or editorial comment were made about the war or America's relation to it. The use of quantitative methods gave precision to part of the history of America's mobilization for war, and opened up a series of questions about the relation between the ups and downs in the New York *Times* and corresponding fluctuations in New York newspapers reaching different social groups, and in newspapers published in cities of different sizes throughout the country.[10]

More exact methods give us a means of clarifying certain categories that have been at the root of many past evils in the work of historians and social scientists. For a century, controversy has raged over the relative weight of "material" and "ideological" factors in the social and political process. This controversy has been sterile of scientific results, though the propaganda resonance of "dialectical materialism" has been enormous.

Insofar as sterility can be attributed to technical factors in the domain of scholarship, the significant factor is failure to deal adequately with "ideological" elements. The usual account of how material and ideological factors interact upon one another leaves the process in a cloud of mystery. It is as though you put people in an environment called material—and presto!—their ideas change in a predictable way; and if they do not, the failure is ascribed to an ideological lag of some kind. But the relations, though assumed, are not demonstrated. So far as the material dimensions are concerned, operational methods have been worked out to describe them; not so with the ideological. We are amply equipped to describe such "material" changes as fluctuations in output or amount of machinery employed in production; but we can not match this part of the description with equally precise ways of describing the ideological. The result is that the historical and social sciences have been making comparisons between patterns, only a few of which are handled with precision. The other dimensions remain wholly qualitative, impressionistic and conjectural.[11]

We have undertaken to clear up some of the confusion that has long beset the analysis of "environment" by introducing basic distinctions: the first between the "attention frame" and "surroundings," and the second between the "media frame" and the "non-media frame." The attention frame or "milieu" is the part of an environment reaching the focus of attention of a person or group; the surroundings do not reach the focus. The media frame is composed of the signs coming to the focus of attention (the press which is actually read, for instance). The non-media frame includes the features of an environment that, although not signs, reach attention, such as conspicuous buildings, or persons. Whether any given set of surrounding does affect the structure of attention is to be settled by observing the phenomena, not by assumption.

The fundamental nature of these relations is evident when we reflect upon the requirements for a scientific explanation of response. Two sets of factors are involved: the environment and predispositions. R (response) is a function, in the mathematical sense, of E (environment) and P (predisposition); and we have shown that the part of the environment immediately affecting response is what comes to the focus of attention (the attention frame). Information about surroundings is pertinent only to the degree to which it can be shown that the surroundings determine attention. In deciding whether any feature of the environment comes to the focus, it is necessary to demonstrate that a minimum (the threshold level) has been elicited. We do not consider that radio programs which are blacked out by static have come to the attention of an audience. A threshold level has not been reached. (The threshold is not part of the R in the formula of explanation used above; only changes above the threshold are called "effects"—response to what is brought into the attention field.)

The procedures of "content analysis" of communication are appropriate to the problem of describing the structure of attention in quantitative terms.[12] Before entering upon technicalities, it may be pointed out that quantitative ways of describing attention serve many practical, as well as scientific, purposes. *Anticipating the enemy* is one of the most crucial and tantalizing problems in the conduct of war. The intelligence branch of every staff or operations agency is matching wits with the enemy. The job is to out-guess the enemy, to foretell his military, diplomatic, economic and propaganda moves before he makes them, and to estimate where attack would do him the most harm. A principal source of information is what the enemy disseminates in his media of communication.

The Global War introduced a new source of information about the enemy—radio broadcasts under his supervision. When the enemy speaks to his home population, it is possible to listen in. We overhear what the

253

enemy says to his allies, to neutrals and to his enemies. At the outbreak of the Global War, belligerent governments set monitors to work, listening, recording and summarizing the output of enemy and enemy-controlled stations. In Great Britain a group connected with the British Broadcasting Corporation subjected this enormous body of material to systematic examination and began forecasting Nazi policy. These estimates have since been restudied.[13] The same procedures have also been applied to the press and to every other channel of communication. The full plan of the enemy often appears only when the entire stream of communication is interpreted as a whole.

As we improve our methods of describing public attention and response, our results become more useful for another practical purpose—the *detecting of political propaganda*. During World War II, the U.S. Department of Justice employed objective propaganda analysis to expose and prosecute enemy agents, like the Transocean Information Service (Nazi-controlled) and "native Fascists." The Federal Communications Commission described in Court the Axis themes recognized by experts who monitored and analyzed short-wave broadcasts emanating from Germany, Japan and Italy. Objective procedures had been applied in discovering these themes. Objective procedures were also used to analyze the periodicals published by the defendants, and to reveal the parallels between them and the themes disseminated by Axis propagandists.[14]

Quite apart from the use of legal action, it is important that members of the public be informed of the behavior of those with access to the channels of communication. In deciding how much we can rely upon a given newspaper, it is important to know if that newspaper ceases to attack Russia when Germany and Russia sign a non-aggression pact, and then returns to the attack as soon as Germany and Russia fall apart. Under these conditions, we have grounds for inferring a pro-German propaganda policy. By studying the news, editorial and feature material in a medium of communication under known German control, we can check on this inference. We may find that the two media distribute praise and blame in the same way among public leaders and the political parties; and that they take the same stand on domestic and foreign issues. If so, our inference is strengthened that the channel is dominated by pro-German policies.[15]

In the preceding paragraphs, we have said that policy may be served by objective procedures used to anticipate the enemy and to detect propaganda. Also, as scientific knowledge increases, the possibility of control improves; hence, a third contribution of objective research to policy is *skill*.[16] Skill is the most ecomonical utilization of available means to attain a goal. Appraisals of skill are among the most difficult judgments to establish on a convincing basis, since they depend upon exhaustive knowledge of concrete circumstances and of scientific relations. To say that A is more skillful than B in a given situation is to allow for all factors being "equal."

It is not easy to demonstrate that the two sets of environing and predisposing factors are strictly comparable. The simple fact that the Nazis won out in Germany against the Socialists and other parties does not necessarily warrant the conclusion that the Nazis were more skillful propagandists than their antagonists. Or the failure of the French to hold out against the Germans longer in 1940 was not necessarily because French propagandists were lacking in skill. The "skill" factor can be separated from the others only when a very comprehensive view can be gained of the context. Did the responsible heads of state choose the most suitable personnel to conduct propaganda operations? Were the most effective symbols chosen? The most useful media? In each case, the question must be answered with reference to alternatives available in the original situation.

That content analysis has a direct bearing on the evaluation of skill is evident, since such methods introduce a degree of precise description at many points in the propaganda process. Directives can be described in detail; so, too, can material released through the propaganda agencies and disseminated through various media controlled by, or beyond the control of, the propagandist. Indeed, as we pointed out in our analysis of the attention factor in world politics,[17] every link in the chain of communication can be described when suitable methods are used; quantitative procedures reduce the margin of uncertainty in the basic data. (There is, of course, no implication that non-quantitative methods should be dropped. On the contrary, there is need of more systematic theory and of more luminous "hunches" if the full potentialities of precision are to be realized in practice. As the history of quantification shows [in economics, for instance], there is never-ending, fruitful interplay between theory, hunch, impression and precision.)

A fourth contribution relates not to policy as a whole, but to the special objectives of humane politics. The aim of humane politics is a commonwealth in which the dignity of man is accepted in theory and fact. Whatever *improves our understanding of attitude* is a potential instrument of humane politics. Up to the present, physical science has not provided us with means of penetrating the skull of a human being and directly reading off his experiences. Hence, we are compelled to rely upon indirect means of piercing the wall that separates us from him. Words provide us with clues, but we hesitate to take all phrases at their face value. Apart from deliberate duplicity, language has shortcomings as a vehicle for the transmission of thought and feeling. It is important to recognize that we obtain insight into the world of the other person when we are fully acquainted with what has come to his attention. Certainly the world of the country boy is full of the sights and smells and sounds of nature. The city boy, on the other hand, lives in a labyrinth of streets, buildings, vehicles and crowds. A Chinese youth of good family has his ancestors continually thrust upon his notice; an American youth may vaguely recall his grandparents. The son of an English ruling family may be reared on the anecdotes of centuries of imperial history, while the son of an American business man recalls that there was a Revolution and that Bunker Hill had something to do with it.

The dominant political symbols of an epoch provide part of the common experience of millions of men. There is some fascination in the thought of how many human beings are bound together by a thread no more substantial than the resonance of a name or the clang of a slogan. In war, men suffer pain, hunger, sorrow; the specific source of pain, the specific sensation of one's specific object of sorrow, may be very private. In contrast, the key symbol enters directly into the focus of all men and provides an element of common experience.[18]

It is obvious that a complete survey of mass attention will go far beyond the press, the broadcast or the film. It will cover every medium of mass communication. Further, a complete survey would concentrate upon the most active decision-makers, disclosing the milieu of the heads of states, the chiefs of staff, diplomats and all other groups. An exhaustive inventory would describe the entire intelligence process.[19]

Why, then, be quantitative about communication? Because of the scientific and policy gains that can come of it. The social process is one of *collaboration* and *communication;* and quantitative methods have already demonstrated their usefulness in dealing with the former. Further understanding and control depend upon equalizing our skill in relation to both.

NOTES

1. Kegan Paul, London, and Knopf, New York, 1927; reprinted by Peter Smith, New York, 1938.

2. See Ralph Haswell Lutz, "Studies of War Propaganda, 1914–33," *Journal of Modern History*, 5: 496–516 (December, 1933).

3. Cotta'sche Buchhandlung Nachfolger, Stuttgart and Berlin.

4. Stanford University Press, Stanford.

5. *Die Englische Presse zum Ausbruch des Weltkrieges,* Verlag "Hochschule und Ausland," Charlottenburg, 1928.

6. *Kriegsziele und öffentliche Meinung Englands, 1914–16,* W. Köhlhammer, Stuttgart, 1929.

7. Macmillan, London, 2 vols., 1886.

8. "The American Newspaper," *Annals of the American Academy of Political and Social Science*, 16: 56–92 (1900).

9. *Foreign News in American Morning Newspapers,* Columbia University Press, New York, 1930.

10. "How America Became Belligerent: A Quantitative Study of War-News, 1914–17." *American Journal of Sociology*, 40: 464–76 (January, 1935). See also studies summarized in Quincy Wright, *A Study of War,* University of Chicago Press, Chicago, 2 vols., 1942. Note especially Chapter XXX.

11. See Harold D. Lasswell, "Communications Research and Politics," in *Print, Radio, and Film in a Democracy*, edited by Douglas Waples, University of Chicago, Chicago, 1942 pp. 101–117.

12. For a review of the research situation at the outbreak of the war (1939), consult Douglas Waples, Bernard Berelson, and Franklyn R. Bradshaw *What Reading Does to People*, University of Chicago Press, Chicago, 1940. More recent developments are noted in Harold D. Lasswell, "Content Analysis," in Bruce L. Smith, Harold D. Lasswell and Ralph D. Casey, *Propaganda, Communication and Public Opinion*, Princeton University Press, Princeton, 1946. (Modified from *Document* II, Experimental Division for the Study of Wartime Communications, Library of Congress, 1942.)

13. Ernst Kris, Hans Speier and Associates, *German Radio Propaganda; Report on Home Broadcasts During the War*, Oxford University Press, New York, 1944. See also *Propaganda by Short Wave*, edited by Harwood L. Childs and John B. Whitton, Princeton University Press, Princeton, 1942; and the valuable essay by Charles Siepmann, *Radio in Wartime*, Oxford University Press, 1942. A survey of the situation in 1939 is by Thomas Grandin, *The Political Use of Radio*, Geneva Research Centre, Geneva, 1939; for a later period, Arno Huth *Radio Today; The Present State of Broadcasting in the World*, Geneva Research Centre, Geneva, 1942. Concerning the news and documentary film, the most penetrating inquiry to date, is by Siegfried Kracauer, *Propaganda and the Nazi War Film*, Museum of Modern Art Film Library, New York, 1942.

14. *United States of America* vs. *William Dudley Pelley* (and others), tried in the U.S. District Court for the Southern District of Indiana, Indianapolis Division, summer, 1942; conviction affirmed on appeal to the U.S. Circuit Court of Appeals, Southern Circuit, October Term, 1942. A writ of certiorari denied by the U.S. Supreme Court. Government witnesses included Harold N. Graves, Jr., of the Federal Communications Commission, and Harold D. Lasswell.

15. The historians of literature have relied upon quantitative analysis as one of the chief means at their disposal in the many "detection" problems that confront them. They must detect corrupt texts, decide among competing attributions of authorship, arrive at the true order in which works were composed, determine the sources relied upon by the author and the influences affecting authorship. As Yule points out, th technique of word-counting goes back many centuries, at least to the "Masoretes," who, after the destructruction of the Jewish state, A.D. 70, devoted themselves to preserving the text of the Bible and the correct manner of pronunciation. It is curious to see that, despite the ease and amount of word-counting, first-class statisticians have only begun to concern themselves with the problems involved—notably G. Udny Yule, *The Statistical Study of Literary Vocabulary*, Cambridge University Press, Cambridge, Eng., 1944. Although word-counting is involved in the study of communication, not all quantitative procedures are necessarily "content analysis." This term can legitimately be applied only when "counts" are undertaken with reference to a general theory of the communication process. In this sense, "content analysis" is quite recent.

The literary historians have occasionally been stimulated by the methods of crytography, and they have also made direct contributions to the subject. One example of the influence of this art is Edith Rickert, long associated with J. M. Manly in Chaucerian research, who worked in the "Black Chamber" during World War I, and subsequently devised new ways of studying style:

257

New Methods for the Study of Literature, University of Chicago Press, Chicago, 1926. A brief example of differences in the handling of political material by different authors is revealed by a simple study of Scipio's alleged speech to the mutineers in 206 B.C. In Polybius "The speech contains 520 words, in which pronouns or verbal forms of the first person singular occur 14 times—i.e., once in every 37 words. In Livy the speech occupies about 1025 words, and there are no less than 64 occurrences of *ego* or *meus* or verbs in the first person singular—i.e., one word in very 16—a frequency of more than double." (R. S. Conway, *The Portrait of a Roman Gentleman, from Livy, Bull. of the John Rylands Library,* Manchester, 7 (1922–23: 8–22.)

An absorbing mystery has been written in which detection depends upon content analysis and engineering: Brett Rutledge (pseud. of Elliott Paul), *The Death of Lord Haw Haw,* Random House, New York, 1940. On certain problems see Wladimir Eliasberg, "Linguistics and Political Criminology," *Journal of Criminal Psychopathology,* 5 (1944): 769–774.

16. Hypotheses or assumptions about skill have been stated or implied in quantitative studies of many channels of expression. Special attention has been given to oratory, from this point of view, and especially to such quantifiable characteristics as length of sentence. The language of Rufus Choate so greatly impressed his contemporaries that the chief justice of the highest court in Massachusetts, Joseph Neilson, was among those who gave it special study (*Memoirs of Rufus Choate,* Houghton Mifflin, 1884). Choate was given to long sentences, averaging no fewer than 37 words in one of his most famous cases. Nearly an eighth of all his sentences, in this instance, contained more than 80 words. Consult John W. Black, "Rufus Choate," in *A History and Criticism of American Public Address,* prepared under the auspices of The National Association of Teachers of Speech, William Norwood Brigance, Editor, McGraw-Hill, New York, 1943. Vol. 1, pp. 455–456. More technical investigations are conducted by modern specialists on public speaking. Howard L. Runion, for example, concentrated on fifty speeches by Woodrow Wilson, and counted many features, including the use of figures of speech. (Unpublished dissertation, University of Wisconsin, 1932. For more detail see Dayton David McKean, "Woodrow Wilson," in *op. cit.* Vol. 2, pp. 968–992, Brigance, editor.) It is perhaps unnecessary to remark that studies of classical orators are researches into the style of classical historians. See, for instance, Grover Cleveland Kenyan, *Antithesis in the Speeches of Greek Historians,* University of Chicago Libraries, Chicago 1941.

17. See Harold D. Lasswell in Lyman Bryson (ed.) *The Communication of Ideas,* Harper's, New York, 1948, Chapters IV and XV.

18. The use of key symbols in Quantitative analysis of comparative literature is exemplified by Josephine Miles, "Some Major Poetic Words," *Essays and Studies* (by members of the Department of English, University of California), University of California Publications in English, Vol. XIV, University of California Press, Berkeley and Los Angeles, 1943, pp. 233–239. ". . . the trend of change through five hundred years of main consistencies may be justly observed, and may be summarized in these three ways: First, in term of parts of speech, it may be said that all the verbs to be stressed by more than one poet were established by Donne or sooner; the adjectives, by Burns, or sooner; the last noun, not until Poe. Second, in terms of new subject matter, the direction is clear from *making* to *thinking,* from *good* and *great* to *high* and *sweet* and *wild,* and from *heaven* and man to *soul* and *heart,* to *eye* and *hand,* and then to *day, sun, dream, night;* it is the direction from

action to thought, and from conceived to sensed. Third, in terms of contrast between first and last, the prevailing strength of the three main words, *man*, *love*, and *see*, stands out, mainly the simple verbs are lost, and *heart*, *day*, and *night* are the fresher forces. These three views, as we have seen, add up strongly to one: the view of a general stability in the language of major English poetry, tempered by the shift, gradual in all save Collins, from action and concept toward feeling and sensing."

Expertly conducted studies in expressive media other than literature can throw a light on the changing outlook of peoples. The ruling classes of Delft, for instance, early retired from the brewing industry to live upon investments in the East India Company, and remained retired generation after generation. As they shrank from all forms of commercial activity, no other outgoing mode of life attracted them. Max Eisler has been able to demonstrate a remarkable parallel between Delft's paintings and the quietism of Delft life. First, they found landscapes too breezy and, withdrawing indoors, bought church interiors. Presently these seemed too expansive, and they took to cozy home interiors. Vermeer was the culminating artist in this development, and we see in his paintings the citizens of Delft in unvarying sunshine lounging at table, staring at their reflections in a mirror, or at their jewels; sometimes they have passed from lethargy to sleep. And in these paintings the walls are seen coming closer and closer. Year by year, the world of the Delft rentiers grows narrower and narrower, though always in perpetual sunshine (Max Eisler, *Alt-Delft*, Vienna, 1923. Put in perspective by Miriam Beard, *A History of the Business Man*, Macmillan, New York, 1938, p. 306).

19. Special studies eventually to be made public have been completed by some of our associates in the World Attention Survey: Professor Richard Burks, Wayne University; Dr. Heinz H. F. Eulau; Dr. Bruno Foa, formerly University of Turin; Doris Lewis; Dean James J. Robbins, American University; Professor David N. Rowe, Yale University; Professor Douglas Waples, University of Chicago.

BERNARD BERELSON

Content Analysis in Communication Research

IN THE COMMUNICATION PROCESS a central position is occupied by the content. By communication content is meant that body of meanings through symbols (verbal, musical, pictorial, plastic, gestural) which makes up the communication itself. In the classic sentence identifying the process of communication—*"who* says *what* to *whom, how,* with *what effect"*— communication content is the *what*. This book deals with the analysis of what is said in communications of various kinds.

Since the content represents the means through which one person or group communicates with another, it is important for communication research that it be described with accuracy and interpreted with insight. Communication content is so rich with human experience, and its causes and effects so varied, that no single system of substantive categories can be devised to describe it. However, a scientific *method* has been developed —and is being developed further—for describing various facets of communication content in summary fashion. That method is called content analysis. It has been used to answer such diverse questions as these:

How have the slogans of May Day propaganda in the U.S.S.R. changed during the Soviet regime?

What are the dominant images in Shakespeare's plays?

How is the writer's personality structure reflected in what he writes?

How do the values in American plays differ from those in German plays of the same time? How do the values in Boy Scout literature in the United States differ from those in *Hitlerjugend* literature?

What are the major trends in the use of research literature by chemists and physicists since 1900?

Reprinted from *Content Analysis in Communication Research* (1952), pp. 13–20, by permission of the author and the publisher. (Copyright, 1952, Bernard Berelson.)

How are minority ethnic groups treated in short stories in popular magazines?

How can communications suspected of subversion be tested for their "propaganda" component?

How do newspapers and radio compare in their treatment of a sensational murder case?

What makes writing readable?

In what ways do motion pictures reflect popular feelings and desires?

What are the similarities and differences in the political symbols which come to the attention of people in the major power states?

What happens to a "good book" when it is made into a movie?

What intelligence data can be secured from analysis of enemy propaganda?

This is a report on the technique of content analysis, which has been used with increasing frequency in recent years. This report attempts critically to survey the applications of content analysis through 1950, to relate it to marginal developments in other fields, to note the major types and categories of analysis, and to review certain technical problems. After a general introductory section, the report discusses the major uses of content analysis, the nature of "qualitative" analysis, the units and the categories of analysis, and such technical matters as sampling, reliability, presentation, and modes of inference.

Definition of Content Analysis

What is meant by the term "content analysis"? Review of several definitions which have appeared in the technical literature will serve to identify the major characteristics of content analysis.

Systematic content analysis attempts to define more casual descriptions of the content, so as to show objectively the nature and relative strength of the stimuli applied to the reader or listener (Waples & Berelson, 1941, p. 2).

A social science sentence may be called one of 'content analysis' if it satisfies all of the following requirements: 1) it must refer either to syntactic characteristics of symbols ... or to semantic characteristics. ... 2) it must indicate frequencies of occurrence of such characteristics with a high degree of precision. One could perhaps define more narrowly: it must assign numerical values to such frequencies. 3) it must refer to these characteristics by terms which are general. ... 4) it must refer to these characteristics by terms which occur ... in universal propositions of social science. One may consider adding to this definition another requirement: 5) a high precision of the terms used to refer to the symbol characteristics studied (Leites & Pool, 1942, pp. 1–2).

The content analyst aims at a quantitative classification of a given body of content, in terms of a system of categories devised to yield data relevant to specific hypotheses concerning that content (Kaplan & Goldsen, 1943, p. 1).

'Content analysis' may be defined as referring to any technique for the *classification* of *sign-vehicles;* which relies solely upon the *judgments*—which, theoretically, may range from perceptual discriminations to sheer guesses—of an analyst or group of analysts as to which sign-vehicles fall into which cate-gories; on the basis of *explicitly formulated rules;* provided that the analyst's judgments are regarded as the reports of a *scientific observer.* The results of a content analysis state the frequency of occurrence of signs—or groups of signs—for each category in a classification scheme (Janis, 1943, p. 429; his emphasis).

. . . The technique known as content analysis . . . attempts to characterize the meanings in a given body of discourse in a systematic and quantitative fashion" (Kaplan, 1943, p. 230).

This group of definitions provides six distinguishing characteristics of content analysis:

1. It applies only to social science generalizations: Leites & Pool

2. It applies only, or primarily, to the determination of the effects of communications: Waples & Berelson

3. It applies only to the syntactic and semantic dimensions of language: Leites & Pool

4. It must be "objective": Waples & Berelson, Leites & Pool, Janis, Kaplan

5. It must be "systematic": Leites & Pool, Kaplan & Goldsen, Kaplan

6. It must be quantitative: Waples & Berelson, Leites & Pool, Kaplan & Goldsen, Janis, Kaplan

And we shall see, the first and second of these characteristics define the field of content analysis too narrowly. The review of the literature will show that it has been applied successfully in other fields than the social sciences and for other purposes than the description of the effects of communications upon readers and listeners. But the other four character-istics are required for a proper definition of content analysis.

The *syntactic-and-semantic requirement* is meant to rule out the analysis of communication content for the pragmatic dimension of lan-guage (the third branch of semiotic, the general science of signs, as developed by Charles Morris). That is, content analysis is ordinarily limited to the manifest content of the communication and is not normally done directly in terms of the latent intentions which the content may express nor the latent responses which it may elicit. Strictly speaking, con-tent analysis proceeds in terms of what-is-said, and not in terms of why-the-content-is-like-that (e.g., "motives") or how-people-react (e.g., "appeals" or "responses"). Three reasons have been given for this delimitation: 1) the low validity of the analysis, since there can be little or no assurance that the assigned intentions and responses actually occurred, in the absence of direct data on them; 2) the low reliability of such analysis, since differ-ent coders are unlikely to assign material to the same categories of inten-tion and response with sufficient agreement; and 3) the possible circularity involved in establishing relationships between intent and effect on the one hand, and content on the other, when the latter is analyzed in terms referring to the former.[1]

The *requirement of objectivity* stipulates that the categories of analysis should be defined so precisely that different analysts can apply them to the same body of content and secure the same results.[2] Like the first requirement, this ordinarily limits content analysis to the manifest content. This requirement, of course, is necessary in order to give some scientific standing to content analysis.

The *requirement of system* contains two different meanings. In the first place, it states that *all* of the relevant content is to be analyzed in terms of *all* the relevant categories, for the problem at hand. This requirement is meant to eliminate partial or biased analyses in which only those elements in the content are selected which fit the analyst's thesis. Thus "system" means that if some occurrences of the category are taken into consideration, within a specified body of content, then all occurrences must be—or the definition of the problem changed.

The second meaning of "system" is that analyses must be designed to secure data relevant to a scientific problem or hypothesis. The results of a content analysis must have a measure of general application. Thus a tabulation simply reporting the numbers of books of different kinds acquired by a particular library in a given year would not represent a content analysis study (unless the results were used for a trend or comparative analysis, or for some other generalization).[3] By this requirement, content analysis is designed for the establishment of scientific propositions.

The *requirement of quantification,* the single characteristic on which all the definitions agree, is perhaps the most distinctive feature of content analysis. It is this characteristic of content analysis which goes farthest toward distinguishing the procedure from ordinary reading. Of primary importance in content analysis is the *extent* to which the analytic categories appear in the content, that is, the relative emphases and omissions. Now this requirement of quantification does not necessarily demand the assignment of *numerical* values to the analytic categories. Sometimes it takes the form of quantitative words like "more" or "always" or "increases" or "often." Although results of this kind may be appropriate for certain studies, it should be recognized that such terms are just as "quantitative" as the terms 37 or 52%; they are only less exact and precise. (This is discussed at some length in the section on "qualitative" analysis.) In most applications of content analysis, numerical frequencies have been assigned to occurrence of the analytic categories.

This review of the distinguishing characteristics of content analysis, then, results in the following definition: *Content analysis is a research technique for the objective, systematic, and quantitative description of the manifest content of communication.*[4]

Assumptions of Content Analysis

This definition of content analysis implies certain assumptions which should be made explicit. Different types of content analyses and particular studies have their own specific assumptions, but we are not concerned with them here. At this point we are concerned only with those general assumptions which apply to all studies of content analysis. There are three such general assumptions.

1. Content analysis assumes that inferences about the relationship between intent and content or between content and effect can validly be made, or the actual relationships established. We say "inferences" (i.e., "interpretations") because most studies utilizing content analysis have been limited to inferences; there have been extremely few studies which concretely demonstrate the nature or the extent of the relationship between communication content, on the one hand, and intentions or effects, on the other. This assumption that knowledge of the content can legitimately support inferences about non-content events is basic to a central contribution of content analysis, namely, to illuminate certain non-content areas. Content analysis is often done to reveal the purposes, motives, and other characteristics of the communicators as they are (presumably) "reflected" in the content; or to identify the (presumable) effects of the content upon the attention, attitudes, or acts of readers and listeners. The nature of such inferences is discussed in the section on technical problems.

2. Content analysis assumes that study of the manifest content is meaningful. This assumption requires that the content be accepted as a "common meeting-ground" for the communicator, the audience, and the analyst. That is, the content analyst assumes that the "meanings" which he ascribes to the content, by assigning it to certain categories, correspond to the "meanings" intended by the communicator and/or understood by the audience. In other words, the assumption is that there is a common universe of discourse among the relevant parties, so that the manifest content can be taken as a valid unit of study.

This requirement that the analysis deal with manifest content raises the question of whether, in a psychological sense, there is such a thing as "manifest content." The argument runs like this: the only sense in which "manifest content" exists is in the form of black-marks-on-white. As soon as meanings are attached to the symbols, the psychological predispositions of the reader become involved and to some degree they distort his comprehension of the "manifest content." Thus there is no guarantee that the meanings in the "manifest content" are the same as the meanings actually understood by the different readers or intended by the writer; and thus only latent content can exist wherever meanings are involved. To some degree the argument goes, every reader takes his own peculiar meanings away from the common content. Without going into the meta-psychology of this argument, we suggest that there are various kinds of "levels" of communication content and that analysis of the manifest content for meanings can apply to some and not to others. If one imagines a continuum along which various communications are placed depending upon the degree to which different members of the intended audience get the same understandings from them, one might place a simple news story on a train wreck at one end (since it is likely that every reader will get the same meanings from the content) and an obscure modern poem at the other (since it is likely that no two readers will get identical meanings from the content).[5] Other kinds of content will fall at various points along this continuum. The analysis of manifest content is applicable to materials at the end of the continuum where understanding is simple and direct, and not at the other. Presumably, there is a point on the continuum beyond which the "latency" of the content (i.e., the diversity of its understanding in the relevant audience) is too great for reliable analysis. In general, then, content analysis must deal with relatively denotative communication materials and not with relatively connotative materials. Under such conditions, analysis of the manifest content of communications takes on a certain uniformity of comprehension and understanding.

3. Content analysis assumes that the quantitative description of communication content is meaningful. This assumption implies that the frequency of occurrence of various characteristics of the content is itself an important factor in the communication process, under specific conditions. Whenever one word or one phrase is as "important" as the rest of the content taken together, quantitative analysis would not apply. It does apply only when the content units have a more or less equal weight, for purposes of the analysis. To some extent, but not entirely, this is simply a matter of selecting the important categories for analysis. In any case, content analysis should be undertaken only when relative frequencies of content categories are relevant to the problem at hand.

(There are two related considerations which are *not* involved in this assumption: 1) the assumption does not imply that different items of the same length—e.g., a front page newspaper story and a story on an inside page—are necessarily given the same "weight" in the final quantitative formulation; and 2) the assumption does not imply that all the members of the audience, or the typical members of the audience, necessarily expose to the communication content in the proportions in which the categories appear; that is, there is no assumption that audience exposure and content emphasis are necessarily parallel.)

265

References

Janis, Irving L., "Meaning and the Study of Symbolic Behavior," *Psychiatry*, 6, 1943, 425–39.

Kaplan, Abraham. "Content Analysis and the Theory of Signs," *Philosophy of Science*, 10, 1943, 230–47.

Lasswell, Harold D. *Analyzing the Content of Mass Communication: A Brief Introduction.* Library of Congress, Experimental Division for Study of War-Time Communications, Document no. 11. Washington, D.C., 1942.

Leites, Nathan C., and Pool, Ithiel de Sola. *On Content Analysis.* Library of Congress, Experimental Division for Study of War-Time Communications, Document no. 26, Washington, D.C., 1942.

Schutz, William. Theory and Methodology of Content Analysis. PhD. dissertation, UCLA, 1950.

NOTES

1. For an extended discussion of the problem, see Janis, 1943. See also the following section on the assumptions of content analysis.

2. For the fulfillment of this requirement in actual content analysis studies, see the section of this report on reliability.

3. For a discussion of this point, see the distinction between "topical" analysis and "presentation" analysis in Lasswell, 1942.

4. It should be made explicit here that content analysis can be applied to private communications like conversation or the psychoanalytic interview just as it can be applied to public or "mass" communications like newspapers and radio programs. One proposal suggests enlarging the scope of the definition beyond communication content: ". . . description of human behavior, particularly linguistic" (Schutz, 1950, p. 3).

5. The poem might still be analyzed for certain nonmeaning categories, e.g., use of certain terms.

ERNST KRIS AND NATHAN LEITES

Trends in Twentieth Century Propaganda

IN SPEAKING of propaganda, we refer to the political sphere and not to promotional activities in general. We define acts of propaganda, in agreement with H. D. Lasswell[1] as attempts to influence attitudes of large numbers of people on controversial issues of relevance to a group. Propaganda is thus distinguished from education which deals with non-controversial issues. Moreover, not all treatments of controversial issues of relevance to a group fall under the definition; they are not propaganda if they aim at the clarification of issues rather than at the changing of attitudes.

In the following, we deal mainly with propaganda by agents of government and exclusively with propaganda using the channels of mass communication, i.e., principally print, radio and film.

However, neither the potentialities of any one medium, nor the variety of promotional devices used by all will be discussed here. We are concerned with the place of propaganda in Western civilization. Our general hypothesis is that responses to political propaganda in the Western world have considerably changed during the last decades; and that these changes are related to trends in the sociopsychological conditions of life in the twentieth century.

We shall not be able to offer conclusive proof for the points we wish to make. We do not know of the existence of data comprehensive and reliable enough to demonstrate in quantitative terms broad hypotheses about changes in responses to propaganda. We start out from changes in content and style of propaganda, assuming that they reflect the propagandist's expectation as to the response of his audience. The propagandist

Reprinted from *Psychoanalysis and the Social Sciences*, Vol. I (1947), pp. 393–409, by permission of the authors and the publisher. (Copyright, 1947, by the International Universities Press.)

may be mistaken in his expectations, but finally he will be informed to some extent about his audiences' response, and adapt his output, within limit, to their predispositions.

We choose two situations in which propaganda was directed towards comparable objectives: the two World Wars.

Wartime propaganda is enacted in a situation with strictly limited goals. Under whatever conditions, the objective of propagandists in wartime is to maximize social participation among members of their own group and to minimize participation among members of the enemy group. Social participation is characterized by concern for the objectives of the group, the sharing of its activities, and the preparedness to accept deprivations on its behalf. High "participation" is therefore identical with high "morale." Its psychological dynamics are mutual identifications among group members, and identification of individual members with leaders or leading ideals of the group, strong cathexis of the goal set by the group, and decreased cathexis of the self; processes that at least in part are preconscious and unconscious. Low participation may manifest itself in two ways: first, participation may be shifted partly or totally from one group to another. In this case, one may speak of a split in participation. Second, low participation may manifest itself as a withdrawal of individuals from the political sphere; in this case, we speak of privatization[2] (H. Speier and M. Otis).[3]

The psychological dynamics of a split in participation are obvious: one set of identifications and objectives has been replaced by another. The only dynamic change consists in the fact that, as a rule, the old group has not lost its cathexis, but has become the target of hostility.

The dynamics of privatization are more complex: withdrawal of cathexes from the group of its objectives leads to a process comparable to, but not identical with a narcissistic regression. Concern with the self becomes dominant. Since the striving for individual indulgence is maximized, the individual becomes exceedingly vulnerable to deprivation.

Modern warfare is distinguished from older types of warfare by the fact that it affects larger numbers of individuals. In total war "nations at arms" oppose each other with all their resources. Hence participation becomes increasingly important. To the extent that preparedness for war infringes upon life in peace, the problem continues to exist in peacetime.

Participation of whole nations was more essential during World War I than during any previous war; and yet it was somewhat less essential than during World War II; the first World War, especially at its onset, was "less total" than the second. On the other hand, the media of mass communication were less developed; radio and film had hardly been tested. Three areas of difference between the propagandas of the two wars seem particularly relevant in our context:

1. Propaganda during the second World War exhibited, on the whole, a higher degree of sobriety than propaganda during World War I; the incidence of highly emotionalized terms was probably lower.

2. Propaganda during the second World War was, on the whole, less moralistic than propaganda during the first World War; the incidence of preference statements as against fact statements was probably lower.

3. Propaganda during the second World War tended to put a moderate ceiling on grosser divergences from presently or subsequently ascertainable facts, divergences that were more frequent in propaganda during the first World War. Also, propaganda during the second World War tended to give fuller information about relevant events than propaganda during World War I.

In summarizing the psychological aspects of these differences, we might say that propaganda appeals were less frequently directed to id and super-ego, more prominently to the ego.

In this respect, these areas of difference are representative of others. At least two qualifications to the points mentioned above are essential: first, most of the differences we stress became ever clearer the longer the second World War lasted; second, they were more accentuated in the propaganda of the Western democracies than in that of Germany and Russia.[4]

The use of emotionalized language was, at the outset of World War II, almost completely absent in British propaganda. When, in the autumn of 1939, Mr. Churchill, then First Lord of the Admiralty, referred to the Nazis as "Huns," thus using the stereotype current during World War I, he was publicly rebuked. Basically, that attitude persisted throughout the war in Britain and the United States. "We don't want to be driven into hate" was the tenor of opinion. There were modifications of this attitude: in the United States in regard to Japan, in Britain after the severe onslaught of bombing. However, hate campaigns remained largely unacceptable. In Germany, a similar attitude persisted: attempts of German propaganda to brandish the bombing of German cities by British and later by American planes as barbarism, to speak of the crews of these planes as "night pirates" and of German raids against British as retaliatory largely failed to arouse indignant hate.

The waning power of *moral* argumentation in propaganda is best illustrated by the fact that one of the predominant themes of propaganda during World War I played no comparable part in World War II. The theme "Our cause is right; theirs is wrong" was secondary in the propaganda of the Western powers; its part in German propaganda was limited; only in Russian propaganda was its role presumably comparable to that it had played in World War I propaganda. In the democratic countries and in Germany, the moral argumentation was replaced by one in terms of indulgence and deprivation (profit or loss): "We are winning; they are losing"; and: "These will be the blessings of victory; these the calamities of defeat." There is evidence indicating that both in the democracies and in Germany this type of appeal was eminently successful. In other words: success of propaganda was dependent on the transformation of superego appeals into appeals to the ego.[5]

269

The third area of difference, the increased concern for some agreement between the content of propaganda and ascertainable facts, and the increased concern for detailed information was to some considerable extent related to technological change. Thus, during the first World War, the German people were never explicitly (and implicitly only much later) informed about the German defeat in the battle of the Marne in September 1914. A similar reticence during the second World War would not have proved expedient, since in spite of coercive measures, allied radio transmissions were widely listened to by Germans. However, technological progress was not the only reason for the change. The concern with credibility had increased, independently of the technology of communication. The tendency to check statements of one's own against those of enemy governments existed both in Germany and in the democracies; while it was limited in Germany, it was widely spread in Britain and the United States.

The differences of propaganda during World Wars I and II are epitomized in the treatment of a theme related to all three areas discussed —enemy atrocities. As far as we know, only Russian propaganda on German atrocities, and German propaganda on Russian atrocities gave to this theme about the same importance in World War II that all propagandists had given it during World War I. But German reports on allied atrocities were rather timid, if compared to the inventiveness of German propaganda in other areas; and German propaganda about Soviet atrocities was largely designed to create fear and defensive combativeness rather than hate and indignation. In the democracies, however, the "playing down" of reports on enemy atrocities was a guiding principle of propaganda, at least until 1945. While during World War I, allied propagandists did not refrain from exaggerating and even inventing atrocities, uncontestable evidence of enemy atrocities was, for a long time, withheld during World War II. It is needless to say that the atrocities to which this documentation referred and which, at the end of the war and after the war became manifest to the soldiers of armies traversing Europe, were of a kind totally different in horror from anything the world of the earlier twentieth century had known. The purposeful reticence of the democratic governments becomes thereby even more significant.

No adequate understanding of these propaganda trends is possible, unless we take two closely related trends in the predispositions of the public into account. Our thesis is that the differences between the propaganda styles during both World Wars are largely due to the rising tendencies towards *distrust* and *privatization*—tendencies that we believe to have existed in the Western democracies as well as in Germany.

Distrust is directed primarily against the propagandist and the authority he represents, secondarily also against the "suggestibility" of the "propagandee."[6]

The first mentioned manifestation of distrust can be traced back to the last war. Propaganda operated then on a new level of technological perfection; the latent possibilities of the mass communication media became suddenly manifest; in all belligerent countries, outbursts of enthusiasm for war occurred. Propagandists, like children playing with a new toy, charged their messages with many manufactured contents. After the war, they reported on their own achievements—sometimes exaggerating the extent to which they had distorted events. These reports helped to create the aura of secret power that ever since has surrounded propagandists. In Britain and the United States, some of this prestige was transferred from the propagandist to the public relations counsel; some of the men who had successfully worked in government agencies became pioneers of modern advertising. Beliefs in the power of propaganda led to a phobia of political persuasion; propaganda became "a bad name," an influence against which the common man had to guard himself.

The political and economic failures of the postwar era, the futility of the idealistic appeals which had helped to conclude the first World War, reinforced this distrust. Its spread and influence on the political scene, however, was sharply different in different areas. In Germany, the distrust of propaganda was manipulated by the nationalist, and later, the national-socialist movement. Propaganda was identified with those allied propaganda efforts that had accompanied German defeat.[7] While distrust was directed against one side, nationalist and national socialist propaganda could operate more freely under the guise of anti-propaganda. In the Western democracies, the propaganda phobia rose during the Great Depression. It became a lasting attitude both in the United States and possibly to a lesser degree, in the United Kingdom; and it took years of experience to discover a propaganda style that would at least not provoke distrust. While the disdain of propaganda had been initiated by the upper strata, it was during the second World War more intense with lower socioeconomic groups.

At this point, it becomes essential to supplement our analysis of the distrust of propaganda by a discussion of contemporary privatization tendencies. Many motivations contribute to such tendencies. Some of them are not taken up here.[8]

Individuals in the mass societies of the twentieth century are to an ever increasing extent involved in public affairs; it becomes increasingly difficult to ignore them. But "ordinary" individuals have ever less the feeling that they can *understand* or *influence* the very events upon which their life and happiness is known to depend.[9] At the same time, leaders in both totalitarian and democratic societies claim that decisions ultimately rest upon the common man's consent, and that the information supplied to him fully enables him to evaluate the situation. The contrast between these claims and the common man's experience extends to many areas. Thus in economic life ever more depends upon state interference. But, on the other hand, people increasingly regard economic policy as a province in which the professional specialist is paramount and the common man incompetent. The increasing "statification" of economic life has been accompanied by a rising mass reputation of scientific economies as a specialty. The emotional charges of simple economic formulae such as "free enterprise" or "socialization of the means of production" seem to have decreased (one might speak, at least in certain areas, of the silent breakdown of "capitalism" and "socialism" as ideologies). While the economic specialist is to fulfill the most urgent demand of the common man, that for security of employment, the distance between him and his beneficiary grows; he becomes part of a powerful elite, upon which the common man looks with a distrust rooted in a dependency.

This is but one instance of the experience of disparity—of insight as well as power—between the common man and the various political organizations into which he is integrated. That disparity counteracts the feeling of power which accompanies the manipulation of increasingly effective machinery, whether of production or destruction: the common man is usually acutely aware of the fact that the "button" he is "pushing" belongs to an apparatus far out of the reach of any unorganized individual.

This feeling of disparity greatly affects the common man's attitude to foreign policy. The potential proximity of total war produces situations that not only seem inherently incomprehensible, but that he, the common man, feels cannot be made comprehensible to him by his government. "Security considerations," he infers, are the reason why the "real dope" is kept away from him. Thus the distance between the common man and the policy maker has grown to such an extent that awe and distrust support each other.

The common man feels impotent in a world where specialized skills control events that at any moment may transform his life. That feeling of impotence bestows upon political facts something of the solidity of natural events, like weather or hurricane, that come and go. Two attitudes result from this feeling: First, one does not inquire into the causation of the events thus viewed; second, one does not inquire into their morality.[10]

The feeling that politics as such is outside the reach of morals is an extreme form of this attitude. Probably moral indignation as a reaction to political events has been declining since the turn of the century. One may compare the intense reactions to injustice against individuals under comparatively stable social conditions—the Dreyfus affair, the cases of Ferrer, Nurse Cavell, Sacco and Vanzetti—with the limited reactions to Nazi terror and extermination practices as they gradually became notorious. In the case of the Nazis, public reaction went through a sequence of frank disbelief, reserved doubt, short lived shock and subsequent indifference.

The psychological dynamics operating the interplay of distrust and privatization can now be formulated more sharply. We here distinguish in the continuum of distrustful attitudes, two cases: One we call critical distrust; the other projective distrust.[11] In the child's development, the former arose not independently from the latter. Critical distrust facilitates adjustment to reality and independence; it is at the foundation of scientific thought, and is an essential incentive in the battle against what Freud called the prohibition of thinking in the individual. Critical distrust has gained a decisive importance in modern society, since technology has played havoc with many kinds of magic. Projective distrust, on the other hand, is derived ultimately from ambivalence; it is an expression of hostility, in which aggressive tendencies against others, frequently against authority, are perceived as tendencies of others, frequently as attitudes of authority.

We allude to these complex questions only in order to round off our argumentation; in the world of the twentieth century, the exercise of critical distrust by the common man meets with many obstacles; it is at the

272

same time increasingly stimulated and increasingly frustrated. He therefore regressively turns to projective distrust: He fears, suspects and hates what he cannot understand and master.

Privatization is, amongst other things, a result of the hostility between the individual and the leadership of the group: We mentioned that it is comparable to what is known as a narcissistic regression. In order to maintain this attitude in which self-interest predominates over group interest—the self in this case may include "primary" groups such as the family—projective distrust is set into operation. Scepticism becomes the guarantor of privatization: scepticism here acts as a defense. If the individual, for instance, were to accept available evidence on atrocities, his emotional involvement in politics might rise; he might hate or experience enthusiasm. Thus privatization could not be maintained. The propagandist's concern in wartime is therefore to reduce such scepticism.

That concern, we said, was more clearly expressed in the democracies than in Germany or Russia. In order fully to understand this difference, we turn to a more detailed discussion of the relationship between propagandist and "propagandee." Every propaganda act occurs in such a relationship; in the case of propaganda by agents of governments, it is the relationship between the individual and his government.

We discuss this relationship in regard to two types of political organization: the totalitarian state with the charismatic leader and democracy. In both cases, the propagandists speak for the leaders, who are the chief propagandists. In both cases, propaganda presupposes, and attempts to strengthen identifications of the propagandees with the propagandists. These identifications, however, have a different character under the two regimes.

In a totalitarian state these identifications concern, to a large extent, id and superego functions. These identifications facilitate the gratifying completion of impulses, as superego functions have been projected upon the propagandist, and as he is idealized in an archaic sense: omnipotence, omniscience and infallibility are attributed to him.

In democratic states, the corresponding identifications concern, to a large extent, ego functions which are delegated to the propagandist. Amongst these functions, the scrutiny of the existing situation and the anticipation of the future are of predominant importance. While the propagandee relies upon the propagandist for the fulfillment of these functions, he retains a critical attitude in relation to him.

Superego and ego identifications, of course, constantly interact. The distribution of their intensities, however, is clearly dependent upon the institutionalized relationship between propagandist and propagandee. In this sense, we may say that the one is typical of totalitarian, the other of democratic propaganda relations.

That difference is reflected in the devices of propaganda. Totalitarian propaganda tries to sway the audience into participation; its preferred setting is the visible leader talking to the masses; it is modeled after the relations between the hypnotist and his medium. Democratic propaganda gives weight to insight as basis for participation; it is to a greater extent modeled after the principles of guidance or education.

The nature of the two propaganda situations accounts for the fact that for each of the two kinds of propagandists different goals are difficult to reach. The totalitarian propagandist finds it arduous to stimulate initiative among his followers. When German propaganda was faced with the task of stimulating cooperative action "from below" among the citizens of bombed towns, that difficulty became apparent: the devices then adopted were plain imitations of the techniques of British propagandists in a similar situation. Democratic propagandists meet a comparable difficulty when faced with the task of manifestly denying information on reasons for government action, that is, of demanding implicit trust for a limited time. The impasse in which allied leadership found itself when faced with a public demand for the opening of a second front, especially in 1943, is an example.

The two types of propagandists react to the impact of distrust and privatization in different ways; these tendencies show a different incidence under the two political orders. In a totalitarian state, privatization grows with deprivation. Then the latent cleavage of the totalitarian state becomes manifest, the cleavage between the faithful, from whose ranks elite and sub-elite are recruited, and the indifferent, who are controlled by the faithful. Their mounting privatization renders this control more difficult. Superego identifications cease to function with ever more individuals, and finally they function only with the fanatics. When that situation crystallized in Germany with the approach of defeat, two devices were adopted: First, a gradual revision of propaganda policy. Appeals to superego identifications became less and less important and increased weight was given to the stimulation of fear: ego interests should now motivate continued allegiance. But this did not prevent further privatization. Thus the central method of all totalitarian social control was applied ever more consistently: violence. In its last phases, Nazi propaganda hardly fulfilled the purpose of gaining participation in the present; building the Nazi myth, it addressed its appeals to future generations.

Democratic propaganda is better equipped to deal with the tendency towards privatization, since it puts greater emphasis on the creation of insight. Its appeals are better in tune with a high level of distrust. In totalitarian regimes, there is a polarization between the politicized and the privatized, which is, however, difficult to perceive from the outside. In democratic states, tendencies towards privatization are clearly perceptible but their distribution within the society is less clear cut.

There are periods when this tendency decreases: in America after

Pearl Harbor, in Britain after May 1940. While enthusiasm was kept at a low level, determination prevailed and sacrifice was willingly sustained.

What was the part of the propagandist in such situations? It may be illustrated by turning to one specific situation, in which democratic propaganda reached its greatest success.

We refer to Churchill's propaganda feat during the spring of 1940. The series of speeches he made in May, June and July of 1940 are remembered for the singular depth of feeling and the heroic quality of language. But these qualities were only accessories to the major political impact of these speeches. Their function was a threefold one—to warn Britain of the danger, to clarify its extent, and to indicate how everyone could help to meet it. In order to illustrate this point, we refer to one topic only: the announcement of the Battle of Britain.

The first intimation was made on May 12th, three days after Churchill's appointment, when the Battle of Flanders had not yet reached its climax. After having described the battle on all fronts, Churchill added that "many preparations had to be made at home." On May 19th, after the surrender of Holland, and during the climax of the Belgian battles, he devoted well over one-third of his speech to announcing "that after this . . . there will come the battle for our island." And after demanding full mobilization of production, he gave for the first time the "box score": he reported that the R.A.F. had been downing three to four enemy planes for each of their own. This, he inferred, was the basis of any hope. On June 4th, in his famous speech after Dunkirk, the theme was taken up anew and an elaborate account of the chances of the fighter force in a battle over the homeland was given. Churchill went into technical details; at a time when France seemed still vigorously to resist, he acquainted the British people with the chances of their survival. While the enemy had broken through the allied front with a few thousand armored vehicles, he forecast the future by saying: "May it not also be that the course of civilization itself will be defended by the skill and devotion of a few thousand airmen. And while he discussed the necessity of ever increasing production, he spoke at this time of imminent defeat of "the great British armies of the later years of war."

In the later speeches of that unforgettable spring, he elaborated on the subject. Every one could understand how his own behavior was related to the total situation, and how this situation was structured; how supplies were needed for the repair and construction of fighter planes, and how in this matter every detail, even the smallest one, could contribute to the final result. All this information was released well in advance of any German attack.

Thus Churchill had not only given the "warning signal" and mobilized "emergency reactions." His detailed analysis of the situation also contributed to the prevention of an inexpediently large and rapid increase in anxiety: unknown danger was transformed into a danger known in kind and extent. He fulfilled those functions of leadership that can be compared to those fulfilled in the life of the individual by the organization of the ego.[12] At the same time, Churchill offered his own courage as a model: "If you behave as I do, you will behave right." He not only spoke of Britain's "finest hour" but was careful to add that in this hour "every man and woman had their chance."

The propagandist thus seems to fulfill a double function: first that of structuring the situation so that it can be anticipated and understood, and second, that of offering himself as a model.

It is essential to understand the difference between the democratic leader who functions as a model and the charismatic leader.[13] The latter offers himself as an object that replaces superego functions in the individual. The model function of leadership implies that in identifying with the leader, the individual will best serve the ideals he shares with him. But the understanding of the situation is a precondition for such moral participation.

The general problem which we here finally approach concerns the relation between ego and superego functions. One might tentatively formulate the hypothesis that in a situation in which the ego functions smoothly, the tension between ego and superego is apt to be low. In fact, we find in the study of superego formation in the child some evidence in support of such a formulation.[14] However, other evidence is contradictory. Frequently, successful ego performance is accompanied by intense conflicts between ego and superego. We therefore reject this formulation and substitute another: unsuccessful ego functions endanger the positive relationship between ego and superego. They tend to encourage regressive trends. Individuals who feel impotent in the face of a world they do not understand, and are distrustful of those who should act as their guides, tend to revert to patterns of behavior known from childhood, in which an increase of hostility against the adults and many neurotic or delinquent mechanisms may develop. The incidence of such maladjustments may increase in a society in which privatization tendencies have become dominant.[15]

Little can be said here about what conclusions can be drawn for the future of democratic propaganda from these considerations. They clearly point to the desirability of sharp and wide increases of insight into events in the world at large among the citizens. Briefly, the trend towards distrust and privatization among the audience of the propagandist should be turned into a trend towards increase of insight. That trend would find a parallel in changes of related techniques: psycho-therapy and education, largely under the influence of psychoanalysis, have substituted or are substituting insight for pressure. If the appropriate education, on a vast enough scale and at a rapid enough rate is not provided for, the distrust and privatization of the masses may become a fertile soil for totalitarian management.

NOTES

1. Lasswell, H. D. *Propaganda Techniques in the World War,* New York, Alfred A. Knopf, 1927. Smith, B. L., Lasswell, H. D. and Casey, R. D. *Propaganda, Communication, and Public Opinion,* Princeton Univ. Press, 1946.

2. Two kinds of decreased participation in the direction of privatization

can be distinguished: first, a decrease of active attitudes towards the political sphere, in favor of passive or merely adjusting attitudes; in this case, one must speak of a decrease of attitudinal participation; second, a decrease of the actual sharing in political action; in this case, one might speak of a decrease of behavioral participation.

3. Speier, H. and Otis, M. "German Radio Propaganda to France during the Battle of France," in: *Radio Research*, 1942/43 eds. P. F. Lazarsfeld and F. N. Stanton, New York, Duell, Sloan & Pearce, 1944, pp. 208–247.

4. In the following, we shall in the main limit ourselves to examples from American, British and German propaganda, and some data on response; information on reactions of Russian and Japanese audiences is not accessible.

5. Masserman, J. H. *Principles of Dynamic Psychiatry*, Philadelphia, W. B. Saunders, 1946. He makes a similar point (p. 219). He speaks of "resonance with personal incentives."

6. Kris, E. "The Danger of Propaganda," *American Imago*, 2, 1941, pp. 1–42. Kris, E. "Some Problems of War Propaganda." A Note on Propaganda, Old and New, *Psychoanalytic Quarterly*, 2, 1943, pp. 381–99.

7. For the question of the actual contribution of propaganda to this defeat and generally for the question of the limited influence of propaganda on warfare, see Kris, E., Speier, H. and Associates, *German Radio Propaganda*, New York, Oxford Univ. Press, 1944.

8. For instance, we do not propose to discuss how privatization is related to changes in values.

9. Mannheim, K. *Man and Society in an Age of Transition*, K. Paul, Trench, Trubner & Co., London, 1940. Kecskemeti, P. and Leites, N. *Some Psychological Hypotheses on Nazi Germany*, Washington, D.C. Library of Congress, 1945 (multigraphed).

10. American soldiers during the second World War were frequently explicitly opposed to discussion of its causation: going into its pre-history was frequently regarded as futile and somewhat "out of this world."

11. We do not propose here to discuss in detail their genetic interrelation, nor their pathological manifestations, especially in obsessional neuroses and paranoid syndromes. (See H. Deutsch's classical expositions. "Zur Psychologie des Misstrauens," *Imago*, 7, 1921, pp. 71–83.) A fuller treatment would also have to consider the question of retaliatory and self-punitive distrust.

12. Kris, E. "Danger and Morale," *American Journal of Orthopsychiatry*, 14, 1944, pp. 147–155.

13. Redl, F. "Group Education and Leadership," *Psychiatry*, 5, 1942, pp. 573–596.

14. Friedlander, K. "Formation of the Antisocial Character," *The Psycho-Analytic Study of the Child*, New York, International Universities Press, I, 1945, pp. 189–204.

15. We here note that the traditional discussion of the applicability of "individual" psychological hypotheses to "social" events lacks substance, since events dealt with in the empirical analysis of human affairs, "psychological" or "sociological," occur in individuals. We deal with frequencies of incidence.

KURT LANG AND GLADYS ENGEL LANG

The Unique Perspective of Television

THIS PAPER aims to investigate a public event as viewed over television or, to put it differently, to study in the context of public life, an event transmitted over video. The concern is not with the effects of television on individual persons, irrespective of the spread of this effect. Our assumption is, on the contrary, that the effect of exposure to TV broadcasting of public events cannot be measured most successfully in isolation. For the influence on one person is communicated to others, until the significance attached to the video event overshadows the "true" picture of the event, namely the impression obtained by someone physically present at the scene of the event. The experience of spectators may not be disseminated at all or may be discounted as the biased version of a specially interested participant. Or, again, the spectator's interpretation of his own experience may be reinterpreted when he finds the event in which he participated discussed by friends, newspapermen, and radio commentators. If the significance of the event is magnified, even casual spectatorship asssumes importance. The fact of having "been there" is to be remembered—not so much because the event in itself, has left an impression, but because the event has been recorded by others. At the opposite extreme, privately significant experiences, unless revived in subsequent interpersonal relations, soon recede into the deeper layers of memory.

By taking MacArthur Day in Chicago,[1] as it was experienced by millions of spectators and video viewers, we have attempted to study an event transmitted over video. The basis of this report is the contrast between the actually recorded experience of participant observers on the scene, on the one hand, and the picture which a video viewer received by way of the television screen, and the way in which the event was interpreted, magni-

Reprinted from *American Sociological Review*, Vol. XVIII, (February 1953), pp. 3–12, by permission of the author and the publisher. (Copyright, 1953, *American Sociological Review*).

fied, and took on added significance, on the other. The contrast between these two perspectives from which the larger social environment can be viewed and "known," forms the starting point for the assessment of a particular effect of television in structuring public events.

The Research Design

The present research was undertaken as an exploration in collective behavior.[2] The design of the communications analysis differs significantly from most studies of content analysis. The usual process of inferring effect from content and validating the effect by means of interviews with an audience and control group is reversed. A generally apparent effect, i.e., the "landslide effect" of national indignation at MacArthur's abrupt dismissal and the impression of enthusiastic support, bordering on "mass hysteria," given to him, was used to make inferences on given aspects of the television content. The concern was with the picture disseminated, especially as it bore on the political atmosphere. To explain how people could have a false imagery (the implication of participant observational data), it was necessary to show how their perspective of the larger political environment was limited and how the occasion of Chicago's welcome to MacArthur, an event mediately known already, was given a particular structure. The concern is how the picture of the events was shaped by selection, emphasis, and suggested inferences which fitted into the already existing pattern of expectations.

The content analysis was therefore focused on two aspects—the selections made by the camera and their structuring of the event in terms of foreground and background, and the explanation and interpretations of televised events given by commentators and persons interviewed by them. Moreover, each monitor was instructed to give his impression of what was happening, on the basis of the picture and information received by way of television. The monitors' interpretations and subjective impressions were separately recorded. They served as a check that the structure inferred from the two operations of "objective" analysis of content were, in fact, legitimate inferences.[3] At the same time, utilizing the categories of the objective analysis, the devices by which the event was structured could be isolated, and the specific ways in which television reportage differed from the combined observations could be determined.

Thirty-one participant observers took part in the study. They were spatially distributed to allow for the maximum coverage of all the important phases of the day's activities, i.e., no important vantage point of spectatorship was neglected. Since the events were temporally distributed, many observers took more than one station, so that coverage was actually based on more than 31 perspectives. Thus the sampling error inherent in individual participant observation or unplanned mass-observation was greatly reduced. Observers could witness the arrival at Midway Airport and still arrive in the Loop area long before the scheduled time for the parade. Reports were received from 43 points of observation.

Volunteers received instruction sheets which drew their attention to principles of observation[4] and details to be carefully recorded. Among these was the directive to take careful note of any activity indicating possible influences of the televising of the event upon the behavior of spectators, e.g., actions specifically addressed to the cameras, indications that events were staged with an eye towards transmission over television, and the like.

Summary of Findings

THE PATTERN OF EXPECTATIONS

The mass-observation concentrated on discerning the psychological structure of the unfolding event in terms of present and subsequent antici-- pations. Certainly the crowd which turned out for the MacArthur Day celebration was far from a casual collection of individuals: the members *intended* to be witnesses to this "unusual event." One may call these intentions specific attitudes, emergent acts, expectations, or predispositions. Whatever the label, materials on these patterns of expectations were taken from two sources: (1) all statements of spectators recorded in the observer reports which could be interpreted as indicative of such expectations (coded in terms of the inferences therein); (2) personal expectations of the 31 study observers (as stated in the personal questionnaire).

Though not strictly comparable—since the observations on the scene contained purely personal, very short-range and factually limited expectations—both series of data provide confirmation of a basic pattern of observer expectations. The persons on the scene *anticipated* "mobs" and "wild crowds." They expected some disruption of transportation. Their journey downtown was in search of adventure and excitement. Leaving out such purely personal expectations as "seeing" and "greeting," the second most frequent preconception emphasizes the extraordinary nature of the preparations and the entertaining showmanship connected with the spectacle.

As a result of an unfortunate collapsing of several questions regarding personal data into one, the response did not always focus properly on what the observers "expected to see." In some cases no evidence or only an incomplete description of this aspect was obtained. Of those answering, 68 per cent expected excited and wildly enthusiastic crowds. But it is a safe inference from the discussion during the briefing session that this figure tends to underestimate the number who held this type of imagery. The main incentive to volunteer resided, after all, in the opportunity to study crowd behavior at first hand.

To sum up: most people expected a wild spectacle, in which the large masses of onlookers would take an active part, and which contained an element of threat in view of the absence of ordinary restraints on behavior and the power of large numbers.

THE ROLE OF MASS MEDIA IN THE PATTERN OF EXPECTATIONS

A more detailed examination of the data supports the original assumption that the pattern of expectations was shaped by way of the mass media. For it is in that way that the picture of the larger world comes to sophisticated as well as unsophisticated people. The observers of the study were no exception to this dependence on what newspapers, newsreels, and television cameras mediated. They were, perhaps, better able than others to describe the origin of these impressions. Thus Observer 14 wrote in evaluating his report and his subjective feelings:

I had listened to the accounts of MacArthur's arrival in San Francisco, heard radio reports of his progress through the United States, and had heard the Washington speech as well as the radio accounts of his New York reception. . . . I had therefore expected the crowds to be much more vehement, contagious, and identified with MacArthur. I had expected to hear much political talk, especially anti-Communist and against the Truman administration.

These expectations were completely unfulfilled. I was amazed that not once did I hear Truman criticized, Acheson mentioned, or as much as an allusion to the Communists. . . . I had expected roaring, excited mobs; instead there were quiet, well ordered, dignified people. . . . The air of curiosity and casualness surprised me. Most people seemed to look on the event as simply something that might be interesting to watch.

Other observers made statements of a very similar content.

Conversation in the crowd pointed to a similar awareness. Talk repeatedly turned to television, especially to the comparative merit of "being there" and "seeing it over TV." An effort was consequently made to assess systematically the evidence bearing on the motives for being there in terms of the patterns of expectations previously built up. The procedures of content analysis served as a useful tool, allowing the weighing of all evidence *directly* relevant to this question in terms of confirmatory and contrary evidence. The coding operation involved the selection of two types of indicators:

1 general evaluations and summaries of data; and

2 actual incidents of behavior which could support or nullify our hypothesis.

Insofar as the observers had been instructed to report concrete behavior rather than general interpretations, relatively few such generalizations are available for tabulation. Those given were used to formulate the basic headings under which the concrete evidence could be tabulated. The generalizations fall into two types; namely, the crowds had turned out to see a great military figure and a public hero "in the flesh"; and—its logical supplement—they had turned out not so much "to see *him*, as I noticed, but to see the spectacle (Observer 5)." Six out of eleven concretely stated propositions were of the second type.

An examination of the media content required the introduction of a third heading, which subdivided the interest in MacArthur into two distinct interpretations: that people had come to find vantage points from which to see the man and his family; or, as the official (media and "Chicago official") version held, that they had come to welcome, cheer, and honor him. Not one single observer, in any generalized proposition, confirmed the official generalization, but there was infrequent mention of isolated incidents which would justify such an interpretation.

The analysis of actual incidents, behavior, and statements recorded is more revealing. A gross classification of the anticipations which led people to participate is given (according to categories outlined above) in Table 1.

Table 1—Types of Spectator Interest

Form of Motivation	Per Cent
Active hero worship	9.2
Interest in seeing MacArthur	48.1
Passive interest in spectacle	42.7

A classification of these observations by area in which they were secured gives a clear indication that the Loop throngs thought of the occasion *primarily* as a spectacle. There, the percentage of observations supporting the "spectacle hypothesis" was 59.7. The percentage in other areas was: Negro district, 40.0; Soldiers Field, 22.9; Airport, 17.6; University district, 0.0. Moreover, of the six generalizations advanced on crowd expectations in the Loop, five interpreted the prevalent motivation as the hope of a wild spectacle.

Thus, a probe into motivation gives a confirmatory clue regarding the pattern of expectations observed. To this body of data, there should be added the constantly overheard expressions—as the time of waiting increased and excitement failed to materialize—of disillusionment with the particular advantage point. "We should have stayed home and watched it on TV," was the almost universal form that the dissatisfaction took. In relation to the spectatorship experience of extended boredom and sore feet, alleviated only by a brief glimpse of the hero of the day, previous and similar experiences over television had been truly exciting ones which promised even greater "sharing of excitement" *if only one were present.* These expectations were disappointed and favorable allusions to television in this respect were frequent. To present the entire body of evidence bearing on the inadequate release of tension and the widely felt frustration would be to go beyond the scope of this report, in which the primary concern is the study of the television event. But the materials collected present unequivocal proof of the foregoing statements, and this—with one qualified exception—is also the interpretation of each one of the observers.

Moreover, the comparison of the television perspective with that of the participant observers indicates that the video aspects of MacArthur Day in Chicago served to *preserve* rather than disappoint the same pattern of expectations among the viewers. The main difference was that television remained true to form until the very end, interpreting the entire proceedings according to expectations. No hint about the disappointment in the crowd was provided. To cite only one example, taken from what was the high point in the video presentation, the moment when the crowds broke into the parade by surging out into State Street:

The scene at 2:50 p.m. at State and Jackson was described by the announcer as the "most enthusiastic crowd *ever* in our city. . . . You can feel the tenseness in the air. . . . You can hear that crowd roar." The crowd was described as pushing out into the curb with the police trying to keep it in order, while the camera was still focusing on MacArthur and his party. The final picture was of a bobbing mass of heads as the camera took in the entire view of State Street northward. To the monitor, this mass of people appeared to be pushing and going nowhere. And then, with the remark, "The whole city appears to be marching down State Street behind General MacArthur," holding the picture just long enough for the impression to sink in, the picture was suddenly blanked out.

Observer 26, who was monitoring this phase of the television transmission, reported her impression:

. . . the last buildup on TV concerning the "crowd" (cut off as it was, abruptly at 3:00 p.m.) gave me the impression that the crowd was pressing and straining so hard that it was going to be hard to control. My first thought, "I'm glad I'm not in that" and "I hope nobody gets crushed."

But observers near State and Jackson did not mention the event in an extraordinary context. For example, Observer 24 explained that as MacArthur passed:

Everybody strained but few could get a really good glimpse of him. A few seconds after he had passed most people merely turned around to shrug and to address their neighbors with such phrases: "That's all," "That was it," "Gee, he looks just as he does in the movies," "What'll we do now?" Mostly teenagers and others with no specific plans flocked into the street after MacArthur, but very soon got tired of following as there was no place to go and nothing to do. Some cars were caught in the crowd, a matter which, to the crowd, seemed amusing.

THE STRUCTURE OF THE TV PRESENTATION

The television perspective was different from that of any spectator in the crowd. Relatively unlimited in its mobility, it could order events in its own way by using close-ups for what was deemed important and leaving the apparently unimportant for the background. There was almost complete freedom to aim cameras in accordance with such judgments. The view, moreover, could be shifted to any significant happening, so that the technical possibilities of the medium itself tended to play up the dramatic. While the spectator, if fortunate, caught a brief glimpse of the General and his family, the television viewer found him the continuous center of attraction from his first appearance during the parade at 2:21 P.M. until the sudden blackout at 3:00 P.M. For almost 40 minutes, not counting his seven minute appearance earlier in the day at the airport and his longer appearance at Soldiers Field that evening, the video viewer could fasten his eyes on the General and on what could be interpreted as the interplay between a heroic figure and the enthusiastic crowd. The cheering of the crowd seemed not to die down at all, and even as the telecast was concluded, it only seemed to have reached its crest. Moreover, as the camera focused principally on the parade itself, the crowd's applause seemed all the more ominous a tribute from the background.

The shots of the waiting crowd, the interviews with persons within it, and the commentaries, had previously prepared the viewer for this dramatic development. Its resolution was left to the inference of the individual. But a sufficient number of clues had already come over television to leave little doubt about the structure. Out of the three-hour daytime telecast, in addition to the time that MacArthur and party were the visual focus of attention, there were over two hours which had to be filled with visual material and vocal commentary. By far the largest amount of time was spent in anticipatory shots of the crowd. MacArthur himself held the picture for the second longest period; thus the ratio of time spent viewing MacArthur to time spent anticipating his arrival is much greater for the TV observer than for the spectator on the scene.

The descriptive accounts of the commentators (also reflected in the interviews),[5] determined the structure of the TV presentation of the day's events. The idea of the magnitude of the event, in line with preparations announced in the newspapers, was emphasized by constant reference. The most frequently employed theme was that "no effort has been spared to make this day memorable (eight references). There were seven direct references to the effect that the announcer had "never seen the equal to this moment" or that it was the "greatest ovation this city had ever turned out." The unique cooperative effort of TV received five mentions and was tied in with the "dramatic" proportions of the event. It was impossible to categorize and tabulate all references, but they ranged from a description of crowded transportation and numerical estimates of the crowd to the length of the city's lunch hour and the state of "suspended animation" into which business had fallen. There was repeated mention that nothing was being allowed to interfere with the success of the celebration; even the ball game had been cancelled.[6] In addition to these purely formal aspects of the event, two—and only two—aspects of the spectacle were *stressed:* (1) the unusual nature of the event; (2) the tension which was said to pervade the entire scene. Even the references to the friendly and congenial mood of the waiting crowd portended something about the change that was expected to occur.

Moreover, in view of the selectivity of the coverage with its emphasis on close-ups,[7] it was possible for each viewer to see himself in a *personal* relationship to the General. As the announcer shouted out: "Look at that chin! Look at those eyes!"—each viewer, regardless of what might have been meant by it, could seek a personal interpretation which best expressed, for him, the real feeling underlying the exterior which appeared on the television screen.[8]

It is against the background of this personal inspection that the significance of the telecast must be interpreted. The cheering crowd, the "seething mass of humanity," was fictionally endowed by the commentators with the same capacity for a direct and personal relationship to MacArthur as the one which television momentarily established for the TV viewer through its close-up shots. The net effect of television thus stems from a convergence of these two phenomena; namely, the seemingly extraordinary scope of the event together with the apparent enthusiasm accompanying it and personalizing influence just referred to. In this way the public event was interpreted in a very personal nexus. The total effect of so many people, all shouting, straining, cheering, waving in personal welcome to the General, disseminated the impression of a universal, enthusiastic, overwhelming ovation for the General. The selectivity of the camera and the commentary gave the event a personal dimension, non-existent for the participants in the crowds, thereby presenting a very specific perspective which contrasted with that of direct observation.

OTHER INDICES OF THE DISCREPANCY

In order to provide a further objective check on the discrepancies between observer impressions and the event as it was interpreted by those who witnessed it over television, a number of spot checks on the reported amount of participation were undertaken. Transportation statistics, counts in offices, and the volume of sales reported by vendors provided such indices.

The results substantiate the above finding. The city and suburban lines showed a very slight increase over their normal loads. To some extent the paltry 50,000 increase in inbound traffic on the street cars and elevated trains might even have been due to rerouting. The suburban lines had their evening rush hour moved up into the early afternoon—before the parade had begun.

Checks at luncheonettes, restaurants, and parking areas indicated no unusual crowding. Samplings in offices disclosed only a minor interest in the parade. Hawkers, perhaps the most sensitive judges of enthusiasm, called the parade a "puzzler" and displayed unsold wares.

Detailed Illustration of Contrast

The Bridge ceremony provides an illustration of the contrast between the two perspectives. Seven observers witnessed this ceremony from the crowd.

TV perspective: In the words of the announcer, the Bridge ceremony marked "one of the high spots, if not the high spot of the occasion this afternoon. . . . The parade is now reaching its climax at this point."

The announcer, still focusing on MacArthur and the other participating persons, took the opportunity to review the ceremony about to take place. . . . The camera followed and the announcer described the ceremony in detail. . . . The camera focused directly on the General, showing a close-up. . . . There were no shots of the crowd during this period. But the announcer filled in. "A great cheer goes up at the Bataan Bridge, where the General has just placed a wreath in honor of the American boys who died at Bataan and Corregidor. You have heard the speech . . . the General is now walking back . . . the General now enters his car. This is the focal point where all the newsreels . . . frankly, in 25 years of covering the news, we have never seen as many newsreels gathered at one spot. One, two, three, four, five, six. At least eight cars with newsreels rigged on top of them, taking a picture that will be carried over the entire world, over the Chicagoland area by the combined network of these TV stations of Chicago, which have combined for this great occasion and for the solemn occasion which you have just witnessed.

During this scene there were sufficient close-ups for the viewer to gain a definite reaction, positive or negative, to the proceedings. He could see the General's facial expressions and what appeared to be momentary confusion. He could watch the activities of the Gold Star mothers in relation to MacArthur and define this as he wished—as inappropriate for the bereaved moment or as understandable in the light of the occasion. Taking the cue from the announcer, the entire scene could be viewed as rushed. Whether or not, in line with the official interpretation, the TV viewer saw the occasion as *solemn*, it can be assumed that he expected that the participant on the scene was, in fact, experiencing the occasion in the same way as he.

Actually, this is the way what was meant to be a solemn occasion was experienced by those attending, and which constitutes the crowd perspective. The dedication ceremony aroused little of the sentiment it might have elicited under other conditions. According to Observer 31, "People on our corner could not see the dedication ceremony very well, and consequently after he had passed immediately in front of us, there was uncertainty as to what was going on. As soon as word had come down that he had gone down to his car, the crowd dispersed." Observer 8 could not quite see the ceremony from where he was located on Wacker Drive, slightly east of the bridge. Condensed descriptions of two witnesses illustrate the confusion which surrounded the actual wreath-laying ceremony (three other similar descriptions are omitted here).

It was difficult to see any of them. MacArthur moved swiftly up the steps and immediately shook hands with people on the platform waiting to greet him. There was some cheering when he mounted the platform. He walked north on the platform and did not reappear until some minutes later. In the meantime the crowd was so noisy that it was impossible to understand what was being broadcast from the loud-speakers. Cheering was spotty and intermittent, and there was much talk about Mrs. MacArthur and Arthur . . . (Observer 2).

Those who were not on boxes did not see MacArthur. They did not see Mrs. MacArthur, but only her back. MacArthur went up on the platform, as we were informed by those on boxes, and soon we heard some sound over the loudspeakers. Several cars were standing in the street with their motors running. . . . Some shouted to the cars to shut their motors off, but the people in the cars did not care or did not hear. . . . The people in our area continued to push forward trying to hear. When people from other areas began to come and walk past us to go toward the train, the people in our area shrugged their shoulders. "Well, I guess it's all over. That noise must have been the speech." One of the three men who had stood there for an hour or more, because it was such a good spot, complained, "This turned out to be a lousy spot. I should have gone home. I bet my wife saw it much better over television" (Observer 30).

Regardless of good intentions on the part of planners and despite any recognition of the solemn purpose of the occasion by individuals in the crowd, the solemnity of the occasion was destroyed, if for no other reason, because officials in the parade were so intent upon the time-schedule and cameramen so intent upon recording the solemn dedication for the TV audience and for posterity that the witnesses could not see or hear the ceremony, or feel "solemn" or communicate a mood of solemnity. A crowd of confused spectators, cheated in their hopes of seeing a legendary hero in the flesh, was left unsatisfied.

Reciprocal Effects—There is some direct evidence regarding the way in which television imposed its own peculiar perspective on the event.

287

In one case an observer on the scene could watch both was was going on and what was being televised.

> It was possible for me to view the scene (at Soldiers Field) both naturally and through the lens of the television camera. It was obvious that the camera presented quite a different picture from the one received otherwise. The camera followed the General's car and caught that part of the crowd immediately opposite the car and about 15 rows above it. Thus it caught that part of the crowd that was cheering, giving the impression of a solid mass of wildly cheering people. It did not show the large sections of empty stands, nor did it show that people stopped cheering as soon as the car passed them (Observer 13).

In much the same way, the television viewer received the impression of wildly cheering and enthusiastic crowds before the parade. The camera selected shots of the noisy and waving audience, but in this case, the television camera itself created the incident. The cheering, waving, and shouting was often largely a response to the aiming of the camera. The crowd was thrilled to be on television, and many attempted to make themselves apparent to acquaintances who might be watching. But even beyond that, an event important enough to warrant the most widespread pooling of television facilities in Chicago video history, acquired in its own right some magnitude and significance. Casual conversation continually showed that being on television was among the greatest thrills of the day.

Conclusion

It has been claimed for television that it brings the truth directly into the home: the "camera does not lie." Analysis of the above data shows that this assumed reportorial accuracy is far from automatic. Every camera selects, and thereby leaves the unseen part of the subject open to suggestion and inference. The gaps are usually filled in by a commentator. In addition the process directs action and attention to itself.

Examination of a public event by mass-observation and by television revealed considerable discrepancy between these two experiences. The contrast in perspectives points to three items whose relevance in structuring a televised event can be inferred from an analysis of the television content:

1. Technological bias, i.e., the necessarily arbitrary sequence of telecasting events and their structure in terms of foreground and background, which at the same time contains the choices on the part of the television personnel as to what is important;

2. Structuring of an event by an announcer, whose commentary is needed to tie together the shifts from camera to camera, from vista to close-up, helping the spectator to gain the stable orientation from one particular perspective;

3. Reciprocal effects, which modify the event itself by staging it in a way to

288

make it more suitable for telecasting and creating among the actors the consciousness of acting for a larger audience.

General attitudes regarding television and viewing habits must also be taken into account. Since the industry is accustomed to thinking in terms of audience ratings—though not to the exclusion of all other considerations—efforts are made to assure steady interest. The telecast was made to conform to what was interpreted as the pattern of viewers' expectations. The drama of MacArthur Day, in line with that pattern, was nonetheless built around unifying symbols, personalities, and general appeals (rather than issues). But a drama it had to be, even if at the expense of reality.

Unlike other television programs, news and special events features constitute part of that basic information about "reality" which we require in order to act in concert with anonymous but like-minded persons in the political process. Action is guided by the possibilities for success, and, as part of this constant assessment, inferences about public opinion as a whole are constantly made. Even though the average citizen does, in fact, see only a small segment of public opinion, few persons refrain from making estimates of the true reading of the public temper. Actions and campaigns are supported by a sense of support from other persons. If not, these others at least constitute an action potential that can be mobilized. The correct evaluation of the public temper is therefore of utmost importance; it enters the total political situation as perhaps one of the weightiest factors.

Where no overt expression of public opinion exists, politicians and citizens find it useful to fabricate it. Against such demonstrations as the MacArthur Day, poll data lack persuasiveness and, of necessity, must always lag, in their publication, behind the development of popular attitudes. For the politician who is retroactively able to counter the errors resulting from an undue regard for what at a given time is considered overwhelming public opinion, there may be little significance in this delay. The imagery of momentary opinion may, however, goad him into action which, though justified in the name of public opinion, may objectively be detrimental. It may prevent critics from speaking out when reasoned criticism is desirable, so that action may be deferred until scientific estimates of public opinion can catch up with the prior emergence of new or submerged opinion.

Above all, a more careful formulation of the relations among public opinion, the mass media, and the political process, is vital for the understanding of many problems in the field of politics. The reports and telecasts of what purports to be spontaneous homage paid to a political figure assume added meaning within this context. The most important single media effect coming within the scope of the material relevant to the study of MacArthur Day was the dissemination of an image of overwhelming public sentiment in favor of the General. This effect gathered force as it was incorporated into political strategy, picked up by other media, entered into gossip, and thus came to overshadow immediate reality as it might have been recorded by an observer on the scene. We have labelled this the "landslide effect" because, in view of the wide-spread dissemination of a particular public welcoming ceremony the imputed unanimity gathered tremendous force.[9] This "landslide effect" can, in large measure, be attributed to television.

Two characteristics of the video event enhanced this effect (misevaluation of public sentiment). (1) The depiction of the ceremonies in unifying rather than in particularistic symbols (between which a balance was maintained) failed to leave any room for dissent. Because no lines were drawn between the conventional and the partisan aspects of the reception, the traditional welcome assumed political significance in the eyes of the public. (2) A general characteristic of the television presentation was that the field of vision of the viewer was enlarged while, at the same time, the context in which these events could be interpreted was less clear. Whereas a participant was able to make direct inferences about the crowd as whole, being in constant touch with those around him, the television viewer was in the center of the entire crowd. Yet, unlike the participant, he was completely at the mercy of the instrument of his perceptions. He could not test his impressions—could not shove back the shover, inspect bystanders' views, or attempt in any way to affect the ongoing activity. To the participant, on the other hand, the direction of the crowd activity as a whole, regardless of its final goal, still appeared as the interplay of certain peculiarly personal and human forces. Political sentiment, wherever encountered, could thus be evaluated and discounted. Antagonistic views could be attributed to insufficient personal powers of persuasion rather than seen as subjugation to the impersonal dynamics of mass hysteria. The television viewer had little opportunity to recognize this personal dimension in the crowd. What was mediated over the screen was, above all, the general trend and the direction of the event, which consequently assumed the proportion of an impersonal force, no longer subject to influence.

This view of the "overwhelming" effect of public moods and the impersonal logic of public events is hypothesized as a characteristic of the perspective resulting from the general structure of the picture and the context of television viewing.

NOTES

1. "MacArthur Day in Chicago" includes the following occasions which were televised: arrival at Midway Airport, parade through the city including the dedication at the Bataan-Corregidor Bridge, and the evening speech at Soldiers Field.

2. This paper reports only one aspect of a larger study of MacArthur Day in Chicago. A report of the larger study is nearing completion. This writeup is limited to drawing together some of the implications concerning the role of television in public events, this particular study being considered as a pilot study for the framing of hypotheses and categories prerequisite for a more complete analysis of other such events in general. The present study could not test these categories, but was limited to an analysis of the television content in terms of the observed "landslide effect" of the telecast. The authors wish to express their indebtedness to Dr. Tamatsu Shibutani (then of the Department of Sociology, University of Chicago) for lending his encouragement and giving us absolute freedom for a study which, due to the short notice of MacArthur's planned arrival in Chicago, had to be prepared and drawn up in three days, and for allowing his classes to be used for soliciting volunteers. No funds of any sort were at our disposal. Dr. Donald Horton was kind enough to supply us with television sets and tape recorders. In discussions of the general problems involved in the analysis of television content, he has indirectly been of invaluable aid. Finally, we are indebted to the other twenty-nine observers, without whose splendid cooperation the data could never have been gathered.

3. That this check together with our observation of the general impression left by MacArthur Day constitutes only a very limited validation is beyond question. Under the conditions of the study—carried on without financial support and as an adjunct to other research commitments—it was the best we could do.

4. Analysis of personal data sheets, filled out by participants prior to MacArthur Day, revealed that "objectivity" in observation was not related to political opinion held, papers and periodicals subscribed to, and previous exposure to radio or TV coverage of MacArthur's homecoming. The significant factor in evaluating the reports for individual or deviant interpretation was found to reside in the degree to which individual observers were committed to scientific and objective procedures. Our observers were all advanced graduate students in the social sciences.

5. An analysis of televised interviews is omitted in this condensation. Interviews obtained for the study by observers posing as press representatives elicited responses similar to those given over TV. Without exception, those questioned referred to the magnitude, import, and other formal aspects of the event. These stand in contrast to results obtained through informal probes and most overheard conversation. One informant connected with television volunteered that television announcers had had specific instructions to emphasize that this was a "dramatic event." Another of Chicago's TV newsmen noted that throughout the telecast the commentary from each position made it sound as if the high points of the day's activity were about to occur or were occurring right on their own spot.

6. The day's activities at a nearby race track were not cancelled. At one point in the motorcade from the airport to the Loop, a traffic block resulted in a partially "captive audience." An irritated "captive" remarked, "I hope this doesn't make me late for the races."

7. In a subsequent interview, a TV producer explained his conception of the MacArthur Day coverage as "being the best in the country." He especially recalled bracketing and then closing in on the General during the motorcade, the assumption being that he was the center of attraction.

8. During the evening ceremonies, MacArthur's failure to show fatigue in spite of the strenuous experiences of the day received special notice. A report

from a public viewing of the evening speech indicates the centering of discussion about this "lack of fatigue" in relation to the General's advanced years (Observer 24).

9. It must be re-emphasized that there was no independent check—in the form of a validation—of the specific effect of TV. However, newspaper coverage emphasized the overwhelming enthusiasm. Informal interviews, moreover, even months later, showed that the event was still being interpreted as a display of mass hysteria.

HAROLD L. WILENSKY

Mass Society and Mass Culture

SEVERAL MAJOR QUESTIONS about the social impact of affluence have come to dominate intellectual discussion concerning the shape of modern society. Some of them involve the nature, extent, and impact of mass culture and mass leisure. Everyone agrees that abundance everywhere brings a rise in mass communications, through radio, television, and press; the development of mass education and the concomitant spread of literacy; and, finally, mass entertainment on a grand scale. I propose to deal with these trends in the context of ideas about the "mass society." I will:

1 analyze the interplay of high culture and mass culture, with special attention to the structural roots of cultural standardization and heterogeneity in rich countries;

2 present data on the quality of media exposure in a variety of occupational groups and strata in the Detroit metropolitan area—so that we may both gauge the extent of cultural uniformity and locate the sources of resistance to mass culture. My general aim is to fill in gaps in theories of the mass society and to arrive at a more valid vision of modern society.

Theories of Mass Society and the
Functions of the Mass Media

Traditional theorists of "urbanism" or of the "mass society" tend to be pessimistic in ideology and macroscopic in sociology; their empirical critics tend to be optimistic—some would say fatuous—in ideology and microscopic in sociology. Both seek to interpret the impact of industrial-

Reprinted from *American Sociological Review*, Vol. xxix (April 1964), pp. 173–197, by permission of the author and the publisher. (Copyright, 1964, *American Sociological Review*.)

ism and urbanism on social structure and culture. Together they have given us most of the imagery with which we construct our picture of the affluent society.

From Tocqueville to Mannheim[1] the traditional theorists have been concerned with one or both of two problems: (1) the debilitation of culture-bearing elites (and of the core values they sustain) brought on by their diminishing insulation from popular pressures; (2) the rise of the masses, who, for various reasons, are increasingly susceptible to demagogues and extremist movements.[2] These scholars are said to believe that the mobility, heterogeneity, and centralization of modern society destroy or weaken the ties that bind men to the common life, rendering the mass manipulatable, leaving mass organizations and the mass media in control. Although they vary in their depiction of the generating forces, they tend to accent either the atrophy of primary and informal relations or the atrophy of self-governing secondary groups and associations.[3]

Now the empirically-minded critics—a later generation studying a more industrialized society—have countered with these propositions: Primary groups survive, even flourish. Urban-industrial populations have not stopped participating in voluntary associations, which in America and perhaps in other pluralist systems, continue to multiply. Moreover, in every industrial society, whether pluralist or totalitarian, there are potent limits to the powers of the mass media, the big organizations, and the centralized state.[4]

I count myself as one of the critics,[5] but I am restive about the way the debate has progressed.[6] The parties talk past one another and ideological blinders obstruct the vision far more than in other areas of sociological investigation. Nowhere is this more true than in the sketchy treatment of mass culture in theories of the mass society and in the almost ritualistic recital of the "two-step flow" slogan by the students of media ineffectiveness.

The main theme of the theorists is this: the *mass society* develops a *mass culture*, in which cultural and political values and beliefs tend to be *homogeneous* and *fluid*. In the middle and at the bottom—in the atomized mass—people think and feel alike; but thoughts and feelings, not being firmly anchored anywhere, are susceptible to fads and fashions. At the top, poorly-organized elites, themselves mass-oriented, become political and managerial manipulators, responding to short-run pressures; they fail to maintain standards and thereby encourage the spread of populism in politics, mass tastes in culture—in short, a "sovereignty of the unqualified."[7]

The empirically-minded critics of such theories are impressed by the diversity of modern life. Concerning the leveling and fluidity of culture, they point to an extraordinary variety of cultural products, assert that it is easier to prove that mass tastes have been upgraded than that such tastes have been vulgarized, and protest that high culture has not declined but merely become more widely available. Concerning the role of the mass media in politics and culture, the critics cite considerable diversity of media content as well as persistence in habits of exposure. And where diversity of *content* falls short, they argue, there is everywhere enormous diversity in *response*. While the optimists are well aware of the limits of their studies, they seem always to come to the same punch line: the burden of evidence indicates that the media are not omnipotent; they are absorbed into local cultures via the two-step flow from media to local group to person; and this absorption involves a self-selection of exposure corresponding to previous attitude.[8]

It is a pity that these students of the media who know mass communications best are not more ideologically sensitive and not more concerned with general characterizations of society; equally unfortunate is it that the theorists, at home in the world of ideologies and utopias, are not more sophisticated in the handling of data. For systematic observation and theoretical problems must be brought together if we are to understand the interplay of social structure, high culture, and mass culture.

MASS CULTURE AND HIGH CULTURE

For my purposes here the most useful definition that distinguishes high culture from mass culture is one that emphasizes the social context of production. "High culture" will refer to two characteristics of the product:

1 It is created by or under the supervision of a cultural elite operating within some aesthetic, literary, or scientific tradition (these elite are the top men in the sphere of education, aesthetics, and entertainment who carry the core values and standards of that sphere and serve as models for those working in it);

2 critical standards independent of the consumer of the product are systematically applied to it. The quality of thought or expression of the cultural object and the social milieu in which it is produced define high culture. This definition has the advantage of leaving open questions about the organization and recruitment of cultural elites, the social controls to which they are subject (e.g., pressures from patron, market, or mass), the conditions under which a high-quality product—a Shakespearian play, a Mozart symphony—can become popular, the ways in which the product is or is not absorbed into the culture of the consumer.

"Mass culture" will refer to cultural *products manufactured solely for a mass market*. Associated characteristics, not intrinsic to the definition, are *standardization* of product and *mass behavior* in its use. Mass culture tends to be standardized because it aims to please the average taste of an undifferentiated audience. Common tastes shape mass culture; critical standards sustained by autonomous producing groups shape high culture. Another frequent but not inevitable correlate of mass culture is a high rate of mass behavior—a uniform and direct response to remote symbols.[9] It is expressed in strong attachment to and dependence on distant public objects and concerns—e.g., acts, thoughts, and feelings regarding the nation (hyperpatriotism and xenophobia), class (Marxian class consciousness), race (racism). The definition leaves open questions about the relation of mass culture to high culture; the conditions under which a product of mass culture can meet the standards of high culture; the degree to which mass culture is fluid or, like folk culture, stable (characterized by little original creation in each generation); whether traditions of expression and performance develop in it; the extent to which the impact of the mass media is mediated by audience standards and the extent to which those very standards are themselves anchored in the media.

In short, these concepts permit sociological analysis of cultural products in the social contexts in which they are created and used. They have the disadvantage of being difficult (but not impossible) to apply in empirical research.

THEORETICAL PROBLEM AND ASSUMPTIONS

Our problem is the relation of the main structural trends associated with abundance to the form and content of high culture and mass culture. The main research question is, "which groupings of modern populations acquire a 'mass' character and which do not—with what net effect on culture, high and low?" More precisely, will the heterogeneity of culture rooted mainly in the division of labor give way to the homogeneity of culture rooted mainly in the centralized state, mass education, the mass media, and mass entertainment?

Five assumptions about modern society have guided my approach to this question: (1) social differentiation persists, even increases; (2) cultural uniformity also grows; (3) in rich countries there is more independent variation of social structure and culture than in poor ones, although some of this incongruity is due to imprecise measures of structure; (4) developments in the aesthetic-recreational sphere as well as the political sphere may remain isolated from those in the economy and locality for some time, so that in the short run mass behavior in one sphere may not become mass behavior in another; but (5) over several generations, and as rich countries grow richer, there is a strain toward consistency between structure and culture and between behavior in one institutional sphere and that in a second.

1. Social Differentiation Persists, Even Increases—It is rooted first in specialization by job and occupation and by the corporate and occupational communities that develop from work. It is rooted second in society-wide age-grading systems and in individual stages of the life cycle. (As sources of alienation from work and community, for instance, age and life cycle stage, which are fixed in both biological and social nature, are invariably more important than family income, which tends toward equalization.) Finally, differentiation is rooted in religious institutions, which everywhere mesh with kinship and friendship and often form a basis for wider but separate networks of affiliation. (The labor-leisure study shows that religion is a far stronger anchor for close friendships than occupation or workplace—as measured, for instance, by the religion, occupation, and place of employment of one's three best friends.) Of course, racial and ethnic groups do assimilate, but only slowly. If they serve as a basis for variants of religious communities, as among Catholics of diverse origin, or Jews, or for protest movements, as among Negroes, such groups maintain a tenacious hold, which is often reinforced by residential segregation. The ties of locality doubtless diminish, despite the evidence of occasional communities in the metropolis (again ethnic, racial, or class "neighborhoods" or at least "blocks").

There is, in short, no evidence that the bonds of economy, age, religion, and the nuclear family (with family and church often meshed with extended kin) are weakening in the rich countries, although the quality of those relationships may be changing and their influence in particular social contexts is still problematic. In much of the discussion of "mass" society or "totalitarian" society, the persistence and stability of such ties are underestimated. The masses have nowhere in any developed country been kept "atomized," "available," "unattached," "in motion."[10] Many writers, shocked by the barbarity of the Stalinist and Nazi regimes, have generalized a vocabulary appropriate to brief historical episodes or, in the case of the Nazis, selected populations, and have thereby missed the main trend. The limits of terror have been encountered by every totalitarian elite committed to economic progress. Even the most monolithic industrial societies are forced to supplement coercion with persuasion and manipulation, and to attend to problems of morale and motivation. This is especially true when they confront skilled workers at every level, including cultural elites, and is most evident when persons in these categories are in short supply. The argument is both familiar and accurate: some tasks cannot be mastered without the development of more-or-less autonomous groups—crafts, professions, scientific disciplines, and other private enclaves. Such groups cultivate technique and celebrate it, motivate disciplined work, provide stable careers and professional conviviality. The arts and sciences that flourish in the Soviet Union are not merely those which are politically safe; they are the ones which prior to the rise of Bolshevism were characterized by a high degree of skill and organization and either an aristocratic tradition (music, the ballet) or a tradition of intellectual achievement (mathematics, linguistics).[11] In short, the necessity of mobilizing social support for the performance of complex tasks sets practical limits on the baiting of intellectuals and professionals.

While the "professionalization" of occupations is often no more than a struggle for the rewards of exclusive jurisdiction, and while there are many organizational and political threats to the autonomy of professional groups, the number of occupations that are given some freedom to organize their work seems to be increasing in every rich country. And while the freezes and thaws in the intellectual climate make it difficult to assess the persistence of cultural elites under political attack, here, too, autonomy based on social differentiation persists. Groups that could be expected to carry high culture maintain considerable social insulation, which stems from their unique training and jobs (and related differences in religion and family background). The separate worlds of work multiply.

2. Nevertheless, cultural uniformity grows—Even without the obliteration of social differences, modern society tends toward cultural standardization—a widespread sharing of beliefs, values, and tastes, cross-cutting groups and categories.The forces at work are well known: popular education and mass literacy; high rates of social and residential mobility; the emergence of national markets and a national politics, both making use of nationwide media of mass communication and entertainment. Of course rich countries vary in the level of these modern developments and none has yet experienced their full impact. Even in the richest of them all, the United States, a really mass education system has existed for less than two generations,[12] hardly time for its cultural influence to be felt. Nevertheless, it seems likely that on its production side, modern society displays increasing diversity of structure; on its consumption and leisure side, increasing standardization of culture.

3. Structure and Culture Change at Varying Rates in All Societies, but Their Independent Variation is Greatest at the Highest Levels of Modernization—The relevance here is that "mass culture" (and its correlates, standardization and fluidity of tastes in consumption and media content) can vary independently from "mass structure" (in which the mass lack firm ties to the social order and are easily mobilized into mass movements). This follows from my first two assumptions—the simultaneous growth of structural differentiation and cultural uniformity. In fact, the closest meshing of mass society and mass culture may appear neither in modern pluralist countries nor in modern totalitarian countries but instead in the new nations of Africa and Asia, where demagogic politicians, on radio, on television, in the village square, inveigh against imperialists and colonialists, manipulating a population torn loose from traditional tribal ties. As Shils suggests, "the availability of the media of mass communication is an invitation to their demagogic use—even more pronouncedly so where the populace is illiterate and scattered in many not easily accessible villages, and where there is the belief that the members of the populace must be 'mobilized' for the progress of the country."[13] Where intellectual elites have achieved only embryonic development, the prominence of modern communications also means that all culture, as it moves away from traditional patterns becomes mass culture.

The characteristics of mass society and mass culture exist in some degree in every country undergoing rapid social change, but they are most compatible in the emerging nations, however they may blend with traditional ways of life. Because the level of economic and political development conditions the effect of "mass" structures on mass culture and high culture, we cannot assume any straight-line trend from simple, poor, and non-massified, to complex, rich, and massified.

4. Not only are structure and culture divergent in modern society as it has thus far developed, but *there is considerable independence among the separate institutional spheres.* Behavior in the aesthetic-recreational sphere as well as in the political sphere may for some time remain isolated from that in the economy and the locality. In my study I assumed the independent variation of patterns of work, social participation, exposure and response to mass culture, and vulnerability to mass politics; I took as problematic the conditions under which their influence is reciprocal. My data show that a modern population can display fluid politics or high susceptibility to media manipulation, propaganda, and advertising, and yet simultaneously evidence stable patterns of social relations at work and in the community. And for some men the gap left by impoverished social relations is filled by vicarious participation in television programs, vicarious involvement with media heroes, a symbolic sharing in the national non-political life which acts to constrain both apathy and mass politics. The data also demonstrate, however, that much behavior spills over from one sphere to another, and therefore are consistent with my fifth assumption.

5. *There is in the long run a strain toward consistency (1) among values and beliefs in diverse institutional spheres;*[14] *(2) among behavior patterns in diverse spheres; (3) between culture and social structure.*

The congruence of values in spheres as diverse as kinship, politics, and aesthetics—e.g., "idealistic" and "authoritarian" political values and child-rearing philosophies as reflected in literature—is well illustrated in a careful, sophisticated content analysis of the 45 most popular new plays in Germany and the United States in 1927.[15] In 44 per cent of the 45 German plays and only 4 per cent of the 45 American plays, *"idealism"* was a basic theme: a central character, standing above the masses, pursues high principle and is compelled to sacrifice conventional morality (as is the case of the patriot who, for the sake of his country, murders his beloved). The level of action was 51 per cent *ideological* in Germany, 96 per cent *personal* in America: the American hero must struggle against immoral or antisocial tendencies in himself or in others which block the achievement of personal happiness; the German hero, pursuing an ideal goal, must struggle against the normal practices of society itself. Personal ambitions and satisfactions, expressed within the bounds of conventional morality, are positively sanctioned in the American plays; such strivings are often portrayed as the root obstacle in the German plays, the "materialism" and "Philistinism" against which the idealist must fight. Literature and art are not mirror images of society, but in the rare case where the data are most solid and comparative, the congruence is striking.

Concerning consistency of behavior in the diverse spheres of modern life, a nation probably cannot forever have both high rates of mass behavior in consumption and low rates in politics (Britain) or rate low on mass consumption and high on mass politics (France). I assume that mass behavior in politics, consumption, and media exposure are correlated—that voting for Ike's personality is like responding to undiscussed gasoline ads, and the two can reinforce one another. Data reported elsewhere support this notion.[16]

Similarly, with respect to the congruence of structure and culture, I assume that a modern nation cannot forever have both an elite educational system and continued growth in mass culture (as in France, where the paid circulation of the Reader's Digest now exceeds a million, which, in proportion to population, is almost a third of its penetration in the United States), or high rates of mobility and stable, insulated leisure styles (class sub-cultures in Britain, ethnic sub-cultures in America). And the formulation sometimes advanced by students of American culture[17] that we have made progress by moving on from a concern with "politics" to a concern with "culture" and "conformity," obscures the most interesting challenge —to discover the complex connections between them. Mr. Minow's travail suggests that cultural homogeneity is rooted in the political structure as well as the market place.[18]

Thus, we may assume that the influence of mass education, the media, and the centralized state will in the long run overcome the influence of variations in work, religion, age, and locality as sources of cultural values and leisure styles and we can expect mass culture in both Europe and America to penetrate structures now more or less insulated from it.

Educational institutions are strategic in linking structure and culture and the diverse institutional spheres. The education system is locality bound, but brings wider worlds to view; its curricula are highly differentiated, reflecting the specialized occupations for which it trains youngsters, but it is the central transmitter of core values and beliefs. Universities and colleges are the main source of what high culture there is, and to some extent they innoculate against mass culture; at the same time mass education uses the media, incorporates them into its content and technique and helps train the next generation in a style of leisure permeated by the great din of the media.[19]

Clearly, to understand the impact of abundance on culture and the limits and possibilities of public policy in overcoming cultural uniformity, we need to contrast the cultural life of countries whose governments differ in policy regarding education and the media of mass communication.[20]

Social Structure, High Culture, and Mass Culture: An Empirical Approach

Let us apply the larger debate about modern society to the mass media and mass entertainment in America. We must first grasp the fact that the mass media are the core of American leisure and that television has become the core of media exposure. The sheer arithmetic is striking. Nine in ten American homes average five to six hours daily with the TV set on. And it is not just turned on; it is generally being watched. Eight in ten Americans spend at least four hours a day viewing television, listening to the radio, or both.[21] Additional time goes to reading newspapers and magazines.

The trend is up. An increasing fraction of the daily routine is devoted to the products of the mass media. Mainly due to the rise of television. the media together and on the average now take up almost as much time as work; substantial minorities log more hours a year in TV viewing alone than in working.

Both cause and consequence of this trend is the development of an enormous machinery of promotion. Today, our outlays for advertising are almost equal to our current expenditures on public schools (elementary and secondary)—about 11 billion annually.[22] Additional billions go to PR and the like. The more abundance, the more activity to increase the desire for it.

So far we are on safe ground. The size of this frenzied promotion effort and the astonishing amount of exposure are well known. The *impact* on the quality of American culture, however, is difficult to judge.

In tackling the problem I have tried to be specific: in approaching the *standardization* of culture I have looked for media exposure and response cross-cutting social classes, educational levels, age grades, and religious and nativity categories. In handling the *heterogeneity* of culture I have searched for variations in media exposure and response with special attention to structural facts obscured by these traditional categories of sociological analysis—e.g., the quality variations within broad levels of education; the variations in tasks, work schedules, occupational groups, workplaces, and job patterns within broad occupational strata. The picture that emerges is more complicated than the assertions and counter-assertions of theorists and critics, but it is also a more realistic reflection of modern life.

I will first present findings bearing on the structural roots of cultural heterogeneity, and then findings that suggest the perhaps more powerful roots of cultural uniformity. I will draw from data on the quality of media exposure among 1,354 men ranging from highly-educated professors, lawyers, and engineers and executives matched for age and income, through a cross-section of the lower middle and upper working classes (the "middle mass") of the Detroit area, and down through 186 men unemployed and on relief.[23] We listed all their favorite TV shows, periodicals and newspapers read regularly, and all books they could name which they had read in the last two months. We then classified each program, each magazine, and each book in three "brow" levels—high quality, trash, or neither.

In coding for quality we were tolerant. The aim was to classify according to some fixed aesthetic standard, applicable to the medium, the more-or-less best performances and the clearly worst. Thus, the bias was that of Gilbert Seldes' *Seven Lively Arts*—sympathetic to the media. The product does not have to be aggressively educative to get by as highbrow, but if it is drama, the contrast is "Playhouse 90" vs. the most stereotypical detective, western, and adventure shows; if it is a paperback mystery, the contrast is Agatha Christie or Chandler vs. Spillane.

On *television programs* our staff made an effort to keep in touch with critical opinion and pooled judgments.

On *books, periodicals,* and *newspapers,* we compiled an initial classification and checked with experts. For the book code, for instance, two English professors reputed to have opposing views about the modern novel independently agreed on 97 per cent of the 200-odd high-quality titles. (That this code, like the others, is tolerant is suggested by the reaction of a literary critic who judged that perhaps half of the highbrow books would better be labeled "middling" or "upper middle;" clearly the list would not withstand the scrutiny of a Dwight MacDonald. But by that token it has the advantage of not understating the fallout from the "cultural explosion" as it appears in these samples—which, as it turned out, was scanty.)

In general these codes do *not* reflect a snobbish understatement of quality exposure, and there is less disagreement at the extremes than one would expect.[24]

To establish the coherence, independence, and economy of my measures, I combined all samples and carried out two factor analysis—one of the content, social context, and psychological functions of exposure; the other, of media uses as part of leisure style. A resulting factor from each analysis will be used as a dependent variable below.

1. "Much exposure to poor TV" is a strong factor (12 per cent of the variance) in the media analysis. It is defined by: (*1*) high number of hours per week of television viewing; (*2*) many westerns as "favorite TV programs—the ones you almost always watch;" and (*3*) many detective and adventure programs as favorites. These defining items not only go together in the media experience of our 1,354 men but they are independent of such other factors as "privatized TV-viewing," "vicarious participation via television," and a variety of uses of print. The men who score high here are neither ardent sports fans nor devotees of panel, quiz, giveaway, audience participation, and general entertainment shows. But so far as one can become involved with the western-detective-adventure triumvirate, these men are: when they watch, they watch with others; when they are away from home they are likely to discuss television often with friends or relatives.

2. *"Low leisure competence"* (*or "compulsive absorption of much poor TV as a time filler"*) is a strong factor (22 per cent of the variance) in the analysis of leisure style, which included data from all areas—social participation, consumption, politics, as well as media exposure and response. It is defined by (*1*) much exposure to poor TV (above); (*2*) absorption of media, especially television, into groups beyond the nuclear family; (*3*) compulsive TV-viewing (when watching he often feels he'd rather do something else, but he just can't tear himself away); and (*4*) much restless, aimless, aggressive leisure (he "blows his top" often, does a great deal of aimless Sunday driving, says he would not watch TV more if the day were 26 hours long, but meanwhile names the late show or the late-late show as TV favorites).

Other correlates of this factor are: *deviance* (the man who is low in leisure competence is likely to be a McCarthyite, a cross-class identifier, have a deviant perception of his standard of living—i.e., he is a blue-collar worker who thinks he is better off than office workers or a white-collar worker who thinks he is worse off than blue-collar workers—and he hangs on to his cars longer than most people); *leisure malaise* (often feels he has time on his hands, doesn't know what to do with himeslf); subjectively *weak attachments to secondary associations* and *fluid friendships;* and, as I shall show below, a *short work week.*[25]

The most precise summary phrase I can think of to describe the psychology of this leisure style is, "coping with restless malaise by an unsatisfying retreat to violent, escapist television." Students of the media who stress the absorption of television into the warm bosom of family and peer group should ponder what is being absorbed most effectively by whom with what effect.

Other, simpler measures of media behavior will be self-evident as I use them. I now turn to the sources of variation in the quality of exposure.

Structural Roots of Cultural Heterogeneity—The paradox of structural differentiation and cultural homogeneity is in part a spurious product of our weak concepts and measures of the attributes of social organization. If we pinpoint the groups and events that grip men in the daily round, some of the cultural phenomena which at first blush appear standardized turn out to be somewhat differentiated.

This can be seen in an analysis of the sources and correlates of (1) the number of media areas (television, newspapers, magazines, books) in which our respondents were exposed to any high-brow material and (2) their score on "much exposure to poor TV." In each case, 17 variables were related to these two media exposure variables. (See Table 1.) To determine the relative effect of each variable and to locate the incidence of high- and low-brow exposure within each class of each variable, I used a regression technique called "multiple classification analysis" which permits the use of non-continuous variables like religion and does not assume linearity in their effect (see APPENDIX ON METHOD).

Only 85 of these men were exposed to any high-brow material in three or four areas; 157 score in two areas, 305 in one; 807 men reported no quality exposure in any area. At the other extreme 138 men reported very high exposure to poor TV—25 and 30, even 35 hours of westerns, detectives, and adventure programs a week; 524 have medium scores; 692 avoid large doses of this type of program.

Although the main story is the general scarcity of quality exposure, which I will explore in detail later, Table 1 tells us something important:

Table 1—Rank Order of 17 Sources and Correlates of Quality of Media Exposure and Adjusted Means for Subclasses in a Multiple Classification Analysis[b]

| | | Quality of Media Exposure | | | |
| | | NO. AREAS HIGH-BROW | | MUCH EXPOSURE TO POOR TV | |
	N	Adjust. Mean	Rank as Predictor	Adjust. Mean	Rank as Predictor
I. Pre-Adult Socialization					
A. Generation American, Religion, and Status of Religious Preference					
Protestant					
Above average status of religious preference and four grandparents born in U.S.	98	.752		49.046	
Above average status of religious preference and three or fewer grandparents born in U.S.	133	.807		49.454	
Average or below average status of religious preference and four grandparents born in U.S.	144	.719		48.779	
Average or below average status of religious preference and three or fewer grandparents born in U.S.	217	.702		49.239	
Catholic					
Average or below average status of religious preference and four grandparents born in U.S.	70	.895		49.608	
Average or below average status of religious preference and three or fewer grandparents born in U.S.	351	.700		49.990	3
Jewish	77	.922		48.337	
No Preference	66	.943	2	49.774	

Table 1—(Continued)

	N	Quality of Media Exposure			
		NO. AREAS HIGH-BROW		MUCH EXPOSURE TO POOR TV	
		Adjust. Mean	Rank as Predictor	Adjust. Mean	Rank as Predictor
B. Early Farm Isolation (number of years lived on farm, nature and number of activities while in school, and teen-age club memberships)[a]					
Non-farm activist (40–49)	693	.772	17	49.754	4
Mixed farm-non-farm, isolation-non-isolation (50–59)	373	.751		49.093	
Much farm isolation (60–79)	90	.710		48.105	
C. Level and Quality of Formal Education (degree of exposure to liberal arts)					
Less than high school graduate	235	.278		53.004	1
High school graduate	255	.303		52.391	
Some college (1–3 years)	124	.409		50.745	
Baccalaureate degree, low quality	173	.722		48.344	
Baccalaureate degree, high quality	63	1.040		46.865	
Graduate or professional degree, low quality	152	1.502		44.805	
Graduate or professional degree, high quality	154	1.729	1	44.707	
II. Work Context, Schedule, and Attachment					
A. Size of Workplace					
Less than 49 employed	249	.655		48.475	
50–499 employed	194	.748		49.558	
500 or more employed	543	.940	3	49.306	
Self-employed	170	.337		50.950	2
B. Work Schedule					
Has orthodox work schedule	1039	.767	15	49.547	7
Has deviant work schedule	117	.696		48.206	
C. Long Hours: Chooses Work Over Leisure (many hours per week and weekends, and has control over work schedule)[a]					
Short work week (30–49)	575	.660		49.626	8
Medium work week (50–59)	446	.812		49.464	
Long work week (60–69)	135	1.013	4	48.320	
D. Work Alienation					
None	979	.755		49.362	
Some	126	.728		49.401	
Much	51	.928	10	50.377	13
III. Age, Aspirations, Mobility, and Career					
A. Age of Respondent					
21–29	121	.609		50.196	6
30–39	478	.818	6	49.710	
40–55	557	.744		48.981	
B. Worklife Mobility Pattern					
Up	385	.726		48.967	10
Stable	420	.776		49.672	
Fluctuating	335	.780	14	49.650	
Down	16	.727		48.238	

Table 1—(Continued)

	N	Quality of Media Exposure			
		NO. AREAS HIGH-BROW		MUCH EXPOSURE TO POOR TV	
		Adjust. Mean	Rank as Predictor	Adjust. Mean	Rank as Predictor
C. Intergenerational Climbing of Couple (Respondent's father's occupational stratum → respondent's; respondent's father-in-law's occupation → respondent's; and educational level of respondent compared with father's)[a]					
Much status loss of couple (20–39)	99	.695		50.131	12
Little or no status loss of couple (40–49)	407	.753		49.327	
Some status gain of couple (50–59)	484	.800	9	49.347	
Much status gain of couple (60–69)	166	.700		49.375	
D. Occupational Aspirations (past, present, and for the next generation)[a]					
Low aspirations (30–39)	52	.670		48.659	
Medium-low aspirations (40–49)	398	.737		49.450	
Medium-high aspirations (50–59)	505	.778		49.466	16
High aspirations (60–69)	201	.784	13	49.390	
IV. Participation, Community Attachment, and Miscellaneous Leisure Correlates					
A. Primary Range (index of range of values, interests, and status levels represented by relatives, neighbors, friends from workplace or in same line of work, and other friends.[a]					
Low primary range (00–04)	158	.706		49.006	
Medium primary range (05–12)	764	.738		49.500	15
High primary range (13–19)	234	.867	8	49.395	
B. Effective Mediating Attachments (much time and wide range of contacts in formal assns.; numerous assns. clearly attached to; and high political affect and strong mediation of campaigns)[a]					
Weak mediating attachments (30–39)	183	.766		49.391	
Medium-weak mediating attachments (40–49)	251	.778	12	48.966	
Medium-strong mediating attachments (50–59)	492	.775		49.443	
Strong mediating attachments (60–79)	230	.702		49.844	11
C. Community Attachment, Good Citizen Style (voted in recent elections; voted for school taxes; gives high percentage of family income to churches and charity; feels neighborhood is "real home" and reasons show local attachment)[a]					
Weak local citizen (30–39)	61	.820	7	49.310	
Somewhat weak citizen (40–49)	354	.792		49.370	
Somewhat strong citizen (50–59)	676	.760		49.478	17
Strong local citizen (60–69)	65	.531		49.030	

Table 1—(Continued)

	N	Quality of Media Exposure NO. AREAS HIGH-BROW Adjust. Mean	NO. AREAS HIGH-BROW Rank as Predictor	MUCH EXPOSURE TO POOR TV Adjust. Mean	MUCH EXPOSURE TO POOR TV Rank as Predictor
D. Leisure Malaise: Time on Hands					
Never have time on hands	610	.793	11	49.009	
Not very often	461	.720		49.743	
Fairly or very often	85	.741		50.500	5
E. Leisure Style as a Status Criterion: Taste (mentions manners and speech, books, music and art, and refinement of taste in defining class differences)[a]					
Few references to taste (40–49)	376	.692		49.411	
Some references to taste (50–59)	649	.754		49.520	14
Many references to taste (60–69)	131	.985	5	48.871	
F. Leisure Style as a Status Criterion: External Symbols (mentions houses, amount of money, clubs and organizations, and clothing in defining class differences)[a]					
Few references to external symbols (40–49)	637	.748		49.080	
Some references to external symbols (50–59)	425	.765		49.848	9
Many references to external symbols (60–69)	94	.817	16	49.678	
Total N	1156				

[a] Items are combined in a factor score; the cutting points for scores are in parentheses.
[b] For explanation see "Appendix on Method." For details on measures which are not self-explanatory, see text. For participation measures (e.g. of the range of values, interests, and status levels represented by the respondent's social relations) see "Orderly Careers . . . ," op. cit.

with sensitive measures of social position we can go far in explaining what cultural variation we do uncover. *The 17 variables explain over 46 per cent of the total variance in the number of areas in which quality exposure is reported and 25 per cent of the variance in exposure to poor TV.*

Both the measures and samples of the larger study were designed to permit projections of social and cultural trends in the affluent society based on comparisons of vanguard and rearguard groups at the same stage of the life cycle and the same social level. Does modernization increase the level of education? Then compare college graduates of growing mass institutions with those of elite colleges, which produce a declining percentage of the educated. Does economic development bring rising levels of mass aspiration? Then compare the aspiring with the less aspiring. Does it bring the dominance of large, complex organizations? Then compare the self employed with men in work-places of various sizes and structures. Does it make for an uneven distribution of leisure? Then compare the long hours men with the short. Does modernization change the social composition of elites? Then compare established Protestant elites with rising Catholic populations.

My findings underscore the importance of education and the persistence of older bases of differentiation—descent (religion and nativity), age and work situation. When we really peg the meaning of these as indicators of social position and discover their variable effects, however, we cannot help but be struck with the difficulty of predicting their future functions for the maintenance or decline of cultural diversity.

The three top predictors of quality of exposure in both "number of areas of highbrow exposure" and in amount of poor TV are:

1. an index of level and quality of formal education which I interpret as degree of exposure to the liberal arts—by far the single most important variable in both cases;

2. an index of "generation American, religion, and status of religious preference;"

3. work context (size of workplace and self-employment status). The more education, and within educational levels, the higher the quality, the higher the level of taste. Among religious-nativity categories Jews, those with no preference, and established Catholics (four grandparents born in the U.S.) stand out in taste while the most ardent consumers of low-brow TV are Catholics of more recent American vintage (three or fewer grandparents born in the U.S.); however, two of those same high-brow categories—established Catholics and men with no preference—also produce more than their share of enthusiasts for the Western-detective-adventure shows. Jews and established high-status Protestants tend to avoid big doses of poor TV. As for work context, the good-taste categories are salaried men employed in big organizations; the poor-taste categories are self-employed or are employed in medium-sized workplaces. Long hours, a factor measuring choice of work over leisure, ranks fourth as a predictor of high-brow media exposure; short hours ranks eighth as a predictor of low-brow television exposure. Men 21–29 years old (all in the middle mass) stand out in low-brow exposure; men 30–39 stand out in high-brow exposure.

What can we make of such findings? We began with the macroscopic assumption that the division of labor, religious institutions, and age-grading systems persist as powerful sources of cultural differentiation and that mass education is a source of standardization. Now that we have pinpointed the effect of these variables, slicing things a bit finer, the picture is not so simple. Take one of our favorite sociological clues to social structure: education. Will rising education levels bring an upgrading of taste, or will mass education mean an efflorescence of *kitsch?* In answering such questions, the distinctions I have made are crucial.

Table 1 (variable I-C) reports the mean scores (for each of seven categories of education) for number of media areas in which the respondent reports any high-brow exposure and for much exposure to poor television. To take account of the increasing diversity of higher education,[26] the colleges and universities from which degree holders had graduated were divided into two quality levels. For professors, the top 20 graduate schools in the 1957 Keniston rating[27] were coded high quality, the rest, low. For lawyers and engineers, faculty in a position to reflect professional consensus were given the complete lists and asked to rank leading schools, second-line schools, and others. The ten leading and second-line law schools, and 17 leading and second-line engineering schools, were counted as high quality; the rest were coded low.[28] The aim, again, was to capture as much of the variation in exposure to the liberal arts as possible and to explore the cultural impact of the rise of mass education.

The main findings are these:

1. For the number of media areas in which high-brow exposure is reported, *amount* of education makes little difference from grade zero through "some college;" thereafter, both quality of education and sheer level count heavily. The biggest jump in mean scores is between baccalaureate level and graduate level (.462), but the difference between men with high- and men with low-quality undergraduate education (.318) is greater than the differences between less than high school vs. high school (an infinitesimal .025), high school vs. some college (.106) or even some college and low-quality baccalaureate degree (.313).

Ultimately the mere rise in the average education level will do little for the cultivation of taste in reading and in the broadcast media; what counts is the number who complete college, and especially the number fortunate enough to go through a few favored colleges.

2. For the avoidance of big slugs of poor TV, sheer level of education counts slightly more than quality, although the differences are tiny until we come to college populations. Here the three largest differences are between "some college" and the low-quality baccalaureate (2.401), high-quality baccalaureate and low-quality graduate school (2.060), and low-quality and high-quality baccalaureate (1.479).

In sum: when we conceptualize "education" even at this crude level of "exposure to the liberal arts" and devise measures to match, we can gauge the cultural impact of abundance with more precision. These data suggest that the rising average level of education will protect against enervating amounts of the very shoddiest media content but it will not cause large populations to break the mediocrity barrier. As for the graduates of quality institutions, they will decline as a percentage of the educated and, as I shall show below, their exposure to quality print has declined and perhaps will continue to decline as a fraction of their leisure routine.

A final demonstration of the ambiguous effects of education and of the structural roots of cultural heterogeneity is in Table 2, which shows the impact of the organization of work and the level and quality of education on "leisure competence." In modern economies, group propensity and opportunity to work vary greatly even among occupational groups at the same social level; Table 2 ranges my samples in columns according to the proportion of the group or stratum usually working 44 hours or less a week. You will recall that the measure of "low leisure competence" is a factor score tapping a style best described as the compulsive absorption of much poor TV as a time filler.

The table shows first that a simple structural fact—group schedules of work—is a powerful source of diversity in leisure style. "Low" leisure competence ranges from 17 per cent in long hours groups to 65 per cent in short hours groups. The underdogs are similar to short-hours engineers and blue-collar workers: 61 per cent score low competence. Within various work contexts, how does the education of the individual affect his leisure competence? Exposure to the liberal arts has a heavy effect, which increases with shorter hours. For instance, among the short hours groups, a high-quality bachelor's degree brings the low competence rate down to 25 per cent; a low-quality bachelor's degree yields 45 per cent incompetence; some college or less yields a whopping 73 per cent. The 343 men comprising that 73 per cent are the largest group and have the lowest rate of competence in the table. Among men not accustomed to the wider universe made available by demanding work, it takes a long, expensive education to avoid an impoverished life. For students of American culture who look forward to the leisure-oriented society, in which we retreat from work to the more diversified joys of ever-shorter hours, the moral is that those who have most leisure have least resources for its creative use.

Structural Roots of Cultural Homogeneity—So far I have asked, "who in all these samples is exposed to high culture and who avoids the very worst of mass culture?" I have not dealt with the *extent* of high-brow exposure, the effects of diverse *types of media,* and above all, the *interaction between high culture and mass culture.* How much do men who could be expected to have cultivated tastes expose themselves to high culture? To what extent are intellectuals insulated from mass culture? Which media of communication have most and least impact on the standards of cultural elites and educated laymen?

Not everything that is wrong with our intellectuals, as Shils reminds us, can be attributed to the media or to mass culture; high culture has always been precarious.[29] But what *is* new, unique to our time, is a thorough interpenetration of cultural levels; the good, the mediocre, and the trashy are becoming fused in one massive middle mush.

Structural trends in the organization of intellectual life are at the root of the problem; among *intellectuals* and their educated publics we see:

Table 2—Short-Hours Groups and Men on Relief Are Prone to Compulsive Absorption of Much Poor Television as a Time Filler; Groups on Long Work Weeks Display Higher Leisure Competence. Quality and Level of Education Increase Leisure Competence Most Among Short-Hours Groups

Group Propensity and Opportunity to Work:a	Long-Hours Groups			Medium-Hours Groups				Short-Hours Groups				Unemployed Underdogs on Relief			
Level of Education: Quality of Education:	PROFESSIONAL OR GRADUATE DEGREE			BA OR MORE		Some College or Less		BA OR MORE		Some College or Less					Sample
	High %	Low %	Total %	High %	Low %	%	Total %	High %	Low %	%	Total %	Negro %	White %	Total %	Total %
Leisure Competenceb															
High	89	78	83	64	55	33	42	75	55	27	34	33	43	39	47
Low	11	22	17	36	45	67	57	25	45	73	65	67	57	61	52
Total	100	100	100	100	100	100	99	100	100	100	99	100	100	100	99
N	(141)	(134)	(275)	(44)	(127)	(271)	(442)	(32)	(64)	(343)	(439)	(81)	(105)	(186)	(1342)

a. Long-hours groups are "Urban U." professors and all lawyers, solo or firm; only 17 to 22 per cent work 44 or fewer hours per week. Medium-hours groups are "Church U." professors, Unico engineers, and white-collar men of the middle mass, any age; 32 to 38 per cent have short work weeks. Short-hours groups are Diversico engineers, blue-collar men of the middle mass, any age; 52 to 59 per cent work short work weeks. Men on relief provide extreme contrast.

b. A factor score: 47 men scoring 20–30 on "Low Leisure Competence" and 599 scoring 40–49 were combined to form the high competence; 89 men scoring 60–79 and 619 men scoring 50–59 comprise the low competence category. Twelve unemployed in the middle mass are excluded from this table. For details on measures, see text.

large numbers, spatial scattering, intense professional specialization, and a loss of a sense of autonomy and intellectual community (America, with more college graduates than any other nation in the world, does not have a first-rate intellectual weekly like the *Observer* in Britain). For both *intellectuals and the general population*, as I have suggested earlier, the cultural atmosphere is permeated by the mass media.

These are all in some measure requisites or consequences of abundance. Hundreds of thousands, eventually millions, of specialized experts and intellectuals are indispensable in a complex society. And the spread of higher education to the average man is both a manpower requirement of modern economies and a great achievement in equality.

The problem is not that the taste of the masses has been debased, but rather that the creators and maintainers of high culture in the humanities, the arts, the sciences, have an increasingly difficult time doing their proper work. Intellectuals are increasingly tempted to play to mass audiences and expose themselves to mass culture, and this has the effect of reducing their versatility of taste and opinion, their subtlety of expression and feeling.

There is little doubt from my data as well as others' that educated strata—even products of graduate and professional schools—are becoming full participants in mass culture; they spend a reduced fraction of time in exposure to quality print and film. This trend extends to the professors, writers, artists, scientists—the keepers of high culture themselves—and the chief culprit, again, is TV.[30]

You will remember that media researchers emphasize the limited power of mass communications by invoking the idea that the audience sorts itself out according to predisposition. By that formula, we should find the highly-educated listening to Gerry Mulligan, watching Channel 9, and reading the *Partisan Review* (or at least *Harper's*); and the less educated should be listening to Elvis Presley, watching "Gunsmoke," and reading *True Detective*. The evidence is that the educated display, on balance, a mild tendency toward more discriminating tastes.

Studies consistently demonstrate that college graduates compared to the less educated have somewhat less exposure to the broadcast media, which are more uniform in their content, and somewhat more to print, which is more diversified. They are a bit more choosey in the regular programs they watch on television; they definitely read more quality magazines and newspapers; and they listen to more serious music.[31] Table 3, emphasizing the efforts of educational and occupational groups to be selective in their use of newspapers, periodicals, and television, confirms this picture. For instance, over two-fifths of the professors, a third of the lawyers, and a tenth of the engineers compared to one in a hundred of the middle mass and none of the underdogs read a quality newspaper. And in reading the newspaper, the professional groups are somewhat more cosmopolitan and serious; they include world and national news as sections important to them more often than do the middle mass or underdogs. Similar differences appear for quality magazines read regularly. But the differences in exposure to print among my samples, as well as those in other studies based on broader samples, are not great. Table 3 deliberately reports measures yielding the largest differences in media exposure one can get. Even here, if we pinpoint the groups and take interest in political news as a clue to wider perspectives, the most privileged, well-educated firm lawyers have only a 10 per cent edge over the middle mass; and engineers are about the same as lower white-collar workers. In his interest in world news, the solo lawyer has only a 7 per cent edge over the younger blue-collar worker. The differences in the proportion of diverse groups who rank local news as important to them in their daily reading are similarly small.[32]

Even more uniform from group to group are media habits tapped by more subtle measures of involvement with mass culture not shown in Table 3—being a loyal rooter for sports teams, rating comics as an important daily experience, becoming deeply involved with media heroes. And when we come to television, at least in America, the constraint of structural differentiation seems doomed: uniformity of behavior and tests is the main story. Nowhere else has a "class" audience been so swiftly transformed into a "mass" audience.

A recent nationwide survey of TV-viewers, sponsored by CBS, reports that those with more than four years of college average about 3 hours a day of viewing compared to the 4.3 hours of those with only grammar school education.[33] Admitted prime-time viewing is unrelated to education. When the CBS survey asked them to name their favorite programs (those watched regularly), over half of those at the top of the educational range named light entertainment shows, the overwhelming preference of everyone else. Comedy, variety, and action (i.e., western, adventure, crime, police, private eye)—these were only slightly less common favorites among the college educated than among the less privileged.

Unfortunately, the actual record of viewing—in diaries, for instance—reveals even fewer differences.[34] Education has a lot more to do with how people *feel* about TV than what they *do* with it. College graduates criticize TV programming, but they choose to watch extensively, and in doing so, find themselves in Mr. Minow's wasteland, unable, because of the limited high-brow fare available, to exert much more selectivity than the general population. They clearly display more signs of guilt and uneasiness at this state of affairs, but apparently it's not so punishing that it makes them flick the dial to "off."

Perhaps the most telling data demonstrating the interpenetration of brow levels, not merely in television viewing but also in reading, come from my sample in the Detroit area. Most of those who read at least one high-brow magazine, also read middle- or low-brow magazines. Only

Table 3—Efforts to be Discriminating in Media Exposure, by Occupational Group and Stratum, in Percentages

| | LAWYERS | | | PROFESSORS | | | ENGINEERS | | | Middle Mass | | | | | UNDERDOGS | | |
| | | | | | | | | | | AGE 21-29 | | AGE 30-55 | | | | | |
N	Solo (100)	Firm (107)	Total (207)	Church (31)	Urban (68)	Total (99)	Diversico (93)	Unico (91)	Total (184)	WC (69)	BC (54)	WC (251)	BC (304)	Total (678)	Negro (81)	White (105)	Total (186)
Daily Newspaper[a]																	
Reads at least one quality paper	22	50	36	26	50	42	10	12	11	0	0	2	1	1	0	0	0
Does not read a quality paper	78	50	64	74	50	58	90	88	89	100	100	98	99	99	100	100	100
Rating of "Serious" Content in Newspapers																	
Mentions world news as important	55	67	61	81	87	85	76	65	71	41	48	41	36	39	41	31	35
Mentions national news as important	66	84	75	68	85	80	76	65	71	52	33	43	36	40	28	33	31
Mentions local news as important	56	42	49	29	22	31	51	58	54	57	35	50	45	47	37	25	30
Mentions political news as important	40	29	34	61	62	62	23	24	23	10	9	24	18	19	4	6	5
No. of Quality Magazines Read Regularly[b]																	
Three or more	5	13	9	67	64	64	8	2	6	0	0	1	0	0	0	0	0
One or two	31	34	33	25	13	17	51	60	56	7	0	5	1	3	0	0	0
None	64	52	58	3	1	2	39	37	38	93	100	94	99	96	100	100	100
Missing data	0	0	0	3	22	16	2	0	1	0	0	0	0	0	0	0	0
Cultural, "Educational," Selected "Special" TV Shows																	
No favorite	72	58	65	42	51	49	66	70	68	83	83	75	83	80	96	91	94
One favorite	10	22	16	16	16	16	18	19	18	7	7	10	12	11	4	5	4
Two or more	18	21	19	42	32	35	16	11	14	10	9	15	5	9	0	4	2

Table 3—(Continued)

| | LAWYERS | | | PROFESSORS | | | ENGINEERS | | | Middle Mass | | | | | | UNDERDOGS | | |
| | | | | | | | | | | AGE 21-29 | | AGE 30-55 | | | | | | |
	Solo (100)	Firm (107)	Total (207)	Church (31)	Urban (68)	Total (99)	Diversico (93)	Unico (91)	Total (184)	WC (69)	BC (54)	WC (251)	BC (304)	Total (678)	Negro (81)	White (105)	Total (186)
Indiscriminate TV-viewing (lets whatever comes on the channel stay, from one show to another)																	
Never	55	64	60	74	60	65	28	29	28	28	41	37	29	33	15	19	17
Seldom	23	21	22	19	10	13	41	35	38	35	33	36	33	34	36	30	32
Occasionally, often, or almost always	17	11	14	6	7	7	12	23	17	17	9	11	15	13	16	19	18
Missing data incl. "no TV" and "never watches")	5	4	4	0	22	15	2	2	2	4	6	4	3	3	4	12	9
Clear Theme of Cultural Criticism Appears in the Interview																	
Clear cultural criticism	38	50	44	74	76	76	32	32	32	9	7	21	8	13	0	5	3
No clear cultural criticism	62	50	56	26	24	24	68	68	68	91	93	79	92	87	100	95	97

a. New York Times, Herald Tribune, Washington Post, Christian Science Monitor, Manchester Guardian, St. Louis Post-Dispatch, Wall Street Journal.
b. Includes 41 non-professional periodicals, plus major law reviews, professional journals of engineering societies, and, for professors, all learned and professional journals.

3 per cent of all these men read only high-brow magazines. How about books? *Among college-educated professionals, only one in four claimed to have read a high-brow book in two months.* Only about three in five of the professors and lawyers, the most highly educated, entirely avoid low-brow TV favorites. The typical professor crosses one or two levels of TV exposure. The engineers and executives, middle mass, and the under-dogs on relief are quite similar in their TV-viewing habits. Television, again, appears to be a powerful force for cultural standardization, since these groups include men making more than $100,000 and others who have been unemployed for years. The department chief at GM, his foremen, and the unemployed autoworker on relief are bound together in the common culture of Huntley-Brinkley, "Restless Gun," and Mr. Clean.

If we consider magazines, books, newspapers, and TV together, what portion of these groups are exposed to any quality product in more than two areas? The answer: a minority of each group. Forty-three per cent of the professors score high on at least one item in each of three or four areas, 13 per cent of the lawyers, 5 per cent of the engineers and executives, 1 per cent of the middle mass, none of the underdogs.

The fact that the professors did so well in this generally dismal picture encouraged me to carry out a special analysis of deviant cases—those who use print and television for enlightenment and stimulation, and seek the quality product for entertainment.

Portrait of the Media Purist—Who are the media purists—men who insulate themselves fully from mass culture? We could not find one case in 1,354 who was not in some area exposed to middle- or low-brow material. By relaxing the definition, however, we located 19 men who make rather heroic efforts to cultivate the best in the media. They either (1) report some high-brow exposure in all four media areas (magazines, books, newspapers, TV) *and* are exclusively high-brow in one or more reading areas; or (2) have no TV set or never watch TV, have some high-brow exposure in the three reading areas, and are exclusively high-brow in one reading area.

The characteristics of the 19 men suggest that one must be a very odd fellow in America to avoid mass culture. All but two were educated in high-quality liberal arts colleges and graduate schools or were educated abroad—a very rare pattern. In occupation, 16 were professors (13 of high rank, especially in the humanities, mathematics, and physics); three were prosperous corporation lawyers. As a group, the media purists have inherited higher occupational status than their colleagues (their parents tend to be established professionals and executives)—which suggests that it may take rather close family supervision over more than a generation to inculcate a taste for high culture. In religion they are more often Jewish or have no preference or are inactive Protestants. Several are intermarried or in other ways have experienced cultural discontinuity. In origin, training, and position, then, this group is at once high status and marginal.

What constitutes the style of life of media purists? In consumption, they are almost ascetic; among the professors, their relatively high incomes are spent only minimally for luxury possessions, homes, cars, vacations, or charity. They are apartment-dwellers more often than home owners. They tend to be ambitious, independent-minded, like to "go-it-alone." Their media exposure is not only more high-brow; it is more extensive.

Although these media purists stand outside American society ideologically, they are well-integrated socially and politically. As one would expect, they are to a man highly critical of the media. They are also generally estranged from the major power centers in the United States—except for the federal courts, Which they feel are doing an excellent job. In participation patterns, however, they belong to more organizations and are attached to more than their colleagues. The professors among them are almost all active, liberal Democrats; the lawyers are conventional, moderate Republicans.

In short, it takes such an unusual set of experiences in family, school, and career to produce a media purist that they are practically nonexistent.

Implications for Sociological Theory

In applying the larger debate about the shape of modern society to the mass media and mass entertainment in America, I have brought systematic survey data to bear on the problem of the interplay of social structure, mass culture, and high culture. I have tried to resolve the paradox of a simultaneous growth of structural differentiation and cultural uniformity by re-examining the structural roots of media exposure and response. These data point up the need for a merger of the main characterizations of modern society—"mass," "industrial," and "urban." Specifically, three lessons can be learned.

1. The sketchy treatment of mass culture in theories of the mass society and the very limited idea of the two-step flow of mass communications, which accents the healthy absorption of the media into local cultures, demand more sophisticated treatment of the social structures in which the media are received. My data suggest that we need to slice up social structure in ways that capture both the persistence of older divisions (age, religion, occupation) and the emergence of newer ones (the quality and content of education) and to do it more precisely than usual. To say "white collar" or "working class" is to obscure most of what is central to the experience of the person and the structure of society. To say "profes-

317

sional, technical, and kindred" captures more of social life but not much more. "Lawyer" and "engineer" move us closer to social reality, for these men develop quite different styles of life, rooted in diverse professional schools, tasks, work schedules, and organizational contexts. To say "independent practitioner" is to say even more, and finally, to particularize the matter with "solo lawyer" vs. "film lawyer" is to take account of the sharp contrasts in recruitment base (social origins, religion, quality of professional training), career pattern and rewards which divide the two.

In general, data both here and in other studies suggest that as predictors of life style variables—especially cultural tastes and ideology—sex, age, and social-economic stratum are far weaker than religion, type of education, work and career—variables that represent positions in established groups. The implication is clear: return to the study of group life.

2. Television, the most "massified" of the mass media, the one with the largest and most heterogeneous audience, has become central to the leisure routine of majorities at every level. The usual differences in media exposure and response among age, sex, and class categories—easy to exaggerate in any case—have virtually disappeared in the case of television. Even here, however, where we pinpoint social groups—an occupation supported by an occupational community, a religion buttressed by a religious community—some differences do remain. And among the printed media, where most competition prevails, the chance of such groups to stylize their uses of mass communications remains strong.

3. The paradox of the simultaneous growth of structural differentiation and cultural uniformity is thus partly a matter of our weak concepts and measures of social structure and our consequent failure to spot group-linked variations in life style. But it may also reflect the state of an affluent society in transition. In order to pin down the cultural impact of continued economic growth, we require data not now in hand. For countries at similar levels of economic development, having diverse cultural traditions and systems of education and communications, we need data on levels of mass taste, organization and self-conceptions of cultural elites, distance between educated and less educated in exposure to mass culture and high culture. Until we have such systematic comparisons, I will assume that structure and culture are congruent and massified in rapidly developing new nations and that they become increasingly *in*congruent at levels of development thus far achieved. Finally, as rich countries grow richer, homogenizing structures in politics, education, and mass communications combine with an already high level of cultural uniformity to reduce the hold of differentiating structures of age, religion, work, and locality, and bring about greater consistency of structure and culture—a new combination of "mass" society and "industrial" society, mass culture and high culture.

4. Many leads in my data point to the need for synthesis not only of

318

ideas about industrial society and mass society but also the ideas about pluralism and totalitarianism. I can here merely indicate the direction of these findings. Briefly, what takes place in the economy and the locality—work, consumption, and participation in formal associations—forms coherent styles of life, one of which I have come to label "Happy Good Citizen-Consumer." The style includes these pluralist-industrial traits: strong attachment to the community (supporting increased school taxes, contributing generously to churches and charity, thinking of the neighborhood as one's "real home," voting in elections); consumer enthusiasm (planning to buy or to replace many luxury possessions); optimism about national crises; a strong belief that distributive justice prevails (feeling that jobs are distributed fairly). It also involves long hours at gratifying work, little or no leisure malaise; wide-ranging, stable secondary ties and, to some extent, wide-ranging, stable primary ties—the very model of a modern pluralist citizen. But this benign pattern of work, consumption, and participation is independent of participation in and feelings about mass culture. And both happy good citizenry and the uses of the mass media are more or less independent of approaches to national politics—or at least go together in ways not anticipated in received theory. Thus, the good citizen-consumers tend to be unusually prone to personality voting (party-switching, ticket-splitting), dependent on the media for opinions on issues, susceptible to advertising and to mass behavior generally (e.g., they score high on a measure of susceptibility to manipulation by the media in politics and consumption). Men who have confidence in the major institutions of American society distrust "TV and radio networks"; men who trust the media distrust other institutions. Finally, men whose social relations are stable tend to have fluid party loyalties. *To be socially integrated in America is to accept propaganda, advertising, and speedy obsolescence in consumption.* The fact is that those who fit the image of pluralist man in the pluralist society also fit the image of mass man in the mass society. Any accurate picture of the shape of modern society must accommodate these ambiguities.

Appendix on Methods

To determine the relative effect of each variable and to locate the incidence of high- and low-brow exposure within each class of each variable, I used a technique of multivariate analysis ("multiple classification analysis") which is a simple extension of multiple correlation to situations in which the explanatory factors may be either membership in subclasses like religion or continuous variables divided into classes. The computer program was developed by Vernon Lippitt and the General Electric Company. The rationale is described in Daniel Suits, "Use of Dummy

Variables in Regression Equations," *Journal of the American Statistical Association*, 52 (December, 1957), pp. 548–551, and J. N. Morgan *et al.*, *Income and Welfare in the United States*, New York: McGraw-Hill, 1962, Appendix E. The main advantage is that no assumptions are made about the linearity of the effect. The main restriction is the assumption that the effects of various factors are independent or additive; interaction among the independent variables is ignored.

I dealt with this limitation by:

1. Eliminating variables with the most obvious overlap. Occupational group was eliminated because it is highly correlated with level and quality of formal education.

2. Running three- and four-variable cross tabulations where interaction effects might be likely. For instance, one such table shows that weak community attachment (IV-C), which ranks only seventh as a predictor of number of areas of high-brow exposure in Table 1, is strongly associated with high-brow exposure among men with graduate or professional degrees, especially those from elite schools; community attachment has little effect in other educational strata. Scoring low on "good citizen" strengthens the already strong relation between a good education and high-brow exposure; alienation from the local community goes with cultivation of the better products of print and television, and both are rooted in long exposure to the liberal arts.

3. As a further way to avoid reliance on the beta weights in the regression analysis I gave primary attention to the mean of each pattern of media exposure for each subclass of each variable. The several classes of one variable may together rank low as a predictor (II-D ranks 10th on "number of areas high brow") but one subclass based on a small N (51 cases of "much" work alienation) may be very deviant (much high-brow exposure, and, if we look at "Poor TV," much low-brow exposure, too).

Table 1 reports (*1*) the subclass means adjusted simultaneously for the effects of all the other variables and the intercorrelations among them; and (*2*) the rank order of the beta coefficients for 17 variables thought to be sources or correlates of media exposure. The categories, grand means, multiple correlation coefficients, variance explained, and "adjusted variance" for the two dependent variables follow:

Number of Media Areas in Which Respondent Reports Any High-Brow Exposure	Much Exposure to Poor TV (High Number of Hours of Viewing; Favorites Include Many Western, Detective, and Adventure Shows)
Index Number	Factor Score
0. None	40–49. Least poor TV
1. One media area	50–59.
2. Two	60–69.
3. Three	70–72. Most poor TV
4. Four	
$x = .760$	$x = 49.411$
$R = .698$	$R = .530$
$R^2 = .487$	$R^2 = .281$
$R_a = .682$	$R_a = .500$
$R_a^2 = .465$	$R_a^2 = .250$
$p < .001$	$p < .001$

Because my hypotheses here included work milieu and feelings about work, the underdogs and 12 unemployed men of the middle mass were eliminated, leaving 1,156 men for this regression analysis.

Subclass means above the grand mean represent more than the average number of areas of high-brow exposure (.760) or more than the average exposure to poor TV (49.411) for these 1,156 men; subclass means below that are below average. The importance of a variable can be judged both by its rank order and by the size of differences between subclass means and their deviations from the grand mean.

The interpretation can be illustrated by considering variable IV-D, "leisure malaise." The three classes of malaise rank fifth as a predictor of low-brow media exposure. The adjusted means tell us that, holding constant all other classes of all other variables, there remains a moderate difference of 1.491 between (1) the above-average amount of poor TV (50.500) of the men who "fairly often" or "very often" feel they have "time on their hands" when they're not at work and "just don't know what to do" with themselves, and (2) the below-average amount of poor TV (49.009) of men who report they "never" have time on their hands. This variable is a weak predictor of high-brow exposure, however; the men without malaise have only a slight edge in high-brow exposure.

Why is the difference of 1.491 in exposure to poor TV among malaise categories "moderate?" The difference is moderate compared to the difference, say, between the bottom and top classes of education (I-C), the leading predictor. There the subclass "less than high school" scores a very high average of poor TV (53.004) and the subclass "graduate or professional degree high quality" scores a very low average (44.707)—a difference of 8.297. The discussion of education in the text is based on differences in subclass means in Table 1; the cross-tabulation in Table 2, which uses a different measure of work context and another qualitative measure of television exposure, is consistent with the results of the regression analysis. For instance, the differences in adjusted means of the hours groups, variable II-C in Table 1, are larger between long and medium than between medium and short—the same pattern presented by percentage differences among hours groups in Table 2.

The present study represents an intensive search for cultural differences among subclasses; these differences, typically small, should not obscure the generally high absolute level of mass exposure in every subclass.

NOTES

1. Alexis de Tocqueville, *Democracy in America,* New York: Alfred A. Knopf, 1948, 2 vols.; Karl Mannheim, *Man and Society in an Age of Reconstruction,* London: Routledge & Kegan Paul, 1940.

2. Cf. William Kornhauser's treatment of "accessible elites" and "available masses" in *The Politics of Mass Society*, Glencoe, Ill.: The Free Press, 1959.

3. Cooley, Mayo, and their students emphasize the functions of primary groups in the maintenance of social order, and cite reasons for their declining functions and authority. Since the primary group is the training ground for good citizenship, its decline, they felt, would produce mass men who would produce a "mass society," "anomie," or "social disorganization." Charles H. Cooley, *Social Organization*, New York: Charles Scribner's Sons, 1927; Elton Mayo, *The Human Problems of an Industrial Civilization*, Cambridge: Harvard University Press, 1933, esp. pp. 122 ff. and *The Social Problems of an Industrial Civilization*, Cambridge: Harvard University Press, 1945, Chs. 2 and 5. Tocqueville, among other 19th-century observers, and Lederer, Neumann, and DeGré, among modern students of totalitarianism, tend to emphasize the functions of secondary associations in the maintenance of social order or democratic political systems, or both. Alienation from work, politics, and community, and a related susceptibility to mass movements, they argue, are mainly due to the weakness of independent organizations lying between the nuclear family and the state. Tocqueville, *op. cit.*; Emil Lederer, *State of the Masses*, New York: W. W. Norton, 1940; Franz L. Neumann, *Behemoth*, New York: Oxford University Press, 1942; and Gerard DeGré, "Freedom and Social Structure," *American Sociological Review*, 11 (October, 1946), pp. 529–536. Cf. Robert A. Nisbet, *The Quest for Community*, New York: Oxford University Press, 1953. Emile Durkheim was aware of the possible links of both primary and secondary groups to the level of social integration. He tended to stress the atrophy of primary group life as a source of anomie and expressed the hope that larger secondary associations (especially the occupational group or workplace) could emerge as new bonds of solidarity, new sources of civic virtue. *The Division of Labor in Society*, trans. by George Simpson, Glencoe, Ill.: The Free Press, 1947, pp. 1–31. (In later writings, Durkheim increasingly emphasized the second point.)

4. In evidence, the critics say, look at the following studies: Fritz J. Roethlisberger and William J. Dickson, *Management and the Worker*, Cambridge: Harvard University Press, 1939; Paul F. Lazarsfeld, Bernard Berelson, and Hazel Gaudet, *The People's Choice*, New York: Columbia University Press, 1948; Morris Janowitz, *The Community Press in an Urban Setting*, Glencoe, Ill.: The Free Press, 1952; Scott Greer, "Urbanism Reconsidered: A Comparative Study of Local Areas in a Metropolis," *American Sociological Review*, 21 (February, 1956), pp. 19–25; Marvin B. Sussman, "The Help Pattern in the Middle Class Family," *American Sociological Review*, 18 (February, 1953), pp. 22–28; J. Smith, W. H. Form, and G. P. Stone, "Local Intimacy in a Middle-Sized City," *American Journal of Sociology*, 60 (November, 1954), pp. 276–284; Charles R. Wright and Herbert H. Hyman, "Voluntary Association Memberships of American Adults: Evidence from National Sample Surveys," *American Sociological Review*, 23 (June, 1958), pp. 284–294; Daniel Miller and Guy E. Swanson, *The Changing American Parent*, New York: John Wiley and Sons, 1958; E. Katz and Paul F. Lazarsfeld, *Personal Influence*, Glencoe, Ill.: The Free Press, 1955; Michael Young and Peter Willmott, *Family and Kinship in East London*, Glencoe, Ill.: The Free Press, 1957; Joseph T. Klapper, *The Effects of Mass Communication*, Glencoe, Ill.: The Free Press, 1960; etc.

5. See Harold L. Wilensky and Charles N. Lebeaux, *Industrial Society and Social Welfare*, New York: Russell Sage Foundation, 1958, Ch. 5.

6. For an assessment of the evidence on the vitality of social participation

see Harold L. Wilensky, "Life Cycle, Work Situation, and Participation in Formal Associations," in R. W. Kleemeier (ed.), *Aging and Leisure*, New York: Oxford University Press, 1961 and "Social Structure . . . ," *op. cit.*; for an empirical study of the integrative potential of various types of social relations see Harold L. Wilensky, "Orderly Careers and Social Participation," *American Sociological Review*, 26 (August, 1961), pp. 521–539.

7. Cf. Philip Selznick, "Institutional Vulnerability in Mass Society," *American Journal of Sociology*, 56 (January, 1951), pp. 320–331; Bernard Rosenberg and David Manning White (eds.), *Mass Culture*, Glencoe, Ill.: The Free Press, 1957; and Kornhauser, *op. cit.*

8. See e.g., Klapper, *op. cit.*; and Raymond A. and Alice H. Bauer, "America, 'Mass Society' and Mass Media," *Journal of Social Issues*, 16 (1960), pp. 3–56.

9. Following Blumer and Wirth, the "mass" is a collectivity which is big, heterogeneous (dispersed geographically and cross-cutting many groups and sub-cultures), and socially-unstructured (comprised of individuals who do not share norms and values relevant to the situation—individuals who are unattached for a time, not in role, and can therefore behave in a uniform, undifferentiated way). Herbert Blumer, "Elementary Collective Behavior," in Alfred McClung Lee (ed.), *New Outline of the Principles of Sociology*, New York: Barnes & Noble, 1964, pp. 185 ff.; and Louis Wirth, "Urbanism as a Way of Life," *American Journal of Sociology*, 44 (July, 1938), pp. 1–24. On the public, see also Robert E. Park, *Masse und Publikum: Eine Methodologische und Soziologische Untersuchung*. Inaugural-Dissertation der Hohenphilosophischen Fakultaet der Ruprecht-Karls-Universitaet zu Heidelberg, Bern: Lack & Grunau, 1904.

10. A major theme in Kornhauser, *op. cit.*, a creative synthesis of literature on sources of extremism, is that totalitarian control depends on the institutionalization of "high availability" of the mass (p. 62). Totalitarian regimes deliberately atomize the mass (via forced migration, pudges, terror), but since mass behavior is unpredictable, they need to "keep the masses in a state of constant activity controlled by the elite" (p. 123) and so, these regimes take steps to remain with their subjects "one gigantic movement" (p. 62). Three questions about this argument may be raised. First, the implication that Bolshevik power, as a key case, depends on "massification" and the latter makes the regime vulnerable, runs counter to the apparent stability of Soviet society. Second, if totalitarian nations had to keep the masses in a constant state of mobilization, we would expect them to become increasingly terror-ridden. Although the variable use of terror thus far does not provide sufficient evidence on long-run trends, much totalitarian terror has seemed to give way to other means of control. Finally, the treatment of mass "availability" is tautological. Availability is indicated by (1) a high rate of mass behavior and (2) lack of attachment to independent groups. Here the hypothetical causes of mass behavior are confused with the idea of mass behavior itself (cf. 40–41, 61–62). I have dealt with this in my study by maintaining a distinction between mass behavior as particular acts in time an space (e.g., responding to a gasoline ad or a demagogue without reference to group norms) and persistent structures that presumably give rise to it (e.g., a pattern of impoverished social relations).

11. Within the general framework of a policy of strenuous intervention (even in strictly philosophical matters) the Soviet regime has alternated application and relaxation of controls over intellectual life. J. M. Bochenski in A. In-

keles and K. Geiger, (eds.), *Soviet Society*, Boston: Houghton Mifflin, 1961, pp. 454 ff. Despite these ups and downs, Soviet commitment to modernization has forced some liberalization. In the short run (e.g., during the period of maximum Stalinist terror) the regime can do pretty much what it likes with particular disciplines: it can wipe out genetics by persecuting Mendelian deviationists; it can proscribe quantum mechanics as inconsistent with dialectical materialism. But over the long pull, some disciplines stand up better than others. For instance, some disciplines once purged now flourish in relative freedom (linguistics, poetics); others do not (genetics, history, literary history and criticism, economics). To demonstrate such variable resistance, however, we would need data on the degree of vulnerability to the purge in each case (number put to death, imprisoned, removed from any office, removed from top office only, merely forced to recant, etc.) and on the persistence of each group beyond the purge (men and resources devoted to the discipline, quality of output, success of efforts to maintain autonomy). To demonstrate further that resistance to state penetration is a function of the pre-existing organization and tradition of the discipline as well as the indispensability of its contribution to Soviet power would require the same systematic comparisons.

12. Richard H. Bolt in a National Science Foundation study has analyzed numbers of baccalaureate and first professional degrees expressed as a percentage of the college-graduating-age cohort (median about 22 years). The ratio increased slowly from about 1.3 per cent in 1870 to about 2 per cent in 1910, and then increased roughly logistically to nearly 20 per cent by 1960. A similar acceleration of high school graduates had already markedly set in by 1900 and by 1960 high school graduates exceeded 70 per cent of the relevant age cohort. Unpublished manuscript, 1963.

13. Edward A. Shils, "Demagogues and Cadres in the Political Development of the New States," in Lucien W. Pye (ed.), *Communications and Political Development*, Princeton, N.J.: Princeton University Press, 1963, p. 67.

14. William Graham Sumner, *Folkways*, Boston: Ginn, 1906, pp. 5–6.

15. Donald V. McGranahan and Ivor Wayne, "German and American Traits Reflected in Popular Drama," *Human Relations*, 1 (1948), pp. 429–455.

16. Wilensky, "Social Structure . . ." *op. cit.* p. 21. Tabulations based on 678 interviews with a cross-section of white males in the middle mass (upper working class and lower middle class) of the Detroit area, aged 21–55, show that our indicators of susceptibility in advertising and politics are indeed correlated. We assumed that candidate switchers—Democrats who went for Ike, the (less numerous) Republicans for "Soapy" Williams—were responding to personality appeals in recent campaigns. Then we asked those who own cars and notice gas ads, if, when they hear claims made in these ads, they "ever try a tankful or so to see how true the ads are." We also asked everyone how often he had bought something because he saw it advertised and then found he'd been stuck. Among those who never completed high school (whatever their income), and among young high-school grads with low family incomes (in this sample that means $5,000–8,000), it is the loyal party men who try a tankful; but among the vanguard populations—higher-education, higher-income men—it is the candidate switcher or ticker-splitter who takes a flier, especially among middle-aged, upper-income, high school grads and young college men (whatever their income). Incidentally, these same college-educated Eisenhower Democrats report that they get stuck in the product market quite often. The link between mass behavior in consumption and politics is most visible among men of the future.

17. Winston White, *Beyond Conformity*, New York: Free Press of Glencoe, 1961, and the early writings of David Riesman.

18. If there is more independent variation of politics and culture in the United States than in other rich countries, it may stem from our greater gap between intellectuals and the government, the split that Tocqueville noted between intelligence and action. In several parts of Europe, notably Britain and Scandinavia, the media to some extent feel compelled to reflect the work of the intellectuals—the statesman, the educator, the serious artist. In the United States, the media reflect more the work of the businessman as advertiser, the artist as entertainer, the politician as demagogue; they are typically managed and staffed by anti-intellectual intellectuals. Cf. Reuel Denney, *The Astonished Muse*, Chicago: The University of Chicago Press, 1957, p. 216; and Richard Chase, *The Democratic Vista*, Garden City: Doubleday, 1958, *passim*.

19. The reciprocal influence of the mass media and mass education has received little serious attention. A few of the obvious possibilities are: (1) Extensive exposure in the home accustoms the child to visual and oral communication of the simplest sort; teachers and curriculum planners respond by using the media to make education more entertaining, using the child's television experience (e.g., current events) as the basis for class discussion—generally displacing time otherwise devoted to a more systematic treatment of history or geography. (2) The average college receives students unaccustomed to disciplined reading and adapts assignments and techniques accordingly. (3) In school and college alike, manners, morals, and speech are more subtly influenced—with self-display becoming a new ideal, and publicity-consciousness a new set of mind. The "show and tell" sessions of our elementary schools, like the audience participation and panel shows of television, combine both. Whether the post-Sputnik spurt in "hard" subjects (a product of Cold War competition) together with the oversupply of youngsters (a product of the changing age distribution, which increases competition for college entrance) will offset the penetration of mass culture into the schools is unknown. As all these forces converge, the cultural tests of the average college professor, like those of the school teacher, will weigh in the outcome.

20. For some lines of inquiry, see Pye, *op. cit.*

21. G. A. Steiner, *The People Look at Television*, New York: Alfred A. Knopf, 1963, pp. 4, 112; and citations in footnote 30 below.

22. Fritz Machlup, *The Production and Distribution of Knowledge in the United States*, Princeton, N.J.: Princeton University Press, 1962, p. 104.

23. The analysis is based on detailed interviews with probability samples or universes of six professional groups (100 solo lawyers; 107 firm lawyers in the 19 Detroit firms with ten or more partners and associates; 31 professors at "Church University;" 68 professors at "Urban University;" 91 engineers at "Unico" and 93 at "Diversico"—generally research and development specialists, supervisors, or executives); a probability sample of the middle mass (N = 678); and, as a sharp contrast, two samples of underdogs, 81 Negro and 105 white, who were severely deprived. The interviews took place in the first half of 1960. Only males who were in the labor force, 55 years old or younger, and currently or previously married were interviewed. All the professionals had college degrees. The special selection criteria are described in Harold L. Wilensky, "The Uneven Distribution of Leisure: The Impact of Economic Growth on 'Free Time,' " *Social Problems*, IX (Summer, 1961), p. 38; "Orderly Careers . . . ," *op. cit.*, pp. 529–530; and "The Moonlighter: A Product

of Relative Deprivation," *Industrial Relations*, 3 (October, 1963), pp. 106–108. It is important to note that the leading colleges and universities are well represented in the backgrounds of men in the professional samples. Three-quarters of the firm lawyers, for instance, are graduates of one of five elite "national" law schools—Chicago, Columbia, Harvard, Michigan, and Yale. Like the professors—full-time faculty in the humanities and physical sciences (including mathematics) in two arts and sciences colleges—these lawyers may be assumed to have had as much opportunity to acquire discriminating tastes as their counterparts in other cities.

24. Two independent studies, using impressionistic judgments to rank magazines, arrived at results so similar to one another (a rank order correlation coefficient of .93 for 49 magazines) that one is tempted to defend a ranking of the entire range, not merely the validity of three categories. Babette Kass, "Overlapping Magazine Reading: A New Method of Determining the Cultural Level of Magazines," in Paul F. Lazarsfeld and Frank N. Stanton (eds.), *Communications Research: 1948–1949*, New York: Harper, 1949, p. 133, Table 1.

25. These are items whose loadings on the Low Leisure Competence factor rank high, but which are either too weak or appear on two or more factors; they are sufficiently associated with the defining items to be taken as subsidiary meanings of the factor, but they may measure other phenomena as well. The results of this leisure style analysis are reported more fully in Harold L. Wilensky, *Work, Leisure, and Freedom*, New York: The Free Press of Glencoe, forthcoming. Correlation matrices were factor analyzed by the method of principal axes. Factors were rotated according to Kaiser's varimax criterion. In interpretation, loadings below 25 per cent of the average communality of the factors were ignored.

26. The most perceptive treatment is David Riesman, *Constraint and Variety in American Education*, Garden City, New York: Doubleday, 1958.

27. Hayward Keniston, *Graduate Study and Research in the Arts and Sciences at the University of Pennsylvania*, Philadelphia: University of Pennsylvania Press, 1959, p. 119.

28. Respondents are coded according to the highest degree attained. The category, "baccalaureate degree, low quality," includes 121 engineers plus the 53 men of the middle mass who have a degree; the 63 men with a high-quality baccalaureate are all engineers. I assumed that the best graduate and professional schools draw from the best liberal arts colleges.

29. Edward A. Shils, "Mass Society and Its Culture," *Daedalus*, 89 (Spring, 1960), pp. 288–314.

30. Any assertion about long-term trends is inferential; we lack good baseline data. My position rests on three considerations. First, there is scattered evidence that the broadcast media in competition with print generally win out—in attraction, number of hours, perhaps persuasiveness, too. Reading, especially of books and magazines, declines. T. E. Coffin, "Television's Impact on Society," *The American Psychologist*, 10 (October, 1955), p. 633; L. Bogart, *The Age of Television* (2nd ed.), New York: Frederick Ungar, 1958, pp. 133 ff.; James N. Mosel, "Communications Patterns and Political Socialization in Transitional Thailand," in Pye, *op. cit.*, pp. 184–228; and Klapper, *op. cit.*, pp. 107 ff. Second, among the educated, total exposure to broadcast media has recently increased. Before television, radio listening among set owners averaged 4.9 hours daily; evening listening averaged 2.6 hours for all, 2.4 hours for college graduates. Program preferences did not vary much by education. P. F. Lazarsfeld, *The People Look at Radio*, Chapel Hill, N.C.: The University of North Caro-

lina Press, 1946, pp. 97–98, 136. Today, even excluding highbrow FM, radio listening has not declined to zero. (The typical radio family that acquired a television set cut radio listening from four or five hours to about two hours a day. Bogart, *op. cit.*, p. 114.) Meanwhile, television viewing for the average product to a graduate or professional school rose from zero to three hours daily. Steiner, *op. cit.*, p. 75. If we assume no major increase in the work week of the educated, and no change in life style that can remotely touch television in sheer hours, their exposure to undifferentiated broadcast media has risen as a portion of the daily round while their exposure to serious print has declined. And the small differences in amount and quality of television exposure reported in the text indicate that the educated are not especially discriminating. Finally, the argument about the effect of intellectuals' participation in mass culture on their standards of performance and appreciation proceeds through example and counter example without the benefit of much systematic evidence. "Raymond Aron's thought," says Edward Shils, "does not deteriorate because he occasionally writes in the *New York Times Magazine*." *Op. cit.*, p. 306. Unfortunately, we cannot know what the quality of Aron's thought would have been if as a young man he had been watching "situation comedies" instead of reading books. As a master of ambiguous polemic, Shils presents the best defense of the view that mass culture has little effect on high culture; but in listing the structural forces that threaten high culture, he gives inadequate weight to them and no weight at all to the major problem we confront here—central tendencies in the life styles of educated strata.

31. Cf. Paul Lazarsfeld, *Radio and the Printed Page*, New York: Duell, Sloan, and Pearce, 1940; B. Berelson and M. Janowitz, *Reader in Public Opinion and Communication*, Glencoe, Ill.: The Free Press, 1953, Part 7; L. Bogart, "Newspapers in the Age of Television," *Daedalus* (Winter, 1963), pp. 116–127, and other essays in that issue; and the citations in footnote 30 above.

32. If you are inclined to use the British as a case on the other side, you will receive little support from Mark Abrams' careful study of the media habits of the socio-cultural elite of Great Britain. "The Mass Media and Social Class in Great Britain," paper presented at the Fourth World Congress of Sociology, Stresa, Italy, September, 1958. The upper 1 per cent in education and occupational status (from a random sample of 13,620 adults, aged 25 and over) reported media habits so similar to those of the mass public, that one is reluctant to use the label "cultural elite." More of them read the *Daily Express* and *Daily Mail* than the *Times* or *Guardian;* their movie habits—both in frequency of attendance and choice of films—are hardly differentiated from those of the rest of the population. The only real gap between mass tastes and elite tastes is the preference of the latter for no TV or BBC programs over commercial programs. A qualification is in order: while prestige dailies lag in circulation, good Sunday papers—the *Observer*, the *Times*, the *Telegraph*—show a marked increase. Further, the recent return to BBC of large television audiences once lost to commercial competition tells us that a speedy decline in mass tastes is not inevitable, although it does not challenge the proposition that the interpenetration of brow levels threatens high culture.

33. Steiner, *op. cit.*, p. 75.

34. *Ibid.*, p. 161.

7

Communication Audiences

THE FIELD of audience research includes not only those studies aiming at accurate description of the audience to various media, channels, or items of communication. In addition, it deals with the factors responsible for the types of communication exposure which do exist, as well as the motivations for seeing, reading, and listening. As in the case of public opinion measurement, there is a considerable body of literature on the technical aspects of audience research; and as in that case, we have not attempted to represent such technical matters here.

The first selection presents an overview of the structure of the American mass media audience. Gary Steiner, on the basis of national survey data, describes patterns of reaction of the American audience to television. Audience analysis also involves intensive study of the communication behavior of selected and especially elite groups. Raymond Bauer, Ithiel de Sola Pool, and Lewis Dexter, present an analysis of the media sources used by American businessmen to inform themselves generally and specifically about matters concerning international tariffs and trade. Communications audiences also involve international media and international organization in support of political objectives. Students of mass communication have set for themselves the task of analyzing the strategy and assumptions of such efforts. Barghoorn's study of Soviet foreign propaganda is a case in point where the structure of the audience is related to the propagandist's objectives and ideology.

GARY A. STEINER*

The People Look at Television

* Under a grant from the Columbia Broadcasting System, a national survey of 2,498 adults was conducted in 1960 on public attitudes toward television
by Gary A. Steiner. The following selection summarizes some of the main
findings on the structure of the television audience.

The "average American viewer"

THE AVERAGE AMERICAN VIEWER spends hours a day in front of his TV
set and finds it a relaxing and pleasant—now an integral—part of his daily
life: certainly not without important costs, but by and large, in his judgment, well worth them. TV's contributions to home life, on balance, are
somewhat more apparent than the other forms of family interaction it
may replace; and its advantages for the children and for him (especially
her), as parent, outweigh the dangers and problems it poses in this regard.

Though he has come to depend a great deal on routine, daily viewing
—or perhaps *because* he has—television is not often terribly exciting. In
the beginning, it was "really something to talk about"; today, the viewer
gives little evidence of extreme response in either direction. He is not
often overwhelmed by what he sees; nor is he often bored or disgusted.
When he does tend to use superlatives in his discussion of television, it is
less likely to be about the programs than about the good or evil that stems
from viewing *per se*.

The programs, on the whole, he considers good—somewhat better
than satisfactory; and among them he finds many favorites that are extremely enjoyable. There is no reservoir of specific unfulfilled desires; nor
does he find an oversupply or an imbalance in what the industry offers
him. Accordingly, he watches pretty much what happens to be on the

Reprinted from *The People Look at Television: A Study of Audience Attitudes*, (1963), pp. 228–236, by permission of the publishers and author. (Copyright, 1963, by the Bureau of Applied Social Research).

air, as he must do to sustain the number of hours he spends at it: how selective can one be when total consumption approaches a substantial proportion of what is available?

There have been some memorable serious moments in his viewing history, especially some original television dramas, but by and large he recalls the comedy stars that TV has made: Caesar, Gleason, Desi and Lucy, Berle, *et al.* And this, of course, is consistent with the principal use to which he now puts the medium—easy, relaxing entertainment. Accordingly, his favorites in the current season are most likely to fall into "action" and "comedy-variety" categories; he finds these shows entertaining, interesting, and relaxing—but by no means especially original or creative.

He would like TV to be more informative and educational but certainly not at the expense of entertainment. Aside from the day's news and weather—which he watches regularly—he rarely uses the set as a deliberate source of information, and he is extremely unlikely to turn on serious and informative public affairs presentations, even if he is watching while they are on the air.

All of this reflects the present division of labor between the various media. Television, among the home sources of mass communication, has its greatest comparative advantage in the field of entertainment. According to the average viewer, and no doubt in reality, newspapers presently provide more thorough reports of the important happenings on the local and larger scene; radio is quicker with frequent, capsule summaries; and magazines best provide for limited, specialized interests. It is television, and by a wide margin, that is turned to for relaxation and diversion.

This division is certainly not complete, but rather one of relative emphasis. Nor is it the necessary, *a priori* allocation of function: newspapers *could* carry more entertainment and television *could* devote more time to news and editorials. And if that occurred, there would probably be some shifts in what the public expects from these media and seeks in them. But this is where we stand at the moment.

TV brought moving sight-and-sound—the nation's number-one pastime for twenty years—from the theater into the living room, from fee to "free." It seems unlikely that a medium more restricted in its sensory dimensions will displace television as the principal source of mass amusement. Conversely, and by complement, print has clear advantages in the transmission of serious material that requires concentration or self-pacing.

The problems and frustrations that surround television in the average home are several. They deal principally with how the viewer regards himself and his use of the set. But there are two notable exceptions that deal directly with content:

1. The average viewer thinks that programs depict too much imitable violence that children see both in "their shows" and in those de-

signed for adults. This problem he places squarely on those in charge of programming. True, parental acquiescence is a necessary ingredient, he feels, but why should broadcasters put parents on that spot? There should be less need for vigilance to keep the children from potentially dangerous material, particularly since the parents usually enjoy and often benefit from the children's hours in front of the set.

2. He also thinks that there are too many commercials, and especially too many that are boring, repetitious, and/or irritating. Here, again, the responsibility is not that of the viewer; and he wishes that those in charge would do something to improve the situation.

But his most serious and pervasive hesitations are not so easily disposed of. They rest at home—precisely, in part, because *he* rests, so often and so long, at home.

Television wastes so much time! Which means, of course, that he often wastes time watching it. To watch TV is to be not "doing" anything, except relaxing; and to be doing nothing for so many leisure hours (and perhaps, for women, many "working hours") arouses some ambivalence.

There may be an inherent conflict between extensive and time-consuming "passive" amusement and the stress on achievement among mobile Americans. Television, unlike many other pastimes, does not come with a ready-made set of justifications. Golf is healthful; reading, admirable; sleep, restorative. Even liquor helps to combat those dangerous daily tensions. Keeping informed and learning something may be potential counterparts—but this particular ambivalence and its resolution reach greater significance in the case of the non-average, better-educated viewer, and we turn to him in a moment.

Some underlying "laziness" is not the only disquieting concomitant of daily viewing in the average American home. Many families have a sometimes vague, sometimes well-articulated feeling that television replaces other past or potential family activities. It does tend to keep them at home and together, but by the same token it curtails conversation, visiting, going out.

In addition, family viewing often creates conflict between what adults enjoy (and, in most cases, the children also) and what the parents think is good or appropriate for the youngsters. The issue is usually resolved in the predictable way; at the cost of some qualms about the "effects" on the children, and perhaps an accompanying annoyance at the broadcasters who provided the seductive but dangerous alternative.

But real as these and other hesitations are, they certainly do not overshadow the basic satisfaction that the television set provides. That was apparent from the beginning, in the ubiquitous and extensive consumption the medium enjoys. All things considered, television is among the most significant contributions to everyday pleasure that modern technology has produced. The average viewer would not give it up if he could—as, of course, he *could* if he wanted to. When the house is temporarily without television, as it sometimes is for mechanical reasons beyond his control, he sees to it that it is temporary indeed.

This average American viewer in the average American home is a concept of convenience, which enables us to summarize the most common patterns in personal terms. But he is not a statistical artifact, "average" only in the arithmetic sense: that is, he is not the result of adding an enthusiast to an indifferent viewer and dividing by two. He exists, and in the largest numbers.[1]

He has no more than a high-school education, an annual income of less than $8000, and he accounts for over three quarters of all television homes and a still higher percentage of the effective audience at any given time because he watches somewhat more often than those with higher social-economic standing. Thus, the thoughts and reactions we have attributed to him are broadly characteristic of the major segment of the American television audience.

2. *The average nonaverage viewer.* The higher-educated, higher-income, big-city viewer shares many of the above responses, but departs notably in others. In general, his verbal focus shifts visibly to the negative: he finds the same basic satisfactions in television but he takes its costs more seriously.

He too turns to television principally for relaxation and entertainment. More than the rest, he has other sources of serious information available to him—especially magazines—and only slightly more often than the common man does he select information from what is available when he watches. He too has been most impressed by the comic greats of past seasons and would like to see them return. He too watches a great deal of television—quite a bit less than the average, but that is still quite a bit. And he too generally finds the programs he watches "extremely enjoyable"; indeed, his own favorites get even more glowing praise than the mass audience lavishes on its own.

On the other hand, he is far less impressed with "television in general" and its "programs in general." Accordingly, he is especially likely to put great emphasis on the related issues of "productive" programming and selective viewing.

Selectivity is a matter of some importance in his personal approach to the subject of TV: he may claim a bit more than he exercises but probably no more than he would like to. He does tend to be attracted to specific, outstanding dramatic programs, but they account for an infinitesimal share of his television week. That, as with the average viewer, is devoted mostly to light entertainment.

Thus, his consistent call for more informative television is possibly the clearest finding with the least clear interpretation. To summarize the survey results is simple: the more educated and informed the viewer, the more education and information he says television should provide—to the point where this becomes the number-one criticism or suggestion of the number-one educational group.

But why does he say it, and what does he mean? Apparently not that he, personally, would like to see more programs like the present informational ones on the air. He has a long way to go before he comes close to exhausting those—even on the commercial channels, let alone the educational outlets. He takes little of the first and still less of the second, when he *has* the opportunity to do so.

Perhaps he means something else by information and education; something different, or better, than what now goes by that name. But if so, he fails to tell us about it when he has the chance. On the contrary, he often lists current informational shows as his favorites, and he has little else to suggest when we get to specifics.

Is it just a matter of response bias—of saying what is appropriate, approved, expected of a well-educated, sophisticated respondent? Probably in large part; certainly not entirely. There are at least two other possibilities.

First, he may be sincerely convinced that television should be more informative *beyond* the extent to which he himself needs or wants more enlightenment from it. Social, not personal criteria may be involved. Listen again to Academicus, for a clear exposition of the extreme position:

. . . precisely my complaint about the mass media arises from the fact that they do occupy the center of attention in America . . . television itself gets more hours of attention each week than anything but home and work, and perhaps it rivals them. You can't get people to think about the great values because they're watching TV. So the media *are* reaching vulnerable people who, from our standpoint, do not give attention to other things. With that huge slice of attention, then, goes responsibility for our values. And what values are they serving?"[2]

Academicus obviously watches little if any television himself, and certainly does not depend on it for serious information. His chief concern is with the social and cultural implications of so much television "escape" among the masses. To him, the country *need*s a more informative and educational schedule, as it needs speed limits, better public schools, and racial integration—not necessarily for his personal benefit or use, but for the common good when adopted by others.

This argument is not reduced to "hypocrisy" by the intellectuals' own neglect of TV information; in fact, it is entirely untouched by whatever they do or fail to do. If it is to be met, it must be met on its own ground; and we will give both sides a platform in the next section.

Or, his call may be for information *with*, not *instead of*, entertainment, so as to make his own relaxation more rewarding or at least more psychologically comfortable. Recall that, in large numbers, he refused to choose between the two and asked, instead, for "both"—for programs at once enjoyable and intellectually satisfying.

As a middle-class, striving American, he more acutely feels the need to spend time usefully than his less ambitious counterparts; and his formal schooling has placed a high value on reading and serious study. This combination attaches more than a little uneasiness to the hours he spends being entertained without effort by materials he regards of little intrinsic worth. "Waste," which probably tends to be an issue with him in many areas, seems especially evident here in the case of time, his most valuable resource.

If he could only learn something—historical, political, scientific, cultural—that would justify this otherwise unproductive use of time. Maybe he asks for "more information" partly out of the desire for such a justification.

There is at least some evidence in that direction: first, in the widespread agreement that TV is educational for children—which increases with parental schooling only among those who admit to using the set as a baby-sitter; secondly, in the far greater intellectual benefits the educated viewer already attributes to his favorites, even when these come from the "action" or "light drama" categories.

(The best rationalizations, of course, are the true ones. The psychological functions of a belief say nothing of its validity, just about the reasons for clinging to it. Television may *be* highly educational for children; and a more informative adult schedule *would* reward the mind as well as salve the conscience—but only if it were watched.)

Finally, our "class" viewer has financial and cultural resources which make "more meaningful" alternatives psychologically available, if not always actually so. He "could have" gone to the opera or read something provocative instead. Whether he actually would have, except for television, is another matter. The mere presence of these more highly sanctioned and probably more satisfying alternatives raises the issue; and its expression may often take the form of dissatisfaction with the seductive "influence" of the easier time-killer.

Who or what is really to "blame," if evenings at home with television are sometimes or even generally preferred to more worthwhile ways of spending time? This is not an empirical question—but investigation does point out that there are at least two components in the decision: the presence of the television alternative, and its actual selection by those who prefer it. As we have said, watching television is not, like outdoor advertising, imposed or interposed between the viewer and better things by an industry; it is, after all, an activity initiated by those who have the final option in the matter. If the TV set "intrudes," it is by invitation.

In sum, then, the great mass of the American television audience divides roughly into two major segments according to the social-economic standing of the household, with formal schooling the single factor that makes the most difference. The number of slices on this continuum is of course arbitrary; but on most matters we do little violence to the data by dividing the public into those with and those without college training.

These two groups differ markedly in what they have to say about television, but not so markedly in how they use it and what they choose to see. There are significant differences in taste, but most tastes are already represented in the present range of television programming, though not in equal proportions. The behavioral distinction (not the verbal one) is between *Gunsmoke* and nondescript westerns; between Sid Caesar and the canned comedy; between *Play of the Week* and anthology light drama. It is *not* between occasional selective viewing of a few outstanding presentations and daily hours of escape. To see that contrast, we must sample not the college-educated but the teachers of their teachers.[3]

The big and real difference seems to lie not in what they do but how they feel about it. What the majority accepts as a legitimate use of television, the minority may think of as abuse of it (or *its* abuse of *them*). The mass audience is more likely to thank TV for keeping the family together, physically; the class viewer is more apt to blame it for keeping them apart, socially. The large segment concentrates on the help it gives them in keeping their children out of mischief; the small, on the fact that it (also) keeps them out of books or bed.

But while they focus on different sides, all examine the same coin. In the average and non-average home alike, we have seen at least as much concern with *how* people watch as with *what* they watch. Thus, the audience itself is aware of what sociologists might call the "structure" (as against the content) of television, and in this awareness, isolates the unique effects of TV. For the content is not unique: westerns did not originate with television and do not end with it, and neither, of course, does Shakespeare.

So it is that one commentator can say today of the video tube:

We have triumphantly invented, perfected, and distributed to the humblest cottage throughout the land one of the greatest technical marvels in history, television, and have used it for what? To bring Coney Island into every home. It is as though movable type had been devoted exclusively since Gutenberg's time to the publication of comic books.[4]

precisely what another said one hundred years ago about that movable type:

Communications has just about reached the lowest point, with respect to its importance; and contemporaneously the means of communications have pretty nearly attained the highest point, with respect to quick and overwhelming distribution. For what is in such haste to get out, and on the other hand, what has such widespread distribution as . . . twaddle? Oh, procure silence![5]

But, watching at the dinner table, pre-school children engrossed quietly for hours, the family at the movies in the living room—these things did originate less than fifteen years ago. They are the effects of the medium itself, as against the more general implications of the type of content found before and at present in other channels of mass communication.[6]

Interestingly, too, the popular critics and observers (as against the professional ones) seems to have trained their sights mainly on such issues. As both class and mass cartoons illustrate, satirists have treated television largely in terms of its demands on us, and ours on it. Programming, as such, has been far less important.

None of this is to deny the significance of programming, its level and its diversity. In the last analysis, that is in large measure responsible for the way television *is* used. The point is that the relationship is clearly two-way: the actual uses of the medium influence programming (by determining what fare will be most appropriate and thus most popular) and they certainly affect how the public regards its shows and what it says about them. But to understand popular praise and popular criticism and to know how much stock to put in each, they must be read against the criteria the public actually applies—the criteria not readily admitted as well as those held with pride.

NOTES

1. In this sense, technically, he is modal, not mean.

2. In Berelson, Bernard, "The Great Debate on Cultural Democracy," in Donald N. Barrett, ed., *Values in America* (University of Notre Dame Press, 1961).

3. The extremes, at either end, account for relatively few people; but on matters of policy their voices are perhaps the most and least important, respectively.

The true upper-crust intellectual—the thought leader at the national level—certainly accounts for a negligible portion of the audience, but hardly a negligible portion of the effective critical voice. He writes the articles, teaches the classes, and runs the government agencies that direct attention to the shortcomings of television—as well as those of the other media, and indeed American society in general. And he has by far the least rosy picture of the state and effects of today's TV.

At the opposite extreme, we have a larger number of unqualified enthusiasts (some argue, in both senses of unqualified), with neither the articulation, the platform, or the power—not even the consumer dollar—to make themselves heard.

4. From an address delivered by Robert M. Hutchins, Center for the Study of Democratic Institutions, Washington, D.C., June 1, 1961.

5. Kierkegaard as quoted in Berelson: op. cit.

6. And here, also, we know precisely which is chicken and which egg, unlike content considerations, which are always subject to such argument: do the values portrayed in programming reflect, produce, or just reinforce the general cultural norms and trends? For example, to what extent does TV violence or immorality foster such behavior; to what extent does it simply express our national acceptance of these patterns?

RAYMOND A. BAUER, ITHIEL DE SOLA POOL,
AND LEWIS DEXTER

American Business: Channels of Information

(Editor's Note: The data for this analysis is based on a survey of a sample of 903 business leaders who represent a sample of heads of firms with more than 100 employees. These businessmen were interviewed by the National Opinion Research Center in 1954 as part of a study on the politics of foreign trade policy.)

AMERICAN BUSINESS LEADERS are a generally well educated group of men in highly responsible posts.[1] Since they must, if only to do their jobs well, keep posted on what is happening in the world, they are avid information seekers. But they are extraordinarily busy with the daily affairs of their firms. News of the political world must compete for their attention with that of the economy and technology and problems of their own company.

What an executive can learn about public or international affairs depends on the way channels are set up to brief him. What he needs to learn depends on whether his firm is small or a nationwide, diversified giant. The structure of the staff which feeds him information varies with the firm's size. His job thus makes a difference in what a man learns about world affairs, a greater difference even than does his education. By the time he has become the head of a company, a man has become a certain type of individual. His chances of getting there are better if he has had a college education, but, if he is the exceptional man who has got there without such an education, he has long since made up the deficiency. He has become indistinguishable from his more formally educated colleagues. It was role more than background which controlled what our respondents learned about the world.

On matters not closely bearing on their own businesses, executives rely heavily on conventional printed media. Despite the other demands on

Reprinted from *American Business and Public Policy*, (1963), pp. 154–178, by permission of the authors and the publisher. (Copyright, 1963, Atherton Press.)

their time, they do much reading of newspapers and magazines. As a matter of fact, a study made by Bursk in 1957 (described below) indicates that in the business world they are the men with most responsibility and hence with the greatest pressure on their time who do the most reading.

On matters that touch their business more closely than the news in a magazine or daily paper, our respondents learned a great deal from conversation. To a surprising degree, the American business communication system is oral or by memorandum. In many instances, requirements for information are so technical that the businessman must rely on specialists to brief him. Specialized reading can be made almost impossible by the pressures of other demands. On the other hand, highly informed advisers are readily available. American businessmen thus get a considerable amount of their information face-to-face, on the telephone, or in the form of letters or condensed memorandums.

International information comes to our respondents via one more major channel, foreign travel. Travel supplements the standard American news media and the oral advice of experienced colleagues. Our respondents traveled abroad often, and, when they did, their travels had a profound effect on their views.

In this article, we shall try to document these conclusions. The data on which they are based come from a series of questions on the NORC survey concerning the reading and travel experience of our respondents as well as from our informal interviews. We shall also include certain comparable data from studies by Bursk and by Erdos and Morgan, the latter being referred to as "E. and M."[2]

Reading Habits

Regular reading of one or more newspapers is virtually unanimous,[3] and a majority of our respondents say they read two or three regularly. Among the newspapers cited, the most important numerically are local papers.[4] Second is *The Wall Street Journal*, which was mentioned by almost one-half of the group (Bursk, 75 per cent, E. and M., 49.8 per cent). In third and fourth places were *The New York Times* (about one in three; Bursk, 33 per cent; E. and M., 26 per cent) and the *Herald Tribune* (about one in six; E. and M., 16.6 per cent). General business newspapers (not trade papers) other than *The Wall Street Journal* were read by about one person in ten.

The Times, Herald Tribune, and to some extent *The Wall Street Journal* may be viewed as substitutes for each other. They are means for keeping currently informed at a level of detail above that possible with an ordinary local daily alone. It is significant that relatively few of our respondents used none of these superior daily sources. Only 37 per cent of our sample did not read either *The Times* or the *Herald Tribune* on the other hand or *The Wall Street Journal* plus a local paper on the other.

There are, of course, great regional differences in newspaper-reading. In each locality, local newspapers predominated. In New York, where one-fifth of our sample of American corporate heads was located, *The New York Times* and the *Herald Tribune* served as both national and local papers, and one or both were read by 90 per cent of the executives. Those two papers also enjoyed a considerable national readership; 33 per cent of non-New Yorkers read them (and that was before the West Coast edition of *The New York Times* existed). *The Wall Street Journal* was read explicitly as a national newspaper. As one proceeds away from New York, readership of *The Wall Street Journal* in one of its three editions (New York, Chicago, San Francisco) increased in comparison to the New York papers. The regional distribution is presented below in Table 1.

Table 1—Regional Patterns in the Reading of "National" Newspapers

PERCENTAGE OF RESPONDENTS WHO READ:

	New York Times	Herald Tribune Per Cent	Wall Street Journal	Regional Distribution of the Sample Per Cent
New York	71	40	43	21
Northeast	38	19	44	25
North Central	19	6	38	29
South	28		50	13
West	6	2	53	12
				100

Thus we find not only that business leaders are habitual newspaper readers but also that the majority read a newspaper of relatively broad scope giving them adequate coverage of both national and general business news. If they lived in New York—or for that matter in the same-day-delivery area around New York, from Boston to Washington—they tended to rely on the two New York papers which gave them national, general business, and local news simultaneously. The farther they lived from New York, at least in 1954, the more they relied on *The Wall Street Journal* in combination with local papers. Improving air mail delivery and the publication of national editions of leading papers will undoubtedly change the details of the picture.

Magazine-reading was not as pervasive as newspaper-reading. It was nevertheless general. At least three out of four men checked one or more national news magazines which they read. Although half the heads of firms with more than 10,000 employees said they read two or more news magazines regularly, this proportion drops off for the smaller firms, and we find only 33 per cent of the men in this group saying that they read two or more. Among news magazines, *Time* was read most often by slightly over half the men; Bursk, 53 per cent; E. and M., 44.7 per cent); *U.S. News and World Report* was second (approximately one in three; Bursk, 44 per cent; E. and M., 26.5 per cent); and *Newsweek* was third (about one in four; Bursk, 31 per cent, E. and M., 20.6 per cent). Only about one business leader in ten read any of the liberal magazines of commentary, such as *The Reporter, The Nation*, and *The New Republic*.

General business magazines were read about as often as news magazines, and about one-half of the men in our sample read two or more. Readership was concentrated mainly on two magazines: *Business Week* (45 per cent; Bursk, 46 per cent; E. and M., 29 per cent) and *Fortune* (25 per cent; Bursk, 38 per cent; E. and M., 16.8 per cent). The *Harvard Business Review* (Bursk, 24 per cent; E. and M., 3.2 per cent) and *Kiplinger Letter* (Bursk, 48 per cent; E. and M., negligible) were mentioned by about one in ten.[5] The residual reading of general business magazines was scattered.

Journals devoted to the problems of specific businesses and industries were almost as widely read as newspapers. Nine out of ten respondents said that they read at least one, and two out of three cited two or more.

Whereas businessmen tended to read news and business magazines with considerable frequency, this was less true of their readings of less serious material. Among general magazines, *Life* was clearly first, with one-fourth of the men from the largest firms and more than one-third among those from the smallest firms citing it (E. and M., 29.7 per cent). The *Saturday Evening Post* came next, with about one fourth of all the men mentioning it (E. and M., 17.5 per cent). Finally, *Reader's Digest* was checked with some frequency by the heads of the smallest firms (23 per cent), but only infrequently by the men from the largest (6 per cent). Only about one-sixth of the men said that they read any of the "high-brow" magazines, such as *Atlantic Monthly, Partisan Review, National Geographic, New Yorker*, and others.

SOME SIMILARITIES AND DIFFERENCES IN READING HABITS

Viewed in the perspective of the over-all population, the business leaders whom we interviewed constituted a remarkably homogeneous group with respect to reading habits. Even the most diverse subgroups in our sample were more like each other in their choice of reading material than they were like the rest of the population. For example, in the population at large it can be taken for granted that the higher educated will read more of most categories of materials than will the less educated. For certain publication there will, of course, be a reversal; highly educated people will read relatively and sometimes absolutely fewer tabloid newspapers, confession magazines, and the like. Although our business-leader group was quite highly educated, a quarter had not attended college, and one in ten or twelve had not completed high school.[6] Surprisingly enough, the differences in reading habits that are associated with these educational differences were exceedingly small. For those who became leading officers of good-sized businesses, factors of selection, experience, and responsibility substantially wiped out any disparity based on early education, at least insofar as reading of newspapers and business and news magazines is concerned.

The homogenizing effect of role on our sample was most clearly brought home to the authors by an episode which concerned the data on foreign travel, rather than that on reading. As with reading, we found no over-all difference between our better-educated and less-well-educated respondents in propensity to travel abroad. More accurately, we found, as Table 2 shows, that, among the heads of small firms, the better-educated

Table 2—Education and Communication Behavior

Larger Firms Per Cent	No College	Some College	College Graduate	Postgraduate
Much Traveled	59	50	56	54
Read News Magazines	84	84	85	87
Read Trade Publications	93	95	89	85
Read Hi-brow Magazines	5	8	16	23
Read Readers Digest	16	13	12	9
Smaller Firms Per Cent	No College	Some College	College Graduate	Postgraduate
Much Traveled	26	36	43	52
Read News Magazines	71	71	85	67
Read Trade Publications	93	97	97	87
Read Hi-brow Magazines	9	9	15	29
Read Readers Digest	22	25	24	19

men, as expected, traveled more. But among the larger firms the difference disappeared, and, if statistically unreliable differences are to be treated as plausible, it may indeed be the other way around. We queried an intelligent big-business informant about these results, which did not surprise him at all. "In those [top finance] circles, one is expected to know that little street off the Champs Elysées, and, if a man comes from a background where he doesn't, he will seize the first free forty-eight hours to hop over there." At that level, the cost is no obstacle, but it still is for the man with 100 to, say, 400 employees. The latter may have a harder time leaving his plant for even a few days. His reference group consists of less-widely traveled persons. At the big-business level, travel was a means of demonstrating achieved status by those who needed to show it. The man who had risen to the top despite the fact that he had not gone to the right schools is a man of energy, prone to seize every opportunity to acquire the status symbols of his colleagues. Travel is one of the easiest of these symbols for him to acquire and one which a wife, married early, can also share as she rises with him. Thus, in our sample, which was defined by achieved status, educational background, which normally correlates well with symbols of status, was no longer predictive of them.

Reading for self-education, like travel, could be a way to establish one's identity with a social group into which one has risen. Indeed, as we have already noted, the successful though uneducated executive did behave exactly like his more privileged colleagues in regard to business- and news-reading. But changing one's reading habits is a more arduous way to establish one's status than is travel. Thus we find that, in sophisticated reading, education did make a difference. For businessmen of any given size of firm, there was a positive correlation between the amount of education a man had and his reading of such high-brow magazines as *The New Yorker, Harper's,* and the like. Among the heads of larger firms, there was a negative correlation between education and reading of the *Reader's Digest.*

Some variations in reading habits depend on the size of the firm which a man heads. The representatives of the larger firms, when contrasted with those from smaller firms, showed a concern for national as opposed to local affairs and for broad business matters as opposed to the problems of their own industry. In Table 3, we present some of the data on reading

Table 3—Reading Habits of Heads of Firms of Various Sizes

| | PER CENT REPORTING REGULAR USE | | | | | | |
Size of Firm	New York Times	Herald Tribune	Wall St. Journal	General News Mg.	General Bus. Mg.	Trade Journals	Local Papers
Large	43	31	64	88	91	83	62
Medium	39	17	54	84	88	84	70
Small	33	15	42	75	79	90	73

habits which reflect this trend. In general, the heads of the larger firms read more and were exposed to more of all sorts of communications. However, they were the heads of the smallest firms who read the most local newspapers[7] and the most trade journals.

The larger the firm he represents, the more must a man see things with what may be called "the broad view," the wider the variety of information he must have. The general level of the communications behavior of the smaller businessman was lower and concentrated relatively on matters concerning his local community and his own industry. In these areas, his reading actually exceeded that of his opposite number from larger companies. As we note repeatedly in this study, the concern of the head of a big business is largely with the external environment, whereas that of the head of a small business is with internal management.[8] Their reading corresponded with this difference.

Such differences in reading habits between large and small businessmen are not of extraordinary magnitude. When viewed in the perspective of the American population as a whole, these men are alike in their communications behavior. For example, it would be difficult to find another occupational group in the United States comparable in size to the business community—unless it be physicians—in which at least 40 per cent read any one paper (*The Wall Street Journal*) and 80 per cent read a small group of general occupational magazines.

Foreign Sources of Information

American foreign-trade policy is an issue which is in large part involved with information about events outside the United States. It is therefore relevant and interesting to note that the reading of our respondents was confined almost exclusively to domestic sources. We found that our respondents had two main sources of information about foreign affairs: the American media which report foreign news and their own foreign travel. They read scarcely any foreign printed material. Even though our questioning about news sources concluded an interview which had been largely focused on foreign affairs, only thirty-five of our 903 respondents listed foreign publications among the newspapers and periodicals which they read regularly. (Cf. Table 4.) These thirty-five men cited a total

Table 4—Reading of Foreign Publications

Country of Origin	Number of Publications Read	Number of Respondents (Out of 903)
Great Britain	36	26
Canada	4	3
Latin America	3	2
France	1	1
Australia	1	1
Unspecified	2	2
	47 publications	35 respondents

of forty-seven sources, most of which (thirty-six) were British. *The Economist*, London, was the source most often mentioned (fifteen times) and was the only one mentioned with any frequency.

This overwhelming reliance on domestic as opposed to foreign printed material for information does not stem from indifference to foreign affairs. A fair portion of our respondents' firms were involved in foreign operations. Among the largest firms, 60 per cent had foreign subsidiaries, as did 37 per cent of the medium and 13 per cent of the smallest firms. (And, as we shall see shortly, American businessmen as a group do a great deal of traveling abroad.)

More surprising than that the top men in American firms do not read foreign newspapers and magazines is that this was true also of their aides who are directly responsible for overseas business.

We interrogated a number of import-export managers in unstructured interviews. An interview with the export manager of a fair-sized American chemical company was typical. There was, he said, a tremendous amount of travel from headquarters to other countries, and vice versa. Much of the company's information about conditions abroad came from its own men overseas and from the observations of home-office men when they went on trips. He himself read American newspapers, magazines, trade journals, and bank letters. When pressed for foreign sources, he named a publication of the American Foreign Trade Council.

Another respondent, an importer who himself traveled often, stated that, when he was in this country, he relied mainly on the foreign division of the Big City Bank[9] for information on developments in foreign countries. This bank exemplifies those few organizations which act as transmission belts for foreign information to the American business community. When we interviewed the head of the bank's foreign division and asked him where it got information about what was going on abroad, he said, "First of all, from foreign banks." For example, a bank in Europe might write him, saying that it had a textile manufacturer who wanted to find a market for a certain kind of fabric. He in turn would approach an American organization that might be interested. A certain amount of economic and political information is picked up via such correspondence. He added that bank personnel keep in touch with foreign affairs, mainly through the important dailies, of which he mentioned *The New York Times*. One man in the office, the only one of foreign birth, read the *Neue Zücher Zeitung;* another read the London *Economist*.

Among the most international-minded of American business leaders, one had a staff member who read foreign sources and called his attention to items which might be of interest to him. But this practice was, to the best of our knowledge, exceptional. More often, specialized organizations, such as foreign-trade departments of banks; the Foreign Trade Council; export associations for particular industries; foreign investment, marketing, and public-relations consultant firms; or international editors of business publications were the direct consumers of foreign printed matter. They then relayed part of the contents to a wider segment of the business community. In most instances, however, materials did not exceed two or three titles.

Aside from such "gatekeepers," who have direct contact with foreign sources and who process them for the American consumer, American businessmen paid negligible attention to foreign printed matter.

Failure to use foreign printed media did not entirely deprive American businessmen of direct exposure to foreign attitudes. Whereas the average American is unusual if he has traveled outside the United States once in his lifetime, one of our respondents was very unusual if he had not done so. The travel experience of the interviewees is summarized in Table 5.

Table 5—Travel Experience of American Businessmen

	LARGE FIRMS	Heads of MEDIUM FIRMS Per Cent	SMALL FIRMS
A. Extent of travel			
Number of trips abroad:			
None	7	11	14
1 trip	9	9	13
2–4 trips	18	20	28
5–9 trips	21	22	19
10–24 trips	20	21	18
25 trips or more	14	10	2
Many, unspecified	6	5	3
No answer	5	2	3
	100	100	100
B. Recency of last trip abroad			
Last trip was within:			
Last year	58	52	43
1–5 years	25	31	31
Over 5 years ago	17	17	26
	100	100	100
C. Purpose of last trip abroad			
Business only	55	41	22
Vacation only	28	39	55
Business and vacation	8	12	12
Other[a]	9	8	11
	100	100	100

a. Includes military service and study abroad.

Even among the smallest firms, six out of seven had made at least one trip abroad. The men from the larger firms were even more active travelers; most of the heads of the largest firms had made five or more trips. About half of the sample had been out of the United States in the preceding twelve months. Three-fourths had been in the preceding five years.

The countries most often visited on the last trip were Great Britain and Canada (about equally), followed by Western Europe and other European countries, South America, and Mexico. Other areas of the world were visited by only small minorities.[10] Communist countries were virtually unvisited at the time of our 1954 survey, a situation which has now presumably changed.

Our respondents traveled abroad for both business and pleasure, often for both at once. Motives for travel are not easy to assess.[11] Often a traveler himself cannot tell you the exact proportion of these two motives. And, even if he does know, the Bureau of Internal Revenue discourages him from saying. In general, statistics on purposes of travel are highly artificial. Those based on visa applications are biased in favor of tourist travel, for it is simpler to get a tourist visa than any other type. Those based on U.S. passport or other application forms may be biased, for tax purposes, in favor of business travel. But, then, how does one classify a trip in which a man meets and talks socially to leading businessmen in other lands while he also visits cathedrals? Who can say what social contact may eventually provide a client or associate? At the business level, as in the free professsions, private and business life merge into an indistinguishable whole in a way which it is hard for a salaried man or wage-earner to grasp. Everything the executive does may promote or injure the business in which he serves as guide and symbol, be it activity in the Community Chest; membership on the board of a college; participation in politics; establishing social friendships; or expanding his own areas of experience, information, and expertise.

But, whatever vagueness there is about the statistics on travel motives, they do measure something. Our respondents were able to cut the continuum of motives in some way, and replies show important differences. Among the heads of the largest firms, 66 per cent of the most recent trips were stated to have been for business or for business in combination with vacation. This was true of only 34 per cent of the most recent trips made by men from the smallest firms. The men from the smaller firms not only traveled somewhat less frequently but also were proportionately less likely to travel for business. Note the parallel between the figures on traveling abroad for business and the proportions of firms with subsidiaries abroad (60 and 13 per cent for large and small firms, respectively). The heads of larger business organizations are more often directly involved in business abroad.

We must also note the small but important proportion of businessmen who traveled abroad for reasons other than business or pleasure and more particularly that very small minority whose reason was government service, especially in connection with the Marshall Plan. A great deal has been said in recent years about the sobering and broadening effect of government experience on business leaders. Many of these executives have served in foreign areas on technical-aid and other missions.

The theory of the business community being educated by such experiences is not without validity, but it is easy to overstate. Only a minority, though among big businessmen a very substantial minority, of

our respondents had ever held policy-level government jobs. (See Table
6.) Except among the heads of small companies, these jobs were overwhelmingly federal.[12] Most of them were domestic, but close to half were

Table 6—Public-Affairs and Foreign-Affairs Experience

Type of Job	AMONG RESPONDENTS FROM		
	LARGE FIRMS	MEDIUM FIRMS	SMALL FIRMS
		Per Cent	
Policy-level government job	20	10	3
Foreign-affairs government job			
(e.g., FOA, ECA, UN, consul)	8	6	—
Overseas government job	4	4	—

concerned with foreign affairs, and some of those—four per cent of top
executives of both large and medium firms—had worked for the government abroad.

Although those businessmen who had once had to look at foreign
affairs from a role of responsibility for national interest were few in
numbers, the part they played in the leadership of the organized liberal-
trade effort was enormous. We have reason to note such names as Clarence
Randall, who had been involved in technical assistance to Turkey, and
Ralph Straus, George Ball, Gen. William Draper, and William C. Foster,
all of whom had played significant roles in the Marshall Plan and all of
whom participated actively in the reciprocal-trade controversy and, with
one exception, in the formation of the Committee for a National Trade
Policy, the low-tariff organization. These men with deep foreign-affairs
involvement were transmitters of information to the rest of the business
community.

But foreign observation came not only through gatekeepers. A well-
traveled group, our respondents had all in all a good deal of opportunity
to observe events abroad with their own eyes.

We may ask ourselves what kinds of effect such travel experiences
had upon them. Travel abroad is a quite different source of information
from the mass media. Travel is for all except a small minority an intermittent matter, and it is selective in that each man visits only one or a few
of the many possible sectors of the globe.

Yet, travel is a deeply personal experience which turned out to have
a profound impact on the frame of reference in which our respondents
viewed foreign affairs. Few of them went to gain political insight or to
study foreign relations. But, whatever happened as they bathed on the
Lido, bought souvenirs, or transacted business turned out to be politically
important, too.

Summarized in a sentence, the political effect of travel on tariff attitudes was to counteract the force of self-interest. It made a man see the trade issue in national terms, rather than in the parochial terms of his own industry.[13]

The highly traveled respondents—those who had made five or more trips abroad and at least one in the previous five years—were not in general more liberal on trade matters than their less-traveled colleagues, nor were they more protectionist. However, they differed in one important way. Their view on tariff policy was less predictable—from knowing the industry in which they were engaged—than was that of their more provincial colleagues.[14] (See Table 7.) For those businessmen who had not

Table 7—Travel and Self-Interest[a]

	High Tariff Self-Interest		Mixed Self-Interest		Low Tariff Self-Interest	
	MUCH TRAVELED	THE REST	MUCH TRAVELED	THE REST	MUCH TRAVELED	THE REST
Smaller Firms			Per Cent			
Opposed to Own Self-Interest	45	27	52	27	56	45
In Line with Own Self-Interest	55	73	48	73	44	55
	High Tariff Self-Interest		Mixed Self-Interest		Low Tariff Self-Interest	
	MUCH TRAVELED	THE REST	MUCH TRAVELED	THE REST	MUCH TRAVELED	THE REST
Larger Firms			Per Cent			
Opposed to Own Self-Interest	27	100	37	22	49	27
In Line with Own Self-Interest	73	100	63	78	51	73

a. Definitions:

Own self-interest is:	Reply in line with own self-interest is:	Reply opposed to own self-interest is:
High tariff	Raise or leave as is	Lower
Mixed	Raise or leave as is	Lower
Low tariff	Lower	Raise or leave as is

traveled much, if we knew what their firm made, we could make a reasonable prediction of where they as individuals would stand on tariff policy. For those who had traveled, a better prediction could be made, not by knowing what they manufactured, but by knowing the nation's foreign policy. From either atypical extreme, the travelers moved to support that norm.

Foreign travel introduced international political problems and America's relationship to them increasingly into the businessman's conscious-ness. As he traveled, he found himself being role-cast, not as the repre-sentative of a particular industry, but as an American. He found himself playing at being secretary of state and talking for his country, not for his firm.

The influence of travel was not primarily to bring European or other foreign ideas to the traveler, leading him to diverge from his national norm. On the contrary, it moved him toward that norm. There was a shift in center of gravity away from narrow parochial interests *toward* inter-national interests, but with views quite close to the national standard. Thus, foreign travel broadened the frame of reference in which the businessman considered the foreign-trade issue to one which took account of world political and economic circumstances. But the responses he gave to the facts that he learned abroad were ones that his own domestic reference group would approve. The reference group perceived as rele-vant changed from a parochial to a national one, but it remained a domestic one.

Thus the very partial and often irrelevant experiences of foreign travel, either on the Lido or in an office, could affect a man's broad foreign-policy conclusions. Whether the traveler acquired his sense of responsi-bility to an American role in an argument with a perverse waiter or in a study of foreign production costs made little difference. The effect was to shake his established convictions and to make him see himself in a more statesmanlike role, defined, it is true, as the American business community sees that role.

The way in which foreign travel related to public-affairs attitudes was illustrated in a most striking way by data on political party affiliation of our respondents. Our theory postulates that, if any shift of opinion on matters of substance occurs as a result of travel, its direction should be toward the standard business position—in this case, toward the Republican Party. Though this prediction follows from our theory, we cannot claim advance wisdom. Like most of our colleagues, we expected that travel would liberalize and that liberals would be less often Republicans. We were wrong. We find, as our theory should have led us to expect, that the most traveled businessman are most uniformly Republican.

This finding deserves a little more elucidation. Virtually no business-man switched from the Republican to the Democratic Party. Those who switched party were switching from an ancestral Democratic affiliation to a Republican affiliation more appropriate to their career role. Thus, the Republican homogeneity of the highly traveled business executives simply means that a larger proportion of the travelers who chanced to be both Democrats had abandoned their ancestral party than did so among the nontravelers. Those who were born Democrats, if they exposed them-selves to new and unsettling experiences, moved away from that "deviation" toward the central ideology of their group. Those who continued to hold a more sectional (for example, Southern), familial, or otherwise particularistic traditional stand, which is what being a Democrat means if one is head of a company, are found among the nontravelers.

Table 8—Travelers More Solidly Republican Than Nontravelers[a]

| | Larger Firms | | Small Firms | |
	MUCH TRAVELED	THE REST	MUCH TRAVELED	THE REST
		Per Cent		
Democrats	14	25	22	36
Republicans	86	75	78	64

a. The findings hold up separately for both Democrats and Independents, but the numbers are small. In the graph, they are combined.

The same kind of shaking-up which appeared in party politics explains our findings about travel and foreign-trade attitudes. Although travel shook men loose from their industry stands, its net result was to permit them by changing to solidify, not weaken, their bonds to their decisive domestic reference group. Attention to foreign attitudes, to foreign reactions to American trade policy, and to varied foreign facts became greater among those respondents who had traveled much than it was among those who had not. But we must not confuse this increased awareness of foreign views with acceptance of them.

Although much-traveled men were not more likely to favor lower tariffs, they differed from the less-well-traveled men in what they thought were the best arguments for a low-tariff policy. We see in Table 9 that

Table 9—Best Argument for Low Tariffs

| | Larger Firms | | Small Firms | |
	MUCH TRAVELED	THE REST	MUCH TRAVELED	THE REST
		Per Cent		
A Domestic One	26	43	29	47
No Good Argument	7	7	9	11
An International One	67	50	62	42

men who had been frequently abroad were more likely to favor low-tariff arguments with an international orientation than were those who had done less traveling.

An interesting instance of broadened perception has to do with the ideas our respondents had for increasing foreign trade. When asked what actions might result in an increased volume of foreign trade, the much-traveled respondents more often than the less-traveled cited actions by foreign agencies (Table 10). They blamed foreigners more often than

Table 10—Which Actions Would Increase Foreign Trade

Large and Medium Firms	Per Cent Citing Action by, or Stability of, Foreign Country or People
Much-traveled	25
All others	17
Small Firms	
Much-traveled	19
All others	10

did the less-well-traveled respondents for existing difficulties in international trade.

At first glance, that might suggest that our well-traveled respondents were more isolationist in the sense that they were more likely to lay blame abroad. However, there is independent evidence that they are neither more nor less isolationist than are those who have traveled less. The groups are identical in their attitudes toward United States participation in world affairs. These data represent, instead, a direct manifestation of the greater familiarity with foreign facts among the frequent travelers. They knew what obstructions there were to trade abroad as well as to that at home.

We have said that foreign travel—except for a very few men who spend a very high proportion of their time abroad—is not to be regarded as a regular news source for events abroad. True, men who travel abroad do return with a certain amount of specific information, both concerning their own particular businesses and also concerning general economic and political conditions. However, it seems clear that the major day-to-day impact of foreign travel is on the man's reaction to the news which he gets from domestic American sources. He is enabled to bring a broader background of experience to bear on the interpretation of what he reads in the American press.

Sources of Information on the Reciprocal-Trade Controversy

Considering the reading habits of our respondents and the media coverage given the reciprocal-trade controversy in the years 1953–1954, the men we interviewed had ample opportunity to become acquainted with the general features of the controversy. Although most newspapers and practically all national magazines favored the extension of the Reciprocal Trade Act, there was also adequate reportage of the statements of protectionist spokesmen. There was quite frequent reporting of the complaints of injury on the part of the watch, textile, coal, chemical, and other industries.

Granting that it is difficult to judge just what is "adequate reporting" and granting also that the general run of local papers paid only sporadic attention to the reciprocal-trade debate, it nevertheless seems safe to say that *The New York Times, Herald Tribune*, and *Wall Street Journal* (at least one of which 72 per cent of our respondents read), the national news magazines, and the general business magazines reported the controversy adequately, certainly to the point where everyone could know that it existed and what its general alignment was.[15]

Perhaps the coverage was inadequate on one point, the concern of foreign countries over whether American trade barriers were going to increase or decrease. News stories on reciprocal trade tended to originate in Washington. Foreign correspondents wrote about more salient subjects. Anyone who had access to foreign sources at that time perceived a greater sense of involvement and urgency on the part of foreigners than was conveyed by the American press on the whole, although Swiss reaction to United States tariffs on watches was effectively reported. However, about half of our respondents had been abroad in the preceding year and would in all probability have been exposed to foreign attitudes on this subject. So, even on this point, our respondents had access to substantial information.

But access to copious information does not guarantee its assimilation. Selective attention, perception, and recall among businessmen, as among any other human beings, assured that those who learned about a controversy were those with specific interest in it.

We now look at the impact of two events which were thoroughly covered in the public press, namely, the Randall Commission report and the President's message. The Randall Commission report, which had been delivered some months before our interviews, was well covered at that time in the local press, as well as in the prestige papers and news magazines and to some extent on radio and television. It was the subject of considerable later debate, too. The Randall report was also sent by the Committee for a National Trade Policy to its entire mailing list, which included businessmen from virtually all the larger firms in our sample. The President's message was delivered the day before we began interviewing, and, although there was therefore not time for it to become the topic of wide discussion, it should have been fresh in the minds of our respondents if they had been following the ordinary domestic news sources. In Table 11 are presented the proportions of men in each size of firm who had heard or read about either of these reports.

Since the President's message had been delivered so recently before our interviews began, there had been little time for it to be discussed or reported in trade journals or even in the general business or news magazines. Accordingly, most respondents who said that they had read or heard about the President's message had read about it in a newspaper. This was true of a minority of the people who said they had heard or read about the Randall Commission report. General news magazines, general business magazines, and trade journals—all having a longer time lag in reporting than do newspapers—were somewhat more often mentioned as sources of information about the Randall report.

One difference between the sources of information for the President's message and the Randall report is especially interesting. That difference is in the reading of quite specialized documents—either the report itself or other items that we have lumped under the heading of special communications. The latter are communications from one's trade associations, industry representatives, lobbyists, or even one's congressman in a few instances. What such materials have in common is that they do not come to the respondent as part of a regular media flow to which he subscribes, but come to his desk episodically and more often on the initiative of the communicator than that of the recipient. The special communications may be viewed as a second wave, activated by the first wave of reporting in the general media. Ironically, the Randall report itself or the President's message may most often be viewed as part of this second wave. For, though they actually start the media flow and though a few of our most influential and involved respondents may have had copies at the moment of release or earlier, for most of our respondents the act of looking at the full text which someone had mailed to them was a follow up to being informed through the newspapers that this was an important document and worth pulling out of the pile of incoming printed material.

The second wave material is specialized in its points of origin, its content, and its selection of audience. The second wave also takes time to get organized and heard, even though the major documents themselves are mailed out as quickly as possible after release. For that reason, if for no other, such special communications had come to constitute at the moment of interviewing but a small proportion of the sources of knowledge concerning the President's message. They accounted for a much larger proportion of the sources concerning the Randall report.

Such specialized communications are more likely to be directed at the men in the largest firms, apparently because the latter are publicly more visible and have better lines of communication. It will be seen in Table 11 that the spread between the largest and the smallest firms in knowledge of the President's message is but 15 percentage points, whereas in knowledge of the Randall report the spread is 44 percentage points. The President's message being still the news of the week, the difference in awareness of it

355

among large and small firms was not great and reflected above all individual differences in competence, political interest, and cosmopolitanism, rather than in communication exposure. The Randall report, however, was far enough in the past to have fallen out of the news, to have been for-

Table 11—Proportion of Men Having Heard or Read about Randall Report and Eisenhower Message

	Randall Report			Eisenhower Message		
	LARGE FIRMS	MEDIUM FIRMS	SMALL FIRMS	LARGE FIRMS	MEDIUM FIRMS	SMALL FIRMS
			Per Cent			
Had not	10	25	54	26	38	41
Had Heard or Read	90	75	46	74	62	59

Table 12—Sources of Information on Randall Report and Eisenhower Message[a]

	Large firms		Medium firms		Small firms	
	RANDALL	PRESIDENT	RANDALL	PRESIDENT	RANDALL	PRESIDENT
			Per Cent			
Newspapers	36	60	43	57	39	61
News magazines	16	7	29	13	17	15
General business magazines	9	3	6	3	7	5
Trade journals	10	1	8	2	11	5
Special communications[b]	24	5	15	3	13	3
Saw report or message itself	29	7	22	5	11	3

a. Adds to more than 100 per cent because some gave more than one source. Only those who had heard of report or message are included in this table.

b. Includes communications from men in own business, trade associations, lobbyists, congressmen, etc.

gotten by those who did not care about it, and to have been maintained in the focus of attention above all for those businessmen who continued to receive specialized follow-up communications. Those were largely the heads of larger firms.

This analysis suggests that the media of general communication play a dual role in the transmission of information to the business community. They convey initial news of events, and they stimulate a secondary wave of specialized communications, which have a delayed and relatively selective effect.

The general communications media are also somewhat selective in effect. Such events as the Randall report and the President's message, though universally reported, were not universally read. Selective perception is a pattern found in every study of news-reading. We have seen that men from larger firms, presumably having a wider range of interests, were consistently better informed and more active in communicating about foreign-trade policy.

Size of firm was but one of the factors which affected which news businessmen read and remembered. Self-interest, or, more particularly, fear of loss, was another. For example, among the heads of the smallest firms, only 25 per cent of those men who had said that foreign competition affected their firms had not heard of the Eisenhower message, but as many as 46 per cent of the men who had said that their businesses were not affected were ignorant of it. Again it turns out that those who saw a threat to themselves in foreign imports informed themselves about foreign-trade news.

Table 13—Proportion of Men Having Heard or Read about Randall Report and Eisenhower Message Related to Objective Tariff Interest

Larger Firms

	RANDALL REPORT				EISENHOWER MESSAGE			
Tariff Interest	High Per Cent	Mixed Per Cent	Low Per Cent	None Per Cent	High Per Cent	Mixed Per Cent	Low Per Cent	None Per Cent
Had not Had Heard	18	17	18	32	18	21	31	41
or Read	82	83	82	68	82	79	69	59

Small Firms

	RANDALL REPORT				EISENHOWER MESSAGE			
Tariff Interest	High %	Mixed %	Low %	None %	High %	Mixed %	Low %	None %
Had not Had Heard	31	43	60	55	27	39	39	42
or Read	69	57	40	45	73	61	61	58

Thus we find that either fear of foreign competition or an externally oriented business role was a force which would lead a businessman to select foreign-trade news for attention from among the flood of items available to him in the general media.

NOTES

1. Even among the small firms, 50 per cent were college graduates, and, among the other firms, 61 per cent.

2. Edward C. Bursk, "New Dimensions in Top Executive Reading," *Harvard Business Review*, 35 (September–October 1957), 93–112, and Erdos and Morgan Research Service, "The Reading Preferences of Corporate Officers and Executive Personnel" (1957; private circulation). Both studies were done on a sample of executives drawn from *Poor's Register of Directors and Execu-*

tives. The samples which were drawn in both studies consisted of "top execu-tives," but were not as much confined to heads of firms as was our sample.

The Bursk study was done in 1957, three years after ours. The E. and M. report gives results of surveys done in 1952, 1954, and 1957. Both studies were done by mail questionnaire. The Bursk study was supplemented by 100 tele-phone follow-ups on nonrespondents. Bursk used aided recall giving respond-ents a list of publications from which to check those which they read for business purposes. The Erdos and Morgan study, done for *The Wall Street Journal*, asked respondents to indicate spontaneously, without the aid of a list, the newspapers and the magazines they read "regularly for general or business news."

There are certain obvious differences between these two studies and ours. (1) The samples were somewhat different. (2) Ours was a personal, oral inter-view, and the others were mail questionnaires. (3) Each of the three studies put the question somewhat differently. (4) The other studies report findings for years other than 1954. Yet, when all this is taken into account, the picture drawn from each of the three studies is remarkably similar. Only if one had an interest in selling space in one of the media concerned would he be inclined to quarrel over the differences in the findings. The precise findings on reading habits are so inevitably a function of the details in design of study and question-wording that it has been our policy not to emphasize the precise figures, but only the over-all patterns. However, where the Bursk and the E. and M. studies report on the same newspapers or magazines as we do, the comparable figures are inserted for the reader's guidance. The Bursk figures refer to 1957, the E. and M. figures to the 1954 portion of their findings.

It will be seen that Bursk, using aided recall, generally reports higher reader-ship for specific media. This should be expected from the difference in method. However, it should be remembered that aided recall has a tendency to produce overreporting, though data introduced by Bursk indicate that his own study may not have produced such overreporting. On the other hand, E. and M., using spontaneous recall, tend to report lower readership than we do. This would be expected on a self-administered questionnaire in comparison to an oral interview, in which the interviewer can keep probing. It is probably also a function of the limited number of spaces provided in the questionnaire. This discourages the really active reader from listing all his sources. (Cf. the discus-sion of the *Harvard Business Review*, below.) Finally, the E. and M. question is more restrictive, specifying reading for news. Bursk has shown that much of the disparity between his and the E. and M. figures disappears when one cor-rects for this difference in question-wording—a correction he was fortunately able to make by virtue of further questions which he asked.

3. Respondents were asked about the newspapers and magazines they read. Apparently some, in concentrating on magazines, overlooked mentioning news-papers. The total proportion of men who did not mention reading some news-paper was slightly over 5 per cent. A look at their interviews indicates that most and probably all of the limited number of men who reported no news-paper actually were newspaper-readers. We are assuming that newspaper-reading was for practical purposes universal.

4. Outside New York, 83, 68, and 76 per cent of large, medium, and small businessmen, respectively, mentioned local newspapers.

5. Our own method did not limit the respondent to any specific number of titles or any specific subject matter, but it also did not provide a list. The respondent's own tendency to name four or five titles and then stop or his

sense of fitness probably tended to reduce mention of less salient titles. For these reasons, there are marked disparities in these findings, with ours falling midway between the other two. The Bursk method of aided recall detected a much higher proportion of readers of the *Harvard Business Review* and *Kiplinger Letter*. (Bursk produces very convincing evidence that these men were actually readers of the *Harvard Business Review*.) The E. and M. study, on the other hand, may have discouraged the reporting of these relatively specialized sources by virtue of the limited number of lines it provided for the listing of magazines. Also, the specification "general or business news" may have affected the reporting of these two relatively special sources. We would be inclined to accept the Bursk findings over either our own or those of E. and M. for at least occasional readership.

6. For the statistics on education by size of firm, see Raymond A. Bauer and Ithiel de Sola Pool, *American Businessmen and International Trade* (Glencoe, Ill.: The Free Press, 1960), pp. 66 f.

7. This result is accounted for by the concentration of large firms in New York. Taking only firms outside New York, the citing of local papers occurred among 83 per cent of large, 68 per cent of medium, and 76 per cent of small businessmen. Whether the explanation is the geographical structure of small and large businesses or the psychology of each of them, the fact remains that the reading habits of small businessmen were more parochial.

8. Cf. Carroll L. Shartle, *Executive Performance and Leadership* (Englewood Cliffs, N.J.: Prentice-Hall, Inc., 1956), which shows public relations to be the single most time-consuming activity in the big-business executive's day.

9. This name is a pseudonym.

10. Bauer and Pool, *op. cit.*, p. 77.

11. Cf. Ithiel de Sola Pool, Suzanne Keller, and Raymond A. Bauer, "The Influence of Foreign Travel on Political Attitudes of American Businessmen," *The Public Opinion Quarterly*, XX (Spring 1956), No. 1, 161–175.

12. Cf. Bauer and Pool, *op. cit.*, pp. 104 ff.

13. These results are more fully reported in Pool, Keller, and Bauer, *op. cit.*

14. We might briefly note some qualifications at this point. Among the much-traveled, a small group had been abroad twenty-five or more times. These continuous travelers were mostly in businesses where foreign trade is life and death. They therefore tended to line up fairly well behind their firms' self-interest. Among the little-traveled, there was one particularly interesting group, those who had made their first trip abroad recently. There were only sixteen of them who also had an identifiable tariff interest. These few were the most extreme in defense of their self-interest: eight defended it in extreme form, only two opposed it. This is in line with our hypothesis about the contrary effects of much and little travel. One trip may provide ammunition for one's previous views. Time and more experience may shake them. However, the data are too sparse for reliance.

15. *The New York Times Index* had 12.5 column inches of entries under "Reciprocal Trade Act" in 1954 and 35 column inches in 1955. Stories appeared on about 60 days during 1954 and 110 days during 1955.

FREDERICK BARGHOORN

Soviet Doctrine
on the Role of Propaganda

WORDS AND PICTURES have played a more continuous, and perhaps a more vital role than bullets or rubles in Moscow's struggle to undermine the social order of capitalism and to reconstruct society on "Marxist-Leninist" foundations. Lenin and his followers were convinced that they had an historic mission to transform human relations and ultimately shape a "new" communist man. The conviction that only they are privy to the "truth" has given communists confidence in the righteousness of their cause. It has not, however, rendered them at all indifferent to the necessity of exercising the utmost skill in shaping the outlook and firing the imagination of their audiences. Communists know it is their duty to master the legacy of Lenin, who, like other successful propagandists, taught that the success of a social movement depended as much on use of the art and strategy of persuasion as on firmness of convictions. Communist propaganda is formidable because it combines crusading zeal with professional skill. Today, to these sources of strength it adds the material achievements of the "socialist camp," most spectacularly manifested in the feats of Russian astronauts. Selected aspects of Soviet achievements are highlighted by Moscow as proof of the success of socialism.

Understanding of the contemporary significance of propaganda as an instrument of Soviet foreign policy requires some acquaintance with the writings of V. I. Lenin on the instrumentalities of politics. Perhaps the salient characteristic of Lenin's version of Marxism, especially of his conception of the disciplined hierarchical revolutionary organization out of which grew the bolshevik party, the Soviet state, and the international communist movement, was his emphasis upon the power of political communication. It is noteworthy that in his central contribution to the

Reprinted from *Soviet Foreign Propaganda*, (1964), pp. 3–19, 300–11, by permission of the author and the publisher. (Copyright, 1964, Princeton University Press.)

bolshevik theory of strategy and tactics, *What Is To Be Done?*, Lenin paid close attention to urging the establishment of an all-Russian political newspaper. Its staff was to act as his agents in propaganda, intelligence, and organizational work.[1] In this work, Lenin exhorted his followers to "go to all classes of the population" in the capacity of "theoreticians, propagandists, agitators and organizers." Lenin thus stressed the political significance of communication.

Also, like Trotski and other left-wing Russian Social Democrats, Lenin defined, in terms broader than those which western European Marxists had usually used, the social targets for his party's revolutionary mission. In this way he helped to provide a basis for rationalizing what was to become the bolshevik predilection for various forms of limited collaboration between Leninists and other political groups. Lenin's emphasis on the breadth of his movement's short-run goals reflected his realization that bolshevism could not gain power in a backward and still largely agrarian society unless the "party of the proletariat" won over to its side at least substantial portions of the peasantry, and the still weak but rapidly developing middle classes. Most important for our interests in this study is the fact that Lenin established a tradition within which bolshevik "professional revolutionaries" and, later, specially trained functionaries of the Soviet state and of foreign communist parties, have systematically employed modern communications techniques in a continuing effort to bring about "the radical transformation of the conditions of life of all of mankind."[2]

Obviously, the present leadership of the Soviet Union shares Lenin's concern regarding the significance of propaganda as a political instrument. Indeed, an intensification of emphasis on the role of political communication has been a conspicuous feature of the post-Stalin era. Continuous reissuing of Lenin's complete works—a fifth edition is now in process of publication—is one of many indications of continuity in outlook between Lenin and those who proudly proclaim themselves his pupils and successors. Such "classics" of Leninism as *What Is To Be Done?* are studied and re-studied in both the general educational and the special political training institutions which shape the outlook of Soviet citizens, especially those aspiring to elite status.[3]

The major addresses delivered at congresses of the Communist Party of the Soviet Union by Lenin, Stalin, Khrushchev, and other important leaders, or at special meetings of the ruling CPSU devoted to problems of propaganda and political education, have always emphasized that the party regards agitation, propaganda, and other forms of "ideological work" as one of its central tasks. Such ideological work is also deemed a significant function of the subordinate "mass organizations," such as the Young Communist League, the Soviet trade unions, and others. This concern with mass communication was emphasized in an article published in a Soviet reference work in 1939, which stated that "the problem of propaganda has always been the center of attention of all party congresses and conferences."[4]

A particularly interesting indication of the importance attached to propaganda by the CPSU leadership in the post-Stalin era was contained in a speech given by Leonid F. Ilichev (now, next to Khrushchev, perhaps the leading Soviet policymaker in all fields of political communication) at a conference held in Moscow in September 1960. As quoted in *Pravda* for September 14, 1960, Ilichev stated that the CPSU had "now raised ideological work and the communist education of the working people to the level of the central task of the party, the trade unions, the Young Communist League and other public organizations." Continuing, Ilichev asserted that "the need to step up ideological-educational work derives from the present-day domestic and international situation and is objectively dictated by the laws of socialist construction." He stated further that the building of communism in the USSR was not merely an internal Soviet affair. It was also a decisive factor in the competition of two social systems in the world. The Soviet people, he went on to say, looked upon their struggle to build communism as an obligation to the working people of the whole world. Ilichev thus stressed two major themes which have normally been prominent in Soviet statements regarding political communication, and which, since the death of Stalin, have been vigorously reemphasized. One theme, as already indicated, is that the success and very survival of communism as a movement depend largely upon the energy and skill of communists as communicators. Secondly, Ilichev's references to the international situation and the struggle of "two systems" reminded his audience that today, despite the changes in—some would say, the degeneration of—Russian Marxism since the period when Lenin first demanded the establishment of a party of professional revolutionaries, communist propaganda is devoted, ultimately, to a political-ideological mission. This mission is overthrowing "capitalism" and first establishing "socialism," and, eventually, "communism" throughout the world.

Contemporary Soviet doctrine reaffirms a well-established pattern by also emphasizing the foreign propaganda significance of the internal economic development of the USSR. A resolution passed by the Twentieth CPSU Congress, in 1956, called for "a closer link between propaganda and agitation and the task of establishing the material-productive base of communism."[5] It is clear from the context of this and later similar statements that they relate to foreign as well as to domestic Soviet policy.

Since this study is concerned primarily with the role of propaganda as an instrument of the foreign policy of the Soviet state, it may be well at the outset to remind ourselves that Moscow's appreciation of the political significance of propaganda does not imply any underestimation of the role of other instruments of domestic and international politics. Harold D. Lasswell has cogently observed that the aim of Soviet propaganda has been "to economize the material cost of world dominance."[6] However, Moscow—not to mention Peking—has never explicitly repudiated Lenin's dictum that great political problems are decided, in the last analysis, by force.[7] It is clear, however, that in our era of super-weapons the Soviet communists prefer more than ever before to achieve their ends by persuasion rather than by force, and that they share, to a high degree, the fear of the consequences of nuclear war which bulks so large in the policy calculations of Washington and London.

In a period of "competitive coexistence" the significance of propaganda may be great indeed. Professor Henry L. Roberts of Columbia University a few years ago raised the question whether under conditions of a military stalemate "of sorts," the "whole weight . . . of these two tremendous political and ideological systems will be brought to bear on one of the few areas of relative mobility and change—the realm of ideas and of cultural activities."[8] Professor Roberts' question seems as pertinent today as in 1958. Indeed, it may be more pertinent if the conclusion of a partial nuclear test ban treaty in 1963, while mitigating weapons competition, puts an even greater premium upon skill in persuasion.

The Soviet communists are, then, dedicated to an energetic, systematic, and persistent propaganda effort, both at home and abroad. How does the Soviet approach to foreign propaganda compare with the "western" approach? What have been the major elements of continuity and of change in the perception by the Soviet leadership of the functions of propaganda as an instrument of foreign policy? Before seeking answers to these questions in major Soviet writings and statements, it might be useful for us to establish a basis for comparison by examining some non-Soviet interpretations of the nature and functions of political propaganda. Robert T. Holt and Robert W. van de Velde note that there are almost as many definitions of propaganda as there are writers on the subject, but they identify it as "the attempt to influence behavior . . . by affecting, through the use of mass media of communications, the manner in which a mass audience perceives and ascribes meaning to the material world." Lasswell, in a study already referred to, describes political propaganda as "the management of mass communications for power purposes," while E. H. Carr, stressing Soviet success in the use of mass communications for foreign policy ends, defines propaganda as "a process organized and carried out by officials . . . as part of the normal conduct of foreign policy." Lindley Fraser traces the use of propaganda in political and religious struggles to the Old Testament, observing, however, that the American Civil War was the first important struggle during which propagandists "regarded it as a major part of their task to persuade outsiders—in particular, Great Britain—that their cause was good and would prevail. . . ."[9]

The above definitions tend to emphasize the elements of manipulation, or even of deception, in propaganda. They reflect the generally suspicious attitude toward the manipulation of symbols for political ends which has been typical of modern western political thought. Western students of politics, and especially of mass communications, are inclined, on the whole, to agree with Dovring's negative characterization of propaganda as "biased communication." Democratic governments, except perhaps in periods of acutely felt international crisis, are more inhibited than are totalitarian states from the employment of propaganda as a major instrument of foreign policy. The high degree of voluntary consensus that prevails in prosperous democracies fosters tolerance and skepticism. The lack of continuity of office and policy characteristic of democracy, especially in the United States, also militates against a systematic government-organized foreign propaganda program of the kind that seems to be a logical concomitant of totalitarianism.

However, the propaganda weaknesses of a democracy are more apparent than real. The unwillingness to attempt to impose its values and organizational patterns on the world that characterizes the government of a mature democratic society bespeaks a broad basis of agreement on fundamental values that is lacking in the outwardly confident but perhaps inwardly seething totalitarian regime. Still, the vigorous propaganda of totalitarianism, with its air of certitude regarding values and goals, has often proved persuasive to disillusioned, alienated, or politically unsophisticated audiences. The communists are at least partly correct in assuming—as they so evidently do—that facts will speak for themselves only if those who communicate them perform their function forcefully and competently.

By way of contrast with western usage, Soviet writers, nurtured in a tradition of what one might call political messianism, have tended to use the term "propaganda" in a highly positive sense, as more or less equivalent to education. Their approval, of course, is restricted to communist propaganda—that disseminated by the "international bourgeoisie" is invariably denounced as the essence of mendacity. Soviet communicators are generally unwilling to admit, except implicitly and infrequently, that they employ propaganda in the sense in which the term is pejoratively used in the west. Moreover, they are vague and usually reticent regarding the foreign propaganda activity of the Soviet state. This reticence has gradually replaced the frank exhortations to political missionary activity of the first few years of the bolshevik regime, and has tended to complicate the task of government officials and scholars seeking clues to Kremlin objectives and tactics in overt Soviet communications.

Reticence, even extreme secretiveness, was Moscow's response from the early post-revolutionary years, to the often exaggerated but not unjustified accusations in foreign countries that Soviet Russian was seeking, by propaganda, to subvert the established social order wherever it saw any possibility of so doing. Almost from the inception of the Soviet regime, foreign governments began to be frustrated and exasperated by what George F. Kennan has called "that ambiguity and contradictoriness of Soviet policy which has endured to the present day: the combination of the doctrine of co-existence—the claim, that is, to the right to have normal outward relations with capitalist countries—with the most determined effort behind the scenes to destroy the western governments and the social and political systems supporting them."[10] Yet, there have also been many occasions when foreign communists, and some Soviet communists, have felt that Moscow was not doing everything in its power to support the cause of social revolution.[11]

Lenin and his followers were acutely aware of the impossibility of inducing more than a tiny fraction of even that most "advanced" social class, the proletariat, to understand, assimilate, and, above all, act in accordance with the complex Marxist system of beliefs and values to which they subscribed. After all, a central tenet of bolshevism always has been that the workers, peasants, and other underprivileged strata of "bourgeois" society, given the influence exerted on their thinking by the machinery of propaganda in the hands of the bourgeois "ruling class," could never elevate their understanding of political and social forces above the level of mere "labor union consciousness" without the guidance of full-time "professional" revolutionaries.[12] The articles on propaganda and related topics in Soviet encyclopedias and other authoritative sources over a period of some forty years have continued to quote and paraphrase Lenin's prescriptions for overcoming the influence of "bourgeois" propaganda on the "masses" and for awakening the victims of "capitalism" to an awareness of their true interests.[13] According to the Leninst theory of opinion formation a few intelligent and dedicated individuals, drawn from all social classes, could be converted by means of propaganda to the "correct" Marxist, or Marxist-Leninist, point of view, and eventually some of these individuals might become fully trained party leaders. However, most people, including most members of the "working class," could best be influenced, and even then usually only temporarily, by what in Leninist doctrine is known as "agitation." In Lenin's original conception, agitation consisted of simple, concrete, forceful illustrations of the general principles of Marxism. In one example given by Lenin an agitator discussing the problem of economic crises took as a starting point the death from starvation of a worker's family. This illustration could be used to drive home the idea of "the senseless contradiction between the increase of wealth and the increase of poverty." A more complete explanation, according to Lenin, should be left to the propagandists.[14]

With the passage of time, and particularly since the consolidation of power in Russia by the bolsheviks after 1917, the concrete, agitational element in Soviet political communication has tended to overshadow the more abstract theoretical or propagandistic element. Also, agitation has tended to become more and more demagogic. As Alfred G. Meyer has observed, agitation rather early became largely synonymous with the activity of inciting the masses to action by playing on their instincts and passions.[15]

It will be useful now to examine some typical Soviet statements on the subject of agitation, especially since, as Inkeles was the first to point out, this form of Soviet political communication has been relatively unstudied in the west. The 1928 article in the *Small Soviet Encyclopedia* on the work of the party in the fields of agitation and propaganda asserted that its basis was the inculcation of "the idea of revolutionary internationalism and the task of strengthening the Communist International as the leader of the revolutionary struggle on a world scale." This article, however, also stated that since 1921 the main content of domestic agitation had been defined by tasks connected with the reconstruction of the Russian national economy.[16] The 1937 article on agitation, in the second edition of the same source, asserted that the "bolshevist organization of agitation requires that all the working people be subjected to ideological influence," but it quoted both Lenin and Stalin concerning the necessity of tying agitation closely to the current policies of the party. Interestingly, the article also pointed out that the success of agitation was dependent upon its adaptation to the particular social stratum to which it was addressed.[17] These statements reflected the increasingly pragmatic spirit of the Soviet approach to political communication, especially after the consolidation of Stalin's totalitarian rule.

The 1949 article on agitation contained in the second edition of the *Large Soviet Encyclopedia* defined it as political activity designed to influence by dissemination of ideas and slogans the "consciousness and mood" of the "broad masses." It added that agitation was an important instrument in the struggle of classes and parties, conducted by means of press, radio, speech, posters, leaflets, cartoons, and the like. Regarding the international aspects of agitation, this article declared that agitation conducted by communist parties in capitalist countries was directed toward "the revolutionary training of the working class, and the working people generally, in the spirit of Marxism-Leninism." Such agitation, besides exposing "fascists and warmongers," played an important role in consolidating the ranks of the international labor movement, combatting Titoists, and exposing lies and slander about the USSR.[18]

It is interesting to compare this 1949 article with an article published in 1955 in the same encyclopedia—after a considerable change of the Soviet political "line." This article asserted that the communists of all countries successfully utilized the experience of the USSR "in the struggle for peace, democracy, and socialism." Indicating the determination of the post-Stalin leaders to exploit nationalist, anti-colonialist, sentiments, it declared that "bourgeois" propaganda not only sought to shake the faith of the working people in the possibility of achieving socialism, but, in its efforts to keep the masses in the capitalist countries enslaved, such propaganda also preached the "dogma of the domination of certain peoples over others." In contrast, the communists, the article stated, disseminated the concept of "proletarian internationalism," as well as "the ideology of the friendship of peoples and real patriotism," and, of course, "the struggle for peace in the whole world."[19]

It is probably sensible to assume that from the Kremlin's standpoint most Soviet messages addressed to non-communist foreign audiences, including speeches and interviews by Khrushchev and other top leaders, and statements made by Soviet representatives at the United Nations, fall within the category of agitation. On the other hand, literature for Marxist-Leninist "study groups," which were found by Royal Commissions in Canada in 1946 and in Australia in 1954 to have been among the instruments for recruitment of susceptible intellectuals into communist "cells," might reasonably be classified as propaganda in the Leninist usage.

We should point out, at this stage of our discussion, that Soviet political communication—hereafter, we will usually use the term propaganda to cover all aspects of such communication—presents both an ideological aspect and a manipulative aspect. By the ideological element in Soviet communication we refer to indications of the faith of Soviet communists that their system of beliefs and their way of life represent an appealing, convincing, model for all of mankind, which will eventually, if its virtues are effectively disseminated, become universal. They can contribute to the adoption of communism by humanity in general by means of exhortation, persuasion, pressure, and, if need be, by violence. Despite the obvious—to a "bourgeois" outsider at least—weaknesses and vulnerabilities of Soviet communism, and also despite the growth of the pragmatic, expediential element in Soviet strategy and tactics, this ideological, almost "religious," but somewhat ritualistic aspect, has never disappeared from the content of Soviet propaganda. Indeed, the persistence of the phraseology of political messianism over a period of more than sixty years in the official documents of Russian Marxism is rather impressive. Looking backward, we find that the first manifesto of the Russian Social-Democratic Labor Party, adopted in 1898, referred to "the great historical mission of the proletariat," namely, the establishment of "a social order in which there will be no place for the exploitation of man by man."[20]

The program adopted sixty-three years later by the CPSU, at its Twenty-second Congress in October 1961, boasted that one-third of mankind was "building a new life under the banner of scientific communism" and it made bold to claim that "The socialist world is expanding; the capitalist world is shrinking." In these ways the program buttressed its position that "communism accomplishes the historic mission of delivering all men from social inequality, from every form of oppression and exploitation." Thus, in remarkably similar language, it echoed the messianic claim of 1898.[21]

The vision of the glorious society of the future, free of coercion and exploitation, which is allegedly being built in the Soviet Union, has normally played a conspicuous role in Soviet propaganda. This "utopian" aspect of communism bulks large in the Soviet form of what Dyer has called the propaganda of "conversion"—which he contrasts to general propaganda, which seeks "relevant political action."[22] The process of ideological conversion, in turn, "produces revolutionaries and makes possible both the party and its hope for eventual success."[23]

Even in the communist propaganda of conversion and political recruitment, manipulative as well as purely ideological elements are present. As Almond points out, "The process of recruitment into the communist movement has at least two stages. The first is that of attraction to one of the many agitational representations. The second stage, that of training and testing in action screens out those elements who have suitable qualities and potentialities." And, as Almond further notes, recruits "at the point of admission into the movement," perceive only dimly the "inner doctrine and practice of the party."[24] Certainly there is a wide gulf between communist demonology as presented in such mass media as the British *Daily Worker* or the French communist newspaper *L'Humanité*, and the power calculus set forth—though not fully systematized or explicated—in the "classics" of Leninism. Individuals are recruited into communist parties through appeals to personal, ethnic, class, or national aspirations and frustrations. Once under party discipline, they are given the political education and the ideological indoctrination that the party leadership regards as appropriate at a particular historical stage.

The utopian-ritualistic aspects of Soviet propaganda are still important. Like the sacred tenets of any belief system, these aspects bolster the sense of righteousness of those who profess to believe in them. They also serve to rationalize the policies of the communist leadership. However, this facet of Soviet propaganda is probably far less important in terms of both domestic and foreign policy than is the manipulative aspect.

By the manipulative aspect of Soviet propaganda we mean the practice of associating, either explicitly or implicitly, the goals and policies of the CPSU and the Soviet state with non-communist symbols and sentiments in order to secure for Soviet policies the maximum possible support of non-communists. Often those influenced by this process of manipulation are unaware of the motives or even the identity of the manipulators. Of course, the tactical flexibility and capacity for manipulation, even of Soviet propaganda, is not and never has been unlimited. To be sure, Soviet propaganda, particularly since about 1934, has been characterized by a high degree of what Lasswell and Blumenstock refer to as "adaptiveness," or the association of key symbols with the aspirations, grievances, and prejudices of the audience to which propaganda is directed. However, as the same authors point out, effective propaganda always requires an element of "distinctiveness." Certain symbols must be "distinctive in meaning and style; otherwise the propagandist will not be able to keep control of the attitudes which he fosters."[25]

Even during World War II, when the Soviet leadership sought to maximize military cooperation with the "capitalist" United States and Great Britain against Nazi Germany, *Pravda* continued to carry on its masthead the traditional appeal, "Proletarians of all countries, unite!" Of course, *Pravda* was not widely available outside the Soviet Union, and what was being said in Russian to Soviet communists was balanced during the period of the "Anglo-Soviet-American Coalition" by soothing assurances, in messages intended for non-communist audiences, of a community of interests and goals between the Soviet Union and the western democracies.

While demanding the exercise of adaptiveness in the interests of effective propaganda, Soviet leaders have usually been alert to the risks of flexibility. Lenin's warning in *What Is To Be Done?* that any deviation from "socialist ideology" signifies a strengthening of "bourgeois ideology" has been cited again and again by his successors whenever they felt it necessary to warn that the limits of flexibility in political strategy and propaganda were being approached.[26] Communists are frequently urged to combine ideological consistency with flexibility, as in Stalin's formula of "the greatest adhesion to principle (not to be confused with sectarianism) with a maximum of contacts and connections with the masses (not to be confused with 'tailism'!)...."[27]

Effectiveness and Limitations of Soviet Propaganda

What is signified, after all, by the sound and fury of Soviet foreign propaganda? How effective is it? Can it create political parties, topple governments, subvert the social order? Or does it have merely a nuisance value for the Kremlin, the capability of influencing or even converting some alienated intellectuals, who may then become either cogs in the Soviet espionage machine, or rather ineffectual and probably temporary propagandists for the Soviet "line"? Or, finally, is it a significant but supplementary instrument of Soviet foreign policy, which reinforces and is congruent with military, economic, and diplomatic instruments?

A qualifiedly affirmative answer would appear to be appropriate for most of the above questions. With the possible exception of Russia itself, in

1917–1918, when Lenin's promises of bread, peace, land, and national self-determination proved overwhelmingly persuasive, propaganda has probably not played the decisive role in communist seizures of power. It has, however, been an important or even crucial Soviet instrument of power. It has made, or helped to make, converts to communism. It has pushed many individuals far enough along the road to conversion to win at least their benevolent neutrality toward Soviet policies and designs. Others, basically hostile to Marxist-Leninist ideology, have either naively believed Soviet promises or have thought, mistakenly, that they could use the communists rather than be used by them in alliances against "capitalists" or "imperialists."

Most important of all, Soviet propaganda has succeeded in intensifying and channeling in directions desirable to the Kremlin attitudes such as fear of war, anti-colonialism, and anti-western nationalism. Soviet propaganda, as Paul Kecskemeti has noted, has been most successful when it has been in a position to project an image of the Soviet Union as being bent on combatting a "manifest evil." In such situations, it has made a significant impact, and has been able to win helpers or at least benevolent neutrality toward Soviet policy.[28] Kecskemeti has identified four historical situations in which the Soviets were able to employ what he called the "universalistic argument." These were : (1) the First World War; (2) the rise of Nazi Germany; (3) the fear of war in the late 1940's; (4) the decline of colonialism in Asia and Africa. It will be noted that three of the four situations identified by Kecskemeti as exceptionally favorable to the success of Soviet foreign propaganda were concerned with the effects or the fear of war.

Kecskemeti's analysis is useful both because it indicates the difficulties confronting Soviet propagandists and points to some of the major factors influencing the effects of Soviet propaganda efforts. Kecskemeti correctly emphasized the essentially negative character of Soviet foreign propaganda. However, he wrote before the full development of certain major features of post-Stalin foreign propaganda which we have sought to analyze in this study. In recent years, the Soviet leadership has made increasingly successful efforts to project important positive propaganda themes, especially to the peoples of the less-developed countries and the newly emerging nations of the world. As Dyer noted, in commenting on Soviet propaganda handling of the launching in 1957 of Soviet artificial earth satellites, the Soviet Union "proclaimed a right to leadership on the ground that its knowledge was superior."[29] Soviet propaganda regarding such matters as educational and scientific progress, economic development, and the alleged Soviet solution of the "nationality problem" has told the peoples of the developing areas that by following the Soviet path of economic, social, and political development, they could most effectively realize their own legitimate aspirations.

"Positive" and affirmative Soviet propaganda, while often resting in part on a foundation of facts—as in the case of Soviet scientific achievements—can be in its way as demagogic as the negative propaganda identified by Kecskemeti.[30] Soviet propagandists frequently offer solutions to urgent problems, such as disarmament, which seem plausible but which in the opinion of western experts cannot be implemented and which they themselves would refuse to put into effect were their propaganda bluff to be called.

In many economically underdeveloped countries Soviet propaganda has guided and reinforced the efforts of local communist parties to exploit peasant poverty and land hunger. As in Russia, peasants have often supported leaders who have promised to give the land to those who till it. But the leaders conceal from their followers their Marxist-Leninist goal of collectivizing farming and turning the farmer into a cog in a state-directed economic machine. Cuba, Vietnam, and many other examples come readily to mind. Soviet propaganda has inspired moods or generated pressures within foreign states which have tended to lessen the ability of their governments to oppose Soviet policies. Soviet "ban the bomb" propaganda, for example, probably was an important factor in enabling the USSR to simultaneously pursue an expansionist foreign policy and limit the effectiveness of western countermeasures during the years when the United States had a monopoly of atomic weapons. Also, Soviet anti-western propaganda may have played a sufficient part in shaping the attitudes of individuals in "neutralist" countries to influence the policies of their governments in a pro-Soviet, anti-western direction. Of course, the Suez crisis, the Algerian conflict, the situations in the Congo and Angola, among many, were exploitable and Moscow did its best to fan the flames.

However, the effectiveness of Soviet propaganda regarding, for example, Algeria or Angola, may have been limited because while Moscow talked it did little to aid the groups it professed to support. One wonders whether many a Latin-American radical did not feel at least temporarily let down or even betrayed when Khrushchev in October 1962 agreed to remove Soviet "offensive" ballistic missiles from Cuba. Moreover, the Soviets have usually been remarkably parsimonious in offering positive programs for the correction of the evils they decry and denounce. The self-seeking line followed by the Russians could not fail, one would think, in the long run, to be disappointing to all but communists. However, we must recognize the fact that many intellectuals and would-be intellectuals in underdeveloped countries feel that Soviet policy, because it is "socialist" must be constructive. Soviet propaganda in the last few years, despite improvement in the quantity and quality of its informational support, as well as increased use of promotional devices, such as radio quiz shows, a philately department in the magazine *USSR*, and recently the placing of advertisements in major American newspapers, has not been strikingly

371

original or imaginative. For example, the Kremlin seems to have neglected to exploit propaganda opportunities inherent in differences of emphasis among the western allies on such matters as the degree and kind of inspection necessary for a workable agreement banning nuclear weapons tests.

It should be borne in mind, nevertheless, that in terms of careful briefing and coordinated action for the purpose of quickly marshalling data necessary to support their government's policy line, Soviet UN personnel —and Soviet participants in international scientific and other kinds of conferences and organizations—are probably at an advantage, and operate more effectively, than their British or American counterparts. In part, these observations are prompted by conversations with American and African diplomats serving at the UN.

There is increasing evidence that with the growth in Soviet self-confidence occasioned by the expanding world role of the USSR, and, perhaps also reflecting the relatively relaxed post-Stalin domestic situation, Soviet personnel serving abroad, especially at the United Nations, are less reluctant than formerly to participate in various social activities on a more or less informal basis, especially with nationals of the less-developed countries. But, in connection with Africa, it is worth remembering that no African state has yet become communist, and even in leftist-oriented Guinea the Soviets, in 1961, failed dismally in their efforts to organize an actively subversive movement, and have apparently been losing rather than gaining influence ever since.

It appears that Soviet communicators, like others, have found face-to-face contact a more effective instrument of influence than the printed page or the radio broadcast. It is probably in connection with this superiority of "primary contact" as a propaganda tool that Moscow derives the greatest benefit from the existence of a network of foreign communist parties that present the Soviet line as fellow-countrymen of those to whom they speak.

The success of Khrushchev in projecting his personality and using himself as an instrument of propaganda access has been considerable, and the same can probably be said, though to a far lesser degree, about Mikoyan, Kozlov, Mukhitdinov, Brezhnev, and other leading Soviet agitator-politicians. However, the nature of Soviet totalitarianism imposes limits on Soviet use of face-to-face communication. Many instances have been reported to this writer, and he has personally observed some, in which the inflexible, phonograph-like presentation of the official Soviet foreign policy position by Soviet representatives, either at home or abroad, has proved to be a source of irritation rather than persuasion. In addition, Soviet fear of easy intimacy and informality often interposes barriers to easy communication. Generally speaking, Soviet success in the area of cultural diplomacy and exchanges of persons are more likely to occur when carefully staged spectacles and regimented masses—as in youth and sports festivals—can be employed, than in the smaller, more intimate type of gathering, where communist aversion to spontaneity is likely to strike a jarring note.

Also, Moscow achieves an impact with some of its dramatic propaganda spectacles, such as the youth and students' festivals, partly because of the failure of the United States and other free nations to develop positive programs to demonstrate the values of democracy. Why not a democratic world youth festival? In connection with the 1962 communist youth festival in Helsinki, the American State Department had no clear policy regarding its attitude toward participation by American youth—and participation by some curious, idealistic, and in some instances highly competent American young people was inevitable, with or without official encouragement or discouragement. It is to be hoped that the efforts of various groups of young Americans to exploit for democratic purposes this Soviet-organized propaganda spectacle did not go unappreciated by American policy-makers. A noncommittal, evasive attitude such as the United States Government has sometimes taken toward communist efforts to exploit the idealism of youth or the legitimate grievances of peasants and workers furnishes no basis for countering Soviet propaganda, let alone for developing an effective positive program of democratic action. The same can be said about the tendency of American officials serving in many countries to associate mainly, sometimes solely, with members of the entrenched local elites, and to neglect contacts with leaders of reform movements and even with artists, scientists, and other persons outside of government. In addition, the American image has of course suffered from the ethnocentrism, cultural parochialism, and ignorance—for example, of foreign languages—still too often displayed by otherwise well educated Americans. Obviously, we cannot cultivate whatever favorable predispositions exist toward democracy if we lack knowledge of them and are unable to establish rapport with those who possess them.

Some characteristics of the Soviet foreign propaganda effort stand out with particular clarity. The hostility and aggressiveness underlying it, though relatively mild in comparison with Peking's output, are patent. However, the road to world domination is not necessarily paved with craving for power. It is certain that the Soviet effort is a big and an expensive one. It is not, perhaps, as big an effort, in terms of financial support, as some of us, including this writer, have in the past been inclined to believe. Still, it is large and growing. According to information received by the author from a well-informed United States government source, in March 1962 it was estimated that as of 1957 the total communist bloc foreign propaganda effort amounted, in terms of American dollars, to something between four hundred and seventy-five million and seven hundred million. As of 1962, the range of estimates was between something under a billion and something more than one hundred million. The Soviet part of this total effort was estimated to be about forty per cent. A reflection of communist fear of free communication can be seen from the estimate the USSR alone was spending about one hundred and fifteen million dollars a year, as of 1961, for the jamming of foreign radio broadcasts. This figure was in excess of the estimated Soviet expenditure for transmitting radio broadcasts to foreign countries.[31]

The questions posed at the beginning of this article could be better answered if the government agencies concerned, as well as private scholars, undertook, on a much bigger scale than at present, to produce the necessary descriptive, historical, analytical, and statistical studies of the impact of Soviet propaganda on different geographic regions and social strata. The most sophisticated and balanced study of communist influence which has so far been published is Gabriel A. Almond's *The Appeals of Communism*. This study, however, deals primarily with the activities of four major western communist parties, namely, the American, British, French, and Italian parties, rather than with the foreign political activity of the Soviet Union. A difficult problem, only partially explored as yet in the literature on the Soviet Union or on foreign communist parties, is that of distinguishing between the influence of Soviet propaganda and that of the various national communist parties. Of course, even with an abundance of good case studies, the evaluation of the effectiveness of Soviet propaganda would remain formidably difficult. It is often impossible to perceive accurately or fully the relationship between a particular political act and a given, identifiable propaganda stimulus. As Lerner has indicated, the four main types of evidence of propaganda effectiveness—responsive action, participant reports, observer commentaries, and indirect indicators—are all difficult to obtain and require caution and subtlety of interpretation to be useful.[32]

It is well to strike a cautious note in any general appraisal of the effectiveness of Soviet propaganda. The tendency of the American public is to attribute almost superhuman cunning, skill, and effectiveness to Soviet propaganda. This is indicated, for example, by such typical press items as the headline in the *New York Herald Tribune* for January 31, 1962, "Gallup Poll Gives Reds Four-Three Edge in War of Ideas." The public tendency, as well as that of some experts on communism, is to attribute the growth of communist power exclusively to communist cunning, and to ignore the complex situations which predispose individuals, groups, and sometimes nations to respond to the appeals of communism. It is useful to have the warnings about the effectiveness of Soviet propaganda produced by Suzanne Labin and Stefan T. Possony.[33] Labin argues that Soviet and French communist propaganda was responsible for the defeat of EDC in France in 1954. She also asserts that "European universities are so contaminated that the Communist and para-Communist movements of Asia and Africa can be said to have been nurtured in them."[34]

There is a grain of truth in such assertions, but of course they represent gross exaggerations. The danger in being guided exclusively by estimates of Soviet propaganda influence such as the foregoing, is two-fold. On the one hand, excessive emphasis on the role of propaganda in Soviet policy can blind one to the importance of such factors as education and scientific research that enable the USSR to build the power which makes its propaganda impressive. Perhaps more important, the alarmist view of Soviet propaganda may lead us to think that all that is required to combat communist influence is American counter-propaganda.

We must constantly keep reminding ourselves that ours is an era of disturbing and puzzling social and cultural change. The unsettling effects of rapid social change have been compounded by the destruction and disillusionment resulting from wars. Add to all this the anxieties induced by the existence of nuclear weapons and there is a situation pregnant with potential for propaganda manipulation. Unfortunately for Moscow, however, the extremism of the Chinese communists may have rendered it difficult for the international communist movement to exploit the "peace" theme as effectively as Khrushchev might desire. This is indicated, for example, by the fact that in his already-cited speech of December 12, 1962, in which he defended Soviet Cuban policy against the "Trotskyite" policy of his "Albanian"—a thinly veiled reference to Chinese—critics, Khrushchev said that their willingness to risk the "destruction of millions of human beings" could "repel millions and millions of people from the communist movement."

Emphasis on the factors in the international environment which foster susceptibility to the appeals of communism is in no sense defeatist. If we are to limit the effectiveness of these appeals, we must first perceive their dimensions as clearly as possible. In some situations, awareness of the predispositions which favor communist influence may stimulate action designed to alter the circumstances which foster pro-communist attitudes. It may also prevent us from falling into the trap of indiscriminately labeling all social protest movements as "communist." Finally, it may facilitate refutation of communist propaganda by enabling us to point to incompatibilities between standard communist operating procedures and the promises communists often make to persons unaware of the gulf between Soviet propaganda and the reality of Soviet international practices.

The main purpose of this study has been to demonstrate the energy with which Soviet propaganda has exploited both the negative and the positive sentiments generated by the revolutionary social-political and psycho-cultural developments of the twentieth century. It is sensible to assume that continued existence of the favorable predispositions toward Soviet claims and promises of some strata of the contemporary world propaganda audience combined with systematic, intensive Soviet cultivation of these attitudes will tend to foster Soviet influence. This will be particularly true in the absence of effective free world concern. However, direct evidence of Soviet propaganda effectiveness is extremely scanty. There have been, of course, a few studies which strongly suggest that Soviet achievements in outer space, for example, have had a powerful impact on many sectors of world opinion.[35] However, it is a real question to what extent the impact of Soviet achievements in this or other fields can be considered evidence of the effectiveness of Soviet propaganda exploitation of these achievements and to what extent it is merely a reflection of the fact that they occurred. Perhaps it is not irrelevant to remind ourselves here that if the positive example of Soviet achievements can influence world opinion, so also can knowledge of western shortcomings, such as unjust treatment of ethnic minorities.

Khrushchev evidently regards Soviet scientific and technical progress as one of the main instruments for the victory of communism in the world today. Beginning in 1956, he has increasingly emphasized the crucial significance of victory in the "battle of production" for the world triumph of communism. This conviction is also indicated by current stress, in Soviet articles regarding propaganda and ideology, on the priority of the propaganda of production.[36]

NOTES

1. V. I. Lenin, *Izbrannye proizedeniya v dvukh tomakh*, Vol. I (Moscow, 1943), pp. 157, 176, 186.

2. *Ibid.*, p. 252.

3. See, for example, Alex Inkeles, *Public Opinion in Soviet Russia* (Cambridge, Mass., 1951), Part 1; John A. Armstrong, *The Soviet Bureaucratic Elite* (New York, 1959), Chaps. 3 and 7; *Programma po kursu zhurnalistiki*, published by the Higher Party School of the CPSU central committee (Moscow, 1958); *Aspirantura, spravochnik dlya postupayushchikh v aspiranturu i soiskatelei uchenykh stepenei* (Moscow, 1960). The latter indicates the works of Lenin, Stalin, Marx, Khrushchev, etc., which must be studied in the political courses taken by Soviet graduate students. See also *Lenin-zhurnalist i redaktor* (Moscow, 1960), in which Lenin's activities and techniques as political journalist and editor are held up as models for present-day Soviet practitioners in these fields; and *Lenin o propagande i agitatsii* (2nd edition, Moscow, 1962); a handbook of selected statements by Lenin on propaganda. E. Adamov, in his pamphlet, *O masterstve rechi propagandista* (Moscow, 1962), quotes Lenin frequently—but quotes Khrushchev even more frequently, perhaps.

4. *Malaya sovetskaya entsiklopediya*, 2nd ed., Vol. 8 (Moscow, 1939), cols. 726–731. The article also briefly summarized Lenin's activities as a propagandist, referring, for example, to the school for training party propagandists organized by Lenin in Paris, in 1911, Lenin's sloganeering during World War I, and his role after the bolshevik revolution of 1917 in helping to establish the Soviet network of propaganda agencies.

5. *XX sezd kommunisticheskoi partii sovetskogo soyuza, stenograficheski otchet*, Vol. II (Moscow, 1956), p. 426. This resolution was also referred to in *Politicheski slovar* (Moscow, 1958), p. 456.

6. Harold D. Lasswell, "The Strategy of Soviet Propaganda," in Wilbur Schramm, ed., *The Process and Effects of Mass Communication* (Urbana, Ill., 1954), p. 538.

7. Lenin, *Izbrannye proizvedeniya*, Vol. I, p. 436.

8. *Columbia University Forum*, Spring, 1958, p. 29. See also Abraham Brumberg, "New Formula for Soviet Propaganda," *New Leader*, August 15–22, 1960.

9. Robert T. Holt and Robert W. van de Velde, *Strategic Psychological Operations and American Foreign Policy* (Chicago, 1960), pp. 26–27; E. H. Carr, *The Soviet Impact on the Western World* (New York, 1947), p. 69; Lasswell, *op. cit.*, p. 538; Lindley Fraser, *Propaganda* (London, 1957), p. 30. Other studies which provide particularly valuable insights or concepts useful in the analysis of Soviet propaganda include the following: Gabriel A. Almond, *The Appeals of Communism* (Princeton, 1954); Frank S. Meyer, *The Moulding of Communists* (New York, 1961); Neal Wood, *Communism and British Intellectuals* (London, 1959); Karin Dovring, *Road of Propaganda* (New York, 1959); and Murray Dyer, *The Weapon on the Wall* (Johns Hopkins Press, 1959).

10. George F. Kennan, *Russia and the West under Lenin and Stalin* (Boston & Toronto, 1960, 1961), p. 166.

11. See Alexander Dallin, "The Use of International Movements," in Ivo J. Lederer, ed., *Russian Foreign Policy* (New Haven & London, 1962), Chap. 10.

12. Lenin, *Izbrannye proizvedeniya*, pp. 175, 186.

13. See, for example, *Malaya sovetskaya entsiklopediya*, 1st ed., Vol. I (Moscow, 1928), col. 103; *ibid.*, Vol. 6 (Moscow, 1930), cols. 931–932; *Bolshaya sovetskaya entsiklopediya*, Vol. 24 (Moscow, 1953), pp. 495–496; 2nd ed., Vol. 35 (Moscow, 1955), pp. 30–33; *Politicheski slovar* (Moscow, 1958), p. 456.

14. Inkeles, *op. cit.*, p. 39. A full understanding of Lenin's distinction between "propaganda" and "agitation" requires the study of a number of Lenin's works, especially *What Is To Be Done?*

15. Alfred G. Meyer, *Leninism* (Cambridge, Mass., 1957), p. 50. Meyer strongly emphasizes the manipulative element, even in early Leninism.

16. *Malaya sovetskaya entsiklopediya*, Vol. I, col. 103.

17. *Malaya sovetskaya entsiklopediya*, 2nd ed., Vol. I, (Moscow, 1937), cols. 126–127.

18. *Bolshaya sovetskaya entsiklopediya*, 2nd ed., Vol. I (Moscow, 1949), pp. 295–301.

19. *Bolshaya sovetkaya entsiklopediya*, 2nd ed., Vol. 35 (Moscow, 1955), p. 73.

20. *KPSS v rezolyutsiyak i resheniyakh. Tizdanie sedmoe* (Moscow, 1953), Vol. I, p. 13.

21. The 1961 program is available in a number of good English translations, of which perhaps the most useful is that edited by Jan F. Triska, under the title *Soviet Communism, Programs and Rules* (San Francisco, 1962). Above material on pp. 24–25. The original Russian text of the program, as adopted, appeared in *Pravda* for November 2, 1961, while a slightly different "Draft" was published in *Pravda* for July 31, 1961; the differences are indicated by Triska.

22. Murray Dyer, *The Weapon on the Wall* (Johns Hopkins, 1959), p. 14.

23. Lucian W. Pye, *Guerrilla Communism in Malaya* (Princeton, 1956), p. 40.

24. Almond, *op. cit.*, pp. 5 and 93.

25. Harold D. Lasswell and Dorothy Blumenstock, *World Revolutionary Propaganda* (New York, 1939). See especially pp. 247–358 and also comment in David D. Truman, *The Governmental Process* (New York, 1951), p. 229.

26. A recent example of such warnings is contained in the preface to the sixth volume of the fifth edition of the complete works of Lenin. See V. I. Lenin, *Polnoe sobranie sochinenii*, Vol. 6 (Moscow, 1959), ix.

27. Quoted by Georgi Dimitroff in the *Communist International*, Nos. 17–18, 1935 (New York: Workers' Library Publishers, September 20, 1935), p. 1207, from an article by Stalin in *Pravda* for February 3, 1925.

28. Paul Kecskemeti, "The Soviet Approach to International Political Communication," *Public Opinion Quarterly*, Vol. XX (Spring, 1956), No. 1, pp. 299–308. Quoted material on p. 305.

29. Dyer, *op. cit.*, p. 3.

30. However, propaganda about Soviet scientific and economic achievements serves as a powerful instrument of psychological pressure upon the non-Soviet world. Needless to say, the impact of this pressure depends not only upon the material realities involved, but also upon the accuracy of information and maturity of judgment of the publics to whom Soviet claims regarding material achievements are directed. For this reason, among others, such studies as Nicholas DeWitt's monumental work, *Education and Professional Employment in the USSR*, Washington, D.C., 1961, are useful.

31. The figures on Soviet foreign propaganda expenditures given in this author's *Soviet Cultural Offensive, op. cit.*, p. 158, may have been somewhat inflated. For additional data on the logistics of the Soviet program, see the already-cited works of F. Bowen Evans and Evron Kirkpatrick, as well as the 1957–1958 *Fact Book*, distributed by the United States Information Agency.

32. Daniel Lerner, "Effective Propaganda: Conditions and Evaluation," in Schramm, *op. cit.*, pp. 485–487.

33. Madame Labin's study, "The Technique of Soviet Propaganda," was distributed in a pamphlet under that title by the Subcommittee to Investigate the Administration of the Internal Security Act and Other Internal Security Laws, of the Committee on the Judiciary, U.S. Senate, 86th Cong., 2nd Sess., Washington, D.C., 1960; see also Stefan T. Possony, "Language as a Communist Weapon," distributed by the House Committee on Un-American Activities, under date of March 2, 1959.

34. Labin, *op. cit.*, p. 7.

35. See the study by Gabriel A. Almond, "Public Opinion and the Development of Space Technology."

36. It is significant that the first, in order of listing, of the duties prescribed for members of the CPSU by the statutes, adopted at the Twenty-second Congress is to "work for the creation of the material and technical basis of communism," etc., and that both Khrushchev's major speech of December 12, 1962, and the foreign policy declaration published in *Pravda* for January 7, 1963 emphasized the centrality, for the world victory of communism, of victory in the US–Soviet production contest. Also, a decree of the CPSU issued in 1957 prescribed that Soviet trade unions should disseminate, among foreign trade unionists, information regarding the economic-scientific achievements of the Soviet Union. The text of this decree is available on pp. 160–176 of *Spravochnik sekretary a pervichnoi partiinoi organizatsii* (Moscow, 1960).

8

Communication Effects

THE EFFECTS of communication are many and diverse. They may be short-range or long-run. They may be manifest or latent. They may be strong or weak. They may derive from any number of aspects of the communication content. They may be considered as psychological or political or economic or sociological. They may operate upon opinions, values, information levels, skills, taste, or overt behavior.

The variety and the complexity of the effects of communications makes difficult the research procedures for studying communication effects. While in the past these topics have been relatively neglected, there has been during the last decade more of a concerted effort to attack these problems. Most studies have dealt with short-run effects upon opinion because the available research methods seemed most applicable to this particular problem. However, by the use of interrelated procedures and more adequate theoretical formulations, distinct advances have been made toward the objective of rigorous, systematic research in this field.

The first selection is taken from Charters' summary of the Payne Fund pioneer investigations of the effects of motion pictures upon children. This review indicates the various techniques which were employed

379

in the parent study; "before and after" attitude testing, educational testing, analysis of personal documents and case histories, and physiological measurement. Although carried out over three decades ago, it is most contemporary in its underlying research strategy. Then follows an example of a careful experimental study of communication effects taken from a series of studies by Hovland and associates who developed the "before and after" method into a refined type of investigation. Alternatively, greater understanding of the impact of communication messages is possible when the researcher employs deeper psychological tools of analysis, such as intensive interviews and projective tests. While no such example is included, the bibliography makes reference to a variety of such studies.

Likewise, a fuller understanding of the processes of communications effects derives from the use of more than one research standpoint, and especially where the institutional context is taken into account. The prototype for this approach is presented in a portion of the study by Shils and Janowitz on "Cohesion and Disintegration in the Wehrmacht." On the basis of various research techniques, they probe the organizational structure of the German military as a context for understanding the impact of Allied propaganda messages. Their theoretical frame of reference, which focuses on the linkages between primary group contacts and mass communications, has become a standard theoretical approach. In a related fashion, Himmelweit's study of the effect of television on children and young people represents the combined use of survey techniques, diaries, personality tests, educational achievement measurements, and teachers' ratings, in order to ascertain more precisely the impact of this medium.

As a result, the main thrust in this field has been toward analysis and synthesis which would present us with more broadly explanatory models of the long-term impact of mass communications. Katz and Lazarsfeld present some empirical data about a "two step" flow, in which the impact of the mass media is seen as the result of a flow of communications to opinion leaders who in turn influence the populations involved. Lang and Lang, on the basis of a variety of studies, use the voting decision as an example, where communication impact is seen to involve also direct and relatively unmediated reactions. Finally, Klapper presents a synthesis of the field designed to identify the conditions under which the mass media are effective in producing change.

Motion Pictures and Youth

Developing Attitudes

BECAUSE A CLOSE RELATIONSHIP between the attitude of an individual and his actions may be assumed, the study of the effect of motion pictures upon the attitude of children toward important social values is central in importance.

Peterson and Thurstone by the use of different techniques isolated the influence of specific pictures upon groups of children while keeping constant the factors of community standards, habits of children, school, influence, home training, and the like. They assumed that these had not materially influenced the children in the brief period between their first and second tests of attitudes; the factor that had changed during the period was exposure to a specific film.

These investigators used eleven highly sensitive instruments to discover changes in attitude toward or against the following eight social objects: the Germans (a scale and a paired comparison), war (two scales), crime, prohibition, the Chinese, capital punishment, the punishment of criminals (two scales), and the Negro. The instruments were scales which consisted of approximately thirty statements each expressing an attitude toward an object. These statements varied in intensity of position from one extreme of attitude against the object to the other extreme of attitude in favor of the object. The statements were weighted according to techniques described in the study[1] and a total score was computed for each individual to express his attitude toward an object.

The scales were given to high-school children shortly before a picture was seen and the position of the group upon the scale was computed. The picture (which in all cases the children had not seen before) was shown

Reprinted from *Motion Pictures and Youth* (1933), pp. 18–25; 35–43, by permission of the author and the publisher. (Copyright, 1933, by Macmillan Co.)

and approximately the day after the showing the scale was given again. The new position of the groups was computed and the resulting change in position noted. In some cases the scale was again checked by some of the groups after two and one-half, five, eight, and nineteen months had elapsed to determine the permanence of the changes which were noted the day after the showing of the picture.

Approximately 4,000 individuals participated in the study as subjects. Most of the subjects were junior and senior high-school students. The exceptions were three in number. In one study 246 college students were used and in another about 100 fourth- and fifth-grade children checked the scale while in three other studies sixth-grade children were included with the junior and senior high-school students. The children were located in the schools of small towns in the neighborhood of Chicago and at Mooseheart, the children's home supported by the Loyal Order of Moose. Small towns were chosen primarily because of the ease of selecting pictures which had not been seen by the children.

Thirteen pictures were selected which met three criteria: they definitely pertained to the issues to be studied, they were free enough from objectionable matter so that high-school principals could be asked to send their students to see them, and they were sufficiently recent to eliminate distractions caused by fashions or photography. Between 600 and 800 pictures of all kinds were reviewed and from them the thirteen used in the studies were selected. This selection represents an attempt to secure films which would in the judgment of the reviewers be likely to produce a noticeable change in attitude if changes were produced by any pictures. All, however, were well-known films. The titles and issues were: "Four Sons" (on the Germans and war); "Street of Chance" (gambling); "Hide Out" (prohibition); "Son of the Gods" (the Chinese); "Welcome Danger" (the Chinese); "The Valiant" (capital punishment); "Journey's End" (war); "All Quiet on the Western Front" (war); "The Criminal Code" (punishment of criminals); "Alibi" (punishment of criminals); "The Birth of a Nation" (the Negro); "Big House" (punishment of criminals); and "Numbered Men" (punishment of criminals).

The outstanding contribution of the study is the establishment of the fact that the attitude of children toward a social value can be measurably changed by one exposure to a picture. An outstanding picture of potency in its influence upon attitude was "Son of the Gods," a picture selected because it was thought to be favorable to the Chinese. Prior to the showing of the picture the mean attitude of a population of 182 children from grades 9 to 12 inclusive stood at 6.72 on a scale in which the extreme positions were approximately 3.5 at the favorable end of the scale and 9.5 at the unfavorable end. After the children had seen the picture the mean shifted 1.22 steps in a favorable direction from 6.72 to 5.50 and this difference was 17.5 times the probable error of the differences. The shift in attitude is "very striking." "The Birth of a Nation" was shown to 434 children of grades 6 to 12 inclusive. Prior to the showing the mean position of this population was 7.41 with extremes of approximately 2.5 at the unfavorable end of the scale to approximately 9.5 at the favorable end. After exposure to the picture the position shifted in an unfavorable direction to 5.93 with a difference of 1.48, which was 25.5 times the probable error of the differences. This was the largest shift obtained in the studies. "All Quiet on the Western Front" produced in 214 junior and senior highschool students a shift against war 14.98 times the probable error of the differences and "The Criminal Code" a shift against the punishment of criminals 12.2 times the probable error of the difference with 246 college students and 11.7 times against the same issue with 276 high-school students. These were the outstanding cases. Significant results were obtained, also, from the showing of "Four Sons" upon attitude toward the Germans, "Welcome Danger," "The Valiant," and "All Quiet on the Western Front." Statistically important changes did not result from single showings of "Four Sons" upon the attitude toward war, of "Hide Out" toward prohibition, of "Journey's End," with one group, toward war, and "Alibi," "Big House," and "Numbered Men" toward the punishment of criminals. In all of these cases but one the differences, however, were in the expected direction. In "Street of Chance" the investigators expected to discover a change of attitude favorable to gambling but a significant change against gambling was recorded.

The range of influence of the motion picture is sensibly broadened by a second fact which these attitude studies have discovered. The investigators found that the effect of pictures upon attitude is cumulative. They demonstrated the fact that two pictures are more powerful than one and three are more potent than two. At Mooseheart, when "Big House" was shown to 138 junior and senior high-school children and "Numbered Men" to another group of 168, neither produced a statistically significant shift in attitude toward the punishment of criminals. When both pictures were seen by a group the change became significant. The shift was then 3.0 times the probable error of the differences. When to these two exposures was added exposure to a third film on the same subject, "The Criminal Code," the shift was still greater and amounted to 6.7 times the probable error.

Again at Mooseheart "Journey's End" and "All Quiet on the Western Front" were shown separately and in combination. These pictures had individual potency. "Journey's End" alone caused a shift of 5.07 times the probable error against war and "All Quiet on the Western Front" produced one of 6.07 times in the same direction. When the former was followed by the latter the shift was increased to 8.07 times the probable error and when the latter was followed by the former the amount of change was increased to 8.26 times.

This pair of studies indicates a significant hypothesis, namely, that even though one picture related to a social issue may not significantly affect the attitude of an individual or a group, continued exposure to pictures of similar character will in the end produce a measurable change of attitude. What the range and limits of such influence may be we do not know. Whether or not it is true in this area that the repetitions of exposure would increase indefinitely is a subject worthy of investigation. Whether or not there is a threshold of personal sensitivity in children above which many pictures do not rise in power and influence we can not say. But it is worth while to know that under the conditions of these studies at least, the cumulative effect of pictures upon attitudes is unmistakably indicated.

To these two leads into the influence of motion pictures upon attitudes Peterson and Thurstone have added a third. They have shown that the shifts created by exposure to a film have substantial permanence. In six localities the attitude scales were repeated at varying intervals and changes in average positions of the groups were computed. The case of the high school at Geneva, Illinois, is typical. Before seeing the film, "Son of the Gods," the children's position on a scale of attitude toward the Chinese was 6.61 and promptly after seeing the film it was 5.19—a shift in favor of the Chinese. Five months after seeing the film there was a recession to 5.72 toward the original position of 5.19 and nineteen months later the position was 5.76. That is to say, the effect of the film had not worn off in a year and a half. In none of the six localities was the recession complete except in one. At Paxton, Illinois, the original position was 4.34 on the scale of attitude toward war before exposure to the film, "All Quiet on the Western Front." After viewing the picture the group shifted to 3.74, indicating a less favorable attitude toward war. Eight months later the position had changed to 4.64 which is more favorable to war than was the original attitude. Probably other influences had played upon the children during these eight months. In all other cases residual traces of the exposure were in evidence at the end of periods of two and one-half, four, six, or eight months.

The principle of permanence is indicated by these investigations. One cannot say that the effects of pictures disappear rapidly. And this position is supported in numerous cases reported by Blumer from the movie autobiographies of his subjects, where hundreds of memories of the influence of specific pictures are related in later years by adults. In other cases Blumer's autobiographers, however, attest to the short-lived influence of movies upon conduct.

This trio of conclusions has great significance for education. We can conclude on the basis of fact that single pictures may produce a change in attitude, that the influence of pictures is cumulative, and that their effects are substantially permanent. This is the second link in the chain of evidence.

How to interpret the social significance of these changes is an interesting consideration. One clue is given in the scores upon the scales. For instance, to select one of the more powerful films, before the picture "Son of the Gods" was shown there were individuals in the group at one extreme position of unfavorableness marked 9.5 upon the scale—meaning roughly: "There are no refined or cultured Chinese," "I don't see how any one could ever like the Chinese," or "There is nothing about the Chinese that I like or admire." Six steps to the other extreme in this group were those who held: "I like the Chinese" and "I'd like to know more Chinese people." The mode of the group and the average were slightly unfavorable at 6.72, which is slightly beyond the neutral point of 6 and toward the unfavorable end. The mode (the most common position taken by the individuals in the group) was: "I have no particular love nor hate for the Chinese." After the picture was shown the same spread of six units was in evidence, from 3.5 to 9.5, but there were fewer children at 9.5 and more at 3.5. The change was 1.22 indicating a shift of about 20 per cent of the distance between the positions of the most extreme and the least extreme individuals in the group. The mode had shifted from neutrality to a point between "The Chinese are pretty decent" and "Chinese parents are unusually devoted to their children."

Influencing Conduct

Conduct is a product of many factors. Of these factors the preceding investigations have explored four. We may assume the obvious position that information is a factor in behavior: what one knows determines in part what one does. We may also assume that attitudes toward social objects affect conduct: if one is friendly toward an objective of action in a situation he will be influenced to build one behavior pattern; if unfriendly, to build another. It may also be fairly assumed that experiences which are accompanied by excitement and emotion have a more powerful effect upon conduct than do those which are placid and uninteresting. Likewise, we may assume that fatigue expressed either by increased or decreased sleep motility results in producing a tone of behavior by which conduct patterns are affected. We have seen that motion pictures have an influence upon all of these factors.

We were able to check the validity of these assumptions, which square with common sense, by a mass of evidence from the studies of Blumer and his associates. Here it was possible to secure hundreds of cases in which the information and attitudes acquired in the motives were directly operative in the conduct of children.

Blumer, Thrasher, and their associates[2] supplemented the foregoing indirect studies of conduct by investigating the direct relationships existing between movies and conduct. Blumer used an autobiography technique, supplemented by interviews, accounts of conversations, and questionnaires. His major study was based upon the case reports of 634 students in two universities, 481 college and junior-college students in four colleges, 583 high-school students, 67 office workers, and 58 factory workers. After studying many biographies written without specific directions and discovering the patterns into which they unconsciously fell, he formulated a few questions to guide the writers as follows: trace the history of your interest in the movies; describe how motion pictures have affected your emotions and your moods; write fully about what you have imitated from the movies; describe your experience with pictures of love and romance; write fully about any ambitions and temptations you have gotten from the movies. Unusual care was taken to preserve the anonymity of the writers. Interviewers were held with 81 university students who had previously written autobiographies and 54 high-school students who had not. Careful accounts of conversations were secured from several fraternities, several sororities, and girls' groups and from several cliques of high-school boys and girls, from conversations of high-school boys and girls at parties, and from boys' gangs, play groups, office girls, and factory workers. Direct questionnaires were administered to 1,200 children in the fifth and sixth grades of 12 public schools in Chicago distributed between schools in high, medium, and low delinquency areas. One set of questionnaires was filled out by a special school for truants and boys with behavior problems. Direct observations were made of children while in attendance at small neighborhood theaters.

From these sources a huge mass of materials was collected. The materials were analyzed to discover trends and significant facts. The main use of the material "has been to show and illuminate the different kinds of ways in which motion pictures touch the lives of young people." Experiences which recurred with a high rate of frequency in the separate documents were selected and samples of each type were presented in the report.

Obviously the validity of personal reports is an issue that has a bearing upon the conclusions of the investigators. Upon this question Blumer took all known precautions against error and presents the following facts about the safeguards which they threw around the investigations: (1) Machinery was set up to demonstrate in an obvious manner the anonymity of the written accounts. (2) The utmost care and attention were devoted to gaining full coöperation from the students in securing their frank, honest, and unexaggerated statements. (3) The interviews held six months after the autobiographies were written were used in the cases of some 60 students with their consent but without this previous knowledge as a check against agreement between the content of the written report and the substance of the interview; no discrepancy of importance was discovered. (4)

The accounts were checked for internal consistency and some twenty which showed contradiction were discarded. (5) Conversations were checked against the written reports. (6) Individuals were asked to write only about those experiences which they recalled vividly.

The chief means of checking the character of the experiences given in the written documents was "in the comparison of document with document. The accounts were written independently by students in different schools and localities. . . . The comparison of large numbers of documents coming from different groups of people with no knowledge of each other made it possible to ascertain the general run of experiences. The contents of documents coming from different sources yielded substantially the same general kind of experiences."

In short the validity of the report is determined by the care taken to secure valid materials and by the mass and consistency of testimony bearing upon significant issues. This mass and consistency protect the validity of the conclusions.

Foremost among the contributions of these reports is the elaboration of the phenomenon of "emotional possession" which is characteristic of the experience of children before the motion-picture screen. Watching in the dark of the theater, the young child sits in the presence of reality when he observes the actors perform and the plot of the drama unfold. He sees the actions of people living in a real world—not of actors playing a make-believe rôle. His emotions are aroused in ways that have been described. He forgets his surroundings. He loses ordinary control of his feelings, his actions, and his thoughts. He identifies himself with the plot and loses himself in the picture. His "emotional condition may get such a strong grip on him that even his efforts to rid himself of it by reasoning with himself may prove of little avail." He is possessed by the drama.

The intensity of child experience in viewing pictures cannot be fully appreciated by adults. To adults the picture is good or bad, the acting satisfactory or unsatisfactory, the singing up to or not up to standard. To them a picture is just a picture. They may recall memories of thrills they used to have but the memories are pale in comparison to the actual experience. They get a more vivid impression of this excitement by watching a theater full of children as a thrilling drama unreels. They see the symptoms of keen emotion. But even in the presence of these manifestations they miss the depth and intensity of the child's experience.

Several factors contribute to emotional possession. The actions and the setting are concrete. When in the fairy story the child is told that the prince led his troops into battle he has to provide his own imagery; but in the picture he sees the charming prince at the head of a band of "real" men. Every significant visual image is provided before his eyes in the motion picture. He does not have to translate the words in which the story is conveyed. He sees machines; he does not hear about them. He visits the islands of the southern seas in a real ship; he does not have to listen to a narrator describe the scenes in words alone. The motion picture tells a very concrete and simple tale in a fashion which makes the story easy to grasp.

Emotional possession is also caused by the dramatic forms of the picture. One of the objectives of drama is to arouse the emotions. Indeed, the weakness of many "teaching firms" is the absence of dramatic elements— often necessarily omitted because of the nature of the content to be taught. But in the commercial movies and in teaching films of action, the dramatic flow of the story stirs the emotions and produces that intensity of experience which Blumer calls "emotional possession."

A third factor which contributes its influence to this condition is the attractiveness of the pictures—beautiful and thrilling scenes, interesting people, attractive persons moving on the stage, stimulating color, expert lighting, and the like. The child wants to be a part of such a bit of life. He does not pull back from the experience; he hurls himself into it.

All of these factors and probably others produce a condition that is favorable to certain types of learning. This is the quality of authority. Children accept as true, correct, proper, right what they see on the screen. They have little knowledge. The people on the screen are confidence-producing. Everything works to build up a magnificent and impressive world. Holaday and Stoddard found the children accepting both fact and error as fact. Blumer indicates the power of movie patterns upon conduct. The authority of the screen may account for some of the striking change of attitude of children found by Peterson and Thurstone.

All of these considerations lead inevitably to the increasing strength of the conclusion that the motion picture is an extremely powerful medium of education.

A second conclusion drawn from the report is that the range of influence of movies is very wide. Blumer found in studying two thousand children what every parent knows about his own child—that the movies dominate the patterns of play of children in a wide variety of forms. He presents scores of cases to show that the world of phantasy of young children and adolescents and of both sexes is ruled by movie subjects Dozens of cases are presented to show the effects of the movies in stimulating emotions of fright, sorrow, love, and "excitement." Cases are presented to illustrate how the movies give children techniques of action in situations which are of interest to them ranging from the trivial techniques of the playground to disturbing cues for the delinquent. And most far-reaching of all he indicates how they stir powerful ambitions, good and bad; develop permanent ideals, high and low; and crystallize the framework of life careers. In most unexpected quarters the influence of the movies is discovered in the reports of Blumer and Thrasher and their associates.

A third concept which supplements emotional possession and range of influence is the guidance concept which grows out of the preceding paragraph. Children are born into a world of which they know nothing. They are little individuals who have laboriously to learn how to fit into social groups. They possess impulses, instincts, wishes, desires, which drive them on to seek experience, adventure, and satisfaction. They are avidly interested in everything that seems to them to be able to provide what they want.

Yet they know so little and are so anxious to learn. They seek information, stimulation, and guidance in every direction. They are often confused, frequently maladjusted, and sometimes without confidence. In this situation the motion picture seems to be a godsend to them. While they are being entertained they are being shown in attractive and authoritative fashion what to do. They are guided in one direction or another as they absorb rightly or wrongly this idea or that one. Sometimes the guidance is good, at other times it is bad. Sometimes it lies in a direction opposed to the teachings of the home or the school; at other times it reinforces them. But always the motion picture is potentially a powerfully influential director. Not the only guide which leads them, to be sure: the community, chums and playmates, the home, the school, the church, the newspapers, all are used by these omnivorous seekers after the kinds of experience they want. But among them the motion picture possesses potency so substantial that society must not fail to understand and see that it is used beneficently in the guidance of children.

One means of helping the child to dominate his movie experiences rather than be possessed emotionally by them is a fourth product of these investigations. It is possible to increase control of movie experiences by developing what Ruckmick calls adult discount and Blumer describes as emotional detachment. Blumer describes one interesting series of cases to show the stages of growth of this maturer attitude. Certain fourth graders showed in the most undisguised fashion a great interest in serial thrillers and particularly in one. They talked freely and spoke with frank enthusiasm. The sixth graders were reluctant to talk. They admitted interest yet felt some shame at their interest in a "childish" picture. Their attitude was one of affected sophistication. The attitude of the eighth graders was, however, one of spontaneous and frank disapproval, dislike, and disgust at serials. The steps were three in number, frank approval, affected sophistication, and mature disapproval.

Three methods of developing adult discount or emotional detachment are mentioned by Blumer. The one most commonly present in the evolution of children's attitudes is the response to the attitude of slightly older groups or the "sophisticated" members of one's own group—as just indicated. The child is quick to put away childish things when his group frowns upon them as childish and he enjoys exhibiting superiority and

389

sophistication. In later years and with older experience adult discount may be produced by a second factor: the conviction that the pictures are not true to life. "In real life things aren't that way." This is a normal method of developing sophistication. The third method is to give children instruction about the movies. Sometimes Blumer found that talks with parents, or suggestions that "this is only make believe" from older people, helped the children to develop emotional detachment. Particularly, however, detachment comes with learning how pictures are made, how effects are secured, what to look for in pictures, what makes pictures artistically good or bad. Dale's appreciation study contributes to this end.

In summary of the direct influences of motion pictures on conduct: they owe their power over children chiefly to the factor of emotional possession; the range of influence of commercial movies is very wide; the motion picture because of its potency in many directions plays a substantial and significant rôle in the informal guidance of children; and the influence of pictures can be controlled in considerable measure by the development of emotional detachment and the application of an adult discount. In producing this intelligent attitude toward the movies, instruction in motion-picture criticism and appreciation provides a promising lead.

With this section, we have concluded a description of the studies which essayed to measure the influence of the motion picture as such. We see that as an instrument of education it has unusual power to impart information, to influence specific attitudes toward objects of social value, to affect emotions either in gross or in microscopic proportions, to affect health in a minor degree through sleep disturbance, and to affect profoundly the patterns of conduct of children.

NOTES

1. *Motion Pictures and the Social Attitudes of Children*, by Ruth C. Peterson and L. L. Thurstone.
2. *Movies and Conduct*, by Herbert Blumer; *Movies, Delinquency, and Crime*, by Herbert Blumer and Philip M. Hauser; *Boys, Movies, and City Streets*, by Paul G. Cressey and Frederick M. Thrasher.

CARL I. HOVLAND, ARTHUR A. LUMSDAINE
AND FRED D. SHEFFIELD

Short-Time and Long-Time Effects
of an Orientation Film

IN CONNECTION with the use of the orientation films, the question arose as to how well the effects of the film were retained over a long period of time. The practical significance of this question lay in judging the need for later supplementary material covering the same ground as the films. In the experiments with orientation films presented earlier, the effects were determined at time intervals ranging from four to seven days after the film showings. In the present study, effects were determined at two time intervals after the film showing, one at five days and another at nine weeks. The primary objective of the study was to discover the extent to which the "short-time" (five-day) effects, endure, as evidenced by the extent to which they were still present after a nine-week interval had elapsed.

The phrasing of the practical question to be answered by the study carries the implication that a decrement in effects is to be expected after a lapse of time. A more general question is to ask what is the influence of passage of time on the effects produced by the film. From this standpoint one need not anticipate only decrements with time; rather, in some cases the effect of time may be to enhance the initial effects of the film. Thus, some of the effects of the film may be "sleepers" that do not occur immediately but require a lapse of time before the full effect is evidenced. It should be realized, of course, that in making a controlled-variation study of the influence of time, it is not time per se that is the variable under study but rather the events which occur during the lapse of time.

The film used in this study was "The Battle of Britain." This film was

Reprinted from *Experiments in Mass Communications* (1949), pp. 182–190; 197–200, by permission of the authors and the publisher. (Copyright, 1949, by Princeton University Press.)

chosen partly because its initial effects, as determined from a previous study, were relatively large, providing a better base for measuring retention than would be the case with a film having small initial effects.

The before-after experimental design was used. The "before" Questionnaire was given to ten Infantry Replacement Training Companies during the first week of the study (April 1943). During the second week, the film was shown to five of the ten companies. The other five companies were controls and did not see the film during the study. Five days after the film showings, three of the film companies and three of the control companies were given the "after" questionnaire. These six companies were used to determine the *short-time* effects of the film. The remaining four companies (two controls and two experimental) were used nine weeks after the film showings to determine the *long-time* effects of the film. A nine-week interval was used because it was the longest period during which the companies would retain the same personnel. The experimental design is outlined below.

WEEK OF STUDY	SHORT-TIME GROUPS		LONG-TIME GROUPS	
	Experimental (3 Companies)	Control (3 Companies)	Experimental (2 Companies)	Control (2 Companies)
First Week	"Before" Questionnaire	"Before" Questionnaire	"Before" Questionnaire	"Before" Questionnaire
Second Week	Film Showing	....	Film Showing	....
Third Week	"After" Questionnaire	"After" Questionnaire	....	....
Eleventh Week	....	....	"After" Questionnaire	"After" Questionnaire

It will be observed in the experimental design that the same sample of men was not used at the two different times after the film. A design involving a short-time and long-time measure on the same men was avoided on the grounds that the first "after" measure might affect the results obtained on the second. It must also be observed that more men were used in the short-time measurement of effects than the long-time measurement. The reason for this was that an incidental purpose of the study was to make a more detailed analysis of the short-time effects of the film than was possible with the after-only procedure that had been used at the first camp at which "The Battle of Britain" had been studied. To get a sizable number of cases for this analysis, the greater number of men were concentrated in the short-time measurement.

After the equating of the film and control groups, the resultant samples were 900 for the short-time effects (450 film and 450 control) and 500 for the long-time effects (250 film and 250 control).

Results with Fact-Quiz Items

The results for the ten fact-quiz items (which were included only in the "after" questionnaire) are shown in Table 1. The items in the table are arranged in descending order of magnitude of *short-time* effect.

Table 1—Short-Time and Long-Time Effects of "The Battle of Britain" on Fact-Quiz Questions

Fact-Quiz Items	Control	Short-Time Film	Diff.	Control	Long-Time Film	Diff.	Difference (Long-Time Minus Short-Time)
1. RAF not destroyed on ground because kept planes at edge of fields	23%	80%	57%	21%	53%	32%	−25%
2. First targets of Luftwaffe were ports and ships	13	58	45	13	20	7	−38
3. Luftwaffe ten times as large as the RAF	24	56	32	19	33	14	−18
4. Nazi plan was to destroy RAF, then invade England	30	58	28	26	40	14	−14
5. British Navy could not operate in channel because of danger of air attacks	41	60	19	37	44	7	−12
6. After fall of France British could equip only one modern division	5	21	16	3	8	5	−11
7. Famous statement "Never . . . was so much owed by so many to so few" referred to the RAF	23	34	11	17	28	11	0
8. Goering the head of the German Force	58	65	7	51	58	7	0
9. "Luftwaffe" the name of the German Air Force	66	72	6	65	70	5	−1
10. Germans lost about 2000 planes in the Battle of Britain	49	54	5	49	58	9	+4
Mean	33.2%	55.8%	22.6%	30.1%	41.2%	11.1%	−11.5%

It can be seen in Table 1 that all of the items showed a decrement with passage of time except some of the items with very small short-time effects. The long-time mean score on the fact quiz was slightly less than half as great as that obtained in the short-time measurement. Thus retention was about 50 per cent after nine weeks. If the results in Table 1 are recomputed excluding the last three items, where the obtained "effects" are of questionable reliability, the means are 29.7 per cent and 12.9 per cent for short-time and long-time effects, respectively, giving a retention value of 12.9 divided by 29.7 or 43 per cent.

Results with Opinion Items

In contrast with the foregoing findings for fact-quiz items, the results for opinion items did not show an overall decrement during the interval of nine weeks. Instead, some items showed the expected decrement while others showed reliable increment, with a mean effect that was slightly greater for the long-time measurement than for the short-time. For the entire group of opinion items used in the after questionnaire, the range was from a decrement of -17% to an increment of $+14\%$, with a mean of $+1.9\%$.[1] The variance of the differences between the short-time and the long-time "effects" was 40.3.%. By contrast, when the groups were compared before the film showing, the range of the second-order differences was only from -7% to $+7\%$ with a variance of 14.6%.

Comparison of Short-Time and Long-Time Effects on Individual Opinion Items Showing a Reliable Effect at Either Time Interval

The foregoing comparisons were based upon all opinion items included in the questionnaire and therefore included many items for which no reliable effect of the film was demonstrated. Of special interest are the items which individually exhibited reliable effects of the film. In Table 2 the results at the two time intervals are shown for the 15 opinion items for which a reliable effect was obtained at either or both of the two time intervals.

The criterion of reliability used for the selection of items in Table 2 required a 10 per cent difference between film and control after the film showing. In terms of the empirical distributions of film-minus-control differences before the film, a difference of 10 per cent was beyond the 1 per cent level of confidence at either time interval. (The standard deviations of the distributions of "before" difference between film and control were 2.7 per cent and 3.5 per cent, respectively, for the short-time and long-time groups.) In the table the content is indicated for each of the 15 items, as well as the film and control percentages for each interval. The items are arranged in descending order of magnitude of *short-time* effect.

As can be seen from Table 2 the average for the 15 items was about the same for short-time and long-time effects, with a slight advantage (2.4 per cent) in favor of the long-time effects.

However, Table 2 brings out clearly the fact that the near equality of

Table 2—Short-Time and Long-Time Effects of "The Battle of Britain" on Significantly Affected Opinion Questions

Content of Opinion Item	Control	Short-Time Film	Diff.	Control	Long-Time Film	Diff.	Difference (Long-Time Minus Short-Time)
1. RAF gave Nazis first real defeat	21%	45%	24%	20%	27%	7%	−17%
2. RAF most important in preventing German conquest of England	54	78	24	46	69	23	−1
3. Nazi invasion attempt failed because of determined resistance of British	51	71	20	54	68	14	−6
4. Battle of Britain was a real invasion attempt	32	46	14	30	40	10	−4
5. England's refusal to surrender saved U.S. cities from bombing	62	74	12	67	74	7	−5
6. RAF has done about the best job of fighting in the war	49	60	11	42	45	3	−8
7. British more democratic than before Battle of Britain	55	65	10	59	62	3	−7
8. American workers in war plants should not work longer hours	48	52	4	42	54	12	8
9. America and Allies can still lose the war (disagree)	34	37	3	35	48	13	10
10. We would be fighting on American soil if Britain had not held off Nazis	52	55	3	50	62	12	9
11. British are doing their fair share of the fighting	71	73	2	61	77	16	14
12. Better just to defend U.S. rather than going overseas to fight	83	84	1	79	90	11	10
13. If England had been conquered the U.S. would have been attacked next	23	24	1	22	32	10	9
14. The war will probably end in less than one year	11	10	−1	12	22	10	11
15. The British not to blame for America's having to get into the war	56	54	−2	44	55	11	13
Mean	46.8%	55.2%	8.4%	44.2%	55.0%	10.8%	2.4%

the averages is a balance of some effects that were larger in the short-time measurement and others that were larger in the long-time measurement rather than approximate equality of individual effects at the two time intervals. This trend is perhaps somewhat exaggerated in Table 2 owing to the selection of effects that met the criterion of 10 per cent at either time interval. Thus borderline instances that just barely met the criterion at only one of the time intervals would be expected to regress somewhat in a replication of the experiment.

These findings are of considerable significance both from the standpoint of methodology of research on educational films and from the standpoint of theory as to the effects of educational programs on attitudes. Methodologically, they raise the problem as to the point in time at which effects of a film or other educational device are to be measured. From the standpoint of theory they raise the possibility of "sleeper" effects in the case of opinions and the implications of such effects for theory of attitude or opinion changes. From the standpoint either of educational film research or of the use of educational films it would be very desirable to know how generally this finding holds for documentary films of this type and also to know what factors determine whether the effects will show a loss or a gain with time. Unfortunately, studies of long-time effects were not made on any of the other orientation films, so no evidence can be given as to the generality of the results.

An analogy may be drawn between the findings reported here and the finding in studies of retention that "substance" is better retained than verbatim learning.[2] Thus the general ideas in a passage of verbal material are retained with little loss over periods in which memory for the actual wording has dropped markedly. In the present study retention for opinions—which correspond to the substance—averaged better than 100 per cent whereas memory for detailed facts dropped to only half of its initial value.

However, this analogy is somewhat superficial in view of the fact that the average for opinions was a mixture of some gains and losses on particular items of "substance" (if opinions can be regarded as "substance"). In this connection it may be pointed out that another familiar phenomenon in learning studies—the phenomenon of "reminiscence," in which more rather than less of the original content is recalled after a lapse of time—is more frequently found in the case of substance material than in the case of detailed verbal content.[3] Thus the present results may be regarded as a mixture of the greater retention of general ideas plus "reminiscence" for part of the material.

One hypothesis as to the source of the "sleeper" effects involving a purely methodological artifact was checked but was not supported by the data. This hypothesis was that the before-after procedure may cause a "consistency reaction" which would occur when the two questionnaires are close together in time but which could not be present for two questionnaires separated by an interval as long as eleven weeks. (The possibility of a "consistency reaction" is discussed in Appendix C of *Experiments in Mass Communication* along with other methodological aspects of the before-after procedure.) The effect of the "consistency reaction," if present, would be a tendency for the respondent, having given a particular answer to a question on one occasion, to give the same answer when questioned in a similar context a short time later. Hence the true magnitude of the change effected by the film would not be revealed at the short-time interval. Since some of the questions in the present study were asked only in the "after" questionnaire and others both before and after, it was possible to check whether after-only questions show the normal forgetting decrement with time and only the before-after questions show an increment. This finding would be expected if the "consistency reaction" were reduced where an 11-week interval is allowed between before and after tests.

However, no significant relation was found between whether the question was an after-only or a before-after question and whether it showed a decrement or an increment with time. In Table 2 the after-only questions were numbers 2, 7, 8, 11, 14, and 15. Of these six after-only items, it can be seen that two showed a decrement and four showed an increment in effects as a function of time. Of the remaining nine questions, asked both before and after, five showed a decrement and four showed an increment. Thus while the hypothetical "consistency reaction" may have functioned to some extent to reduce the size of the decrement, the data do not at all support it as the factor responsible for the delayed or augmented effects. As can be seen in Table 3 the results are in the opposite direction from the prediction of the consistency hypothesis. (The apparent difference in retention of the after-only items is not significant.)

Table 3—Mean Effect (Film Per Cent Minus Control Per Cent)

	Short-Time	Long-Time
For six after-only items	6.2%	12.5%
For nine before-after items	9.9	9.7

Other Hypotheses

A number of other hypotheses may be advanced suggesting possible factors contributing to the increments on some of the opinion items. These hypotheses could not be checked in the present experiment but they are presented below because they may provide useful areas for future study.

1. FORGETTING OF AN INITIALLY DISCOUNTED SOURCE

One hypothesis that could explain the results would be that some of the themes of the presentation were initially accepted and others were initially discounted as having a biased source. According to this hypothesis, forgetting is the rule but the *source* of an item of information is more quickly forgotten than the material presented. Thus the men might have retained a feeling that the British did well in the war long after they have forgotten about seeing the film, "The Battle of Britain." The factors involved in this hypothesis would be maximized in situations where the content was very well persented but where the source was suspect, so that the main factor preventing an attitude change is nonacceptance of the trustworthiness of the source. In this case, what is remembered and what is believed may be kept separate at first, but if the content "sticks" after the source is forgotten, it may no longer be discounted. Content would of course be subject to some forgetting, so that the net result would be a decrement of effect with passage of time for those contents which are *immediately* accepted contents, but an increment of effect for those contents for which forgetting of the suspected source proceeded more rapidly than forgetting of the content.

2. DELAYED INTERPRETATION IN A RELEVANT CONTEXT

Another hypothesis is that while forgetting of content is the rule, the implications of the initially learned content may not be apparent to the audience at the outset but may become more clear later when the material learned in the film becomes relevant to some new experience. Thus the film, "The Battle of Britain" showed the defeat of the Luftwaffe by the much smaller RAF and the frustration of the Nazi plans for the capitulation of Britain. Initial effects on fact-quiz and attitude items indicated that this content was learned. However, the film in no way presented the idea that the Nazi military machine was weak or that their strategy and tactics were inferior, and nothing in the initial effects indicated that this was a conclusion immediately drawn by the men as a result of seeing the film. However, if the men were later forced to consider the implications of these facts as to the likelihood that the Nazis could defeat the Allies, they might conclude that if the Germans could not defeat little Britain they have little chance of winning the war, as in the delayed effect on item number 14 in Table 2.

An expectation from this second hypothesis is that material directly related to the content of the film would tend to show a decrement with time in correspondence with the forgetting curve, whereas increments would occur only for indirect implications of the content that could be initiated at a later time while a fair amount of the content was still retained. However, a differentiation between direct and indirect implications is one which it was not feasible to make clearly with these films.

3. Conversion of Details into Attitudes

A third hypothesis to account for the results involved a possible factor that would, if it actually functions, be of more general significance for theory concerning attitude formation. According to this hypothesis, forgetting is accompanied by loss of specificity of content—the details drop out and the "general idea" that is retained is in a more generalizable form, so that the individual has a greater tendency to go beyond the facts initially learned. In this sense attitudes are to a certain extent "general ideas" that lack specificity and generalize more broadly than is justified by the evidence.

An example of the interpretation from this hypothesis in the case of the film, "The Battle of Britain," would be that initially the men learned specific facts about the performance of the British, particularly the RAF, during the Battle of Britain, but as the specific facts were forgotten all that was remembered was that the British had performed well in the war. In this form the "general idea" applies to all British rather than just the RAF and to the entire war rather than just the Luftwaffe attack on England. Any opinions that dealt with specific contents would show a decrement with time, whereas those dealing with generalizations beyond the evidence would show an increment with time.

Delayed Effects on Orientation Objectives

One final question raised by the findings in this comparison of long-time and short-time effects of an orientation film is the extent to which delayed effects were found in the orientation objectives of the film. This is a question of methodological importance in the evaluation of an educational program designed to affect attitudes, because the evaluation may provide a different answer depending on the point in time at which the program is evaluated. The findings in the present study indicate a real possibility that at least in the case of the film, "The Battle of Britain," greater effects on orientation attitudes were obtained after a nine-week lapse of time than after only five days. The relevant findings are presented below.

The orientation objective most relevant to the film was that of increasing confidence in our ally, Britain. While many items about Britain were included to test the effects of the film, only six items were used for the specific purpose of determining general orientation attitudes toward

Britain. The short-time and long-time effects for these items are shown in Table 4. The effects are measured as differences between before-after changes for all questions used in both questionnaires.

Results on other standard orientation items not specific to opinions

Table 4—Effects on the Orientation Objective of Increasing Men's Confidence in the British

Content of Item	EFFECT OF FILM Short-Time Effect	Long-Time Effect
British are doing all they can to help in the war	7%	3%
British will try to work out a just peace after the war	9	7
British are taking it easy in hope that U.S. will win the war for them disagree)	2	9
British are doing their fair share of the fighting	2	16
British will fight on to the end (rather than seek a separate peace)	1	4
British are to blame for America's entry into war (disagree)	−2	11
Mean	3.2%	8.3%

of the British are shown in Table 5. These items are of lesser relevance to the film than the above items concerning Britain as an ally. Specific contents of individual items are not shown; only the general area of the items is given. In the case of each area, however, the results given are the averages for all of the standard items used in that area.

Table 5—Effects on Generalized Orientation Objectives

Content of Area	AVERAGE EFFECT OF FILM Short-Time	Long-Time
The U.S. had to fight—war was unavoidable (3 items)	0.3%	6.0%
Resentment against the enemy (2 items)	−2.0	5.0
Confidence in home support (4 items)	−1.0	2.0
Willingness to serve (2 items)	1.5	0.5
Mean	0.5%	3.4%

In both Tables 4 and 5 the mean effect is larger at the long-time interval. This indicates that a greater effect of the film in achieving its orientation objectives was present after nine weeks than after one week. However, the results are not highly consistent from item to item in Table 4 nor from area to area in Table 5. In neither case is the result reliable at the 5 per cent level if we treat the questions used as a sample from the population of relevant items.

While inconclusive, the results have a bearing on two important problems:

1 they support the hypothesis that changes in opinions of a general rather than specific nature may show increasing effects with lapse of time, and

2 they focus attention on the methodological problem of selecting the point in time at which measurements should be made after a presentation in order to detect its full effects. At the outset of the present studies it was more or less assumed that deterioration of effects with time would be the rule; it now appears that this assumption is not warranted in the case of opinions of a general nature.

NOTES

1. This included all opinion items except those involving ranking of enemy and allied strength and two questions about branch of service that could not be scored individually.

2. Cofer, C. N. "A Comparison of Logical and Verbatim Learning of Prose Passages of Different Lengths." *Amer. J. Psychol.*, 1941, *54*, 1–20.

3. English, H. B., Wellborn, E. L., and Killian, C. D. "Studies in Substance Memorization." *J. gen. Psychol.*, 1934, *11*, 233–60. See also Buxton, C. E. " 'Reminiscence' in the Studies of Professor English and His Associates." *Psychol Rev.*, 1942, *49*, 494–504.

EDWARD A. SHILS AND MORRIS JANOWITZ

Cohesion and Disintegration in the Wehrmacht in World War II

(INTRODUCTORY NOTE: The analysis of the German army as a social group from which the following selection was drawn emphasize the crucial importance of primary group organization in the maintenance of fighting effectiveness and morale. It appears that the immediately present agents and symbols of authority—junior officers, NCO's, and conceptions of soldierly honor—were effective because of their consistency with the personality system of the individual soldier. The excerpt which has been reprinted deals with the effectiveness of more remote or secondary symbols, in German military morale: on the one hand, those of indoctrination by the Nazis, and, on the other hand, the propaganda appeals employed by the Allied Expeditionary Forces in Europe.)

STRATEGIC ASPECTS OF THE WAR

For the mass of the German Army, the strategic phases of the war were viewed apathetically. The ignorance of the German troops about important military events, even on their own front, was partly a result of the poverty of information about the actual course of the war—itself a part of Nazi policy.[1] But the deliberate management of ignorance need not always result in such far-reaching indifference as the German soldiers showed. Deliberately maintained ignorance would have resulted in a flood of rumors, had the German soldiers been more eager to know about the strategic phases of the war. As it was, there were very few rumors on the subject—merely apathy. Three weeks after the fall of the city of Aachen,

Reprinted from *The Public Opinion Quarterly*, Vol. XII (1948), pp. 300–306; 308–315, by permission of the authors and the publisher. (Copyright, 1948, by Princeton University Press.)

there were still many prisoners being taken in the adjoining area who did not know that the city had fallen. For at least a week after the beginning of von Rundstedt's counter-offensive, most of the troops on the northern hinge of the bulge did not know that the offensive was taking place and were not much interested when they were told after capture. Of 140 Ps/W taken between December 23–24, 1944, only 35 per cent had heard of the counter-offensive and only 7 per cent said that they thought it significant.[2]

Some exception to this extensive strategic indifference existed with respect to the Eastern front. Although the German soldiers were extremely ignorant of the state of affairs on that front and made little attempt to reduce their ignorance, still the question of Russians was so emotionally charged, so much the source of anxiety, that it is quite likely that fear of the Russians did play a role in strengthening resistance. National Socialist propaganda had long worked on the traditional repugnance and fear of the German towards the Russian. The experience of the German soldiers in Russia in 1941 and 1942 increased this repugnance by direct perception of the primitive life of the Russian villager. But probably more important was the projection onto the Russians of the guilt feelings generated by the ruthless brutality of the Germans in Russia during the occupation period. The shudder of horror which frequently accompanied a German soldier's remarks about Russia was a result of all these factors. These attitudes influenced German resistance in the West through the shift of soldiers from East to West and the consequent diffusion of their attitudes among their comrades. They also took effect by making soldiers worry about what would happen to their families if the Russians entered Germany. Of course, it should also be mentioned that this fear of the Russians also made some German soldiers welcome a speedier collapse on the Western front in the hope that a larger part of Germany would fall under Anglo-American control.

Before the actual occupation, only a small minority expressed fear of the consequences of an Anglo-American occupation. The continuing monthly opinion poll conducted by the Psychological Warfare Branch, mentioned elsewhere, never showed more than 20 per cent of the prisoners answering "yes" to the question, "Do you believe that revenge will be taken against the population after the war?" Those who feared retribution were confirmed Nazis. Yet the general absence of fear of revenge did not cause a diminution of German resistance.

Neither did expectations about the outcome of the war play a great role in the integration or disintegration of the German Army. The statistics regarding German soldier opinion cited below show that pessimism as to final triumph was quite compatible with excellence in fighting behavior. The far greater effectiveness of considerations of self-preservation, and their vast preponderance over interest in the outcome of the war and the

403

strategic situation, is shown by German prisoner recall of the contents of Allied propaganda leaflets (see Table I). In the last two months of 1944 and the first two months of 1945, not less than 59 per cent of the sample of prisoners taken each month recalled references to the preservation of the individual, and the figure rose to 76 per cent in February of 1945. On the other hand, the proportion of prisoners recalling references to the total strategic situation of the war and the prospect of the outcome of the war seldom amounted to more than 20 per cent, while references to political subjects seldom amounted to more than 10 per cent. The general tendency was not to think about the outcome of the war unless forced to do so by

Table 1—Tabulation of Allied Leaflet Propaganda Themes
Remembered by German Ps/W

	Dec. 15–31 1944	Jan. 1–15 1945	Jan. 15–31 1945	Feb. 1–15 1945
Number of Ps/W	60	83	99	135
Themes and appeals remembered:				
a. Promise of good treatment as Ps/W and self-preservation through surrender	63%	65%	59%	76%
b. Military news	15	17	19	30
c. Strategical hopelessness of Germany's position	13	12	25	26
d. Hopelessness of a local tactical situation	3	1	7	7
e. Political attacks on German leaders	7	5	4	8
f. Bombing of German cities	2	8	6	—
g. Allied Military Government	7	3	—	—
h. Appeals to civilians	5	4	2	—

(The percentages add up to more than 100% since some Ps/W remembered more than one topic. Only Ps/W remembering at least one theme were included in this tabulation.)

direct interrogation. Even pessimism was counter-balanced by the reassurances provided by identification with a strong and benevolent Führer, by identification with good officers, and by the psychological support of a closely integrated primary group.

The Ethics of War and Patriotism

Quite consistently, ethical aspects of the war did not trouble the German soldier much. When pressed by Allied interrogators, Ps/W said that Germany had been forced to fight for its life. There were very few German soldiers who said that Germany had been morally wrong to attack Poland, or Russia. Most of them thought that if anything had been wrong about the war, it was largely in the realm of technical decisions. The decision to extirpate the Jews had been too drastic not because of its immorality but because it united the world against Germany. The declaration of war against the Soviet Union was wrong only because it created a two-front war. But these were all arguments which had to be forced from the Ps/W. Left to themselves, they seldom mentioned them.

The assumption underlying these arguments was that the strong national state is a good in itself. But it was not, in fact, the highest good for any but the "hard core." In September 1944, for example, only 5 per cent of a sample of 634 Ps/W said that they were worried about anything other than personal or familial problems, while in the very same survey, more than half of the Ps/W said they believed that Germany was losing the war or that they were at best uncertain of the war's outcome. In brief, fear for Germany's future as a nation does not seem to have been very important in the ordinary soldier's outlook and in motivating his combat behavior. As a matter of fact, as the war became more and more patently a threat to the persistence of the German national state, the narcissism of the German soldier increased correspondingly, so that the idea of national survival did not become an object of widespread preoccupation even when it might have been expected to become so.[3]

Ethical-religious scruples seem to have played an equally small role. Although there were a few interesting cases of Roman Catholic deserters, Roman Catholics (except Austrians, Czechs and Polish nationals) do not seem to have deserted disproportionately. Prisoners seldom expressed remorse for Nazi atrocities, and practically no case was noted of a desertion because of moral repugnance against Nazi atrocities.

POLITICAL IDEALS

The significance of political ideals, of symbols of political systems, was rather pronounced in the case of the "hard core" minority of fervent Nazis in the German Army. Their desire for discipline under a strong leader made them enthusiasts for the totalitarian political system. Their passionate aggressiveness also promoted projective tendencies which facilitated their acceptance of the Nazi picture of an innocent and harmless Germany encircled by the dark, threatening cloud of Bolsheviks, Jews, Negroes, etc., and perpetually in danger from inner enemies as well. But for most of the German soldiers, the political system of National Socialism was of little interest.

The *system* was indeed of very slight concern to German civilians also, even though dissatisfaction increased to a high pitch towards the end of the war. Soldiers on the whole were out of touch with the operation of the Party on the home front. Hence the political system impinged little on their consciousness. Thus, for example, of 53 potential and actual deserters in the Mediterranean theater, only one alleged political grounds for his action. The irrelevance of party politics to effective soldiering has already been treated above: here we need only repeat the statement of a German soldier, "Nazism begins ten miles behind the front line."

Nor did the soldiers react in any noticeable way to the various attempts to Nazify the army. When the Nazi Party salute was introduced in 1944, it was accepted as just one more army order, about equal in significance to an order requiring the carrying of gas masks. The introduction of the *National Socialistiche Führungsoffiziere* (Guidance, or Indoctrination Officer), usually known as the NSFO, was regarded apathetically or as a joke. The contempt for the NFSO was derived not from his Nazi connection but from his status as an "outsider" who was not a real soldier. The especially Nazified Waffen SS divisions were never the object of hostility on the part of the ordinary soldier, even when the responsibility for atrocities was attributed to them. On the contrary, the Waffen SS was highly esteemed, not as a Nazi formation, but for its excellent fighting capacity. Wehrmacht soldiers always felt safer when there was a Waffen SS unit on their flank.

Devotion to Hitler

In contrast to the utterly apolitical attitude of the German infantry soldier towards almost all secondary symbols, an intense and personal devotion to Adolf Hitler was maintained in the German Army throughout the war. There could be little doubt that a high degree of identification with the Führer was an important factor in prolonging German resistance. Despite fluctuations in expectations as to the outcome of the war the trust in Hitler remained at a very high level even after the beginning of the serious reverses in France and Germany. In monthly opinion polls of German Ps/W opinion from D-Day until January 1945, in all but two samples over 60 per cent expressed confidence in Hitler,[4] and confidence in January was nearly as high as it was in the preceding June. During this same period considerably more than half of the German soldiers in seven out of eight polls said they believed that it was impossible for the German Army to defeat the Allies in France. Only when the German Army began to break up in the face of overwhelming Allied fire power and deep, communications-cutting penetrations, did confidence in Hitler fall to the unprecedentedly low level of 30 per cent. Even when defeatism was rising to the point at which only one-tenth of the prisoners taken as of March 1945 believed that the Germans had any chance of success, still a third retained confidence in Hitler.[5]

Belief in the good intentions of the Führer, in his eminent moral qualities, in his devotion and contributions to the well-being of the German people, continued on an even higher level. This strong attachment grew in large part from the feeling of strength and protection which the German soldier got from his conception of the Führer personality.

For older men, who had lived through the unemployment of the closing years of the Weimar Republic and who experienced the joy of being reinstated in gainful employment by Nazi full-employment policies, Hitler was above all the man who had provided economic security. This attitude extended even to left wing soldiers of this generation, who denounced the Nationalist Socialist political system, but found occasion to say a good word for Hitler as a man who had restored order and work in Germany. For men of the generation between 22–35, who had first experienced Hitler's charisma in the struggles to establish their manliness during late adolescence, Hitler was the prototype of strength and masculinity. For the younger Nazi fanatics, he was a father substitute, providing the vigilant discipline and the repression of dangerous impulses both in the individual and in the social environment; for them he had the additional merit of legitimating revolt against the family and traditional restraints.

Prisoners spoke of Hitler with enthusiasm, and even those who expressed regret over the difficulties which his policies had brought on Germany by engendering a two-front war and by allowing the Jews to be persecuted so fiercely as to arouse world hatred—even these men retained their warm esteem for his good intentions. They found it necessary to exculpate him in some way by attributing his errors to dishonest advisors who kept the truth from him, or to certain technical difficulties in his strategic doctrines which did not in any way reflect on his fundamental moral greatness or nobility.

It was difficult for German soldiers, as long as they had this attitude toward Hitler, to rebel mentally against the war. Time after time, prisoners who were asked why Hitler continued the war when they themselves admitted it was so obviously lost, said he wouldn't continue the war and waste lives if he did not have a good, even though undisclosed, strategic reason for doing so, or if he didn't have the resources to realize his ends. Nazis as well as non-Nazi answered in this way. Or else they would say, "the Führer has never deceived us," or, "he must have a good reason for doing what he does."

There was obviously a fear of rendering an independent judgment of events among the German soldiers and a desire for some strong leader to assume the responsibility for determining their fate. American and British soldiers often complained that the complexity of the army organization and strategy was so great and their own particular part was so small that they could not see the role of their personal missions. Their failure to see the connection made them miserable because it reduced their sense of personal autonomy. In the German Army, on the other hand, there was no difficulty for soldiers who were used throughout their lives to having other persons determine their objectives for them.

It is also possible that the very high devotion to Hitler under conditions of great stress was in part a reaction formation growing from a hostility against lesser authorities, which emerged as the weakness of these authorities became more manifest. In the last year of the war, hostility and contempt on the part of the German soldiers toward Nazi Party functionaries and toward Nazi Party leaders below Hitler (particularly Goebbels and Goering) was increasing. After the *Putsch* of July 20, hostility toward senior Wehrmacht officers also increased somewhat, although it never reached the levels of hostility displayed by civilians against local civilian Party officials and leaders. It is possible, therefore, that guilt created in ambivalent personalities by giving expression, even though verbally, to hostility against subordinate agents of authority, had to be alleviated by reaffirmed belief in the central and highest authority.

WEAKENING OF THE HITLER SYMBOL

As the integral pattern of defense was broken down, however, and as danger to physical survival increased, devotion to Hitler deteriorated. The tendency to attribute virtue to the strong and immorality to the weak took hold increasingly, and while it did not lead to a complete rejection of Hitler, it reached a higher point than at any other stage in the history of National Socialism. The announcement of Hitler's death met an incapacity to respond on the part of many soldiers. There seemed to be no willingness to question the truth of the report, but the great upsurge of preoccupation with physical survival as a result of disintegration of the military primary group, the loss of contact with junior officers and the greatly intensified threat of destruction, caused a deadening of the power to respond to this event. For the vast horde of dishevelled, dirty, bewildered prisoners, who were being taken in the last weeks of the war, Hitler was of slight importance alongside the problem of their own biological survival and the welfare of their families. For the small minority who still had sufficient energy to occupy themselves with "larger problems," the news of Hitler's death released a sort of amorphous resentment against the fallen leader whose weakness and immorality had been proven by the failure of his strategy. But even here, the resentment was not expressed in explicit denunciations of Hitler's character or personality. The emphasis was all on technical deficiencies and weaknesses.

The explanation of the deterioration and final—though probably only temporary—hostility toward Hitler may in part be sought in the average German soldier's ambivalence toward the symbols of authority. This psychological mechanism, which also helps to explain the lack of a significant resistance movement inside Germany, enables us to understand the curve of Hitler's fame among the German people. Hitler, the father symbol, was loved for his power and his great accomplishments and hated for his oppressiveness, but the latter sentiment was repressed. While he remained strong it was psychologically expedient—as well as politically expedient—to identify with Hitler and to displace hostility on to weaker minority groups and foreigners. But once Hitler's authority had been undermined, the German soldiers rejected it and tended to express their hostility by projecting their own weakness on to him.

Thus the only important secondary symbol in motivating the behavior of the German soldiers during the recent war also lost its efficacy when the primary group relations of comradeliness, solidarity and subordination to junior officers broke down, and with it the superego of the individual, on which the effective functioning of the primary group depends.[6]

PROPAGANDA THEMES

The most striking aspect of Nazi indoctrination of their own men during combat was the employment of negative appeals and counter-propaganda, which attempted less to reply directly to the substance of our claims than to explain the reasons why the Allies were using propaganda.

The Nazis frankly believed that they could employ our propaganda efforts as a point of departure for strengthening the unpolitical resolve of their men. They had the legend of the effectiveness of Allied propaganda in World War I as a warning from which to "conclude" that if the Germans failed to be tricked by propaganda this time, success was assured. A typical instance of this attitude was contained in a captured order issued by the Officer in Command of the garrison of Boulogne on September 11, 1944, in which he appealed to his men not to be misled by Allied propaganda. The German order claimed that the propaganda attack in the form of leaflets was in itself an expression of the weakness of the Allied offensive, which was in desperate need of the port for communications. During the same period, an NSF (political officer) issued an elaborate statement in which he reminded the garrison at Le Havre that the "enemy resorts to propaganda as a weapon which he used in the last stages of the first world war," in order to point out that German victory depended on the determination of the German soldier to resist Allied propaganda.

In the fall and winter of 1944, the campaign to counteract Allied propaganda by "exposing" it was intensified and elaborated. (This method had the obvious advantage that direct refutations of Allied claims could largely be avoided.) *Mitteilung für die Truppe* (October 1944), a newspaper for officer indoctrination, reviewed the major weapons in the "poison offensive." They included: attacks against the Party and its predominant leaders ("this is not surprising as the enemy will, of course, attack those institutions which give us our greatest strength"); appeals to the Austrians to separate themselves from the Germans ("the time when we were split up in small states was the time of our greatest weakness"); sympathy with the poor German women who work in hellish factories ("the institution must be a good one, otherwise the enemy would not attack it").

Other themes "exposed" in leaflets were: the enemy attempts to separate the leaders from the people ("Just as the Kaiser was blamed in 1918, it now is Hitler who is supposed to be responsible"); the enemy admits his own losses in an exaggerated way in order to obtain the reputation of veracity and to lie all the more at the opportune moment.

Even earlier in the Western campaign, the Germans followed the policy of stamping Allied leaflets with the imprint, "Hostile Propaganda," and then allowing them to circulate in limited numbers. This was being carried out at the same time that mutually contradictory orders for the complete destruction of all enemy propaganda were being issued. The explanation, in part, is that the Nazis realized that it would be impossible to suppress the flood of Allied leaflets, and therefore sought to clearly label them as such and to employ them as a point of departure for counter-propaganda.

The procedure of overstamping Allied leaflets was linked with follow-up indoctrination talks. Such indoctrination lectures, which were conducted by the Nazi NSFO's, became towards the end of the war one of the main vehicles of Nazi indoctrination of their own troops. Ps/W claimed, although it was probably not entirely correct, that they usually slept through such sessions, or at least paid little attention, until the closing *Sieg Heil* was sounded. At this late date in the war, emphasis on oral propaganda was made necessary by the marked disruption of communications. Radio listening at the front was almost non-existent due to the lack of equipment; when in reserve, troops listened more frequently. Newspapers were distributed only with great difficulty. More important were the leaflets which were either dropped by air on their own troops or distributed through command channels.

"STRENGTH THROUGH FEAR"

Major lines of the negative approach employed by these leaflets in indoctrination talks, in the rumors circulated by NSF officers, stressed "strength through fear," particularly fear of Russia and the general consequences of complete destruction that would follow defeat.

Because of the German soldier's concern about the welfare of his family living inside Germany, Nazi agencies were constantly issuing statements about the successful evacuation of German civilians to the east bank of the Rhine.

Equally stressed in the strength through fear theme were retaliation threats against the families of deserters, mistreatment of prisoners of war in Anglo-American prison camps, and the ultimate fate of prisoners. The phrase *Sieg order Sibirian* (Victory or Siberia) was emphasized and much material was released to prove that the Anglo-Americans planned to turn over their prisoners to the Russians. When the U.S. Army stopped shipping German Ps/W to the United States, Nazi propaganda officers spread the rumor among German soldiers "that the way to Siberia is shorter from France than from the United States."

Statements by Ps/W revealed that shortly before the Rundstedt counter-attack, speeches by NSFO's were increased. One of the main subjects seems to have been weapons. In retrospect, the intent of the directives under which they were working was obvious. Attempts were made to explain the absence of the Luftwaffe, while the arrival in the near future of new and better weapons was guaranteed.

Psychological preparation for the December counter-offensive was built around the Rundstedt order of the day that "everything is at stake." Exhortations were backed up with exaggerated statements by unit commanders that large amounts of men and material were to be employed. Immediately thereafter, official statements were issued that significant penetrations had been achieved; special editions of troop papers were prepared announcing that 40,000 Americans had been killed.

Such announcements received little attention among the troops actually engaged in the counter-offensive because of the obvious difficulties in disseminating propaganda to fighting troops.

Nevertheless, after the failure of the counter-attack, the Nazis felt called upon to formulate a plausible line to explain the sum total result of that military effort, especially for those who felt that better military judgment would have resulted in a purely defensive strategy against Russia. On January 25, *Front und Heimat* announced that the December offensive had smashed the plan for a simultaneous onslaught: "The East can hold only if the West does too. . . . Every fighting man in the West knows that the AngloAmericans are doing all they can, although belatedly, to start the assault on the Fortress Germany. Our task in the West now is to postpone that time as long as possible and to guard the back of our Armies in the East."

Despite the obvious limitations on the efficacy of propaganda during March and April 1945, the Nazis continued to the very end to keep up their propaganda efforts. Due to the confusion within the ranks of the Wehrmacht and the resulting difficulties of dissemination, the task devolved almost wholly on the NSFO's who spent much of their time reading to the troops the most recent orders governing desertion. Leaflets called largely on the Landser's military spirit to carry on. One even demanded that he remain silent (*zu schweigen*). The Nazis taxed their fancy to create rumors as the last means of bolstering morale. Here a favorite technique for stimulating favorable rumors was for CO's to read to their men "classified" documents from official sources which contained promises of secret weapons or discussed the great losses being inflicted upon the Allies.

The Impact of Allied Propaganda on Wehrmacht Solidarity

The system of controls which the social structure of the Wehrmacht exercised over its individual members greatly reduced those areas in which symbolic appeals of the Allies could work. But the millions of leaflets which were dropped weekly and the "round-the-clock" broadcasts to the German troops certainly did not fail to produce some reactions.

The very first German Ps/W who were interrogated directly on their reactions to Allied propaganda soon revealed a stereotyped range of answers which could be predicted from their degree of Nazification. The fanatical Nazi claimed, "No German would believe anything the enemy has to say," while an extreme attitude of acceptance was typified by a confirmed anti-Nazi who pleaded with his captors: "Now is the moment to flood the troops with leaflets. You have no idea of the effect sober and effective leaflets have on retreating troops." But these extreme reactions of soldiers were of low frequency; Nazi soldiers might admit the truth of our leaflets but usually would not accept their conclusions and implications.

The fundamentally indifferent reaction to Allied propaganda was most interestingly shown in an intensive study of 150 Ps/W captured in October 1944 of whom 65 per cent had seen our leaflets and for the most part professed that they believed their contents. This was a group which had fought very obstinately, and the number of active deserters, if any, was extremely small. Some forty of these Ps/W offered extended comments as to what they meant when they said they believed the contents of Allied leaflets.

Five stated outright that they believed the messages and that the leaflets assisted them and their comrades to surrender.

Seven declared they believed the leaflets, but were powerless to do anything about appeals to surrender.

Eight stated that they believed the contents, but nevertheless as soldiers and decent individuals would never think of deserting.

Twenty-two declared that events justified belief in the leaflets, but they clearly implied that this had been of little importance in their battle experiences.

In Normandy, where the relatively small front was blanketed with printed material, up to 90 per cent of the Ps/W reported that they had read Allied leaflets, yet this period was characterized by very high German morale and stiff resistance.

Throughout the Western campaign, with the exception of periods of extremely bad weather or when the front was fluid, the cumulative percentage of exposure ranged between 60 and 80 per cent. (This cumulative percentage of exposure was based on statements by Ps/W that they had seen leaflets sometime while fighting on the Western front after D-Day. A few samples indicated that penetration during any single month covered about 20 per cent of the prisoners.) Radio listening among combat troops was confined to a minute fraction due to the lack of equipment; rear troops listened more frequently. In the case of both leaflets and radio it was found that there was widespread but desultory comment on the propaganda, much of which comment distorted the actual contents.

412

Not only was there wide penetration by Allied leaflets and newssheets, but German soldiers frequently circulated them extensively among their comrades. A readership study of *Nachrichten für die Truppe*, a daily newssheet published by the Allied Psychological Warfare Division, showed that each copy which was picked up had an average readership of between four and five soldiers—a figure which is extremely large in view of the conditions of combat life. Not only were leaflets widely circulated, but it became a widespread practice for soldiers to carry Allied leaflets on their person, especially the "safe conduct pass" leaflets which bore a statement by General Eisenhower guaranteeing the bearer swift and safe conduct through Allied lines and the protection of the Geneva convention. There is evidence that in certain sectors of the front, German soldiers even organized black-market trading in Allied propaganda materials.

It is relevant to discuss here the differences in effectiveness between tactical and strategic propaganda. By tactical propaganda, we refer to propaganda which seeks to promise immediate results in the tactical situation. The clearest example of this type of propaganda is afforded by "cross the lines" loudspeaker broadcasts, which sometimes facilitated immediate capture of the prisoners of war—not by propaganda in the ordinary sense, but by giving instructions on how to surrender safely, once the wish to surrender was present.

No sufficiently accurate estimate is available of the total number of prisoners captured by the use of such techniques, but signal successes involving hundreds of isolated troops in the Normandy campaign have been credited to psychological warfare combat teams. Even more successful were the loud-speaker-carrying tanks employed in the Rhine River offensive, when the first signs of weakening resistance were encountered. For example, the Fourth Armored Division reported that its psychological warfare unit captured over 500 prisoners in a four-day dash from the Kyll River to the Rhine. Firsthand investigation of these loudspeaker missions, and interrogation of prisoners captured under such circumstances, establish that Allied propaganda was effective in describing the tactical situation to totally isolated and helpless soldiers and in arranging an Allied cease fire and thereby presenting an assurance to the German soldier of a safe surrender. The successful targets for such broadcasts were groups where solidarity and ability to function as a unit were largely destroyed. Leaflets especially written for specific sectors and dropped on pin point targets by fighter-bombers were used instead of loudspeakers where larger units were cut off. This method proved less successful, since the units to which they were addressed were usually better integrated and the necessary cease fire conditions could not be arranged.

Less spectacular, but more extensive, was strategic propaganda. Allied directives called for emphasis on four themes in this type of propaganda:

(*1*) Ideological attacks on the Nazi Party and Germany's war aims, (*2*) the strategical hopelessness of Germany's military and economic position, (*3*) the justness of the United Nations war aims and their unity and determination to carry them out (unconditional surrender, although made known to the troops, was never stressed), (*4*) promises of good treatment to prisoners of war, with appeals to self-preservation through surrender.

Although it is extremely difficult, especially in view of the lack of essential data, to assess the efficacy of these various themes, some tentative clues might be seen in the answers given to the key attitude questions in the monthly Psychological Warfare opinion poll of captured German soldiers.[7] Thus, there was no significant decline in attachment to Nazi ideology until February and March 1945. In other words, propaganda attacks on Nazi ideology seem to have been of little avail, and attachment to secondary symbols, e.g., Hitler, declined only when the smaller military units began to break up under very heavy pressure.

Since the German soldier was quite ignorant of military news on other fronts, it was believed that a great deal of printed material should contain factual reports of the military situation, stressing the strategical hopelessness of the German position. As a result, the third most frequently recalled items of our propaganda were the military news reports. It seems reasonable to believe that the emphasis on these subjects did contribute to the development of defeatist sentiment.

Despite the vast amount of space devoted to ideological attacks on German leaders, only about five per cent of the Ps/W mentioned this topic—a fact which supported the contention as to the general failure of ideological or secondary appeals. Finally, the presentation of the justness of our war aims was carried out in such a way as to avoid stressing the unconditional surrender aspects of our intentions, while emphasizing postwar peace intentions and organizational efforts; much was made of United Nations unity. All this fell on deaf ears, for of this material only a small minority of Ps/W (about 5 per cent) recalled specific statements about military government plans for the German occupation.

As has been pointed out previously, the themes which were most successful, at least in attracting attention and remaining fixed in the memory, were those promising good treatment as prisoners of war. In other words, propaganda referring to immediate concrete situations and problems seems to have been most effective in some respects.

The single leaflet most effective in communicating the promise of good treatment was the "safe conduct pass." Significantly, it was usually printed on the back of leaflets which contained no elaborate propaganda appeals except those of self-preservation. The rank and file tended to be favorably disposed to its official language and legal, document-like character. In one sector where General Eisenhower's signature was left off the leaflet, doubt was cast on its authenticity.

414

Belief in the veracity of this appeal was no doubt based on the attitude that the British and the Americans were respectable law-abiding soldiers who would treat their captives according to international law. As a result of this predisposition and the wide use of the safe conduct leaflets, as well as our actual practices in treating prisoners well, the German soldier came to have no fear of capture by British or American troops. The most that can be claimed for this lack of fear was that it may have decreased or undercut any tendency to fight to the death; it produced no active opposition to continued hostilities.

As an extension of the safe-conduct approach, leaflets were prepared instructing noncommissioned officers in detailed procedures by which their men could safely be removed from battle so as to avoid our fire and at the same time avoid evacuation by the German field police. If the Germans could not be induced to withdraw from combat activity, Allied propaganda appealed to them to hide in cellars. This in fact became a favorite technique of surrender, since it avoided the need of facing the conscience-twinging desertion problem.

As a result of psychological warfare research, a series of leaflets was prepared whose attack was aimed at primary group organization in the German Army, without recourse to ideological symbols. Group organization depended on the acceptance of immediate leadership and mutual trust. Therefore this series of leaflets sought to stimulate group discussion among the men and to bring into their focus of attention concerns which would loosen solidarity. One leaflet declared, "Do not take our (the Allies) word for it; ask your comrade; find out how he feels." Thereupon followed a series of questions on personal concerns, family problems, tactical consideration and supply problems. Discussion of these problems was expected to increase anxiety. It was assumed that to the degree that the soldier found that he was not isolated in his opinion, to that degree he would be strengthened in his resolve to end hostilities, for himself at least.

Conclusion

At the beginning of the second world war, many publicists and specialists in propaganda attributed almost supreme importance to psychological warfare operations. The legendary success of Allied propaganda against the German Army at the end of the first world war and the tremendous expansion of the advertising and mass communications industries in the ensuing two decades had convinced many people that human behavior could be extensively manipulated by mass communications. They tended furthermore to stress that military morale was to a great extent a function of the belief in the rightness of the "larger" cause which was at issue in the war; good soldiers were therefore those who clearly understood the

415

political and moral implications of what was at stake. They explained the striking successes of the German Army in the early phases of the war by the "ideological possession" of the German soldiers, and they accordingly thought that propaganda attacking doctrinal conceptions would be defeating this army.

Studies of the German Army's morale and fighting effectiveness made during the last three years of the war throw considerable doubt on these hypotheses. The solidarity of the German Army was discovered by these studies—which left much to be desired from the standpoint of scientific rigor—to be based only very indirectly and very partially on political convictions or broader ethical beliefs. Where conditions were such as to allow primary group life to function smoothly, and where the primary group developed a high degree of cohesion, morale was high and resistance effective or at least very determined, regardless in the main of the political attitudes of the soldiers. The conditions of primary group life were related to spatial proximity, the capacity for intimate communication, the provision of paternal protectiveness by NCO's and junior officers, and the gratification of certain personality needs, e.g., manliness, by the military organization and its activities. The larger structure of the army served to maintain morale through the provision of the framework in which potentially individuating physical threats were kept at a minimum—through the organization of supplies and through adequate strategic dspositions.

The behavior of the German Army demonstrated that the focus of attention and concern beyond one's immediate face-to-face social circles might be slight indeed and still not interfere with the achievement of a high degree of military effectiveness. It also showed that attempts to modify behavior by means of symbols referring to events or values outside the focus of attention and concern would be given an indifferent response by the vast majority of the German soldiers. This was almost equally true under conditions of primary group integrity and under conditions of extreme primary group disintegration. In the former, primary needs were met adequately through the gratifications provided by the other members of the group; in the latter, the individual had regressed to a narcissistic state in which symbols referring to the outer world were irrelevant to his first concern—"saving his own skin."

At moments of primary group disintegration, a particular kind of propaganda less hortatory or analytical, but addressing the intensified desire to survive and describing the precise procedures by which physical survival could be achieved, was likely to facilitate further disintegration. Furthermore, in some cases aspects of the environment towards which the soldier might hitherto have been emotionally indifferent were defined for him by prolonged exposure to propaganda under conditions of disintegration. Some of these wider aspects, e.g., particular strategic consideration, then tended to be taken into account in his motivation and he was more likely to implement his defeatist mood by surrender than he would have been without exposure to propaganda.

It seems necessary, therefore, to reconsider the potentialities of propaganda in the context of all the other variables which influence behavior. The erroneous views concerning the omnipotence of propaganda must be given up and their place must be taken by much more differentiated views as to the possibilities of certain kinds of propaganda under different sets of conditions.

It must be recognized that on the moral plane most men are members of the larger society by virtue of identifications which are mediated through the human beings with whom they are in personal relationships. Many are bound into the larger society only by primary group identifications. Only a small proportion possessing special training or rather particular kinds of personalities are capable of giving a preponderant share of their attention and concern to the symbols of the larger world. The conditions under which these different groups will respond to propaganda will differ, as will also the type of propaganda to which they will respond.

NOTES

1. Nazi propagandists, with their hyperpolitical orientation, tended to overestimate the German soldier's rseponsiveness to politics.

2. The fact that the High Command made no attempt to explain away the defeat of the counter-offensive may have been due, among other things, to its conviction of the irrelevance of strategic consideration in the morale of the ordinary soldier.

3. The proposition often asserted during the war that the Allies' refusal to promise a "soft peace" to the Germans was prolonging the war, i.e., that German military resistance was motivated by fear of what the Allies would do to Germany in event of its defeat, scarcely finds support in the fact that in October 1944, when the German front was stiffening, 74 per cent of a sample of 345 Ps/W said they did not expect revenge to be taken against the German population after the war.

4. See Gurfein, M. I., and Janowitz, Morris, "Trends in Wehrmacht Morale," The Public Opinion Quarterly, Vol. 10, No. 1 (1946), p. 78.

5. Much of the reduction of trust in Hitler which occurred in this final period was simply a diminution in esteem for Hitler's technical skill as a strategist and as a diplomat.

6. The mixture of apathy and resentment against Hitler persisted through the first part of the demobilization period following the end of the war, but as life began to reorganize and to take on new meaning and the attitudes toward authority, which sustain and are sustained by the routines of daily life, revived, esteem for Hitler also began to revive. It is likely to revive still further and to assume a prominent place in German life once more, if the new elite which is being created under the Allied occupation shows weakness and lack of decisiveness and self-confidence.

7. Cf. Gurfein, M. I., and Janowitz, Morris, op. cit.

HILDE HIMMELWEIT

Television and the Child

(EDITOR'S NOTE: *Television and the Child* is a report of a research study on the "impact of television on children and young people" in Great Britain. The data were collected in 1955 following a research design in which a group of viewers, those who had television at home, were compared with another group of controls, who had no television at home and were not regular viewers. The groups were matched on four variables: sex, age, intelligence and social class. The study was carried out in four English cities, London, Portsmouth, Sutherland, and Bristol, and a total of 4,500 children were studied.

The survey concentrated on two age groups: 10–11 and 13–14 year olds. The basic data were collected by means of questionnaires and the children were asked to keep a diary privately at school for each day for one week. The second batch of questionnaires were used six weeks later. In addition, measures of children's personality were obtained, as well as ratings by the teachers of the children's behavior and personality characteristics.)

This chapter is designed to give a general picture of the main findings. It divides into two main sections. Section I gives the effects for each area in turn, while Section II provides the broader picture of the way different factors determine children's reactions. To keep the presentation brief, we may on occasions sound more categorical than the evidence warrants. This summary should, therefore, be read in conjunction with the main report, where the evidence is presented with its necessary qualifications and where the implications of the findings are more fully discussed. The relevant chapters are indicated in brackets throughout this summary. Unless specifically stated otherwise, the findings refer to children with access to BBC television only and are based on the results obtained from 10–11 and 13–14 year old children.

Who Are the Early Viewers?—Apart from various social and economic determinants, we found that the first people to buy television were those with the strongest need for ready-made entertainment. In the United

States research among adults has shown that the early set buyers were originally more avid cinema-goers and radio listeners. Our work with children also indicates that those from homes which bought television early were more dependent on outside stimulation—they had an unusually high interest in comics, radio, and clubs, and their taste in book reading tended to be narrower. All this suggests a home atmosphere which would seek the stimulation of outside entertainment rather than rely on its own resources.

Section I

THE AMOUNT CHILDREN VIEW

How Many Hours Per Week do Children View Television?—At the time of our survey, viewers in both age groups watched television for an average of 11–13 hours a week, or just under two hours a day; they spent more time on television than on any other single leisure activity. While older and younger children devoted about the same amount of time to television, the time was in each case differently distributed; the 10–11 year olds watched more children's television and less evening television than the adolescents. On average, children's television was watched by grammar, secondary modern, and primary school children respectively for four, five, and six hours a week. Viewing was fairly regular throughout the week, Saturday being the favourite viewing night.

The popular image of the child glued to the television set, watching whatever is on, did not fit the facts. Most children viewed reasonably selectively, turning to other things when something was on which they did not like. Many also consulted the *Radio Times* or the newspapers before they settled down to viewing, despite the fact that in many of the homes —two-thirds, according to the children—the set was left on for most of the evening. This happened as often in middle- as in working-class homes.

What Factors Reduce Interest in and Time Spent on Viewing?—The single, most important background factor was undoubtedly intelligence; the higher the child's intelligence, the less his viewing. This difference was already clear cut among the 10–11 year olds and became more pronounced in early adolescence—where the grammar school pupils, of all the children tested, proved the least interested and the least prepared to spend a lot of time on television.

In both age groups boys and girls spent roughly the same amount of time in front of the set.

Viewing seemed to become a habit on which the child fell back when nothing more interesting was available. Consequently, the child with many interests, the active child, and the outdoor type tended to view less than

419

the other children. But for all children, outdoor play and (in adolescence in particular) social activities proved television's strongest rivals. For the average child, viewing took second place to these.

The social level of the home (whether it was a middle- or a working-class home) proved of little importance in affecting how much children viewed. Only among the younger children was there any difference. Middle-class children tended to view a little less than working-class children, largely because of their earlier bedtimes. What proved much more important was parental example, and to a lesser extent, parental control. In homes where the parents themselves were selective and moderate viewers, the children also tended to view relatively little. While this was the general pattern, we also found much individual variation between members of the same family.

It would appear that the amount a child views depends in the first instance on his intelligence, secondly on his personality and on how full and active a life he had led before television came on the scene, and thirdly on parental example.

How Does the Amount of Viewing Change (a) Over Time and (b) With the Introduction of a Second Channel?—Viewing rapidly becomes a habit—within the first three months the children settled to a routine in keeping with their age, intelligence, and personality, and one which seemed relatively independent of how long they had had television. The veteran viewers (those with television for over three years), compared with recent viewers, reduced their viewing by only two hours a week although they were more critical and less attached to television.

Even the attractions of an alternative channel, offering many more of the children's favourites, did not change this pattern. A study carried out with children who had access to both channels showed that the average number of hours they viewed was about the same as for children with access to BBC alone.

Do the Children Watch Many Programmes Designed for Adults?— From the age of 10 onwards, at least half the children watched adult programmes in the first part of the evening (until 9 P.M.). Even after 10 P.M. one-third of the 13–14 year olds was still watching. On evenings not followed by school days, the children viewed until a later hour.

An assessment of the effects of television on children which did not take evening programmes into account would, therefore, be seriously misleading.

CHILDREN'S TASTE IN TELEVISION

What Kinds of Programme do Children Like Best?—Three-quarters of the votes for the most favoured programme went to adult programmes, particularly to crime thrillers and, to a lesser extent, to comedies, variety programmes, and family serials. Westerns were much favoured by the younger children. Other types of programme—such as puppets, nature and animal programmes, and how-to-make programmes—were not especially popular. Only among the 8–10 year olds did children's television programmes or *Watch with Mother* appear among the top five favourites.

As with time, so with taste. We found that age and intelligence affected preferences, while the social level of the home made little difference. A child's liking for a given programme is a function of his sex, emotional and intellectual maturity, and of his own idiosyncratic needs.

The preferences of adolescent girls and boys differed more than did the tastes of the younger boys and girls. Rather unexpectedly, girls seemed as much interested as boys in crime and detective series.

Adult political programmes, documentary and discussion programmes such as *Panorama* or the *Brains Trust* held little appeal, even for the more intelligent grammar school children.

One finding was of special interest; even the most popular programme or programme type was mentioned by no more than one-third of the children. Within any given age and intelligence group there is thus a great deal of variation in taste, a fact which seems to be considerably underestimated in popular discussion.

Do Children's Tastes in Television Reflect Their Tastes in Other Mass Media?—On the whole we found they did. Children liked similar types of programmes whether they occurred on television, or radio, or in the cinema, or whether they formed the content of a book. Tastes in television were further linked with interest in other activities. Children have a general underlying pattern of preferences, and it is therefore possible to predict (within limits) a child's television likes and dislikes from a knowledge of his age, intelligence, and taste in other mass media.

Can Children's Tastes be Developed by Seeing Programmes which Are Not on the Whole Popular with Children?—When programmes such as *Science Review; Animal, Vegetable, or Mineral?; Meet the Commonwealth; From Tropical Forests; Have You a Camera?* come on the screen, children with access to one channel only must either stop watching or view programmes which they do not expect to be very interesting. Under these circumstances, quite a number of children chose to see such programmes and in fact enjoyed them. Children with access to one channel only get the chance to discover such programmes, but those with two channels hardly ever.

The more the child can follow his favourite choices by switching from channel to channel, the less likely is he to come in contact with programmes which, from an educational viewpoint, would prove more worthwhile and which would enable him to experience new things and so broaden his taste.

How is Taste Affected by Access to a Second Channel?—While the amount of viewing did not increase, children now tended to concentrate more on their favourites, switching from channel to channel. They therefore saw other kinds of programmes less often. Thus, child audiences for adult crime and detective series, panel games, Westerns, drama and variety programmes remained high, while information and documentary programmes suffered a disproportionate loss (from 48 per cent down to 13 per cent). Once there is a choice of channels, with programmes as at present distributed, those with educational value or those which have been especially produced for children are most likely to suffer.

Family conflict over the choice of channel was rare; only about 10 per cent of the children on any one day could not watch a programme they wanted to see because (they said) the rest of the family preferred to view something else on the other channel.

On the whole, children in homes where a second channel had recently become available much preferred ITV. It offered more of their favourites, and many liked the advertisements. This was particularly true of the 10–11 year olds; the older and the more intelligent children tended to be more critical both of the advertisements and of the interruptions they cause.

What Constitutes Television's Appeal for Children?—The interviews with the children suggest that part of television's appeal lies in its easy availability and its consequent value as a time filler.

Television offers the satisfaction of being in the know, of going behind the scenes and of learning about the world and about people. On the emotional side, television appeals in different ways to different children. It offers security and reassurance through the familiar format and themes of many of its programmes, notably the family serials and the Westerns. It offers constant change, excitement, and suspense. It provides escape from everyday demands with lightheartedness, glamour, and romance, and permits the child to identify himself with different romantic heroes.

Television also offers the appeal of personalities, presented more intimately and in more everyday terms than the stars of the cinema. The personalities of television seemed to be liked by the children in particular for their warmth and friendliness.

As a preliminary step in the study of the effects of television on the child's values and outlook, a content analysis was made of the programmes on both channels, first when ITV had only just come on the air and again about nine months later.[1] The allocation of time to different types of programme was charted and a detailed analysis made of the themes, motives, values, and characterisation of adult plays (excluding comedies) and of children's Westerns.

What Does Television Offer to the Child in Terms of Programme Content?—Taking both children's and evening television together, the staple fare consisted of plays—chiefly Westerns, crime, and adventure. Without overstaying his bedtime the child with access to both channels could watch well over twenty-five plays a week. In one rather typical week, between 5 and 9 P.M., eighteen plays were shown which dealt with one or other aspect of lawbreaking and retribution,[2] fourteen of them on ITV (nine of these were designed for adults). In the same week, the BBC during these hours offered four programmes of this kind (two designed for children).

In the evening, ITV offered twice as many plays or playlets as the BBC, half of them episodes from crime, adventure, and adult Western series; the BBC devoted about one-fifth of its plays to such episodes, the remainder being comedies or problem plays.

In children's television the BBC allotted about one-third of its time to information programmes and one-third to plays. On ITV, plays occupied first 50 then 73 per cent of the time. While both channels offered mainly adventure plays, in the case of ITV these amounted to 96 per cent. They consisted of Westerns, swashbuckling adventure and animal adventure series, most of them produced in America. Seventy-three per cent of BBC children's plays were adventure plays; they covered a wider range of topics than those shown on ITV, with more of them being live productions.

That such programme uniformity is not an inevitable by-product of commercial television is seen in comparison with New York television; where programme output for children proved more varied, even though New York has seven stations competing for audiences.

In consequence, children's information programmes on ITV compared with BBC were fewer, shorter, and covered a smaller number of topics. There were no programmes to correspond to the BBC programmes on foreign countries, fewer 'making and doing' programmes, and fewer programmes about the ways of life of people in different occupations. Apart from current affairs programmes like *This Week* and the news, children missed nearly all ITV evening information programmes, as these were on too late. In the case of the BBC, information programmes were more uniformly spread over the evening, so that children could see more of them; but even so they would miss most of the BBC science programmes (which might well appeal to children) and all the programmes on art.

In the course of the last year, ITV programmes for children have become more varied.

EFFECT OF TELEVISION ON VALUES AND OUTLOOK

What View of Life and What Values do Adult television Plays Offer the Child?—Analysis of the content of randomly selected adult plays from both channels (excluding comedies, crime and detective series), showed the values put over to be remarkably consistent from play to play. Since children see and enjoy a great number of plays, we set out to discover how far there was a cumulative effect on their outlook and values.

The world of television drama tends to be that of upper middle-class urban society. The occupations of people of this social level are depicted as worth-while, while manual work is presented as uninteresting. Television plays teach that self-confidence and toughness are needed to achieve success—goodness of character is not enough; that life is difficult, especially for women; that marriages are frequently unhappy, and parent–child relationships often strained. Events rarely turn out satisfactorily and virtue seldom brings happiness in its train. Violence is an inevitable part of life, and good people often resort to it. For the adult observer a hackneyed view of life emerges, similar in many ways to that offered in films or in the theatre; for the child television may afford a glimpse of adult life which he would otherwise gain less often and only at a later age.

To What Extent is the Child's Outlook Coloured by What He Sees on Television?—We have found a number of instances where viewers and controls differed in their outlook, differences which did not exist before television came on the scene. There was a small but consistent influence of television on the way children thought generally about jobs, job values, success, and social surroundings. In their wishes about jobs the viewers proved more ambitious than children not exposed to television; in their job values they were more 'middle class,' and in their assessment of the factors making for personal success they more often stressed the need for self-confidence. Some of their descriptions of the homes of rich people reflected the hall-marks of wealth depicted on television.

Adolescent girl viewers proved more concerned than their controls about growing up and marrying—possibly a reaction to the difficulties of adult life of which television made them aware at an age when they are much in need of reassurance.

Probably as a result of BBC programmes about foreign (and especially European) countries, viewers made fewer value judgements about foreigners; where stereotypes were given, they tended to reflect those offered by television.

Television tended to make no impact where the child could turn for information to his immediate environment, parents, and friends; it had little effect on the jobs children expected to do, as distinct from their wish dreams about them.

The most affected were the less intelligent 13–14 year olds. The lesson of television was not absorbed by a child bright enough to be well informed, or critical of what he viewed, or by one too young to perceive or to take an interest in the implied values.

All in all, the values of television can make an impact if they are consistently presented in dramatic form, and if they touch on ideas or values for which the child is emotionally ready. Extrapolating from these findings, one would expect that in the crime and detective series the constant

424

display of aggression by both the criminal and the upholder of the law would also make an impact on those children sensitised to such cues.

REACTIONS OF FEAR AND ANXIETY

What Frightens Children on Television?—Westerns tended to frighten only the very young or the insecure; it is likely that the majority of children can enjoy them without fear by the time they are about 7. On the other hand, detective, murder and crime thrillers were often mentioned as frightening by adolescents as well as by the 10–11 year olds. Violence in these plays, unlike Westerns, is realistic, not stylised, and forms less often part of a stereotyped plot sequence.

Many children were frightened by incidents in horror programmes, space fiction, and even such dramatisations as *Jane Eyre*. On the other hand, real events of a violent nature seen on newsreels were rarely mentioned as frightening. Fiction made a deeper impact than reality.

Where children mentioned incidents that had frightened them, they often spoke of nightmares and of difficulty in falling asleep. It is in such effects as these that the disturbance caused by frightening programmes can best be seen.

Children tended to be more readily frightened when viewing in the dark, and when watching programmes in the evening without an adult present. Television in so far as it is more of a family activity than radio listening is likely to arouse less fear, but television's visual impact in darkened rooms could well make up for this. In general, television emerged from our survey as very similar to the cinema and radio, both in the amount of fear it engendered and in the types of programmes which children found frightening.

What Types of Aggression Prove Most Disturbing to Children?— Guns and anything to do with guns, proved least and daggers and sharp instruments most disturbing, with swords somewhere in between. Fist-fights and fighting on the ground were disturbing only when they occurred in sports programmes, i.e. in real life, rather than in fictional programmes.

We found young children unmoved by a scene in which polecats devoured a rat; but they were very disturbed by danger to animals like the dogs in *Lassie* and *Rin-Tin-Tin*, for which they had a particular attachment or which had been cast in a special role.

Verbal acts of aggression, reprimand, and ridicule sometimes occasioned more unease than physical aggression, particularly when they occurred in real-life situations, in panel games, or sports programmes. Children were disturbed by situations with which they could identify themselves; this is a more important factor than the sheer amount of force of the physical violence shown.

Children enjoy being a little frightened; they like suspense for the sake

425

of the relief that follows. There is a narrow margin between pleasurable suspense and intolerable fear. The children themselves made a clear distinction between exciting and frightening programmes, enjoying the former and not the latter.

THE EFFECT OF WESTERNS, AND OF
CRIME AND DETECTIVE SERIES

Do These Programmes Make Children Aggressive?—We did not find that the viewers were any more aggressive or maladjusted than the controls, television is unlikely to cause aggressive behaviour, although it could precipitate it in those few children who are emotionally disturbed. On the other hand, there was little support for the view that programmes of violence are beneficial; we found that they aroused aggression as often as they discharged it. We also found that they taught the one-sided lesson that to offend against the law is bad, without teaching its positive counterpart.

By taking up such a disproportionate amount of viewing time, these programmes prevent the showing of more varied types of programmes that could offer children a broader view of life.

Do These Programmes Fill an Urgent Demand?—While *Fabian of Scotland Yard* was the first favourite, as many as two-thirds of the children mentioned quite different programmes as their favourites. Also, when asked to plan an ideal evening's entertainment, only 10 per cent of the adolescents and 26 per cent of the younger children mentioned these programmes in their bill of fare. It would seem, therefore, that the number of these programmes could safely be reduced without fear of losing the child audience.

TELEVISION'S EFFECT ON GENERAL KNOWLEDGE
AND SCHOOL PERFORMANCE

Does Television Improve Children's General Knowledge?[3]—On the whole the gain was very slight, but varied with the type of child. Children can undoubtedly learn from television; but viewing takes time, some of which might be spent with books or other sources of information. It incurs, therefore, both gain and loss. We found a net profit only for the younger, duller children.

There were several reasons for the absence of gain. Documentaries and the discussion programmes offered a good deal of information; but the type of information contained in programmes designed especially for children is also readily available to the controls from other media, so that there is little advantage to be gained from viewing. Adult information programmes were not very popular and did not always get their points across even to adolescents. In any case, younger children do not remember the

426

content for any length of time, so that there is little storing of information. Paradoxically, our results suggest that gains in general knowledge come mostly from adult non-information programmes; these contain useful details of plot and circumstance which are more readily remembered because of their dramatic content.

For most children in our survey, television proved neither a help nor a hindrance as far as general knowledge was concerned, except for the younger or duller children (as yet able to read very little), for whom it proved a real advantage. Their gain in knowledge proved the equivalent to what a child would normally gain in the course of four to five months of intellectual development. For these children, television provided information in the form and the pace best suited to them—in dramatic and above all in visual form. Grammar school viewers, on the other hand, did not gain; in fact they proved a little less knowledgeable than their controls. Viewing offered them little that was new and took time away from other sources of knowledge, such as reading or radio.

Although children remembered nature programmes well, they carried over little of such programmes into their general knowledge of this subject or into their performance in related subjects taught at school. Gain in knowledge of current affairs was negligible because children had little interest in these programmes. There was equally little gain in cultural interests. Few children, for example, went to a museum after seeing exhibits from it in a children's programme.

How Does Television Affect Children's School Work?—On the whole, viewers more or less held their own with class mates of similar age, sex, social class, and intelligence; but the brighter children in both age groups tended to fall a little behind.

Television created no particular interest in any school subject, nor were viewers markedly better or worse at any of them.

Viewers and controls also spent much the same amount of time on homework. But the closing of the transmission gap between 6 and 7:30 may well make a difference here, and a repeat inquiry is needed under these new conditions.

Does Television Make Children Listless and Lead to Poor Concentration at School, and Reduce Interest in School?—Our findings suggest that it does not. There was no difference between viewers and controls in children's subjective assessments of tiredness in the morning, nor in ratings by class teachers of each child's concentration.

On the other hand, half the teachers, when asked for their opinion, said that one of the three most important effects of television was the children's tiredness in the morning and consequent lack of concentration. Their views reflected their general attitude to television and their classroom experience with viewers; our findings were likely to be more valid since they were derived from a comparison of viewers and controls, taking into account the number of children without television who nevertheless lacked concentration and felt tired.

Children's interest in school or school societies did not seem to be affected. Viewers and controls differed neither in the age at which they would like to leave school, in the frequency with which they took part in extra-curricular activities, nor in their attitude to school as judged by their class teachers.

THE EFFECT OF TELEVISION ON LEISURE

Are Children's Lives Dominated by Television?—This proved true in only a minority of cases—just as only a minority of children are obsessed with the cinema or radio. Children gave much of their time to television, but far less of their interest. There was an age difference here: the 10–11 year old in the survey proved more attached to television than the adolescent and, within each age group, the child of below average intelligence more than the bright child.

How much television is wanted depends on the relative emptiness of the child's life before he had television and also on his emotional needs. For a minority of cases the vicarious companionship and excitement offered through television is very important, and in such cases television occupies a central place in their lives. But about half the children said they would not very much miss television if they had to do without it, and most children on most ordinary days of the week had other activities which they enjoyed more than viewing.

What Makes Room for Viewing?—Viewing takes up a good deal of children's time—on average just under two hours a day. Something, then, must make room for viewing. We consider first the two mass media which are most closely akin to television: cinema and radio; then reading; and finally other leisure activities.

How Has Television Changed Children's Interest in the Cinema?— Cinema and television are seen by many children as interchangeable. Both provide entertainment, one with the added advantage of convenience and of not having to pay. Younger viewers therefore reduced their cinema visits and continued to go less often even after viewing for some years. More among them only went once a fortnight rather than once or twice a week. The cinema, however, is also a social occasion, a way of meeting friends away from home. This proved more important for the adolescents than for the younger children; recent adolescent viewers went to the cinema only a little less often than before, but those who had already been viewing for a year had returned to the number of cinema visits characteristic of the adolescent control group.

Individual films made less impact on viewers than controls, accustomed as the former were to the rapid panorama of television programmes with their juxtaposition of emotion and content. But admiration for film stars

428

continued undiminished—television here helps with the many personal appearances of film stars that it features.

How Has Television Affected Listening to the Radio?—Children with access to television listen very little to the radio. While future viewers were keener listeners than their controls, once they had television they stopped listening almost completely. Half the older and a third of the younger viewers still spent a little time with the radio—on average, about one hour a week. One exception here were the frequent viewers who were also relatively heavy consumers of whatever other ready-made entertainment was available; when television was off the air, they would turn to radio. However, for the majority of children, there is a limit to the amount of ready-made entertainment they require—given enough of one mass medium, they cut down severely on the others.

Children who had been viewing for several years showed a very slight revival of interest in the radio. Where listening to the radio continued, viewers assigned it a specialist role. They listened to sports commentaries, discussions, panel games, and musical programmes, rather than to plays; these they enjoyed more on television.

What Is the Effect of Television on Reading and Skill in Reading?—Children, once they started viewing, certainly read less than before, by how much depended on the type of child and on how long he had been viewing; it also differed for book- and comic-reading.

The future viewer read more comics than his control, but once he had been viewing for a time his comic-reading came down to the level of that of the control children. Ultimately, then, viewers read no fewer comics than their controls, although before they had television they read more. Books, on the other hand, were read equally often by future viewers and their controls (even though the quality of books read by the former tended to be lower); but with the arrival of television, the viewers reduced their book-reading more severely than their comic-reading. This reduction was most marked among older children and those of medium intelligence; the bright children were little affected and the dull children read very little in any case.

At first, television decreased the proportion of books to comics read. But as children got used to viewing they gradually reverted to books; so that after a few years the viewers were once again reading as many books as the controls, and the duller children had even increased their share. Ultimately, therefore, television favours book- —rather than comic- —reading.

Book-reading comes into its own, not despite television but rather because of it. Television stimulated interest in reading, through its serial dramatisation of books; it also aroused the child's interest and curiosity so that he became interested in a wider range of books than before, including non-fiction.

Television may reduce children's reading skill at first, but not in the long run. The present generation of children, who first meet with television at a crucial stage of development, come off worst in this respect, especially since those who reduce their book-reading most tend to be most in need of reading practice. But it must be remembered that book-reading (and therefore reading practice) revives after several years of viewing, and that duller children come to read more than their controls. Ultimately, when television sets have become as commonplace as radio and children grow up accustomed to viewing, there is likely to be no loss in reading skill.

Does Television Reduce Social Contacts Outside the Family?—Entertaining at home tended to increase with the acquisition of a television set, but visiting other children was not affected. What did suffer somewhat was the time spent in casual companionship with other children; this is in line with other effects we have noted, the more clearly defined activities being the least affected.

As a result of television, children's lives become more structured; less time is spent on doing 'nothing in particular' either alone or with other children. There is less time "to stand and stare."

Whether this is desirable or not will depend on the use to which such time is put and how much of it a child has. A distinction needs to be made here between aimless, bored loafing, on the one hand, and 'healthy' idleness on the other, which enables the child to draw on his own resources rather than on ready-made entertainment.

Effect on Family Life

Does Television Keep the Family Together?—Television does keep members of the family at home more. But it is doubtful whether it binds the family together in more than this physical sense, except while the children are young. As they grow older, their viewing becomes more silent and personal. Also, as children grow into adolescence, the increased time spent with the family may set up strains, since it runs counter to their need to make contacts outside; they may therefore do less in the way of other joint activities with their parents than formerly.

Does Television Cause Conflict in the Family?—Conflict about television does occur, especially over bedtimes, mealtimes, and the banning of certain programmes. But in many cases this conflict is only indirectly due to television; it may arise from existing poor parent–child relations, from unwise handling by the parents of problems thrown up by television (failure, for instance, to understand the child's absorption in what he views), or from emotional disturbance within the child. In all this television does not create conflicts, although it may precipitate them; it provides a whole new range of situations about which conflict can occur—

but the root cause of the conflict normally goes much deeper than television.

Do Parents Control Their Children's Viewing?—Many parents are greatly in favour of television, even to the point of being defensive about it. To some extent television helps them to keep an eye on the children. Also, if they themselves enjoy television and view a lot, they have a vested interest in defending it. Perhaps for these reasons many parents do not admit to a need to control the amount and content of children's viewing. Also, of course, when parents view unselectively themselves, such control becomes difficult to enforce. Two-thirds of the children we questioned said that the television set was left on all the evening in their homes.

There were also signs—though many children and parents tended to deny it—that television is used as an instrument of discipline, for punishment and reward.

PASSIVITY AND STIMULATION

Does Television Make Children Passive?—In the opinion survey, as many as a quarter of the teachers (and an even higher number among those who disliked television) believed that television made children more passive.

This vague term 'passivity' seems to be used in five different senses; taking each sense in turn and comparing the viewers' behaviour with that of the controls, we found no evidence whatsoever of increased passivity.

1. Children, it is said, absorb television like a sponge; this view (in which physical and mental inactivity are confused) proved untenable, judging from the observations of mothers and the subjective reports by children of their reactions to programmes. Inherent in this view is a confusion between what to the adult may appear poor entertainment, and the way such programmes may appear to the less sophisticated child.

2. Viewing, it is argued, leads children to prefer an edited version of life to the 'real thing', since they can have the screened version without effort. We found no evidence of this.

3. It is also said that viewing leads to loss of initiative. But both viewers and controls enjoyed the same types of activity; and in fact children mainly tended to make room for viewing by cutting down on other ready-made entertainments, notably the cinema and radio, rather than on hobbies and play. Similarly, teachers' ratings of the children's initiative were identical for the two groups.

4. A fourth assertion is that television leads to a jaded palate; we found if anything that the opposite was true, especially among dull adolescents and bright 10–11 year olds; as a result of viewing, they had become interested in a wider range of subjects than their controls.

5. Finally, it is thought that viewing dulls the imagination. Yet when the teachers in our survey were asked to rate each child as 'unusually' or 'moderately' imaginative or as 'unimaginative', no difference emerged between viewers and controls.

The consistently negative results obtained for each one of these five aspects give confidence in our findings. Children's love of activity and exploration is very strong. When there was a choice between sports or hobbies and viewing, television was often the loser.

Can Television Broaden and Stimulate Children's Interests?—The power of television in this respect is most evident in relation to reading. We found that future viewers, before they got their sets, showed less interest than controls in specialised and non-fiction subjects, but that after they had been viewing for a time their interests expanded. This change seemed to occur most often among children of a mental age of about 12; the duller 13–14 year olds and the brighter 10–11 year olds proved most receptive to television's benefit.

Does Television Make Children More Enterprising, or Stimulate Them to Make Things, Enter Competitions, Visit Places of Interest, or Develop New Hobbies?—On the whole it does not. We found few children had made anything after seeing it modelled on television, and those who did tended to be the hobby-minded, generally alert children—the ones least in need of stimulation. Only 2 per cent of the older and 3 per cent of the younger children had made and sent things to the BBC Television Centre for a competition.

The under-nines, according to their mothers' accounts, became interested in things shown on television and tried to copy them more often than did the older children. Apart from an increased interest in sport, children of nine years and older proved little responsive.

Visits to museums and art galleries increased little after the viewing of specific programmes.

Viewing, it seems, stimulates interest rather than activity. This may be due to the methods of presentation and choice of topics; but it is probably in large measure due to the nature of television entertainment—a rapid succession of programmes allowing little time for reflection and so only stimulating children with initially strong interest in a given topic. Serialised dramatisations of books are effective possibly because each episode ends on a note of suspense, so retaining the children's interest after the programme has finished.

EFFECT OF TELEVISION ON NIGHT REST AND EYESIGHT

Do Child Viewers Get Less Sleep than Their Controls, and Have More Trouble in Falling Asleep?—Within the two age groups studied, viewing caused a slight postponement of bedtime on weekdays; on average not more than twenty minutes a night. Moreover, the controls spent more time than viewers playing or reading in bed, before they turned out the lights; there was, therefore, very little difference between viewers and non-viewers in effective sleeping time.

Bedtimes were postponed especially among those who would otherwise go to bed early, that is girls and younger children from middle-class homes. Contrary to popular belief, really late bedtimes occurred as often among controls as among viewers; they reflect not so much the lure of television as the general home atmosphere, of which excessive viewing may be just another facet. In fact, the Norwich findings suggested that more relaxed parental control of bedtime was characteristic of parents who were among the first to buy television sets.

We had many reports of difficulties in falling asleep, and of nightmares after some specially frightening programme. But, in general, viewing did not seem to over-excite children; viewers had no more difficulty in falling asleep and reported no more frightening dreams than their controls. Younger children may, however, be more seriously affected than the two age groups we studied.

Is There More Defective Eyesight among Viewers Than Controls?— Defective eyesight was no more frequent among viewers than controls, at least when assessed in terms of the number wearing glasses or complaining of eyestrain. In fact, adolescent girls without television—those who read most—complained of eyestrain more often than the viewers. Of course, some children with poor eyesight may find that their eyes hurt after viewing. Our findings suggest, however, that if these children had used their eyes in other ways (as in reading) the effect would have been much the same.

Do Children View under Optically Suitable Conditions?—A fair proportion viewed under poor conditions. Children often sat on the floor with the screen above eye level; and as many as one in four viewed in the dark, thus maximizing the glare. Viewing in the dark, we found, had a further disadvantage: it enhanced the emotional impact of potentially frightening programmes. There is need for more education of parents and children on the correct conditions for viewing, so as to lessen the possibility of eyestrain for those predisposed to it.

THE CHARACTERISTIC OF THE TELEVISION ADDICT—THE EFFECTS OF HEAVY VIEWING

What Type of Child Becomes a Television Addict?—It is difficult to characterise the television addict or heavy viewer, since addiction is, of course, not simply a matter of heavy viewing. For classification purposes, however, we have been forced to treat it in these terms and have defined as addicts or heavy viewers the 30 per cent in each age group who viewed the most. Of the different factors that correlate with amount of viewing, the most important was intelligence, the duller children viewing more than those of high intelligence; in addition, in the younger age groups, heavy viewing occurred rather more frequently among working-class children.

But personality make-up tends to be at least equally important, and here an addict type emerged who is not exclusive to television; his emotional insecurity and maladjustment seem to impel him towards excessive consumption of any available mass medium. If television is available to such a child, he will view excessively; if not, he will go very often to the cinema, listen a great deal to the radio, or become a heavy reader of comics (but not of books). Such children were characterised by lack of security, by being ill at ease with other children. Their teachers often described them as shy and retiring.

The television addicts in our sample showed less initiative than occasional viewers. They preferred plays of two escapist types—adventure or mystery, and family serials. The first type of play offers them the vicarious pleasure of an active, dangerous life, while the family serial facilitates identification with a happy and united family, offering them reassurance.

While the occasional viewers cut heavily into radio listening and cinema-attendance, the addict managed to fit in something of them all. He listened to the radio when there was no television to watch, and went to the cinema as often as two or three times a week in spite of spending over half his free time in front of the television set.

A comparison of television addicts with control children who were frequent cinema-goers showed that both groups need a great deal of ready-made entertainment; both were insecure and afraid of striking out for themselves. These characteristics are more likely to be the cause than the result of heavy viewing, but the intensive viewing which addiction entails can only make matters worse. With escape through television so readily available, the heavy viewer's outside contacts become more restricted still. Such contacts demand much effort and offer little promise of success; they therefore compare unfavorably with the certain, undemanding companionship of television.

Within a given intelligence level, social class, and age group, the amount a child views gives an indication of the degree to which his life is satisfactory; heavy viewing is a symptom of unsatisfactory adjustment or of inadequate environmental facilities.

Section II

THE WAY IN WHICH DIFFERENT CHILDREN REACT TO TELEVISION

Throughout the summary we have discussed each effect in turn and indicated how it varied for different types of children. Here we shall look at the picture from the other point of view and attempt to show how the

434

various factors of intelligence, age, sex, social class, personality and home background determine television's role in the child's life.

Effects on Children of Different Intelligence—The relationship between intelligence and the effects of television is complex, depending on the one hand on the ability to comprehend what is offered, and on the other hand on the level of programme content, compared with that of other sources of information with which children are likely to come into contact.

In this survey intelligence emerged as the single most important determinant. This is shown both in the amount children view and in their interest in viewing; the more intelligent the child, the less inclined he will be to watch television and the less interest in it will he show.

In the case of the 13–14 year olds the picture is clear-cut, irrespective of the effects examined; grammar school children, compared with the less intelligent children of the same age group, proved the less interested, devoted less time to viewing, and also were the less affected by what television offered in the form of values or knowledge. This was partly because for these children television offered little that was new; also because in the case of knowledge, television even hampered intelligent adolescents by reducing the time they might otherwise spend on different sources of information, such as books or the radio, for instance.

In general, we found that the 13–14 year olds of average and below average intelligence and the bright 10–11 year olds were the most responsive both in terms of gaining wider interests (though not activities) and also in terms of their absorption of the values television offered. It would, of course, also follow that they would be similarly affected by inadequate or harmful values, if these were consistently presented. These two groups of children have approximately the same mental age of about 12 years, an age at which television still offers sufficient that is new to the children and where at the same time other sources of stimulation are unlikely to be more adequate than television.

The 10–11 year old of average or below average intelligence can absorb only the simplest of values from television entertainment. However, it is this group—whose reading and access to other sources of knowledge is the most limited—who has gained most from television as far as general knowledge is concerned.

In the matter of gaining knowledge, television has narrowed the gap between the more and the less intelligent 10–11 year olds; in the case of values and outlook it has brought about the same equalising process between the more and the less intelligent older children.[4]

When a child of relatively low intelligence views a great deal, this has quite a different significance than with a child of about average intelligence. With the former, television provides his main source of stimulation; such a child tends to have few hobbies, and often comes from a home with equally few interests; television for him takes the place of the newspaper and the book; it becomes his main source of information, offered in a manner and at a pace which suits him.

In the case of the intelligent child, the same amount of viewing would more often be a sign of an environment poorly equipped in resources, or else of personal problems within the child himself. Such a child can read and engage in hobbies; under these circumstances, with the majority of children television occupies a less central role.

Effects on Children of Different Ages—At adolescence, television becomes less important; this is not so much because its content no longer interests the children, but rather because viewing occurs among the family at home and so fails to meet the adolescent's social needs. For this reason, the cinema, for instance, by providing opportunities for meeting friends as well as entertainment, gains in popularity as children grow older.

Tastes also change; some of this change comes from increased intellectual maturity, some from changing emotional needs and circumstances. The adolescent ceases to be interested in Westerns (so popular with the 10–11 year olds) with their stereotyped plots and straightforward action; he prefers the more varied action and more complex motivation of detective and other adult plays.

At all ages, children respond to the programmes in terms of their own needs and of their personal capacity for understanding; in adolescence this involves greater responsiveness to information about personal relationships, and about adult life. About to leave school, the adolescent responds to cues about the type of jobs and about the social values contained in much television drama, which as yet make no impact on the younger child. Similarly, only the older children reacted, and some of them with anxiety, to the problem-laden view of adult life that inevitably forms part of so many evening television plays.

The younger child likes action; his capacity for perceiving motives, unless they are explicitly stated, is as yet limited. Consequently, he responds to episodes or incidents rather than to the overall theme (unless through repetition the theme has been learnt, as in Westerns). This factor must be borne in mind in evaluating the manner in which a child will respond to a given programme; the younger the child the greater the tendency to respond to particular incidents rather than to the story as a whole. He prefers clear-cut characterisation, provided there is also excitement and suspense; as a result he enjoys both the stereotyped Western and the less stereotyped detective series. At the same time he likes family serials and shares with the older child enjoyment of programmes which invite laughter.

In their enjoyment of funny programmes and in their susceptibility to the fear potential in various programmes, no age difference was found.

The older child, because he is more concerned with problems of inter-personal relationships and able to understand a wider range of situations, can be as readily disturbed as younger children, albeit by different types of situations. This is important; particularly since older children compared with younger ones are less ready to admit fear or disturbance.

Effects on Boys and Girls—Girls, especially among the adolescents, proved more responsive than boys to television's impact even though they gave no more time to viewing. Girls were more often influenced in their outlook, and also more often than boys admitted to fears and disturbances after seeing certain television programmes.

Television's impact on girls may be stronger than on boys because they tend to be the more interested in plays dealing with problems of human relationships; also because television tends to reinforce girls' feelings of insecurity (characteristic of adolescence) by failing to provide them with reassuring models. The sympathetic female characters in television plays tend to be unhappy and troubled, and to be dominated by events of which they are unable to take command.

Considering that half the child audience consists of girls, it is indeed surprising to see how few children's plays seem to take account of this factor; their themes tend to relate to boys' rather than to girls' interests, providing adequate heroes for the former, but inadequate heroines for the latter.

Yet, this survey evidence provides little support for the popular view that girls compared with boys are more squeamish about violence. Westerns appealed to girls a little less than to boys, but they were just as, indeed more, interested in the detective series *Fabian of Scotland Yard*.

Effects on Children from Middle- and Working-class Homes—Contrary to popular opinion, social background exercised an almost negligible influence on children's reactions to television.[5]

It must be remembered that when we looked at social-class differences, we held intelligence constant, that is, we ensured that there were as many bright medium, and dull children in the working- as in the middle-class sample.

Under these circumstances, social-class differences were still found; many examples of them, in terms of the children's behaviour and outlook, have been cited in this report, but not usually in relation to amount of viewing or to children' taste in programmes. In the case of cinema visits, for instance, social-class differences were found; paradoxically, social background was less influential in respect of the home-bound media (radio and television); the children's use of these readily accessible media depends less on social conventions and more on personal choice.[6]

The same would seem to be true for adults; we found that as many children in middle- as in working-class families claimed that their television sets were left on all the evening; nor was there any class difference in the amount of parental viewing reported. Social conventions would seem to enter more into those activities which take place outside the home, and into such traditional patterns of upbringing as are expressed in the selection of appropriate bedtimes rather than into the use to which children put this new and readily available medium.

Effects on Children of Different Personalities—One important factor determining the amount of time a child watches television and the importance viewing assumes for him, lies in the personality of the child, in the quality of his relationships with his friends and family, and in the general home atmosphere.

The active child, socially at ease and with a happy home background, is the least likely to become preoccupied by television. On the other hand, children who view a great deal do so (particularly the intelligent ones) because they have difficulties in making friends or problems in their family relationships. They retreat into viewing or into ready-made entertainment of other types. A vicious circle is then set up whereby the ready access to television aggravates those problems of the children which led them to view heavily in the first instance.

The child's personality also affects his reactions to the content of television programmes; the extent to which these frighten and disturb him and the extent to which he identifies himself with the characters on the screen.

Equally important in this context is family atmosphere and parental example. Where parental viewing is high the children will tend to adopt a similar pattern.

Principles and Generalizations

For some of television's effects we have been able to arrive at a set of principles which would help to predict, for instance, what would happen if television, or some other medium, were newly introduced into a community comparable to our own; or if at some time in the future a medium capable of satisfying three, instead of two, senses were to make its appearance.

These principles can be grouped into four main categories:

1. The principles of leisure displacement.
2. The principles underlying television's effects on children's outlook and values.
3. Generalisations about taste.
4. The principles which determine what types of incident arouse fear and emotional disturbance.

THE PRINCIPLES OF LEISURE DISPLACEMENT

With television available, the child finds himself in a conflict situation: consciously or unconsciously, he has to decide how much to view, and how to make room for viewing. The resulting compromise seems to be made on the basis of three principles: first, he will sacrifice most readily those activities which satisfy the same needs as television but less effectively—those activities which are *functionally similar*. Secondly, some activities will be so thoroughly cast in the shade by television that in order to continue with them at all children will come to use them in a specialised way so that they do not overlap with viewing: these are the *transformed* activities which must either change in character or cease to exist. And thirdly, the child will tend to make room for television at the expense of activities on which he places little value, or of those which are of an unspecific, indefinite character (the *fringe* or *marginal* activities).

Functional similarity: the first of these principles concerns functional rather than objective, similarity, or equivalence. For instance, cinema visits are considerably reduced by the younger viewers, for whom cinema and television are relatively interchangeable; but amongst adolescent viewers cinema visiting is little affected—and then only temporarily—because for the adolescent the cinema represents an opportunity to meet friends and to develop a social life away from home, a need which television cannot gratify.

Other activities are little affected by viewing, because they are of great importance to children and yet functionally different from viewing, as, for example, outdoor play, and activities which permit self-expression. When there is competition between viewing and activities of this kind, viewing often turns out to be the weaker rival.

Transformed Activities—there were two examples of transformed activities. Radio, in particular, comes to take on a specialised role for those viewers who turn to it at all. To a lesser extent, something of the same kind happens with reading: the circulation figures for adult magazines in general have dropped but not for the specialised and non-fiction ones.[7] Among children, interest in non-fiction subjects increases under the impact of television, turning reading slightly away from the well-trodden paths of television.

Marginal or Fringe Activities—we found that in so far as outdoor activities or social pastimes are affected at all, the more casual, unstructured activities are the ones that suffer, rather than the organised or more clearly purposive ones. There is a consequent reduction of *leisure itself* as children's lives inevitably become more crowded.

These two basic principles are illustrated particularly well in the case of reading. Book-reading is most severely reduced among those children who start off with only a marginal interest; and comic-reading, it will be remembered, was permanently reduced by television. But whereas television can provide an effective substitute for a good deal of comic-reading, in the case of books the position is very different. Book-reading is temporarily reduced because the satisfactions offered by books and viewing at first seem similar. In the long run, viewing cannot offer the same freedom of choice or diversity of subject matter; as a result, after a few years, both viewers and controls are once again reading a similar number of books.

THE PRINCIPLES UNDERLYING TELEVISION'S EFFECTS ON CHILDREN'S OUTLOOK AND VALUES

Gradually, almost imperceptibly, television entertainment brings about changes in children's outlook and values, even though the programmes that achieve this do not deliberately set out to influence. It is rather that the similarity of views and values conveyed in television programmes, particularly in plays, make their cumulative impact.

The following principles indicate the conditions under which maximal effect is likely to occur (i.e. from the cumulative impact of a number of programmes rather than from the impact of a particular programme):

1. If the values or views recur from programme to programme;
2. If the values are presented in dramatic form so that they evoke primarily emotional reactions;
3. If they link with the child's immediate needs and interests;
4. If the viewer tends to be uncritical of and attached to the medium;
5. If through his friends, parents, or immediate environment the viewer is not already supplied with a set of values which would provide a standard against which to assess the views offered on television.

Provided these conditions are fulfilled, values may be taken over from the main themes of plays or programmes, and also from the subsidiary touches used in presenting them. Children have an inconvenient way of responding to isolated incidents rather than to overall themes.

These same principles apply equally whether the views and values are worth-while or worthless. The process is likely to be a slow and gradual one, reflecting not so much the impact of individual programmes as the cumulative effect of them all. Over and above this slow effect (composed of the accumulation of minute influences from many programmes) individual programmes also make their impact, either because of their dramatic excellence or because they touch on something of specific importance to the child. For most children both types of effects are likely to operate.

GENERALIZATIONS ABOUT TASTE

Five generalizations can be made on the basis of our findings:

1. Taste in one medium is linked, not only to taste in other media, but to the child's interests generally. Already by the age of 10, children have a fairly integrated set of taste patterns.

2. Children tend to prefer adult to children's programmes and watch more of them; it may therefore be adult rather than children's programmes which have the larger share in forming tastes.

3. Children appear to be quite capable of enjoying programmes without understanding them fully.

4. When children are brought inadvertently into contact with programmes which do not, 'in anticipation', interest them, they often like them and may later even seek them out again. To develop children's tastes, it is therefore important to provide in programme planning for such experiences. It is possible to achieve this in a one-channel situation where the choice lies between watching such a programme and switching off, but it is more difficult where there is access to two channels—under these circumstances the child can more easily limit himself to his favourite types of programme. This will ultimately lead to a narrowing of taste.

5. The diversity of taste among children of the same sex, age, and intelligence is so great that in our survey even the most popular programme was the first favourite of no more than 30 per cent of children in any one age or intelligence group. It follows that firm predictions about what children will like or reject cannot be easily made; this is even more so when considering favourite television personalities.

THE PRINCIPLES WHICH DETERMINE
WHAT TYPES OF INCIDENT AROUSE FEAR
AND EMOTIONAL DISTURBANCE

In the last resort, children's fears are idiosyncratic, determined by the nature of the stimulus (or programme), by the child's own needs, and also by the extent to which particular incidents touch on personal preoccupations. Nevertheless, certain general principles can be laid down about the type of incidents which tend to arouse fear. Emotional disturbance of this kind is not only aroused by episodes of killing, wounding, and lethal weapons; fist-fights are also disturbing (whether in plays or in the boxing-ring), and incidents of verbal aggression such as quarrelling and one person telling another off. Children can also be upset by portrayal of adult relationships where unhappiness is stressed more than violence. Finally, the uncanny may frighten, as, for instance, the sleep-walking of the mad wife of Mr. Rochester in *Jane Eyre* or the invasion from outer space in *Quatermass*.

In general, we found that violent or aggressive episodes tend to cause far *less* disturbance where the following conditions are fulfilled:

1. If the presentation of violence is stylised, as in Westerns.

2. If the programme forms part of a series, so that the child can become familiar with the conventions; if the ending falls into an accepted

pattern; and if there is a hero figure who appears in each of the episodes.

3. If the setting in which the violence occurs is unfamiliar, so that children are the less likely to imagine that similar events might occur in their own home or street. But at the same time the setting and violence should not be so unfamiliar as to be uncanny (as in the case of *Quatermass*).

4. If the characters are black and white rather than grey. Detective plays, with their emphasis on the psychological exposition of character, often arouse sympathy with the criminal; this is absent in Westerns, whose villains usually remain shadowy, unsympathetic figures.

5. If the child can feel sure that the events are make-believe rather than real; although it must be remembered that with smaller children this distinction tends not to be clear-cut.

6. In general, children tend to be less concerned about the magnitude of the disaster or the seriousness of its consequences, than about the prospect of hurt to *someone with whom they can identify*. For this reason, disasters in newsreels may be less disturbing than a heated discussion on television in which one person may be made to look foolish, or the threat of injury to the dogs in *Lassie* and *Rin-Tin-Tin* (the same children, however, remained quite undisturbed by the sight of animals in nature programmes being attacked and eaten by other animals). Differences were also found with regard to the type of physical aggression. Fighting on the ground proved no more disturbing than other kinds of fighting. Any gun fight, whether 'real' or fictional, was enjoyed, probably because children play at shooting, and see so much of it in Westerns, that they treat gun fights as spectacles, whatever the context in which they are shown. On the other hand, knives, used at close quarters, quite often proved disturbing.

Finally, there are the differential effects of violent and disturbing programmes. While familiarity with the series tends to reduce emotional impact, familiarity with viewing does not; we found that children who had been viewing for many years were as readily affected as those who had as yet little experience of television entertainment. Moreover, programme impact was no greater for heavy viewers than for those who saw less television.

Nor does susceptibility to fear decrease with age, although the types of situation capable of arousing fear do undergo change. Equally, susceptibility to fear does not appear to be related to intelligence: even though the intelligent children viewed less and were more critical of programmes than the other children, they were as readily disturbed by them.

Perhaps most important of all, television does not seem to induce fear any more readily than sound radio. There is, however, evidence to suggest that the emotional impact of reading may be slighter than those of radio and the two visual media—television and films.

HILDE HIMMELWEIT: Television and the Child

The final picture of the influence of television on children's leisure, interests, knowledge, outlook, and values proves to be far less colourful and dramatic than popular opinion is inclined to suppose. Effects occur in each one of the various fields, but not to such a degree that the children would have been fundamentally changed.

Television, then, is not as black as it is painted, but neither is it the great harbinger of culture and enlightenment which its enthusiasts tend to claim for it. If television is a window on the world, it gives a view not very different from that provided in book, comics, films, and radio programmes. Similarly, its capacity for broadening a child's horizons is not spectacularly different from that of any of the other mass media.

Part of the reason why popular opinion produced a picture considerably at variance with the facts lay in each observer's tendency to generalise from the children he knew. Part, however, stems from the distrust with which people tend to view new technical inventions (particularly in the field of culture): the radio, the cinema, and now television. Each tends to be seen as bringing about a change for the worse, a lowering of standards and behaviour. In such an atmosphere of distrust three things combine to distort the picture of television's true effects; the intrinsic power of the medium is exaggerated, the resilience of the children tends to be seriously underestimated, while at the same time the past is idealised. The same factors operate in reverse with those people who welcome the medium and are among the first to use it.

With each new medium the experience gained from the introduction of the previous one counts for little. Each time the attractions of the new technique loom so large that once again its potential effects are exaggerated.

It is important to gain a proper perspective, not only for correct understanding and recording of contemporary events, but also for finding the best ways of effecting change. Unless the effects are known to be undramatic, there is the danger that untoward reactions (such as very heavy viewing, very late bedtimes, loss of concentration or interest at school)—aspects which have to do with the child and his environment rather than with the lure of television—may be mistakenly passed off as the inevitable by-product of having television in the home.

In the course of this inquiry we have often been asked to sum up briefly what we have found, particularly to evaluate whether television is good or bad for children. It will be clear from the findings reported in the preceding chapter that any answer to such a question would require innumerable qualifications in order to be even approximately accurate.

In fact, this question makes no more sense than asking a doctor 'Are injections good or bad for children?' He will answer that it depends on the type of injection, the dosage, the particular condition and age of the child, the appropriateness of the injection to the illness, and the context in which it will be administered. Similarly, whether television is good or bad for children depends on the programmes, the amount the child views, the type of child, the type of effects to be examined, and the context in which viewing takes place. In the last resort, it is an individual matter with the effects varying from child to child. Nevertheless, just as in immunology it is possible to lay down certain rules or broad guiding principles as to when injections should or should not be used, so here we have been able to make certain generalisations.

At *best*, television can implant information, stimulate interests, improve tastes, and widen the range of the child's experience so that he gains some understanding of people in other walks of life; this can make him less prejudiced and more tolerant. It can make him less susceptible to over-simplified value judgments; it can raise the level of his aspirations. At *best*, viewing can reduce the child's less worth-while activities (such as comic-reading), whilst leaving the more worth-while ones intact.

At *worst*, on the other hand, viewing can lead to a reduction in knowledge (in that it takes up time which could be spent more profitably), keep children from relatively worth-while activities (like outdoor play and book-reading), and implant or accentuate one-sided, stereotyped value judgments—if the content of television is such as to convey this kind of attitude. Depending on content, television can frighten and disturb, particularly those who are emotionally insecure or those who are preoccupied with a particular problem.

While the majority of children are not drastically affected, it must nevertheless be remembered that each minority group represents a large section of the child population, whose needs must be considered.

Lastly, two further generalisations can be made. First, the extent to which the introduction of a new medium forces a greater differentiation into the existing ones—radio and to some extent reading show signs of taking on specialised roles. We have signs of this in our survey, and also a good deal of confirmatory data from surveys in the United States (19).

Secondly, the introduction of any new element into an existing structure requires assimilation and integration. We have shown that this takes place smoothly in the majority of cases; but with children who have problems, families which have conflicts, or (for example) clubs which have a decreasing membership, television may just tip the scale.

NOTES

1. The analysis was based on programmes put on the air by the BBC and by the two programme companies serving the London region (Associated Rediffusion and Associated Television); for brevity's sake these will be referred to as ITV. The analysis was carried out in 1956.

2. These figures were obtained in May 1958 and are similar to those of 1956.

3. We were examining the increase of knowledge obtained not from school's television, but from general television entertainment.

4. In the study of teachers' opinions, some teachers from schools for educationally subnormal children mentioned that television had helped their pupils not only in providing them with a common talking point with the rest of the family, but also by offering them a source of information which they could easily comprehend.

5. Social background is defined here in terms of differences in parental occupation. The group of 'working-class' children consisted of children whose fathers engaged in manual work. The middle-class sample, since it was restricted to state schools, included only a few children whose fathers did professional work or held higher executive posts.

6. There was similarly no difference among the controls between middle- and working-class children listening to the wireless.

7. Bogart shows that in the United States this trend has gone much further, with specialised magazines flourishing, and magazine articles increasingly dealing with informational topics. Fiction is more and more left to television. Between 1946 and 1955 there was a much increased demand for non-fiction books (19).

ELIHU KATZ AND PAUL F. LAZARSFELD

Personal Influence

ONE OF THE SPECIFIC HYPOTHESES with which this study set out is the hypothesis of "the two-step flow of communication." Formulated first in *The People's Choice*, the hypothesis suggests that "ideas often flow *from* radio and print *to* the opinion leaders and *from* them to the less active sections of the population."[1] But since this formulation, and the evidence to substantiate it, were based only upon one kind of opinion leader— people who were influential for others during the course of an election campaign—we do not know whether the hypothesis is applicable to opinion leadership in other realms as well. In this article we want to compare the media behavior of opinion leaders and non-leaders to see whether the leaders tend to be the more exposed, and the more responsive group when it comes to influence stemming from the mass media. In general, we shall find that the hypothesis is substantiated in each of the arenas of influence with which we are concerned. In addition we shall try to refine and further specify our understanding of the workings of this interesting phenomenon by introducing one further aspect of the "relay" role which opinion leaders play.

Opinion Leadership and Exposure to the Mass Media

The kind of information it takes to be an opinion leader in marketing is quite different, of course, from the kind required for influentiality, say, in public affairs. We shall not expect, therefore, that opinion leaders in each of the different realms will consistently outdo the non-leaders in

Reprinted from *Personal Influence*, (1955), pp. 309–320, by permission of the authors and the publisher. (Copyright, 1955, Free Press, New York.)

exposure to every single medium of mass communication. Yet, on the other hand, considering the vast span of interest encompassed by such broad categories as "magazines" or "radio," we should not be surprised either if opinion leaders, no matter what their spheres of influence, do actually exceed non-opinion leaders in mass media exposure in general. We shall find, in varying instances, that both generalizations are true. For a first example, let us look at the data on magazine readership, comparing the extent of readership of each of the brands of opinion leaders with those who are not influential at all.[2]

It is plain from the table that influentials of every type read a larger number of magazines than those who are not influential. Thus, the non-leader group includes in its ranks many fewer readers of five or more magazines; and this is true, too, the table shows, when education is taken into account.[3] In other words, then, opinion leaders in each arena—whether it be marketing, fashions, politics or movie-going—tend to have greater contact than non-leaders with the features and advertisements in America's magazines.

Table 1—Opinion Leaders Read More Magazines than Nonleaders

Number of Magazines	LOW EDUCATION				
	Marketing Leaders	Fashion Leaders	Public Affairs Leaders	Movie Leaders	Non-Leaders
5 or more	41%	58%	60%	58%	30%
less than 5	59	42	40	42	70
100% =	(91)	(79)	(30)	(64)	(270)
	HIGH EDUCATION				
	Marketing Leaders	Fashion Leaders	Public Affairs Leaders	Movie Leaders	Non-Leaders
5 or more	65%	69%	63%	71%	53%
less than 5	35	31	37	29	47
100% =	(75)	(80)	(50)	(58)	(146)

When we turn from magazines to other media, we find that, as a rule, the same phenomenon holds true; that is, opinion leaders exceed non-leaders in exposure. But at the same time, these other media begin to reveal some idiosyncrasies of the different leader types as well. Consider book reading, for example.

Again, on both levels of education, all the leaders are more likely to read at least one book per month than are the non-leaders. Again, too, this is true on both high and low levels of education. Notice, however, that on both educational levels the marketing leaders exceed the non-leaders by only very little, while each of the other leader types seems to be more clearly differentiated. This, of course, is as we might have expected; intuitively at least, one would not say that the "requirements" for market-

Table 2—Opinion Leaders Read More Books than Nonleaders

Number of Books per Month	LOW EDUCATION				
	Marketing Leaders	Fashion Leaders	Public Affairs Leaders	Movie Leaders	Non-Leaders
1 or more	25%	47%	38%	38%	20%
less than 1	75	53	62	62	80
100% =	(81)	(76)	(29)	(61)	(270)
	HIGH EDUCATION				
	Marketing Leaders	Fashion Leaders	Public Affairs Leaders	Movie Leaders	Non-Leaders
1 or more	39%	42%	57%	51%	34%
less than 1	61	58	43	49	66
100% =	(74)	(79)	(49)	(55)	(146)

ing leadership include the reading of a greater number of books, whereas a case could be made for the relationship between reading books and leadership in the other three areas.

Leaders tend to exceed non-leaders in number of hours of radio listening, too, although the differences are quite small and not always consistent. The movie leaders of both educational levels seem to be particularly attentive to radio, together with the lower-educated marketing and fashion leaders. However, the well-educated leaders in the latter two realms, plus the political leaders on both educational levels, do not exceed the non-leaders in time spent listening to the radio.[4] The political leaders, furthermore, are the only group which does not exceed the non-leaders in movie-going; all other leaders do.[5]

In sum, it can safely be stated that the opinion leaders in every realm tend to be more highly exposed to the mass media than are the non-leaders. But while we have begun to talk about these variations, that is, about the different media habits of one kind of leader as compared with another, we have not yet talked explicitly about the relationship between such variations and the different *content* of the several media.

Opinion Leadership and the Content of Mass Communications

Within each of the media, of course, there is a world of variation. The name "radio" includes both the soap opera and the Metropolitan Opera; the category "magazines" has an almost incredible range; and the same is true for all of the other media. So far, we have seen only that opinion leaders are, as a rule, more exposed to the media *in general* than non-leaders. But we also have begun to see that the marketing leader or the movie leader may be more or less exposed to a given medium than the fashion leader, say, or the public affairs leader. Our intention now is to inquire more specifically into the kinds of media content with which different sorts of leaders are more likely to be in touch.

One of the first studies of opinion leadership—in fact, it was a study of what we are now calling public affairs leadership—discovered that it was important to distinguish between two kinds of public affairs leaders in a community: those who are influential in local affairs, and those who exert influence concerning national and international affairs.[6] It was found that the "cosmopolitans"—those who were concerned particularly with news of the world outside their community—typically had access to news media which originated outside and brought them such news, while the "locals"—the experts on township affairs—were local in their communications habits, too. In the present study, we cannot distinguish between "local" and "cosmopolitan" leaders within the one realm we call political affairs, but we can compare the media habits of our several leader types, this time to see which is more "local" and which is more "cosmopolitan" in its readership of news. In other words, while we shall not distinguish between two types of public affairs leaders as the earlier study did, we shall compare the leaders in each of our four arenas to see how they differ from each other on this matter of "cosmopolitan" and "local" news orientation.

To make this comparison, we have combined the answers to two questions relating to newspaper and magazine readership. Those who said that they read newspapers which were published out of town as well as news or news analysis in the national magazines were classed as "cosmopolitans"; those who maintained neither of these contacts with the world outside (but who did have access to local papers) were labeled "locals"; and those who qualified either on out-of-town newspapers or on magazine news were labeled "intermediate." Here we shall compare the proportion of "cosmopolitans" among each of the leader types as well as between the leaders and non-leaders in each arena, thus modifying somewhat the procedure in the last few tables above:

Table 3—The "Cosmopolitans" Among the Opinion Leaders Are in Fashions and Public Affairs

Per Cent Who Read Both Out-of-Town Newspapers and News in National Magazines

| | MARKETING | | FASHION | | PUBLIC AFFAIRS | | MOVIE | |
	Leaders	Non-Leaders	Leaders	Non-Leaders	Leaders	Non-Leaders	Leaders	Non-Leaders
Low Ed'n	27%	20%	39%	17%	50%	20%	25%	24%
100% =	(88)	(324)	(79)	(330)	(30)	(381)	(64)	(159)
High Ed'n	48%	43%	53%	41%	55%	41%	45%	47%
100% =	(77)	(219)	(81)	(218)	(51)	(247)	(58)	(148)

First, let us read along the top line. Among these low educated groups, it is quite evident that the movie leaders do not exceed non-movie leaders in "cosmopolitan" exposure, and that the marketing leaders are only slightly more oriented to the outside world than the non-marketing leaders. The arenas of fashions and of public affairs, however, show striking differences. In these two realms, the leaders far exceed the non-leaders in "cosmopolitan" communications exposure. Smaller differences, but essentially the same story, hold true also for the well educated groups. Again, the movie and marketing leaders are indistinguishable from non-leaders, while the leaders in fashions and public affairs markedly exceed the non-leaders.

The explanation for these differences seems apparent to us: neither the movie leaders nor the marketing leaders have much "need" for out-of-town papers or magazine news in order to exert their particular brand of influence; as a matter of fact, there is no reason to supose that these groups should be more interested in news in general than are the non-leaders. Obviously, however, the metropolitan press means much more for influentials in political affairs and in fashions. The advertisements and the features of the metropolitan press and the news in the national magazines provide a channel for these small-city residents to keep up with "big city" fashions and world-wide news, and this information, in turn, bolsters their respective types of influentiality.

Another illustration of the relationship between media content and the readership choice of varying types of leaders is provided by the magazines. Earlier, we observed that leaders of all four types tended to read a larger number of magazines than their followers. But we did not look there to see which magazines which leaders tend to read. Comparing the magazines read by fashion leaders and non-leaders, for example, we find that on both levels of education, the leaders are more likely to read a fashion magazine. Thus on the low education level, 9 per cent of the fashion leaders but only 2 per cent of the non-leaders read one or more fashion magazines while among upper educated woman, 30 per cent of the leaders compared with 15 per cent of the non-leaders report fashion magazine readership. In the same way, it can be shown that public affairs leaders exceed non-leaders in their readership of one or another of the national news weeklies; 22 per cent of the former, compared with 14 per cent of the latter do so. This finding becomes even more convincing when it is pointed out that in no realm other than public affairs is opinion leadership associated at all with news magazine readership.

Continuing along the same line, let us look at the arena of movie-going. As Table 4 indicates, movie magazine readership clearly distinguishes between movie leaders and non-leaders.

On both levels of education, movie leaders are more likely that non-leaders to read movie magazines. They are also more likely to purchase these magazines themselves than are the non-leaders; in other words, the movie leaders don't rely as much as the non-leaders on borrowing, or on second-hand copies, or on beauty parlor reading. They are more likely to go out and buy a copy directly.[7] Again, an examination of each of the other types of leaders—in fashions, marketing and public affairs—reveals that none of these particularly exceeds the corresponding non-leaders in readership of movie magazines. And so it appears evident that the specialized interests which are associated with leadership in one area rather than another go hand in hand with some kinds of media content and not with others.

Table 4—More Movie Leaders Read Movie Magazines

Reads Movie Magazines	LOW EDUCATION		HIGH EDUCATION	
	Movie Leaders	Non-Movie Leaders	Movie Leaders	Non-Movie Leaders
Yes	56%	34%	50%	42%
No	44	66	50	58
Total (= 100%)	(66)	(157)	(58)	(151)

Opinion Leadership and Mass Media Effect

So far we have seen that the opinion leaders tend to be both more generally exposed to the mass media, and more specifically exposed to the content most closely associated with their leadership. Presumably this increased exposure then becomes a component—witting or unwitting—of the influence which such influentials transmit to others. As a result of these findings, the idea of the "two-step flow of communication" gains credence.

That is as far as the idea of the "two-step flow" takes us. Yet it would seem worthwhile to proceed one step further, to see whether opinion leaders actually make more "use" of their greater media exposure in their own decisions. We want to see whether opinion leaders are not only more *exposed* to the media—which is all that the two-step flow hypothesis claims—but, compared with non-leaders, whether they are relatively more *affected* by them as well.

Actually, there is no need to expect that this will necessarily be true. Take marketing, for example. We have seen that marketing leaders are exposed to the media generally somewhat more than non-leaders. The advice they pass on to others may incorporate this greater exposure; yet, there is little reason to expect that their own decisions will be based, much more than others, on the content of the media which we have studied. It would seem much more reasonable to assume that marketing leaders, like non-leaders, will also base their decisions primarily on personal contacts with others—with other marketing leaders, perhaps—and "use" the media only in a supplementary way.

In fashions, on the other hand, or in public affairs, there would be more reason to expect the leaders to be relatively more influenced by the media in their own decisions. In these arenas, unlike marketing, the relevant "environment" with which the opinion leader must bring his group into contact is much less immediate and much more dependent on the media for transmission. Thus, the media carry the fashion word from the big city, and politics—at least cosmopolitan politics—also comes from the world "outside." And opinion leaders, presumably, are looked to for precisely such information.

Let us consider this possibility in the case of fashions. Specifically, we can assess the relevant influences that went into the making of the opinion leaders' decisions and compare them with those factors which were influential for non-leaders. Thus, Table 5 is a comparison of those fashion leaders and non-leaders who, upon reporting some recent change in their clothes, hairdo, make-up style, etc., were asked: "Who or what suggested this change to you?" For each level of education, the table reports the percentage of all influences named which were personal influences and the percentage which were mass media influences:

Table 5—Fashion Leaders Are Influenced More by Mass Media and Less by Other People Than Are Non-Leaders[8]

| "Who or What Suggested Change?" | Per Cent of All Influences Mentioned (Recent Changes Only) | | | |
| | LOW EDUCATION | | HIGH EDUCATION | |
	Fashion Leaders	Non-Fashion Leaders	Fashion Leaders	Non-Fashion Leaders
Heard or Saw Somebody	40%	56%	37%	47%
Mass Media	42	31	42	33
Other	18	13	21	20
Total Influences (= 100%)	(164)	(308)	(135)	(250)

On each level of education, Table 5 clearly indicates that fashion leaders who recently made some change were more influenced in their decisions by the mass media, and less by other people, than recent changers among the non-leaders. Although not very large, the differences in the table are consistent throughout.[9]

As we expected, the data for marketing and also for movie-going are inconclusive; that is, the several channels of influence impinge on the leaders in much the same way as they do upon the non-leaders. Contrary to our expectations, however, the public affairs leaders do not behave like the fashion leaders either. If anything, these leaders are more likely than non-leaders to report personal influence as the more significant component of their recent opinion changes. In other words, although each of the leader types is more exposed to the media than non-leaders—and, presumably, therefore more likely to incorporate media content into the influences they pass on—nevertheless when it comes to crediting the media with impact on personal decisions, only the fashion leaders significantly exceed the non-leaders in this.

It is interesting to ask why the public affairs leader, whom we expected to make more use of her greater media exposure in her personal decisions, tends to rely less, not more, on the media than non-leaders. It may be, perhaps, that our sample contains a disproportionately large numbers of "local" rather than "cosmopolitan" leaders, and that the latter—if our data permitted us to examine them separately—would in fact show greater media impact in their decisions. Or, it may be that the effect of the media in public affairs would be more clearly visible if we traced the networks of interpersonal influence further back; in other words, we might find that the next step—that is, the opinion leaders of the opinion leaders—are the ones who form opinions in more direct response to the media. Or, it might be that we would have to go back several steps before we found the link between the interpersonal networks of public affairs opinion and disproportionate mass media effect. Compared with the realm of fashions at any rate, one is led to suspect that the chain of interpersonal influence is longer in the realm of public affairs and that "inside dope" as well as influencing in specific influence episodes is much more a person-to-person affair. In any event, the different combinations of media and personal influence which go into the several opinion leader roles we have examined, seem to corroborate much that, to date, has been merely speculative as well as pointing to new lines of research on the flow of influence.

There is one final point that deserves mention. We have just learned that movie leaders are not necessarily more likely than one-leaders to attribute influentiality to the mass media; in fact, we did not expect them to. But we have been limiting our discussion in movies, as in the other realms, to "decisions"—in this case, decisions concerning which movie to see. We have been asking, in other words, where leaders and non-leaders in this realm get their ideas about what movies to see but we have not yet asked, apart from such decisions, what people get from the movies themselves. This, of course, is a full scale investigation in its own right but we should like to introduce only one set of findings from our data which is relevant to the concern of this article: movie leaders say that movies are helpful in their daily lives. Stated otherwise, movie leaders "get more out" of the movies than non-leaders.

For example, we asked, "Have you ever happened to get any ideas about what clothes to wear or how to fix your hair from the movies you see?" Leaders, both young and old and with high and low education, answered affirmatively more than matched groups of non-leaders. Similarly, we asked, "Do the movies help you to deal better with the problems in your own everyday life?" and again the leaders answered "yes" more often than non-leaders. And the same pattern reveals itself in answer to, "Do you think the movies make you more contented or less contented with your own life?"

In sum, there is need to inquire not only into the media exposure patterns of opinion leaders and the extent to which their own opinions and decisions are shaped by the media, but also into the different kinds of "uses" to which the media are put by leaders in each realm, as compared with non-leaders.

NOTES

1. Lazarsfeld, Berelson and Gaudet (1948), p. 151. It is important to distinguish between the flow of *influence* and of *information*. The roles of media and interpersonal sources in the spread of a news event is considered, for example, in Bogart (1950), Larsen and Hill (1954). See Whyte (1954) for an example, paralleling our own, of the role of word-of-mouth in the flow of consumer *influence* together with suggestions concerning linkages with mass media.

2. To simplify the presentation of Table 1, we present the data for each leader group separately and then for the group which is not influential at all in any area (the "non-leaders"). In an area-by-area comparison, the readership of the non-leaders would increase slightly because the non-leaders in any given area would also include women who are leaders in other areas. Nevertheless, the leader-non-leader difference persists very clearly in each area. It should be noted, too, that the leadership groups presented in this table are not mutually exclusive, that is, a woman will reappear in every area in which she is a leader; only the non-leader group is exclusive.

3. "High education" begins with high school graduates; "low education" includes all who have less than a complete high school education.

4. The study was completed before the general introduction of television.

5. These tables are not shown here.

6. Merton (1949B).

7. Among the low educated, 74% of the leaders and 52% of the non-leaders personally purchase movie magazines; among the well educated, it is 52% to 48%.

8. This table is based only on those who reported a recent fashion change (in clothes, hairdo, makeup, etc.). The base figures under each column represent the total number of *influences* mentioned by each group in connection with their fashion decisions.

9. Controlling level of interest—that is, comparing equally interested leaders and non-leaders on each level of education—the differences still persist as markedly as when education alone is controlled.

KURT LANG AND GLADYS ENGEL LANG

The Mass Media and Voting

AFTER EACH NATIONAL ELECTION students of political behavior comment on how little effect the mass media appear to have had on the outcome. Franklin D. Roosevelt and Harry S Truman won *in spite of* the press. The personal nature of the Eisenhower victory in 1952 showed that the campaign was so much shouting and tumult; the election was won before the campaign had even begun. Still, all of us—politicians, candidates, public servants, symbol manipulators, members of the Great Audience, and even students of political behavior in our private capacities as interested and partisan citizens—much as we may publicly belittle what the mass media do, act most of the time *as if* we believed in their potency. Republican members of the faculty pay for a newspaper ad supporting their candidate; the Democrats must counter with their own publicity. The vagaries of research leads us away from a principal concern with the impact of press, radio, television, and magazines, but nothing would seem to have banished our not yet empirically demonstrated beliefs that the mass media are more influential than we would sometimes wish. Outcries against certain political television shows during and between campaigns, as well as the enduring and enthusiastic acceptance accorded to George Orwell's *1984*, indicate vividly that our research may not tell us what our common sense reveals is there to be told.

At first glance recent research on voting behavior appears to go along with this emphasis on *how little* the mass media determine the vote. The reader's attention is called to influences that intervene between the content itself and the individual's voting decision. Emphasis also moves away from a concern with the power once attributed to mass communications to the personal dispositions and group influences that circumscribe it.

None of the three voting studies—Elmira, 1948; Bristol North-East,

---

Reprinted from *American Voting Behavior*, (1959), pp. 217–235, by permission of the authors and the publisher. (Copyright, 1959, Free Press of Glencoe.)

1951; the U.S. national survey in 1952[1]—draw any explicit conclusions to the effect that mass communications are *not* an important influence in voting behavior. They all point to their own methodological inadequacies, and in the most recent of the three studies the problem of mass-media impact has actually been avoided.[2] At many points, the importance of the mass media is stressed; nowhere is their role in connection with the vote actually belittled. Yet there may be a difference between the author's own interpretations and more or less popular understandings of what their findings mean.

Mass Communications During the Campaign

Exactly what do we learn about the influence of mass communication on voting behavior by studying its effect within the scope of a single campaign?

Both the Elmira and the Bristol studies reiterate findings of earlier research. In Elmira the group who changed their voting intentions during the campaign, compared with those who followed through, included fewer people who were interested in the election. They were less "exposed" to the mass media, and they arrived at their decision later. Likewise in Bristol, "floaters [those inconsistent either in their intentions or in their vote], no matter what their final party, listened to fewer broadcasts and read fewer national newspapers than the regular voters."[3] These observations are consistent with the most widely accepted finding on mass-media impact: "Media exposure gets out the vote at the same time that it solidifies preferences. It crystallizes and reinforces more than it converts."[4]

Accordingly, then, the election period serves less as a force for change than as a period for reclarification. There are several concrete circumstances in a campaign which severely circumscribe opportunities for observing the influence of mass-media propaganda.

Most obvious in this connection is the observation, confirmed in different contexts and by different methods, that the minds of most voters are closed even before the campaign officially opens. At various places and at different times, this figure has been set at anywhere from 50 to 84 per cent of the voters.[5] But even if a voter arrives at his decision late in the campaign, he is not necessarily in a constant quandary, endlessly pulled in opposite directions by conflicting propaganda. Evidence from panel studies indicates that in most cases where the final decision comes late in the campaign, prior learnings are crystallized into a firm intent. The impregnability of voting intentions as a whole limits drastically the number of people who are, so to speak, potential converts.

Moreover, during a campaign, people cannot help but be aware, however unhappily, that they are the targets of deliberate propaganda. Neither side enjoys a monopoly of available space or time, and so propaganda is almost always exposed as such. Expecting attempts at persuasion, voters come prepared with stereotyped meanings. It is not altogether unusual to hear speeches discounted as so much campaign talk. People, being aware of the intent of the messages, tend to avoid views contrary to their own. They tend to believe their own side and to question the arguments of the other. As long as old loyalties are activated, selective perception will serve as an effective screen.

Campaigners themselves limit the conversion potential of their propaganda. While their aim is to activate partisan loyalties and to persuade the small undecided group, their speeches and political shows must not alienate anyone disposed to be on their side. The lore of politics is replete with the terrible specter of candidates who lost elections because of a few ill-chosen words.[6]

The campaign period, then, would seem inherently to be less a period of potential change than a period of political entrenchment, a period in which prior attitudes are reaffirmed. This may well be a real paradox of political life: We are accustomed to think of campaign periods as the dynamic times when political passions are aroused and wholesale changeover results, and of periods between as the quiescent years, when people tend to forget about politics and are less attentive to the larger political environment. Yet changes in political opinion and in the general political climate may be less characteristic of the days of arousal than of the "quiescent" times between campaigns.

At any rate, the number of people who have already "made up their minds" before the campaign begins, the overwhelming importance of "filtering" effects resulting from self-selection and selective perception of media content, and the awareness of the intent with which all campaign statements are phrased all work together to make "conversion" through any medium particularly difficult during an election. But, in addition, there is something in the way the problem is approached which may obscure certain ways in which the mass media are effective.

Let us briefly review how the impact of the mass media is detected in the panel studies.[7] The authors of these studies investigate the initial voting intention and how it crystallizes and changes during the course of the campaign. They record individual "exposure" to the campaign—mostly in terms of attention paid to campaign materials, sources relied on, and the operation of self-selection. Then, by relating the voting intention to "exposure" within a framework of contextual factors, they infer the impact of that exposure. But among all the relevant "exposures," specifically what influences a vote cannot be easily inferred. More direct evidence about the content of that "exposure" and what it signifies to the consumer is necessary. To this end the researchers did ask at least one open-ended question that might (and did) elicit reports of particular speeches, news events, and broadcasts that helped voters "make up their minds." Yet the authors attribute no high validity to these retrospective answers. Consequently, the over-all amount of attention paid to the campaign remains the main index from which to infer mass-media impact.

This approach allows the authors of these studies to relate generally "high" exposure to a rising interest in the campaign and to a strengthening of partisan conviction.[8] Milne and Mackenzie point to a "hardening of opinion" after the campaign, which they find it "not unreasonable" to attribute to "persistent and concentrated propaganda."[9]

But to relate "exposure" to interest and partisanship is not to explain why people vote as they do. For such explanation the authors of the panel studies revert to an examination of people's prior political predispositions, their group identifications, and other variables which, by comparison with mass-media exposure, can be deemed relatively impermeable. These group measures, used in *Voting* and *Straight Fight* to "explain" voting decisions, are analogous to, though less explicit than, the set of "motivational" variables[10] which the more recent Survey Research Center study focuses upon. To be sure these generalized motivational variables—issue orientation, party identification, and candidate orientation—allow for the comparison of elections but still unexamined are the processes by which "weights" come to be assigned to various elements involved in the voting decision.

As long as the loyalties and imagery of the electorate are treated as "givens," as they have been, rather than as themselves in need of explanation, the probability of understanding the nature of mass-media impact is duly minimized. The very emphasis on change *within* the span of a campaign makes it almost inevitable that whatever realignments occur are limited by the more permanent identifications and loyalties existing at the time the study is started. In the same way, both the amount of attention paid to campaign materials and the sources on which people rely follow motivational and social dispositions as they follow prior political opinions. All of these habits and orientations have their roots outside the campaign.

To sum up, whether the "strain toward consistency" which characterizes the campaign period is observed on the *individual* level as bringing attitudes into line with motivations or as the adjustment of a voting decision to the local pressures emanating from the *social* environment immediately relevant to the voter does not much matter. In either case, examination of change within this short span fails altogether to account for the cumulative impact of media exposure which may, over a period of time, lead to such changes in the motivational patterns as differentiate one election from another or to a breaking away of many "primary" groups from older allegiances.

Political Change

The study of long-range effects leads us to a comparison of elections and especially to a second look at the occasional election in which long-standing habits seem to be upset.

What, we have to ask, do the results of any election mean? What is a "vote of confidence" for a party in power returned to govern, and what marks a political turnover? The vote recorded at the polling place, though a climactic and discrete act, is after all but a summary measure. "Whatever we may not know about the act of voting itself, we do know that it is highly complex, the net result of influences from many other activities in which voters are engaged and of other experiences than those directly associated with political campaigns."[11] We cannot explain the vote unless we know the influences that are at work during the so-called "quiescent" times. What do the mass media contribute to political stability and to political turnover?

Underlying the "strain toward consistency" observed in election periods is the basic stability of the vote. This stability also extends over longer periods. There is a high correlation between a person's first vote and his subsequent choices. Moreover, geographic, demographic, and social groups often display surprisingly consistent (over time) voting rates and patterns. Such consistent loyalties are fostered, above all, through the linkage of party images which class (and other status) symbols and the reinforcement of these loyalties through the relatively homogeneous political environment in which a majority of voters appear to move.

The study of the Bristol constituency highlights this basic stability. It indicates the importance of party images and the relative insignificance in British politics of "candidate appeal." Only 19 per cent of the respondents admitted that, in any of three elections since 1945, they had voted for a party other than the one they were supporting in 1951.[12] Indeed, in 1951 not a single candidate in all of Britain was able to win for Labour a previously Conservative seat and reverse what was a slight (though politically decisive) shift toward the Conservatives. This may be attributed, in part, to the fact that candidates considered valuable to a party may be run in "safe" constituencies. Yet it principally reflects the decisive role of the national party struggle and the importance that must be attached to the efficacy of party images as such. "However unthinking many electors may be," a British scholar writes, "their votes do seem on balance to represent a general judgment between the merits of the national parties."[13]

What seems to matter in British politics is the party image—what the party stands for. As economic and social conditions change, so do the self-images of voters. Inasmuch as party loyalties reflect class loyalties, the successful party must manage to alter its image even if ever so slightly to

459

take account of these shifts. The role of the mass media in disseminating the "appropriate" party image is apparent in *Straight Fight*. It is the national news sources that largely serve to channel to the electorate the party image with the pertinent symbols and clichés. Although the processes by which and the conditions under which these images are successfully communicated remain to be explained, Milne and Mackenzie conclude that national propaganda sources (as contrasted with local sources) have more "powerful direct effects."[14]

Such party images are obviously not the product of a single campaign; they are in existence, ready-made, long before the official contest begins. Their reinforcement through local pressures helps to give the vote its fundamental stability and to make much of voting a highly institutionalized and conventionalized activity, especially when, as in Great Britain, the party ties are closely linked with class organizations, trade unions, and the like. But it is not only stability that we have to understand. Also to be explained is how long-standing habits are upset, and upset among many divergent local groups. The mass media would seem to play an indispensable role in producing the cumulative changes that are given expression in a turnover at the polls.

A possible turnover in the United States was forestalled in 1948. A rally back to the Fair Deal "decided" the outcome of the presidential vote in Elmira that year. In particular, the "waverers," strays from the Democratic fold, returned largely because of the salience of class issues, exactly those issues stressed by Truman during his campaign. National surveys confirm this Fair Deal rally as a nationwide phenomenon. Truman's benefits from those who in the early part of the campaign had been "undecided" or did not follow through on their original voting intention were twice as great as Dewey's.[15] These late changers were 1944 Democrats switching back to the administration.

The importance of the mass media for the Fair Deal rally is flatly stated in the Elmira study. (The "salience of class issues was brought home through the mass media.")[16] Though the image of Truman did *not* change, the image of what was important in the campaign did change. As the campaign progressed, socioeconomic issues became dominant. The change was most noticeable among persons high in mass-media exposure. The Fair Deal rally, based on renewed attentiveness to class issues which was helped along by the mass media, enabled the Democrats to chalk up still another victory. Not very much attention has been paid to this finding on the mass media.

Legend already has it that Truman, as he whistle-stopped across the nation, took his own case to the people and won despite a hostile press. What Truman actually did, it would seem, was to make "news." The press—or magazines or radio—could editorialize against the administration; their presentation of the news that Truman was making could be more or less subtly biased through headlines, spacing, choice of words, and the like. But since what Mr. Truman said was news, his appeal to class interests commanded attention and helped bring the strays back into the fold.

Nevertheless, the Truman victory in 1948 called attention primarily to what the mass media could *not* do. The results in 1952 surely have led us to reconsider the assumption that people will not, on the whole, cross party lines. The proportion of voters who did cross was undoubtedly small. But there were enough of these, together with previous nonvoters, to produce the Republican landslide. Primary group pressures, local influences, latent dispositions of voters throughout the country failed to reinforce wavering allegiances to the Democratic party. The motivational pattern of the vote was different. If 1948 was largely a party year, in 1952 the "more variable factors of issues and candidates" assumed unusual importance.[17] Some analysts have pointed to the long-term trends underlying these cyclical changes, such as the general prosperity prevailing, the upward mobility of minority groups, the trek to the suburbs, the industrialization of the South, and the general change from "interest" to "status" politics.[18]

That the mass media were a significant force in defining and structuring the decisive issues of the 1952 campaign and in "projecting" the candidates' personalities should be beyond dispute. The extent of this influence can unfortunately only be inferred. The campaign may have reactivated old loyalties, but, if it did, they were not the same old loyalties as in 1948. The issues were drawn differently. Where socioeconomic issues had invoked Democratic loyalties, the issue of national security, especially the Korean war, exercised a new attraction which worked in favor of the GOP. And, along with this, the public personality of General Eisenhower appealed to Democrats and Republicans alike, though not always for the same reasons.

Plausible as it may seem to impute a great impact to advertising techniques employed during the political war, to the novel role played by TV, and especially to the saturation of TV with filmed "spots," there is no evidence that the official campaign propaganda, as such, changed many votes.[19] The "turnover" away from the Democrats had taken place before the official campaign opened. The campaign found the Republicans with a number of issues ready-made. From a postelection perspective, it appears evident that, in order to win, the Republicans had but to bring these vividly before the public. The real influence of the mass media, then, is to be sought in the play given communism and corruption in government and the controversies over Korea. These had been spelled out on front pages and in radio bulletins for some time. How, during the weeks of the campaign, the stalemated Korean war was restored from the back to the front pages of newspapers has been duly noted, though not yet systematically treated.[20]

The campaign talk on Korea may not actually have "converted." It nonetheless kept open the psychological wound inflicted by a peacetime war. Straight news and campaign oratory were joined to keep attention on what could, it seemed, only redound to the benefit of Republicans. Only in this sense may the campaign talk have "converted" by preventing the return of Democrats to their party.

We can inquire similarly about media influence on the Eisenhower image. He was, in 1952, not simply the "man of the year." Already in 1945, Eisenhower enjoyed an immense popularity, though for a war hero not a popularity without precedent. The political appeal of the General seems to have resided less in what he stood for than in what he did not stand for. Few Democrats or Republicans, who, as early as 1948, were advocating an Eisenhower candidacy, seem to have been familiar with his views on important issues. His political ("partisan") leanings were not on public record, and what was on the record had not been publicized.

Neither, for that matter, do early Eisenhower enthusiasts seem to have placed any emphasis on his political views. It was the "personal character" that counted. Eisenhower seemed to appeal most to those voters who "placed less emphasis on ideology and more emphasis on personal qualities in their choice of a candidate."[21] Yet, at that time very few people had met Eisenhower "intimately" via TV and there is no evidence that the personal image of Eisenhower originated with or was most prevalent among veterans of the European theater. But the image was there, ready for political exploitation, and it must be understood as a mass-media-built image.

Personal Influence and Mass Influence

The mass media, then, exert some of the influence they do because they are more than a channel through which national party policy is brought before the local electorate. In filtering, structuring, and spotlighting certain public activities, the media content is not confined to conveying what party spokesmen proclaim and what the candidates say. All news that bears on political activity and beliefs—and not only campaign speeches and campaign propaganda—is somehow relevant to the vote. Not only during the campaign but also in the periods between, the mass media provide perspectives, shape images of candidates and parties, help highlight issues around which a campaign will develop, and define the unique atmosphere and areas of sensitivity which mark any particular campaign. Any long-run view, therefore, reveals certain differences among elections which make clear that in each case voters, much as they may respond to traditional allegiances, also respond to a unique historical situation.

The scheme of analysis outlined in *Voting* barely touches upon the role of the mass media in creating a secondhand reality, through which public policy is elaborated and the effects of that policy on the voter clarified and made tangible. The "main concern," we are told, "is with the electorate itself. How many individuals pay *direct* attention to the campaign via the mass media?"[22] In this scheme the mass media act primarily as transmitters of content supplied by the national parties and by their candidates and subsequently consumed, in one way or another, by the electorate. The personal network of communications within the community hooks onto and makes use of the mass media. Opinion leaders usually pay more attention to the mass media than their peers, and they relay relevant information to those less firm in their partisan convictions.

In this transmission system which passes along arguments and information required in voting decisions, personal influence often seems more crucial and persuasive than mass-media content. The reasoning seems to go as follows: The opinion leader can induce compliance not only through *what* he says; he can exert his influence in a flexible fashion and also provide gratifications that go with compliance.[23] The prestige of opinion leaders is often interposed between the mass-media content and those who, on their own, pay no direct attention (or only very little attention) to the content itself. It is in aligning voters with their peers that personal contacts reactivate latent dispositions.

Opinion leaders thus seem often to counter the possible impact of counterpropaganda and to make effective the propaganda favoring their own side. This signal discovery of the ubiquity of opinion leaders has led many to pit the measure of personal influence against that of the mass media. Nothing could obscure the real character of mass-media impact more than to pose the problem in this way. Personal and mass-media influence do not act in the same way. Personal influence may govern a larger segment of any individual's behavior than do the mass media—and it may be easier to demonstrate how a husband influences his wife's voting decision than to demonstrate what the mass media have to do with her voting behavior—but from the viewpoint of the larger society, it is the influence of the mass media which is the most potent.

The persons generally designated by social scientists as "opinion leaders" prepare the ground for mass-media impact. They translate the mass-media reality into the experience of local groups. Some persons may enjoy informal status as opinion leaders precisely because they attend to the relevant mass-media content. Or it may be that in order to wield influence a man may have to be especially knowledgeable about what the mass media do and say. In either case, the opinion leaders exhibit greater responsiveness to the mass media, channeling for their peers—to whose dispositions they are particularly sensitive—that which the mass media have already made significant.

463

Theirs is essentially a transmission function and through them the views and interests of persons not directly exposed to the content of the mass media are involved. Yet these leaders select what they will transmit, and hence such influentials need not act only as a stabilizing influence. An emergent local leadership at odds with the official party may make use of whatever prestige or credibility the mass-media content has per se to subvert older loyalties.

The short-run frame of reference, with its primary concern with the electorate and how it lines up within the course of a single campaign, has perhaps exaggerated the dominant role of personal influences and the effectiveness of "normal" social pressures. For it puts the accent on the type of changer who is most susceptible—perhaps by a sort of default—to such influences, that is, it draws attention almost exclusively to changers who are converted or whose decision crystallizes only *during the campaign*. In the first place, such persons are, quite logically, those with a relatively low interest in politics and for whom political loyalties are not ordinarily salient; second, they are further characterized by low mass-media exposure.

Moreover, people who do *not* vote with their peers as well as people who do *not* vote in accord with their predispositions appear only as deviant cases among the over-all consistencies found in the panel studies. Deviants somehow get lost in the concern with how A influences B and how both A and B vote in line with their basic predispositions. Yet in order to understand the nature and extent of mass-media influence—and especially their impact on the larger political trends that often mark off one election from another—it is precisely these deviants upon whom we may be forced to concentrate.

By way of brief explication, take the situation described in the Elmira study: Women as a group are less interested in the campaign than men. In their voting decisions, they tend to follow their husbands. Yet at the same time, the "women's vote" is less clearly linked to social class than the male vote. To put it more succinctly, women from the higher socio-economic levels are less Republican than the men from those classes, whereas women among the working and lower classes are less strongly Democratic.[24] Somehow or other women follow their husbands' leads and yet, by comparison with their husbands, vote less in accord with their class interests. Many plausible explanations commend themselves, but clearly the pattern of the "women's vote" cannot be explained as the simple outcome of personal influence, however helpful this approach is in explaining individual vote changes.

The Bristol study does distinguish the "waverer" from the "changer." And a follow-up of this distinction may serve to sharpen our knowledge of influences upon voting behavior. The "waverer," although consistent in his vote over time, may move into the "undecided" column during any particular campaign or his "intentions" may (judged by what he tells us) appear inconsistent. The "changer" is one whose vote "at present" differs from that of the past, whether or not such a change is recorded within the span of a single campaign. We would contend that there is nothing in the Bristol or other data to indicate that the short-run regularities that mark campaigns reflect accurately the patterns associated with party turnover between elections and over longer periods of time. "Waverers," for instance, may mostly be political indifferents who give way under the pressure of the campaign. But is this true of "changers"? Especially if their conversion occurs during the "quiescent" times between campaigns, when personal pressures are least likely to be deliberately exerted in a politically partisan way, it raises the possibility that such change, or the disposition to change, follows from their private communions with the mass media and the trickle of news reports. During a campaign, women will in all likelihood move toward greater agreement with their husbands. But when the political battle is less obviously joined, the influences weaning women as a group away from the class loyalties of their husbands may well be of a different sort.[25]

The significant question at issue is, then, the pressures that cause people to vote out of accord with their local surroundings and out of accord with their group-anchored attitudes. No speculative answer can be accepted as adequate. Nonetheless, the response of individuals in the mass audience to certain nonlocal influences, however vaguely or indirectly they are perceived, is a problem with which research must contend. Voters, much as they interpret their secondary and symbolic environment in terms of their local milieu, do as individuals acquire certain general political perspectives that shape their responses during campaigns. Notions of politics, of parties, of issues, of candidates, and of their own roles as participating citizens cannot be satisfactorily explained by study of local communication networks. Along these lines, more than along others, ideas are affected by what the mass media present.

Secondhand Reality and the Mass Audience

Persons in the mass society are, as we all know, members of many more or less formally organized groups. Some of these memberships are, of course, more politically relevant than others. Trade unionists in the United States tend to vote Democratic; in England they most often side with Labour. Some minority groups "stick together" politically, and some organizations formed to defend "majority" interests have their own characteristic voting patterns. We know a considerable amount about the political perspectives that derive from such memberships and about the cross-pressures exerted by multiple allegiances.

We are also aware that most of what people know about political life comes to them secondhand—or even thirdhand—through the mass media. The media do structure a very real political environment but one which, even in these days of TV, we can only know "at a distance." Because of the way people select from the political content of the mass media and interpret what they select, the political communication system serves to transmit materials peculiarly relevant to persons in various milieus. Beyond this, however, the mass media also structure a larger, nonlocal reality from which it is hard to escape. The content filters through, even though people are not directly exposed to it or do not claim to be paying a great deal of attention.[26] There is something obtrusive about what the mass media present, something that makes their influence cumulative.

The mass media have, then, another function. They not only transmit materials that feed into the political perspectives of relevant groups; they leave an impress of their own. There are political perspectives that rise out of an individual's position as a member of a mass, as the object of direct and indirect stimuli coming from the mass media. The relationships between voting behavior and the perspectives developed by virtue of one's position in the mass have as yet been inadequately investigated, perhaps because of the very real methodological difficulties involved, perhaps because we over-estimate the difficulties or fear to risk criticism of our results.

The subsections that follow outline briefly *some* ways in which the media shape the perspectives of voters, so to say, en masse. Whether individuals accept the media content as "authentic" or discount it as "propaganda," they nonetheless respond to it. The relationship of the following three areas of mass-media impact to voting, however apparent their relevance to politics, has so far not been systematically investigated.

THE DISSEMINATION OF DISTRUST

The mass media, by the way in which they structure and present political reality, may contribute to a widespread and chronic distrust of political life. Such distrust is not primarily a mark of sophistication, indicating that critical "discount" is at work. It is of a projective character and constitutes a defensive reaction against the periodic political crises known to affect a person's destiny as well as against what are defined as deliberate efforts to mobilize political sentiment.

How, we may ask, do the media encourage such distrust? Who is most prone to it? And how is it counteracted? The answers must be sought in the way in which the mass media tend to emphasize crisis and stress it in lieu of the normal processes of decision-making. Such distrust also has its roots in the complexity of events and of problems in which the mass audience is involved. For instance, since viewers bring little specialized knowledge to politics, even full TV coverage of major political events does not allay this distrust. In fact, it may abet it. The efforts of telecasters, in 1952, to let the viewer in on everything happening at the conventions sometimes boomeranged.[27] Viewers, being overwhelmed, often felt less that they were being "let in on the inside" than that they were being kept out. People low in political competence and those who tended to take a sinister view of politics were especially prone to such hostile stereotypy.[28]

THE CHANNELING OF TRUST

How does this distrust express itself in voting or nonvoting? After all, people, in order to act politically, must form some credible picture about political questions. If we knew more about who trusts what mass-media sources and how this trust is channeled, this knowledge would be a springboard for assessing how persons who withdraw from political mass-media materials may periodically be stirred out of their apathy.

To study this, we might start with the characteristics of the consumers rather than those of the media. Certainly not all consumers of mass-media materials approach the political content with the same orientations. Persons with above-average political sophistication (and therefore less subject to a "chronic distrust" of politics) are in the habit of checking one source of information against another. While, like all others, dependent on the mass media for information, they have a sort of natural immunity to the news slant of any particular medium. They are a "high" interest group and usually firm in their voting decisions.

But what about those others who feel disbarred from channels of political influence and who would also seem most suspicious of politics in general? Will they distrust all mass-media sources and believe only what their friends tell them? Paradoxically, the withdrawal of "interest" from political mass-media materials may go hand in hand with high reliance on some particular trusted "medium" somehow exempted from the contamination imputed to the mass media as a whole. This would seem to put a high premium on "sincerity" and "honesty" and on a public personality radiating confidence. And, thus, under certain conditions, it would make those most distrustful of politicians most susceptible to mobilization.

The relation between chronic distrust and reliance on TV as a source of political information seems a particularly rewarding avenue for investigation. Pilot research suggests that television has an especially strong appeal for the chronically distrustful. Members of the audience feel themselves taken "to the scene of the crime," free to explore and follow their own clues. Inherently, TV is therefore the most authentic of the media. The viewer is ready to believe that he "sees for himself," though what he imputes to the picture often originates in other news sources. The immediate and apparently "firsthand" experience of television makes seem as direct experience what may be the end product of a careful build-up. If politicians employing TV can find a successful formula for channeling the trust of persons usually apathetic to and distrustful of politics, the newly mobilized might become a dynamic force in politics, highly volatile and acting with great conviction at election time, but not necessarily out of sustained interest in public policy.

THE DICTATION OF PUBLIC IMAGINATION

The mass media force attention to certain issues. They build up public images of political figures. They are constantly presenting objects suggesting what individuals in the mass should think about, know about, have feelings about. There is implied in the way they address their audience, moreover, an appropriate way of looking at politics. By the materials they choose, the media may give us the semblance of an "acquaintance with" the political world, though most of us have but a most indirect knowledge of what it is all about.

The media can also stifle debate and criticism by defining certain elements in a situation as not *actually* subject to controversy. This is most easily done in relation to public personalities and "moral" issues. For example, during the Truman-MacArthur controversy in 1951, the press reported a striking unanimity of public sentiment. In addition to the official hero's welcome for the ousted General, they reported many minor public demonstrations aimed against the Truman administration and indicating sympathy for MacArthur. In retrospect, the unanimity of this sentiment appears to have been misstated.[29] For some months, however, public discussion took its cues from this assumed sentiment, and only the brave politician dared to raise his voice publicly against MacArthur. Most waited until the storm "blew over" and MacArthur was no longer headline news. In much the same way, Democratic criticism of the Eisenhower administration appears to have foundered on the rocks of the unimpeachable hold of his personality on public imagination. How much, we may inquire, has the assumption of reporters about this unshakable popularity prevented them from featuring less popular images of the Eisenhower personality and thus helped to maintain the popular public image as such? This is one type of impact study which we need.

Such definitions of overwhelming public sentiment—"landslide perceptions"—tend to be cumulative. They influence political strategy; they inject a tone into news reporting; they seem to produce a certain reserve in personal discussion, since much conversation revolves around what is assumed to be held in common (like views on the weather). Politicians themselves believe in the importance of band-wagon effects in victory or defeat, and there have been attempts to assess the impact of election forecasts on election results. But this is not merely a matter of confidence or wanting to be on the winning side. For the communicator, assumptions about the public temper "legitimate" what is communicated to the mass. These assumptions likewise "legitimate" omissions. If the assumption about the unanimity of a public mood is erroneous, omissions of news about dissenting views or dissenting imagery make the unanimity much more marked than it is. For it tends to withdraw from personal discussion the very stuff that can be assumed as common political experience and, conversely, leaves uncriticized what everyone else is believed to approve. By influencing both public and private discussion, the saliency of what is at stake is affected, and where this influence enters campaigns, the election itself may be determined.

Individuals in the mass are likely to imagine what others in the mass are believed to be imagining.[30] Thus not only local influences but the beliefs imputed to nameless others exercise their pressure in the mass. Surely, one of the more interesting approaches to mass-media impact on political participation must be the study of private and public imaginations in relation to each other, and their joint relation to what we consider group-relevant reasons for casting a vote.

Conclusion

In this article we have set ourselves the task of exorcising the currently prevalent emphasis on *how little* mass media determine votes. We all are constantly exposed and sometimes concerned about mass-media influence, and yet this influence escapes our research endeavor.

Studies in voting behavior have dealt with both long-run trends and short-run changes. In either case, since voting rates and voting decisions can be determined with a high degree of validity, we seek inferences about antecedent conditions influencing these end products of political activity. Such influences as age differences, regional locations, and traditional political affiliations which may affect voting habits can with relative ease be isolated for examination. When we come to deal with mass-media influences, however, these are much more difficult to single out. They operate among a multitude of other factors and their effects do not always take tangible shape. Consequently, the measures of mass-media exposure are usually crude and the effects looked for are relatively specific and short run.

Quite naturally, campaign studies such as we have been considering, have focused on the short-range influences operating during the period of active electioneering and on how these culminate in a final voting decision. It so happens, as we have tried to point out, that this approach to the problem, with its emphasis on individual conversion during the "official" campaign, minimizes the important cumulative influences of the mass media and emphasizes instead how political communications are transmitted through personal networks and how latent tendencies are activated. In this way, attention has been focused on the limits to mass-media influence.

Where the question for study is "What makes the electorate tick?" research is naturally shaped to fit the problem; the mass media become just one among many concerns. On the other hand, experts in mass communications have not in recent years distinguished themselves by probing the long-range influence of mass media on political life—and more particularly on voting behavior. The cumulative and society-wide effects about which we often talk vaguely as shifts in public moods or drifts in political opinion are hard to demonstrate; yet, if we would further our knowledge of political behavior, such effects are much in need of clarification. And they can only be clarified through research specifically designed to get at them.

In turning attention to the continuous, and not only the intermittent, aspects of mass-media influence, we must deal, first, with the role of *mass* communications as such, focusing not only on the communicator's job as a transmitting agent for party propagandists but on the direct impress the communications have on what individuals in the mass society know of the larger political world. We have to get at the political perspectives that rise out of the individual's remote participation in politics as a member of the mass and at the relationships between voting behavior and these perspectives.

Moreover, we must develop a more apt definition of relevant changes and "changers." In place of turnover during a campaign, changes in party allegiances between one election and the next, together with discrepancies between "fundamental dispositions" and voting decisions, ticket splitting, and the like, are suggested.

A few specific problems for study have been directly outlined or indicated. The imagery made especially relevant by the mass media—the imagery of the "public imagination," of public personalities, of what politics is really like—and the relationship of such imagery to party alignments seem noteworthy. Among other subjects, the specific role of television, its authenticity and the exploitation of that authenticity by public officials and publicity directors, and the impact of such exploitation on voting participation constitute important areas for inquiry.

NOTES

1. B. R. Berelson, P. F. Lazarsfeld, and W. N. McPhee, *Voting* (Chicago: University of Chicago Press, 1954); R. S. Milne and H. C. Mackenzie, *Straight Fight* (London: The Hansard Society, 1954); and Angus Campbell, Gerald Gurin, and W. E. Miller, *The Voter Decides* (Evanston, Ill.: Row, Peterson, 1954).

2. In a separate article, the authors have discussed the role of television but qualify their data in stating that they had "no clear evidence" on how it affected the voting. Cf. Angus Campbell and others, "Television and the Elections," *Scientific American*, 188 (1953), 46–48.

3. Milne and Mackenzie, *op. cit.*, pp. 96 ff.

4. Berelson, Lazarsfeld, and McPhee, *op. cit.*, p. 248.

5. In Erie County, Ohio (1940), roughly one half were precampaign deciders. Cf. P. F. Lazarsfeld, B. R. Berelson, and Hazel Gaudet, *The People's Choice* (2d ed.; New York: Columbia University Press, 1948), p. 53. According to a "Gallup" poll before nomination day, 84 per cent of the British electorate were already decided. Cited by R. B. McCallum and A. Readman, *The British General Election of 1945* (London: Oxford University Press, 1947), p. 201. British figures seem to hover around the 80 per cent mark, with American figures, perhaps because of the more protracted campaign period, on the whole closer to two-thirds.

6. Best known among these are the famous "rum, Romanism, and rebellion" phrase so successfully used during the 1884 contest; and Charles Evans Hughes's alienation of Hiram Johnson, which lost him California and, consequently, the election.

7. There are important differences between the Elmira and Bristol studies. But our basic interest here is in the logic of their approach, not in a detailed methodological evaluation.

8. Berelson, Lazarsfeld, and McPhee, *op. cit.*, pp. 246 ff.

9. Milne and Mackenzie, *op. cit.*, p. 104.

10. Namely, "attitudes, perceptions, and group loyalties which mediate between the external environmental facts and the individual response." Campbell, Gurin, and Miller, *op. cit.*, pp. 7 ff.

11. D. B. Truman, "Political Behavior and Voting," in Frederick Mosteller and others, *The Pre-Election Polls of 1948* (New York: Social Science Research Council, 1949), p. 225.

12. Milne and Mackenzie, *op. cit.*, p. 26.

13. D. E. Butler, *The Electoral System in Britain 1918–1951* (Oxford: The Clarendon Press, 1953), p. 201.

14. Milne and Mackenzie, *op. cit.*, p. 121.

15. Campbell, Gurin, and Miller, *op. cit.*, p. 12.

16. Berelson, Lazarsfeld, and McPhee, *op. cit.*, p. 264 n.

17. Campbell, Gurin, and Miller, *op. cit.*, p. 184.

18. Cf. S. A. Lubell, *The Future of American Politics* (New York: Harper, 1951); Louis Harris, *Is There a Republican Majority?* (New York: Harper, 1954); and Richard Hofstadter, "The Pseudo-Conservative Revolt," *The American Scholar*, Winter 1955, pp. 9–27.

19. As far as the campaign is concerned, Stevenson, if anyone, gained more in personal appeal than Eisenhower. Cf. Harris, *op. cit.*, pp. 52 ff.; and *The Influence of Television on the 1952 Election* by the Oxford Research Associates, Oxford, Ohio, Dec. 1954.

20. Apparently such an analysis was conducted, but results have not yet come to our attention.

21. H. H. Hyman and P. B. Sheatsley, "The Political Appeal of President Eisenhower," *Public Opinion Quarterly*, XVIII (Winter 1953–54), 459.

22. Berelson, Lazarsfeld, and McPhee, *op. cit.*, p. 235. Italics supplied.

23. Elihu Katz and P. F. Lazarsfeld, *Personal Influence* (Glencoe, Ill.: The Free Press, 1955), p. 185. Also J. T. Klapper, *The Effects of Mass Media* (New York: Columbia University, Bureau of Applied Social Research, 1949).

24. Berelson, Lazarsfeld, and McPhee, *op. cit.*, p. 61.

25. Harris, *op. cit.*, Chap. 7, shows that women as a group gave a larger majority to Eisenhower than did men and that, especially, the wives of union members voted contrary to their husbands.

26. Berelson, Lazarsfeld, and McPhee, *op. cit.*, report this "unexpected" finding: "More people showed signs of exposure than claimed to be paying 'attention'."

27. "Political Participation and the Television Audience," paper read by the authors at the annual meeting of the American Sociological Society, Washington, D.C., 1955.

28. Cf. G. D. Wiebe, "Responses to the Televised Kefauver Hearings," *Public Opinion Quarterly*, XVI (Summer 1952), 179–200, for a discussion of the phenomenon of "social impotence."

29. R. H. Rovere and A. M. Schlesinger, Jr., *The General and the President* (New York: Farrar, Strauss, and Young, 1951), and Kurt and G. E. Lang, "The Unique Perspective of Television and Its Effect," *American Sociological Review*, XVIII (Feb. 1953), 3–12.

30. Gabriel Tarde referred to this phenomenon of contagion in his *L'opinion et la foule* (Paris: F. Alcan, 1901).

JOSEPH T. KLAPPER

The Effects of Mass Communication

TWENTY YEARS AGO, writers who undertook to discuss mass communication typically felt obliged to define that then unfamiliar term. In the intervening years, conjecture and research upon the topic, particularly in reference to the *effects* of mass communication, have burgeoned. The literature has reached that stage of profusion and disarray, characteristic of all proliferating disciplines, at which researchers and research administrators speak wistfully of establishing centers where the accumulating data might be sifted and stored. The field has grown to the point at which its practitioners are periodically asked by other researchers to attempt to assess the cascade, to determine whither we are tumbling, to attempt to assess, in short "what we know about the effects of mass communication."

What we know of course varies, depending on whether we are discussing one type of effect or another. In regard to some points, the evidence is remarkably consistent. In regard to others, the data contain apparent anomalies or apparent outright contradictions. These characteristics of the data are by now well known, and they have given rise to a widespread pessimism about the possibility of ever bringing any order to the field.

The author acknowledges and will here briefly document the pessimism, but he neither condones nor shares it. He will rather propose that we have arrived at the brink of hope. More specifically, he will here propose that we have reached the point at which certain empirical generalizations may be tentatively formulated. A few such generalizations will be presented, and it will be further proposed that they are capable of ordering a good deal of the data, of resolving certain apparent anomalies, and of indicating avenues for new and logically relevant research.

The Bases of Pessimism

The pessimism, at present, is widespread, and it exists both among the interested lay public and within the research fraternity.

Some degree of pessimism, or even cynicism, is surely to be expected from the lay public, whose questions we have failed to answer. Teachers, preachers, parents, and legislators have asked us a thousand times over these past fifteen years whether violence in the media produces delinquency, whether the escapist nature of much of the fare does not blind people to reality, and just what the media can do to the political persuasions of their audiences. To these questions we have not only failed to provide definitive answers, but we have done something worse: we have provided evidence in partial support of every hue of every view. We have claimed, on the one hand, and on empirical grounds, that escapist material provides its audience with blinders and with an unrealistic view of life,[1] and, on the other hand, that it helps them meet life's real problems.[2] We have hedged on the crime and violence question, typically saying, "Well, probably there is no causative relationship, but there just might be a triggering effect."[3] In reference to persuasion, we have maintained that the media are after all not so terribly powerful,[4] and yet we have reported their impressive success in promoting such varied phenomena as religious intolerance,[5] the sale of war bonds,[6] belief in the American Way,[7] and disenchantment with Boy Scout activities.[8] It is surely no wonder that a bewildered public should regard with cynicism a research tradition which supplies, instead of definitive answers, a plethora of relevant but inconclusive and at times seemingly contradictory findings.

Considerable pessimism, of a different order, is also to be expected within the research fraternity itself. Such anomalous findings as have been cited above seemed to us at first to betoken merely the need of more penetrating and rigorous research. We shaped insights into hypotheses and eagerly set up research designs in quest of the additional variables which we were sure would bring order out of chaos and enable us to describe the process of effect with sufficient precision to diagnose and predict. But the variables emerged in such a cataract that we almost drowned. The relatively placid waters of "who says what to whom"[9] were early seen to be muddied by audience predispositions, "self-selection," and selective perception. More recent studies, both in the laboratory and the social world, documented the influence of a host of other variables including various aspects of contextual organization;[10] the audiences' image of the sources;[11] the simple passage of time;[12] the group orientation of the audience member and the degree to which he values group membership;[13] the activity of opinion leaders;[14] the social aspects of the situation during and after exposure to the media,[15] and the degree to which the audience member is forced to play a role;[16] the personality pattern of the audience member;[17] his social class, and the level of his frustrations;[18] the nature of the media in a free enterprise system;[19] and the availability of "social mechanism[s] for implementing action drives."[20] The list, if not endless, is at least overwhelming, and it continues to grow. Almost every aspect of the life of the audience member and the culture in which the communication occurs seems susceptible of relation to the process of communication effect. As early as 1948, Berelson, cogitating on what was then known, came to the accurate if perhaps moody conclusion that "some kinds of *communication* on some kinds of *issues*, brought to the attention of some kinds of *people* under some kinds of *conditions*, have some kinds of *effects*."[21] It is surely no wonder that today, after another decade at the inexhaustible fount of variables, some researchers should feel that the formulation of any systematic description of what effects are how effected. and the predictive application of such principles, are goals which become the more distant as they are the more vigorously pursued.

But, as has been said, the present author takes no such pessimistic view. He rather proposes that we already know a good deal more about communication than we thought we did, and that we are on the verge of being able to proceed toward more abundant and more fruitful knowledge.

The Bases of Hope

This optimism is based on two phenomena. The first of these is a new orientation toward the study of communication effects which has recently become conspicuous in the literature. And the second phenomenon is the emergence, from this new approach, of a few tentative generalizations.

In describing the new approach, and in presenting the generalizations, the author submits rather than asserts. He hopes to be extremely suggestive, but he cannot yet be conclusive. And if these pages bespeak optimism, they also bespeak the tentativeness of exploratory rather than exhaustive thought. Explicit note will in fact be taken of wide areas to which the generalizations do not seem to apply, and warnings will be sounded against the pitfalls of regarding them as all-inclusive or axiomatic.

THE "PHENOMENISTIC" APPROACH

The new orientation, which has of course been hitherto and variously formulated, can perhaps be described, in a confessedly oversimplified way, as a shift away from the concept of "hypodermic effect" toward an approach which might be called "situational" or "functional."[22] Because of the specific, and for our purposes sometimes irrelevant, connotations attached to these two terms, we will here use a word coined by the present author in an earlier publication and refer to the approach as "phenom-enistic."[23] Whatever it be called, it is in essence a shift *away* from the tendency to regard mass communication as a necessary and sufficient cause of audience effects, toward a view of the media as influences, working amid other influences, in a total situation. The old quest of specific effects stemming from the communication has given way to the observation of existing conditions or changes, followed by an inquiry into the factors, *including* mass communication, which produced those conditions and changes, and the roles which these factors played relative to each other. In short, attempts to assess a stimulus which was presumed to work alone have given way to an assessment of the role of that stimulus in a total ob-served phenomenon.

Examples of the new approach are becoming fairly numerous. The so-called Elmira[24] and Decatur[25] studies, for example, set out to determine the critical factors in various types of observed decisions, rather than to focus exclusively on whether media did or did not have effects. The Rileys and Maccoby focus on the varying functions which media serve for different sorts of children, rather than inquiring whether media do or do not affect them.[26] Some of the more laboratory-oriented researchers, in particular the Hovland school, have been conducting ingeniously de-signed controlled experiments in which the communication stimulus is a constant, and various extra-communication factors are the variables.[27]

This new approach, which views mass media as one among a series of factors working in patterned ways their wonders to perform, seems to the author already to have been extremely useful, and to have made pos-sible a series of generalizations which will very shortly be advanced.

Before the generalizations are advanced, however, a few words of preliminary warning about the phenomenistic approach seem highly in order. For that approach, despite its usefulness, may, if relied upon too exclusively, tend to obscure the very issues it is intended to elucidate.

It is possible that the phenomenistic approach may so divert our at-tention to the factors with which mass communication is in interplay, or to the fact that interplay exists, that we forget our original goal of de-termining the effects of mass communication itself. For example, we shall see, that the effects of mass communication are likely to differ, depending upon whether the communication is or is not in accord with the norms of groups to which the audience members belong. In a later chapter, we shall see that the effects of fantasy and of media depictions of crime and violence are likely to have different effects among children who are primarily oriented toward different types of groups. This is valuable in-formation which contributes greatly to our knowledge of the processes and types of mass communication effect. But if research is to provide socially meaningful answers to questions about the effects of mass com-munication, it must inquire into the relative prevalence of these different conditions under which mass communication has different effects. Unfortunately, communication research has not often addressed itself to such questions, and this book will necessarily reflect that limitation. It may, however, be noted that if the phenomenistic approach thus tends to delay the provision of definitive answers, it does so in the interests of the eventual answers being the more meaningful.

It must also be remembered that though mass communication seems usually to be a *contributory* cause of effects, it is often a major or necessary cause and in some instances a sufficient cause. The fact that its effect is often mediated, or that it often works among other influences, must not blind us to the fact that mass communication possesses qualities which distinguish it from other influences, and that by virtue of these qualities, it is likely to have characteristic effects. Neither the phenomenistic approach nor the proposed generalizations deny these possibilities; they are, in fact, explicitly stated in the third and fourth generalizations below. But there seems some danger that attention may at times become too exclusively focused on the other factors to which the phenomenistic approach points, and the dangers of such neglect must be kept in mind.

Precautions can, of course, be taken against such dangers as have here been outlined, and given such precautions, the phenomenistic approach seems to the present author to offer good hope that the disarray of communications research findings may to some degree be ordered. He feels, as has already been noted, that the approach has in fact made possible a series of generalizations which will now be advanced. They are submitted very gingerly. They seem to the author at once extremely generic and quite immature; they seem on the one hand to involve little that has not been said, and on the other hand to be frightfully daring. They do seem, however, to be capable of relating a good deal of data about the processes, factors, and directions of communication effects, and of doing this in such a way that findings which hitherto appeared to be at best anomalous, if not actually contradictory, begin to look like orderly variations on a few basic themes. . . .

Concluding Note

It would seem desirable to conclude this reading with an evaluative note on the five generalizations which were proposed in the introduction. What follows is, like the various notes on the subject sprinkled throughout the text, a purely subjective and personal offering. As in all previous such contexts, the author here submits rather than asserts.

On the positive side, the generalizations appear to have served three major functions.

First, as the various notes on "theoretical considerations" have been at some pains to demonstrate, the generalizations have permitted us in some measure to organize, or to "account for," a considerable number of communications research findings which have previously seemed discrete and anomalous. The author submits, tentatively, that the set of generalizations has in fact made possible organization of several different orders:

It has enabled us to relate the *processes* of effect and the *directions* of effect. Put another way, it has provided us with a concept of the process of effect in which both reinforcement and change are seen as related and understandable outcomes of the same general dynamics. This concept enabled us to account for the relative incidence of reinforcement and change in reference to attitudes on specific issues, and provided an orientation which was found to be applicable in one or another degree to reinforcement and change in regard to a wide variety of audience orientations.

It has enabled us to view such diverse phenomena as audience predispositions, group membership and group norms, opinion leadership, personality patterns, and the nature of the media in this society, as serving similar functions in the process of effect—as being, so to speak, all of a certain order, and distinct from such other factors as the characteristics of media content.

It has enabled us to view other seemingly unrelated phenomena, such as the efficacy of the media in creating opinions on new issues and the effect of role-playing, as manifestations of the same general process—as specific combinations of known variables, the outcomes of which were predictable.

So much for the organizational capabilities of the generalizations. But note that this organization of existing data, even within so sketchy a framework as these generalizations provide, permitted us to see gaps—to discover, for example, that certain presumed outcomes have to date been neither documented nor shown not to occur. This points to a second contribution: the generalizations seem capable of indicating avenues of needed research which are logically related to existing knowledge. But virtually *any* set of generalizations, or any theoretical framework, will point to gaps and needed research. The fact that these generalizations do so thus in no way gainsays the fact that future thought and research must inevitably change the generalizations themselves. As presently formulated, they constitute only a single tentative step forward, and it may reasonably be hoped that their refinement or emendation would enlarge rather than reduce the area of their applicability.

Finally, it is in the extent of the applicability of the generalizations, coupled with their present primitive nature, that the author finds particular basis for hope. Sketchy and imperfect as they are, these propositions regarding the process and direction of effect seem applicable to the effects of persuasive communications and to the effects of various kinds of nonpersuasive media content upon a wide range of audience orientations and behavior patterns. Futhermore, the mediating variables to which the generalizations point—variables such as predispositions, group membership, personality patterns, and the like—seem to play essentially similar roles in all these various kinds of effects. Even if the generalizations turn out to be wholly in error, they seem nevertheless sufficiently useful and sufficiently applicable to justify the faith that *some* generalizations can in due time be made. And the author has indicated, from the outset, that he is "less concerned with insuring the viability of these generalizations than he is with indicating that the time for generalization is at hand."

For certainly these particular generalizations do not usher in the millennium. They are imperfect and underdeveloped, they are inadequate in scope, and in some senses they are dangerous.

They do not, for example, cover the residuum of direct effects, such as the creation of moods, except to note that such effects exist. They recognize, but in no way illuminate, the dynamism of the variety of effects stemming from such contextual and presentational variables as order, timing, camera angles, and the like. They are less easy to apply, and are conceivably inapplicable, to certain other broad areas of effect, such as the effect of the media upon each other, upon patterns of daily life, and upon cultural values as a whole. To be sure, we have spoken of cultural values as a mediating factor which in part determines media content, but certainly some sort of circular relationship must exist, and media content must in turn affect cultural values.

Such concepts suggest what is perhaps the greatest danger inherent both in these generalizations and in the approach to communications research from which they derive. And that danger, which has been mentioned in the Introduction but is well worth repeating, is the tendency to go overboard in blindly minimizing the effects and potentialities of mass communications. In reaping the fruits of the discovery that mass media function amid a nexus of other influences, we must not forget that the influences nevertheless differ. Mass media of communication possess various characteristics and capabilities distinct from those of peer groups or opinion leaders. They are, after all, media of *mass* communication, which daily address tremendous cross-sections of the population with a single voice. It is neither sociologically unimportant nor insignificant that the media have rendered it possible, as Wiebe (1952) has put it, for Americans from all social strata to laugh at the same joke, nor is it insignificant that total strangers, upon first meeting, may share valid social expectations that small talk about Lucy and Desi, or about Betty Furness, will be mutually comprehensible. We must not lose sight of the peculiar characteristics of the media nor of the likelihood that of this peculiar character there may be engendered peculiar effects.

We must remember also that under conditions and in situations other than those described in this volume, the media of mass communication may well have effects which are quite different and possibly more dramatic or extensive than those which have here been documented.

For example, the research here cited which bears upon mass communication as an instrument of persuasion has typically dealt with non-crucial issues and has been pursued either in laboratories or in naturalistic situations within a relatively stable society. Little attention has here been given to the potentialities of persuasive mass communication at times of massive political upheaval or in situations of actual or imminent social unrest. Given the rumblings of serious social malcontent—or, in terms of our current orientation, given individuals with predispositions toward change, unstructured as the envisaged change may be—mass communication would appear to be capable of molding or "canalizing" the predispositions into specific channels and so producing an active revolutionary movement. Some such process, in miniature, appears to have occurred in the previously cited cases of Nazi and North Korean soldiers who, upon the dissolution of their primary groups, became susceptible to Allied propaganda. A similar process of greater social width may well have occurred in under-developed countries in which the Communist party has recently become a major political force. Mass communication in such areas has of course been deliberately and carefully abetted by personal influence and by the formation and manipulation of reinforcing primary and secondary groups. Although it cannot therefore be said to have been a sufficient cause of the observed social changes, it may well have been an extremely important or even a crucial cause. Its effects may have been largely restricted to the activation and focusing of amorphous unrest, but these effects appear to have had consequences far beyond those normally associated with the reinforcement of pre-existing and specific attitudes. The fear that a similar activation process may occur, or that the media might actually create new attitudes, presumably lies behind the totalitarian practice of denying media access to voices of the political opposition.[28]

Even within a relatively stable social situation, the media of mass communication may well exercise extensive social effects upon the masses by the indirect road of affecting the elite. Particular vehicles of mass communication (e.g., The New York Times) and other vehicles directed toward a more specialized audience (e.g., The Wall Street Journal or U.S. News and World Report) may reasonably be supposed to affect the decisions and behavior of policy-making elites. Individual business and political leaders may or may not be "opinion leaders" in the sense in which the term is used in communications research—i.e., they may or may not critically influence a handful of their peers. But their decisions and their consequent behavior in themselves affect society at large, and the mere fact of their taking a particular stand frequently serves to make that stand and the issue to which it pertains a topic of media reporting and debate, and a topic in regard to which personal influence, in the more restricted sense of the term, is exercised. The media may, in short, stimulate the elite to actions which affect the masses and which incidentally restimulate and so affect both the media and channels of interpersonal influence.

It has also been suggested that the classic studies of how voters make up their minds—e.g., Lazarsfeld, Berelson, and Gaudet (1948) and Berelson, Lazarsfeld, and McPhee (1954)—provide an incomplete picture of the total effects of mass communication because they concentrate only on effects which occur *during* the campaign itself. Lang and Lang (1959), for example, point out that although most of the voters observed in such studies apparently kept to a decision made before the campaign began, shifts in voting behavior sufficient to produce changes of administration do occur. They suggest that such changes take place slowly *between* the campaigns, as new issues arise and as the images of the parties change or fail to change. Mass communication, they propose, makes these issues salient and builds the party images, and may thus exercise a much more extensive effect than is revealed in the classic voting studies. The Langs call for research designed to investigate the possibility of such effects and of various other types of effect which they believe mass communication may exercise upon political opinion.

Some elections, furthermore, may be more "critical" than others. Key (1955), for example, notes that there is "a category of elections," including those of 1896 and 1928, in which

> . . . voters are, at least from impressionistic evidence, unusually deeply concerned, in which the extent of electoral involvement is relatively quite high, and in which the decisive results of the voting reveal a sharp alteration of the pre-existing cleavage within the electorate. Moreover, and perhaps this is the truly differentiating characteristic of this sort of election, the realignment made manifest in the voting in such elections seems to persist for several succeeding elections.[29]

The elections on which the classic voting studies focus are not "critical" by these criteria, but are rather occasions on which previously manifested alignments held more or less stable. What role mass communication may play in determining voter's decisions before a "critical" election is not yet known.

Mass media may also have extensive but as yet undocumented effects of various non-political sorts. We have already alluded, for example, to the probable but unmapped interplay between the mass media and cultural values. To look more closely into one aspect of this matter, one might postulate that the media play a particularly important role in the socialization and acculturation of children. Such studies of children as are cited in this volume have dealt with children aged five and older, and have focused on highly specific attitudes or patterns of behavior. But to what degree do the media structure, even for younger children, the society and the culture which they are entering? The influence of the media in these respects is no doubt modified by the influence of the family, of the school, and of peer groups; but the question of ultimate media effect is complicated, perhaps beyond the possibility of simplification, by the fact that the persons comprising these very sources of extra-media influence are themselves exposed to and affected by the media. The role and the effects of the media in the socialization of the child can perhaps no longer be accurately assessed, but some concept of its possible scope may be obtained by performing the mental experiment of imagining the process of socialization occurring in a society in which mass media did not exist. Our knowledge of primitive cultures and of pre-media years suggests that the present social system and the present culture are at least in part a product of the existence of mass communication, and may be dependent upon such communication for their continued existence.

One may also speculate on the possibility that some of the functions served by mass communication may, perhaps indirectly and perhaps only after a long period, have certain effects both upon the audience as individuals and upon integral elements of the social structure. We have noted, for example, that certain light media material, such as comic strips, serves certain audience members by providing a common ground for social discourse. It is interesting to speculate on what alternative systems of serving the same function may be thereby replaced, may be reduced in importance, or may simply fail to develop for lack of being needed. If no comic strips or other mass media material existed to serve the conversational needs of the adult males observed by Bogart (1955), might they and others like them perhaps be more actively interested in each other's real life goals and problems? Do mass media, by providing an easily available and common ground for chit-chat, perhaps reduce or retard the development of interest in one's fellow men? And to what degree, if any, has the serving of such functions by mass media affected the functions previously served by such institutions as the neighborhood bar and barber shop?

Other situations and conditions which are not covered in this volume in which mass communication may have extensive effects may be readily imagined. For many of these situations and conditions, the primitive theoretical framework we have sketched may prove to be an inadequate model. It is to be hoped that its shortcomings may serve to stimulate the development of other models, at once refined and more widely applicable.[30]

The phenomenistic approach, which our generalizations suggest, also has its dangers and limitations. As we have noted, the identification of conditions under which mass communication has different effects is only a step in the direction of answering the basic questions about the incidence of such effects. If the influence of mass communication is to be described in socially meaningful terms, research must also inquire into the relative prevalence of the conditions under which the several effects occur.

The need of recognizing such limitations and of taking precautions against such dangers does not seem to the author, however, to compromise the usefulness of either the generalizations or the phenomenistic approach. The most fruitful path for communications research appears to him to be neither the path of abstract theorizing nor the path, which so many researchers have deserted, of seeking simple and direct effects of which mass communication is the sole and sufficient cause. The author sees far greater hope in the new approach which begins with the existing phenomenon—an observed change of opinion, for example—and which attempts to assess the roles of the several influences which produced it. He sees similar hope in the pursuit of logically related controlled experiments in which the multifarious extra-media factors being investigated are built into the research design. These are the paths which seem to him to have brought us to the point of tentative generalization and which seem likely to lead further toward the still distant goal of empirically-documented theory.

REFERENCES

Arnheim, Rudolf (1944) "The World of the Daytime Serial," in Lazarsfeld, Paul F. and Stanton, Frank N., eds., *Radio Research, 1942–43*. New York: Duell, Sloan and Pearce.

Berelson, Bernard (1948) "Communications and Public Opinion," in Schramm, Wilbur, *Communications in Modern Society*, Urbana, Ill.: University of Illinois Press.

Berelson, Bernard, Lazarsfeld, Paul, and McPhee, William (1954) *Voting: A Study of Opinion Formation in a Presidential Campaign*. Chicago: University of Chicago Press.

Bogart, Leo (1955) "Adult Talk about Newspaper Comics," *American Journal of Sociology*, LXI, 26–30.

Bogart, Leo (1956) *The Age of Television*. New York: Frederick Ungar Publishing Company.

Cooper, Eunice and Jahoda, Marie (1947) "The Evasion of Propaganda," *Journal of Psychology*, XXIII, 15–25.

Ford, Joseph B. (1954) "The Primary Group in Mass Communication," *Sociology and Social Research*, XXXVIII, 3.

Freeman, Howard E., Weeks, H. Ashley, and Wertheimer, Walter I. (1955) "News Commentator Effect: A Study in Knowledge and Opinion Change," *Public Opinion Quarterly*, XIX, 209–15.

Friedson, Eliot (1953) "The Relation of the Social Situation of Contact to the Media of Mass Communication," *Public Opinion Quarterly*, XVII, 230–38.

Herzog, Herta (1944) "What Do We Really Know About Daytime Serial Listeners," in Lazarsfeld, Paul and Stanton, Frank, eds., *Radio Research, 1942–43*. New York: Duell, Sloan and Pearce.

Hovland, Carl I. (1954) "Effects of the Mass Media of Communication," in Lindzey, Gardner, ed., *Handbook of Social Psychology*. Cambridge, Mass.: Addison-Wesley Publishing Company, Inc., II, 1062–103.

Hovland, Carl I., *et al.* (1957) *The Order of Presentation in Persuasion.* New Haven: Yale University Press.

Hovland, Carl I., Lumsdaine, Arthur A., and Sheffield, Fred D. (1949) *Experiments on Mass Communication.* "Studies in Social Psychology in World War II." Vol. III. Princeton: Princeton University Press.

Hovland, Carl I., Janis, Irving L., and Kelley, Harold H. (1953) *Communication and Persuasion.* New Haven: Yale University Press.

Hovland, Carl I. *et al* (1959) *Personality and Persuasibility.* New Haven: Yale University Press.

Hovland, Carl I., and King, B. T. (1954) "The Influencing of Role-Playing on Opinion Change," *Journal of Abnormal and Social Psychology,* XLIX, 211–18.

Janis, Irving L. (1954) "Personality Correlates of Susceptibility to Persuasion," *Journal of Personality,* XXII, 504–18.

Katz, Elihu (1957) "The Two-Step Flow of Communication," *Public Opinion Quarterly,* XXI, 61–78.

Katz, Elihu and Lazarsfeld, Paul (1955) *Personal Influence.* Glencoe, Ill.: The Free Press.

Kelley, Harold H., and Volkart, Edmund H. (1952) "The Resistance to Change of Group Anchored Attitudes," *Americal Sociological Review,* XVII, 453–65.

Kelman, Herbert C. (1953) "Attitude as a Function of Response Restriction," *Human Relations,* VI, 185–214.

Key, V. O. (1955) "A Theory of Critical Elections," *Journal of Politics,* XVII, 3–18.

King, B. T. and Janis, Irving L. (1953) "Comparison of the Effectiveness of Improvised Versus Non-Improvised Role-Playing in Producing Opinion Changes." Paper presented before the Eastern Psychological Association.

Klapper, Joseph T. (1948) "Mass Media and the Engineering of Consent," *American Scholar,* XVII, 419–29.

Klapper, Joseph T. (1949) *The Effects of Mass Media.* New York: Bureau of Applied Social Research, Columbia University.

Klapper, Joseph T. (1957–58) "What We Know About the Effects of Mass Communication: The Brink of Hope," *Public Opinion Quarterly,* XXI, 4.

Lang, Kurt and Lang, Gladys E. (1959) "The Mass Media and Voting," in Burdick, Eugene and Brodbeck, A., *American Voting Behavior.* Glencoe, Ill.: The Free Press.

Lazarsfeld, Paul F., (1942) "The Effects of Radio on Public Opinion," in Waples, Douglas, ed., *Print, Radio and Film in a Democracy.* Chicago: University of Chicago Press.

Lazarsfeld, Paul F., Berelson, Bernard and Gaudet, Hazel (1948) *The People's Choice.* New York: Columbia University Press.

Lazarsfeld, Paul F., and Merton, Robert K. (1948) "Mass Communication, Popular Taste and Organized Social Action," in Bryson, Lyman, ed., *The Communication of Ideas.* New York: Harper and Bros.

Maccoby, Eleanor E. (1954) "Why Do Children Watch TV?" *Public Opinion Quarterly,* XVIII, 239–44.

Merton, Robert K. (1946) *Mass Persuasion*. New York: Harper and Bros.

Michael, Donald N. and Maccoby, Nathan (1953) "Factors Influencing Verbal Learning from Films Under Varying Conditions of Audience Participation," *Journal of Experimental Psychology*, XLVI, 411–18.

Riley, John W., Jr., and Riley, Mathilda White (1959) "Mass Communication and the Social System," in Merton, Robert K., Broom, Leonard, and Cottrell, Leonard S., Jr., eds., *Sociology Today: Problems and Prospects*. New York: Basic Books.

Riley, Mathilda White and Riley, John W., Jr., (1951) "A Sociological Approach to Communication Research," *Public Opinion Quarterly*, XV, 444–60.

Smith, Bruce L., Lasswell, Harold D., and Casey, Ralph D. (1946) *Propaganda, Communication and Public Opinion*. Princeton: Princeton University Press.

Warner, Lloyd and Henry, William (1948) "The Radio Day Time Serial: A Symbolic Analysis," *Genetic Psychology Monographs*, XXXVII, 3–71.

Wiebe, Gerhardt D. (1951) "Merchandising Commodities and Citizenship on Television," *Public Opinion Quarterly*, XV, 679–91.

Wiebe, Gerhardt D. (1952a) "Mass Communications," in Hartley, Eugene, and Hartley, R. E., *Fundamentals of Social Psychology*. New York: A. A. Knopf, Inc.

Wiebe, Gerhardt D. (1952b) "Responses to the Televised Kefauver Hearings," *Public Opinion Quarterly*, XVI, 179–200.

NOTES

1. e.g., Arnheim (1944) and Herzog (1944).
2. e.g., Warner and Henry (1948).
3. This is a typical conclusion of surveys of pertinent literature and comment, e.g., Bogart (1956), pp. 258–74.
4. e.g., Lazarsfeld and Merton (1948); Klapper (1948).
5. Klapper (1949), pp. II–25, IV–52.
6. Merton (1946).
7. The efficacy as well as the limitations of media in this regard are perhaps most exhaustively documented in the various unclassified evaluation reports of the United States Information Agency.
8. Kelley and Volkart (1952).
9. Lasswell proposed in 1946 (Smith, Lasswell, and Casey, p. 121) that communications research might be described as an inquiry into *"Who* says *what,* through what *channels* (media) of communication, *to whom,* [with] what . . . results." This now classic formulation was widely adopted as an organizational framework for courses and books of readings in communications research and greatly influenced research orientations as well.
10. e.g., Hovland (1954); Hovland *et al* (1957).
11. e.g., Merton (1946), p. 61 ff.; Freeman, Weeks and Wertheimer (1955); Hovland, Janis, and Kelley (1953), chap. ii, which summarizes a series of studies by Hovland, Weiss, and Kelman.
12. Hovland, Lumsdaine, and Sheffield (1949) *in re* "sleeper effects" and "temporal effects."

13. e.g., Kelley and Volkart (1952); Riley and Riley (1951); Ford (1954); Katz and Lazarsfeld (1955) review a vast literature on the subject (pp. 15–133).

14. Katz (1957) provides an exhaustive review of the topic.

15. e.g., Friedson (1953). For an early insight, see Cooper and Jahoda (1947).

16. Janis and King (1954), King and Janis (1953), and Kelman (1953), all of which are summarized and evaluated in Hovland, Janis, and Kelley (1953); also Michael and Maccoby (1953).

17. e.g., Janis (1954); Hovland, Janis and Kelley (1953), chap. vi; Janis et al (1959).

18. e.g., Maccoby (1954).

19. e.g., Klapper (1948); Klapper (1949), pp. IV–20–27; Wiebe (1952–B).

20. Wiebe (1951).

21. Berelson (1948), p. 172.

22. See Berelson, Lazarsfeld, and McPhee (1954), p. 234, for "hypodermic effect."

23. Klapper (1957–58).

24. Berelson, Lazarsfeld, and McPhee (1954), p. 234.

25. Katz and Lazarsfeld (1955).

26. Riley and Riley (1951), and Maccoby (1954).

27. e.g., the experimental programs described in Hovland, Janis, and Kelley (1953), Hovland et al (1957), and Janis et al (1959).

28. Monopoly propaganda as practived by totalitarian governments, and a kind of unwitting monopoly propaganda practiced in democracies in favor of certain cultural values, are believed by some authors to be in themselves very effective persuasive procedures. See, for example, Lazarsfeld (1942), Lazarsfeld and Merton (1948), and Klapper (1948) and (1949, IV–20–27). In general, these writers suggest that the monopoly propaganda continually reinforces the attitudes it espouses, while simultaneously handicapping the birth and preventing the spread of opposing views. The argument is logically appealing and has been advanced as a conjectural explanation of various attitude and opinion phenomena, but it has been neither substantiated nor refuted by empirical research.

29. Key (1955), p. 4.

30. A particularly provocative and already well developed model for the study of mass communication as a process occurring within a social system has been recently provided by Riley and Riley (1959).

9

Public Opinion, Communication, and Democratic Objectives

SINCE THE problems of public opinion and communication are concerned with the "marketplace of ideas" in a democratic society, questions of social and political values cannot and should not be neglected. The problems of social control, political processes, and social objectives are interlarded with considerations of the proper conduct of the communication media, as well as with considerations of the state and quality of public opinion upon basic issues. The study of the processes of public opinion and mass communication is not only an intellectual end in itself. The goal of such analysis includes a better understanding of the dynamics of democratic institutions. The idea of the "Great Enlightenment" is no longer generally accepted—namely, that public opinion and the extension of the mass media would automatically strengthen democracy. Likewise, empirical research has undermined the notion that the mass media are responsible for the political difficulties of an advanced industrial society. Berelson seeks to attack these problems in his analysis of the public opinion requirements for a democratic society. Shils pushes the analysis further as he explores the dimensions of mass society and the role of the media in strengthening and weakening democratic institutions.

With the conviction that the matter of communication and public opinion is too important to be left to the researchers, men of good will have devoted themselves, in the United States and in Britain, to the problems of the communication media. From these two bodies—the Commission on the Freedom of the Press in this country, and the Royal Commission on the Press in Britain—have come definite statements of the standards of performance by which the press should be evaluated. While both of these statements are more than a decade old, they still represent the most penetrating thinking on the subject.

BERNARD BERELSON

Democratic Theory and Public Opinion

THE FIELD of public opinion research has had a number of intellectual godparents. Psychologists have contributed their experience with attitude and intelligence tests and measurements, as well as substantive concepts and propositions. Sociologists have provided experience with field and community studies and ideas about social structure and the place of opinion within it. Market research has developed new techniques and furnished a variety of practical problems on which to try them. The statisticians have worked on such problems as sampling and scaling. But my subject is the claim of political theory to contribute to the character of public opinion research.

It would be too much to say that it has played no role thus far. For a good many years the political scientists have been discussing the nature of public opinion and the role it plays in the political process. But somehow, in recent years, we have tended to overlook the related facts that there is a political content in what we call public opinion; that there exists a long and elegant intellectual tradition (in the form of the political theory of democracy) for dealing with opinion problems; and that this theory provides a helpful framework for the organization and conduct of opinion studies. The normative theory of political democracy makes certain requirements of the citizen and certain assumptions about his capacity to meet them. The tools of social research have made it possible, for the first time, to determine with reasonable precision and objectivity the extent to which the practice of politics by the citizens of a democratic state conforms to the requirements and the assumptions of the theory of democratic politics (insofar as it refers to decisions by the electorate). The closer collaboration of political theorists and opinion researchers should

Reprinted from *Public Opinion Quarterly*, Vol. XVI (Fall 1952), pp. 313–330, by permission of the author and the publisher. (Copyright, 1952, Princeton University Press.)

contribute new problems, new categories, and greater refinement and elaboration to both sides.

The theorists tell us how a democratic electorate is supposed to behave and we public opinion researchers claim to know something about how the democratic electorate in this country actually does behave. The task I have taken on myself is figuratively to confront the one with the other. Such an analysis should be useful not only in organizing the results of opinion studies in terms of an important body of theory, but also in revealing neglected and promising areas for further investigation. I bespeak the interest of both theorists and researchers in extending, refining, and, in general, improving this formulation. For even on the basis of my preliminary exploration, I am convinced that each side has a good deal to learn from the other and that joint work on this common problem can be valuable both for social science and for public policy.

Such collaboration, like most cross-disciplinary work, is not easy, but it is necessary since neither side can solve the problem alone. In this connection, the deficiencies of the present formulation on the theoretical side will be particularly clear to the political theorist; I can only hope that the representation of theory, drawn as it is from a variety of sources, has not been caricatured, and that the theorists will themselves undertake the indicated corrections.

What, then, does democratic political theory assume or require of the democratic citizen, and to what extent are the assumptions or requirements realized? There are a number of ways of identifying and classifying the requirements, depending upon which political philosophers are given primary consideration. It has seemed most appropriate in this preliminary analysis to present a composite set of requirements, even though they may overlap at various points and thus not present a coherent system. While not all of them may be required in any single political theory of democracy, all of them are mentioned in one or another theory.

The Prerequisites of Electorate Decisions

There appear to be two requirements in democratic theory which refer primarily to characteristics demanded of the electorate as it initially comes to make a political decision. These are the preconditions for electorate decisions.

The first is the possession of a suitable *personality structure:* within a range of variations, the electorate is required to possess the types of character which can operate effectively, if not efficiently, in a free society. Certain kinds of personality structures are not congenial to a democratic society, could not operate successfully within it, and would be destructive of democratic values. Others are more compatible with or even disposed toward the effective performance of the various roles which make up the democratic political system. Among the characteristics required—and this is not intended as anything more than an illustrative list—are a capacity for involvement in situations remote from one's face-to-face experience; a capacity to accept moral responsibility for choices; a capacity to accept frustration in political affairs with equanimity; self-control and self-restraint as reins upon the gross operation of self-interest; a nice balance between submissiveness and assertiveness; a reasonable amount of freedom from anxiety so that political affairs can be attended to; a healthy and critical attitude toward authority; a capacity for fairly broad and comprehensive identifications; a fairly good measure of self-esteem; and a sense of potency.

The distribution of such personality characteristics in the population, let alone their relationship to political behavior, is not known. What is more or less known is only a beginning of the problem. We know, for example, that contrary to common belief the incidence of psychosis has not increased in this country over the past century (Goldhamer and Marshall); on this score, at least, we are not less capable than past generations of governing ourselves. We know that the authoritarian personality is associated with social prejudice and restrictive politics (the Berkeley study of Adorno, Frenkel-Brunswick, *et al.*); that neuroticism limits attention to political matters (Elmira study); that a wide discrepancy between aspiration and achievement leads some persons to over-aggressive acts against the political environment and lowers their respect for political leaders (Bettelheim and Janowitz); that the "democratic character" is more flexible and adaptable than the authoritarian character (Lewin and Lippitt).

There is a great deal of work to be done on this problem; and it is here particularly that the psychologists can make an important contribution to the study of political behavior. The influence of character on political democracy has been perceived in general terms by a number of theorists, and some psychologists and sociologists have begun to work on the topic. The dependence of democratic processes upon the "democratic character" seems clear in general, but the nature of this relationship has been only slightly documented in the literature. Without doubt, a sympathetic and imaginative study of the literature of democratic theory will generate many important hypotheses for empirical investigation.

The second requirement is not only a prerequisite but also an outcome of electorate decisions. This is the factor of *interest and participation;*[1] the electorate is required to possess a certain degree of involvement in the process of political decision, to take an appropriate share of responsibility. Political democracy requires a fairly strong and fairly continuous level of interest from a minority, and from a larger body of the citizenry a moderate-to-mild and discontinuous interest but with a stable readiness to respond in critical political situations. Political disinterest or apathy is not permitted, or at least not approved.

Here the descriptive documentation provided by opinion studies is relatively good. The amount of political interest in the community, its fluctuations through time, its incidence among various population groups, its causes and its consequences—on all these topics we have reasonably systematic data. Less than one-third of the electorate is "really interested" in politics, and that group is by no means a cross-section of the total electorate. The more interested people are more likely to affect others and thus to exercise a greater influence upon the outcome of elections. The decreasing political interest in the population, viewed with alarm by some people who are distressed by the fact that a smaller proportion of eligible people vote now than did fifty years ago, is to some extent due to the increasing feeling people have that they are impotent to affect political matters in the face of the complexity and magnitude of the issues. Participation in the actual election is not only segmental but also partial; if everybody eligible to vote actually did vote, the distribution of support in recent national elections would have been measurably different. Finally, interest is not a simple unidimensional factor. A recent analysis identified three kinds of interest: spectator interest (regarding the campaign as a dramatic spectacle); citizen interest (deciding how to vote); and partisan interest (securing the election of one's own candidate). Of these, only the second is "pure" interest according to some theorists.

The major question raised by this requirement, both for political theory and for opinion research, is the fundamental one of its universality and intensity. People have always argued whether the vote is a duty or a privilege, and there have always been advocates of an unlimited and continuous requirement of interest. As early as the Athenian democracy it was said that "we regard a man who takes no interest in public affairs not as a harmless but as a useless character." But is he really so useless to the operation of democracy? Some recent theorists and studies have suggested that a sizable group of less interested citizens is desirable as a "cushion" to absorb the intense action of highly motivated partisans. For the fact is that the highly interested are the most partisan and the least changeable. If everyone in the community were highly and continuously interested, the possibilities of compromise and of gradual solution of political problems might well be lessened to the point of danger. It is an historical axiom that democracy requires a middle class for its proper operation. Perhaps what it really requires is a body of moderately and discontinuously interested citizens within and across social classes, whose approval of or at least acquiescence in political policies must be secured.

492

The Components of Electorate Decisions

The political theory of democracy also makes requirements regarding the components of electorate decisions; that is, the content of the decision.

The first requirement of electorate decisions is the possession of *information and knowledge;* the electorate must be informed about the matters under consideration. Information refers to isolated facts and knowledge to general propositions; both of them provide reliable insight into the consequences of the decision. This is a requirement nearly everyone sets down for a democratic electorate; politicians and statesmen, adult educators, journalists, professors of political science—all of them pay deference to the need for "enlightened public opinion."

This is another factor on which opinion researchers have assembled a good deal of data. What do they show? One persistent conclusion is that the public is not particularly well informed about the specific issues of the day. A recent survey of the current status of American public opinion states that "tests of information invariably show at least twenty per cent of the public totally uninformed (and usually the figure is closer to forty per cent)." And at that, most of the studies have been based upon simple and isolated questions of fact (i.e., information) and only seldom, if at all, upon the historical and general propositions (i.e., knowledge) which underlie political decisions. Perhaps the proportion of the knowledgeable would be even lower than the proportion of the informed. At the same time, it must be recognized that there is a significant middle ground—a kind of vaguely perceived impression which reveals to the possessor certain relationships which are very "real" to him, which form "reasonable" bases for his decision, yet which cannot be explicitly articulated by him in any detail. An obvious example is the difference between the Republican and Democratic parties, a difference visible to many partisans of both.

Thus it often appears that people express opinions on issues when they seem to know very little about them. Lack of information may be a bar to the holding of an opinion in the minds of the theorists but it does not seem to be among the electorate (where, of course, it is not experienced as lack of information at all). In most campaigns, whether political or informational, the people best informed on the issue are the ones least likely to change their minds. Much of this represents attitudinal stability; some of it may represent rigidity.

Information and knowledge are required of the electorate on the assumption that they contribute to the wisdom of the decision; informed citizens make wiser decisions. In this country it is clear that the better-educated people are the best informed and most knowledgeable, yet it is also clear that other variables are involved in the development of wise decisions, e.g., flexibility of predispositions, a wide range of identifications, a low level of aggressiveness, etc. Finally, it appears from most studies that information and knowledge are sought and used more often as rationalization and reinforcer than as data to be used in making what might be called a free decision.

The requirement thus does not seem to be met in any direct way. But this is really an oversimplified statement of the requirement. How can an electorate be expected to be informed on the wide range of issues which confront the modern public? For example, the front page of *The New York Times* for one day alone recently contained stories on the following events, in each of which is embedded an issue on which the public might be expected to inform itself: price ceilings, the Korean war and the British position in it, the American defense build-up, Communist riots in France, the Berlin crisis, a new disarmament proposal, American military aid to France, official Soviet spies in this country, and the Mutual Security Aid Bill. Clearly there is too little time for simply getting the relevant information, let alone digesting it into a generalized system of political opinions. Actually the major decisions the ordinary citizen is called upon to make in a modern representative democracy involve basic simplifications which need not rest upon a wide range of information so long as they are based upon a certain amount of crucial information, reasonably interpreted. After all, the voter's effective choice is limited; he can vote Republican, he can vote Democratic, or he can refrain from voting, and becoming informed on a number of minor issues usually does not tip the scales against the weight of the few things that really matter—employment, social security, the cost of living, peace.

If the theoretical requirement is "full" information and knowledge, then democratic practice does not conform. But for some theorists the requirement is more differentiated than that. Representative government with large-scale political organization does not require that everyone be equally informed on everything all the time. To such a differentiated standard, actual practice may conform reasonably well. Opinion studies should not only document this requirement, but also refine their inquiries into the actual ways in which information and knowledge are held and used by the citizen in his vote decision. At the same time, theorists should differentiate and elaborate their conceptions of the intellectual requirements for a democratic citizenry.

The second component required of decisions is the possession of *principle;* the electorate is required to possess a body of stable political principle or moral standards, in contrast with fluctuating impulses or whims, to which topical questions can be referred for evaluation and decision.

Such principles are of two kinds. In the first place, there are the principles which refer to democratic procedures (as distinguished from the content of democratic decisions) and on them there must be consensus. Everyone, or nearly everyone, must agree on the rules of the political game and accept them in advance of the controversy so that they will obtain even in defeat. Among such principles are the rules that violence must not be involved in the making of electoral decisions; that the majority decision must be accepted as final in any particular instance, until legitimately appealed to a court, a legislative body, or the citizenry; that the citizen must have due respect for constituted authority; that the citizen must share respect with other parts of the community and thus be ready for political compromise. Few data on such questions have been collected in opinion studies, perhaps because their wide observance seems so obvious. It would be instructive to describe more precisely the citizenry's image of desirable and actual processes of democracy and to analyze the factors responsible for it.

The other kind of principle refers to the substantive bases of political decisions—the underlying moral or political ends in terms of which particular issues are determined at particular times. Just what they are for different parts of the population is difficult to say in the absence of more systematic research devoted to this purpose. At this time, however, it would seem at least likely that the *same* avowed principles underlie political positions at every point on the continuum from left to right. Full employment, a high standard of living, freedom, a better life for one's children, peace—these are the types of answers we have now, and we get them from persons of every political persuasion. Now this is not so empty as it sounds. Democratic theorists have pointed out what is often overlooked because too visible, namely, that an effective democracy must rest upon a body of political and moral consensus. If splits in the population are too sharp or too great, democratic processes cannot be maintained because of actual, threatened, or suspected conflict among partisans. In this circumstance, a seeming consensus which is accepted at its face value is far better than no consensus—and a seeming consensus is sometimes reflected in loyalty to the same symbols even though they carry different meanings. A sense of homogeneity is often an efficient substitute for the fact of homogeneity. Thus it is not an empty assertion to say that the role of substantive principles—like that of some information—is both to rationalize and to guide the choice simultaneously. Rationalization has a social function, too. What this means, then, is that the selection of means to reach agreed-upon ends is more likely to divide the electorate than the selection of the ends themselves.

At the same time, however, the principles must be applicable to current political life. Political decisions made today in the light of principles which support or oppose the major social reforms identified as the "New Deal" or the "welfare state" are relevant. But decisions made *simply* in conformity to an historical regional loyalty or to a primary group loyalty are of dubious relevance; and those made *only* in conformity to an ancestral loyalty or a religious loyalty are of no relevance at all. When theorists insist that public decisions in a democracy must be based upon principle and doctrine, they mean principle and doctrine which can confront and cope with the major problems of the age. Yet the studies show that a large proportion of the party vote today is by this test unprincipled.

If it is nothing more, then, the requirement of principle or doctrine means that the electorate must genuinely accept the procedures and rules involved in democratic processes, that it must at least share the symbols describing the substantive ends to which political action is directed and in terms of which it is justified, and that it must make political decisions on the basis of relevant standards. The first two requirements are met to a greater extent than the third.

The Process of Electorate Decision

The third set of essentials in democratic theory refers to the process by which decisions are made. Here there seem to be three requirements.

The first of the requirements relates to the process of perception of which information and knowledge are the end products. This is the requirement of *accurate observation;* the electorate is required to perceive political realities clearly and objectively, with an absence or only a small amount of subjective distortion. It is difficult indeed to see life steadily and see it whole, and in politics clarity of perception is made doubly hard on the one hand by the predispositional strength which the citizen brings to the matter and, on the other, by the deliberate and in many cases inevitable ambiguity which the political leader brings there.

There is no need to labor this point. Walter Lippmann made a reputation for himself thirty years ago by elaborating the differences between the "world outside and the pictures in our heads." For the most part, he said, "we do not first see and then define, we define first and then see." Recent studies provide some documentation which refines this general observation. According to data from the Elmira study, not only is the citizen's image of the candidate and the campaign subject to the influence of preconception, but so is his view of group support for the candidates and even of the candidates' stand on political issues. Given just a minimum of ambiguity to work with—and that is usually available—people tend to think their candidate agrees with them, or at least they manage not to know where he stands on the particular issue when they stand on the other side. The stronger the party affiliation, the greater the misperception.

The consequences of such misperception are interesting to speculate about. It seems to decrease the tension within the individual since it enables him to bring his opinions into an internal consistency without disturbing his basic position. At the same time, it increases the internal solidarity of the parties and thus increases political tension within the community by seeming to sharpen the differences between the parties, particularly under the stress of a political campaign. Thus political perception is by no means simply a matter of concrete observation; it also involves protective coloration from a total position. And hence, that democratic theory which assumes clarity and objectivity of political perception must be qualified at the outset.

The second important requirement of democratic process is *communication and discussion;* the electorate is required to engage in discussion and communication on political affairs. Democratic decision-making requires free examination of political ideas, and this means discussion. Democratic citizens are supposed to listen to their political leaders arguing with one another, to listen to them when they speak directly to the electorate, to talk back to them, and to discuss among themselves the public issues of the day. According to many modern theorists, this requirement stands at the heart of the democratic process. "Above all, if it is to be true to its own peculiar nature, democracy must enlist the effective thought of the whole community in the operation of discussion."

Now here again, as in the case of information, public opinion researchers have assembled a sizable body of data, not only on the amount and kind of communication and discussion within the community but also on the conditions under which it takes place. The overall picture presented by the opinion studies looks something like this: There is a 20 per cent nucleus of people who are active and regular political discussants, another group of 25 per cent who engage in political discussion on occasion, another 25 per cent who are activated into discussion only by dramatic political events, and a residual group of 25 or 30 per cent who do not engage in political discussion at all. Furthermore, it is particular groups within the community that give most attention to politics: the better-educated, the men, the "joiners"—in short, those groups most subject to social pressure translated into expectations of how "our kind of people" should behave in this respect. And the people who read and listen to political content in the mass media also talk and listen to other people, and thus the concentration of political communication and discussion is carried one step further.

To complete the picture we need to ask two other questions which together bring into consideration another aspect of this requirement. Democratic citizens are required not simply to discuss politics, but to discuss political alternatives in a genuine effort to clarify and refine public policy. The first question is, "Who talks to whom?", and the answer is that people mostly discuss politics with other people like themselves—"like" in such characteristics as social position, occupation, and attitude. Mainly this goes on inside the family, but even outside it there is a clear tendency for political discussions to be carried out in intra- rather than inter-social groups. The second question is, "What do they see and hear and talk about?" The broad answer is, "What pleases them"; i.e., what is congenial to their own point of view. People usually read and listen to their own side. In person-to-person discussion of politics, about a third or more of the talk centers upon topics not directly involving political preferences —for example, predictions of and arguments about who will win an election—and the remainder consists overwhelmingly of exchange of mutually agreeable remarks. What this all means—and this is clearly documented —is that the people who do the most reading and listening and talking are the people who change their minds the least. Lowell did not say it first but he said it well: "To a great extent, people hear what they want to hear and see what they want to see. They associate by preference with people who think as they do, enter freely into conversation with them, and avoid with others topics that are controversial, irritating or unpleasant. This is not less true of what they read. To most people, that which runs counter to their ideas is disagreeable, and sought only from a sense of duty."

In summary, then, genuine political discussion—not acrimonious argumentation on the one hand or mutual admiration for right thinking on the other, but free and open discussion devoted to finding a solution to a problem through the clarification and modification of views—this is not marked by its magnitude. Perhaps it is naive to point this out once more; perhaps it is naive to require it in the first place. We cannot inquire here into what the requirement of discussion can really mean in a modern democracy; whether self-interested argument is improper, whether genuine discussion goes on a different level in the political process. But certainly democratic practice does not conform fully to the requirements of some theorists: "The person or party formulating political principles or policies in advance of discussion, and refusing to compromise under any circumstances; or settling such principles or policies before the process of discussion is completed and refusing to compromise further; renders discussion a farce in the first place, and in the second, limits its usefulness."

The third requirement under process is *rationality;* the electorate is required to exercise rational judgment in political decisions.

Philosophers and economists still talk professionally about "rational behavior," but sociologists never really used the concept, psychologists have given it up, and political scientists seem to be in process of doing so. The problem of giving the term a clear meaning acceptable to others is partly responsible for this state of affairs. The term, says a recent writer on rational conduct, "has enjoyed a long history which has bequeathed to it a legacy of ambiguity and confusion. . . . Any man may be excused when he is puzzled by the question how he ought to use the word and in particular how he ought to use it in relation to human conduct and to politics."

The difficulty, of course, is not that there is no reasonably clear definition for the term but that there are several definitions describing several

498

different kinds of rationality. And the conformity of democratic practice varies with each definition. Let us review a few major meanings and their relationship to democratic practice. In the first place, we may distinguish between the rational decision as outcome and the rational decision as process. In the former case we speak of rationality as equivalent to a "right" decision. This assumes that there is one right answer to every problem, and that the power of reason can arrive at truths of policy which should be evident to all—all, that is, except those ruled by prejudice or emotion. When this is not simply a euphemism for describing decisions of which we approve, it presumably refers to a decision taken in conformity with an estimate of desirable ends (it thus assumes a valid analysis of whose interest lies where) and also in conformity with a correct estimate of which means will achieve the given ends. If we leave determination of self-interest up to the individual involved, then virtually all electorate decisions are rational by this definition; if we leave it up to the "objective observer" then the proportion will vary arbitrarily with his estimate of the present situation and the future. Even in philosophy, this meaning appears to be so ambiguous that it is difficult to see how we can design empirical research to test the extent of its observance by the electorate.

If we take rationality as referring to the process of decision—a more likely definition—then various possibilities are available. One meaning requires a certain independence of the rational process from the influence of predispositions broadly defined. Here rationality becomes the "free decision"—free from coercive imposition; free from blinding institutional loyalties; free from personal position (such as class or race); free from passions and impulses; free, in short, from any distorting or distracting pressures which prevent clear observation and calm, sober reflection. Here the term refers to logical, syllogistic ratiocination. But this seems to be an impractical, untenable, undesirable, and quite unreasonable definition; it takes the content heart out of politics and leaves the voter with no real basis on which to evaluate political proposals. By this standard, at least in its extreme version, there are almost no rational voters. As a social philosopher says, "individuals who on their own initiative form or change their fundamental beliefs through genuine critical reflection are so rare that they may be classed as abnormal."

A second meaning of rationality is close to, if not identical with, our requirement of information and knowledge: the voter should be aware of the correct state of public affairs at the present and of the "reasonable" consequences of alternative proposals for action. By this definition someone who made up his political mind on the basis of ends for which there are no present means of attainment would be making a non-rational decision, and so would the person whose estimates of the present situation or of the future were wrong. Also by this meaning the voter should be capable of indicating some relevant grounds for his decision, and most voters can cite such grounds. Here we meet the difficult question of rationalization, as against rationality, but we can suggest a partial answer. Rationality is limited by the individual's incapacity to deal with the real world in all its complexity, so it must allow for the legitimacy of dealing with simplified models of reality. In politics, the voter may "really" decide on the basis of one or two issues which are dominant for him (for example, peace or the New Deal) and use other issues as reinforcing rationalizations (for example, the military background of a candidate or corruption in the Federal administration).

A third definition requires the presence of convincibility or open-mindedness in consideration of political issues. This does not require the citizen to change his mind but only to be genuinely open to a change of mind. Here the time involved seems crucial. If this means, for example, that the citizen should be open-minded between June and November of an election year, then probably fewer than half the electorate is rational, and very few indeed in the South and parts of New England. If it includes the four years of a presidential administration or the "natural history" of a major political issue, from birth in controversy to death in near-unanimity, then the figure would become quite higher. It is hard for the researcher to be more specific because of the difficulty of determining just when "genuine consideration," as against rationalization, goes on.

Still another meaning of rationality as process requires that the decision be made in a state of low psychic tension; that is, that the decision not be an emotional one but be marked by a certain amount of detachment and freedom from passion. This poses a nice democratic dilemma; the people most rational by this definition are the people least interested in the political process and least involved in its outcome. The more interested people are the more emotional, in this sense, and the least detached; they are the ones who ascribe important consequences to the outcome of the decision and thus find enough psychic energy to be active about the matter. Here the rational voter is the independent voter, that is, the one without sufficient interest or investment in the election to get excited about it.

Still other meanings are available. There is the meaning in which rationality refers to the presence of deliberately directed behavior to consciously formulated purposes. Here again, almost all voters could qualify. There is the meaning in which rationality refers to a choice of behavior that is optimal in some sense, and this definition can be readily satisfied on the grounds of a subjective optimum if nothing more. There is the meaning in which a rational decision is a self-consistent decision. There are undoubtedly other meanings.

If it is not easy to say what is meant by a rational decision, it is somewhat easier to say what is not meant by it. A rational decision is not a capricious decision, or an impulsive one, or an unprincipled one, or a decision guided by custom or habit or tradition or sentiment alone. But the central problem is to relate the demand of rationality to the analysis of decision-making in terms of such sociopsychological concepts as the reference group; that is, to see the "rational decision" as imbedded in a social context which limits it at the same time that it gives it political meaning. While the types of rationality are not easy to define and while they are certainly never present in a pure or extreme form, they can be isolated empirically, clarified, and investigated as to their frequency, their functions, and their preconditions.

The Outcome of Electorate Decisions

Finally, there is one basic requirement which might be included under the need for principle but which seems to deserve independent treatment in view of its central importance with reference to the outcome of the decision. This is the requirement of *community interest;* the electorate is supposed to come to political decisions on consideration of the common good rather than, or in addition to, self-interest.

In several formulations of democratic theory, the electorate is required to devote thought to what is good for the community as a whole instead of relying exclusively upon calculation of what is good for oneself or one's own group. The classical formulation comes from John Stuart Mill: "In any political election . . . the voter is under an absolute moral obligation to consider the interests of the public, not his private advantage, and give his vote, to the best of his judgment, exactly as he would be bound to do if he were the sole voter, and the election depended upon him alone."

Now here again the problem of definition is a central one. How is the researcher to distinguish between honest conclusion and forced rationalization, as in the slogan, "What's good for me is good for the country"? How distinguish the "immediate and apparent interest" from the "ultimate and real interest"? Does self-interest refer only to the criterion of direct self-gain or to that of benefit to one's group or class, and over what period of time? Does community interest refer to agreement on procedures, or to an outside criterion (and if so, what), or to the residual decision after the various self-interests have balanced themselves out, or to genuine concern for other groups, or to restraint upon self-interest, or to deviation from the predominant vote of one's group? The more one looks into the matter, the more it appears that one man's self-interest is another man's community interest, and that many people sincerely identify the one with the other. Nor have the theorists overlooked this. "Men come easily to believe that arrangements agreeable to themselves are beneficial to others," said Dicey. "A man's interest gives a bias to his judgment far oftener than it corrupts his heart." And from Schumpeter: "To different individuals and groups the common good is bound to mean different things. This fact, hidden from the utilitarian by the narrowness of his outlook on the world of human valuations, will introduce rifts on questions of principle which cannot be reconciled by rational argument."

In a current study of opinion formation (the Elmira study), we concluded that it is more satisfactory to analyze this question in terms of the forces making for political cleavage and political consensus within the community. The health of a democratic order depends on achieving a nice balance between them: enough cleavage to stimulate debate and action, enough consensus to hold the society together even under strain. Political parties in a democracy should disagree—but not too much, too sharply, nor too fundamentally. The evidences of cleavage are clear to everyone. Cleavage along class and religious and regional lines in addition to direct attitudinal differences on basic issues of foreign and domestic policy— these are so familiar as to require no elaboration. At the same time there are important evidences of consensus, of political cohesion, which deserve more attention than they usually get. In the first place, there is the basic fact that group memberships and identifications overlap political choices; sizable political minorities are found in various social groups and this provides a kind of glue to hold the community together. In addition, even at the height of a presidential campaign there are sizable attitudinal minorities within each party and each social group on political issues, and thus sizable attitudinal agreements across party and group lines. Such overlappings link various groups together and prevent their further estrangement. All of this means that democratic politics in this country is happily not total politics—a situation where politics is the single or central selector and rejector, where other social differences are drawn on top of political lines. Cross-pressures in political allegiances, based upon a pluralistic system of values, are thus highly important to the society.

So the question of self and community interest may best be seen as the question of cleavage and consensus. The multiplicity and the heterogeneity of identifications and associations in the great society develop an overlapping, pluralistic social organization which both sharpens and softens the impact and the consequences of political activity.

Conclusion

The political theory of democracy, then, requires that the electorate possess appropriate personality structures, that it be interested and participate in public affairs, that it be informed, that it be principled, that it correctly perceive political realities, that it engage in discussion, that it judge rationally, and that it consider the community interest.

Now this combination of requirements sets a high—an ideal—standard for the political process. And since this is a composite list, from a variety of sources, it is not necessarily a matter for disillusionment or even disappointment that the democratic electorate does not conform to every requirement in the full degree. There is always an appropriate observation from Lord Bryce:

"Orthodox political theory assumes that every citizen has, or ought to have, thought out for himself certain opinions, for example, ought to have a definite view, defensible by arguments, of what the country needs, what principles ought to be applied in governing it, of the men to whose hands the government ought to be entrusted. There are persons who talk, though certainly very few who act, as if they believed this theory, which may be compared to the theory of some ultra-Protestants that every good Christian has or ought to have, by the strength of his own reason, worked out for himself from the Bible a system of theology."

Opinion studies in recent years have done much to fill in the picture of what actually happens in democratic decision-making. As is evident even from this brief survey, they have done so in three ways: first, by documenting the theoretical assumptions with facts about actual political behavior; second, by clarifying the concepts and assumptions of democratic theory, if in no other way simply by insisting upon researchable formulations; and third, by differentiating and reformulating the general theoretical propositions in more exact terms. Further systematic exploration of this subject within a sharper, more valid, and more sophisticated framework of political theory should make a rich contribution to each side. The difficulties of collaboration between political theorists on the one hand and opinion researchers on the other must not be allowed to stand in the way of joint work, for the theorists can provide a systematic statement in terms of which public opinion studies can be meaningfully organized, and the empirical researchers can document the theoretical requirements. The theorists can suggest new concepts and hypotheses to the researcher, and the researcher can force the theorists to sharpen and differentiate—yes, and quantify—their formulations.

Of course there are problems but they should be negotiated or overcome. For example, the theorists tend to use descriptive categories (e.g., rationality) and the researchers prefer predictive categories (e.g., group memberships) in "explaining" political preferences. Hard and joint thinking on such problems should bring returns.

The investigation of the realities of democratic processes at the level of the electorate is a useful service and it should be carried forward. Opinion studies can help a democracy not only to know itself in a topical and immediate way but also to evaluate its achievement and its progress in more general terms. In this framework, the study of public opinion can make a telling contribution in the basic, continous struggle to bring democratic practice more and more into harmony with the requirements and the assumptions—that is, with the ideals—of democratic theory.

NOTES

1. Included here is acceptance of the political sphere as one of the legitimate elements of social life. In a democratic society the political sphere must not be widely viewed as unclean or degraded or corrupt. Opinion studies have produced some data on the image of politics and of politicians among the citizenry.

EDWARD A. SHILS

Mass Society and Its Culture

Mass Society: Consensus, Civility, Individuality

A MASS ORDER of society has taken form since the end of the World War
I in the United States, above all, but also in Great Britain, France,
Northern Italy, the Low and Northern European countries, and Japan.
Some of its features have begun to appear in Eastern and Central Europe,
though in a less even manner; more incipiently and prospectively so, in
Asian and African countries. It is the style to refer to this new order as
the "mass society."

This new order of society, despite all its internal conflicts, discloses
in the individual a greater sense of attachment to the society as a whole,
and of affinity with his fellows. As a result, perhaps for the first time in
history, large aggregations of human beings living over an extensive
territory have been able to enter into relatively free and uncoerced association.

The new society is a mass society precisely in the sense that the mass
of the population has become incorporated *into* society. The center of
society—the central institutions, and the central value systems which guide
and legitimate these institutions—has extended its boundaries. Most of the
population (the "mass") now stands in a closer relationship to the center
than has been the case in either premodern societies or in the earlier
phases of modern society. In previous societies, a substantial portion of the
population, often the majority, were born and forever remained "outsiders."

The mass society is a new phenomenon, but it has been long in gesta-

Reprinted from *Culture for the Millions*, Norman Jacobs, editor, (1959) pp.
1–27, by permission of the author and the publisher. (Copyright, 1959, D.
Van Nostrand.)

tion. The idea of the *polis* is its seed, nurtured and developed in the Roman idea of a common citizenship extending over a wide territory. The growth of nationality in the modern era has heightened the sense of affinity among the members of different classes and regions of the same country. When the proponents of the modern idea of the nation put forward the view that life on a contiguous, continuous, and common territory—beyond all divisions of kinship, caste, and religious belief— united the human beings living within that territory into a single collectivity, and when they made a common language the evidence of that membership, they committed themselves, not often wittingly, to the mass society.

An important feature of that society is the diminished sacredness of authority, the reduction in the awe it evokes and in the charisma attributed to it. This diminution in the status of authority runs parallel to a loosening of the power of tradition. Naturally, tradition continues to exert influence, but it becomes more open to divergent interpretations, and these frequently lead to divergent courses of action.

The dispersion of charisma from center outward has manifested itself in a greater stress on individual dignity and individual rights. This extension does not always reach into the sphere of the political, but it is apparent in the attitudes toward women, youth, and ethnic groups which have been in a disadvantageous position.

Following from this, one of the features of mass society I should like to emphasize is its wide dispersion of "civility." The concept of civility is not a modern creation, but it is in the mass society that it has found its most complete (though still very incomplete) realization. The very idea of a *citizenry* coterminous with the adult population is one of its signs. So is the moral equalitarianism which is a trait unique to the West, with its insistence that by virtue of their sharing membership in the community and a common tongue men possess a certain irreducible dignity.

None of these characteristic tendencies of mass society has attained anything like full realization. The moral consensus of mass society is certainly far from complete; the mutual assimilation of center (i.e., the elite) and periphery (i.e., the mass) is still much less than total. Class conflict, ethnic prejudice, and disordered personal relations remain significant factors in our modern mass societies, but without preventing the tendencies I have described from finding an historically unprecedented degree of realization.

Mass society is an industrial society. Without industry, i.e., without the replacement of simple tools by complicated machines, mass society would be inconceivable. Modern industrial techniques, through the creation of an elaborate network of transportation and communication, bring the various parts of mass society into frequent contact. Modern technology has liberated man from the burden of physically exhausting labor, and has given him resources through which new experiences of sensation, conviviality, and introspection have become possible. True, modern industrial organization has also been attended by a measure of hierarchical and bureaucratic organization which often runs contrary to the vital but loose consensus of mass society. Nonetheless, the fact remains that modern mass society has reached out toward a moral consensus and a civil order congruous with the adult population. The sacredness that every man possesses by virtue of his membership in society finds a more far-reaching affirmation than ever before.

Mass society has aroused and enhanced individuality. Individuality is characterized by an openness to experience, an efflorescence of sensation and sensibility, a sensitivity to other minds and personalities. It gives rise to, and lives in, personal attachments; it grows from the expansion of the empathic capacities of the human being. Mass society has liberated the cognitive, appreciative, and moral capacities of individuals. Larger elements of the population have consciously learned to value the pleasures of eye, ear, taste, touch, and conviviality. People make choices more freely in many spheres of life, and these choices are not necessarily made for them by tradition, authority, or scarcity. The value of the experience of personal relationships is more widely appreciated.

These observations are not meant to imply that individuality as developed in mass society exists universally. A part of the population in mass society lives in a nearly vegetative torpor, reacting dully or aggressively to its environment. Nonetheless, the search for individuality and its manifestations in personal relations are distinctly present in mass society and constitute one of its essential features.

The Culture of Mass Society

The fundamental categories of cultural life are the same in all societies. In all the different strata of any given society, the effort to explore and explain the universe, to understand the meaning of events, to enter into contact with the sacred or to commit sacrilege, to affirm the principles of morality and justice and to deny them, to encounter the unknown, to exalt or denigrate authority, to stir the senses by the control of and response to words, sounds, shapes, and colors—these are the basic elements of cultural existence. There are, however, profound variations in the elaboration of these elements, for human beings show marked differences in capacity for expression and reception.

No society can ever achieve a complete cultural consensus: there are natural limitations to the spread of the standards and products of superior culture throughout society. The tradition of refinement is itself replete with antinomies, and the nature of creativity adds to them. Creativity is a modification of tradition. Furthermore, the traditional transmission of superior culture inevitably stirs some to reject and deny significant parts of it, just because it is traditional. More fundamental than the degrees of creativity and alienation is the disparity in human cognitive, appreciative, and moral capacities. This disparity produces marked differences in the apprehension of tradition, in the complexity of the response to it, and in the substance of the judgments aroused by it.

Thus a widely differentiated "dissensus" has become stabilized in the course of history. The pattern of this "dissensus" is not inevitably unchanging. The classes consuming culture may diminish in number, their taste may deteriorate, their standards become less discriminating or more debased. On the other hand, as the mass of the population comes awake when its curiosity and sensibility and its moral responsiveness are aroused, it begins to become capable of a more subtle perception, more appreciative of the more general elements in a concrete representation, and more complex in its aesthetic reception and expression.

THE LEVELS OF CULTURE

For present purposes, we shall employ a very rough distinction among three levels of culture, which are levels of quality measured by aesthetic, intellectual, and moral standards. These are "superior" or "refined" culture, "mediocre" culture, and "brutal" culture.[1]

Superior or refined culture is distinguished by the seriousness of its subject matter, i.e., the centrality of the problems with which it deals, the acute penetration and coherence of its perceptions, the subtlety and wealth of its expressed feeling. The stock of superior culture includes the great works of poetry, novels, philosophy, scientific theory and research, statues, paintings, musical compositions and their performance, the texts and performance of plays, history, economic, social, and political analyses, architecture and works of craftsmanship. It goes without saying that the category of superior culture does not refer to the social status, i.e., the quality of their attainment, of the author or of the consumers of the works in question, but only to their truth and beauty.

The category of mediocre culture includes works which, whatever the aspiration of their creators, do not measure up to the standards employed in judging works of superior culture. Mediocre culture is less original than superior culture; it is more reproductive; it operates largely in the same genres as superior culture, but also in certain relatively novel genres not yet fully incorporated into superior culture, such as the musical comedy. This may be a function of the nature of the genre or of the fact that the genre has not yet attracted great talent to its practice.

At the third level is brutal culture, where symbolic elaboration is of a more elementary order. Some of the genres on this level are identical with those of mediocre and refined culture (pictorial and plastic representation,

508

music, poems, novels, and stories) but they also include games, spectacles (such as boxing and horse racing) and more directly expressive actions with a minimal symbolic content. The depth of penetration is almost always negligible, subtlety is almost entirely lacking, and a general grossness of sensitivity and perception is a common feature.

The greatest difference among the three levels of culture, apart from intrinsic quality, is the tremendous disparity in the richness of the stock available in any society at any given time. What any given society possesses is not only what it creates in its own generation but also what it has received from antecedent generations and from earlier and contemporaneous generations of other societies. Superior culture is immeasurably richer in content because it contains not only superior contemporary production but also much of the refined production of earlier epochs. Mediocre culture tends to be poorer, not only because of the poorer quality of what it produces in its own generation, but because these cultural products have a relatively shorter life span. Nevertheless, mediocre culture contains much that has been created in the past. The boundaries between mediocre and superior culture are not so sharp, and the custodians of superior culture are not so discriminating as always to reject the mediocre. Furthermore, a considerable amount of mediocre culture retains value over long periods; and even though mediocre taste varies, as does superior taste, there are stable elements in it, too, so that some of the mediocre culture of the past continues to find an appreciative audience.

At the lowest cultural level, where the symbolic content is most impoverished and where there is very little original creation in each generation, we come again to a greater, if much less self-conscious, dependence on the past. Games, jokes, spectacles, and the like continue traditional patterns with little consciousness of their traditionality. If the traditional element in brutal culture has been large, this is due to the relatively low creative capacities of those who produce and consume it. Here, until recently, there has been little professional production, machinery for preservation and transmission is lacking, and oral transmission plays a greater part in maintaining traditions of expression and performance than with superior and mediocre cultures.

THE MAGNITUDES: CONSUMPTION

The quantity of culture consumed in mass society is certainly greater than in any other epoch, even if we make proper allowance for the larger populations of the mass societies at present. It is especially at the level of mediocre and brutal culture that an immense expansion has occurred, but the consumption of superior culture has also increased.

The grounds for this great increase, and for the larger increase in the two lower categories, are not far to seek. The most obvious are greater availability, increased leisure time, the decreased physical demands of work, the greater affluence of the classes which once worked very hard for long hours for small income, increased literacy, enhanced individuality, and more unabashed hedonism. In all these, the middle and the lower classes have gained more than have the elites (including the intellectuals, whatever their occupational distribution).

The consumption of superior culture has increased, too, but not as much as the other two categories, because the intellectual classes were more nearly saturated before the age of mass society. Moreover, the institutions of superior culture—the collections of connoisseurs, academies, universities, libraries, publishing houses, periodicals—were more elaborately and more continuously established in the pre-mass society than were the institutions which made mediocre and brutal culture available to their consumers.

Thus in mass society the proportion of the total stock of cultural objects held by superior culture has shrunk, and correspondingly the share of mediocre and brutal culture has grown.[2]

NOTE ON THE VALUE OF MEDIOCRE AND
BRUTAL CULTURE

Mediocre culture has many merits. It often has elements of genuine conviviality, not subtle or profound perhaps, but genuine in the sense of being spontaneous and honest. It is often very good fun. Moreover, it is often earnestly, even if simply, moral. Mediocre culture, too, has its traditions; many of the dramas and stories which regale the vulgar have a long history hidden from those who tell and enjoy them. Like anything traditional, they express something essential in human life, and expunging them would expunge the accumulated wisdom of ordinary men and women, their painfully developed art of coping with the miseries of existence, their routine pieties and their decent pleasures.

There is much ridicule of *Kitsch*, and it *is* ridiculous. Yet it represents aesthetic sensibility and aesthetic aspiration, untutored, rude, and deformed. The very growth of *Kitsch*, and of the demand which has generated the industry for the production of *Kitsch*, is an indication of a crude aesthetic awakening in classes which previously accepted what was handed down to them or who had practically no aesthetic expression and reception.

The Reproduction and Transmission of Culture

In medieval society, the church and, to a less effective and more limited degree, the schools (which were immediate or indirect adjuncts of the church) brought the culture of the center into the peripheral areas of a very loosely integrated society.[3] Protestantism and printing led to a pronounced change which showed the direction of the future. The cheapened access to the printed word and the spread of a minimal literacy (which became nearly universal within European societies only at the beginning of the present century) resulted in an expansion of each of the three strata of culture. In this expansion, the chief beneficiaries were mediocre and brutal culture.

The increased wealth, leisure, and literacy of the lower classes, and the flowering of hedonism which these permitted, would undoubtedly have produced the great expansion in mediocre and brutal—as well as superior—cultural consumption, even without the further technological developments of communication in the twentieth century. This technological development did, however, supply a mighty additional impetus. The popular press of the last decades of the nineteenth century showed the way. The development of new methods of graphic reproduction in lithography and in both still and moving pictures, new methods of sound recording and the transmission of sound and picture, increased the flow of communication from the center to the periphery. Where previously the custodians of superior culture and its mediocre variants had nearly a monopoly—through their quasi-monopoly of the institutions of transmission—the new methods of mass communication have transformed the situation.

The quest for a larger audience, which would make it feasible to obtain a subsidy (in the form of advertising) to cover the difference between what the consumers pay and what it costs to produce cultural objects, has been of the greatest importance to the interrelations of the various strata of culture. The dependence of the subsidy on greatly extended consumption would in itself have required a reaching-out toward a heterogeneous audience. The increased overhead of communication enterprises in television, for example, as compared with book printing, has intensified the need for large and heterogeneous audiences.

Before the emergence of the most recent forms of mass communication, with their very large capital requirements, each stratum of culture had its own channels and institutions. As long as books were the chief means of impersonal cultural transmission, the cultural segregation of the classes could be easily maintained. The drive toward a maximum audience has helped change this, and the change has had momentous repercussions. The magazine is the embodiment of this new development. The form of the magazine is an eighteenth-century phenomenon; but the enlargement of its role in the reproduction and transmission of culture is the product of the latter-day need to gain the maximum audience, one in its turn impelled by the economic necessity of the subsidy. To speak to the largest possible audience, it has been necessary to make the content of what is transmitted in a single issue as heterogeneous as the audience sought.

The general principle of providing something for everyone in the family became well established in the first decades of the popular press. The principle was developed to the point where every class which could possibly increase the total audience was offered something. This principle has not succeeded in dominating the entire field. There are still specialized organs and institutions which seek to please only one particular stratum of consumers, and in Europe the tradition of a unitary public still persists— but even there not without making very substantial concessions to the new principle. Even the universities (which do not necessarily seek large numbers) in Europe, although not as much as in America, have also diversified their programs in order to meet the diversified demand. In popular periodicals like *Time, Life, Look, Picture Post, Match, Der Spiegel, Esquire*, and in distinguished daily newspapers like *The New York Times*, and recently, even in a cumbersome way, *The Times* of London, there is an intermixture of superior, mediocre, and brutal culture which is historically unique. The same can be observed in television and, of course, in the film: a single network presents a wide variety of levels, and films of genuinely high artistic and intellectual merit may be produced in the same studio which produces numerous mediocre and brutal films.

The Consumption of Culture

In modern society, the number of consumers of superior culture has never been very large; in premodern societies, it was even smaller. The chief consumers of works of superior culture are the intellectuals, i.e., those whose occupations require intellectual preparation, and in practice, the application of high intellectual skills. In the contemporary world this category includes university teachers, scientists, university students, writers, artists, secondary-school teachers, members of the learned professions (law, medicine, and the church), journalists, and higher civil servants, as well as a scattering of businessmen, engineers, and army officers.

Outside the intellectual occupations, where the largest number are found, the consumers of superior culture are spread thin and at random. This situation has probably never been different, even in periods when the princes of the church were patrons of painting and sculpture, or when in most grand-bourgeois households one coud find sets of Goethe, Nietzsche, Fielding, the memoirs of Sully, or the letters of Mme. de Sévigné.

The political, technological, military, ecclesiastical, and economic elites have not usually been intellectuals, even though their members have had intellectual training and followed intellectual careers before entering their particular profession. Politician and intellectual come closest in regimes just established by revolution or by a successful nationalist movement (their quality as intellectuals, however, is usually not particularly distinguished). In established political regimes, although there may be a significant number of politicians who were once intellectuals of a respectable level, over a long period the demands of the profession of politics leave little time, strength, or sensitivity for the continued consumption of intellectual goods.

Among the leading Western countries, it is in the United States that the political elite gives a preponderant impression of indifference toward works of superior culture. The situation is probaby not very different in Great Britain, France, Germany or Italy—though there, the political elite, living amidst aristocratic and patrician traditions, possesses an external gloss of intimacy with high culture. In the United States, however, despite Woodrow Wilson, Franklin Roosevelt, the Plutarch-reading Harry Truman, and the *De re metallica*-editing Herbert Hoover, the political elite gives a definitely unintellectual impression.

The same is true of the American plutocracy: as a body of collectors of the works of painting and sculpture and as patrons of learning, it will take an outstanding place in the history of the great Maecenases. Yet the dominant impression is one of indifference and inhospitality to intellectual work. The great industrial system of the United States has required a large corps of engineers and applied scientists, men of great imagination and even high creativity; yet their cultural consumption (not only of superior culture but also of mediocre culture) is rather small. The vigor and pre-eminence of these sectors of the American elite, and the conventions of the media of information through which their public image is formed, fortify intellectuals with the sense that they alone in their society are concerned with superior culture.

Among the middle classes the consumption of the traditional genres of superior culture is not large. Popular periodicals, best-selling novels, political books of transient interest, inferior poetry, inspirational works of theology and moral edification and biographies—these made up and still make up the bulk of their consumption. More recently, the films and radio, and most recently, television, have provided the substance of their cultural consumption. Their fare is largely philistine—mediocre culture and brutal culture. Nonetheless, because of exposure to the "mass media," e.g., periodicals like *Life* and a narrow band of the output on television, film, and radio, a large section of these classes has come into contact with and consumed a larger quantity of extra-religious, superior culture than has been the case throughout the course of modern history.

Finally, the industrial working class and the rural population remain to be considered. Together, these classes consume almost nothing of the inheritance and current production of superior culture. Very little mediocre culture of the conventional genres reaches them except in such periodicals as *Life, Look,* and *The Reader's Digest.* Much of their culture as transmitted by mass media is brutal—crime films and television spectacles, paperbacks of violence, pornographic oral and printed literature, and the culture of the world of sports.

It would be a mistake, however, to think that the culture possessed by these classes is exhausted by what comes to them through the mass media. A large amount of traditional religious culture (and of sectarian variants of traditional religious culture) flourishes in all the nonintellectual classes. Much of regional and class culture, maintained by family, by colleagues, neighbors, and friends and by local institutions, survives and is unlikely to be supplanted by the larger culture which emanates from the center. This places limits on what is incorporated from the current flow of the mass media.[4]

A special stratum of the population that cuts across all classes and gives a particular tone to mass society is the younger generation, the maligned and bewildering "youth." The coming forth of youth in contemporary society rests on primordial foundations which exist in all societies. In most societies, however, the institutional structure and the niggardliness of nature have kept youth in check. In modern times, romanticism and increased wealth and (more deeply) the expanding radius of empathy and fellow-feeling have given youth opportunities never before available. The enhanced productivity of the economy of Western countries has, on the one hand, allowed young people to remain outside the hard grind of work for a longer time; it has given them opportunities to earn and spend substantial individual incomes. The resulting cultural manifestations are largely responsible for what is called "mass culture."

Before the advent of mass society, a small proportion of the youth were rigorously inculcated with superior culture; the rest were exposed to the brutal culture of their seniors. It is one of the marks of mass society, however, that youth has become a major consumer of the special variants of mediocre and brutal culture that are produced for transmission through the mass media. An extraordinary quantity of popular music, mediocre and brutal films, periodical literature, and forms of dance is produced for and consumed by youth. This is something unprecedented, and this is the heart of the revolution of mass culture.

Most of the "youthful mass" comes from strata of society which have had little connection except through religious education with high or superior culture. Not yet enmeshed in the responsibilities of family and civic life, and with much leisure time and purchasing power, youth constitutes both an eager and a profitable public which attracts the attention of the mass media. The eagerness of youth for the mediocre and brutal culture provided by the mass media, and that youth's own creative poverty are a universal phenomenon. Where the political elite does not grant this eagerness the right of direct expression, but seeks instead to divert it into ideological channels or to dam it up, it still remains powerful and indomitable. Where the political order allows this passionate and uncultivated vitality to find a free expression, the result is what we see throughout the Western world.

The Production of Culture

THE HIGH INTELLIGENTSIA

A differentiated creative intelligentsia is the oldest stratum of Western society with a set of continuous traditions. Such a stratum still exists today, far broader than ever before, far more extended and with international ties exceeding that of any other section of our own or any other society.[5] There is today more internal specialization than in the past: it is impossible for any one man to be fully conversant with the inherited and currently produced stock of cultural objects. The productive intelligentsia is perhaps less intensely like-minded now than in the past, when it was smaller and the body of what it had to master was smaller. Nonetheless, despite changes in society, in the modes of financial support and in the organization of intellectual life, this creative stratum is constantly reproducing and increasing.

THE MEDIOCRE INTELLIGENTSIA

The modern age, however, has seen growing up alongside this creative intelligentsia a much larger stratum of producers of mediocre culture. In the seventeenth and eighteenth centuries, when letters and the arts began to offer the possibilities of a professional career, thanks to the advance of printing and to an enlarging public, there emerged, besides those whose creative capacities achieved the heights of greatness, a wider group of writers, artists, and scholars. From these were recruited the residents of Grub Street, who, while still trying to reach the highest levels, had to live by producing for a less discriminating public. The nineteenth century saw the stabilization of the profession of those who produced almost exclusively for the public that consumed mediocre culture. The popular press, the film, radio, and television have deepened and extended their ranks. The enlargement of university populations and the corresponding increase in the number of university teachers, the increased opportunities for careers in research, in the applied natural and social sciences, have similarly added to the producers of mediocre culture.[6]

The professional practitioner with a mediocre culture has developed traditions, models, and standards of his own. More frequently than in the past he engages directly in the professional production of mediocre culture without first essaying the production of works of superior culture. He can attain an excellence within his own field that often brings him satisfaction and esteem. Indeed, in certain genres of mediocre culture that

515

are new or at least relatively new, he can reach heights of unprecedented excellence, to the point where, if the genre is admissible, his work can take on the lineaments of superior cultural achievement.

Yet despite this approximation to autonomy, the autonomy remains incomplete. The producer of mediocre culture is exposed to the standards of superior culture, and he cannot entirely escape their pressure. If he prospers and his colleagues on the level of superior culture do not, then he is guilt-ridden for having "betrayed" higher standards for the sake of the fleshpots.

This troubling juxtaposition of two consciences is rendered more acute by the physical juxtaposition of the two levels of cultural objects and the social contact of their producers in the media through which mediocre culture chiefly finds its audience, namely, the media of mass communication. The professionals of mediocre culture cannot, even if they would, forget the standards of superior culture, because they mix with persons who often attain them, because the media from time to time present works composed according to those standards, and because critics continually refer to them. These factors provide an increasing stimulus to an awareness of and a concern for high standards, even when they are not observed.

THE BRUTAL INTELLIGENTSIA

The producers of brutal culture confront a quite different situation. They have neither a similarly compelling historical past nor the connections with superior culture which their "colleagues" in the field of mediocre culture possess. They do not, so far as I know, justify their performance by reference to the great masters of their art. There are some exceptions among crime-story writers, boxers, jockeys, and certainly among a few of the best sports writers. But these are new professions. Their practitioners feel no continuity with their forerunners, even though the objects they produce have been produced for a long time. Brutal culture therefore has only recently developed a differentiated professional personnel.

Brutal culture has not shown great potentialities for development. Nonetheless, certain genres of brutal culture have produced works of great excellence, so that these reach through mediocre culture into the outer confines of superior culture. Some works of pornography have found a place in superior culture, some horror stories have done the same, as have the chronicles of sports. Since brutal culture is by no means restricted to the uncultivated classes for its audience, works of brutal culture, which reach a form of high refinement, also make their way upward, and with them, their producers move in the same direction. In the main however, there is a wall which separates the producers of brutal culture from the producers of superior culture. Even where they find the same audience, the tradition of superior culture is such as to erect a barrier to a massive interpenetration.[7]

A few words should be said here about another kind of cultural production: the anonymous production of folk art and literature and linguistic innovation. In their highest manifestations, the production of these arts was probably never very widely spread. They grow on the edge of craftsmanship, of religious worship and of brutal entertainment. Considerable creative talents must have impelled them into existence. Their creators must have been men of genius, working with subterranean traditions that scarcely exist any more, and that had only a small direct connection with the great tradition of superior culture. In so far as they were inspired by craftsmanship, machine production has greatly restricted their emergence; the traditions which sustained them have atrophied.

It is sometimes asserted that the anonymous cultural production of craftsmen and peasants in the Europe of the later Middle Ages and of early modern times has been destroyed by the growth of mass culture. This is possible, but it is not the only possibility. If we assume that the proportion of geniuses and outstandingly gifted intelligences and sensibilities in any population remains fairly constant (not an unreasonable assumption) and that modern Western societies with their increasing cultivation of science, literature, art, enterprise, administration, and technology have been drawing more and more on their reservoirs of talent, then it appears quite plausible to assert that the talents of the type once manifested in the anonymous productions of folk culture have been recruited and diverted into other spheres and are active at different levels of culture and social life.

The Position of Superior Culture in Mass Society

Has the culture created in the past forty years—the approximate age of mass society—deteriorated as much as its detractors claim? The task of assessment is most difficult.

Let us for the moment grant that contemporary refined culture may be poorer than the superior culture produced in any comparable span of years in the past. There may be any number of reasons or causes, totally unrelated to the development and impact of mass society on culture. For example, the distribution and efflorescence of genius are matters that still await full understanding. It is conceivable, if unlikely, that our neural equipment is poorer than that of our ancestors. And even if it is as good, it is also possible that our cultural traditions have passed their point of culmination, that they contain no possibilities of further development, that

517

they offer no point of departure even for creative minds. Another important consideration is whether the alleged deterioration is being evaluated in the light of standards that are applied equally to other periods. We must be sure to comprehend in our assessment the whole range of intellectual and artistic activities. We must remember that the genius which is expressed in refined culture may be of diverse forms, and that it can flow into some domains in one age, and into other domains in other ages.

Yet these might be idle reflections. The evidence of decline is not by any means very impressive. In every field of science and scholarship into which so much of our contemporary genius flows (in physics, chemistry, and in mathematics, in biology and neurology, in logic, linguistics, and anthropology, in comparative religion, in Sinology and Indology), outstanding work is being done, not only in the older centers not yet afflicted by the culture of mass society, but in the United States as well, that most massive of all mass societies. Theology seems to be in a more vital and powerful state than it has been for several centuries. Economics proceeds on a high level, higher on the average than in past periods; sociology, barbarous, rude, and so often trivial, offers at its best something which no past age can match in the way of discovery and penetration. In political philosophy, in which our decay is said to be so patent, we have no Aristotle, Hobbes, or Bentham, but there are probably only a half dozen such masters in all human history. On the other hand, in France and America there are men and women who are at least as deep and rigorous in their analysis of central issues as John Stuart Mill or Walter Bagehot or de Tocqueville were. In the novel, we have no Tolstoy, no Stendhal or Dostoievsky or Flaubert; still, the level of achievement is high. In poetry and in painting, there may indeed have been a falling-off from the great heights; in drama there is no Aeschylus, no Shakespeare, no Racine. But these are among the highest peaks of all human history, and the absence of any such from our two-fifths of a century can scarcely constitute evidence of a general decline in the quality of the products of superior culture in our own time.

That there is, however, a consciousness of decline is undeniable. Intellectuals are beset by a malaise, by a sense of isolation, of disregard, of a lack of sympathy. They feel they have lost contact with their audiences, especially that most important of all audiences, those who rule society. This is nothing new. Romanticism is still far from dead, and it is a cardinal tenet of romanticism that the creative person is cut off from his own society and especially from its rulers. The contemporary romantic intellectual has in addition an acute sense of being cut off from the people.

The noisy, visible, tangible presence of mediocre and brutal culture has heightened his anguish. Whereas intellectuals in earlier ages of modern society could remain ignorant of the cultural preferences of those who consumed cultural objects other than their own, this is not really possible

518

for contemporary intellectuals. By virtue of their own relations to production, the vigor with which mediocre and brutal cultures are promoted,
and the evident enjoyment of their consumers, intellectuals are forced to
be familiar with what takes place on these levels of culture.

But what are the specific threats to superior culture in mass society?
To what extent do they differ from earlier dangers? To what extent do
these dangers derive from mass society itself? For superior culture is and
has always been in danger. Since it never is and never has been the culture
of an entire society, it must necessarily be in a state of tension *vis-à-vis*
the rest of society. If the producers and consumers of superior culture
see further and deeper than their contemporaries, if they have a more
subtle and more lively sensitivity, if they do not accept the received traditions and the acknowledged deities of their fellow countrymen, whatever they say or believe or discover is bound to create tension.

Are intellectuals more endangered in the age of mass society by the
jealousy and distrust of the powerful than in other social eras? Surely,
censorship, arrest, and exile are nothing new. Can the occasional anti-
intellectual flurries of American politicians and businessmen be equated
with the restraints imposed on intellectuals in Soviet Russia, Fascist Spain,
or National Socialist Germany? None of these countries, it should be
noted, are or were mass societies in the sense that the contemporary
United States is, or as the United Kingdom, Western Germany, and
France are becoming. Does the role played by advertising on the television
screen represent a greater intrusion into the creative sphere than did the
prosecutions of Flaubert and Baudelaire in nineteenth-century France, or
the moral censorship which Mrs. Grundy used to exercise so coarsely in
the United States and which she still does in Britain, or the political and
religious censorship practiced in eighteenth-century France? Athenian
society was no mass society, and there were no advertisers there, yet
Socrates was executed. I do not wish to belittle the present or recent
attacks on intellectual or artistic liberty in the United States, but I do wish
to stress that they are not unique to mass society.

It is sometimes asserted that the culture of mass society produces its
insidious effects in roundabout ways that constitute a greater danger than
the crude external pressures employed by the rulers of earlier societies. It
seduces, it is said, rather than constrains. It offers opportunities for large
incomes to those who agree to the terms of employment offered by institutions of mediocre and brutal culture. But does this opportunity, and
even its acceptance, necessarily damage superior culture? The mere existence of the opportunity will not seduce a man of strongly impelled
creative capacities, once he has found his direction. And if he does accept
the opportunity, are his creative talents inevitably stunted? Is there no
chance at all that they will find expression in the mass medium to which he
is drawn? The very fact that here and there in the mass media, on tele-

519

vision and in the film, work of superior quality is to be seen, seems to be evidence that genuine talent is not inevitably squandered once it leaves the traditional refined media.

It is, of course, possible for men to waste their talents, to corrupt themselves for the pleasures of office, for the favor of authority, for popularity, or for income or for the simple pleasure of self-destruction. Qualitatively, the financial temptations of work in the media of mass communication are of the same order as the other temptations intellectuals encounter. Quantitatively, it is difficult to estimate the magnitude of the temptation. There are certainly more opportunities now for intellectuals to earn much money in the production of mediocre and brutal cultural objects than there were before the development of the mass media. It is clear, however, that the large majority of literary men, poets, scholars, painters, scientists, or teachers have not been tempted nor have they yielded to the temptation—even if we concede, which we do not, that their experience in the mass media prevents them from finding creative expression either in the mass media or outside them.

Popularization is sometimes cited as one of the ways in which superior culture is being eroded. Does the contact between mediocre and refined culture which occurs in popularization do damage to refined culture? Raymond Aron's thought does not deteriorate because he occasionally writes in *The New York Times Magazine* and much more frequently in *Le Figaro;* Bertrand Russell suffers no injury from an article in *Look Magazine.* There is no reason why gifted intellectuals should lose their powers because they write for audiences unable to comprehend their ordinary level of analysis and exposition. An intellectual who devotes all his efforts to popularization would soon cease to have anything of his own to popularize and would have to become a popularizer of the works of other persons. But there is no convincing evidence that persons who are capable of refined cultural production and who are strongly impelled to it are being gradually drawn away from their calling by the temptations of popularization. What has been the loss to American, British, and French science in the past forty years from the development of the new branch of journalism which is involved in scientific popularization?

The production of mediocre or brutal culture need not (so the argument goes) destroy superior culture by striking at its producers, either constrainingly or seductively. It can deprive them of their market, and especially of the discriminating appreciation they need to keep their skills at the highest pitch. The corruption of public taste, of those consumers whose natural discriminative powers are not so great that they can dispense with the cultivation which a refined cultural environment provides, is certainly a possibility. In contrast to this possibility, however, is the fact that in the United States today discrimination in a small minority (certainly no smaller than at the end of the nineteenth century or in England today) is as acutely perceptive as it ever was. The quality of literary criticism in *The Partisan Review, The Hudson Review, The Sewanee Review*, and *The New Yorker* is as informed, as penetrating, and as reflective as it was fifty years ago in the best American or British periodicals.

The demand for the products of mediocre and brutal culture certainly affects the market for the products of superior culture. If there were no inferior cultural products available and if the purchasing power were there, there certainly would be a larger body of purchasers of the products of superior culture. This was the situation in Britain during the war, and it is probably the situation in the Soviet Union today. As to whether this represents an improvement in public taste is another matter. In Britain, after the war, once inferior cultural objects became available in larger supply, the prosperity of serious booksellers markedly declined. The same would probably occur in the Soviet Union if a larger range of consumer goods, cultural and other, were to enter the market.

Therefore, when public demand is free to obtain the objects it desires, the market for superior cultural objects, given the present distribution of tastes, is restricted, and enterprisers with capital to invest will not rush in to use their resources in areas of the market where the return is relatively poor. Yet are there many manuscripts of books of outstanding merit lying unpublished today?

The relative unprofitability of the market for superior cultural objects is compensated for in part by the existence of enterprises motivated by other than profit considerations. There is no reason to assume that such uneconomically oriented investors will be fewer in the future than in the recent past. In part, the unprofitability of the market is circumvented by subsidy or patronage.

We often hear the old system of patronage praised by those who bemoan its passing. It is well to remember, however, what misery and humiliation it imposed on its beneficiaries, how capricious and irregular it was, and how few were affected by it during the period from the seventeenth to the nineteenth centuries when intellectuals were growing in numbers. Many more were supported by administrative sinecures in church and state.

The private patronage of individual intellectuals by individual patrons still exists, but it plays a scant role. The place of this older form of subsidy has been taken over by the universities, the state, and the private foundations, and they appear to be more lavish, more generous, and more just than their predecessors were in earlier centuries.

There is, however, a major deficiency in the institutional system of high culture in the United States, one that can be largely attributed to the successful competition among the best of the newer organs of mass communication. America lacks a satisfactory intellectual weekly press, and, ironically, this is in part the achievement of *Time Magazine. The Nation*

521

and *The New Republic*, which thirty years ago provided something quite comparable in journalistic and intellectual quality to *The Spectator*, have declined in quality and influence.

The absence of a passable intellectual weekly[8] does damage to American intellectual life. The country is so large and the intellectuals so scattered that a continuous focus on intellectual concerns (including the evaluation of political and economic affairs in a manner acceptable to a sophisticated, intellectual public) would serve invaluably to maintain standards of judgment and to provide a common universe of discourse.[9] There is a danger in the United States today of a centrifugal force within the intellectual classes, arising from their numbers, their spatial dispersion and their professional specialization. These factors tend to weaken the sense of community among our intellectual classes. Without this sense of community, the attachment to high standards might slacken or even collapse altogether.

Puritanism, Provincialism, and Specialization

If the arguments of those who attribute to mass society the alleged misery of contemporary culture are not sound, there is no gainsaying the fact that the consumption of superior culture does not rest in a perfectly secure position in the United States. The culture of the educated classes, who in America as elsewhere should be its bearers, leaves much to be desired. One is distressed by the boorish and complacent ignorance of university graduates, by the philistine distrust of or superciliousness toward superior culture which is exhibited by university professors in the humanities and social sciences or in the medical and law schools of this country, and by journalists and broadcasters. The political, economic, military, and technological elites are no better. The near illiteracy of some of the better American newspapers, the oftentimes raucous barbarism of our weeklies and our one widely circulated fortnightly, the unletteredness of many of our civil servants, the poverty of our bookshops, the vulgarity of our publishers (or at least those who write their jacket blurbs and their advertising copy) can give little comfort.

There is undeniably much that is wrong with the quality of culture consumed by the more or less educated classes in America. Very little of what is wrong, however, can be attributed to the mass media, particularly to the films, television, radio, and popular magazines.

It is not that the cascade of mediocre and brutal culture which pours out over the mass media is admirable. Quite the contrary. The culture of the mass media is not, however, the reason that the distribution and consumption of superior culture disclose (alongside so many profoundly impressive achievements) many things that are repellent.

522

What is wrong, is wrong with our intellectuals and their institutions and with some of our cultural traditions, which have little to do with the culture created for and presented by the mass media.

The dour Puritanism that looked on aesthetic expression as self-indulgence does not grow out of mass society. Nor does the complacent and often arrogant provincialism that distrusts refined culture because it believes it to be urban, Anglophile, and connected with a patrician upper class. America was not a mass society in the nineteenth century, it was a differentiated society in which pronounced equalitarian sentiments often took on a populistic form. Certain tendencies which have culminated in a mass society were at work in it. However, much of its culture, although mediocre and brutal, was not produced by the institutions or by the professional personnel now producing the culture of mass society.

Refined culture in nineteenth-century America, reflecting the taste of the cultivated classes of New England and the Middle Atlantic States, did not enjoy a hospitable reception in the Middle West, as a result of the usual hostility of province against metropolis and of those who arrived later in America against those who arrived earlier and who became established sooner. American provincial culture in the nineteenth century was a variant of the British provincial dissenting culture that Matthew Arnold criticized unsparingly in *Culture and Anarchy*. Whereas this culture collapsed in England after World War I, in America it has continued powerful almost up to the present.

These are some of the special reasons for the present uncongeniality of superior culture to so many Americans. It springs from a general distrust that superior culture must always encounter in any society. In this country it expresses itself with greater strength, virulence, and freedom because the political and economic elites of American society feel little obligation to assume a veneer of refined culture, as in Great Britain and France.

Against this background of tradition and sentiment, the development of education in the United States in the past decades has created a technical intelligentsia that does not form a coherent intellectual community. While secondary education became less intellectual in its content and undergraduate education dissipated itself in courses of study of very low intensity and little discipline, a very superior and vigorous type of postgraduate education developed. In trying to make up for lost ground and in seeking to make a deep and thorough penetration into a rapidly growing body of knowledge, postgraduate training in each discipline has had to become highly specialized.

This impetus toward specialization has been heightened by the natural development of science and by the growth of the percentage of the population that pursues postgraduate studies. The development of science has greatly increased the volume of literature a student must cover in each discipline; the increasing number of students, and the necessity for each to do a piece of research no one has ever done before have tended to narrow the concentration within the discipline imposed by the internal evolution of the subject.[10]

The product of these educational and scientific developments has been the specialist who is uncultivated outside his own specialty. Except for those strong and expansive personalities whose curiosity and sensitivity lead them to the experience of what their education has failed to give them, even the creative American scientist, scholar, or technologist often possesses only a narrow range of mediocre culture.

The ascent of the universities to preponderance in the life of superior culture in the United States, and increasingly (though still not to the same extent) in Europe, has meant that trends within the university tend to become the trends of intellectual life as a whole to a much greater degree than in earlier periods of modern society. As the universities have become more internally differentiated and specialized, superior cultural life has also tended to become more specialized.

What we are suffering from is the dissolution of "the educated public," coherent although unorganized, with a taste for superior cultural objects with no vocational import. The "universitization" of superior culture—most advanced in America but already visible in Great Britain, too, though not at all a completely realized tendency—is part of this process of the dissolution of the body of consumers of superior culture.

At the same time, it would be disregarding the truth to overlook the extraordinary vitality of the contemporary American university. Vitality by its nature is diffuse and inflammatory. It is possible, therefore, that despite the densely specialized clutter of the postgraduate system and the prevailing pattern of research which is partly a cause and partly a result of that system, this vitality will do more than withstand the pressure; it is possible that it will ignite interest along a broader front than specialized training commands. It is also possible that the waste of undergraduate education will turn into lively cultivation through the vitality of the new generation of college teachers who are at present among the chief consumers and reproducers of superior culture.

Specialization has lessened the coherence of the intellectual community, comprising creators, reproducers and consumers; it has dispersed its focus of attention, and thus left ungratified cultural needs which the mediocre and brutal culture of the mass media and of private life have been called in to satisfy. The consumption of brutal and mediocre culture is the consequence, not the cause, of developments which are quite independent of the specific properties of mass society. As a matter of fact, the vitality, the individuality, which may rehabilitate our intellectual public will probably be the fruits of the liberation of powers and possibilities inherent in mass societies.

The Prospects of Superior Culture
in Mass Society

The problems of superior culture in mass society are the same as in any society. These problems are the maintenance of its quality and influence on the rest of the society.

To maintain itself, superior culture must maintain its own traditions and its own internal coherence. The progress of superior culture (and its continued self-renewal and expansion) require that the traditions be sustained, however much they are revised or partially rejected at any time.

Respect for the traditions in one's own field, together with freedom in dealing with those traditions, are the necessary conditions for creative work. The balance between them is difficult to define, and it is no less difficult to discern the conditions under which that balance can be achieved and maintained. Of great importance is the morale (in its broadest sense) of the intellectuals who take on administrative and teaching responsibilities for the maintenance and advancement of high culture. Within this section of the intellectual class, there must be an incessant scrutiny of every institutional innovation, with regard to its possible impact on intellectual morale. An essential element in this internal state is a balance between respect and freedom in relation to the immanent traditions of each field of intellectual work.

Serious intellectuals have never been free from pressure on the part of sectors of society other than their own. The intellectual sector has always been relatively isolated, regardless of the role of intellectuals in economic and political life. The external world is always jealous of the devotion of the intellectuals to their own gods, and of the implicit criticism which that devotion directs against the ruling values of the other spheres. Intellectuals have always been faced with the task of continuing their own tradition, developing it, differentiating it, improving it as best they could. They have always had to contend with church, state, and party, with merchants and soldiers who have sought to enlist them in their service and to restrict and damage them in word and deed if they did not yield to temptations and threats. The present situation has much in common with the past. The responsibilities of intellectuals also remain the same: to serve the standards they discern and develop and to find a way of rendering unto Caesar what is Caesar's without renouncing what belongs to their own proper realm.

There is no doubt in my mind that the main "political" tradition by which most of our literary, artistic, and social-science intellectuals have lived in America is unsatisfactory. The fault does not lie exclusively with the intellectuals. The philistine Puritanism and provincialism of our elites share much of the blame, as does the populism of professional and lay politicians. Nonetheless, the intellectuals cannot evade the charge that they have done little to ameliorate the situation. Their own political attitudes have been alienated, they have run off into many directions of frivolity. The most recent of such episodes in the 1930's and 1940's were also the most humiliating, and temporarily the most damaging, to the position of intellectuals in American society.

One of the responsibilities implied by their obligation to maintain good relations with the nonintellectual elite is the "civilization" of political life, i.e., the infusion of the standards and concerns of a serious, intellectually disciplined contemplation of the deeper issues of political life into everyday politics. Our intellectuals have in the main lectured politicians, upbraided them, looked down their noses at them, opposed them, and even suspected those of their fellow intellectuals who have become politicians of moral corruption and intellectual betrayal.

The intellectuals who have taken on themselves the fostering of superior culture are part of the elite in any country; but in the United States they have not felt bound by any invisible affiliation with the political, economic, ecclesiastical, military, and technological elites.[11]

The "civilization" of political life is only one aspect of the "process of civilization," which is the expansion of the culture of the center into the peripheries of society and, in this particular context, the diffusion of superior culture into the areas of society normally consuming mediocre and brutal culture.

Within the limits mentioned earlier in this essay, the prospects for superior culture seem to be reasonably good. The overlapping at certain points on the part of the producers of superior culture and those of mediocre culture has resulted in an expansion of the elements of superior culture which reaches persons whose usual inclinations do not lead them to seek it out. Popularization brings a better content, but not all of this expansion is popularization; much of it is the presentation (and consumption) of genuinely superior cultural work. An improvement in our educational system at the elementary and secondary levels, which is assuredly practicable and likely, will also further this process of civilization. A better education of taste, which a richer, less scarcity-harassed society can afford, the opening and enrichment of sensitivity, which leisure and a diversified environment can make possible, and a more fruitful use of available intelligence can also push forward the "process of civilization."

Of course, men will remain men, their capacities to understand, create, and experience will vary, and very many are probably destined to find pleasure and salvation at other and lower cultural levels. For the others, the prospect of a more dignified and richer cultural life does not seem out of the question. It would certainly be an impossible one, however, if all intellectuals devoted themselves to education and popularization. In a short time the superior culture which would be transmitted through the "process of civilization" would fade and dessicate.

Thus, if the periphery is not to be polished while the center becomes dusty, the first obligation of the intellectuals is to look after intellectual things, to concentrate their powers on the creation and reproduction and consumption of particular works of philosophy, art, science, literature, or scholarship, to receive the traditions in which these works stand with a discriminating readiness to accept, elaborate, or reject. If that is done, there will be nothing to fear from the movement of culture in mass society.

NOTES

1. I have reservations about the use of the term "mass culture," because it refers simultaneously to the substantive and qualitative properties of the culture, to the social status of its consumers, and to the media by which it is transmitted. Because of this at least three-fold reference, it tends to beg some important questions regarding the relations among the three variables. For example, the current conception of "mass culture" does not allow for the fact that in most countries, and not just at present, very large sections of the elite consume primarily mediocre and brutal culture. It also begs the important questions as to whether the mass media can transmit works of superior culture, or whether the genres developed by the new mass media can become the occasions of creativity and therewith a part of superior culture. Also, it does not consider the obvious fact that much of what is produced in the genres of superior culture is extremely mediocre in quality. At present, I have no satisfactory set of terms to distinguish the three levels of cultural objects. I have toyed with "high," "refined," "elaborate," "genuine," or "serious," "vulgar," "mediocre," or "middle," and "low," "brutal," "base" or "coarse." None of these words succeeds either in felicity or aptness.

2. This change in the relative shares of the three levels of culture has been distorted by contrast with the preceding epochs. The cultural life of the consumers of mediocre and brutal culture was relatively silent, unseen by the intellectuals. The immense advances in audibility and visibility of the two lower levels of culture is one of the most noticeable traits of mass society. This is in turn intensified by another trait of mass society, i.e., the enhanced mutual awareness of different sectors of the society.

3. A society which was far less "organic" in its structure and outlook than the critics of modern society allege and less "organic" also than the modern society which is so unsympathetically assailed by these critics.

4. Also, it should be added, this persistence of traditional and orally transmitted culture renders fruitless the effort to diagnose the dispositions and outlook of a people by analyzing what is presented to them through films, television, and wireless broadcasts, the press, etc.

5. The internationality of the medieval church and of the European aristocracy in the eighteenth century was thin and parochial in comparison with the scope and intensity of that exhibited by present-day intellectual classes.

6. The increase in numbers of persons in intellectual occupations and those that require intellectual training might well be pressing hard against the supply. The supply of high talent is limited; improved methods of selection and training can somewhat increase it, but they cannot make it limitless or coterminous with the population of any society. Hence as the numbers expand, modern societies are forced to admit many persons whose endowments are such as to permit only a mediocre preformance in the creation and reproduction of cultural works.

7. The bohemian sector of the high intelligentsia, past and present, is an exception to this generalization. The mingling of poets and cut-purses has a long and special history which runs down to the occasional highbrow glorification of the hipster.

8. *Commonweal* exists on a higher intellectual plane than that of our two secular weeklies, but its religious preoccupations restrict the generality of its appeal.

9. The excellent highbrow reviews are no substitute for an intellectual weekly. They are too infrequent, they are too apolitical, and even where they are not, as in the case of the *Partisan Review* or *Commentary*, they cannot maintain a continuous flow of comment and coverage.

10. The romantic idea of originality, which claimed that genius must go its own unique way, has been transposed into one that demands that the subject matter should be unique to the investigator. This led to much specialized triviality in humanistic research.

11. This is not a condition unique to the United States. Only Great Britain has managed to avoid it for most of the period since the French Revolution, yet there, too, the past few years have not provided notable examples of Britain's good fortune in avoiding this separation.

The Requirements

IF THE FREEDOM of the press is freighted with the responsibility of providing the current intelligence needed by a free society, we have to discover what a free society requires. Its requirements in America today are greater in variety, quantity, and quality than those of any previous society in any age. They are requirements of a self-governing republic of continental size, whose doings have become, within a generation, matters of common concern in new and important ways. Its internal arrangements, from being thought of mainly as matters of private interest and automatic market adjustments, have become affairs of conflict and conscious compromise among organized groups, whose powers appear not to be bounded by "natural law," economic or other. Externally, it has suddenly assumed a leading role in the attempt to establish peaceful relationships among all the states on the globe.

Today our society needs, first, a truthful, comprehensive, and intelligent account of the day's events in a context which gives them meaning; second, a forum for the exchange of comment and criticism; third, a means of projecting the opinions and attitudes of the groups in the society to one another; fourth, a method of presenting and clarifying the goals and values of the society; and, fifth, a way of reaching every member of the society by the currents of information, thought, and feeling which the press supplies.

The Commission has no idea that these five ideal demands can ever be completely met. All of them cannot be met by any one medium; some do not apply at all to a particular unit; nor do all apply with equal relevance to all parts of the communications industry. The Commission does not sup-

Reprinted from *A Free and Responsible Press: Report of the Commission on Freedom of the Press* (1947), pp. 20–29, by permission of the publisher. (Copyright, 1947, by The University of Chicago Press.)

pose that these standards will be new to the managers of the press; they are drawn largely from their professions and practices.

A Truthful, Comprehensive, and Intelligent Account of the Day's Events in a Context which Gives Them Meaning

The first requirement is that the media should be accurate. They should not lie.

Here the first link in the chain of responsibility is the reporter at the source of the news. He must be careful and competent. He must estimate correctly which sources are most authoritative. He must prefer firsthand observation to hearsay. He must know what questions to ask, what things to observe, and which items to report. His employer has the duty of training him to do his work as it ought to be done.

Of equal importance with reportorial accuracy are the identification of fact as fact and opinion as opinion, and their separation, so far as possible. This is necessary all the way from the reporter's file, up through the copy and makeup desks and editorial offices, to the final, published product. The distinction cannot, of course, be made absolute. There is no fact without a context and no factual report which is uncolored by the opinions of the reporter. But modern conditions require greater effort than ever to make the distinction between fact and opinion. In a simpler order of society published accounts of events within the experience of the community could be compared with other sources of information. Today this is usually impossible. The account of an isolated fact, however accurate in itself, may be misleading and, in effect, untrue.

The greatest danger here is in the communication of information internationally. The press now bears a responsibility in all countries, and particularly in democratic countries, where foreign policies are responsive to popular majorities, to report international events in such a way that they can be understood. It is no longer enough to report *the fact* truthfully. It is now necessary to report *the truth about the fact*.

In this country a similar obligation rests upon the press in reporting domestic news. The country has many groups which are partially insulated from one another and which need to be interpreted to one another. Factually correct but substantially untrue accounts of the behavior of members of one of these social islands can intensify the antagonisms of others toward them. A single incident will be accepted as a sample of group action unless the press has given a flow of information and interpretation concerning the relations between two racial groups such as to enable the reader to set a single event in its proper perspective. If it is

530

allowed to pass as a sample of such action, the requirement that the press present an accurate account of the day's events in a context which gives them meaning has not been met.

A Forum for the Exchange of Comment and Criticism

The second requirement means that the great agencies of mass communication should regard themselves as common carriers of public discussion.[1] The units of the press have in varying degrees assumed this function and should assume the responsibilities which go with it, more generally and more explicitly.

It is vital to a free society that an idea should not be stifled by the circumstances of its birth. The press cannot and should not be expected to print everybody's ideas. But the giant units can and should assume the duty of publishing significant ideas contrary to their own, as a matter of objective reporting, distinct from their proper function of advocacy. Their control over the various ways of reaching the ear of America is such that, if they do not publish ideas which differ from their own, those ideas will never reach the ear of America. If that happens, one of the chief reasons for the freedom which these giants claim disappears.

Access to a unit of the press acting as a common carrier is possible in a number of ways, all of which, however, involve selection on the part of the managers of the unit. The individual whose views are not represented on an editorial page may reach an audience through a public statement reported as news, through a letter to the editor, through a statement printed in advertising space, or through a magazine article. But some seekers for space are bound to be disappointed and must resort to pamphlets or such duplicating devices as will spread their ideas to such public as will attend to them.

But all the important viewpoints and interests in the society should be represented in its agencies of mass communication. Those who have these viewpoints and interests cannot count on explaining them to their fellow-citizens through newspapers or radio stations of their own. Even if they could make the necessary investment, they could have no assurance that their publications would be read or their programs heard by the public outside their own adherents. An ideal combination would include general media, inevitably solicitous to present their own views, but setting forth other views fairly. As checks on their fairness, and partial safeguards against ignoring important matters, more specialized media of advocacy have a vital place. In the absence of such a combination the partially insulated groups in society will continue to be insulated. The unchallenged assumptions of each group will continue to harden into prejudice. The mass medium reaches across all groups; through the mass medium they can come to understand one another.

Whether a unit of the press is an advocate or a common carrier, it ought to identify the sources of its facts, opinions, and arguments so that the reader or listener can judge them. Persons who are presented with facts, opinions, and arguments are properly influenced by the general reliability of those who offer them. If the veracity of statements is to be appraised, those who offer them must be known.

Identification of source is necessary to a free society. Democracy, in time of peace, at least, has a justifiable confidence that full and free discussion will strengthen rather than weaken it. But, if the discussion is to have the effect for which democracy hopes, if it is to be really full and free, the names and the characters of the participants must not be hidden from view.

The Projection of a Representative Picture of the Constituent Groups in the Society

This requirement is closely related to the two preceding. People make decisions in large part in terms of favorable or unfavorable images. They relate fact and opinion to stereotypes. Today the motion picture, the radio, the book, the magazine, the newspaper, and the comic strip are principal agents in creating and perpetuating these conventional conceptions. When the images they portray fail to present the social group truly, they tend to pervert judgment.

Such failure may occur indirectly and incidentally. Even if nothing is said about the Chinese in the dialogue of a film, yet if the Chinese appear in a succession of pictures as sinister drug addicts and militarists, an image of China is built which needs to be balanced by another. If the Negro appears in the stories published in magazines of national circulation only as a servant, if children figure constantly in radio dramas as impertinent and ungovernable brats—the image of the Negro and the American child is distorted. The plugging of special color and "hate" words in radio and press dispatches, in advertising copy, in news stories— such words as "ruthless," "confused," "bureaucratic"—performs inevitably the same image-making function.

Responsible performance here simply means that the images repeated and emphasized be such as are in total representative of the social group as it is. The truth about any social group, though it should not exclude its weaknesses and vices, includes also recognition of its values, its aspirations, and its common humanity. The Commission holds to the faith that if people are exposed to the inner truth of the life of a particular group, they will gradually build up respect for and understanding of it.

The Presentation and Clarification of the Goals and Values of the Society

The press has a similar responsibility with regard to the values and goals of our society as a whole. The mass media, whether or not they wish to do so, blur or clarify these ideals as they report the failings and achievements of every day.[2] The Commission does not call upon the press to sentimentalize, to manipulate the facts for the purpose of painting a rosy picture. The Commission believes in realistic reporting of the events and forces that militate against the attainment of social goals as well as those which work for them. We must recognize, however, that the agencies of mass communication are an educational instrument, perhaps the most powerful there is; and they must assume a responsibility like that of educators in stating and clarifying the ideals toward which the community should strive.

Full Access to the Day's Intelligence

It is obvious that the amount of current information required by the citizens in a modern industrial society is far greater than that required in any earlier day. We do not assume that all citizens at all times will actually use all the material they receive. By necessity or choice large numbers of people voluntarily delegate analysis and decision to leaders whom they trust. Such leadership in our society is freely chosen and constantly changing; it is informal, unofficial, and flexible. Any citizen may at any time assume the power of decision. In this way government is carried on by consent.

But such leadership does not alter the need for the wide distribution of news and opinion. The leaders are not identified; we can inform them only by making information available to everybody.

The five requirements listed in this chapter suggest what our society is entitled to demand of its press. We can now proceed to examine the tools, the structure, and the performance of the press to see how it is meeting these demands.

Let us summarize these demands in another way.

The chapter of the service required of the American press by the American people differs from the service previously demanded, first, in this—that it is essential to the operation of the economy and to the government of the Republic. Second, it is a service of greatly increased responsibilities both as to the quantity and as to the quality of the information required. In terms of quantity, the information about themselves and about their world made available to the American people must be as extensive as the range of their interests and concerns as citizens of a self-governing, industrialized community in the closely integrated modern world. In terms of quality, the information provided must be provided in such a form, and with so scrupulous a regard for the wholeness of the truth and the fairness of its presentation, that the American people may make for themselves, by the exercise of reason and of conscience, the fundamental decisions necessary to the direction of their government and of their lives.

NOTES

1. By the use of this analogy the Commission does not intend to suggest that the agencies of communication should be subject to the legal obligations of common carriers, such as compulsory reception of all applicants for space, the regulation of rates, etc.

2. A striking indication of the continuous need to renew the basic values of our society is given in the recent poll of public opinion by the National Opinion Research Center at Denver, in which one out of every three persons polled did not think the newspapers should be allowed to criticize the American form of government, even in peacetime. Only 57 per cent thought that the Socialist party should be allowed, in peacetime, to publish newspapers in the United States. Another poll revealed that less than a fourth of those questioned had a "reasonably accurate idea" of what the Bill of Rights is. Here is widespread ignorance with regard to the value most cherished by the press—its own freedom—which seems only dimly understood by many of its consumers.

The Standard by Which the Press Should Be Judged

ANY JUDGMENT of the performance of the Press will necessarily depend upon the standard from which it is derived. At least three distinct standards appear to us to be relevant, and to be implicit in judgments that are commonly made.

The Press as an Instrument of Information and Instruction

The Press may be judged, first, as the chief agency for instructing the public on the main issues of the day. The importance of this function needs no emphasis.

The democratic form of society demands of its members an active and intelligent participation in the affairs of their community, whether local or national. It assumes that they are sufficiently well informed about the issues of the day to be able to form the board judgments required by an election, and to maintain between elections the vigilance necessary in those whose governors are their servants and not their masters. More and more it demands also an alert and informed participation not only in purely political processes but also in the efforts of the community to adjust its social and economic life to increasingly complex circumstances. Democratic society, therefore, needs a clear and truthful account of events, of their background and their causes; a forum for discussion and

Reprinted from *Report of the Royal Commision on the Press, 1947–49*, pp. 100–106.

informed criticism; and a means whereby individuals and groups can express a point of view or advocate a cause.

The responsibility for fulfilling these needs unavoidably rests in large measure upon the Press, that is on the newspapers and the periodicals, which are the main source from which information, discussion, and advocacy reach the public. In recent years this function has been shared with the radio; but the impermanence of broadcasting, together with the limitations on the quantity and character of controversial material which can be diffused over the air, still leaves the Press in a central position. A useful service is being rendered on a small scale by the factual publications of specialist societies and learned bodies, such as the Royal Institute of International Affairs and the British Society for International Understanding; and a number of newsletters of differing value supply information and comment to subscribers; but any shortcomings of the Press in this field are unlikely to be adequately made good by any other agency.

The Press's Standard for Itself

The second standard of judgment which may be applied to the Press is that enunciated by its own spokesmen. It does not differ very greatly from the first, but is somewhat lower.

The proprietors of newspapers gave some indication of the conception entertained by the Press of the functions of newspapers and the standards proper to them in their replies to one of our questionnaires. The questionnaire asked:

Question 2. What is the proper function of a newspaper? What is the character and extent of its responsibility to the public?

Question 1. Do you agree with the American Commission on Freedom of the Press that those who operate the Press have a duty to give expression to ideas which the processes of free speech have brought to public attention, whether or not they agree with them?

Question. 8. Should a paper be a mouthpiece of a particular set of opinions or should it present several points of view on a given topic?

Question 9. Do you believe that news and opinion should be strictly separated?

Question 10. What do you regard as a reasonable standard of accuracy? Does it include not merely the correctness of the facts stated, but also the statement of all revelant facts?

The commonest reply to the first question was, in effect, "to report news and comment upon it," but there was some elaboration of this. For example, Odhams Press Ltd. wrote:

The chief function of a newspaper is to report current events and interpret them to its readers. It is also an important and proper function of the Press to comment on matters of public interest for the guidance of the public, to inform, educate, entertain and enlighten its readers, and to provide a forum for the expression and exchange of opinion.

536

The advertising columns of the modern newspapers have an important function as part of the machinery of commerce, and they are used to an increasing degree by Government departments and national corporations for giving information to the public.

A newspaper has a responsibility to the public to report facts as accurately and as fully as the circumstances of publication allow and to be honest in the expression of opinion.

That news and comment should be given fully and fairly was emphasised by others. London Express Newspaper Ltd. wrote:

Editorial staffs freely assume (in our opinion) the following moral obligations to the public:—

(i) that of giving in the newspaper a correct and balanced account of what is happening,

(ii) that of expressing opinions on controversial matters in such a way as to advance, by fair argument, tendencies, purposes, etc., that appear to be desirable.

Co-operative Press Ltd. (which publishes *Reynolds News*) wrote of a newspaper's responsibility "to strive constantly to report fairly and objectively what is significant while expressing its own opinions clearly and forcibly"; and Associated Newspapers Ltd. of responsibility "to publish all the important news with as much detail as space permits." And the Newspaper Society, representing the proprietors of provincial newspapers, wrote:

The proper function of a newspaper is to report fairly, accurately and objectively local and/or national and/or international news, according to its particular field; to provide, when necessary, fair, accurate and objective background information to enable the public to understand news items; to comment upon important subjects; to diagnose, express and lead public opinion and to give expression to this in the form of letters to the editor; and to further any political opinions it may hold.

Some replies referred to the interests of readers as the criterion of what constitutes news. Daily Mirror Newspapers, for example, said:

A newspaper's function is threefold, to publish news (serious or otherwise) of interest to its readers, to publish opinionative articles and readers' letters on current topics, to express its own opinion.

Kemsley Newspapers Ltd., in the course of a long reply, said:

. . . if a newspaper desires to attain importance and stability it must tell its readers what has happened within the compass over which their interests are spread.

and The Observer Ltd. said:

The space allotted to any subject must be influenced by the judgment of the editorial staff, both on the importance of the subject and consequent willingness to read about it, taking into consideration the particular class of reader which their paper serves.

While there was general agreement that a newspaper has a right, and possibly a duty, to formulate and express its own opinions, there was some difference on the question whether, and to what extent, it should publish those of others. It was generally agreed on the one hand that, in the words of Odhams Press Ltd., "there is no obligation on any of the several units of the Press to provide a universal platform" for the propagation of ideas, and on the other that opinions which by reason either of their importance or of their general interest have become news, ought to be reported whether or not the newspapers agree with them. Some undertakings thought that this was as far as a paper was bound to go and that it was under no obligation in ventilating a particular topic to present opinions upon it other than its own. The Observer Ltd. suggested that it was "preferable that newspapers should make their own standpoint clear and explicit . . . than that they should pretend to an impartiality which is delusive"—a point of view expressed in somewhat similar terms by Odhams Press Ltd. and the Co-operative Press Ltd. On the other hand, The Times Publishing Co. Ltd., referring to the duty of the newspaper to give news, said: "Provision of news certainly includes the presentation of current ideas, whether or not the newspaper approves of them, in reported speeches, published correspondence, articles and book reviews"; and Kemsley Newspapers Ltd., referring to feature and news columns as distinct from leading articles, said: "it is better where there are strong cleavages of view to present the differing opinions."

The replies to Question 10 emphasised the importance attached to accuracy. "The only standard of accuracy which we find tolerable," wrote London Express Newspaper Ltd., "is complete accuracy." But this reply and others suggested that accuracy did not always include the statement of all relevant facts: some would of necessity be omitted, either because they were not available at the time of publication, or because there was no space for them. In the main the replies referred to factual accuracy, but the People's Press Printing Society Ltd. (which publishes the *Daily Worker*) remarked: "Accuracy in a newspaper is not only a matter of the correctness of the news that it carries, but of the accuracy with which the newspaper as a whole reflects the significant news of the day."

There was general, and frequently emphatic, agreement that news and opinion should be strictly separated, qualified in some cases only by the suggestion that, especially in newspapers of the present size, some news may be contained in opinion columns, and by reservations for the articles of specialists such as political or industrial correspondents. It was suggested that it was legitimate for special correspondents to report the news and at the same time comment upon it, provided that their articles were distinguishable from straight news reports. Kemsley Newspapers Ltd., one of the undertakings which made this point, added: "Neither in headlines nor in the text should propaganda be allowed to colour news."

538

The Press as an Industry

The third standard by which the Press may be judged regards the Press less as a public service than as a great industry concerned with the collection and diffusion of news.

The idea of what constitutes news varies from office to office: a paper's standard of news values is one of the most distinctive facets of its personality. There are, however, certain elements common to all conceptions of news. To be news an event must first be interesting to the public, and the public for this purpose means for each paper the people who read that paper, and others like them. Second, and equally important, it must be new, and newness is measured in newspaper offices in terms of minutes. This follows partly from the notion that the public is more interested in what occurred last night than in what occurred yesterday morning, and partly from the fact that a newspaper is created afresh every day. Each issue is designed as something separate and distinct from every other issue and tends inevitably to concentrate on what has occurred since the last was published and to avoid repeating what has already been said.

If news must be both new and interesting, which of the new events occurring every day are held to be of the greatest and most general interest? The replies to a question to this effect in our questionnaire suggest that the answer is: those concerning sport, followed by news about people, news of strange or amusing adventures, tragedies, accidents, and crimes, news, that is, whose sentiment or excitement brings some colour into life. Mr. Francis Williams, an ex-editor of the *Daily Herald*, said: ". . . over the large field of readership of newspapers there is a demand for something bright and interesting, a sort of 'cocktail' before the meal rather than the solid meal"; and a sub-editor on the *Daily Express* added: ". . . we as newspapers are not concerned with what will appear important to posterity. What we have to do is to produce something which will seem, if not important, at least interesting to the man in the street, and to the man in the street the daffodils in Regent's Park are often more important . . . than a massacre in Chungking."

The replies to the questionnaire did not rate interest in public affairs very high, though many undertakings thought that it was increasing, partly as a result of education, but mainly because of the increased impact of politics, and particularly of Government activity, on the lives of ordinary people. The latter point suggests that interest in public affairs is intermittent and varies in intensity with the range of the reader's experience and the relevance to his own affairs of a given event. Explaining the great prominence given in the *Daily Mail* to an announcement of an increase in the price of coal and the paper's comparative lack of interest

539

in the causes of the increase, the editor of the *Daily Mail* said: "I think what would be in the mind of the sub-editor would be this: the public to whom he is selling his newspaper, his readers, are more interested in the fact that the price of coal is going up than that the cost of production is getting more and more difficult." The public's taste in news of public affairs to some extent reflects, or is thought to reflect, its taste in news generally, and the exciting and exceptional features of affairs are considered to have a higher news value than the normal daily events and the background which gives them meaning.

The reader's taste in political news is affected by his own political opinions, especially if they are strong. Members of a political party are naturally more interested in the speeches of their own leaders than in those of the opposing party, and most readers probably prefer news which confirms their own opinions to news which does not. The Co-operative Press Ltd. said in reply to our questionnaire: "If a newspaper does not reflect the limitations and prejudices of at least a considerable section of the public, it will soon cease to exist, for it will find no buyers."

Newspapers are not guided entirely in their conception of news by what the majority wants: most of them feel some obligation to report matters which they believe to be important, even if these interest only a minority. But their judgment, like the reader's, is affected by political opinion. Opponents of the Government will think it important that the public should be informed of the Government's shortcomings, while its supporters will with equal honesty think it more important to inform the public of the Government's achievements.

The Standard to Be Applied

In our view no standard of judgment can be wholly relevant which fails to take some account of the bases both of the first of these standards and of the third. The Press is not purely an agency for the political education of the public, much though democratic society may need such an agency. On the other hand, it cannot be considered purely as an industry: the inescapable fact that it is the main source of information, discussion, and advocacy imposes upon it responsibilities greater than those resting on an industry which does not deal in information and ideas.

The first standard fails to allow for the fact that the primary business of a newspaper undertaking is to sell newspapers. Only by selling newspapers can such an undertaking maintain its existence. Given a free choice people will buy only newspapers which interest them, and a newspaper must consequently either gauge accurately what the public wants and supply it, or persuade the public to accept something different. The latter can be done only slowly and within narrow limits, and while most news-papers do contain material of minority interest, they are bound to cater for the most part for what they believe—on the basis of considerable study—to be the tastes of the majority.

If, however, public demand plays so large a part in determining what a newspaper publishes, it is apparent that a newspaper catering for a mass public will be led to adopt a concept of news nearer to that indicated in paragraphs above than to the clear and truthful account of events and their background and causes which our first standard demands.

The first standard is not therefore, wholly relevant; but if it is set too high, the third may be set too low. Though a newspaper is a com-mercial enterprise it does not follow that it need necessarily pursue com-mercial advantage without limit. A newspaper whose financial position is precarious will, it is true, be compelled to concern itself almost entirely with money-making; but a successful undertaking seldom aims exclusively at profit; it is also interested in its own conception of success, and that con-ception may include a regard for the responsibilities imposed on the Press by the part which it plays in the life of the community.

The statements of the proprietors assume that the acceptance of certain public responsibilities is compatible with the successful conduct of a news-paper as a commercial undertaking. We believe that a standard by which the Press can reasonably be judged can be based on this assumption; but that the standard enunciated by the Press itself is somewhat idealised in relation to practice and tends to make little allowance for the fact that the Press is an industry.

It follows from what we have said about public demand that not all newspapers can perform the same degree of public service, or be expected to observe the same standards. How each paper can best tell the public what it ought to know will depend both on the tastes and education of the particular section of the public to which it is addressed and on the character of the paper itself. If a paper's public looks to it almost entirely for entertainment, the amount of serious information it can communicate is small.

There are, however, two essential requirements which in our view newspapers individually and the Press collectively ought to fulfil, and we propose to take these as as our own standard of judgment. They form a standard more modest and, we believe, more in accordance with reality than the first and second of the three hypothetical standards which we have discussed, but more in accordance with the aspirations of the Press than the third.

The first of these requirements is that if a newspaper purports to re-cord and discuss public affairs, it should at least record them truthfully. It may express what opinions it pleases—and nothing we may say hereafter is intended to criticise the opinions of any newspaper, or to question its right to express them—but opinions should be advocated without suppressing or distorting the relevant facts. If a paper adheres to a political party it should be plain to the reader that it does so, but from the columns of opinion, not from the colouring given to the news. A paper's politics and those of its readers will inevitably and legitimately affect its judgment of the relative interest of certain items of news, but the news it reports it should report truthfully and without excessive bias. The second requirement is that the number and variety of newspapers should be such that the Press as a whole gives an opportunity for all important points of view to be effectively presented in terms of the varying standards of taste, political opinion, and education among the principal groups of the population.

These two requirements are not stated as alternatives: they are complementary. We recognise that even if they are satisfied, the pre-occupation of the Press with the exceptional, and the limited range of interests of the readers of any paper, must continue to throw the picture of events presented by the Press out of focus; but if the Press gives its readers the means of forming judgments on the problems of most immediate interest to them, that is perhaps as much as need be asked of it at present.

10
Toward Comparative Analysis

ONE OF the most ambitious objectives of social research is to deepen our understanding of the processes of social and political change, especially at the level of how nations transform themselves. In the contemporary world, the drive for modernization of the nation state has become universal. As a result, one of the most striking developments in the social sciences is a renewed aspiration to be comparative and cross national in scope. This trend in social research also includes the study of public opinion and mass communications.

But to be truly comparative is a complex, difficult and time consuming task. Almond and Verba have taken a comprehensive step in their five–country comparative survey of political awareness and exposure to the mass media. Inkeles and Bauer make use of systematic interviews with samples of Soviet refugees to record the role of the mass media in the Soviet Union before the period of de-Stalinization. They were able to reconstruct the mechanisms of public opinion that operated under such a regime. In seeking to understand the communications process in Communist China, Schein studied the ideology, the goals, and the tactics, that have emerged in that social and political system. His analysis both describes and gives realistic meaning to the "passion for unanimity" that he encountered. Finally, Pye is concerned with the social and political structure of the so-called new nations and the special problems that they must encounter in nation building. Obviously, mass communication has a central role in the political development of new nations. But given the internal discontinuities in social structure and the weakness of political institutions of these countries, he presents a theoretical analysis of the difficulties their political leaders are likely to encounter as they seek to avoid reliance on force. The comparative study of public opinion and mass communication in the developing nations will certainly be an emerging concern for social scientists in the years ahead.

GABRIEL A. ALMOND AND SIDNEY VERBA

Awareness of Politics:
*Cross-National Comparisons**

* (EDITOR'S NOTE: The following material on comparative exposure to the mass media and political awareness is taken from the study *The Civic Culture* by Gabriel A. Almond and Sidney Verba, which was a study of political attitudes and their relations to democratic practices in five countries. In each nation, United States, Great Britain, Germany, Italy and Mexico, 1,000 survey research type interviews were conducted in a representative national sample. Interviews were carried out in 1959 and 1960, and represent a major effort in systematic cross national research.)

WE MAY ASSUME that if people follow political and governmental affairs, they are in some sense involved in the process by which decisions are made. To be sure, it is a minimal degree of involvement. The civic culture, as we use the term, includes a sense of obligation to participate in political input activities, as well as a sense of competence to participate. Following governmental and political affairs and paying attention to politics are limited civic commitments indeed, and yet there would be no civic culture without them. They represent the cognitive component of the civic orientation.

Table 1 tells us something about the incidence of civic cognition in the five countries. In general, the picture in Table 1 coincides with the one reported in the discussion of subject or output cognition. The United States, Britain, and Germany are high in following political and governmental affairs, and Italy and Mexico are low. But there are two interesting qualifications to this general pattern. First, the Germans more frequently follow political affairs than do the English. And second, the Italians follow political affairs far less frequently than do the Mexicans.

Reprinted from *The Civic Culture*, (1963), pp. 88–100, by permission of the authors and the publisher. (Copyright, 1963, Princeton University Press.)

A similar general pattern is seen in Table 2, which reports data on the frequency with which respondents pay attention to election campaigns. In Italy and Mexico election campaigns are more likely to be ignored than in the other three nations, with the Italians reporting somewhat more frequently that they pay no attention to such campaigns. The proportion of respondents who pay no attention to election campaigns

Table 1—Following Accounts of Political and Governmental Affairs, by Nation[a] (in Per Cent)

Per Cent Who Report They Follow Accounts	U.S.	U.K.	Germany	Italy	Mexico
Regularly	27	23	34	11	15
From time to time	53	45	38	26	40
Never	19	32	25	62	44
Other and don't know	1	1	3	1	1
Total per cent	100	100	100	100	100
Total number	970	963	955	995	1,007

a. Actual text of the question: "Do you follow the accounts of political and governmental affairs? Would you say you follow them regularly, from time to time, or never?"

Table 2—Paying Attention to Political Campaigns, by Nation[b] (in Per Cent)

Per Cent Who Say They	U.S.	U.K.	Germany	Italy	Mexico
Pay much attention	43	25	34	17	15
Pay little attention	44	47	34	25	38
Pay no attention	12	29	27	54	45
Other and don't know	1	0	5	4	2
Total per cent	100	101	100	100	100
Total number	970	963	955	995	1,007

b. Actual text of the question: "What about the campaigning that goes on at the time of a national election—do you pay much attention to what goes on, just a little, or none at all?"

is smaller in America than in any of the other nations, while the percentages in Britain and Germany are quite similar to each other.

The relatively high frequency with which German respondents report that they are cognitively oriented to the governmental input process—a frequency as great as or greater than that in Britain—suggests that at least in the cognitive dimension there may well be civic tendencies in Germany. If democracy does not seem to have struck deep roots in German society, it is not because of lack of exposure to politics or lack of political information.

The Italian and Mexican data present an interesting contrast. On the questions about output cognition and input cognition these two nations scored lower than the other three. But in terms of their cognition of government output, the Italians much more frequently than the Mexicans expressed awareness of such activities. However, in terms of their cognition of government input—their exposure to political affairs and to political campaigns—the Italians much less frequently than the Mexicans indicated such exposure. Thus more than half of the Italian respondents said that the government had an impact on their lives; but almost two-thirds said that they never follow politics or governmental affairs, and more than half said they do not pay attention to election campaigns. In Mexico, on the other hand, a much larger proportion pays attention to campaigns and follows politics than attributes significance to the government.

This Mexican characteristic appears with greater clarity in Table 3. In the other four nations there is a substantial probability that if a respondent is cognitively oriented toward political input, he will also be cognitively oriented toward governmental output. Thus in the United States 89 per cent of those who both follow political and governmental affairs and pay attention to political campaigns also attribute significance to both their national and local governments, while only 3 per cent of those who are high in political exposure are low in attributing significance to their national and local governments. Britain, Germany, and Italy show similar ratios. In Mexico, on the other hand, of those scoring high in exposure to politics 56 per cent attribute significance to neither their national nor local government. The striking character of the Mexican finding is suggested by the fact that in the other four countries the proportion of those who score high in political exposure and low on governmental significance is in every case below 10 per cent. We suggest again, although our evidence has only been partly presented, that Mexico has an individual pattern of political culture: one marked by high output alienation and/or parochialism, along with a high, though diffuse, political involvement in the input structure.

A few comments from our life-history interviews may illustrate the difference between the Mexican and Italian patterns. A Mexican truck driver, when asked whether he was interested in political and governmental affairs, replied, "Very much, because the government can help the general conditions of life of all the Mexicans. At least this is what I wish." Asked when he first became interested in politics, he said, "About ten years ago, when I began to realize that our governors tend to benefit themselves economically without considering the needs of the other citizens." A Mexican shoemaker replied to the same question, "Yes, I like politics. I am very interested in it, because I want to see improvements and also because I want to see that everything goes well, because many political leaders, rather than help the worker, hurt him." And a

Table 3—Awareness of Government Impact, by Nation and Exposure to Politics[a] (in Per Cent)

Per Cent of Who Report They Are Affected by	U.S.			U.K.			GERMANY			ITALY			MEXICO		
	Exposure Low	Med.	High	Exposure Low	Med.	High	Exposure Low	Med.	High	Exposure Low	Med.	High	Exposure Low	Med.	High
Both national and local govt.	57	82	89	54	65	75	45	62	75	33	62	69	14	29	27
Either national or local govt.	21	13	7	21	20	17	24	23	18	23	28	19	18	19	17
Neither national nor local govt.	16	4	3	23	13	6	16	12	6	19	6	8	64	49	56
Other and don't know	7	1	–	3	2	2	15	3	–	23	3	3	3	3	–
Total per cent	101	100	99	101	100	100	100	100	99	98	99	99	99	100	100
Total number	194	315	461	385	290	288	324	231	400	672	173	150	584	257	167

a. As revealed by respondents whose exposure to politics varies in three ways: low exposure to politics means negative responses to both the question on following political and governmental affairs and on paying attention to campaigns; medium exposure means a positive response to one question and a negative to the other; high exposure means two positive responses.

Mexican stenographer commented, "I have an interest in my town that is neglected by its governor. I have compared it with other cities that were at the same level as Pueblo and now they have gone way ahead in culture and beauty." She first became interested in politics when she visited Guadalajara ". . . and saw how it had improved. I remember that last year Pueblo had the second place in the republic for its beauty and now she has lost it because her governors have neglected her."

While there were Italian respondents who described themselves as interested in politics, the more typical reply stressed the danger and futility of interesting oneself in politics:

An Italian Retired Worker, on his interest in politics:
"Reading the paper is the most that I do, and when I read it, I read it very slowly. It takes me a whole day to read it. I don't like to take part in discussions. As I told you before, they are very lively and at times even dangerous."

An Italian Mechanic, on who is interested in politics:
"The fanatics who believe in what they are doing and in their aspirations, or the ignorant people who are behind and pushed by the first."

An Italian Housewife who waits on customers in the family grocery store:
"None! I have an aversion for it, because I feel nothing is just."

An Italian Bookkeeper:
"No! I don't want to get mixed up in it. Who is interested? Educated people. Who is not interested? Peaceful people."

The British responses, though characterized by understatement, reflected relatively high standards of political interest:

A British Housewife:
"I'm not an avid follower of government. I do read newspapers. I do take quite a big interest. As my own party is in, I'm quite happy to let them get on with it. But if Labour were in, I would take much more interest, I suppose."

A British Civil Servant, on who is interested in politics:
"I don't know. The average Tom, Dick and Harry, the ordinary fellow. In the pub, the average bloke used to talk politics. It's fifty-fifty I say. At election nearly everyone, ninety per cent, use their vote. Whether they vote because their father did or what, I don't know. Ninety per cent vote, and fifty per cent are interested in politics."

A British Bartender:
"An average interest. Because you like to know how the country is being run . . . whether for their own good or for the people. . . . Through working ing a bar you hear so many points of view from customers. You get discussions all over the bar. You hear more politics in a bar than anywhere . . . just people talking to you."

A British Housewife working as a Secretary:
"Well, not too much. Sufficient interest. You don't want to waste too much time on it. There are many other things of more interest. . . . You've got to have a certain amount of interest. . . . I think everybody should be interested without being rabid. Everyone must be, because it affects your life."

In the German life-history interviews the participant respondents, in discussing their political obligations, stressed the historical experience of their country:

A German White-collar Worker:
"I am greatly interested in political matters. A good democratic citizen must concern himself with political matters. In a democratic state everyone shares the responsibility for what happens."

A German Baker:
"I have great interest because the kind of government we have concerns me too. Actually, everyone should pay more attention to it."

A German Housewife:
"I am very much interested in politics today. Through the developments since 1914 one sees things quite differently. They should put greater emphasis on the various connections in the schools. You have to have your eye on politics nowadays."

When we use other measures of political cognition, the same national patterns are repeated. Thus when we compare exposure to political communication in the various mass media (Table 4), the Germans come

Table 4—Following Reports of Public Affairs in the Various Media, by Nation[a] (in Per Cent)

Per Cent Who Follow Accounts	U.S.	U.K.	Germany	Italy	Mexico
In newspapers at least weekly	49	43	53	16	31
On radio or television at least weekly	58	36	52	20	28
In magazine (ever)	57	21	45	26	25
Total number	970	963	955	995	1,007

[a] Actual text of the questions: "What about newspapers (radio or television, magazines)? Do you follow (listen to, read about) public affairs in newspapers (radio or television, magazines) nearly every day, about once a week, from time to time, or never?" Only the per cent for those who report exposure are reported here.

out ahead of the British, and the Mexicans better than the Italians.

We have already seen that output cognition is closely related to level of educational attainment and socio-economic position. It also appears that education is strongly correlated with civic cognition (see Table 5).

Table 5—Following Politics Regularly or from Time to Time, by Nation and Education

Nation	TOTAL (%)	TOTAL (No.)[a]	PRIM. OR LESS (%)	PRIM. OR LESS (No.)	SOME SEC. (%)	SOME SEC. (No.)	SOME UNIV. (%)	SOME UNIV. (No.)
United States	80	(970)	67	(339)	84	(442)	96	(188)
Great Britain	68	(963)	60	(593)	77	(322)	92	(24)
Germany	72	(955)	69	(790)	89	(124)	100	(26)
Italy	36	(995)	24	(692)	58	(245)	87	(54)
Mexico	55	(1,007)	51	(877)	76	(103)	92	(24)

a. Numbers in parentheses refer to the bases upon which percentages are calculated.

On the university level almost all respondents in each country follow politics. On the secondary level the countries are, with the exception of Italy, uniformly high in the proportions who follow politics; and even in relation to Italy the difference between secondary-school Italians and secondary-school respondents in other countries is much less than the difference between primary-school Italians and primary-school respondents in other countries. Thus on the higher levels of education one finds in all nations a uniformly high proportion who follow politics. Among those with lower educational attainment the national differences are greater. In the United States, Britain, and Germany, and to a lesser extent in Mexico, those with little education still follow politics; but in Italy few respondents on the lower level are exposed to political communication.

Having Information and Opinions

Our measures of knowledge or cognition of the political system thus far have been subjective estimates of the significance of government and subjective estimates of exposure to political and governmental affairs. We have not yet tried to ascertain the amount of information about government and politics that the respondents actually have. Democratic competence is closely related to having valid information about political issues and processes, and to the ability to use information in the analysis of issues and the devising of influence strategies. Our survey contained two measures of information: one was based on ability to identify the national leaders of the principal parties in each country, and the second was based on ability to identify cabinet offices or departments at the national level of government.

These are simple measures of quantity of a certain kind of information. They tap only a limited aspect of the dimension of knowledge, and they tell us nothing about the capacity to use knowledge intelligently. Furthermore, since the governmental and party structures of the five countries differ, we cannot assume that these quantitative measures of political information are strictly comparable. The ability to identify leaders of the smaller parties in Italy and Mexico may represent a higher order of cognition than the ability to identify a larger number of leaders in the American two-party system. However, when we compare the proportions at the extremes—those having either no correct information or a great deal of information—these structural differences are of less significance and our comparisons are more reliable.

The results in Table 6 show that Germans, English, and Americans have the largest proportion of well-informed respondents by this measure of political information. The high frequency of uninformed Italian respondents is consistent with the high percentage of Italians who describe themselves as not following politics and political campaigns. On the other hand, the Mexican figures are again of great interest. Though reporting with relatively great frequency that they follow politics and political campaigns, the Mexicans show themselves to be the most poorly informed of all our national groups. Approximately half the Mexican respondents—including many who say they follow politics—could not name correctly any political leader or any government department.

If we can demonstrate this Mexican pattern, we shall have added another significant item to our characterization of the Mexican political culture. We have hypothesized that Mexican political culture combines high cognitive self-appraisal with poor cognitive performance. One way

Table 6—Ability to Name Party Leaders and Governmental Ministries, by Nation[a] (in Per Cent)

| | PERCENTAGE OF TOTAL SAMPLE WHO COULD[b] | | | |
Nation	Name Four or More Party Leaders	Name No Party Leader	Name Four or More Ministries	Name No Ministry
United States	65	16	34	28
Great Britain	42	20	34	23
Germany	69	12	40	20
Italy	36	40	23	53
Mexico	5	53	21	47

a. Those with medium levels of information (i.e., who could name one to three in each category) have been left off the table.
b. Percentages in each case are of the total sample.

of testing this would be to determine the extent to which poorly informed respondents in our five countries are ready to express political opinions. We shall use as a measure of readiness to express political opinions a "range of political opinion" index. This index is based upon the frequency with which respondents, rather than saying they did not know, expressed opinions on a series of six general political attitude questions. These questions dealt with such matters as the content of civic obligations, judgments of interest groups and political parties, and the need for political campaigning.[1] That this combination of high cognitive self-appraisal with low information is especially characteristic of Mexico is suggested by Table 7, which reports how frequently respondents answered these opinion questions.

It appears that the Mexicans are almost as frequently willing to express opinions on all six questions as are the Germans, even though the Germans have the largest proportion of persons with high information scores and the Mexicans have the smallest. But to provide further confirmation that Mexico contains a larger proportion of "low infor-

Table 7—Range of Political Opinions, by Nation (in Per Cent)

Per Cent Who	U.S.	U.K.	Germany	Italy	Mexico
Answered all six political questions	63	56	47	26	46
Said "Don't know" to one or two questions	29	37	46	37	35
Said "Don't know" to three or more questions	7	7	7	36	19
Total per cent	99	100	100	99	100
Total number	970	963	955	995	1,007

mation-high opinion" respondents than do any of the other countries, we must ascertain what percentage of respondents in each country *combines* these qualities of low information and high willingness to express opinions. This analysis, expressed in Table 8 brings out a number

Table 8—Willingness to Express Political Opinions among Respondents with Little Political Information, by Nation (in Per Cent)[a]

Nation	Percentage of Total Sample Low on Political Info.[b]	Percentage of Total Sample Low on Info. But Answered Four or More Opinion Questions
United States	13	11
Great Britain	13	10
Germany	8	8
Italy	33	11
Mexico	36	23

a. Percentages in each case are of the total sample.
b. Low on political information means that the respondent could name neither any party leaders nor any government ministerial post.

of points. First, it appears that in all the countries except Italy, persons who score low in information score high in the expression of opinions. Thus two out of three poorly informed Mexicans and almost all of the poorly informed Americans, British, and Germans gave some answer to four or more of the six opinion questions. On the other hand, only one out of three poorly informed Italians expressed opinions in four or more of the questions. This would seem to suggest that in all the countries but Italy, the willingness to express political opinions is widespread, affecting even the uninformed. The striking thing is that the poorly informed Mexicans are in this respect like the Americans, British, and Germans and unlike the Italians. There were almost as many poorly informed respondents in Italy as in Mexico, but most of the former refrained from offering opinions on political questions. Two inferences are suggested: first, Mexico is like the more "developed democracies," for even the cognitively incompetent feel free to express opinions, and, second, there are many more such "aspiring citizens" in Mexico than in any of our other countries. These Mexicans (about one-fourth of the sample) are in almost all cases persons of primary or no education; persons possessing little information about the larger world of public affairs, yet quite willing to take a position on general political questions.[2] Such persons appear in all of our countries, but they appear twice as frequently in Mexico as in any of the other nations. Their existence in such large proportion in Mexico supports our interpretation that the political culture of that country contains a large aspirational component— a tendency to be willing to express opinions—along with poverty of information.

In general our findings on political cognition show the British, Americans, and Germans to be predominantly oriented toward their political systems in both the political and governmental sense. Or to use our jargon, they are cognitively oriented toward the political system in its output and input aspects. The Mexicans and Italians, on the other hand, include large numbers who are alienated or parochial. Table 9

Table 9—Summary of Patterns of Political Cognition, by Nation (in Per Cent)[a]

Nation	Percentage Alienated or Parochial in Terms of Govt. Output[b]	Percentage Alienated or Parochial in Terms of Govt. Input[c]	Percentage Alienated or Parochial in Terms of Both Input and Output[d]
United States	12	20	7
Great Britain	26	33	14
Germany	26	28	13
Italy	42	63	38
Mexico	71	45	35

a. Percentages in each case are of the total national sample.
b. Negative or don't know answers on local government impact.
c. Negative or don't know answers on following politics.
d. Negative or don't know answers on both local government impact and following politics.

provides a convenient summary of much of the argument that has been presented in this chapter. It shows that more than a third of the Italians and Mexicans are fully alienated or parochial, as compared with far smaller proportions for the other three countries. It also brings out quite clearly the imbalances in the Italian and Mexican patterns of orientation, and it summarizes evidence we have thus far presented on the predominance of aspirational tendencies among the Mexicans and of alienated tendencies among the Italians. If to the evidence summarized in Table 9 we add our demonstration of the low political information level in Mexico, combined with an unusually frequent willingness to express political opinions, our theory of Mexican civic aspiration begins to assume a structurally elaborated form.

However, there is more to political culture than knowledge or cognition. How people *feel* about their political systems is an important component of political culture. The state of feeling or political emotion in a country is perhaps the most important test of the legitimacy of its political system. It is also the most important measure of political alienation and aspiration. This is the aspect of political culture to which we now turn.

NOTES

1. The six questions used to compute the "range of political opinion" index were as follows:

"1. One sometimes hears that some people or groups have so much influence on the way the government is run that the interests of the majority are ignored. Do you agree or disagree that there are such groups?

"2. We know that the ordinary person has many problems that take his time. In view of this, what part do you think the ordinary person ought to play in the community affairs of his town or district?

"3. People speak of the obligations that they owe to their country. In your opinion, what are the obligations that every man owes his country?

"4. Some people say that campaigning is needed so the public can judge candidates and issues. Others say that it causes so much bitterness and is so unreliable that we'd be better off without it. What do you think—is it needed or would we be better off without it?

"5. The _____ party now controls the government. Do you think that its policies and activities would ever seriously endanger the country's welfare? Do you think that this *probably* would happen, that it *might* happen, or that it *probably wouldn't happen?*

"6. Same as question 5, but with reference to chief opposition party."

2. It is important to note that we are dealing with the extent to which respondents felt *free* to express opinions, not with the extent to which they actually had opinions. Thus one reason for the infrequency of opinions among Italian respondents may be their greater unease in an interview situation.

ALEX INKELES AND RAYMOND A. BAUER

Keeping Up with the News[1]

CONTRARY TO POPULAR BELIEF, the Soviet regime is by no means uninterested in the state of public opinion. Lenin early introduced the principle that the Soviet state must be based on a balance of coercion *and* persuasion. But the interest of the Soviet rulers is not in adjusting its policies to the wishes of the people. The regime is concerned with molding public opinion to the support of policies established by the Communist Party. In order to effect its goals of mass persuasion, the party has established a special Department of Propaganda and Agitation directly under its main policy-determining organ, formerly the Politburo and currently the Presidium of the Central Committee. While the party and its agencies set policy in the field of communications, operations are in the hands of a series of special government agencies within the Ministry of Culture.[2]

The common goal of the party and the government is to have the most effective network of mass communications, fully geared in structure with the policies of the party. This goal is reflected in the size and structure of the official media and the nature of the controls exercised over them. The official media include not only the pointed sources (newspapers, magazines, and journals), and the radio and a developing television network, but also the theater, movies, the arts and a system of oral agitation. Through the system of oral agitation the regime attempts to capitalize on captive audiences. Two million agitators—and as many as three million in times of special campaigns—regularly carry the message of the party to their fellows at work, play, and even in workers' dormitories and apartments. They gather together their fellow citizens in small groups to hear an article read from the press, to describe some

Reprinted from *The Soviet Citizen*, (1959), pp. 159–188, by permission of the authors and the publisher. (Copyright, 1959, Harvard University Press.)

recent policy decision, to lead a "critical" discussion of the work performance of the group, or to enlist their support in some drive or campaign. Oral agitation is but one manifestation of the official policy of tying communications as closely as possible to the characteristics of the various subgroups to which the party and the government address themselves. There are, for example, about 150 newspapers for the youth of the country, and special newspapers and journals for various occupational and other groups, such as the railroad man, the peasant, and the member of the navy. Not only are there regional and local newspapers, but even a very large factory will have its own regular newspaper, and each office, school, and shop has its own "wall newspaper" with a regularly appointed editor and staff.

The seriousness with which the regime takes the job of getting its message to the public is seen in the efforts made to expand the facilities of communications. In 1939 there were 8,769 newspapers with single issue circulation of under forty million. As a result of postwar consolidations only about 7,200 were operating, but the single issue circulation had risen to forty-nine million.[3] In very broad terms this network compares reasonably well with that in the United States. In 1952 the United States had 229 metropolitan dailies, 1,551 small city dailies, and about 10,000 weekly, semiweekly and biweekly newspapers.[4] At the top of the Soviet hierarchy there were 25 "central" or "All-Union" papers, and about 460 republican and regional papers which are the equivalent of American metropolitan newspapers. The great majority of these are dailies. Smaller cities have about 1,000 dailies. The remainder of under 6,000 small city, district, and local newspapers are published less frequently.

The radio network is not nearly so impressive. In 1952 there were only 125 broadcasting stations in the country, and there were well under 100 receivers per 1,000, 80 per cent of which were not actually radio sets but wired speakers connected with a master receiver. This compared quite poorly with the rate of over 200 receivers per 1,000 in many European countries and was far below the United States rate of 500 per 1,000 of population. As late as 1955, there were only 26 million receivers,[5] still well below Western Europe on a per capita basis. The theater and movies are only partially media of information and will not be considered systematically here. They are generally quite readily accessible in the cities and often inaccessible in the rural areas, with constant shadings and gradations of availability in the towns and cities of intermediate size.

Accessibility to the press is fairly uniform for most citizens except those in the more isolated rural areas. Two thousand newspapers are printed in languages other than Russian in order to reach the national minorities. For most citizens the availability of newspapers is conditioned mainly by their own interest in obtaining them. Radio is fully accessible mainly in urban areas, but has become increasingly available in the countryside through electrification. Television cannot be taken seriously yet as a mass medium, since it is restricted to large cities. Accessibility to the movies and theater parallels closely that of the radio. Of the system of agitation, probably the most pertinent statement that can be made is that there is more difficulty in avoiding it than in making contact with it. In general, the regime has fashioned a technically adequate network of official media for getting its message to the people. Its dimensions, except for the system of agitation, are not as great as those of the United States, but considering the limitations of resources under which the regime operates the magnitude of this system is impressive and is a testimonial to the regime's concern with molding public opinion.

In order to understand the communications behavior which our respondents report, we must know something also of official communications policy. The major premise of Soviet communications policy has been the monopoly of the media of communications. Only the official point of view of the regime may be expressed in the formal media. Very recently we may have observed some breaks in this monopoly. After the "deStalinization" at the Twentieth Party Congress in 1956, opposition viewpoints—notably criticism of Soviet policy made by foreign communists—were in some instances reported in such a way as to define these views as legitimate points for discussion. If this should continue, we will be confronted with a fundamental change of policy. As of 1957, however, the loosening up process was itself still under very tight control, and by 1958 there was evidence of a return to the more stringent pattern typical of the period before the 1956 "thaw."

The system of controls extends to all the media and from central areas out into the remotest regions on the periphery. Because the regime tries to use the media as efficiently as possible to convey its messages, the media, especially the press, are dull, heavy, densely packed, lacking in human interest. In the overwhelming proportion of the press and magazines the tedium of dryly presented news is broken only by occasional satirical pieces. Those of our respondents who worked within the communications system and claim to be in a position to know, say that the regime is fully aware that the media are exactly what the bulk of our respondents, and any foreigner who has read Soviet sources for a time, report them to be—dull, tedious, tendentious, boring. Soviet propaganda operates on a principle of frontal assault by a mass of heavily weighted arguments, rather than by subtle indirection. It believes in presenting one side, the official side, vigorously and repetitively, not in discussing both sides of the question in a detached fashion. These characteristics of official communications policy have a strong influence on the communications behavior of the Soviet citizen.

The Sources of Information

While the regime regards the communications network which it has set up as a means of getting its message across to the citizen, the citizen often regards his own communications behavior primarily as a way of informing himself as to what is going on in the world about him. Even if he is a completely loyal supporter of the regime he is frequently aware of a disparity between its policies and his own sense of curiosity or his need for certain sorts of information. As a result he tries to get information through unofficial channels, which exist despite official attempts at suppression. He also applies certain interpretive principles to the content of the official media in the hope of discovering that which the regime hopes to conceal. "When I read about an event in the paper, by the logic of the question I see what is missing. Then I know what is needed in order to fill the gap," said a postwar refugee. We must therefore think of the system of communications in the Soviet Union as actually two parallel systems, one the official system, and the other a series of devices and media whereby the citizen seeks to supplement, correct, and replace the official media.

In our individual interviews we asked each person: "While you were in the Soviet Union, from what sources did you draw most of your information about what was happening?" This was followed by the probe: "Which of these sources was most important for you? And then?" A medium was scored as a "source" for a person if he seemed to make any meaningful use of it, even if it did not seem particularly important to him, or even if he did not use it frequently.

In dealing with the entire group, as we do for the moment, we tend to overestimate the rate of exposure to all media because of the disproportionate number of highly educated persons in the oral interview sample. In any event, rating a medium as a "source" has a rather ambiguous meaning since it does not indicate any absolute rate of exposure. We therefore restrict ourselves to only the relative frequency with which the various media were cited. The newspaper is the medium our respondents most often report using, and it is cited as a source of information by nine out of ten (Table 1). Next in frequency of mention are radio and word of mouth, each of which is cited by half our sample. "Meetings," which include all agitation activities, were mentioned by only one out of five persons, while personal observation is mentioned by about one in seven. If we use as our baseline the source least often mentioned, namely magazines, the relative importance of each medium is expressed in the ratios: magazines, 1; personal observation, 1.2; meetings, 1.6; radio, 4.2; word of mouth, 4.2; and newspapers, 7.4.[6]

In some respects this pattern is very much what we have come to expect in industrial and "industrializing" countries, but in other respects it may reflect the special nature of Soviet society or of our sample. The most notable similarity between the Soviet pattern and that found in other countries is the widespread use of the newspaper. A national sample

Table 1—Media Cited as Ordinary and as Most Important
Sources of Information[5a]

Media	(1) Per Cent Citing as Source[b]	(2) Per Cent Citing as Most Important	(3) Stability of Salience[c]
Newspapers	89	44	.49
Word of mouth	50	35	.70
Radio	50	13	.26
Meetings	19	2	.11
Personal observation	14	5	.36
Magazines	12	1	.08
Total number of respondents	312	275	

a. From personal interviews.
b. Percentages total more than 100 because more than one source could be cited.
c. Column 3 figures are derived by dividing the per cent in column 2 by that in column 1.

of adults in the United States revealed that 82 per cent looked at one or more newspapers each day.[7] Similar rates of newspaper reading have been reported for the United Kingdom, Germany, and Scandinavia, although in France and Italy substantially lower rates prevailed.[8]

The relative standing of the radio as a major source of news is perhaps lower in our sample than for the United States, and this may reflect the lesser availability of radios in the Soviet Union.[9] It is obvious, however, that the radio is a major source of information. The spontaneous citation of the newspaper by almost everyone, the high number who remembered to cite the radio, and the fact that almost 20 per cent cited agitation and similar meetings to be news sources suggests that our respondents were quite extensively exposed to the official media of communications. They can hardly be thought to be "deviants" or "alien" citizens in this respect.

The relatively low emphasis which these people place on meetings as a source of "information" may be interpreted as an expression of the disparity between the points of view of the government and the people— at least the kind of people we have in our sample. The accounts which people give as to how they learned about specific events or specific policies leads us to suspect that meetings were a more important source of information than this table would indicate. In addition, the "time budget" questionnaire showed that the median for time spent in meetings was an average of one fourth of an hour daily. What this suggests is that the citizen—or at least the refugee ex-citizen—is likely to regard "information" as that which *he* wants to learn, not that which the regime wants him to know. We should perhaps assume that our respondents underestimate the importance of oral agitation as a source of information. Certainly, their attention to it as a source of information underestimates its importance to the regime. We must note, however, that frequent complaints in the Soviet press offer evidence that the agitation meetings generate boredom on a national scale and are not often attended willingly or with genuine interest.

What will most occasion special notice in Table 1 is the fact that half cited word-of-mouth sources (other than official meetings), and that this source was as frequently mentioned as was the radio.[10] The significance of word-of-mouth communication is further accentuated when we consider the proportions of people who cited the various media as their "most important" source of information (second column of Table 1). Newspapers *and word of mouth* are outstandingly the most frequently cited—44 and 35 per cent. Furthermore, they have the most stable saliency (see third column). That is, when they are mentioned as a "regular" source of information the probability is most high for these two media that they will *also* be mentioned as the "most important" source. Word-of-mouth communication has far and away the most stable salience. Two out of three persons who mentioned word of mouth as a regular source also cited it as "most important," whereas this is true of only one tenth of those who mentioned meetings.

The absolute importance of word-of-mouth sources and their relative salience may be mainly a reflection of the special nature of our sample. Since they were alienated people they perhaps more often went *outside* the official channels and relied on informal communications from personally trusted informants. Although this conclusion seems very plausible, we should not jump at it too quickly. Indeed the matter is much more complex than appears on the surface. In general, the less hostile to the Soviet system our respondents were, the *more* likely they were to report exposure to rumor. In the large written questionnaire sample, only 37 per cent of the most anti-Soviet group said they got information through rumors, whereas 64 per cent of the least anti-Soviet subgroup gave this answer.[11] Therefore, to the extent that our sample is anti-Soviet, it ought in general to give us an *underestimation*, not an overestimation, of the use of informal communications.

Of course we do not assert that the nature of our sample in no way colors the picture of Soviet communications with which we emerge. We mean only to caution against treating the picture which develops as if it can all be automatically explained by the nature of our sample. It is obvious that the real conditions of Soviet society encourage the use of informal unofficial sources of information. The absolute monopoly of communications maintained by the regime almost obliges the citizen to look elsewhere to supplement the limited information the regime makes available. The existence of an extensive network of word-of-mouth communications is attested to by the regime itself in its attacks on "rumor mongering" and its attempts over many years to isolate persons—such as those who had contact with the West—who might be the originators of unpalatable opinions and information that would circulate through unofficial channels Foreign observers confirm the ubiquity of rumor in the Soviet Union, and our informants talk about it in many contexts. It is the citizen's device for keeping himself informed in a system of controlled communications.

The two systems of communications, the official and the unofficial, exist side by side and at various points shade off one into the other to the extent that it is difficult to say where one begins and the other ends. For some people the unofficial media serve as a substitute for the official sources and they withdraw almost completely from the use of the latter. Others use the official channels almost exclusively. Most persons, however, use both the official and informal media in a complementary relationship, each utilized as a check on, and as a basis for the interpretation of, the other. The nature of the Soviet Union is such that the communications behavior of the citizen must be regarded as one of the dimensions of his relations with the regime itself.

The Class Patterning of Communications Behavior

Study of communications patterns in European countries has consistently revealed that major subgroups of the population differ markedly in their communications behavior. This seems true for the Soviet Union as well. The main bases for these variations are: (1) a combination of educational and occupational factors which affect interest in what is going on, shape reading and listening habits, determine access to information and the media, and generate situational pressures which put a premium on being well informed; (2) residence, which primarily affects accessibility to sources of information, but must also be presumed to present environments, which vary in degree of intellectual stimulation; and (3) attitudes toward the regime, which are reflected in turn in attitudes toward the media of communication. Obviously, differences on these various dimensions are highly correlated with social class, and the various classes are therefore characterized by marked differences in communications behavior. Except for a few instances, sex and age differences affect communications behavior surprisingly little.[12] Variations in the age and sex composition of the class groups in our sample, therefore, do not significantly affect the class differences which we will discuss in this section.

On the written questionnaire we named eleven different sources of information, and asked our respondents to indicate for each whether they had frequently, seldom, or never utilized the particular source. The resultant pattern of answers produced a series of "exposure types." These types were not deduced on *a priori* logical grounds, but rather were empirically derived. They reflect the natural or "operative" clustering of communications behavior in our sample. Thus, we found that those who frequently read newspapers and magazines also tended to report frequently reading books, *and* frequently listening to the Soviet radio. It did not automatically follow, however, that such a person would be a frequent listener to the foreign radio or would often attend lectures. Those particular habits of communication were in fact associated with other modes in different distinctive clusters.[13] The clusters which emerged from our sorting out of the actual patterns of communications, and the names we assigned them, were as follows:

1. Mass Official: Newspapers and magazines, books and Soviet radio.
2. Aesthetic Official: Movies and theater.
3. Personalized Official: Lectures, agitation meetings, and other official sources.
4. Covert: Discussion with friends, rumor, and foreign radio.

Table 2—Social Class Patterns of Exposure to Communications Media[13a]

Type of Media	Intelli-gentsia	White-Collar Employees	Skilled Workers	Ordinary Workers	Collective Farm Peasants
Official Mass Media Exposure					
High	52%	38%	22%	7%	3%
Medium	45	47	38	32	21
Low	3	15	40	61	76
Personalized Media Exposure					
High	14	7	6	3	2
Medium	33	18	9	6	6
Low	53	75	85	91	92
Aesthetic Media Exposure					
High and Medium	63	44	35	18	8
Low	37	56	65	82	92
Covert Media Exposure					
High	20	11	7	2	1
Medium	26	25	16	10	12
Low	54	64	77	88	87
Total number of respondents	642	679	282	494	387

Table 2 shows the percentage of each social group which received a particular exposure score for each type of media. No matter what type of media is involved, there is an extremely sharp drop in the frequency of exposure as we proceed from the intelligentsia down through the collective farmers.

Thus, 52 per cent of the intelligentsia, but only 3 per cent of the peasantry, reported frequent exposure on all three sources included in the "official mass media" category (Table 2). Even in the case of newspapers, the most widely used individual medium, only 17 per cent of the peasants were "frequent" users—as against 84 per cent of the intelligentsia. Aesthetic media also show a very sharp decline in exposure as we descend the status scale. In the case of both these sets of media, cost, availability, and education probably exert their largest effects. But even in the case of the personal and the covert media, universally available, free of cost and setting no educational qualifications, the peasants are noticeably inactive. Indeed, the intelligentsia is actively exposed to all media, while at the other pole the peasants are markedly withdrawn from participation in the communications network.

Differences in the frequency of exposure are of course not the only measure of the importance of any specific source of news. On the basis of our oral interviews we rated each informant's report to assess which source was *most* important for him regardless of the frequency of his exposure to it (Table 3). Although the number of cases is small, the

Table 3—Information Sources Most Important for Various Social Groups[13b]

Media	Intelligentsia	White-Collar Employees	Skilled Workers	Ordinary Workers	Collective Farm Peasants
Newspapers	47%	59%	30%	35%	18%
Word of mouth	34	23	26	43	60
Radio	9	9	22	14	18
Meetings	2	4	0	2	0
Other	8	5	22	6	4
Total number of respondents	100	56	27	49	27

general pattern seems quite clear and makes good sense. For the better educated intelligentsia and white-collar groups, the printed word carried by the official newspaper was far and away the most important source. Limits on reading ability pull down the importance of the newspaper for the manual classes to a point where it is not much more important than the radio, even though the latter is often inaccessible in the countryside. Most interesting, however, is the shift in the relative importance of word-of-mouth communication. Not only does its relative importance rise as we go from the better placed to the less advantaged, but among the peasants, and to a lesser degree among ordinary workers, it emerges as outstandingly the most important source of information. Thus it appears that as total communications activity decreases, going from intelligentsia to peasant, the relative importance of informal, word-of-mouth communication progressively increases at the expense of the more official, formal, printed sources.

Although status attributes such as education, occupation, or social class membership seem to be the major determinant of the communications patterns, there are individual differences within the classes which seem to exert some independent influence. In particular, the extent to which an individual was politically "involved" played such a role, with those more deeply committed to the system and more actively participating in its development reporting greater exposure. Thus, former members of the Communist Party and Young Communist League, even though closely matched on age, sex, and occupation with nonmembers, scored substantially higher in exposure to official media, including mass, personalized, and "aesthetic" media.

The persistent effect of political sentiment is further strikingly evident when we compare individuals within the same broad occupational categories but differing in their anti-Soviet feeling. In Table 4 there are 55 pairs of figures, and in 45 cases the comparison within each pair reveals that those who were less *hostile* to the Soviet system were the more active "communicators." All of the reversals of the pattern are evidently minor in scale. For the official media the relationship holds cleanly and firmly within each of the several social identification groups. In each instance—press, radio, and books—the less anti-Soviet group gives evidence of higher exposure than does the more anti-Soviet. The relationship is strongest in the intermediate groups, the employees, the skilled workers, and workers, than for the peasants and the intelligentsia. Evidently membership in one of the polar groups puts something of a floor or ceiling on one's communications behavior. There is a limit to how infrequently a member of the intelligentsia will read newspapers no matter how much he may be opposed to the regime and distrust the press. There is similarly a limit to how often a peasant will read them regardless of how favorably inclined he may be toward both the regime and the press. These limitations are clearly more or less imposed by their life situations.

Much the same effect is observed when we compare those who wanted a career with those who did not. To indicate a desire for a career is to suggest that one is ambitious, possibly more alert to opportunity, more in need of the information requisite to success. Under Soviet conditions it also indicates willingness to participate in "the system," from which

**Table 4—Per Cent Frequently Using Various Communications Media:
by Social Group and Anti-Soviet Sentiment Score**[13c]

| | Social group and anti-Soviet sentiment score | | | | | | | | | |
| | INTELLIGENTSIA | | WHITE-COLLAR EMPLOYEES | | SKILLED WORKERS | | ORDINARY WORKERS | | COLLECTIVE FARMERS | |
Communications Media	Low	High	Low	High	Low	High	Low	High	Low	High
Soviet radio	68%	57%	59%	48%	43%	33%	25%	21%	15%	6%
Foreign radio	14	13	12	8	5	7	2	1	1	1
Newspapers and magazines	87	77	77	64	55	37	32	18	27	13
Books	94	90	79	74	54	47	40	23	23	17
Movies	57	50	45	37	38	38	31	14	14	6
Theater	49	43	27	22	19	15	10	5	3	2
Agitation meetings	22	29	19	13	21	9	9	7	13	9
Lectures	43	38	23	17	19	11	11	7	7	6
Rumor	30	30	21	19	16	13	9	6	7	10
Discussion with friends	33	22	24	19	13	14	10	7	5	7
Other	11	10	5	3	5	3	2	2	3	1
Median number of respondents	422	177	370	263	110	133	139	265	93	215

many in our sample claimed to have held back. In every occupational group those who wanted a career are more active in exposing themselves to the communications network. This holds, furthermore, not only for the more formal official sources such as the newspaper and radio, but also applies

**Table 5—Career Desire and Type of Exposure to Communications Media:
by Occupation**[13d]

| | PER CENT FREQUENTLY USING: | | | | | |
Occupation and Career Desire	News-papers & Magazines	Soviet Radio	Movies	Agitation Meetings	Rumor	Median Number of Respondents
Professional						
Wanted a career	92%	71%	65%	31%	40%	(175)
Did not want career	84	61	35	26	35	(191)
Semiprofessional						
Wanted a career	76	69	60	14	25	(183)
Did not want career	76	51	37	21	16	(326)
Skilled workers						
Wanted a career	66	44	49	16	23	(45)
Did not want career	48	36	24	14	15	(102)
Ordinary workers						
Wanted a career	30	32	35	18	12	(123)
Did not want career	26	26	21	9	9	(274)
Collective farmer						
Wanted a career	21	15	12	9	7	(66)
Did not want career	11	5	4	6	7	(177)

to "aesthetic" media like the movies, "personalized" official media like agitation meetings, and even to covert sources like rumor.

Our general theme that communications behavior is independently influenced by the degree of the individual's involvement in the system, seems borne out. The more ambitious and the less anti-Soviet members of our sample consistently report more frequent communications exposure, and in particular exposure to the formal, official media. Such differences, however, work mainly within the class framework and do not override its influence. In most cases, those one class "up," even though more anti-Soviet, still have higher exposure scores than those in the class below, and those far separated by class are far different in communications pattern even when more alike in anti-Soviet sentiment or career desire.

The constellation of factors which affect and accompany these patterns of communications activity can perhaps be grasped more easily from profiles of the two contrasting communications types, the intelligentsia and the peasants. We hope the reader will keep in mind that the phenomena we discuss here are essentially continuous in distribution. The fact that we are discussing polar types should not create the impression of discontinuity between the groups at the poles.

THE PEASANT

Any description of the communications behavior of the peasant must necessarily be something of a stereotype. There are marked variations in the life conditions of the Soviet peasantry depending upon the prosperity of their region, its distance from established urban centers, the type of crop raised, and other factors. In general, however, the life of the Soviet peasant is characterized by isolation from the city, low living standards, long and difficult work days, low levels of education, and poor communications facilities. His environment does little to stimulate intellectual activity, and he has little time or energy for reading. In fact, many of he older peasants exhibited retrogressive illiteracy: they have *forgotten* how to read. Radios are few in the countryside, numbering 650,000 in 1936, and 1,300,000 in 1947. Sixty per cent and more of the population there shared something like 20 per cent of the already modest supply of radios. Newspapers are less accessible as well as less in demand than in the city. Furthermore, the peasant has little need to be well informed in order to carry out his daily work. Finally, the peasantry is outstandingly the most disaffected group in the Soviet system, and, as we have seen, disaffection is directly related to withdrawal from the official media of communication.

By and large, the communications behavior of the Soviet peasant has been similar to that of the peasant in nonindustrialized countries, in his limited access to and slight use of the formal media. A typical description

567

by a tractor driver who left the Ukraine in the summer of 1950 revealed that in a village of a thousand households there were a few regular radios and 80 wired loudspeakers. Yet, his farm was in a prosperous area and must be assumed to be better supplied with radios than was the average kolkhoz. His collective farm subscribed to a newspaper, but only a few members of the farm subscribed individually "and this was mainly for rolling cigarettes." They all liked the well-worn story about the man who goes up to a kiosk to buy a copy of a major newspaper. The woman asks him "Which will you have?" and he answers, "The one with the thinnest paper."

The regime is neither unaware of nor indifferent to the fact that the peasant's voluntary involvement in the system of official communication is remarkably low. The Soviet regime wants no group isolated from its system of propaganda and agitation. But the peasantry is not a key target group, and in fact seems to be quite low on the priority scheme of propaganda effort. Nevertheless, the regime has made appreciable efforts to bring this group into the official network of communications. Advances have been made in extending the facilities of the press and radio, and the regime has tried to stimulate the interest and involvement of the rural groups by oral agitation. Moreover, the educational level of the younger generation has been raised. Despite these measures young and relatively well-educated peasants, as well as the old peasants, remain comparatively untouched by the mass media and express little interest in what is going on in the world around them.

When it is necessary, from the regime's point of view, that the peasants be informed of some event or policy, an official representative conveys the information to them directly. For example, one young woman collective farmer who never read a newspaper or listened to the radio on her collective farm learned about the beginning of the war when the village Soviet convened the fields hands in the evening after work and a spokesman told them of this event. Another collective farmer, when asked how he had learned about new laws and regulations, gave the typical answer that the brigadier or the head of the collective farm told him about such things. In addition, the regime has an organized corps of official opinion leaders on the collective farms, largely in the person of members of the party and Komsomol, who serve as spokesmen for the regime in their informal day-to-day personal contacts. Not only do they convey specific information but they shape the peasants' attitudes and opinions on larger issues. The young woman mentioned above, when asked what her impressions of the Germans were before her farm was overrun, could answer only in terms of what the "party people" on the kolkhoz had told her about them. The task of being such an opinion leader is part of the regular assigned work of many of the white-collar personnel in these rural areas. Teachers, for example, may have to go into the fields during the lunch periods and read to the field hands while they eat their lunch. As one respondent reports, "Teachers used to tell us about things, but they usually said just what they saw in the newspaper. They would read the newspapers at night and then tell us about it in the morning."

The importance of such word-of-mouth communication in American society has been carefully noted by communications specialists in recent years.[14] Increasingly we have come to realize that certain members of society play a major role as intermediaries between the formal media and the great bulk of the people. In the Soviet Union this role has been formalized, and the members of the agitation network are the chief contact that the peasant and many other persons in comparable situations in Soviet society have with the official media. But even though the regime reaches out to the peasant with the "agit-prop" system, he does not necessarily respond actively. When official meetings are called, many of the peasants attend them with reluctance. One peasant reported: "Usually one member of our family went to such a meeting and told the others what was said, not in detail, just a little. . . ." Many other peasants indicated in the personal interviews that they were almost completely indifferent to meetings and other official oral communications.

The most important source of information for the peasant is word of mouth. For him the secondary, *unofficial* network of communications is actually primary. It is this which explains his claim to rely so heavily on word-of-mouth communication, despite his indifference to the official agitation. To a great extent he acquires his information, that is otherwise readily available in the press, via conversations with friends, co-workers, and kin who read and listen to official media or who have heard it from someone who did. One field hand, for example, heard of the Stalin-Hitler pact in a casual conversation with his brigade leader. Additionally, the peasant acquires a good deal of illicit and unofficial news in this manner. Yet, except for information about local events, his sources are very poor. He is very far from the big cities in which most really important events are occurring. The transmission of such information is dependent on someone's physical mobility, and much of the illicit information which the peasant gets about what is happening throughout the country or in the world at large comes from people who are traveling about. One respondent reports:

In the course of conversation with people who came to the kolkhoz to recruit industrial workers you learned something about how people were living in various areas. . . . There were also collective farmers who did seasonal work elsewhere . . . these people have seen living conditions themselves in various areas and were acquainted with them at firsthand.

Other sources of information for the peasant are fellow collective farmers who have gone to city markets, and truck drivers, who are referred to by one respondent as "a genuine rumor factory." But the rank-

and-file peasant seems to be quite passive with respect to the information that comes to him by word of mouth. Thus, we have seen above that he describes this activity as "discussing with friends," rather than hearing "rumors." He takes what comes, but displays little initiative in seeking it out. For the more highly placed rural personnel, however, the geographical isolation of the countryside is a real source of frustration, and the rural-technical and administrative personnel describe themselves as quizzing and cross examining anyone who might have juicy gossip or the inside story on some current event. A rural technician says:

> We were always trying to get information from people who had come from Moscow. The local party secretary always asked me to tell him what I heard in Moscow when I went there. Everybody returning from Moscow used to tell about the rumors he heard there.

As a further result of the geographical isolation of the countryside the peasant is flooded by rumors of a low order of plausibility. In very few instances does he have access to competent, informed sources of information. One respondent reports, for example, that in the summer of 1950 a collective farm in the Ukraine was swept several times by a rumor that the United States had attacked the Soviet Union. As we will see shortly, the low "quality" or plausibility of the rumors he hears is connected with the degree of confidence he has in this source of information.

THE URBAN INTELLIGENTSIA

In marked contrast to the peasants, the urban intelligentsia is very active with respect to all the communications media. Whereas 76 per cent of the collective farmers reported "frequent" exposure to *none* of the three official mass media, only 3 per cent of the urban intelligentsia did so, and more than half reported "frequent" exposure to all three (Table 2). But this high exposure to official mass media is not at the expense of exposure to unofficial sources. While the *relative importance* of unofficial media is equally high for the peasants, the *absolute rate of exposure* to these media is higher for the intelligentsia. The typical member of the urban intelligentsia reads newspapers regularly and probably has a subscription to at least one newspaper, reads books and magazines very often, maybe several of each a month, has a radio, which in a fair proportion of instances can receive foreign broadcasts, and in addition picks up from friends and acquaintances a considerable amount of reliable supplementary information that never appears in official sources.

His attitude towards the official media is more differentiated and discriminating than is that of the peasant or worker. The members of the less educated groups seem either to accept what they read and hear in a rather blanket fashion, or to reject it in an equally categorical manner. The member of the intelligentsia, whether he likes or dislikes the regime, is more likely to assume that what he reads and hears is reliable and complete to varying degrees. Even the loyal member of the urban intelligentsia acknowledges that "policy" dictates the withholding of certain categories of information. Insofar as he believes that there are gaps or direct falsehoods in the information which is given to the public, he seeks to supplement the formal channels via his own resources. He will apply his own interpretation of the official release, reading "between the lines." The intelligentsia uses the official and unofficial networks in a complex and complementary fashion. His attitude toward the relationship of his various sources of information is best exemplified in the fact that he uses word-of-mouth communications as a corrective device for understanding the newspapers. Intelligentsia informants frequently said: "Rumors made it possible to read the newspapers intelligently," or "We read the Soviet newspapers constantly, but here it is necessary to make certain automatic corrections, so our next source was from conversation with people."

Whereas for the peasants the most important source of information is by by word of mouth, for the intelligentsia it is invariably the official media which play this role. Virtually never do they rely on word of mouth to learn something that is readily available in the press. The nature of their work generally made it imperative that they keep in touch with official sources. Indeed our informants sometimes describe going to great efforts to assure themselves of subscriptions to the Moscow papers, as the following comments indicate:

> Most important for me was *Pravda* and then the technical journals, because I needed to know the correct approach to problems, and I also needed to know which author was being criticized so as to get his books off the shelves and the cards out of the catalogue quickly (A librarian).

> I applied for the Moscow *Pravda* on the grounds that in my work I must be informed of all government decrees that might affect my specific field. As long as my work was considered important I was permitted to subscribe (An engineer).

We do not mean to disregard the fact that 31 per cent of the intelligentsia group said in the personal interview that word-of-mouth sources were "most important." They did not seem to mean, however, that these sources were primary in giving them the greatest *volume* of information, but rather that they were important in the sense of being reliable and furnishing the crucial bits of knowledge without which they could not fill in the mosaic. Word-of-mouth information for the intelligentsia is, in other words, qualitatively quite distinct from its role for the peasant. For the peasant it is a substitute for the official media. For the intelligentsia it is a supplement and corrective. They use the official media avidly but they also use the unofficial in conjunction with the official. For the intelligentsia rumor is likely to come directly from reliable sources. Members of the intelligentsia report much more often than members of the lower classes that their word-of-mouth information came from people with special competence. Most frequently these sources are persons inside the party who themselves had legitimate access to esoteric information, or who at least hear the rumors which circulate in such circles. The following quotation from an interview with a nonparty member gives some idea of the range of information which could be obtained from such sources:

I had good relations with the director of the Institute. He explained many questions to me which had been discussed in the party organs. And in talking to party members you could hear very interesting things. In Leningrad, the chief of the planning department . . . informed me about conditions inside the party after the assassination of Kirov. Also, through the members of the party you could learn the party's attitude towards you. For example, in 1938 a general conversation started up on Soviet policy between me and several other plant employees. One very pro-Soviet person expressed herself violently against religion. I pointed out to her that she was not completely right. . . . She attacked me very violently. The next day the director called me and told me that she had asked that I be turned over to the NKVD. He warned me about the impending danger. But finally he exerted influence on this woman, who was his subordinate, and he saved me from the NKVD. . . .

Reliance on word-of-mouth communications as a corrective and supplement for the official media implies a high degree of confidence in one's sources. Throughout their discussions, our intelligentsia respondents refer to the greater reliability of word-of-mouth sources in general, but most especially with reference to news of political import. More striking, however, is the response on our written questionnaire to a question on the reliability of rumor compared with newspapers and magazines. Referring to the bottom row of Table 6 we see that the majority of each class cited rumor as more reliable—which might be expected if we assume the anti-Soviet bias of the sample to be demonstrating itself.[15] But there are vast class differences. Whereas somewhat more than half of the peasants considered rumor as more reliable, 90 per cent of the intelligentsia placed greater reliance on the reliability of rumor. Whatever reservations we may have about the absolute levels of attitude described in these data, it is striking that the urban elite gave so much more credence to rumor than

Table 6—Reliability of Rumor:[a] by Class and Anti-Soviet Sentiment[15a]

PER CENT STATING RUMOR MORE RELIABLE THAN NEWSPAPERS AMONG:

Anti-Soviet Sentiment	Intelligentsia		White-Collar Employees		Skilled Workers		Ordinary Workers		Collective Farm Peasants		All Classes	
None	90%	(147)[b]	86%	(114)	63%	(30)	73%	(22)	70%	(10)	84%	(323)
Low	91	(149)	95	(129)	73	(33)	64	(44)	64	(25)	86	(380)
Medium	90	(82)	89	(95)	83	(35)	63	(53)	49	(35)	80	(300)
High	82	(43)	85	(65)	82	(45)	74	(83)	58	(50)	76	(286)
All levels	90	(421)	90	(403)	76	(143)	68	(202)	57	(120)		

a. This question was asked only of those who reported obtaining some information by rumor.
b. Total number of respondents on the basis of which the percentage is computed.

did the considerably more disaffected peasantry. We presumably see here the consequences of the nature of the rumors heard by the two groups. The peasant generally hears low level rumors of little plausibility, whereas the superiority of the sources on which he drew for rumors apparently enabled the member of the intelligentsia to give them relatively greater credence.

A further note along this line is provided in the main body of Table 48, which indicates that within each class there is no consistent pattern of association between anti-Soviet sentiment and assessments of the reliability of rumor. The most and least anti-Soviet are about equally likely to impute greater reliability to the unofficial media. In contrast, as we will see below in Table 7, the more anti-Soviet of each class are much more likely to say that nothing in the official media was reliable. In other words, one's assessment of the reliability of *official* media is clearly related to one's political attitudes, but one's assessment of the relative reliabilty of *unofficial* media seems to bear no such relationship to political attitudes. Rather, the evaluation of the unofficial media follows mainly from one's class position and remains relatively the same whatever one's political opinion. This also argues that assessment of the unofficial media is a direct reflection of the quality of the word-of-mouth information that circulates within the social environment of the rater. The lower classes, whose sources are of poorer quality than those of the upper classes, reflect this fact by proportionately less often acknowledging the rumors they hear to be reliable.

The communications behavior of the peasant and those in the intelligentsia is a reflection of their different life situations. In most instances a member of the intelligentsia comes from a family with an established cultural tradition of intellectual activity, with a relatively broad horizon which stimulates curiosity in what is going on in the world. He can afford the radio and newspapers, and his urban residence makes them more available. His job places pressure on him to be well informed. He must know about changes in policy and politics, about new and crucial developments in the nation as well as technical problems in his own special area. He uses the official media avidly, but he also uses the unofficial media in conjunction with the official. It is his very involvement in the system, his proximity to people in the know, his active curiosity, the necessity for keeping abreast of developments that make it both possible and necessary for him to get good, reliable information by word of mouth to supplement the official media. The official and unofficial media are used in conjunction with each other. For the peasant this is not so. He uses the word-of-mouth network because he is a rather inert "communicator" who also distrusts the official media and does not want to have too much traffic with them. Word of mouth is for him a substitute for the newspaper, the Soviet radio

573

and magazine. As he withdraws from them he turns to rumor, and more and more uses word-of-mouth communication.

The Impact of the Official Media

Disaffected Soviet citizens are no doubt far from ideal subjects to use in assessing the impact of Soviet propaganda. Their very status as political refugees makes them living proof mainly for the failures rather than the successes of the system. In addition, they all had a period of extended residence in a society outside their original home, and thus acquired other information against which to assess what had been said in the Soviet media. The matter is further complicated because much of their resentment against the Soviet system was channeled toward the propaganda apparatus of the Communist government. Yet even here, in the very process of condemning the media for lying, our respondents reveal the obvious fact that there are many Soviet citizens who believe the press and other official media without major reservations. A typical instance is this statement by a former Red Army officer, who reports:

In the summer of 1940 a *Tass* report said that the Japanese press had false reports that Soviet troops were being transferred to the Polish front. But we saw these troops traveling over the railroad with our own eyes. We were right next to the railroad. That was the first time I began to doubt what I read in the papers.

Although our interviews are replete with similar, and even more frank, acknowledgments of once held faith, the nature of our sample does not permit us to go very far in assessing those effects of Soviet propaganda which, from the regime's point of view, would be "positive." It is our impression that the greatest success was attained in shaping the Soviet citizen's image of the outside world. This applies especially to the foreign policy of "capitalist" countries and the international role of the Soviet Union.[16] Soviet propaganda also apparently had substantial success in selling its version of conditions of life abroad. The relative wealth and affluence of the United States was an image hard to dislodge and one which indeed the Soviet propagandists often inadvertently fostered. But they seem, nevertheless, to have had substantial success in creating the impression that misery and starvation were so much the lot of the European worker that the Soviet Union was almost a worker's paradise by comparison.

The propaganda system also succeeded somewhat in inculcating a series of standard images of the outstanding features of Soviet society—to wit, that it was "democratic," "progressive," "classless," "without conflict," and so on. These images were apparently maintained by people in the face of evident contradictions provided by their own life experience. For example, a twenty-seven-year-old worker who himself had been unable to go on to further education because there was great need for the income he could bring into the household by going to work, nevertheless said: "In the Soviet Union education, even higher education, is equally available to all people, to workers, peasants, and intelligentsia. There are no classes there, you see!"

But beyond these direct and obvious propaganda successes, the most important effect, was the subtle shaping of the whole pattern of human thought which Soviet "agit-prop" attempts. These results, of course, were achieved not by the mass media alone, but also notably by the school. It is probable that the most difficult material to unlearn or to challenge is that which is implicit. Both the interviewers and persons who have read the interviews were struck by the peculiarly Soviet style of thinking, and of formulating problems that the respondents exhibited. By its very nature, this phenomenon is difficult to illustrate. It is almost a matter of flavor. Yet it emerges in the discussion of many topics. One violently anti-Soviet doctor amused the interviewer by referring to the first and second world wars as the First Imperialist War and the Second Imperialist War. Another highly educated man, who claimed to have been highly skeptical of the Soviet press gave a version of the Shakhty trials, in which prominent engineers were in 1928 accused of a "counterrevolutionary plot," which showed that although he himself was an engineer he implicitly accepted the official version of the story. Other respondents exhibited such confusion about events in Soviet history as to suggest that the rewriting of history which took place under Stalin had many of the effects that were intended. Furthermore, the attitudes toward the welfare state, civil liberties, and other issues we take up in later chapters all reveal major influences on basic thought processes arising from the propaganda efforts of the regime.

In addition, Soviet citizens seem to absorb a good deal of the "metaphysics" of Marxism. We do not mean so much that they used the language of Marxism, although they did that, too, but that they couched many of their comments and descriptions in a mold we have come to recognize as distinctive in Soviet Marxist writing. A special study of our personal interviews from this perspective[17] revealed that the concept of the "dialectic" and the idea that "existence determines consciousness" were the two most frequently mentioned. Asked whether religion and atheism should coexist in society, one respondent replied: "Yes, it should be this way. The Marxists are right, probably, in this respect. There should be contradictions and something new developed out of them." Another revealed his indoctrination when, in response to the question as to who believes in the regime, he replied: "The fanatic who doesn't realize the contradiction. They think they can hold them back by force. This can be

575

done, but only up to a certain point. Because man does not make history. History makes man."

It is impossible to be exposed to a system of propaganda as all-pervasive and monopolistic as that of the Soviet regime and escape without some influence. The areas where greatest influence was exerted were precisely those our knowledge of human learning points to, namely the basic values of the individual and the implicit dimensions of his thought. These elements of the mental processes are those which are most often affected by outside forces quite independently of the individual's wishes, and what is acquired is most difficult to unlearn. Here the influence of Soviet media, Soviet education, Soviet culture is most pervasive. This influence becomes more spotty as we move out into areas of more explicit content. It is difficult to say who in the populace is most subject to this influence, since it is virtually impossible to set up a yardstick with the spotty data which we have on this question. We hazard the guess that the influence of the Soviet media in shaping implicit thought patterns is probably most strong on the intelligentsia. They are, after all, the most highly indoctrinated, highly exposed portion of the population, and are forced in their daily life to learn the proper forms of expression and argumentation if only to use them in a *pro forma* fashion.

In any event, the members of the intelligentsia were very much more likely to grant that some (or even most) of the news in the Soviet press was reliable. About 80 per cent of the intelligentsia granted this point, but its acknowledgment falls off sharply until among the peasants we find two thirds asserting that *none* of the news was reliable (Table 7). These

Table 7—Reliability of Soviet Press: by Class and Hostility to Soviets[18]

PER CENT STATING "NOTHING RELIABLE" AMONG:

Hostility to Soviets	Intelli-gentsia		White-Collar Employees		Skilled Workers		Ordinary Workers		Collective Farm Peasants		All Classes	
High	52%	(27)[a]	60%	(60)	45%	(22)	73%	(77)	73%	(59)	65%	(245)
Medium	23	(125)	30	(176)	50	(78)	67	(123)	68	(92)	45	(594)
Low	16	(392)	24	(347)	39	(121)	51	(153)	56	(105)	30	(1118)
All levels of hostility	20	(544)	30	(583)	43	(221)	58	(353)	64	(256)	39	(1957)

a. Total number of respondents on the basis of which the percentage is computed.

data should not be interpreted as indicating the greater gullibility of the intelligentsia, or the greater skepticism of the manual classes, but mainly the characteristic way the different classes handled questions requiring evaluations on a continuum. The more highly educated groups are considerably less likely to give undifferentiated answers to any such question, and obviously regarded a statement that "nothing" in the Soviet press was truthful as an extreme assertion that was *prima facie* nonsense. It is our impression that among the more highly educated groups there are fewer categorical reactions either of acceptance or rejection of the mass media. There is much differentiation and selection of what to believe or disbelieve. Among the lower classes—and again this is an impression based on a variety of scattered bits of evidence—it would seem that there is less differentiation and one tends more either to accept or reject *all* of what he hears and reads from official sources.

Beyond the influence of his class position, however, a man's attitude toward the reliability of the Soviet press was obviously intimately related to his attitude toward the Soviet system at large. In the intelligentsia the percentage who deny that there is anything reliable in the Soviet press increases more than threefold, and among employees it doubles as we go from those who were least to those who were most hostile (Table 7). Among the workers and peasants the impact is also evident, although the effect of hostility is attenuated. The influence of political orientations is strong; sufficiently strong so as water down the influence of class *per se*, and to bring closer together in their assessment of the press people who are quite widely separated by class. In the intelligentsia as a whole, the typical pattern was to allow some reliability to the Soviet press, but those very hostile to the system acted more like the average worker in denying the reliability of the press. To some degree, obviously, the valuation of the press became a target for expressing hostility to the regime in general. The relation was sufficiently strong, in fact, to warrant inclusion of this item on reliability of the press in our "Index of Anti-Soviet Sentiment."

Interpreting the News

Even though the intelligentsia makes the most use of the official media, it nevertheless also most *frequently* utilizes rumor, and has most *confidence* in it. The intelligentsia is also the group which shows the least tendency to distort Soviet reality, the greatest willingness to praise Soviet achievements, the least hostility to the leaders and the system. We feel it not unreasonable to argue on this basis that even those most committed to the Soviet system were aware of the distortions which crept into official Soviet communications, and felt a need to develop informal ways of learning about events and of interpreting the news for themselves. One obvious method was through the use of rumor. Quite another was through the development of subtle interpretative principles whereby the citizen attempted to discern what was *really* going on. Like all peoples whose news sources are censored and controlled, the Soviet citizen tries by inference to detect that which was withheld, or the truth that lies behind what he considers to be an untrustworthy statement.[19] Respondents asserted fre-

577

quently and spontaneously, "You had to read between the lines." The techniques they cite for reading between the lines are based on a combination of the degree of distrust for the official media and a series of implied assumptions about the nature of the Soviet system, particularly as regards its communications policy. The technique favored by a particular individual, and the degree and literalness of its application, was of course a matter of the individual's personality, his life experience and his social position.

The most drastic device suggested was that one should believe exactly the opposite of what the Soviet press said. Obviously, in such a categorical form this is more an expression of hostile sentiment than a serious suggestion of how to read the newspapers. Some respondents went so far as to insist that the Soviet populace initially gave the invading German troops such a warm reception during World War II because the people automatically assumed that any government which had been attacked in the Soviet press was a good one.[20] Certainly there is extensive evidence that even Soviet Jews did not believe stories about the Nazis that later turned out to be quite true. This circumstance demonstrates at the very least that there are a considerable number of Soviet citizens who disbelieve much of what they read in the press, and disbelieve it to the extent of being willing to act on this basis in matters that affect their very lives. As one of Calas' informants says, ". . . it is obvious that the crudest mistakes were made by this method of simply assuming that the reverse of any official statement was necessarily true—to wit, the disbelief in German atrocities."[21]

One relatively sophisticated assumption which leads at times to the acceptance of the opposite of what is found in the Soviet press is that the Soviet government projects its own motives onto foreign governments. Thus, a middle-aged bookkeeper says, "The Soviet press interprets events in Korea as American aggression, when in actual fact the contrary is true and it is really Soviet aggression." Another, a Ukrainian dairy technician, says, "If they wrote that our enemies abroad were arming for war, I knew that the Soviet Union was arming."

Another assumption about Soviet news policy made by our respondents was that the Soviet government would always attempt to prepare the populace in advance to accept unpleasant developments. "If there were going to be a famine in the Ukraine, we always used to hear that there was hunger in Germany and Austria, and that children were picking food out of garbage cans. When I saw such examples I knew that soon we would have a famine." A Ukrainian carpenter says that when he saw a series of newspaper articles deploring the effects of abortion he inferred that legislation controlling abortion was forthcoming. He proved to be right. A cooper of fifty says he always regarded news about social improvements as intended to divert attention from a forthcoming unpleasant event. Some readers will see the parallel between this assumption and the popular belief, common in wartime even in the Western democracies, that the population was always "prepared" for the announcement of a defeat by prior publication of news about some little "victory."

The refugees claim that they learned much from official sources that was quite different from what the regime wanted people to learn. Thus, a middle-aged engineer and former party member stated that if he read in the Soviet press that workers were striking for higher wages in New York City, the main conclusion he would draw would not be that there was industrial unrest, but that American workers could afford to strike *and that they had the right to strike*. A former professor who wrote for the film industry says: "I taught myself to translate the lies of the press into my language of relative truth." He gave these examples:

1. There is a report of a demonstration of dissatisfied workers in Paris. His translation is: "What would Stalin's Chekists do with a similar demonstration in Moscow?"
2. There are reports of the daring and open deeds of Communists in America. Translation: He is surprised at the "childlike naivete of Americans who permitted the most deadly enemies of their country to do whatever they wanted to do."

One story which had wide general circulation in the Soviet emigration suggests the strange mixture of acceptance and rejection of the content of Soviet communications which was typical of the attempts to "interpret" those events the censor permitted to come before the Soviet audience. It concerns a newsreel of race riots in Detroit, shown in the Soviet theaters to demonstrate the degree of racial discrimination in the United States. In one scene a Negro is shown being hurled through the air. There is a pan shot of his shoes as his feet pass the camera. The Soviet audiences, the story goes, noticed the quality of the shoes. *Accepting the official image of the plight of the Negro in America*, they concluded that no *American* Negro would be wearing shoes of the quality shown in this shot. Therefore, they reasoned, the Negro must have been a professional Soviet actor, and the film the propaganda of a Soviet studio. The story may be apocryphal, but it is nevertheless revealing.

Obviously, attempts to "interpret" the news as it appears in official media can backfire. Assuming that everything in the media is false can lead to grotesque errors. The skillful interpreter of the news must have some criteria of what to accept and what to question. In many instances he must use *ad hoc* criteria—the internal coherence of the particular story, or its congruence with other information in which he has a considerable degree of trust. Certain general criteria were advanced, however, by some respondents. Some said that you could believe the "facts" but not the interpretation that the official media put on them. "I must take the facts in an article and assimilate them critically, and I would come to conclusions quite different from the ones written in the article," said a schoolteacher who had served also as an army engineer. Other respondents said they believed stories on topics where the Soviet government had a neutral interest. Still others said they believed only what was unfavorable.

Say there is an article describing a plant; there is disorder, nonfulfillment, spoilage of production. This I believed. But if the article writes about success, for example, that the Astrakhan Fish Trust has overfulfilled by 125 per cent the catching of such and such a fish, and by 130 per cent of some other fish. . . . How can I believe that when I see that there are no fish products in the stores for 2 or 3 months?

This story reflects what was probably the most outstanding difficulty faced by the Soviet propagandist—the glaring contrast between the regime's claim that "life is getting ever easier," on the one hand, and on the other the harsh and grinding poverty of daily life in city and farm. The Soviet worker and peasant could not judge for himself the intentions of a Roosevelt or a Hitler; he could not himself assess the conditions of life of workers in Detroit or farmers in Australia; but he could count the number of families living in his apartment, the number of pants he owned, his wife's dresses, and his children's shoes. He did not have to count very high—one was generally enough—and for the child zero might do, for some items like shoes. Yet the Soviet press continued to picture the workers' paradise. It is not hard to believe that so many Soviet citizens came to distrust the official media.

None of the interpretative devices employed is surprisingly original, nor is the attempt at interpretation *per se* something distinctive of the Soviet system. Even where the media of communication are little subject to political control, there is always a substantial amount of guessing as to what lies behind certain news stories. A prominent public official is sick, but the disease is not mentioned. Is it cancer? The president affirms his faith in a political boss who has been charged with corruption. Does he believe the man is honest, or is this political expediency? The examples could be multiplied. What is distinctive about the Soviet system is the great extent to which these practices were developed and the high degree to which the Soviet citizen was dependent on inference and on interpolation and extrapolation to satisfy his information needs. Some foreign observers have extolled the ability of the Soviet citizen to read between the lines of the official media. It is quite obvious, however, that even though this practice may be productive and worthwhile, it can also produce errors of inference and be quite misleading. With all his reading between the lines, however, the Soviet citizen could not develop the most valuable instrument which he could possibly have for interpreting the news—a good background of reliable information.

580

SUMMARY AND FUTURE PROSPECTS

Under Stalin the Soviet regime, urgently concerned with molding public opinion to the support of the party's policies, developed an elaborate system of official communications media. The system is designed, with respect to structure and controls, to reach a maximum proportion of the population and carry the regime's message in such forms as to convince and exhort the populace to implement the party's wishes. The communications policy of the regime, however, was such as to make even its supporters disatisfied with the coverage of news and the reliability of the information they got via overt means. As a result, there grew up parallel to the official system of communications an unofficial one including word-of-mouth communication, personal observation, and a pattern of interpretative inferences applied to the official media. In one sense, this unofficial system was not different from that which develops in any society. Any social order feels the necessity, and develops the devices with which to withhold certain types of information. The special characteristics of Soviet communications policy, including monopoly over the media and a militant and one-sided presentation of the official point of view, particularly fosters the development of this unofficial system and it has reached distinctive proportions.

The official media, indeed all media, are most extensively used by those higher in education and/or occupational status. Those who are active users of one medium are more likely to be active in the use of others. Distrust of the official media is a function of attitude toward the regime in general. However, some degree of distrust of the official media does not, *per se*, necessarily mean that one is disaffected from the system. Among the intelligentsia a person is quite capable of being a firm supporter of the regime and simultaneously of feeling that the official media cannot be relied on completely. He tends to accept the idea that reasons of "security" and "state interest" make censorship imperative. This does not keep him from seeking out supplemental, covert sources of information such as rumor and word of mouth. Quite to the contrary, his position in society makes this both possible and necessary. He needs such information to survive and advance; he has access to it because he is in contact with people in the know. Members of the lower classes are more categorical in their reaction. The evidence, sparse as it is, suggests that they are more likely either totally to accept or totally to reject what they read and hear from official sources. Acceptance of the regime, involvement in the system, and attention to official media are positively related to the exploitation of the unofficial media among the upper classes. By contrast, the anti-Soviet member of the lower classes withdraws from the system, avoids the official media, and relies primarily on rumor, word of mouth, and other unofficial sources to find out what is going on.

Faced with this picture of the communications process in the Soviet Union, one naturally raises the question of influence: "Quite apart from what they *say* they believe, how much of what they read and hear do they believe *implicitly?*" Obviously, our sample has gross limitations as a source of information for answering that question. It is clear, however, from even our presumably anti-Soviet sample that there are people in all ranks of life who believe implicitly what they read and hear. We have no means of ascertaining what proportion of the population, or of any one group, falls in this category. Our sample may be a limiting case of extreme doubters, and we know our respondents had access to non-Soviet communications for several years. Yet despite this it is striking how the more implicit aspects of Soviet official communications, the mode of thought and the categories in which events are grouped, are reflected in the thought patterns and expression of our informants. This may be most true among the intelligentsia, who, whether they accept or reject the regime must, by virtue of their place in society, learn and repeat the official line to the point where it becomes second nature. There is also evidence of the more direct influence of the official media at a number of particular points. For example, the images of life in the West, and of the policy and intentions of other governments, seem to have been greatly influenced by the official media.

Even the loyal citizen was often frustrated and displeased by the official communications policy. While he may have approved of it in the whole, he chafed at it in detail. The secondary system of unofficial communications served him with information which he might need for the conduct of his job, to save his skin, to satisfy his curiosity; at the least it gave him a little bit of a flesh and blood view of the big shots.

The regime obviously believes in its policy of restricted information or it would not pursue it so vigorously. The unofficial network is a source of irritation to the leaders. But the regime also adapts and accommodates somewhat to the inevitable. Many of our respondents, including some who were in a position to know authoritatively, report that the regime exploits the existing system of word-of-mouth communications in two ways. It plants rumors that it wants circulated, and it taps the rumor network as a method of assessing public opinion.

There is a strong possibility, however, that the system of unofficial communications has certain latent functions of which the regime may not be sufficiently aware. Certainly it effects a modicum of tension reduction by supplying people with information which they desire. Beyond that, the additional information that they acquire may help them to do their jobs better. Like any overly bureaucratized society, the Soviet system tends to be hyper-cautious in the circulation of information that is required for the operation of the system itself. By supplementing these sources *unofficially* people are often better able to perform their official duties.

Very few areas of Soviet life were as totally and distinctively shaped by the impact of Stalin's rule as was the realm of communication. Under his guidance, the Soviet propaganda apparatus was enormously expanded, and the size of the lies and distortions in which it dealt expanded proportionately. Not only current news but history was rewritten to order. Since his death there has been some easing of the controls over mass and private communication. The marked decline in the rate of political arrest will, if the process is not reversed, undoubtedly do much to foster the circulation of critical opinions which earlier no one dared to utter or even to think. The reverberations of such opinions will be important in setting up currents which in time may give rise to the beginnings of genuine, and perhaps mildly influential, public opinion within Soviet society. The chances for the development of such currents seem best in scientific and intellectual circles.

At the same time it would be unduly optimistic to assume that the Soviet leadership is to any major degree moving toward the establishment of free discussion, and least of all that it will permit the use of the official media of communications for the wide dissemination of "private," or "minority," that is, of nonofficial, opinion. The adjustments being made at the moment probably are not an attack on the *principles* of the Leninist and Stalinist methods of thought control. Rather, they are best understood as efforts to remove some of the worst abuses and rigidities which had crept into the system, and were actually interfering with the effectiveness of the propaganda effort as a whole.

What we may, therefore, expect is a continuation, with modifications, of the general patterns sketched in this chapter, rather than a sharp shift in practice. The increasing education of the population and the increasing availability of electric power, and hence radios, in the countryside, will undoubtedly increase the communications activity of the ordinary workers and peasants. Although this should somewhat narrow the gap between the intelligentsia and the manual classes, it can hardly be expected to eliminate it. Neither widespread education nor ready availability of the mass media has had that effect in England or the United States. The better educated, the occupationally more highly placed, the politically more involved, will undoubtedly continue to be much more active "communicators" than will those of lower standing in these regards.

As to the quality of communications activities, it is more difficult to say. We anticipate that continued control and censorship of the Soviet press will foster the kind of reading between the lines in the official media, and the reliance on rumor to supplement them, which we have noted. But, this may decrease over time in certain areas. For a short period at least the startling admissions which the regime made after

Stalin's death about the distortions of news and history which character-ized *his* realm may tend to increase disbelief in and suspicion of the official media. But in the long haul, assuming there is no major retrench-ment, the acknowledgement of *former* distortions should increase con-fidence in the reliability of the *current* communications. In addition, the regime now has less need to lie, and as it lies less the contradiction be-tween propaganda and reality will become less. More than anything else, this should serve to increase confidence in the reliability of the official media.

Furthermore, as the pressures put on managers and others in responsi-ble positions become more reasonable, the need to seek "inside" informa-tion to increase one's security will probably decrease. On the other hand, the sharp controls which continue to exist on free access to information, symbolized by the jamming of foreign radio broadcasts, the uneven pace of Soviet economic development, and the great curiosity and hunger of the Soviet people for information about the outside world, should support extensive use of informal, nonofficial sources of information and wide-spread tendencies to continue to "read between the lines" in the official media.

It is difficult for us to imagine conditions under which Soviet com-munications policy and the reaction of the citizen to it could be more extreme than it was under Stalin. Therefore, almost any change must be for the better. How much improvement there will be will depend on (or be reflected in) the factors noted immediately above.

NOTES

1. Some of the material presented in this chapter was earlier reported on in different form in: Peter H. Rossi and Raymond A. Bauer, "Some Patterns of Soviet Communications Behavior," *Public Opinion Quarterly*, 16: 653–670 (Winter 1952–53); and Raymond A. Bauer and David B. Gleicher, *Public Opinion Quarterly*, 17: 297–310 (Fall 1953).

2. For an extended description of the Soviet communications system and its functioning, see Alex Inkeles, *Public Opinion in Soviet Russia* (Cambridge, 1950).

3. *Narodnoe Khozyaistvo SSSR* (Moscow, 1956) p. 240.

4. F. L. Mott, *The News in America* (Cambridge, 1952).

5. *Narodnoe Khozyaistvo*, p. 184.

5a. Table 1. This table is based on the open-ended questions on com-munications exposure asked during the personal interview. An individual was scored as using a source if he made any mention of his exposure to it, even if it was infrequent. In the table, however, only media cited by 10 per cent or more were included. The other citations were: books, 6 per cent; foreign radio, 6 per cent; other foreign sources, 3 per cent; films, 3 per cent; and other 4 per cent.

Of a total of 329 cases, 17 did not answer the question, or did not use any source. Of the 312 who cited a source, 275 gave sufficient information to permit evaluation of which *particular* source was most important.

6. We use the personal interviews here rather than the larger sample on the written questionnaire because only in the former did we inquire as to "most important" source. The relative standing of the roughly comparable media was, however, very similar for the questionnaire sample. Using as a guide the per cent who claimed to use a source "frequently" the order was: newspapers and magazines, 54 per cent; domestic radio, 42 per cent; discussion with friends, 38 per cent (18 per cent cited "rumor"); and agitation meetings, 16 per cent.

7. From "Public Use of the Library," reprinted Daniel Katz *et al.*, eds., in Public Opinion and Propaganda (New York, 1954), p. 238.

8. Wilbur Schramm, *The Process and Effects of Mass Communication* (Urbana, 1955), pp. 74–83. In France the figure was only 56 per cent and in Italy 39. Such differences in part reflect differences in literacy and levels of education in the different countries. There is in addition the problem of availability, which may in turn also reflect literacy rates. In any event, the number of copies of newspapers per thousand inhabitants, *published* in the various countries varied with the rates of *use*. Thus, in the United Kingdom the number published was 350, in France 259, Italy 98, the rates of daily use approximately 90, 60, and 40, respectively.

The wording of the question, and the meaning of the terms "regular" or "frequent" also varies from country to country and from study to study. In our more precise written questionnaire, for example, it is only by allowing the answer "seldom"—that is, by excluding only those who said that they "never" read a newspaper—that we can classify close to 90 per cent as using the newspaper as an ordinary source. Those who were "frequent" users, which would suggest daily or near daily reading of the newspaper, were only 54 per cent. This rate will be seen to be lower than that for the United States, England, and Scandinavia. This should, however, be of little significance with regard to the main point made in the text, which has to do with the relative importance of the different media for the members of our sample.

9. Materials on the relative importance of the newspaper versus the radio as news sources in the United States are hardly unambiguous in their import. Before World War II the newspaper was generally cited twice as often as a source of news. Apparently, the importance of "flash" news in wartime produced a shift in the opposite direction. For a summary of the survey results up to 1946, see Hadley Cantril, ed., *Public Opinion, 1935–1946* (Princeton, 1951), pp. 523–526.

10. Most American surveys report only 5 or 6 per cent citing "talks with friends or other people" as sources of news (see Hadley Cantril, ed., *Public Opinion*, p. 524). However, the questions put forth tend to stress sources of "news," rather than sources of information or ideas that were important in shaping one's feelings about political issues. There are at least two important American studies which suggest that personal, informal or word-of-mouth communication may under certain circumstances loom as large in the American context as it does on the Soviet setting. Lazarsfeld and his associates asked a question not too different from ours: "From which sources did you get most of the information or impressions that caused you to form your judgment on how to vote?" In Erie County, Ohio, 56 and 52 per cent of the men and women, respectively, cited some personal contact such as relatives, friends, or associates on the job. (See Paul Lazarsfeld, Bernard Berelson, and

Helen Gaudet, *The People's Choice*, New York, 1952, p. 171.) In a second study (Samuel Stouffer, *Communism, Conformity, and Civil Liberties*, New York, 1955) a national sample was asked, with regard to unemployment and hard times, whether "you get your information mostly from what you read or hear on the air, or mostly from what you hear in conversations with other people." Fifty-nine per cent cited "other people" as their source.

11. Hostility is here measured by the distortion index. The "most" anti-Soviet are those with scores of 4, and the "least" those with scores of O.

12. The statement is *generally* true, but has interesting exceptions. Movie attendance, for example, drops off rapidly in the older groups—as it does in the United States.

13. The derivation of these types by means of a modification of certain steps of latent structure analysis is discussed by Peter H. Rossi, in the "Technical Postscript" to "Some Patterns of Soviet Communications Behavior," *Public Opinion Quarterly*, 16:666–670 (Winter 1952–53). Peter Rossi developed these typologies.

13a. Table 2. The exposure to the different types of media is measured according to the Communications Typologies. These exposure types were developed through Latent Structure Analysis by Peter H. Rossi and described by him in the "Technical Postscript" to Peter Rossi and Raymond A. Bauer, "Some Patterns of Soviet Communications Behavior," *Public Opinion Quarterly*, Vol. 16, No. 4, 1952–53. On official mass media: high is a score of 1; medium, a score of 2 or 3; low, a score of 0. On personalized media (legitimate nonmass media): high is a score of 3 or 2; medium, a score of 1; low, a score of 0. On aesthetic media (entertainment media): high is a score of 2 or 1; low, a score of 0. On covert media (nonlegitimate media): high is a score of 3 or 2; medium, a score of 1; low, a score of 0. Social class is based on I–7, excluding 234 cases who were student, other or DK to this question. The N's given at the bottom of the table represent all those in each social class. *For each of the four exposure types separately*, the figures total to 100 per cent, on the base number given for the class.

13b. Table 3. As indicated in note no. 5A (Table 1), 275 individuals gave sufficient information to permit specific scoring of their most important source. Of these, 16 could not be assigned a class, leaving a total of 259 as the total cases considered in this table. "Other" important sources of information include: magazines, personal observation, and others.

13c. Table 4. Social group is based on 1–7 with students, other, and DK (234 cases) omitted. Anti-Soviet sentiment is based on the Index of that name, "Low" indicates a score of 0 or 1; "high" a score of 2, 3, 4, or 5. The per cents indicate the proportion of those of a given social class and a given A.S.S. score who were frequently exposed to the given medium (based on, reading from top to bottom, VIII–1, A, B, C, D, E, F, G, H, VIII–6, VIII–4, VIII–1, I). The base N's are, however, median N's, since for each item there were different numbers who were "no answer" with regard to exposure and these NA's were not included in the base when the percentages were computed.

13d. Table 5. Students, housewives, "other" (702) cases are not included. Desire for a career is based on II–9. "Wanted a career" combines the first three response choices: "did not want a career" combines choices four and five. The last two responses "other" and DK (277 cases) were omitted from consideration. Exposure to media is based on, reading from left to right, VIII–1, parts C, A, E, G, and VIII–6, respectively. In each case, the percentage given represents those who indicated they "frequently" were exposed to the various media. The N's are the median for the five media, since there was some variation in the number not answering for different media.

14. Elihu Katz and Paul F. Lazarsfeld, *Personal Influence* (Glencoe, Ill., 1955).

15. Note that a negatively-toned word for "rumor" (slukhi) was used. This should have had the general effect of lowering the proportions in all classes who rated rumors as more reliable than newspapers and magazines.

15a. Table 6. Social class is based on 1–7. Anti-Soviet sentiment scores; "none" indicates a score of 0, "low" a score of 1, "medium" a score of 2, and "high" a score of 3–5. Reliability of rumor is based on VIII–6, C. Only those who reported hearing rumors are considered here. This eliminated 1133 cases who could not pass on their reliability. In addition, on successive sorts, 234 who were students, other, or DK/NA on Anti-Soviet Sentiment were eliminated. Out of the original 2718 cases, this left a base of 1289 cases for this table.

16. For a fuller discussion, see chapter 14 of *How The Soviet System Works*, Inkeles, Bauer and Kluckhohn.

17. This study was done by John Zawadsky.

18. Table 7. Reliability of the Soviet press is based on VIII–2; social class on 1–7; and hostility to the Soviets on the distortion index. High hostility indicates a score of 3 or 4; medium hostility, a score of 1 or 2; low hostility, a score of 0.

Of 2718 cases, 1957 are represented in this table. The remainder were eliminated on successive sorts as follows: 234 were student, other, or DK on social class; 345 were DK on the distortion index; and 182 were DK on reliability of the Soviet press.

19. The interpretation of news sources by Soviet citizens is discussed by Elena Calas in "Readers' Interpretation of Newspaper Materials in the Soviet Union," *Studies in Soviet Communication*, Center for International Studies, Massachusetts Institute of Technology, 1952. Using similar sources to ours, Mrs. Calas comes to virtually identical conclusions. This section could well have been written exclusively on Mrs. Calas' materials. Our own conclusions on this matter were formed before Mrs. Calas' work was published, and we regard this concurrence of judgment to be a happy coincidence.

20. This particular point is discussed in some detail by Calas, *ibid.*, pp. 59 ff.

21. Calas, *ibid.*, p. 63.

EDGAR H. SCHEIN

The Passion For Unanimity

CHINESE COMMUNIST THOUGHT REFORM is a dramatic instance of the totalitarian passion for unanimity, both in the intensity with which it has been pursued and in the wide range of participation which it has demanded. Is this purely a Chinese phenomenon, or are there forces in any totalitarian society, particularly in a revolutionary period, which can account for the elaborate unanimity rituals like parades, elections with predetermined outcomes, "spontaneous" mass demonstrations, and society-wide campaigns; the extensive proselytizing among the "heretics" or the "infidels"; the purges, programs of re-education, and other repressive measures aimed at deviants; the deep infringement on the part of the government into areas of life ordinarily considered to be private; and the extensive efforts by the leaders to legitimize whatever coercion of overt behavior is present?

We propose to examine this general question by considering what functions ideological unanimity serves for the system as a whole, for the leaders, and for the followers. Most of our examples will deal with Communist society but will highlight those aspects which it shares with other totalitarian societies. Our basic purpose is to show that unanimity pressures can be deduced from many different forces acting in a totalitarian society and that achieved unanimity serves many different functions. In particular we wish to demonstrate the the fallacy of assuming that any single level of analysis—the political, sociological, or psychological—is any more valid than any other level in providing an adequate explanation. Therefore our approach will be to discuss each of the forces which act at these various levels one at a time and as if it were the only one acting. The interaction between the forces, their relative strength, and their degree of interdependence are, of course, important determinants of the final outcome. We

Reprinted from *Coercive Persuasion*, (1961), pp. 62–91, by permission of the author and the publisher. (Copyright, 1961, W. W. Norton.)

have set as our goal, however, only the identification and discussion of the separate forces, considering them to be some of the basic variables of any final theory of the passion for unanimity:

The forces we shall consider can be categorized in the following manner:

Forces deriving from the movement's ideology.

Forces deriving from the goals of the leaders of the movement or state.

1. The necessity of projecting an image of unanimity for external consumption.
2. The necessity of projecting an image of unanimity for internal consumption.
3. Keeping control over any ideas which could become the basis of resistance.
4. Creating or eliciting motivation for social and economic change (rapid industrialization or other pressing goals which the movement or state may wish to attain).

Forces deriving from the definition of the movement or state as being in a state of "combat."

Forces deriving from psychological factors in the leaders of the movement or state.

1. Basic personality traits of the leaders.
2. The psychological consequences of success.
3. The effects of coercing unanimity.

Forces deriving from psychological factors in the followers or citizens of the state.

1. Dependency, alienation from self, need to merge self with larger movement.
2. Effects of crisis or disillusionment.
3. National character factors.
4. Missionary zeal.

A system organized explicitly around an ideology probably shows the effects of the ideology in all areas of its functioning, yet it is usually quite difficult to specify precisely the nature of these effects. In the case of Communist society the difficulty lies partly in our inability to determine precisely the role of classical Marxist ideology in the psychological organization of the leaders; partly in our inability to determine precisely in what manner the ideology enters into the education of the young and integrates itself with existing cultural themes; and partly in the nature of the Communist ideology itself inso far as it is a dynamic philosophical system with a large number of components, many of which are loosely tied together, many of which are susceptible of redefinition as suits the needs of the leaders, and many of which are ethical generalities and platitudes which do not clearly distinguish it from many other ideologies. In the section on ideology we shall present those aspects of classical Marxism-Leninism which bear directly on the question of unanimity, recognizing that the existence of this ideology does not necessarily imply its use by the leaders in actually seeking unanimity; in subsequent sections we shall discuss some of the specific effects of the ideology on the psychology of the leaders and followers in the society.

Communist Ideology

Communist ideology, as a philosophical system, contains a number of features pertaining to unanimity. First, because it is a deterministic, all-encompassing set of beliefs based on pseudo-scientific laws, it cannot, as a religion cannot, admit the possibility of any other truth. Any idea or piece of behavior not in line with Communist principles is *ipso facto* blasphemy, sacrilege, or heresy depending on the nature of the deviance. As Talmon puts it:

> The totalitarian democratic school . . . is based upon the assumption of a sole and exclusive truth in politics. It may be called political Messianism in the sense that it postulates a preordained, harmonious and perfect scheme of things, to which men are irresistibly driven and at which they are bound to arrive. [Talmon, 1952, p. 2]

Second, though the ideology is supposedly based on a scientific analysis of history, it contains in its assumptions the refutation of any competing theory. It is thus completely untestable, while maintaining the appearance of rational truth. For example, the plea on the part of a prisoner to subject an assertion by the interrogator to "scientific" test is immediately refutable on the grounds that the scientific method as conceived of by the Western prisoner is a capitalist invention and therefore, *ipso facto*, not valid. On the other hand, it is asserted that the validity of the Communist point of view can be perceived only by adopting the correct cognitive frame of reference, which means, in effect, the *a priori* acceptance of its basic premises.

Third, the basic goals, i.e., the Communist vision of utopia, are highly acceptable generalities concerning the brotherhood of man, complete harmony of outlook, and a world of freedom and plenty for all. The reiteration of such broad ethical generalities as the justification for the operation of the Communist state not only increases the possibilities of easily obtaining unanimity on a very general level but also sharply decreases the likelihood of successful ideological deviance or resistance. The ideology is too general and broadly acceptable to be vulnerable.[1] However, the acceptability of a broad ethic by no means guarantees that it will be easy to obtain unanimity concerning the means used to achieve the utopia. From the point of view of the leaders of the movement, outspoken unanimity on basic utopian goals is probably important to serve as a set of rationalizations or justifications for a concrete program which, it is anticipated, may lead to strong resistance on the part of the followers or citizens. Whatever resistance arises can be neutralized by affirming the proposed means as the *only* way to achieve the ends that everyone has agreed to already, or can be eliminated by being branded as standing in the way of the achievement of the ultimate goals.

It has been pointed out by Talmon that all utopian ideologies, even those eighteenth-century philosophies which underlie the development of the Western democratic state (e.g., Rousseau's idea of "the general will" as a rational way of integrating separate individual wills), contain the assumptions that make a totalitarian system possible.

It is of great importance to realize that what is today considered as an essential concomitant of democracy, namely, diversity of views and interests, was far from being regarded as essential by the eighteenth century fathers of democracy. Their original postulates were unity and unanimity. The affirmation of the principle of diversity came later, when the totalitarian implications of the principle of homogeneity had been demonstrated by Jacobin leadership. [Talmon, 1952, p. 44]

The very idea of a self-contained system from which all evil and unhappiness have been exorcised is totalitarian. The assumption that such a scheme of things is feasible and indeed inevitable is an invitation to a regime to proclaim that it embodies this perfection, to exact from its citizens recognition and submission and to brand opposition as vice or perversion.

The greatest danger is in the fact that far from denying freedom and rights to man, far from demanding sacrifice and surrender, this system solemnly reaffirms liberty, man's self interest and rights. It claims to have no other aims than their realization. Such a system is likely to become the more totalitarian, precisely because it grants everything in advance, because it accepts all liberal premises *a priori*. For it claims to be able by definition to satisfy them by a positive enactment as it were, not by leaving them alone and watching over them from the distance. When a regime is by definition regarded as realizing rights and freedoms, the citizen becomes deprived of any right to complain that he is being deprived of his rights and liberties. The earliest practical demonstration of this was given by Jacobinism. [Talmon, 1952, p. 35]

The impact of this circumstance on the citizen is described well by Ferreus.

. . . the adoption of the artificial communist creed must produce guilt complexes, as does, within a communist-controlled nation or within the party, party, the negation of the "accepted" code. Many of these guilt complexes are essentially social and political in nature—"I have sinned against my class," "I am a saboteur and exploiter"—and they expose the person to the dangers of nonconformism. Whenever the communists succeed in convincing people that they are a sort of incarnation of humanity's social conscience and that they are history's anointed arbiters of any action undertaken by non-communists, a person will tend to be apologetic about any doubts he may be harboring concerning communism. Opposition to or deviation from communism is tantamount to a negation of mankind's loftiest ideals and of mankind's inevitable future. [Ferreus, 1957, p. 102]

Fourth, in its basic assumptions (and supported by its own semantic rules) the ideology tends to dichotomize the world, reflecting an almost complete lack of tolerance for ambiguity. Thus statements are either absolutely true or totally false; people are either friends or enemies; the world can only be capitalistic or communistic; future developments are either inevitable or impossible; given actions are either prescribed or forbidden; there is in any given situation just one "correct line" of policy, all others tend to lead to ruin; and so on. The philosophical assumption behind this aspect of the ideology is that objective truth is attainable.

When . . . a Party member is given instruction in Marxist ideology, the first thing that is impressed upon him is that there exist, and can exist, only two possible philosophical positions, idealism and materialism. . . . He is told that there are many forms of idealism, but that all assert that mind is primary, and that matter, if it has any reality at all, is secondary. Idealism contends that we can have no *final* knowledge of the world of phenomena, because such knowledge is conditioned by our senses. A knowledge of "things in themselves" is thus impossible. To men born in green or red spectacles the snow will appear green or red, and they have no means of discovering that it is, in fact, neither. On the other hand, materialism insists that reality is not mind but matter; that the existence of matter precedes that of mind; that the material world, so far from existing only in our minds, possesses an objective existence apart from our perception of it; and that we can therefore obtain a knowledge of the world which, though incomplete, like a jigsaw puzzle from which certain parts are missing, contains an indestructible core of absolute truth which is continually growing as our knowledge increases. [Hunt, 1957, p. 36]

Undoubtedly this kind of position creates forces toward unanimity in that any degree of deviation or lack of support can be defined as *total* rejection should the regime choose to apply the definition. Only by complete outspoken acceptance can the citizen guarantee for himself some measure of safety (though, as we shall see later, even this may not be an iron-clad guarantee).

Fifth, the ideology states that it derives its main dynamism from the thought and needs of the proletariat. In fact, it claims to be an expression of the will of the proletariat. It is therefore implied that any member who fits the definition of proletarian ought to think in a Communist manner and support the movement. If he does not, he has been contaminated or infected by incorrect ideas and must be taught the truth. Because it would damage the image of the ideology to have its *a priori* faithfully be heretics, it is clearly justifiable to expend considerable effort to prevent them from becoming or continuing to be unfaithful.[2] For this same reason, perhaps, great emphasis was given by Lenin and others to the Communist Party as the leader and embodiment of the will of the masses (the proletariat). If the masses do not express their own will, the leadership must "make them conscious of it" and express it for them.

For the Chinese Communist Party this ideological problem was exacerbated by the fact that the masses supporting the revolution were primarily drawn from the peasantry instead of the urban proletariat. This circumstance forced Mao to reconsider the correctness of the basic Marxist premise that only the urban proletariat could provide a proper mass base for the revolution. His successful peasant movement validated the concept that people with improper class origins could be re-educated and, in so doing, he laid the foundation for thought reform.

Sixth, the ideology stresses the unity of theory and action. Among other things this concept implies that intellectual knowledge alone is useless and that apathy or lack of support is as evil and intolerable as outright opposition. Hence there results continuous pressure for outspoken, active support.

Marx teaches that . . . sensations, which were held to give us faithful images of the external world, did not provide *immediate* knowledge but only stimuli to knowledge which completed itself in action; for if sensations were purely passive, it was impossible to explain why they should result in conscious activity; and if men were unable to react on their environment and change it, revolutions could no longer be regarded as a form of human activity and were simply incidents in a mechanical process. Hence, he insisted that we only perceive a thing as a part of the process of acting upon it, just as a cat when it sees a mouse immediately pounces on it. . . . Marxists have always insisted that theory and action are one. A theory of which the truth is not confirmed by action is sterile, while action which is divorced from theory is purposeless. The two stand in much the same relation to one another as do faith and works in Christian theology. [Hunt, 1957, pp. 34–35]

In the same vein, Mao said in 1942:

"How can half-intellectuals be transformed into intellectuals with a title corresponding to reality? There is only one way: to see that those with only book knowledge become practical workers engaged in practical tasks, and see that those doing theoretical work turn to practical research. In this way we can reach our goal." [Quoted in Brandt, Schwartz, & Fairbank, 1952, p. 381]

The need for activity as proof of loyalty follows:

Totalitarian terror has not only this negative function to perform (elimination of misfits or deviants). Operating within the context of enforced unanimity, it becomes a stimulant to more enthusiastic expressions of support for the regime. It classified men's behavior according to degrees of loyalty, and mere absence of opposition to the regime becomes insufficient as proof of devotion to it. Positive action is demanded, and men compete in loyalty. It is no accident that secret police files in the USSR stress, first of all, whether a given individual is passive or active. Needless to add, one can be active in a totalitarian society only on behalf of the regime. [Friedrich & Brzezinski, 1956, pp. 135–36]

In China, the pressure for active support has reached even greater intensity:

The regime desires unanimous approval even in the prison camps. We must not imagine that the pariahs can fulminate against the system within their cell walls or under the sun of the Gobi desert. The pressure on them is so great, as we have learned from those who have managed to return from the Chinese prisons to the free world, that the prisoners are zealous to bow to the warders, accusing themselves of all manner of crimes and thanking the People's Republic which has reformed their way of thinking. Unanimity must nowhere be in default, and even Hell itself must echo with approval and praise. [Guillain, 1957, pp. 288–89]

The society, led by the party, must actively work to achieve the utopia, not merely wait for its arrival, and must be willing to use any means to achieve the utopian goals. The dictatorship of the proletariat, excessive terror and coercion, and the combat atmosphere to be described below are all consistent with and justified by this ideological premise. A seventh and final point which should be made about the Communist ideology is that it is an all-inclusive philosophy of life.

It recognizes ultimately only one plane of existence, the political. It widens the thought and action as having social significance, and therefore as falling within the orbit of political action. Its political ideas are not a set of pragmatic precepts or a body of devices applicable to a special branch of human endeavour. They are an integral part of an all embracing and coherent philosophy. Politics is defined as the art of applying this philosophy to the organization of society, and the final purpose of politics is only achieved when this philosophy reigns supreme over all fields of life. [Talmon, 1952, p. 2]

All aspects of life become related to the political, hence all areas of life become the target of political scrutiny, and the demands for unanimity, though they may originate in a purely political sphere, often spill over into the most minute details of daily living. This same all-inclusiveness also operates as one of the powerful appeals of the ideology. In a revolutionary period when traditional values are strongly undermined, or at a time when such values no longer serve to mediate between an individual and the problems he faces in the world, a new ideology which can serve to orient him to all aspects of his external world has more appeal than one which orients him to only a portion of it.

Comment

Having mentioned some general points about the Communist ideology, we should now consider the question of the level at which unanimity is actually demanded in a totalitarian society. We have already made the distinction between behavioral conformity and ideological unanimity, but must further refine the latter concept because the ideology consists of a number of components, not all of which are equally important at all times. These components range from very fundamental premises, philosophical assumptions, and basic goals (the vision of the utopia) to very operational principles which apply to specific situations and may change from day to day. The distinction made by Smith, Bruner, and White (1956) in reference to political attitudes between a person's *basic orientation*, or attitude toward something, and his *policy stand*, or concrete proposals for action in regard to it, can be useful here in considering the components of ideology.

As we have implied before and shall see again, unanimity on basic orientation is often easier to achieve than unanimity on policy stand. From the basic philosophies of most ideologies it is possible to derive several alternative policy stands, each designed to achieve the ultimate goals at which one is aiming. In principle this flexibility also exists in the Communist ideology, but in practice it must often be denied because of the party's position as the only valid formulator of policy stands. If one allowed the possibility of alternatives, then the position of the party as the sole legitimate power would be brought into question. To avoid this possibility the system arrives at a paradoxical conclusion: that unanimity must be shown not only on basic premises but also on any given policy stand (the regime must at all times be publicly upheld as correct); yet that the populace must be prepared to change its mind overnight and become unanimous about new policy stands whenever the party line changes, at the same time pretending that this change has not occurred or that there is no inconsistency at all between the previous and the current position.

In other words, in Communist society certain basic premises and goals must be genuinely accepted by all members of society (including the premise that the party and its leaders are the legitimate leaders of the society), while other principles concerning the day-to-day means of operation must appear to be accepted by all members of the society, regardless of how often they change. It can be seen that for the individual citizen or party member this set of circumstances leads to a difficult psychological situation. He must be committed sincerely to an ideology, but he must not think through the consequences of this ideology for himself; instead he must be prepared ritually to affirm what his leaders dictate and must be able to rationalize his leaders' conclusions in terms of the ideology.[3] The citizen must be prepared to do extensive rationalizing of his leaders' policy in any public situation where he is under the scrutiny of others who have some degree of control over his fate. This kind of pressure to think through and discuss the ideology in various kinds of peer-group situations is, of course, one of the main features of the Chinese Communist approach to producing unanimity.

The components of the ideology also differ in the degree to which their content is relevant for given segments of the population. Certain basic premises must be accepted throughout the society by the masses, the rank and file, the cadres, and the top elite alike. Beyond this, the content of the ideology, and the degree of acceptance required, are tailored to the concerns and needs of each target group and the goals which the leaders have in mind for this group. To the peasants the party brings theories, promises, and programs for land reform; to the workers it brings the theory of the proletariat as the true base of the revolution and promises of labor owning the means of production; to the cadres and party members the leaders bring promises of power and glory for aiding the advancement of the revolution; to the political prisoner or prisoner of war they bring the opportunity of redemption, re-education, and identification with a glorious cause; and so on. Within each group unanimity must be expressed concerning the specific content and program proposed; across groups there must be unanimity about the wisdom of the leadership which has brought these programs into existence, and about the amount of energy, devotion, and loyalty which should be exhibited in their implementation.

From the point of view of the leadership this process not only consists of properly extrapolating from the basic premises of the ideology to a concrete situation but also, more importantly, involves careful diagnosis of the actual demands of a given situation and careful choice of a program (including such details as the language in which to make the ideological appeal).[4]

In summary, it is evident that the Communist ideology has in it many themes which suggest the need for unanimity, but that it is a complex enough philosophical system to preclude the prediction that from its characteristics alone one could specify how the society in which it operates will handle the unanimity problem. The role which ideology plays in the society at a given time, the stage in which a revolution finds itself, and the psychological commitment which the leaders actually feel to it (as contrasted with public commitment which may serve purely political or social functions) all enter into a consideration of how an actual program of creating unanimity may come about and its specific character.

The Goals of the Leaders

MAINTENANCE OF POWER BY PRESENTING A CORRECT EXTERNAL IMAGE

It is a tenable assumption that the leaders of Soviet and Chinese societies, regardless of their degree of commitment to the ideology, have as their primary goal the securing of their own position and the securing of the power position of their nation. Insofar as the leaders see themselves as being in a struggle for survival with other nations in the world, one may expect that they will utilize whatever means are available to give the appearance of being powerful. Therefore the leaders are committed to creating and projecting a certain image of themselves and their society—an image of solidarity, unanimity, and legitimacy.[5] They must show that the society accepts them and their program unanimously and with enthusiasm, and that their citizens will fight to defend the new system. If they can successfully project such an image, two very important functions are served: the solid front which is offered as a proof of strength actually reduces the likelihood of threat from other nations; unanimous popular acceptance as proof of the legitimacy of the regime is a powerful weapon in international bargaining and in proselytizing among neutral national groups.

COMMENT

A regime's need to prove its legitimacy and exhibit its power in the form of unanimity is probably greatest when the society and its leaders are in reality most insecure and least powerful. If the Chinese Communists were in fact at their weakest during the civil war and in the immediate post-takeover days, one would expect to see the greatest pressures toward unanimity at those times. The Chinese Communist leadership relied more from the very beginning on ideological re-education for anyone who came into contact with the movement and did intensify their efforts during the civil war in the *Cheng feng* movement and after the take-over in the thought reform movement.

The importance of unanimity as a means of presenting an image of power to the external world can be seen daily in the impact which Chinese Communist society has on the foreign visitor. Time and again what impresses him is the solidarity and uniformity and the huge numbers of people involved in any public demonstrations.

MAINTENANCE OF POWER BY PRESENTING CORRECT INTERNAL IMAGE

The regime's power position is also supported by an image of unanimity and solidarity projected within Communist society. Such an image serves at least three functions: it isolates the actual potential dissenter psychologically and thus prevents the organization of dissent or resistance; it diverts attention from actual disagreement among members of the ruling groups; and it provides the psychological basis for increased dedication and loyalty to the regime by reassuring the followers that they are indeed part of a powerful and rightful social movement.[6] Many kinds of rituals such as parades, demonstrations, campaigns, and elections seem to have as one of their primary functions the production and dissemination of such an image.

The importance of the first of the above functions can be seen by an examination of the consequences of lifting totalitarian pressure, as in Hungary in 1956, or in the "Let One Hundred Flowers Bloom" speech of Mao Tse-tung. As soon as a few disaffected individuals begin to speak their mind, others discover that they have not been alone in harboring grievances against the regime, leading to a rapid build-up of resistance. In the Hungarian rebellion, once a small group had impulsively initiated resistance action, other disaffected Hungarians risked going into the streets to fight, only to discover that all their neighbors whom they had mistrusted for years were also joining in the fight. The sudden recognition of solidarity and the destruction of the image of a nation solidly standing behind Communism opened the floodgates of rebellion. Of greatest significance is the fact that the image of unanimity, though invalid, had kept hundreds of potential dissenters from ever broaching their dissension to any but their closest friends or family members. Most had believed that their neighbors were Communists and informers.

The regime can prevent the growth of rebellion only by enforcing complete conformity in public utterances, thus insuring that no one will know to whom to turn to seek social support for an anti-regime opinion. Continuing mutual surveillance is also necessary in order to undermine private interpersonal relationships and, in fact, to destroy the concept of a legitimate private world. As close friends and members of the family are seduced into becoming agents of the totalitarian system (e.g., children informing on parents), it becomes increasingly difficult for the citizen to interact with others in anything but a "public" frame of reference. Nothing remains safe from government scrutiny.

. . . perhaps more important than what totalitarianism does to mass communication is what it does to private communication. Mass communication receives a new content, but remains mass, whereas private communication is transformed and ceases to be private. No matter what the context, on the street talking to a stranger or in the intimacy of one's home, one must say only the right thing. And one must say it as publicly as possible. Private communication becomes suspect, for to speak privately implies the desire to speak without being overheard by others. And the wish not to be overheard suggests that one is saying forbidden things—for if they were not forbidden, blasphemous things, would you not be proud to say them aloud for all to hear? In the end, even silence becomes suspect, for it may mean an unwillingness to reiterate the catechism which the mystique requires all to intone, and hence mark one out as an alien, a non-believer, and a potential source of contamination. Thus, private communication becomes public communication, and along with mass communication is subverted to fulfilling the imperatives of the mystique. Communication is communalized. [Inkeles, 1954, p. 102]

As this process takes hold, one may expect that individuals increasingly lose their ability to identify what others really believe, because it becomes increasingly difficult to check the accuracy of their perception. To the extent that the government succeeds in creating an image of the world as a place in which what a person says publicly is taken to be equivalent to what he believes privately, it undermines the individual's confidence in the belief that he and others have a private world or makes him forget how to go about looking for it.[7]

It is an interesting fact that such social isolation can be produced merely by coercing public utterances. It does not matter how disaffected the citizen is privately. As long as he does not speak his mind to others, his disaffection is, in effect, irrelevant to the security of the system.[8] The point is well summarized by Friedrich and Brzezinski:

. . . The atmosphere of fear it creates easily exaggerates the strength of the regime and helps it achieve and maintain its façade of unanimity. Scattered opponents of the regime, if still undetected, become isolated and feel themselves cast out of society. This sense of loneliness, which is the fate of all, but more specially of an opponent of the totalitarian regime, tends to paralyze resistance and makes it much less appealing. It generates a universal longing to "escape" into the anonymity of the collective whole. *Unanimity, even if coerced, is a source of strength for the regime.* [Friedrich & Brzezinski, 1956, p. 137]

The second function of an internal image of unanimity is to obscure actual diversity.

. . . Behind the totalitarian façade, the struggle of the elite formations of Soviet society for power and influence continues to find expression. The Party apparatus, the police, the army, and the administrative bureaucracy vie with one another for preferment, and the local and departmental interests of different sections of the bureaucracy exercise their counterinfluence on the Party. The public affirmations of unanimity on which all totalitarian regimes insist serve to obscure the diversity of interests which they can neither eliminate nor dare openly acknowledge. [Fainsod, 1953, p. 328]

If the regime's legitimacy rests solely on its claim of being the official interpreter of an absolute ideology, it could hardly gain in power by allowing to become public the disagreement among leaders concerning the interpretation of doctrine. As Orwell so well foresaw in his *Nineteen Eighty-Four* (1949), even outright falsification of history, manipulation of statistics and public records, and the faking of elections is justified in the pursuit of an image of unanimity when diversity threatens to become evident.

The third function, that of providing the image of a powerful and righteous social movement, will be discussed in greater detail when we consider the psychology of the follower. Suffice it to say at this point that, if the follower is a person who wishes to lose his sense of self by identifying with a powerful social movement, he will be aided in his quest if the members of the movement are unanimous and outspoken about their unanimity. This result follows both for cognitive and emotional reasons. On the cognitive side, it has been well demonstrated that ease of identification with another person or group is a function of the clarity of that person or group as a model. On the emotional side, the perceived power of the movement, which is again a function of its unanimity, will determine its attractiveness to all those whose desire is to identify with a powerful cause upon which they may become dependent (Hoffer, 1951; Meerloo, 1956).

The compulsive concern with active participation in the thought reform movement obviously aids in the maintenance of the image. The "student" who does not commit himself actively mars the image just as much as if he uttered heresies, for silence can only mean lack of acceptance or unspoken heresy. The student must think out loud and thereby show the manner in which he recognizes the error of his past; he must publicly confess his sins to show to all others who may yet be wavering how the regime is permitting him to become a penitent and redeemable person. Thus he provides a model of how to become part of the movement at the same time as affirming his solidarity with it, a device frequently used by religious mass movements.

MAINTENANCE OF POWER BY CONTROLLING IDEAS

It is a stated assumption of the Communist leaders that correct political behavior is based on correct political ideas. Such an assumption is embodied in Communist ideology (unity of theory and action) and is clearly reflected in Communist law in the concept of guilt for holding ideas which if logically carried out would lead to crimes against the party (Leites & Bernaut, 1954; Berle, 1957). Such an assumption is also reflected in the boundless optimism verbalized by the leaders, especially the Chinese, concerning the malleability of men, and in their energetic program to create "a new man."

Harsh repressive measures against incorrect ideas are justified because, if one can root out such ideas and create a "new man," one can then dispense with coercive controls.

The Chinese Communists have always stressed the importance of ideological homogeneity as a means of control. Believing that action springs from thought, they consider the control of thought even more fundamental than the control of overt behavior. All errors in action, they maintain, are traceable to errors in thinking, or, in other words, to ideological deviations. Consequently, the history of the Communist movement is in part a story of unceasing ideological struggle against tendencies of deviation from the correct orthodoxy sanctioned by the Party leaders. [Chen & Chiu, 1955, p. 177]

Furthermore, permitting incorrect ideas to exist, whether they are in the political area or not, is likely to contaminate loyal citizens and lead inevitably to rival centers of power which must grow from such ideas (Inkeles, 1954).

To achieve ideological homogeneity, the regime controls completely the flow of incoming information, while saturating the mass media of communication with those ideas considered to be correct, and reinforces the correct ideas by thought reform wherever it is considered necessary. This technique was clearly seen in the POW camps where all publications, news broadcasts, movies, mail, and contact with outsiders was carefully filtered for its ideological purity. Western literature and personal mail were permitted only if they supported the Communist ideology or could serve some other important function, e.g., mail was permitted to go through which contained bad news in order to demoralize the prisoner and to undermine the support which he might be getting from identification with reference groups (Schein, 1956). In the political prison the more extreme measure of cutting the prisoner off from all information was sometimes used (Lifton, 1956a, b; Hinkle & Wolff, 1956).

COMMENT

Much of what the Chinese Communists do in reforming a prisoner or citizen is inconsistent with much of what they say theoretically about such efforts, in that the outright coercion of behavior is given at least as much emphasis as the initial control of incoming ideas or persuasion. As we saw in the previous chapter, tremendous overt and covert pressure is brought to bear on everyone to conform publicly, to participate actively, and to work hard, while a façade is maintained that such conformity and dedication is entirely voluntary or the product of successful ideological persuasion. It would appear, then, that the regime not only holds the assumption that correct behavior results from correct beliefs, but also holds the assumption that correct beliefs result from correct behavior. Actually this assumption is also stated explicitly and is strongly supported by ideological underpinnings. The whole concept of reform through labor (learning the attitudes of the proletariat by experiencing directly what the proletarian does), the notion of identifying potential progressives or reactionaries by means of a study of their class origins and what they have done in their lifetime, the rejection of the sophisticated intellectual Communist who has never engaged in political action, all support this assumption.

These apparently inconsistent assumptions can be seen to be consistent if we consider what kinds of ideas or beliefs the good Communist is expected to learn. As we have previously noted, acceptance of the basic utopian premises is one level of idea or belief that everyone is expected to share and which can presumably be inculcated by information control, propaganda, and persuasion alone. But to have correct political beliefs also involves the absolute acceptance of and belief in the party as the official interpreter and implementer of the ideology. This latter class of ideas and attitudes can be taught *only* by coercion,[9] but, once thoroughly learned, does indeed lead ritually to "correct political behavior," i.e., obedience to party directives and policies.

In neither case are we dealing with a class of ideas, beliefs, or attitudes which serve the person as a way of defining his own role in relation to his environment, which express his own needs and personality, which grow and change as his experience changes, or which guide a whole range of overt behavior because of their inner logic. In Communist society, particularly under the impact of the "passion for unanimity," beliefs and attitudes function only as a way of appraising reality and relating to others, particularly to others in positions of authority. To the extent that they cease to express anything about the personality of their holder they become at once coercible and determinative of overt behavior, i.e., they become ritualized. The person who operates in terms of ritualized ideas and beliefs guides his behavior by such ideas or beliefs but is completely dependent on external authority to define for him what his ideas and beliefs should be in any given situation. Thus for the budding Communist his practical training consists of learning how to obey and rationalize party directives in concrete situations or how best to attune himself to what these might be if he is in a situation in which he is cut off from direct party authority.

ELICITING MOTIVATION FOR RAPID SOCIAL
AND ECONOMIC CHANGE

In the period immediately after the take-over, one of the primary goals of a regime is to build up the new society economically, industrially, and socially. In order to accomplish this goal according to the rapid time scale which the regime usually sets for itself, a high degree of motivation and dedication is needed on the part of the citizens. The regime does not have time nor is in a position to earn this kind of loyalty and motivation because it neither has available, nor is willing to produce, the material goods which would serve as real incentives for hard work and loyalty. It must fall back, therefore, on ideological goals and symbolic incentives. However, persuading people of utopian conceptions when their standard of living is only slowly improving is not likely to be successful. Furthermore, with the consolidation of power by the new regime come aspects of life which may be highly unattractive to the citizen: lack of freedom of physical movement, lack of privacy, heavy taxation, longer working hours, and the like. The result may be that the ideology stands in danger of being actually disconfirmed for the man in the street in the immediate post-takeover period.

Under these conditions the regime has two alternatives: to cut back its own programs or time schedules (as in Lenin's New Economic Policy); to tighten discipline and coerce the acceptance of the ideological goals, and the regime's means to achieve them, as a dogma rather than as empirically derived knowledge. The validity of the means and ends is simply stated as a fact not to be questioned, and the unpleasant conditions of the post-takeover period are explained and justified as being an essential stage in the achievement of the ultimate goals (the Dictatorship of the Proletariat), and/or the result of sabotage and counter-revolutionary activity. The all-encompassing and absolutistic nature of Communist ideology makes its conversion from a system of pseudo-scientific knowledge into a dogma a relatively easy matter.

As we have seen at other times in history (e.g., the Papal Inquisition of the Middle Ages, the French Revolution), when faith or knowledge becomes converted into dogma, the passion for unanimity grows apace, for dogma is far more vulnerable than faith or knowledge to the diversity of opinion which rational examination of means and ends entails. When the dogma is a justification for the tremendous self-sacrifice demanded of the citizen in the industrial reconstruction, one may anticipate great pressure against any ideological deviance which could even suggest the possibility of errors in ideological premises or their implementation by the party. Thus we see in totalitarian society the whole coercive apparatus of the state brought to bear on any individual who questions the regime's policy or even advocates that it be subjected to rational discussion.

COMMENT

As the regime is able to build up its industrial base and concentrate on consumer goods, the need for this artificial motivation declines. One may hypothesize that the greatest pressure for unanimity will therefore be present when the maximum rate of industrial and social change is called for and when the fewest alternative motivations such as nationalism or fear of attack are readily available.

Converting ideology into dogma can build some measure of collective motivation, but collective ideological goals do not meet the citizens' personal needs for status, and if such needs are not fulfilled the collective motivation cannot be maintained. To fulfill the needs for status, individual incentives must be provided in the form of reward for and recognition of individual contributions to the collective effort, as have in fact been provided in the Soviet Union and in China in the form of medals, publicity, luxury vacations, extra privileges, and so on.

While at work, the workers are constantly exhorted by their party organizations and by the trade unions to engage in "socialist competition" among themselves, and collectively with the workers of other factories, trusts or institutions. Special rewards are given to those who excel in overfulfilling their norms, the so-called "shock-workers"; since the thirties the successful shock-workers have been known as Stakhanovites, after Stakhanov, a shock-coalminer. The Stakhanovites receive special medals, and badges, as well as financial rewards. They are entitled to certain privileges, such as free railroad travel, while in some cases their children are entitled to free education. It was estimated that in 1948 some 87 per cent of the labor force in the USSR was engaged in "socialist competition." [Friedrich & Brzezinski, 1956, p. 283]

It should be noted that the acceptance on the part of the population of such incentives also tends to deflect attention from a rational examination of the underlying goals of the regime.

By accepting the regime's policies as dogma, the citizen solves a number of problems for himself. He is able to reduce the external pressures impinging on him; he is able to rationalize and justify to himself a course of action which he has reason to believe the regime would impose by force anyway; he can gain some measure of status; and he is able to maintain hope for a better future. It should not be assumed therefore that the citizen's clinging to the dogma is merely an expression of fear. Its acceptance may fulfill a number of psychological needs.

One important limitation of the above argument is that, by itself, it does not explain the tremendous encroachment of the government apparatus on the private lives of the citizens. It does not account for the conformity demands in widespread areas of behavior such as the arts and the manner of dress.

The Communist Movement Defined as a "Combat" Organization

We have alluded in a number of places to the fact that the Communists perceive themselves to be in a struggle for survival with many enemies both inside their movement and in other countries, and to be organized therefore according to military combat standards rather than peacetime standards. The overt emphasis on these conditions is, of course, greatest during and immediately after the take-over, when the actual number of enemies inside and outside the movement may be expected to be greatest. For example, the 1945 Constitution of the CCP states in its preamble:

> The CCP is a unified, combat organization, built on the principle of democratic centralism, and held together by the discipline which all Party members must observe conscientiously and voluntarily. The strength of the CCP rests on its solidarity, unified will, and integral action. The Party cannot tolerate any internal action which deviates from its programme and Constitution or is detrimental to discipline; it cannot tolerate any demand for autonomy within the Party, factionalism, or two-faced deeds which pretend to obey the Party while opposing it in practice. The CCP must constantly purge from its ranks those who violate the programme, Constitution, and discipline of Party membership, and who are incorrigible in their mistakes. [Brandt, Schwartz & Fairbank, 1952, p. 424]

Pye, in commenting on "People's Liberation Movements" in Asia, notes that their reliance on armed struggle is to a degree a reflection of the general importance which armed power has traditionally had in Asian politics. It also reflects the situational demands of a prolonged revolutionary struggle, consisting of the gradual "liberation" of rural areas prior to gaining control of the urban centers.

604

EDGAR H. SCHEIN: The Passion For Unanimity

. . . Conceiving of themselves as existing in an environment dominated by violence and as struggling against enemies who seek to maintain their control by military means, the People's Liberation parties have readily turned to the task of creating their own military forces. [Pye, 1956, p. 27]

"Confronted with such enemies, it is inevitable for the Chinese revolution to take on a 'protracted' and 'ruthless' nature. . . . Confronted with such enemies, the method and principal form of the Chinese revolution must necessarily be militant and not peaceful. . . . It is absolutely correct for Stalin to say, 'One characteristic peculiar to the Chinese revolution is opposition against the armed counter-revolutionaries by the armed revolutionaries.' Hence any tendency to make light of armed struggle, of revolutionary war, of guerrilla warfare, and of the work of the armed forces, is altogether wrong." [Mao Tse-tung, quoted in Pye, 1956, p. 29]

Several general consequences follow from the system's definition of the situation as one of combat which can be found in most post-revolutionary regimes or in non-revolutionary situations where regimes feel themselves to be threatened (e.g., the Papal Inquisition).[10]

1. In a state of combat there is the need for highly centralized authority to achieve efficiency in implementing the goals of the regime and maintain adequate co-ordination among decentralized forces.[11] Highly centralized authority makes possible a greater degree of arbitrariness of decision and thus lays the groundwork for inquisitions and persecutions of deviants.

2. Organizations or regimes which conceive of themselves as being under threat or in combat tend to replace authority by legal process with authority by administrative decision. The source of this trend is probably to be found in the desire of the leaders to maintain as much power in their own hands as possible, but it is also justified as a means of reaching disciplinary decisions rapidly and efficiently, and preserving a solid front by avoiding the full airing of issues which accompanies the usual legal process.

Essentially, the Communist legal system in this respect approximates the situation in other legal systems in States where *Church and State are combined*, and where the law and procedures are assimilated to and governed by ecclesiastical and religious practice. The difference lies in the fact that the Communist system, being materialist, discards any external or transcendental criteria: doctrine is made by the Communist Party of which the State is an expression; there can be, therefore, no principle, let alone law, superior to it. Police, administrative officials and Courts are obliged to adapt the "law" (meaning thereby decrees and regulations, and so forth) to this doctrine, and to handle the accused accordingly. Leaving out the transcendental element, the Communist legal system is probably merely a new version of the practice prevailing in trial of crimes against the State under the Byzantine Empire (in which the Emperor was also dominant in the Church) and of the actual though less rationalized practice in many political cases under the Czarist Empire. [Berle, 1957, p. 649]

There appear to be several corollary effects, particularly as the system operates in Communist China: the automatic assumption of guilt if any member of the administrative apparatus makes an accusation; the inadmissibility of any defense by the accused because such defense constitutes a questioning of the authority and is therefore a revolt against established power; the unavailability of any legal text to which the accused can turn to discover the nature of his crime (which has a striking counterpart in the Papal Inquisition of the twelfth and thirteenth centuries in the outlawing of the Bible for popular consumption [Lea, 1887]; the person in authority defines the law simply by his position); the definition of crime purely in terms of expediency and the demands of the moment, which in turn leads to rather vague categories like "counter-revolutionary activity," "sabotage," "reactionary tendencies," and so on (Berle, 1957); repressive measures which maximize the odds for the government by inferring from a minimum of evidence the actual or probable criminal intent of anyone who is in any way a threat to it.[12]

Given these circumstances, the actual or potential deviant has little chance in the system. If he is accused by anyone, he can quickly be arrested, tried, and convicted by virtually any administrative authority. It is the recognition on the part of the prisoner that the demands for confession and thought reform are backed by completely arbitrary authority which more than anything else creates a hopeless situation for him. Just as the witch or heretic of the Middle Ages could only defend himself or herself by accepting the frame of reference of the inquisitors (which meant accepting at least the validity of the premise that devils and witches do exist), the prisoner of the Communists can survive only by accepting the ideological frame of reference of his captors and the validity of their premise about "struggle," "combat," "ceaseless vigilance against counter-revolutionary activity," and so on.[13] He soon learns that if his judge or interrogator says he is guilty, he is in fact guilty. Bonnichon describes the situation this way:

> Therefore, two ways lie open to you: either you confess and implore the clemency of the government, in which case the government will be lenient, or you resist and subject yourself to the severest of punishments." This speech has been repeated to every accused, both in the field of political crimes and that of ordinary crimes; in each case, it has been repeated many times; it was clear that judges and interpreters alike knew these words by heart. It is understandable, therefore, that to plead innocence is to offend the government; and moreover, you are told so: "So you dare accuse the government of frivolity or injustice!" That is another offence which makes your case worse. Thus, not only is the accused presumed guilty, but he is forbidden to prove the contrary: to try, is to revolt.[14] Not only does the judge have nothing to prove, but he is even dispensed from the necessity of pronouncing a precise accusation: You are guilty; we know it; accuse yourself. When I ask: "Guilty of what?", I am told that it is not for the accused to put questions; there is only one thing he can do: confess and ask the government's pardon.

Thus it is the knowledge on the part of the prisoner that he has absolutely no recourse which forces him ultimately to give in to the system. At the same time, the administrative official knows that his own position depends entirely upon the adequate fulfillment of his superior's orders and this motivates him strongly to produce total conformity in the prisoner at virtually any price (short of losing him by death or psychosis). The combat atmosphere, strongly supported by ideological premises, makes him particularly sensitive to any evidence of crime and deviance, no matter how tenuous or circumstantial; the confessions he finally elicits, of course, confirm his suspicions.

3. Conditions of threat or combat tend to produce a *shift in the frame of reference used to evaluate behavior.* Behavior which under peacetime conditions might be ignored or might result only in mild censure can and does become, under combat conditions, a serious offense punishable by imprisonment or even death. Such severe penalties are applied both for behavior which constitutes failure to achieve a stated goal (such as failing to stay awake on guard duty or to clean one's rifle) and for behavior which increases danger by breaking security (such as telling of a troop ship departure to an unreliable person).

The Chinese Communist definition of such offenses as espionage and sabotage is an excellent example of this kind of shift in frame of reference. As one reads the kinds of charges which have been brought against Western prisoners, one is initially struck by their utter incongruity—a student accused of espionage, a priest or nun accused of sabotage or infanticide, and so on. However, many prisoners in time come to be able to understand the frame of reference from which the conclusion follows that crimes have been committed. This frame of reference, usually called "the people's standpoint," is characterized primarily by the degree to which it attaches serious criminal intent or effect to any action which in any conceivable way could hurt the Communist regime. The justification for this extreme kind of interpretation is the notion of perpetual combat with enemies within and without. For example, a letter to an American friend by a priest who had just traveled through some rural areas, in which he described the landscape and the kind of farming he observed, was espionage according to the judge because, it was pointed out, from the Chinese "people's point of view" combat was not restricted solely to military engagement but included also political and ideological struggle. Hence "intelligence" is not limited to matters of military significance but includes also matters of economic, political, and social significance. If information about a farm in China could conceivably be used as the basis for a psychological warfare campaign against the peasant, for example, it is automatically "intelligence" and its transmitter is deliberately or unwittingly engaging in espionage. The fact that between 1950 and 1953 the United States and Communist China were technically at war with each other supported this logic. It is not at all unlikely that in a situation of comparable threat any nation would adopt a course of maximum security and treat many seemingly innocent actions with suspicion, especially if those actions were committed by members of an enemy nation.

We have belabored this point to establish clearly the distinction between a set of Communist attitudes which derives from their ideology and a set which derives primarily from their preoccupation with struggle, threat, and survival. The point is crucial because many victims of Communist Chinese imprisonment found it much easier to understand and accept the fact that their own behavior was harmful because it represented a threat in a situation which was defined as one of combat than it was for them to accept the ideological premises and rationale that led to such a definition of the situation in the first place. For example, Robert Ford, a British citizen working as a radio operator for the Tibetan government when captured by the Communists, recognized shortly after his arrest that from the Communist point of view he was certainly guilty of espionage (in terms of the circumstantial evidence against him), and that he might as well confess it rather than deny something he could appreciate intellectually. Only much later in his thought reform did the issue of the acceptance of Communist values arise (Ford, 1957).

To generalize the argument: it seems clear that if the Communist regime or any other regime can convince its population that they are under constant threat from enemies inside and outside the system, it is introducing a potent force toward unanimity and conformity because even slight deviance becomes highly suspicious and is severely dealt with. Every person can then be told that his own lack of conformity can be a severe threat to the system as a whole, and that such behavior is therefore not only against his own long-run interests but also gives justification to the harsh repressive measures used by the regime.

Conditions of struggle and combat, particularly in the period prior to take-over, require the recruitment and maintenance of effective fighting forces. If such forces are drawn from politically uneducated masses, and if, as was the case in the take-over of China, these forces have to wage scattered guerrilla warfare as well as to administer "liberated areas," the importance of ideology as a motivating force and guideline for action becomes exceedingly great. Hence, the Communists have placed great emphasis on political education and indoctrination within the armed forces, with the effect of making them more disciplined and providing for their politically untutored audience in the liberated areas an appealing model of the "good life" under Communism.

The ideology operates not only as a unifying force and a guideline to action in ambiguous situations, but also as a *language*, a set of semantic guides, which makes possible rapid and efficient communication of the wishes of the central authorities.[15] For example, if every soldier and cadre understands clearly what is meant by a term like "bureaucratism" (i.e., the slavish obedience to orders without consideration to the local political situation), then a campaign can be launched by the regime against this type of behavior simply by stating that bureaucratism is bad and must be avoided. Everyone knows precisely what is expected of him, what he is to criticize in others, and how to change his behavior in the future. Semantic clarity can be achieved only if unanimity of knowledge and interpretation is strenuously enforced. One function of intensive indoctrination, then, is to insure the widespread sharing of definitions of key terms of the ideology. If this goal can be accomplished, the communication process can to a degree be streamlined and wider active participation can be insured.

REFERENCES

Berle, A. A. (1957) "Legal Background of Communist Methods of Interrogation and Indoctrination." *Bull. N.Y. Acad. of Med.*, 33, 645–53.

Bonnichon, A. (undated) *Law in Communist China*. The Hague: International Commission of Jurists.

Brandt, C., Schwartz, B. I., and Fairbank, J. K. (1952) *A Documentary History of Chinese Communism*. Cambridge: Harvard University Press.

Chen, T. H. and Chiu, S. M. (1955) "Thought Reform in Communist China." *Far Eastern Survey*, 24, 177–84.

Erikson, E. H. (1956) "The Problem of Ego Identity." *J. Amer. Psychoanal. Ass.*, 4, 56–121.

Fainsod, M. (1953) *How Russia Is Ruled*. Cambridge: Harvard University Press.

Ferreus. (1957) "The Menace of Communist Psychological Warfare." *Orbis*, I, 97–121.

Ford, R. W. (1957) *Wind Between the Worlds*. New York: David McKay.

Friedrich, C. J. and Brzezinski, Z. K. (1956) *Totalitarian Dictatorship and Autocracy*. Cambridge: Harvard University Press.

Guillain, R., (1957) *600 Million Chinese*. New York: Criterion Books.

Hinkle, L. E. and Wolff, H. G. (1956) "Communist Interrogation and Indoctrination of 'Enemies of the State.'" *A.M.A. Arch. Neurol. Psychiat.*, 76, 115–74.

Hoffer, E. (1951) *The True Believer*. New York: Harper and Bros.

Hunt, R. N. C. (1957) *The Theory and Practice of Communism*. New York: Macmillan.

Inkeles, Alex (1950) *Public Opinion in Soviet Russia*. Cambridge: Harvard University Press.

Lea, C. H. (1887) *A History of the Inquisition of the Middle Ages*. New York: Harper and Bros.

Leites, N., and Bernaut, Elsa. (1954) *Ritual of Liquidation*. Glencoe, Ill.: The Free Press.

Lifton, R. J. (1956a) "Chinese Communist 'Thought Reform': The Assault Upon Identity and Belief." Mimeographed paper.

——— (1956b) "'Thought Reform' of Western Civilians in Chinese Communist Prisons." *Psychiatry*, 19, 173–95.

Meerloo, J. A. M. (1951) "The Crime of Menticide." *Amer. J. Psychiat.*, 107, 594–98.

Ohlin, Ruth. (1954) "The Passion for Unanimity." Unpublished paper.

Orwell, G. (1949) *Nineteen Eighty-Four*. New York: Harcourt, Brace and Co.

Pye, L. W. (1956) *Guerilla Communism in Malaya*. Princeton: Princeton University Press.

Schein, E. H. (1956) "The Chinese Indoctrination Program for Prisoners of War." *Psychiatry*, 19, 149–72.

Smith, M. B., Bruner, J. S., and White, R. W. (1956) *Opinions and Personality*. New York: Wiley.

Talmon, J. L. (1952) *The Rise of Totalitarian Democracy*. Boston: Beacon Press.

Wei, H. (1955) "Courts and Police in Communist China to 1952." HRRI Research Memorandum No. 43, AFP and TRC, Lackland AFB, Texas.

NOTES

1. Erikson (1958) has pointed out that the ideological utterances of successful leaders of mass movements are often distinguished more by their invulnerability to attack than by their intrinsic appeal. Part of the success of the ideological program lies in the neutralization of potential opposition.

2. Other groups in the society are judged by the ideology to be *a priori* *un*enlightened and in varying degrees to be incapable of re-education (e.g., capitalists, landowners, small shopkeepers, intellectuals, soldiers, etc.). With respect to these groups the government has the alternatives of liquidating them, stripping them of power and status and tolerating them, imprisoning them, or re-educating them.

3. It is probably for this reason that the intellectual communist, the man who believes in all portions of the ideology and thinks it through for himself, is often considered to be the real enemy of the system. His "formalism," to use the phrase Mao used in condemning certain factions in the Chinese Communist movement (Brandt, Schwartz, & Fairbank, 1952), makes him unreliable as an obedient citizen and makes him ineffective if he has to adapt the ideology to a situation for which no formal solution has as yet been worked out or promulgated, a situation which arose often in the Chinese case.

4. Mao, for example, said the following in a speech on "Opposing Party Formalism": "As soon as a man talks with another man he is engaged in propaganda work. If he is not mute, he always will have a few words to say. Therefore, our comrades must all study languages. In studying various languages [they must] pay special attention to the language of the workers, peasants, and soldiers and the masses. If we do not study the language of the masses, we cannot lead the masses." (Brandt, Schwartz, & Fairbank, 1952, p. 400). In another context he says: "The people's language is very rich in expression; it is lively and vigorous and presents life as it is. Many of us have not mastered it, and as a consequence, in writing articles and giving speeches, we do not use lively, vigorous, really effective language; we only have a few varicose veins." (Brandt, Schwartz, & Fairbank, 1952, p. 399)

5. The following news release is a good example:
"London, April 26, 1958 (Reuters)—Following is from the text of President Tito's speech today to the Yugoslav Communist party congress at Ljubljana, as issued by the official Yugoslav news agency Tanyug:

"The seventh congress of the League of Communists of Yugoslavia today finishes its fruitful work.

"We can indeed be pleased and proud of the extraordinary ideological

610

political unity and unanimity which has found full expression during the work of the congress. Whoever has been present at or otherwise followed the work of this congress can no longer have any doubts as to the force which moves and guides the entire process of development of our Socialist society.'"

6. The reassurance which such unanimity provides to the leaders themselves will be discussed below.

7. Inkeles also points out that it is a distinctive feature of totalitarian society to subordinate the individual by first subordinating those social institutions through which he obtains his status and identity as an individual. For example:

"Clearly, if the subordination of the individual cannot be complete without the subordination of his associations, then it follows further that *absolute* subordination of the individual requires absolute subordination of all the human associations which form the web of society. But it is not on these grounds alone that the totalitarian exempts no organization from being measured against his Procrustean rule. The mystique implies a plan of good society. It provides a single metric for all forms of human organization. The totalitarian rejects outright the principle which inheres in the formula 'render unto Caesar the things which are Caesar's.' He accepts no distinction between the sacred and the profane, the public and the private, in social life. The demands of the mystique determine what decision shall be taken in regard to any particular institution, but all institutions are equally subject to review." (Inkeles, 1954, p. 94)

8. Of course, one may expect that such disaffection would have other negative consequences for the regime such as likelihood of low productivity, defection, etc.

9. Except insofar as the person's needs for complete dependency are sufficiently dominant to make him a willing accomplice.

10. In this section in particular, we are shifting our level of analysis. Our purpose is to show that some of the characteristics of totalitarian movements can be explained without explicit considerations of their ideology.

11. High centralization may in fact be the product of the power drive of the leaders, but it is likely to be rationalized and justified in terms of its efficiency.

12. These factors have been noted by a number of students of legal practices in postrevolutionary states. A particularly concise analysis of the Chinese Communist legal system is given by Bonnichon (undated), a jurist who was himself imprisoned. A more detailed discussion can be found in Wei, 1955.

13. The generality of this phenomenon was recently demonstrated in the post-takeover phase of the Cuban revolution in which Fidel Castro set aside the legally arrived-at acquittal of a number of pilots who had fought for Batista, and by administrative act condemned them to life imprisonment on the basis of his personal conviction that they had murdered innocent women and children in their strafing.

14. This presumption is irrefutable to such a degree that the "political instructor" of the prison, assistant to the judge in the "reform of our thoughts," told me one day: "The very fact that you do not see what crimes you have committed makes your case even worse, because it proves your obduracy." [Bonnichon, undated, p. 8]

15. William Griffith, in private conversation, has pointed out the importance of Western studies of Communist ideology as a basis for understanding even what their internal communications mean.

611

LUCIAN W. PYE

Communication Operation in Non-Western Societies

THE EXTENT to which countries in Asia, Africa, and the Middle East are likely to succeed in their experiments with representative government is a question of interest and concern to both the scholar and the policy-maker. The importance of understanding the problems that beset these countries in their attempt to introduce democratic practices hardly needs to be stressed. All of these countries from the Gold Coast in Africa to the newly independent nations of Southeast Asia have their own peculiar problems which stem from their respective cultural heritages and from the circumstances under which they were introduced to institutions and customs which had their origins in the West. However, they also possess many characteristics in common. In particular, they are all societies that are experiencing a profound process of cultural change as a result of their exposure to Western ideas and practices, and their economies are in a state of underdevelopment. Related to those two basic facts are other shared characteristics.

Because of these common features we can speak in general terms of a non-Western type of politics. Indeed, in understanding many of the problems that confront these societies in their attempts to develop viable forms of representative government, it can be helpful to abstract these common feaures and relate them in the form of a conceptual model.

In seeking to foretell the prospects for representative government in non-Western societies, it is particularly important to consider the communication process common to them. In every society, the general communication process performs a key function in structuring the political process. It is a major factor in determining how the vast majority of the

Reprinted from *Public Opinion Quarterly*, Vol. XX (Spring 1956), pp. 249–257, by permission of the author and the publisher. (Copyright, 1956, Princeton University Press.)

people will relate themselves to the sphere of politics, since it gives them a basis for understanding, interpreting, and evaluating political developments. Through the communication process people learn of the moral standards and the intellectual considerations that govern political action in their society.

In two respects the communication process is of critical importance in determining the future of representative institutions in non-Western societies. First, there is the matter of the content of communications. What are the ideas and views about politics that are being most widely disseminated? Are those who are in positions of political influence effectively communicating views that are compatible with democratic practices? In terms of research, such questions as these call for content and survey studies. Secondly, there is the question of how the communication process itself is organized and structured. How are the means of communication related to each other, and how does such a pattern of communication affect the development of representative government? The latter are the questions that concern us here. We shall first briefly indicate the general pattern of communication common to non-Western societies and then examine in greater detail some particular features of the communication processes that influence the character of political life in these societies.

The Atomized Communication Pattern
and the Communal Basis of Politics

We generally find that in non-Western societies the communication pattern possesses two distinct levels: the urban or elite level, and the village or mass level. In the urban centers are the media of mass communication, based on Western technology, serving the most Westernized elements of the society and most closely related to the dominant or national sphere of politics. Outside these centers, the communication process is still largely dependent upon the traditional level of technology, and in its operations it mainly serves the needs of the less Westernized people and a more local and less formally structured political process.

As a consequence of this basic cleavage, ideas and themes that dominate the political communications among an important element in the society may not be reflected in communications among other groups of the population. News about a dramatic event may travel very rapidly throughout the society—the speed with which most Indian villagers learned of Gandhi's death is often cited as an example of the efficiency of a word-of-mouth process of communication—but interpretations that give context to such events are far less effectively communicated. It is true that at the village level there is often a person who receives one of the urban news-papers and thus becomes an important source of information. However, the barrier of illiteracy is great and the frame of reference employed by newspapers in communicating to an urbanized audience is often one that is not meaningful to those in the village.[1] Possibly more significant is the fact that the urban process of communication is generally not very re-sponsive to what takes place in the various village systems. It is often the case that the media of mass communication are far more sensitive to the sphere of international communications. This may not be a surprising fact since the most Westernized groups are the main audience of these media, but it is important for understanding the character of nationalistic senti-ments among many of the urban elements of these countries. Rather than appealing to the vigor and the values of a folk culture and rejecting the values of the foreigner, as is common with extreme nationalists in the West, these groups often express their aspirations by judging the outside world by its own values.

In addition to this fundamental division, the pattern is usually further complicated by the fact that communication at the village level is largely dependent upon a word-of-mouth process which results in countless sub-systems, each limited to the chain of personal contacts of its participants. Villages in different parts of the country may have less communication with each other than they have with the urban centers.

Politically, this isolation of the villages is significant in that it prevents the rural elements from mobilizing sufficient strength to challenge the urban leadership of the country. Thus, in countries in which the vast ma-jority of the population follow a village way of life, the national scene may hardly reflect this fact. Throughout Asia and the Middle East, we find countries in which there are great differences between life in the cities and in the countryside, and yet in their national politics we do not see expressed the clash of interests between city and country, commerce and agriculture, which have been such an important issue in the history of Western politics. To the extent that the rural question arises at all, it usually appears in the form of "village projects" and "rural development programs" which represent essentially an urbanized and bureaucratic defi-nition of the problem. The barriers to communication make it difficult for the rural areas to advance their common interests forcefully and thus become a significant and constant element in the political process. Instead, the various village groupings are usually engaged in independent efforts either to resist the pressures and demands of the central government or to obtain special benefits from it. In cases where the rural areas do have rep-resentation in the national government, their representatives are generally highly urbanized people who may seek to assist their constituents by sup-porting development programs. This, however, this quite different from, say, the role played by Southern and Western leaders during the early phases of the industrialization of America.

Thus the communication process in most non-Western countries does not operate in such a manner as to indicate clearly the extent to which the society is or is not divided on many political issues. Communal groups may be quite unaware that they hold views that are different from those of other groups in the society. As a consequence, these groupings are not comparable to the competing interest groups of Western politics, who all have access to a common communication system, and who each represent a functionally specific interest.

The Merging of the Social
and Political Spheres

If we examine further the communication process common to non-Western societies, we find that it usually does not provide its audiences with a clear picture of a political sphere which is distinct from other aspects of social life. The communication network is generally not so organized as to differentiate "political" from other forms of information. In large part, this is due to the fact that the communication process in these societies is not a highly specialized one, but rather an adjunct of other social functions. The vast majority of the communicators are not "professionals" performing a single role, but men who become communicators because of their other social roles.

Thus the setting in which communication takes place in these societies usually encourages a blurring of what are generally thought of as "political," "social," and "private" considerations. At what we have called the village level, communication usually involves a face-to-face relationship in which the relative social positions and the personal relations of the parties give significance to what is communicated. Those who hold positions of status are expected to be able to provide useful information, while those who can consistently report on the meaning of developments are likely to gain status in the eyes of others.

In a study of the attitudes of Chinese who were former members of the Malayan Communist Party, the present writer found that even though all those interviewed were literates, their concepts about politics were highly colored by the fact that they still relied heavily upon word-of-mouth communications. In talking about what they considered to be their early political experiences, they spoke of what we would consider to be their personal and social relations with various members of their community. They identified those people who could provide them with information about job opportunities, local developments, or world affairs as people

615

with "political power." In accepting or rejecting the views of these informal opinion-makers, they considered that they were acting politically. However, the standards they used in appraising the reliability of the information they received would generally be considered non-political. Thus they would accept the views of information leaders on world developments because they judged them to be "sincere" people and because their own self-interest in the personal relationship made it seem desirable to do so. As a consequence, they tended to relate their private social relations in the local community with national and international developments, but the logic they followed was not guided by how these major developments might affect their self-interest, but rather by how their interests in the local setting might best be advanced. By agreeing with the opinions of their informal leaders and acting on their advice, these former Communists had hoped to improve their own social status and in turn become opinion leaders or, as they would say, "politically" powerful in the eyes of others.

In such situations, the communication process serves a much broader function than just providing information; it helps to define and give cohesion to a wide range of social relations. Any change in the pattern of communication is thus likely to affect the established social relationships in the community. This fact may be of great relevance in helping to explain the difficulties that the Westernized elites have in communicating effectively with the less Westernized masses. It is, of course, true that the acculturation process through which these elites have passed has given them a different outlook on much of life and thus they may find themselves out of touch with the masses, who are still closer to the traditional culture.[2] However, even when members of the urban elite are able to cast their message in a form that is intelligible to the masses, they may still find it extremely difficult to communicate with this larger audience because the existing social relationships at the village level resist the introduction of a channel of communication which would result in a new pattern of social relationships.

This problem can be illustrated by another example taken from Malaya. In the first Johore state elections, one of the candidates carried out an extremely vigorous campaign. In touring the *kampongs*, he put on a remarkable demonstration of how a highly Westernized leader can communicate with the village masses. He was met by large and enthusiastic crowds who appeared to be sympathetic to his message. The election was won, however, by his equally Westernized opponent, who had engaged in little direct campaigning. Subsequent investigation revealed that in appealing directly to the village people the active candidate had by-passed and thus threatened the status of their informal opinion leaders. Seeking to regain their social status after he had left the villages, these men tended to perform their communicator's role in such a fashion as to favor his opponent, who had not challenged their positions in the community.

Under these conditions, political behavior is likely to be influenced more by considerations of the source than by the content of the communications. Ideas and opinion are not generally viewed independently of the source that sponsors them. Thus, the democratic assumption may not hold that people will change their behavior because of the logic or the emotional appeal of statements, and the analogy of the market place for competing ideas can be misleading. Instead, the effort to gain greater acceptance of new ideas is, in a sense, more like an effort to subvert personal and social allegiances. This can be seen most clearly in the cases of those people who in accepting the views of urbanized elites must break many of their traditional community and even family ties.[3] Even among the urban elites, the act of changing one's views may result in changes in one's personal associations.

The Gap Between Language and Action

Since in many non-Western societies the important fact in determining political behavior is the source of communications, there seems to be less need for particular groups to make distinctive public statements. As a result, the language used by politically active groups generally does not provide a clear indication of their policy intentions. It is usually difficult to differentiate among various political groups according to the verbal content of their communications.

The problem of having to employ political oratory both to strengthen national unity and to clarify policy alternatives is generally a peculiarly complex one in non-Western societies. This is because in these societies two very important functions of government have not usually been clearly differentiated. One function is that of providing expressive activities and the other is that of solving questions of public policy. Generally, traditional societies have developed to a very high point the expressive aspect of politics while placing less emphasis upon politics as a means of solving problems. The importance of ritual and ceremony, pomp and display, is an indication of the explicit recognition that traditional societies give to the expressive and dramatic component of politics. Those who have political power are generally seen as leading interesting and exciting lives, free of many of the standards of morality that bind the common people. The problem-solving or decision-making function of government has usually been conceived of as taking place behind the scenes, for much the same reason that traditional Western diplomacy has required secrecy.

Now, as these societies have adopted representative institutions, the expectation is that questions of public policy should be openly debated. At the same time, national leaders must use public oratory as a means for developing new national loyalties. For example, strong international as well as domestic pressures have demanded that the concept of economic development should be a major symbol in the political life of these societies. A language that is customarily associated with policy planning and administration has come to dominate much of the public discourse in these countries; and it has, in turn, come to provide many of the slogans and symbols for essentially expressive activities. Under these conditions, it may be difficult for one who is not involved in the political process to distinguish between political oratory for the sake of creating unity and statements of specific policy intentions. In some cases, the most articulate groups may give the impression that they are primarily concerned with acts of an administrative character, when in fact they are political groups that must devote most of their planning to strategies for the gaining and holding of power.

Thus, in most non-Western societies there has not developed a distinctive type of public discourse which might serve the purpose that, say, Fourth of July oratory did in America. Questions of means often become confused with questions of ends. As a consequence, politicians in these societies cannot easily arrive at their positions on matters of public policy by openly engaging in negotiating and bargaining with a variety of specific interest groups. To do so would make them appear to minimize the value of national unity.

This problem is further complicated by the fact that, as we have seen, the communication process common to these societies does not operate in such a manner as to provide an open forum in which a great variety of specific political interests can be identified. As long as actual or potential interest groups are not actively engaged in publicly communicating their views, the political leaders have few guides for estimating the amount of popular support they can expect to receive for accommodating the particular interests of various groups. Moreover, they cannot readily perform their representative function by identifying themselves with a variety of specific interests. Instead, national leaders generally have to cast themselves in the role of representing a diffuse public, that is, the entire society. As a result, even when seeking to realize limited policy objectives, they may find it necessary to employ expressive oratory in order to mobilize support from an undifferentiated and unstructured public.

This situation reinforces other strong tendencies for political leaders in these societies to seek a highly personal form of recognition and backing. At the same time, the gap between the outlook of the urbanized elites and of the less Westernized masses is often so great that it can only be bridged by judgments about human character and personal motives. Unable to appreciate many of the problems of their leaders, the masses must evaluate those leaders' actions mainly in terms of whether they seem to be "good" or "bad" men and thus whether they should be trusted or not. Conversely, the leaders, finding it difficult to communicate the complexities of national policies, are inclined to seek confidence and trust of a personal nature. These are, of course, conditions which favor the charismatic leader. They are also conditions which make it difficult to determine the extent to which national leaders are divided over issues that are more far-reaching than those of a personal character. That is, the groupings which may appear to be personal cliques in some non-Western countries may in fact be based upon significant policy issues, which, however, are not articulated.

From this analysis, it appears that a key factor in determining the prospects of representative institutions in non-Western countries is the structure of the communication process. When seen in this light, many of the particular problems that beset the development of representative institutions in non-Western societies become more intelligible. For example, the problem of stable and responsible opposition groups in those countries where the national leadership consists of a single, dominant group becomes more than just a scarcity of competent leadership. Instead of being able to seek power on the basis of advancing different specific interests, opposition groups have to adopt the more revolutionary role of challenging the competence of the dominant party to represent the entire society.

It is to be expected that rapid change will take place in the character of the communication process as the media of mass communications come to occupy an increasingly important place in these societies. In some cases, these may lead to a more open political process in which people will act to an increasing extent on the basis of their evaluations of competing statements of public policy. Also, as more specific interests are publicly defined, not only will people find it easier to distinguish a political sphere from their social and personal associations, but political leaders will be able to adopt a more clearly defined representative role. The communal bases of politics may be replaced by more functionally specific groups, as the informal opinion leaders seek to relate the particular interests of members of their communities to the national political process. The role that comparable informal leaders played in assimilating the interests of various immigrant communities to American city and national politics comes to mind. However, it must also be recognized that more efficient mass communication may in some cases only serve to strengthen existing communal tendencies by providing those involved with more complete ideologies. With little communication among such groups, the gap between language and action may persist. The example of French politics comes to mind all too readily.

In employing communication research in order to foretell the prospects of representative government, in particular non-Western societies, it will, of course, be necessary to determine the content of political communications and the views that are being widely disseminated. However, in order to evaluate the political significance of the findings of such studies, it will also be necessary to analyze the general structure or pattern of the communication process.

NOTES

1. Y. B. Damle, "Communication of Modern Ideas and Knowledge in Indian Villages," *Public Opinion Quarterly*, Vol. XX (Spring 1956), pp. 257–298.

2. For an intimate autobiographical account of the personal frustrations of one who has sought to "return to the village" after receiving only an elementary form of Westernized education, see Mahmut Makal, *A Village in Anatolia*. London: Vallentine, Mitchell, 1954.

3. For an excellent discussion of this problem, see David E. Apter, *The Gold Coast in Transition*. Princeton: Princeton University Press, 1955.

11
Research Methods

Analysis of the methodology of public opinion and communication research has produced a voluminous literature during the past fifteen years. Technical advances have been made on many problems. The articles and selections are presented as illustrative of some of the central developments and issues. A number of other problems, notably those relating attitude research to communication research (e.g., audience analysis), have been excluded for lack of space.

It is possible to think of the problems of methodology in these fields as falling into three groups: problems of research design, problems of data collection, and problems of analysis. But often advances are made in such a fashion as to cut across these conventional categories. Moreover, as research in public opinion and communications has developed, the most important methodological advances are those which assist the interplay of empirical technique with theoretical analysis.

Thus, in the first category of research design, there are the contributions by Hyman and Lazarsfeld. Hyman explores basic questions in the strategy of surveys and how research design sets the limits for the analysis of empirical findings. Lazarsfeld deals with the panel technique—the repeated interviewing of a sample—as a research design. Hovland analyzes the difference in findings generated by experimental as compared with survey methodology. As illustrative of problems of data collection, we have included articles on the sources of bias and interview construction. Kornhauser's paper represents a systematic review of the sources of bias in attitude surveys, while Lazarsfeld discusses the advantages and uses of open-ended interviews as compared with the more direct and standardized interviewing approach. Among other problems of data collection facing public opinion researchers, for which we have not included articles, are interviewer bias, the nonrespondent, use of mail questionnaires, the use of projective tests and group interviews, and techniques for classifying attitude data.

The next three contributions represent efforts to refine analysis by the use of mathematical and formal models. Here we are dealing with frontier developments. Osgood presents the semantical differential as a technique for measuring meaning based on a development of factor analysis. Schramm evaluates the potentialities and limitations of information theory in the study of communication processes. McPhee probes the application of simulation to the study of public opinion and communication. While the long term relevance of these procedures remains to be evaluated they constitute devices which are being applied more or less extensively by social researchers.

Developing public opinion and communication research methods is a most active branch of social science. Currently, the interest of research groups in substantive problems is producing efforts to refine techniques of content analysis of sampling, to control interviewer bias, to perfect new methods of scaling, and to apply projective tests. There is also considerable interest in modifying procedures to make them applicable in foreign areas, especially in the so-called underdeveloped countries. Rudolph and Rudolph dramatically report on the problems of public opinion research in one of these countries.

HERBERT H. HYMAN

The Major Types of Surveys

(Editor's note: Herbert Hyman discusses a variety of uses of surveys. One of the major types of survey is designed for sheer description of some phenomenon—Kinsey's inquiry, for example, was concerned with the description of the sexual behavior of the American male. Other types are not concerned with description but rather with seeking an explanation, often taking the form of a test of some specific hypothesis growing out of a larger theory as to a particular determinant of the phenomenon. Explanatory surveys, regardless of type, share a common methodology. The nature of the relationship between one or more phenomena, or dependent variables, and one or more causes or independent variables, is reliably established—although the specific way in which this task is elaborated varies with the type of explanatory survey involved.)

Descriptive Surveys

THE FOCUS *of such an analysis is essentially precise measurement of one or more dependent variables in some defined population or sample of that population.*

Such inquiries may appear pedestrian and the technical problems of analysis too simple to warrant further treatment but the research design and subsequent analysis must have certain essential properties which are often neglected and which reduce the effectiveness of the survey. In brief, the *proper conceptualization* of a phenomenon is a prerequisite to precise measurement. And while this is not difficult for phenomena of a unitary sort in certain sciences, most of the phenomena of descriptive surveys are complex in character and so ambiguous in nature that they are subject to a variety of possible definitions and conceptualizations. In the case of the inquiry into radio, for example, one notes that attitudes about radio is not a narrow problem—it is a wide domain. Shall the analyst describe attitudes

Reprinted from *Survey Design and Analysis* (1955), pp. 68–89, by permission of the author and the publisher. (Copyright, 1955, The Free Press, New York.)

towards the programming, and if so, towards what type of programs? Shall he describe attitudes towards advertising and if so towards what kinds of advertising? Shall he describe attitudes towards such institutional aspects of the American radio industry as commercial sponsorship?

Kinsey's inquiry represents an even more dramatic illustration of this very point. One can readily see that the object of inquiry in the radio survey was of a manifold nature—but sexual behavior appears to be a unitary phenomenon, perhaps presenting serious *technical* difficulties in the process of inquiry but certainly simple to define. But as Kinsey finally conceptualized the problem, it included description of behaviors that might normally be disregarded in the initial thinking about sexual behavior, for example, any behavior that led to orgasm even though it involved less modal patterns such as animal or homosexual contacts. To cover comprehensively the domain of sexual behavior Kinsey had conservatively no less than 300 items of information to cover in the interview, indicating the degree of complexity of the phenomenon.[1]

For a classic sociological example of the problem of definition and conceptualization of the phenomenon in a descriptive survey, we can refer to Durkheim's *Suicide.*[2] We have here a phenomenon apparently unambiguous in meaning and unitary in character. Durkheim himself insists that "the sociologist must take as the object of his research groups of facts clearly circumscribed, capable of ready definition, with definite limits, and adhere strictly to them." He then notes that one of the reasons for his choice of the problem of suicide was that "among the various subjects that we have had occasion to study in our teaching career few are more accurately to be defined." Yet a few pages later, there is a detailed treatment of the difficulties of defining the phenomenon appropriately in which it takes Durkheim approximately 5 pages to examine alternative methods of defining his problem for study and to arrive at a definition that he regards as satisfactory.

Ackoff and Pritzker provide another illustration of how deceptive is the apparent simplicity of the dependent variables that might be the subject of factual descriptive survey. They cite the hypothetical survey in which the problem is "to determine how many chairs people have in their living rooms. To make such a determination we have to define 'chair.' . . . If we define chair in terms of physical properties, such as size, shape, weight, etc., we can always find a chair which does not satisfy these conditions. For example, if 'one or more legs' is taken as a necessary property of chairs, we could point to a chair built into a wall, or built on a solid base, and hence having no legs. A 'chair' is, of course, a functional concept; its essence is its use, not its structure."[3]

Deming makes this point in most general terms by noting that "*no distribution is an intrinsic property of a universe*, but is the result of doing something to it," and what is done in the operations of a survey is dependent on the original conceptualization of the phenomenon. Deming illustrates this with the apparently simple concept of a *dwelling place* in a hypothetical survey with central objective of describing the distribution of inhabitants per dwelling place in a city. The findings would be dependent, for example, on the fact that the definition of a dwelling *place* might have been "an address appearing to the lister to contain not more than three dwelling *units*."[4]

In virtually every descriptive survey, there is considerable theoretical difficulty in the conceptualization of the very phenomenon that shall be described. Moreover, there is considerable problem in *defining the nature of the population* that is most desirable to describe with respect to the phenomenon.

Generally, in descriptive surveys, the aim is to study a population which is *large and heterogeneous*. For what surveys offer through the application of sampling is the opportunity to determine with relative efficiency the state of affairs for a very large number of people. It is easy with other methods or through casual observation to determine the state of affairs for a small number of people or for a homogeneous group, but the need of government administrators or heads of large industrial work forces or huge consumer businesses is to have reliable knowledge of great masses of people. This fact alone has encouraged the growth of survey research of a descriptive sort, for the sample is uniquely geared to these requirements.

There will be rare occasions in applied research of a descriptive sort where the population to be studied is very limited in scope. Such would occur purely where the administrative need is for *very concrete* information for example, on a local or community level, or on a specific type of consumer or occupational group. However, such cases apart, the applied descriptive survey usually tends towards the choice of the large and diverse population. Where the goal of a descriptive survey is of a more academic or theoretical character, the choice similarly will be in the direction of the large and heterogeneous population for this means that the findings have more generality. But granted this usual direction of the decision there is still considerable difficulty in defining the type of population. One can attempt to study everybody in America or limit oneself in some way, for example, to males, to adults, to voters, city dwellers, industrial workers, etc. While there is some restriction on the variability within such groups as compared with the total population of a society, they could still be regarded as relatively heterogeneous. For example, instead of studying industrial workers in one specific type of industry in one community, one might draw a sample of such workers from a variety of areas and industries. Instead of urban dwellers in small cities, one can include cities of all sizes in all parts of the country. The decision as to where to make the choice and still have a rather heterogeneous population is vital, and the basic principle to be followed is that the population have some especial *relevance* to the problem under study.

With respect to one of our cases, the American public's views of radio, for example, are adults the relevant universe, or shall we include children, a sizable part of the radio audience? Shall we limit ourselves to those who own radios and therefore have some experiential basis for their attitudes? Shall we limit ourselves to those who have been exposed to radically other forms of radio programming and therefore have an informed basis for criticism?[5]

The same problem of definition of the population arises in the case of the inquiry on the atom bomb and similar inquiries into political issues.[6] Shall the universe include all adults or be restricted to voters, since they are the individuals whose opinions are backed up by some minimum sense of political responsibility or shall it be those who have still a further political qualification such as high information, habitual voting activity, or some type of influence on the political process?

There are the two major *theoretical* problems in a descriptive survey, the conceptualization of the phenomenon and the decision as to the relevant population. But there are serious *technical* problems which then arise. The conceptualization must then be translated into a *series of operations* which yield data which will ultimately provide accurate measurements or indices of the phenomenon to be described. And here there is much difficulty and perhaps compromise for the concepts may be difficult to translate into operations which are feasible. Moreover, all measurements are subject to some error and there must either be methods developed for the *reduction of errors* or at least for their *estimation* so that the results may be qualified in the light of known error. Effective analysis of a descriptive survey is therefore far from simple and requires considerable training.

By way of illustrating the difficulties in translating a simple problem into research operations, we quote what is, luckily, a *fictional* account of an interview from *Punch*, the British comic magazine.[7]

An Organ of Public Opinion

"Excuse me, sir," said the man in the belted raincoat and beret, "would you mind telling me how you would vote if the General Election were being held today?" He licked the point of his pencil and looked up into the eyes of the Regular Customer.

The regular customer took a pull at his tankard and several shorter tugs at his right ear before replying. "Why," he said, "by puttin' a cross side of the name of the chap I . . . I was goin' to say like *best*, but there's such a thing as the ballot-box, isn't there? By putting a cross side of the name of *one* of the chaps. How's that?"

"Yes, yes, of course," said the investigator, smiling benignly. "I mean which political *party* would you vote for?"

"Today, eh?" said the regular customer as he rubbed his left eye slowly with his knuckle.

"That's right—to-day," said the investigator.

"Bit late though, isn't it," said the regular customer, drawing his watch from a waistcoat pocket and studying it at arm's length. "Booths would be closed up by now, wouldn't they?"

"Well, suppose you'd voted this morning, bright and early," said the investigator.

"Ah, then you mean, 'ow 'ave I *voted*, not 'ow *shall* I vote," said the regular customer.

"All right—how should you have voted?" said the investigator. He licked his pencil again.

"What kind of a choice did I 'ave?"

"Look, sir, I'm sorry I troubled you," said the investigator. "It isn't really fair to take up so much of your spare time. I'll be—"

"No trouble at *all*," said the regular customer. "In fact it's all very interestin'. Carry on."

"Well, let's say there are three candidates—Liberal, Socialist and Tory. Which would you vote for?"

"Which would you?"

"I'm asking you, sir."

"An' I'm asking you. Fair's fair."

"I'm independent, neutral."

" 'Aven't the courage of your confections, eh?"

"It's not that. Now, sir, *how would you vote?*"

"Well, I should 'ave to think, shouldn't I?"

"That's right—Liberal, Socialist, Tory?" said the investigator in a voice entirely devoid of enthusiasm.

"Who's the Socialist chap?"

"What chap?"

"The chap puttin' up, 'course!"

"Does that matter? Can't you give me a rough idea of your preference?"

"I can't very well vote for a chap I don't know nothin' about; now can I?"

"I mean which *party* would you support?"

"Not knowin' what they're proposin' to do, I can't say."

"But you know what they've *done*, their general principles—"

"I knows what they *'aven't* done," said the regular customer.

"Thank you, sir. I'll put you down as 'Don't know.' Thank you very much. Good night!"

"Hey, come back! Don't know what?"

"Which party to vote for," said the investigator wearily.

"Who don't?"

"Well, sir, you said yourself—"

"I said nothin' of the sort. I knows 'ow to use me 'ard-earned vote, me lad. You'll scratch that 'Don't know' out."

"With pleasure, sir, if you'll give me a definite answer."

"Ask me a def'nite question and you'll get a def'nite answer," said the regular customer, tapping the investigator on the chest with his pint.

"Would you vote for the Tories, the Conservatives?"

"Not much choice there, is there? But if I've got to take me pick I'll 'ave the Conservatives."

The investigator's eyes rolled in anguish. He flicked a tick at his pad. "Thank you, sir," he said. "I'm much obliged. Good night."

" 'Arf a sec.," said the regular customer, grabbing at the investigator's raincoat. "You 'aven't asked me yet about the Liberals."

"Some other time, sir. That's quite enough for the moment. I must be pushing." He broke free and walked rapidly out of the saloon.

"Sim'lar, Charlie," said the regular customer.

When the barman returned with the beer he found the regular customer chuckling softly, shaking his head slowly to and fro an inch or two above the counter. "What's the big joke, Bert?" he said.

"That young chap in 'ere just now," said the regular customer. " 'E's gone away with me vote an' 'e's forgotten to take me name. 'E won't 'arf be kickin' 'isself. I reckon 'e'll be back in a bit."

Analytic ability in descriptive surveys is of importance in its own right. Much of applied social research sponsored by government or commercial or action agencies is of this character—for factual knowledge provides a sound basis for administrative actions. Moreover, such descriptive data is central to certain academic disciplines. For example, Lazarsfeld clearly conveys the value that descriptive survey data on the social scene would have for the historian.[8] And on the basis of an inquiry among historians working in the field of modern American history. Parry presents actual data showing the considerable value that historians attach to such current and possible future survey data as an historical source.[9]

But the analytic skills associated with purely descriptive surveys have profound value for the development of skill in treating more explanatory surveys intended to test various kinds of hypotheses. For the essence of such analysis is the establishment of the relationship between some phenomenon or dependent variable and some hypothesized cause or independent variable. In analyzing such surveys, all the sophistication in the manipulation of independent variables, in the invention of fruitful hypotheses as to causes of phenomena, in the techniques of controlling extraneous independent variables, and the like, will be of no avail if the *dependent* variable is not effectively conceptualized. The superstructure of determinants in an explanatory survey must rest on a firm base. Thus, skill in the analysis of descriptive surveys is a prerequisite for effective analysis of explanatory surveys. It is not sufficient to the task, but it is essential. One can, it is true, learn skill in descriptive analysis in the course of more explanatory surveys, for such skill is a component part of such an analysis. But here the complexity is great and many things must be learned at once. The descriptive survey, in other words, permits the learning of a part of the ultimate total array of skills under relatively simplified conditions.

We turn again to the authoritative example of Durkheim's work, *Suicide*, to illustrate the point. We have previously noted the care with which Durkheim conceptualizes the phenomenon of suicide, the dependent variable under study as must be done in any descriptive survey. But Durkheim ultimately was concerned with explanation, with the testing of a general theory, with the determination of causes of suicide. Yet he takes all the pains of elaborate conceptualization of his phenomenon, engages in the most careful descriptive research, for, as he remarks in his introduction, lack of care in conceptualizing the phenomenon creates the risk that "categories of very different sorts of facts are indistinctly combined under the same heading, or similar realities are differently named. . . . We risk distinguishing what should be combined, or combining what should be distinguished, thus mistaking the real affinities of things, and accordingly misapprehending their nature. . . . A scientific investigation can . . . be achieved only if it deals with comparable facts, and it is the more likely to succeed the more certainly it has combined all those that can be usefully compared. . . . Our first task then must be to determine the order of facts to be studied under the name of suicides."[10]

Clarity in the definition and conceptualization of the phenomenon is thus one requirement for effective explanatory analyses. Otherwise the relationship to the independent variable will be obscured. But the descriptive survey involves still another element which is essential to effective explanation in surveys. Clarity in *conceptualization* is no insurance that a relationship can be established—that a theory can be put to test. The later measurements and *operations* may obscure the initial clarity! Any relationship will then be blurred. And as we have noted consideration of procedures for the reduction and estimation of error are central to descriptive surveys, for the sole purpose of such surveys is to provide an *accurate* representation of the phenomenon.

Here again we turn to Durkheim's work to note the persistent emphasis upon the examination of error in the description of the phenomenon when he considers and evaluates and accepts any demonstration of a relationship.[11] We shall note only a small number of the total instances of this recurrent procedure in the work italicizing the argument about errors.

Durkheim's "Suicide"—A Case Study of Recurrent Attention to Error:

In establishing the relationship of age to suicide in various societies, he notes the general finding that it increases regularly with age. Yet he remarks that there are slight exceptions. He considers these and rejects their importance to his theory on the ground that they are "due perhaps to errors of tabulation." (p. 101)

In establishing the relationship to seasonal variations in temperature, he notes that a prior investigator reported one striking exception to the general finding of a maximum incidence in summer. This maximum was demonstrated only once in the autumn season in a series based on data from 18 countries and 34 different time periods. Durkheim evaluates the implication of this inversion and remarks: "This last irregularity, observed only in the Grand-Duchy of Baden and at a single moment of its history, is *valueless*, for it results from a calculation bearing on too brief a period; besides, it never recurred." In three other exceptional instances the maximum occurred in springtime. Durkheim remarks "The other three exceptions are *scarcely more significant.* They occur in Holland, Ireland and Sweden. For the first two countries the available figures which were the base for the seasonal averages are too uncertain for anything positive to be concluded; there are only 387 cases for Holland and 755 for Ireland. In general, the statistics for these two peoples are *not wholly authoritative.* . . . If we consider only the states concerning which there are authentic figures, the law may be held to be absolute and universal." (p. 107)

The student might well raise the question here as to when such considerations as to error factors are applied in an arbitrary manner. An investigator can of course invoke the concept of error to reject any finding he doesn't like. It is a requirement that there be some formal method or logical canon for deciding what is an error-producing procedure and what is not, and that the consideration be applied in an unbiased fashion.[12]

Later in a parallel treatment of the phenomenon of insanity as a function of seasonal variations in temperature, in an attempt to see whether *morbidity in general* is related to temperature, Durkheim remarks on the inadequacy of the primary source data. "The distribution of the cases of insanity among the seasons can be estimated only by the number of admissions to the asylums. Such a standard is very *inadequate;* for families intern invalids not immediately but some time after the outbreak of the disease."[13] (p. 109, footnote)

Later in a treatment of the relationship of the phenomenon of suicide to month of the year, rather than season, Durkheim notes certain irregularities in the general findings. He rejects these on the ground that "the greatest irregularities, moreover, usually appear in series too small to be very significant." (p. 111)

Later in a general discussion of the relation of religion to suicide, manipulated through the procedure of examining suicide rates for nations of different religious compositions, Durkheim notes that England has a low rate among Protestant countries. He remarks, however, that "to be sure, the statistics of English suicides are not very exact. Because of the penalties attached to suicide, many cases are reported as accidental death. However, this inexactitude is not enough to explain the extent of the difference between this country and Germany." (p. 160, footnote)

This particular example strikes home the observation made above about the problem of arbitrariness in evaluating error. Why does Durkheim regard the presence of error in one instance as sufficient to *completely invalidate* the empirical finding, and in the other instance, an *insufficient basis* for rejecting the finding. The thorny problem of *accuracy requirements* is again posed. In the absence of a logical procedure for knowing when something shall be regarded accurate or inaccurate, and how crucial the level of inaccuracy is, there inevitably is some arbitrariness.

Later in establishing the relation of the phenomenon of suicide to sex, Durkheim notes the general finding of a much greater incidence among men with the exception of the Spanish statistics. And he remarks "but not only is the accuracy of Spanish statistics open to doubt, but Spain cannot compare with the great nations of Central and Northern Europe." (p. 166, footnote)

Here again one underscores the problem of arbitrariness in evaluating error components, for the addendum that Spain cannot compare with the great nations seems strangely out of place. Yet, Durkheim may simply not be explicit on the logical grounds for drawing this conclusion about Spanish sources. Elsewhere, his comments are a model of objectivity and care, and he elaborates the exact reason for regarding a datum as artifactual.[14]

Thus far, it might appear that the evaluation of error is introduced as a procedure only in relation to slight irregularities or exceptions or inversions in the general findings, and as a basis for deciding what qualifications must be put upon the general conclusions. But Durkheim in many places considers whether an artifact, an error, is responsible for a very *general* finding. This is of course just as essential a procedure. We cite merely one such instance.

Thus in noting the general negative relation between suicide and wartime conditions, he remarks on the possibility that the finding might be completely artifactual. "It might perhaps be considered due to the drafting of a part of the civilian population in war-time and the fact that it is very hard to keep track of suicides in an army in the field." (p. 205) He is able to reject this possibility on the basis of a particular and ingenious analytic procedure, but he then entertains the possibility that there is still a second artifactual basis for the finding. He speculates as to whether the cause "might not be that the record of suicides was less exactly kept because of the paralysis of (civil) administrative authority." (p. 206) Here again, he derives a logical model of the way other data would have to distribute if the artifact were involved and is enabled to reject the argument.

We have already noted no less than 7 specific instances in which Durkheim makes reference to a possible error factor in the findings. There are at least 13 other instances which we have not reported, which establish the prominence that Durkheim gave to this methodological aspect of survey analysis. Instead of reporting some of these instances, we shall now use them for a problem exercise.

PROBLEM EXERCISE

Durkheim's "Suicide" as an Exercise in the Evolution of Findings in Relation to Artifacts

Find five other instances in Durkheim's *Suicide* where consideration of error factors is introduced in the evaluation of the findings.

Discuss whether there appears to be arbitrariness in the way in which the concept of error is invoked, or whether there is an explicit basis for the decision as to the existence of error and its consequences.

Note whether there is a logical or empirical procedure developed to test the possibility that the finding can be invalidated on the ground of the hypothesized error factor.

Note whether the error applies to the measurement of the dependent or the independent variable.

631

The descriptive survey is thus a training ground for the development of skill in conceptualization of the phenomenon and in the treatment of the findings in relation to error factors, both essential to effective analysis of explanatory surveys. But there is still another feature of the descriptive survey which is especially valuable for ultimate work in the design and analysis of explanatory surveys. Out of the findings of such surveys often comes the basis for the formulation of fruitful hypotheses about phenomena, or at least for some reduction in confusion in theorizing about a phenomenon.

The usual image of the explanatory survey is that there is a hypothesis always waiting to be put to the test, but oftentimes one faces novel problems and phenomena for study and one has little sense of what are the possible determinants. This has always been recognized as a problem and leads to the usual practice of consulting the literature and other informants directly. For example, Ackoff and Pritzker remark with respect to explanatory surveys that "no individual can be aware of *all* the facts, laws, and theories that are potentially useful to him in selecting pertinent variables. There are usually so many things of which we are not aware. . . . Here what we need is the maximum of cooperative effort, for no one person chosen from one scientific discipline is ever in a position to think of all the pertinent aspects of a situation. There should be a realization that the solution to this problem can come about only through the broadest type of social (not individual) experience, and hence it is essential to have wide consultation with people from all sorts of *diverse* fields and backgrounds."[15]

But this solution imputes too much wisdom to our colleagues, past and present, particularly when the survey deals with a novel problem. The alternative is the exploration of the phenomenon directly with the hope that in the experience, one will glean some insight. Thus, Jahoda, Deutsch and Cook remark on the value of an "experience survey," and illustrate various informal or exploratory types of study of the phenomenon leading to the formulation of hypotheses.[16] The descriptive survey, in one sense, represents a more formalized and more elaborate type of exploratory study. But its value in the initial stage of formulating an explanatory survey goes beyond this.

Oftentimes, one faces an apparently significant phenomenon and imposes a huge structure of hypothetical determinants upon this without a second thought as to whether there is sufficient clarity or stability and regularity involved so that a key or explanation can be found. We are addicted to determinism, and find the notion of the ephemeral or unsolvable abhorrent. But it may well be that some of the problems we commit to explanatory surveys should never be undertaken for they are so elusive. The descriptive survey because of its wide sampling can be conceived of as an inquiry into the *uniformity or regularity* of some phenomenon. It permits a better decision as to the wisdom of undertaking any explanatory inquiry at all. Further the descriptive survey by providing data on the *rarity* or *universality* of some phenomenon and its *distribution socially* gives guidance as to what type of determinants might lead to the most fruitful hypotheses. There is, of course, still no assurance that we will pick phenomena that are fruitful to study or invent fruitful hypotheses, but the likelihood is greater.

We may again turn to Durkheim's work to note the way in which these benefits of the descriptive survey are used as a prelude to the more experimental phases of his analysis. Thus early in his work, Durkheim examines the descriptive data on suicide rates for different nations and over a series of years. He notes a *stability* to those data, or even, as he remarks, that they are almost *invariable* for each nation over time. He is thus led to affirm the fact that the phenomenon of national differences is a fact with "its own unity, individuality and consequently its own nature." Because of its regularity over time for each nation, he sees its nature as "dominantly social." (p. 46)[17] In other words, the examination of data such as would be treated in a descriptive survey for their stability and social distribution leads him to support further experimental study and to seek the causes in certain directions.[18] We use his own words to show the conclusion he arrives at:

The suicide rate is therefore a factual order, unified and definite, as is shown by both its permanence and its variability. For this permanence would be inexplicable if it were not the result of a group of distinct characteristics . . . and this variability proves the concrete and individual quality of these same characteristics, since they vary with the individual character of society itself. . . . Each society is predisposed to contribute a definite quota of voluntary deaths. This predisposition may therefore be the subject of a special study belonging to sociology. This is the study we are going to undertake. (p. 51)

He goes on to argue that a phenomenon which has been demonstrated to be so lawful or regular for such a huge entity as a nation "can depend only on extra-social causes of broad generality or on causes expressly social" and thus is guided as to the hypotheses he should test. (p. 52)[19]

The point becomes clearer if we take as a contrasting example, one of our case studies, *The Authoritarian Personality*. We have here an explanatory survey designed to test certain hypotheses as to the causes of a particular ideology. But whereas Durkheim had at his disposal descriptive data on a national level to lead him to the realization that his phenomenon had a regularity at a very macroscopic social level and then to search for this social determinant. *The Authoritarian Personality* study had a relatively homogeneous, although large, sample and could not gain the benefit of knowledge as to whether a phenomenon was frequent or rare in the society. Therefore, on occasion a phenomenon that independent descriptive research shows to be well nigh universal is imputed to an idiosyncratic cause. Hyman and Sheatsley in a long critique of this study make this point under the heading of "the value of national norms."[20]

If the researcher, because of his sampling design, cannot tell whether the given attitude is normative for the general population, he may seek the explanation in the wrong place. We are suggesting that a sample of the heterogeneous total population illuminates the direction for analysis and makes less likely the drawing of broad conclusions which may be unwarranted. We . . . will merely illustrate it . . . with one example.

In discussing the political ideology of ethnocentric individuals, the authors note that such persons are distinguished by an emphasis on the "inevitability of war." The interpretation is then given in individualistic psychodynamic terms: the high scorer has much "psychological passivity," "and underlying sympathy for war-making." . . . When this same question is put to representative samples of the population, one notes that the expectation of war is characteristic of a great many people and not a deviant few; that it fluctuates in a rather orderly fashion according to the objective facts; and that it shows a high negative correlation with education. If one had at his disposal the data from such samples, one might have interpreted the meaning of this sentiment quite differently.

Explanatory Surveys

We have now outlined the central theoretical and technical problems that the analyst will face in the descriptive survey and have pointed to the many values such surveys have. Among these values there is the great benefit in training that the analyst gains for ultimate work in what we have labelled explanatory surveys. The findings of descriptive surveys are a guide to theorizing in explanatory surveys; the skill in conceptualizing a phenomenon, so central to the descriptive survey, is as crucial in the explanatory survey. Here the same power of conceptualization must be extended to the problem of independent variables as well. Technical skill in reducing errors in the procedures or estimating them is required. Otherwise the findings cannot be trusted. But we have not as yet outlined the unique analytic requirements of the explanatory survey. To insure that the obtained relationship of a phenomenon to some particular hypothesized cause is meaningful, one must have confidence that factors operative in the situation other than the hypothesized one are not responsible. This has been a classic problem with which laboratory experimentation has been concerned and methods for ruling out these extraneous factors have been developed which are dependent on the manipulation of the laboratory setting and the initial selection, matching and arrangement of subjects. For example, any differences between laboratory subjects exposed to different values of the independent variable cannot be allocated to other extraneous characteristics since the initial matching or selection and subsequent arrangement of subjects for exposure insures that such is not the case. Moreover, since the independent variable is created and applied at will by the experimentor, it can be separated from other stimulus conditions which might otherwise accompany its operation.

The explanatory survey follows the model of the laboratory experiment with the fundamental difference that it attempts to represent this design in a *natural setting*. Instead of *creating* and manipulating the independent variables whose effect is to be traced the survey analyst must find in the natural setting instances of these factors. By measuring their presence and magnitude, their relationship to the phenomenon can be established in the course of the analysis. But since these variables are not created, but merely found in the natural setting, there is the great danger that a variety of other factors accompany them, and that respondents characterized by particular attributes may vary in other important respects. The influence of these other sources of variability must somehow be reduced. Otherwise any inference about the hypothesized cause may be shaky. *The restriction of the universe which is covered and the design of the sample in the explanatory survey provides the basic technique by which other sources of variation in the phenomenon are excluded.*[21] It is in relation to this problem that the descriptive and explanatory surveys lead to opposing designs. In the descriptive survey, generality is achieved through the study of the heterogeneous universe. But this generality permits the total array of determinants to operate.

In the explanatory survey confidence in the inference as to causality is achieved through restricting the heterogeneity of the universe. We can illustrate the way in which such restriction of the universe is the formal equivalent of the matching in the laboratory experiment by one of our cases and by other examples of explanatory surveys. In the inquiry into the causes of absenteeism, instead of taking the universe of workers throughout the United States, and running the danger that any correlation between some independent variable and absenteeism might be due to almost an infinite number of other operative factors, the universe was restricted. Workers from only 18 plants were studied. Only six industries were represented. By definition, any findings as to the causes of absenteeism could not be invalidated on grounds of the contribution of factors in the wider industrial complex that were excluded. But further, the analysts located workers in such types of plants in two classes of communities, those with good and those with bad community conditions again reducing the sources of variation in the out-plant complex.

We can take as another example of this principle a study from the literature which makes the methodological principle exceedingly explicit. We shall later treat in detail an inquiry by Sewell in which certain hypotheses from psychoanalytic theory about the effect of infantile experience on later personality patterns were tested. We have here a set of independent variables such as whether weaning was abrupt or not, bowel training early or later, feeding by bottle or breast, which obviously cannot

635

be treated in the laboratory setting. Subjects cannot be arbitrarily chosen because they are matched in particular respects and then instructed to rear their children in particular fashions. We can only find subjects who happen to be contrasted with respect to the way in which they were or are being reared and examine the consequences in the personality patterns. But it is obvious that parents who rear their children in contrasted ways may also differ in many other respects, e.g., class, education, ethnicity, which might account for the personality consequences. Sewell attempts to control these sources of variation by the restriction of the universe.

In the design of the study an attempt was made to approximate experimental conditions by the prior control of several factors believed to be associated with personality adjustment. Thus diverse cultural influences were eliminated by selecting only children of old American cultural backgrounds in a predominantly old American community. By selecting children from a single occupational group (farm children), occupational and socio-economic influences were roughly controlled. Age was held constant by selecting only children in the age group five to six. Personal-social experiences were in some measure controlled by the selection of children who had not yet been subject to the socializing effects of school. Only the children of unbroken and never broken unions were selected; consequently, disrupted family situations could not affect the findings.[22]

In both these examples, the absenteeism inquiry and the Sewell study, there remains of course, the possibility that the findings are due to residual factors whose variability has not been controlled by the initial restrictions on the universe and the design of the sample. The natural conditions characteristic of the survey method make for a *very wide* array of factors to be operative, and this fact requires that further protection against the influence of extraneous factors be applied after-the-fact, in the terminal stage of the analysis, by statistical techniques. Such techniques are described in detail in Part III. However, the greater the approximation to the model of an experiment by the initial restriction of the universe, the less is the need for such laborious manipulation and the greater is the confidence in the validity of the obtained explanation. While the restriction of the universe and consequent control of extraneous factors produces these gains, the gain is accompanied by a loss in generality. The reader can see that the explanatory findings naturally only apply under the original restricted conditions. This foreshadows the many conflicts the analyst may experience in the course of designing his survey.

Conflicting Goals and Compromises in Research Design

Thus far it would appear that survey research is relatively simple. The analyst merely decides on the basis of his problem which orthodox type of design to follow and executes it as effectively as his resources will permit.

The analysis follows routinely from the design since the properties built-in at the planning stage insure success. However, the complication that frequently arises is that the goals of a survey are various and the analyst wishes to accomplish a variety of objectives. Under such conditions, he inevitably must compromise and pick a design that is not ideally suited to any single purpose, but perhaps the optimal design considering the multi-purpose character of his research.

Compromises are required by the conflicts in the social setting of the research. Sponsor and analyst may be in opposition about the goals of the survey. The larger controversial aspects of the study exert pressure. Research personnel within the organization may disagree. Practical goals such as economy, speed, and the like militate against the introduction of certain technical safeguards. However, here the analyst's dilemma is clear and while a decision may be unpleasant, it can be made.

The problem is self-evident in the instance of surveys which cover a variety of *content* areas. The high cost of surveys often leads the analyst or research organization to include in one questionnaire a battery of questions on one problem, and other batteries of questions on other problems. Since the overhead costs of field investigation do not change markedly with the length of the questionnaire, each problem is treated at a relatively low expenditure or each client only pays a small portion of the total costs. The gains in economy from such multi-content surveys is considerable, but the loss in quality of research may also be considerable. Where each problem is complex, it may be impossible to treat it comprehensively with a limited number of questions and corresponding measurements. But here again the dilemma is obvious and the choice usually a conscious one.

Quite frequently, however, the analyst experiences no conflict over the content aspects of a survey. Only one content area is to be covered. However, conflict may still arise because there is a desire to study more than one *formal* problem within the content area. Thus, the analyst may be interested in a *descriptive* inquiry—estimating as precisely and comprehensively as possible some state of affairs—and at the same time interested in an *explanatory* inquiry of a theoretical type—testing some particular hypothesis about the determinants of that state of affairs. These respective formal problems might call for opposing features of the research design, and the analyst inevitably compromises.

We can illustrate this very effectively by reference to one of our cases, Centers' inquiry into Class-Consciousness. As noted earlier the main purpose of the inquiry was such as to call for a theoretical and explanatory survey, a test by empirical means of the validity of the theory that certain attitudes arise from a person's economic position. Such an inquiry logically calls for a design of the type we have previously noted as analogous to laboratory experiment. Ideally, groups should have been sampled who varied with respect to their position in the society and attempts should have been made to match these groups initially with respect to other variables so that any obtained differences in attitude could have been allocated to the independent variables with confidence. Such matching would have been achieved as well as possible in advance of the analysis by the principle previously noted of restriction of the universe. Thus, the design for the explanatory survey would have represented the best approximation to the controlled laboratory experiment that was possible under natural field conditions apart from the crudity of measurement and curtailment of the scope of the observations that might accompany the natural setting. However, Centers was interested in a *descriptive* inquiry into class consciousness in addition to his interest in testing a particular hypotheses. From the point of view of a descriptive inquiry, one would seek the most comprehensive and accurate measurement of the phenomenon for some defined large population or sample of that population. To restrict the study to a few contrasted groups within a relatively homogeneous universe would have defeated the purpose since no generalized description of the phenomenon for the entire population would have been possible. And to sample all groups in adequate numbers within the total population apart from prohibitive costs would complicate the inquiry since the description of the state of class consciousness in the aggregate would involve specialized computations. To match the contrasted economic groups *in advance* with respect to other independent variables by restricting the universe severely would have been a mistake for this would not permit any description of the phenomenon as it operated in the natural American setting. This would provide only a description under relatively artificial or restricted conditions. Thus, the better the initial approximation to the laboratory experiment in a survey research design, the less effective is the inquiry as a descriptive one, and this choice is irreversible and irremediable. To use the design of a descriptive inquiry, however, is flexible. One can approximate to the matching of cases after the fact by selecting sub-groups from the original larger number studied who happened to be alike in other respects, and one can hope to find in the mass of the cases a sufficient number of individuals contrasted with respect to the major variable under study. If one is successful in this procedure, one achieves his explanatory findings under conditions where more generality attaches to them because of the wider coverage of the sample. However, it is fortuitous whether the ideal conditions for testing the hypothesis will be present, since the procedure is after-the-fact, and there is much laborious work involved in the manipulation of the constellation of many variables.

In summary, the *choice of a descriptive design permits the later test of a hypothesis by an approximation after the fact to an explanatory design, but the initial choice of an explanatory design precludes any later approxi-*

mation to the design needed for a descriptive inquiry. We can now illustrate this from Centers' text.

Centers' Psychology of Social Classes—A Case Study in Conflicting Goals:[23]

He chose a *descriptive design:*

The method decided upon for the present study was that of a public attitude survey of a *representative cross-section* of the adult white population. Such a method is peculiarly designed to give *macroscopic, over-all results* rather than the kind that might be obtained by *studies of specific populations in limited areas under conditions allowing rigid control of variables*. (p. 34)

The reason is explicit, he stated his theory and indicated his plan to engage in an empirical verification, he now remarks:

The over-all picture (of class consciousness) is still so vague and indistinct that clarification of it is an imperious necessity and certainly logically prior to studies of this latter type. The problem is of such a nature as to demand that great masses of people of every adult age group, of every section of the country, of rural, small town, large town and city residence, and of every socio-economic stratum be represented. (p. 35)

Yet he imposes certain restrictions on the population to be sampled, because of the complications otherwise created for an experimental or explanatory type design.

Because Negroes constitute such a small minority of the population and have in addition a caste-like relationship to the white majority to complicate matters, their class psychology could reasonably be regarded as a problem for later separate study, and hence no Negroes were included in the survey. Women were not included because in a research where stratification is the basic variable, it is important to get definitely placed persons as far as occupation is concerned, and women do not universally have occupations other than that of housewife. (p. 35)

Such restrictions of a universe occasionally occur in a *purely* descriptive inquiry for *practical* reasons of economy or facilitating the research process. But here it is clear that the restrictions are intended to *simplify*, to *make unambiguous*, the comparisons of the ideology of given groups, a purpose compatible with an explanatory survey, but certainly not appropriate in relation to the purposes in the earlier quotation cited above of a description of class-consciousness for groups of *all* types. Moreover, if the inquiry had been purely descriptive there would have been no problem of classifying Negroes or women according to their objective economic position, since one would have been merely interested in the phenomenon of class-consciousness rather than its correlates.

He makes his decision but later he expresses the limitations the descriptive design imposed on his ability to analyze the data effectively for a test of his hypothesis:

The nature of the data obtained in this cross-sectional study imposes limits upon the analytical possibilities. . . . Causal relationships between two given variables can be unequivocally asserted, if they can be asserted at all, only when by rigorous experimental techniques all variables but that to which causal efficacy is to be attributed are held constant—and such control of variables is most difficult to achieve. It is an obvious impossibility in an *exploratory study* of the present type which deals with an entire cross-section of a population that *varies in an almost inexhaustible* fashion. To hold constant everything but occupation, for example, would require a sample several hundred times as large as the present one. Before groups large enough for statistically reliable comparisons and matched for all possibly relevant characteristics save occupation were obtained, such a sample might have to contain fifty or one hundred thousand persons. (p. 162)

Admittedly, the logical problems that Centers imposes in such extreme form could not be solved by any explanatory design. It is of the nature of humans that they vary "in almost inexhaustible fashion" and that holding constant everything is impossible, but certainly some of the variation in extraneous respects could have been reduced by deliberate methods in advance. Centers actually did this in part by excluding women and Negroes, thus implicitly matching respondents of the contrasted classes in sex and color. Moreover, certain groups could have been expanded in size to enhance particular experimental comparisons at the price of dropping out less essential groups.

All this is not intended to imply that Centers should have pursued a *pure* explanatory type of design. Both goals seemed important, and the limitations of each design are made articulate. He made a compromise between these goals, chose a slightly modified design of a descriptive sort and approximated the controls and other properties of the experimental design after the fact by laborious methods of partial correlation, and higher order breakdowns. These procedures were an essential under such conditions. Moreover, some gain does occur by such a decision. Whatever experimental findings are possible are made under conditions of greater generality and less artificiality. The case is merely intended to show the conflicts that the analyst faces frequently and the problems of resolving these conflicts.

Another source of conflict often occurs where *diagnosis* and *testing* are simultaneous goals of an explanatory survey. Testing an hypothesis might call for restriction of the universe. Where the explanatory survey tends towards the *diagnostic*, where the emphasis is less on the test of one specific hypothesis and more on the search for fruitful determinants plus an *ultimate* test, the point earlier noted about the guidance that descriptive data provide for theorizing would lead to the choice of a descriptive design and the attempt to approximate experimental conditions after-the-fact.

Where the explanatory survey is of a *programmatic* or *evaluative* nature, there may also be practical constraints upon the restriction of the universe for study. The universe that might be most desirable for clarifying the operation of an independent variable and providing the most unambiguous experimental test might not be the one that approximates best to the requirements of the action agency. We can illustrate this from the history of the *United States Strategic Bombing Survey*, a case we shall use repeatedly. In this instance, a presidential directive from Franklin D. Roosevelt led to the formation of a special research organization within the military establishment. The explicit directive was that there "be an impartial and expert study of the effects of . . . aerial attack . . . including effects upon the morale and will of the enemy to resist."[24] It is clear by implication that the test of the influence of bombing on morale and will to resist had to provide evidence on the *total* problem, for one specialized finding on the effect of bombing in one city or on a limited group of people would not provide adequate information for the military establishment. Yet, by considering the morale in the total Japanese or German society, and attempting to determine the specific contribution of bombing, one brings into the picture not only the operation of the variables of bombing but also the effect of all other forms of military action as they impinged on the population, and the whole gamut of environmental factors that impinged on the civilian population. But, there was no alternative and the survey had to treat the universe that approximated the total population, and try to abstract during the analysis from the total complex of determinants of morale in wartime the influence of bombing.

The Bombing Survey illustrates one other difficulty in setting up an experimental model for the explanatory inquiry when it is of the evaluative type. Even if the sponsor's needs would have been met by limited findings applicable to the artificially restricted conditions of a few cities or a specialized human population, it would have been *impossible* to locate these ideal conditions anywhere in the society. For example, the analyst in designing such an inquiry might desire to restrict the universe to cities of a certain size and compare the morale changes accompanying different levels of bombing. The populations of cities of different sizes had suffered different degrees of deprivation in wartime, were provided with different degrees of air raid protection and the like and these sources of variation in morale could thus be ruled out. But the original needs of the military establishment were such that bombing was not meted out in accordance with an experimental design, and one could not find zero degrees of bombing within the class of cities that were of large size. For example, among the six largest cities of Japan—Tokyo, Yokohama, Nagoya, Osaka, Kobe, and Kyoto—only one, Kyoto, did not receive a very heavy weight of bombs. For all cities with populations over 100,000 there was only one sub-group of such cities in Japan which were unbombed or lightly bombed and *all* of these were confined to one geographical area, Northeastern Japan.[25] In the programmatic or evaluative survey the needs of the analyst are overriden by the requirements of the action agency and it would be absurd to expect that heavy bombing would occur in unimportant isolated rural areas or that a large and strategically important city would be unscathed.

The frequency of such dual or conflicting purposes—desires to accomplish both a general description and an explanation, to achieve a test but to aim towards generality, to gain diagnostic power from the descriptive data as a prelude to sharpened theory and an ultimate test, to implement an experimental design in the face of the programmatic goals of the sponsor—lead often to the more flexible choice of a descriptive design with some price paid in terms of the laboriousness of the terminal stages of the analysis.

NOTES

1. Kinsey reports that the maximum history for any respondent involved 521 items of information, but our figure does not include those items of inquiry which were intended for classificatory purposes, rather than for description of the actual phenomenon of sexual behavior.

2. E. Durkheim, *Suicide* (English translation) Glencoe: The Free Press, 1951). We shall return again and again to Durkheim's work and present a detailed analysis of its other methodological features as illustrations of some of the problems of descriptive and explanatory surveys.

3. Ackoff and Pritzker, *op. cit.*

4. W. E. Deming, "On Training in Sampling," *J. Amer. Stat. Assoc.*, 40, 1945, 307–316. Italics ours. For another example of an apparently simple phenomenon subject to great complexity in conceptualization, the reader might examine the history of the surveys concerned with measuring "unemployment" or membership in the labor force. See for example, *Labor Force Definition and Measurement* (New York: Social Science Research Council Bulletin #56, 1947).

5. It is not necessary that the decision to restrict the universe of study be followed out in the actual respondents who are enumerated. In some instances it is more desirable or at least more practicable to ask a series of questions which permit the irrelevant groups to be sorted out after-the-fact. On the general problem of relevant populations for study and the procedures for treating this problem, before or after-the-fact, see D. Katz, "The Interpretation of Survey Findings," *J. Soc. Issues*, 2, #2, 35–36.

6. For a treatment of this general problem in relation to the concept of the public in public opinion research surveys see, D. Cahalan, "On the Concepts of Public and Public Opinion," *Int. J. Opin. Attit. Res.*, 1, 1947, #4, 99–102.

7. Cole, W., *The Best Humor From Punch* (Cleveland: World, 1953), pp. 31–34. Reproduced by permission of the Proprietors of *PUNCH*.

8. P. F. Lazarsfeld, "The Obligations of the 1950 Pollster to the 1984 Historian," *Publ. Opin. Quart.*, 14, 1950, 617–638.

9. H. J. Parry, "Historians and Opinion Research," *Int. J. Opin. Attit. Res.*, 2, 1948, 40–53.

10. E. Durkheim, English Translation, *op. cit.*, pp. 41–42.

11. Durkheim's study represents survey method based on *previously collected data* rather than data collected specially for the purpose of the investigation. In such instances, actual procedures for the *reduction* of error are not possible, and instead *estimation and allowance* for error which is in actuality present is the only possibility. One might perhaps advance the general principle that secondary analyses require *extra* attention to error factors. In the case of primary analyses the investigator at least *knows* what cautions were applied in the collection and manipulation of data, if any, but in secondary analyses the original errors may be insidious, since one has little knowledge of the earlier stages of the survey process.

12. This is one reason why so much attention is given in the later text to discussion of the major error factors and to early phases of the survey process, during which phases the errors are generally created, i.e., are artifactual.

13. It might be noted that here the error component is an artifact having to do with the *independent* variable, season of onset of disease, rather than the dependent variable, insanity per se. In the explanatory survey error components must, of course, be evaluated in both these realms. However, the quotation illustrates the general problem of attention to error problems.

14. See, for example the detailed analysis on pp. 175–176 by which he buttresses his categorical statement that certain Swedish statistics are "useless."

15. Ackoff and Pritzker, *op. cit.*

16. *Op. cit.*

17. It should be noted that Durkheim had descriptive data for successive periods of time. A phenomenon may be widespread, but if it is *temporary*, its cause would naturally be sought in the *situational* rather than in some *persistent* social fact. Descriptive surveys *on a trend basis* thus permit the location of determinants more effectively since the transient social can be differentiated from the more permanent social.

18. Of course, one may well argue that this was Durkheim's theoretical orientation to the problem *before* he ever examined these descriptive data. But this does not change the point. He nevertheless examined the data and thereby gained confidence in the direction that more experimental research should take.

19. This same use of descriptive surveys as a basis for the inference as to determinants is, of course, widespread in certain disciplines, although it is not necessarily formulated as an example of descriptive survey method. Thus support for the concept of "culture" as a determinant of behavior derives from descriptive work in Ethnology through the sheer demonstration of uniformities within a society, and differences as between societies.

20. H. Hyman and P. B. Sheatsley, The Authoritarian Personality—A Methodological Critique, in M. Jahoda and R. Christie, ed., *Continuities in Social Research*—Studies in the Scope and Method of the Authoritarian Personality (Glencoe: The Free Press, 1954), pp. 50–122.

21. See D. Katz, "Survey Techniques," *op. cit.* It is vital, however, to distinguish restrictions of the universe which reduce *extraneous* sources of variation from restrictions which reduce the variation in the phenomenon under study. It is well known that a reduction in the range within which a phenomenon can vary affects the magnitude of any correlations that are established, and obviously one wishes to study the phenomenon at all levels. Therefore, one must not impose the latter type of restriction.

22. W. H. Sewell, "Infant Training and the Personality of the Child," *Amer. J. Sociol.*, Vol. 58, 1952, pp. 150–159.

23. Italics ours to emphasize the central points. All quotations are from Centers, *op. cit.*

24. This and all later references are taken from a detailed case study of the Japanese Bombing Survey, an almost unique narrative account of the entire history of the inquiry. See, D. Krech and E. Ballachey, *A Case Study of a Social Survey*, Japanese Survey, United States Bombing Survey, University of California Syllabus Series, Syllabus T G, University of California Press, 1948. The ballot used in the Strategic Bombing Survey of Germany appears in Appendix A.

25. D. Krech and E. L. Ballachey, *ibid*.

PAUL F. LAZARSFELD

The Use of Panels in Social Research

THE FOLLOWING REMARKS are designed to draw attention to a fairly recent development in social research. In its bare essentials, the type of study to be discussed consists of repeated interviews made with the same group of persons. The people participating as subjects in such studies are commonly known as panel members and the whole procedure has become widely known under the name of panel technique.

There are two main types of research problems to which the panel technique is likely to be applied. If the effect of some specific event or series of events is to be studied, then we have the first type of situation in which the panel technique may be used. In one such case, a sample of voters in an Ohio county was kept under observation for six months during the 1940 Presidential campaign, the purpose being to study what effect the propaganda of the two parties had upon the way people made up their minds.[1] In another case, the American Association for the United Nations wanted to find out the best way of getting Americans more interested in the progress of U.N. activities. A sample of persons in a mid-West city of about 800,000 was interviewed about their attitudes towards the United Nations and the actions of the United States in foreign affairs. An intensive informational campaign was conducted by this organization and after the campaign was over the same sample was interviewed again.[2] In a similar way, advertising agencies sometimes use panels to study the effectiveness of their promotional efforts.[3]

The other main type of panel study is somewhat more difficult to describe because no major findings are yet available in the literature. In a society as complex and changing as our own, the individual is continually placed in a situation where he must reconcile the different and

Reprinted from *The Proceedings of the American Philosophical Society*, Vol. 92 (November, 1948), pp. 405–410, by permission of the author and publisher. (Copyright, 1948, by American Philosophical Society.)

variant elements of his experience. A Quaker who is a convinced pacifist sees the country endangered by an enemy. How will he resolve the conflict between his pacifism and his patriotism? A convinced Communist sees the Soviet Union making moves which he considers imperialistic. How will he reconcile his party loyalty and his intellectual judgment on a specific political issue? But we don't need to remain in the area of big issues to look for problems of this kind. In everyday life almost everyone is continuously under cross-pressures of some kind. People belong to different social groups which may have conflicting interests. The individual must make all sorts of choices among his needs, desires, and situational demands, some of which are relatively important, others relatively insignificant.

The study of people under cross pressure is one of the major concerns of social science today. In going through recent social science literature one often comes across the statements of the following sort, "In getting higher education the English Catholic must choose between ethnic affiliation and religion; he generally chooses to study with his Protestant ethnic fellows at McGill University. . . ."[4] The application of the panel technique to problems of this sort allows a greater degree of analytical precision. It would allow us to state, for example, the proportion of English Catholics who go to McGill for their higher education and the proportion who go to Catholic institutions, and to compare intensively those who resolve the conflict between their ethnic affiliation and their religion in one way with those who resolve this conflict in another.

The understanding of what actually transpires in such situations will make for tremendous gains in the understanding of social change. The application of the panel technique to this area of social science interest will be one of its major contributions. By keeping sets of people under repeated observation, we can register the changes they make in their attitudes, affiliations, habits, and expectations. We can learn which of the various attitudes, affiliations, etc., are more basic and hence more constant and which are more superficial and changeable. We hope to determine, if elements change, which element in a psychological or social situation is the more dominant one controlling the changes in the other factors.

The outstanding example of such a study is that undertaken by Theodore Newcomb of the students of a "progressive" college attended by the daughters of well-to-do families. The faculty of this college was quite liberal but the background of the girls quite conservative. For four years the investigators observed the various ways in which one group of girls resolved this conflict.[5]

The reader who is somewhat acquainted with social science literature will at this point raise a justified question especially with reference to the first type of study. If we want to know the effect of a political campaign or a similar event, why do we have to reinterview the same people? Couldn't we interview one group of respondents before the event and a similar one after the event. By comparing the two, the argument runs, we would get a fairly good idea as to the influence which the event had. Numerous examples of this kind come to mind. Many of us have seen public opinion polls taken, for instance, before and after the President made a major public announcement. If people think better of him after the speech then we are sure the speech was a success. Poll data are available which show that the attitude of the average American to the Russians improved every time they were victorious in a battle during the war and slumped every time the Russians, after the war, made a move against one of their neighboring countries. This type of study is undoubtedly of very great value and is usually called a trend study.[6]

It is important to consider the differences between such trend studies and the panel technique. A considerable amount of additional information is obtained by reinterviewing the same people. The most important difference is our ability to single out in a panel study exactly who are the people who change. Once singled out, the changers can be subjected to more intensive study to determine the psychological and social-psychological elements which operated to produce the changes in question. A trend study may show us the net impact of events on opinion. A panel study can allow us to single out the individuals who changed their opinion in the course of the repeated interviewing, to probe for the psychological meaning of the event, and the role played by the various mass media of communication in the change. By interviewing the same people at least twice, we can answer questions such as the following: Are people more likely to change when they are very interested in an event and follow it in great detail; or when they are only slightly concerned and know of it only in a casual way? Some preliminary evidence seems to show that the latter is more likely to be the case. There are many proverbs which claim that men are more apt to shift than women and many others which claim the exact opposite. The panel technique permits us to say whether men or women are more likely to shift their opinions. Incidentally, the results so far do not seem to point to any sex differences.

The study of actual changes often leads to unexpected results. At the time that Senator Black was appointed a judge of the Supreme Court, he was accused of having been at one time a member of the Ku Klux Klan. It happens that there is some information available on who was affected by this allegation which suddenly threatened to change the image of a liberal into that of a reactionary. Although Senator Black received about the same amount of approval before and after the allegation, a kind of game of musical chairs took place. Jews and Catholics turned against him while about an equivalent number of Protestants were more in favor of his appointment than before the storm broke.[7]

The last example points to a second value of the panel technique. Trend studies often indicate that an event has not brought about any net change in opinion. But it might very well be that underneath this apparent constancy, there is a great amount of shifting of positions which can only be found out if the same people and their attitudes are traced over a period of time. At the beginning of the present 1948 presidential campaign, there is some indication of a new development in American politics. As long as Roosevelt was alive, there was a strong feeling in the population that the Democratic Party was the party of the common man whereas the Republicans represented more the interests of the wealthier sections of the population. There are indications that this appraisal of the two parties has changed somewhat and that voters, especially among the working class, are less sure than before which of the two parties represents their interests better.

Suppose that one further development takes place (for which there is no evidence but which we bring in to make our example more dramatic); some sections of the business community might feel that their interest in an active recovery program in Europe is better served by a Democratic administration. Then we might have at this moment an internal shift in the social stratification of the two parties which might go beyond any net change in both which polls or the election might show up. Such a social restratification of the major parties has taken place several times in the political history of the country. The historian looking back over this period many decades hence will not miss such a development. But if we want to know and understand it at the time it happens, we have to make studies of repeated interviews with the same people.

This is not the place to go further into detail on the comparison of panel and trend studies.[8] We shall turn rather to the other type of panel study in order to show briefly some of its considerably more complex technical aspects. The following table (Table 1) exemplifies some of the technical difficulties. It is taken from a small group of people who were interviewed twice during a presidential election. Each respondent was asked two questions: How he intended to vote and whether he felt that the Republican candidate if elected would make a good President. Because both questions were each answered on two different occasions by each respondent we have four pieces of information about each member of the panel. Table 1 classifies these replies first according to whether they were

Table 1

First Interview	SECOND INTERVIEW				
	Dem. Ag.	Dem. For	Rep. Ag.	Rep. For	Totals
Dem. Against	68	2	1	1	72
Dem. For	11	12	0	1	24
Rep. Against	1	0	23	11	35
Rep. For	2	1	3	129	135
Total	82	15	27	142	266

obtained at the first interview or at the second. For each interview we can then sub-classify the respondents into four groups: those who wanted to vote Democratic and who were also personally opposed to the Republican candidate; those who wanted to vote Democratic but personally respected the opposing candidate; those with Republican vote intentions who, however, disapproved of their party's candidate; and, those with Republican vote intentions who also approved of the candidate.

All the information which can be obtained from two questions and two interviews with the same respondents can be represented in the following type of table.

Let us first look at the last column. Most Democrats are against the person of the Republican candidate and most Republicans are for him. But 59 of the 266 respondents have a kind of personal attachment. Twenty-four Democrats think that the opposing candidate is all right while 35 Republicans, although they intend to vote for their party, obviously wish that another candidate had been put up.

Now let us look at the bottom row of figures which come from the second interview. The number of people with such detached views has decreased. Obviously, what the campaign has done is to intensify partisan feeling. Only 15 Democrats now have a good word to say about the Republican candidate and only 27 Republicans have any doubts left about him.

But that is not all that we would like to know from this table. How do people reconcile their vote intention and their opinion on a specific issue? Do the Democrats who like the opposing candidate shift to him or do they remain Democrats and start to see him in a darker light? The answer is given in the second row of our table. There is only one case of the former, but 11 cases of the latter type. And it so happens that similar figures prevail for the Republicans. Let us look at the third row where we find the respondents who at the first interview intended to vote Republican but didn't like their candidate. One of them switched to the Democrats but 11 now feel better towards their candidate. In this one case there is no doubt that more people adjust their cross-pressures in a one-sided direction. If their party loyalties are in conflict with a specific opinion of their own they are rather more likely to maintain their party loyalties and change their opinion.

This is of course just one example from which no general conclusion should be drawn. But it shows the type of problem and the type of procedures which derive from the use of the panel technique. Just for the record it might be mentioned that the statistical analysis of tables like the preceding one is quite difficult and proper procedures are still in the process of development. It can easily be seen how many more problems would arise if we had more than two interviews and more than two questionnaire items to deal with.

Besides the difficulties in analysis discussed above, there is one other drawback of the panel technique. There is a danger that we may change our respondent's attitude by the very fact that we reinterview them repeatedly. In some cases the danger is obvious. Suppose, for example, we interview people during a vaccination campaign. If we repeatedly ask people whether they have been vaccinated, our interviewers will probably act as reminders and speed up the success of the campaign in our panel beyond the performance of the population at large. In this case, then, the results of our study will be quite misleading. It could of course happen that our interviewers antagonize the respondents and as a result they might be less likely to get vaccinated. In other cases the panel bias is not likely to be marked. If interest in an election is high and everyone talks about it, the fact that a respondent has been asked about his vote intentions is not going to influence him very much. In any case this is a matter for concrete study. We cannot tell in advance when bias is likely to exist or not.

Actually, a few such studies of bias have been made. The technique used is fairly simple. At the time the panel is picked out a second group of respondents known as a "control group" is set up as closely matched to the panel as possible. This second group, however, is not interviewed until the whole panel study nears its end. At the time the last interview is made with the panel, the control group is also interviewed. From a statistical point of view the two groups were originally alike and should therefore at the end of the study show the same distribution of attiudes were it not that the panel group was interviewed repeatedly. Whatever significant differences show up between the two groups can be attributed to the effect of the panel bias.

Two examples should give an idea of how much work there is still to be done in this direction. During a presidential campaign it was found that the distribution of opinions in the panel was no different than in the control group. But the panel made up its mind somewhat quicker.

Table 2				
		2ND INTERVIEW		
		Yes	No	Totals
1st Interview	Yes	50	50	100
	No	50	850	900
Totals—		100	900	1000

Table 3				
		2ND INTERVIEW		
		Yes	No	Totals
1st Interview	Yes	400	100	500
	No	100	400	500
Totals—		500	500	1000

Under the impact of the repeated interviews the "Don't Knows" in the end were less numerous in the panel than in the control group. This is a very encouraging result. On the other hand it was found that if people were repeatedly interviewed about their newspaper reading habits the panel group was likely to do more newspaper reading than the control group. The reappearance of the interviewer obviously stimulated the reading interests of the panel members. There was some indication, however, that approximately from the third interview on this effect became less and less marked. It might very well be that if the panel had gone on longer, the panel bias would have disappeared in the end.

There are many operational problems involved in panel studies just as in any other large-scale research operation. How can we get people to participate in a panel and to stick to it? How do we substitute for unavoidable losses? Is it sometimes possible to correspond with panel members by mail rather than to make personal contacts? Should we handle a panel as the American Senate is handled, always substituting part of it by new members?

Finally, there are a number of serious statistical problems to be dealt with. They all center around the concept of turnover. The following two tables exemplify the problem. They each represent one question on which people have been interviewed twice.

In the first question (table 2) 100 people changed their minds one way or another. On the second question (table 3) 200 people did so. One might feel that the turnover on the second question is therefore greater. But one must consider that many fewer people said "Yes" to the first question at the time of the first interview. One therefore cannot expect as many people to change as in the second case. It might be more advisable to compute the turnover as percentage of the people who said "Yes" both times. This would give a turnover of 200 per cent for the first and 50 per cent for the second table and now we would have to say that the first question has the larger turnover. There are obviously still many other ways in which turnover can be described. What index we can use to describe best the turnover in such tables is a very vexing problem, especially because most all of the statistical treatment of panel data goes back to this one point. But this is not the place to deal with such technical matters at length. It is preferable to end up with some more general theoretical considerations which will show the place panel studies are likely to hold in the social sciences in the coming years.

Basically, what we do in a panel study is relate information obtained at one time to information obtained at a subsequent time. We are in the center of what has come to be called dynamic social research. We study changes and we want to explain these changes. We know who changed and we have information on people prior to their change. Explaining the change necessarily means to relate this previous information to the subsequent change. Everything will depend therefore upon how ingenious we are in deciding what information we should gather at different time periods. To exemplify the problem more clearly, let us assume that we are dealing with a panel of people who are about to move into a public housing project where Negroes and whites will live together.[9] If we center our attention on the whites then we know in advance that some of them will get along with their Negro fellow tenants and some will not. Some will improve their ability to get along with people of other races and some will not. What information should we collect from all these prospective tenants prior to the time they move into the housing project to help us explain what shifts in racial attitudes will take place?

We will obviously want to know their race attitudes prior to their entrance into the housing project. But it will also be important to know their *expectations*. It may turn out that the greater their initial uneasiness the more will they be pleasantly surprised by reality. On the other hand we know that some people have a hard time experiencing "reality," and if they enter a situation with apprehension they behave nervously and start trouble. Some sort of index of psychological flexibility is needed.

Pieces of information about the psychological predisposition of the respondents have been called *intervening variables* because they intervene, as it were, between the individual's reaction and the situation in which he is placed.[10] In the example given above, where a group of individuals are about to enter a public housing project, we have people who will be subject to the same external experience. They will, however, react differently. Between the external situation and the individual response there intervene certain psychological and social characteristics which channel the response in an individually characteristic fashion. Social psychologists in recent years have developed out of their experience many hypotheses as to which intervening variables are of importance. We talk of a person's *level of aspiration* or of a person's *expectations*, indicating that we consider that such information will be of value in interpreting how the individuals will react to the situations in which they are placed.

The important intervening variables have to be ascertained before expected changes take place. To follow through with the examples given above, we should know as much as we can about the panel members before they move into the inter-racial housing project. Once they have been living there it is too late to look for such information, for we can never know then whether what we have found has not already been influenced by their new experience. This is, of course, exactly where the importance of the panel technique lies. We periodically study people's attitudes, expectations, and aspirations. We find out what has happened to them between interviews: what they read, with whom they talked, what external events impressed them, etc. Both the situational factors and the intervening variables change continuously. Our analysis would weave back and forth from these two series of data, expressing, in one case, reaction to the situation as a function of some psychological predisposition, and, in another, the psychological predisposition as a function of the changing situation. We would want to know how people's expectations affect the way they react to changes in their environment; and how the environment changes their hopes and concerns.

On more than one occasion it has been said that one of the difficulties which impede the progress of social science is the fact that we cannot experiment with human beings in the same way that the agricultural station experiments with animals and plants. It should not be overlooked, however, that life itself is in a very real sense a continuous series of experiments. In the course of time, almost everything conceivable and sometimes things previously inconceivable happen to one group of persons or another. Although many of these events are, as yet, unpredictable, some events, fortunately for our purpose, occur with sufficient regularity or frequency so that if we know just what sort of persons will be subject to them, we can observe the various ways in which they will respond. Panel studies are conducted, usually, on the impact of events of a given predictable regularity such as voting in a presidential election, exposure to certain advertising, etc. If we find the right statistical technique we will be able to interrelate "stimulus, predisposition, and response" and with time and experience our hope is to understand, predict, and control human behavior more successfully.

NOTES

1. Lazarsfeld, P. F., B. Berelson, and H. Gaudet, *The people's choice*, N.Y., Duell, Sloan and Pearce, 1944.
2. National Opinion Research Center, Report No. 37a, Cincinnati Looks Again.
3. Root, A. R., and A. C. Welch, The continuing consumer study: a basic method for the engineering of advertising, *Jour. Marketing* 7, July 1942.
4. Hughes, E. C. *French Canada in transition*, 86, Univ. of Chicago Press, 1943.
5. Newcomb, T., *Personality and social change*, N.Y., Dryden Press, 1942.
6. Bruner, Jerome S., *Mandate from the people*, N.Y., Duell, Sloan and Pearce, 1944; Cantril, Hadley, *Gauging public opinion*, Princeton Univ. Press, 1944.
7. Lazarsfeld, P. F., The change of opinion during a political discussion. *Jour. Ap. Psychol.* 23: 131–147, 1939.
8. Interested readers will find such a discussion and concrete examples in chapter 10, The panel, in *Say it with figures*, H. Zeisel, N.Y., Harpers, 1946.
9. An especially rich source for explanatory variables will be found in a housing study organized by the Lavanburg Foundation under the direction of Robert K. Merton.
10. The interested reader will find a thoroughgoing discussion of important intervening variables in Sherif, M., *An outline of social psychology*, N.Y., Harpers, 1948.

CARL I. HOVLAND

Results From Studies of Attitude Change

TWO QUITE DIFFERENT TYPES of research design are characteristically used to study the modification of attitudes through communication. In the first type, the *experiment*, individuals are given a controlled exposure to a communication and the effects evaluated in terms of the amount of change in attitude or opinion produced. A base line is provided by means of a control group not exposed to the communication. The study of Gosnell (1927) on the influence of leaflets designed to get voters to the polls is a classic example of the controlled experiment.

In the alternative research design, the *sample survey*, information is secured through interviews or questionnaires both concerning the respondent's exposure to various communications and his attitudes and opinions on various issues. Generalizations are then derived from the correlations obtained between reports of exposure and measurements of attitude. In a variant of this method, measurements of attitude and of exposure to communication are obtained during repeated interviews with the same individual over a period of weeks or months. This is the "panel method" extensively utilized in studying the impact of various mass media on political attitudes and on voting behavior (cf., e.g., Kendall & Lazarsfeld, 1950).

Generalizations derived from experimental and from correlational studies of communication effects are usually both reported in chapters on the effects of mass media and in other summaries of research on attitude, typically without much stress on the type of study from which the conclusion was derived. Close scrutiny of the results obtained from the two methods, however, suggests a marked difference in the picture of communication effects obtained from each. The object of my paper is to consider the conclusions derived from these two types of design, to suggest

Reprinted from *The American Psychologist*, Vol. XIV (1959), pp. 8–17, by permission of the publisher. (Copyright, 1959, *The American Psychologist*.)

some of the factors responsible for the frequent divergence in results, and then to formulate principles aimed at reconciling some of the apparent conflicts.

Divergence

The picture of mass communication effects which emerges from correlation studies is one in which few individuals are seen as being affected by communications. One of the most thorough correlational studies of the effects of mass media on attitudes is that of Lazarsfeld, Berelson, and Gaudet published in *The People's Choice* (1944). In this report there is an extensive chapter devoted to the effects of various media, particularly radio, newspapers, and magazines. The authors conclude that few changes in attitudes were produced. They estimate that the political positions of only about 5 per cent of their respondents were changed by the election campaign, and they are inclined to attribute even this small amount of change more to personal influence than to the mass media. A similar evaluation of mass media is made in the recent chapter in the *Handbook of Social Psychology* by Lipset and his collaborators (1954).

Research using experimental procedures, on the other hand, indicates the possibility of considerable modifiability of attitudes through exposure to communication. In both Klapper's survey (1949) and in my chapter in the *Handbook of Social Psychology* (Hovland, 1954) a number of experimental studies are discussed in which the opinions of a third to a half or more of the audience are changed.

The discrepancy between the results derived from these two methodologies raises some fascinating problems for analysis. This divergence in outcome appears to me to be largely attributable to two kinds of factors: one, the difference in research design itself; and, two, the historical and traditional differences in general approach to evaluation characteristic of researchers using the experimental as contrasted with the correlational or survey method. I would like to discuss, first, the influence these factors have on the estimation of overall effects of communications and, then, turn to other divergences in outcome characteristically found by the use of the experimental and survey methodology.

Undoubtedly the most critical and interesting variation in the research *design* involved in the two procedures is that resulting from differences in definition of exposure. In an experiment the audience on whom the effects are being evaluated is one which is fully exposed to the communication. On the other hand, in naturalistic situations with which surveys are typically concerned, the outstanding phenomenon is the limitation of the audience to those who *expose themselves* to the communication. Some of the individuals in a captive audience experiment would, of course, expose themselves in the course of natural events to a communication of the type studied; but many others would not. The group which does expose itself is usually a highly biased one, since most individuals "expose themselves most of the time to the kind of material with which they agree to begin with" (Lipset et al., 1954, p. 1158). Thus one reason for the difference in results between experiments and correlational studies is that experiments describe the effects of exposure on the whole range of individuals studied, some of whom are initially in favor of the position being advocated and some who are opposed, whereas surveys primarily describe the effects produced on those already in favor of the point of view advocated in the communication. The amount of change is thus, of course, much smaller in surveys. Lipset and his collaborators make this same evaluation, stating that:

As long as we test a program in the laboratory we always find that it has great effect on the attitudes and interests of the experimental subjects. But when we put the program on as a regular broadcast, we then note that the people who are most influenced in the laboratory tests are those who, in a realistic situation, do not listen to the program. The controlled experiment always greatly overrates effects, as compared with those that really occur, because of the self-selection of audiences (Lipset et al., 1954, p. 1158).

Differences in the second category are not inherent in the design of the two alternatives, but are characteristic of the way researchers using the two methods typically proceed.

The first difference within this class is in the size of the communication unit typically studied. In the majority of survey studies the unit evaluated is an entire program of communication. For example, in studies of political behavior an attempt is made to assess the effects of all newspaper reading and television viewing on attitudes toward the major parties. In the typical experiment, on the other hand, the interest is usually in some particular variation in the content of the communications, and experimental evaluations much more frequently involve single communications. On this point results are thus not directly comparable.

Another characteristic difference between the two methods is in the time interval used in evaluation. In the typical experiment the time at which the effect is observed is usually rather soon after exposure to the communication. In the survey study, on the other hand, the time perspective is such that much more remote effects are usually evaluated. When effects decline with the passage of time, the net outcome will, of course, be that of accentuating the effect obtained in experimental studies as compared with those obtained in survey researches. Again it must be stressed that the difference is not inherent in the designs as such. Several experiments, including our own on the effects of motion pictures (Hovland, Lumsdaine, & Sheffield, 1949) and later studies on the "sleeper effect"

(Hovland & Weiss, 1951; Kelman & Hovland, 1953), have studied retention over considerable periods of time.

Some of the difference in outcome may be attributable to the types of communicators characteristically used and to the motive-incentive conditions operative in the two situations. In experimental studies communications are frequently presented in a classroom situation. This may involve quite different types of factors from those operative in the more naturalistic communication situation with which the survey researchers are concerned. In the classroom there may be some implicit sponsorship of the communication by the teacher and the school administration. In the survey studies the communicators may often be remote individuals either unfamiliar to the recipients, or outgroupers clearly known to espouse a point of view opposed to that held by many members of the audience. Thus there may be real differences in communicator credibility in laboratory and survey researches. The net effect of the differences will typically be in the direction of increasing the likelihood of change in the experimental as compared with the survey study.

There is sometimes an additional situational difference. Communications of the type studied by survey researchers usually involve reaching the individual in his natural habitat, with consequent supplementary effects produced by discussion with friends and family. In the laboratory studies a classroom situation with low postcommunication interaction is more typically involved. Several studies, including one by Harold Kelley reported in our volume on *Communication and Persuasion* (Hovland, Janis, & Kelley, 1953), indicate that, when a communication is presented in a situation which makes group membership salient, the individual is typically more resistant to counternorm influence than when the communication is presented under conditions of low salience of group membership (cf. also, Katz & Lazarsfeld, 1955, pp. 48–133).

A difference which is almost wholly adventitious is in the types of populations utilized. In the survey design there is, typically, considerable emphasis on a random sample of the entire population. In the typical experiment, on the other hand, there is a consistent overrepresentation of high school students and college sophomores, primarily on the basis of their greater accessibility. But as Tollman has said: "college sophomores may not be people." Whether differences in the type of audience studied contribute to the differences in effect obtained with the two methods is not known.

Finally, there is an extremely important difference in the studies of the experimental and correlational variety with respect to the type of issue discussed in the communications. In the typical experiment we are interested in studying a set of factors or conditions which are expected on the basis of theory to influence the extent of effect of the communication. We usually deliberately try to find types of issues involving attitudes which are susceptible to modification through communication. Otherwise, we run the risk of no measurable effects, particularly with small-scale experiments. In the survey procedures, on the other hand, socially significant attitudes which are deeply rooted in prior experience and involve much personal commitment are typically involved. This is especially true in voting studies which have provided us with so many of our present results on social influence. I shall have considerably more to say about this problem a little later.

The differences so far discussed have primarily concerned the extent of overall effectiveness indicated by the two methods: why survey results typically show little modification of attitudes by communication while experiments indicate marked changes. Let me now turn to some of the other differences in generalizations derived from the two alternative designs. Let me take as the second main area of disparate results the research on the effect of varying distances between the position taken by the communicator and that held by the recipient of the communication. Here it is a matter of comparing changes for persons who at the outset closely agree with the communicator with those for others who are mildly or strongly in disagreement with him. In the naturalistic situation studied in surveys the typical procedure is to determine changes in opinion following reported exposure to communication for individuals differing from the communicator by varying amounts. This gives rise to two possible artifacts. When the communication is at one end of a continuum, there is little room for improvement for those who differ from the communication by small amounts, but a great deal of room for movement among those with large discrepancies. This gives rise to a spurious degree of positive relationship between the degree of discrepancy and the amount of change. Regression effects will also operate in the direction of increasing the correlation. What is needed is a situation in which the distance factor can be manipulated independently of the subject's initial position. An attempt to set up these conditions experimentally was made in a study by Pritzker and the writer (1957). The method involved preparing individual communications presented in booklet form so that the position of the communicator could be set at any desired distance from the subject's initial position. Communicators highly acceptable to the subjects were used. A number of different topics were employed, including the likelihood of a cure for cancer within five years, the desirability of compulsory voting, and the adequacy of five hours of sleep per night.

The amount of change for each degree of advocated change is shown in Figure 1. It will be seen that there is a fairly clear progression, such that the greater the amount of change advocated the greater the average amount of opinion change produced. Similar results have been reported by Goldberg (1954) and by French (1956).

But these results are not in line with our hunches as to what would

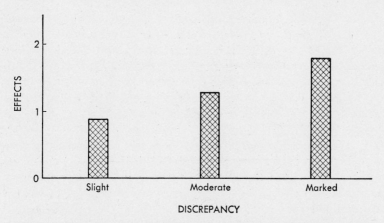

Figure 1—Mean opinion change score with three degrees of discrepancy (deviation between subject's position and position advocated in communication). Adapted from Hovland & Pritzker, 1957.

happen in a naturalistic situation with important social issues. We felt that here other types of response than change in attitude would occur. So Muzafer Sherif, O. J. Harvey, and the writer (1957) set up a situation to simulate as closely as possible the conditions typically involved when individuals are exposed to major social issue communications at differing distances from their own position. The issue used was the desirability of prohibition. The study was done in two states (Oklahoma and Texas) where there is prohibition or local option, so that the wet-dry issue is hotly debated. We concentrated on three aspects of the problem: How favorably will the communicator be received when his position is at varying distances from that of the recipient? How will what the communicator says be perceived and interpreted by individuals at varying distances from his position? What will be the amount of opinion change produced when small and large deviations in position of communication and recipient are involved?

Three communications, one strongly wet, one strongly dry, and one moderately wet, were employed. The results bearing on the first problem, of *reception*, are presented in Figure 2. The positions of the subjects are indicated on the abscissa in letters from A (extremely dry) to H (strongly wet). The positions of the communication are also indicated in the same letters, *B* indicating a strongly dry communication, *H* a strongly wet, and *F* a moderately wet. Along the ordinate there is plotted the percentage of subjects with each position on the issue who described the communication as "fair" and "unbiased." It will be seen that the degree of distance between the recipient and the communicator greatly influences the evaluation of the fairness of the communication. When a communication is directed at the pro-dry position, nearly all of the dry subjects consider it

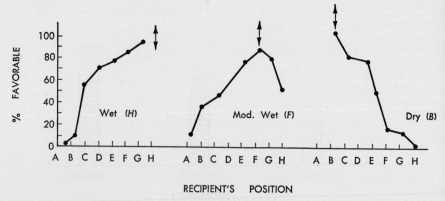

RECIPIENT'S   POSITION

Figure 2—Percentage of favorable evaluations ("fair," "unbiased," etc.) of wet (H), moderately wet (F), and dry (B) communications for subjects from A (very dry) to H (very wet). Position of communications indicated by arrow. Adapted from Hovland, Harvey, & Sherif, 1957.

fair and impartial, but only a few per cent of the wet subjects consider the identical communication fair. The reverse is true at the other end of the scale. When an intermediate position is adopted, the percentages fall off sharply on each side. Thus under the present conditions with a relatively ambiguous communicator one of the ways of dealing with strongly discrepant positions is to *discredit* the communicator, considering him unfair and biased.

A second way in which an individual can deal with discrepancy is by distortion of what is said by the communicator. Thus is a phenomenon extensively studied by Cooper and Jahoda (1947). In the present study, subjects were asked to state what position they thought was taken by the communicator on the prohibition question. Their evaluation of his position could then be analyzed in relation to their own position. These results are shown in Fig. 3 for the moderately wet communication. It will be observed that there is a tendency for individuals whose position is close to that of the communicator to report on the communicator's position quite accurately, for individuals a little bit removed to report his position to be substantially more like their own (which we call an "assimilation effect"), and for those with more discrepant positions to report the communicator's position as more extreme than it really was. This we refer to as a "contrast effect."

Now to our primary results on opinion change. It was found that individuals whose position was only slightly discrepant from the communicator's were influenced to a greater extent than those whose positions deviated to a larger extent. When a wet position was espoused, 28% of the middle-of-the-road subjects were changed in the direction of the communicator, as compared with only 4% of the drys. With the dry com-

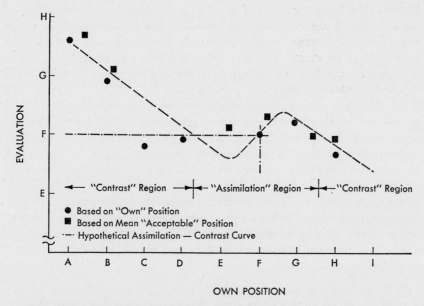

EVALUATION

OWN POSITION

Figure 3—Average placement of position of moderately wet communication (F) by subjects holding various positions on the issue, plotted against hypothetical assimilation-contrast curve. Adapted from Hovland, Harvey, & Sherif, 1957.

munication 14% of the middle-of-the-roaders were changed, while only 4% of the wets were changed. Thus, more of the subjects with small discrepancies were changed than were those with large discrepancies.

These results appear to indicate that, under conditions when there is some ambiguity about the credibility of the communicator and when the subject is deeply involved with the issue, the greater the attempt at change the higher the resistance. On the other hand, with highly respected communicators, as in the previous study with Pritzker using issues of lower involvement, the greater the discrepancy the greater the effect. A study related to ours has just been completed by Zimbardo (1959) which indicates that, when an influence attempt is made by a strongly positive communicator (i.e., a close personal friend), the greater the discrepancy the greater the opinion change, even when the experimenter made a point of stressing the great importance of the subject's opinion.

The implication of these results for our primary problem of conflicting results is clear. The types of issues with which most experiments deal are relatively uninvolving and are often of the variety where expert opinion is highly relevant, as for example, on topics of health, science, and the like. Here we should expect that opinion would be considerably affected by communications and furthermore that advocacy of positions quite discrepant from the individual's own position would have a marked effect.

On the other hand, the types of issues most often utilized in survey studies are ones which are very basic and involve deep commitment. As a consequence small changes in opinion due to communication would be expected. Here communication may have little effect on those who disagree at the outset and function merely to strengthen the position already held, in line with survey findings.

A third area of research in which somewhat discrepant results are obtained by the experimental and survey methods is in the role of order of presentation. From naturalistic studies the generalization has been widely adopted that primacy is an extremely important factor in persuasion. Numerous writers have reported that what we experience first has a critical role in what we believe. This is particularly stressed in studies of propaganda effects in various countries when the nation getting across its message first is alleged to have a great advantage and in commercial advertising where "getting a beat on the field" is stressed. The importance of primacy in political propaganda is indicated in the following quotation from Doob:

> The propagandist scores an initial advantage whenever his propaganda reaches people before that of his rivals. Readers or listeners are then biased to comprehend, forever after, the event as it has been initially portrayed to them. If they are told in a headline or a flash that the battle has been won, the criminal has been caught, or the bill is certain to pass the legislature, they will usually expect subsequent information to substantiate this first impression. When later facts prove otherwise, they may be loath to abandon what they believe to be true until perhaps the evidence becomes overwhelming (Doob, 1948, pp. 421–422).

A recent study by Katz and Lazarsfeld (1955) utilizing the survey method compares the extent to which respondents attribute major impact on their decisions about fashions and movie attendance to the presentations to which they were first exposed. Strong primacy effects are shown in their analyses of the data.

We have ourselves recently completed a series of experiments oriented toward this problem. These are reported in our new monograph on *Order of Presentation in Persuasion* (Hovland, Mandell, Campbell, Brock, Luchins, Cohen, McGuire, Janis, Feierabend, & Anderson, 1957). We find that primacy is often *not* a very significant factor when the relative effectiveness of the first side of an issue is compared experimentally with that of the second. The research suggests that differences in design may account for much of the discrepancy. A key variable is whether there is exposure to both sides or whether only one side is actually received. In naturalistic studies the advantage of the first side is often not only that it is first but that it is often then the only side of the issue to which the individual is exposed. Having once been influenced, many individuals make up their mind and are no longer interested in other communications on the issue. In most experiments on order of presentation, on the other hand, the audience is systematically exposed to both sides. Thus under survey conditions, self-exposure tends to increase the impact of primacy.

Two other factors to which I have already alluded appear significant in determining the amount of primacy effect. One is the nature of the communicator, the other the setting in which the communication is received. In our volume Luchins presents results indicating that, when the same communicator presents contradictory material, the point of view read first has more influence. On the other hand, Mandell and I show that, when two different communicators present opposing views successively, little primacy effect is obtained. The communications setting factor operates similarly. When the issue and the conditions of presentation make clear that the points of view are controversial, little primacy is obtained.

Thus in many of the situations with which there had been great concern as to undesirable effects of primacy, such as in legal trials, election campaigns, and political debate, the role of primacy appears to have been exaggerated, since the conditions there are those least conducive to primacy effects: the issue is clearly defined as controversial, the partisanship of the communicator is usually established, and different communicators present the opposing sides. / *Stop !*

Time does not permit me to discuss other divergences in results obtained in survey and experimental studies, such as those concerned with the effects of repetition of presentation, the relationship between level of intelligence and susceptibility to attitude change, or the relative impact of mass media and personal influence. Again, however, I am sure that detailed analysis will reveal differential factors at work which can account for the apparent disparity in the generalizations derived.

Integration

On the basis of the foregoing survey of results I reach the conclusion that no contradiction has been established between the data provided by experimental and correlational studies. Instead it appears that the seeming divergence can be satisfactorily accounted for on the basis of a different definition of the communication situation (including the phenomenon of self-selection) and differences in the type of communicator, audience, and kind of issue utilized.

But there remains the task of better integrating the findings associated with the two methodologies. This is a problem closely akin to that considered by the members of the recent Social Science Research Council summer seminar on *Narrowing the Gap Between Field Studies and Laboratory Studies in Social Psychology* (Riecken, 1954). Many of their recommendations are pertinent to our present problem.

What seems to me quite apparent is that a genuine understanding of the effects of communications on attitudes requires both the survey and

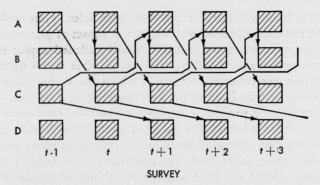

SURVEY

Figure 4a—"Process analysis" schema used in panel research.

Successive time intervals are indicated along abscissa. Letters indicate the variables under observation. Arrows represent relations between the variables. (Adapted from Berelson, Lazarsfeld, & McPhee, 1954)

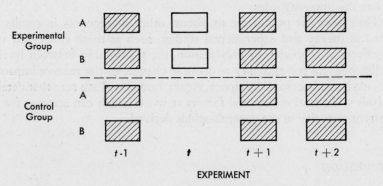

EXPERIMENT

Figure 4b—Design of experimental research.

Letters on vertical axis again indicate variables being measured. Unshaded box indicates experimentally manipulated treatment and blank absence of such treatment. Time periods indicated as in Figure 4a. (Adapted from Berelson, Lazarsfeld, & McPhee, 1954) the experimental methodologies. At the same time there appear to be certain inherent limitations of each method which must be understood by the researcher if he is not to be blinded by his preoccupation with one or the other type of design. Integration of the two methodologies will require on the part of the experimentalist an awareness of the narrowness of the laboratory in interpreting the larger and more comprehensive effects of communication. It will require on the part of the survey researcher a greater awareness of the limitations of the correlational method as a basis for establishing causal relationships.

The framework within which survey research operates is most adequately and explicitly dealt with by Berelson, Lazarsfeld, and McPhee in their book on *Voting* (1954). The model which they use, taken over by them from the economist Tinbergen, is reproduced in the top half of Figure 4. For comparison, the model used by experimentalists is presented in the lower half of the figure. It will be seen that the model used by the survey researcher, particularly when he employs the "panel" method, stresses the large number of simultaneous and interacting influences affecting attitudes and opinions. Even more significant is its provision for a variety of "feedback" phenomena in which consequences wrought by previous influences affect processes normally considered as occurring earlier in the sequence. The various types of interaction are indicated by the placement of arrows showing direction of effect. In contrast the experimentalist frequently tends to view the communication process as one in which some single manipulative variable is the primary determinant of the subsequent attitude change. He is, of course, aware in a general way of the importance of context, and he frequently studies interaction effects as well as main effects; but he still is less attentive than he might be to the complexity of the influence situation and the numerous possibilities for feedback loops. Undoubtedly the real life communication situation is better described in terms of the survey type of model. We are all familiar, for example, with the interactions in which attitudes predispose one to acquire certain types of information, that this often leads to changes in attitude which may result in further acquisition of knowledge, which in turn produces more attitude change, and so on. Certainly the narrow question sometimes posed by experiments as to the effect of knowledge on attitudes greatly underestimates these interactive effects.

But while the conceptualization of the survey researcher is often very valuable, his correlational research design leaves much to be desired. Advocates of correlational analysis often cite the example of a science built on observation exclusively without experiment: astronomy. But here a very limited number of space-time concepts are involved and the number of competing theoretical formulations is relatively small so that it is possible to limit alternative theories rather drastically through correlational evidence. But in the area of communication effects and social psychology generally the variables are so numerous and so intertwined that the correlational methodology is primarily useful to suggest hypotheses and not to establish casual relationships (Hovland et al., 1949, pp. 329–340; Maccoby, 1956). Even with the much simpler relationships involved in biological systems there are grave difficulties of which we are all aware these days when we realize how difficult it is to establish through correlation whether eating of fats is or is not a cause of heart disease or whether or not smoking is a cause of lung cancer. In communications research the complexity of the problem makes it inherently difficult to derive causal relationships from correlational analysis where experimental control of exposure is not possible. And I do not agree with my friends the Lazarsfelds (Kendall & Lazarsfeld, 1950) concerning the effectiveness of the panel method in circumventing this problem since parallel difficulties are raised when the relationships occur over a time span.

These difficulties constitute a challenge to the experimentalist in this area of research to utilize the broad framework for studying communication effects suggested by the survey researcher, but to employ well controlled experimental design to work on those aspects of the field which are amenable to experimental manipulation and control. It is, of course, apparent that there are important communication problems which cannot be attacked directly by experimental methods. It is not, for example, feasible to modify voting behavior by manipulation of the issues discussed by the opposed parties during a particular campaign. It is not feasible to assess the effects of communications over a very long span of time. For example, one cannot visualize experimental procedures for answering the question of what has been the impact of the reading of *Das Kapital* or *Uncle Tom's Cabin*. These are questions which can be illuminated by historical and sociological study but cannot be evaluated in any rigorous experimental fashion.

But the scope of problems which do lend themselves to experimental attack is very broad. Even complex interactions can be fruitfully attacked by experiment. The possibilities are clearly shown in studies like that of Sherif and Sherif (1953) on factors influencing cooperative and competitive behavior in a camp for adolescent boys. They were able to bring under manipulative control many of the types of interpersonal relationships ordinarily considered impossible to modify experimentally, and to develop motivations of an intensity characteristic of real-life situations. It should be possible to do similar studies in the communication area with a number of the variables heretofore only investigated in uncontrolled naturalistic settings by survey procedures.

In any case it appears eminently practical to minimize many of the differences which were discussed above as being not inherent in design but more or less adventitiously linked with one or the other method. Thus there is no reason why more complex and deeply-involving social issues cannot be employed in experiments rather than the more superficial ones more commonly used. The resistance to change of socially important issues may be a handicap in studying certain types of attitude change; but, on the other hand, it is important to understand the lack of modifiability of opinion with highly-involving issues. Greater representation of the diverse types of communicators found in naturalistic situations can also be achieved. In addition, it should be possible to do experiments with a wider range of populations to reduce the possibility that many of our present generalizations from experiments are unduly affected by their heavy weighting of college student characteristics, including high literacy, alertness, and rationality.

A more difficult task is that of experimentally evaluating communications under conditions of self-selection of exposure. But this is not at all impossible in theory. It should be possible to assess what demographic and personality factors predispose one to expose oneself to particular communications and then to utilize experimental and control groups having these characteristics. Under some circumstances the evaluation could be made on only those who select themselves, with both experimental and control groups coming from the self-selected audience.

Undoubtedly many of the types of experiments which could be set up involving or simulating naturalistic conditions will be too ambitious and costly to be feasible even if possible in principle. This suggests the continued use of small-scale experiments which seek to isolate some of the key variables operative in complex situations. From synthesis of component factors, prediction of complex outcomes may be practicable. It is to this analytic procedure for narrowing the gap between laboratory and field research that we have devoted major attention in our research program. I will merely indicate briefly here some of the ties between our past work and the present problem.

We have attempted to assess the influence of the communicator by varying his expertness and attractiveness, as in the studies by Kelman, Weiss, and the writer (Hovland & Weiss, 1951; Kelman & Hovland, 1953). Further data on this topic were presented earlier in this paper.

We have also been concerned with evaluating social interaction effects. Some of the experiments on group affiliation as a factor affecting resistance to counternorm communication and the role of salience of group membership by Hal Kelley and others are reported in *Communication and Persuasion* (Hovland et al., 1953).

Starting with the studies carried out during the war on orientation films by Art Lumsdaine, Fred Sheffield, and the writer (1949), we have had a strong interest in the duration of communication effects. Investigation of effects at various time intervals has helped to bridge the gap between assessment of immediate changes with those of longer duration like those involved in survey studies. More recent extensions of this work have indicated the close relationship between the credibility of the communicator and the extent of postcommunication increments, or "sleeper effects" (Hovland & Weiss, 1951; Kelman & Hovland, 1953).

The nature of individual differences in susceptibility to persuasion via communication has been the subject of a number of our recent studies. The generality of persuasibility has been investigated by Janis and collaborators and the development of persuasibility in children has been studied by Abelson and Lesser. A volume concerned with these audience factors to which Janis, Abelson, Lesser, Field, Rife, King, Cohen, Linton, Graham, and the writer have contributed will appear under the title *Personality and Persuasibility* (1959).

Lastly, there remains the question on how the nature of the issues used in the communication affects the extent of change in attitude. We have only made a small beginning on these problems. In the research reported in *Experiments on Mass Communication*, we showed that the magnitude of effects was directly related to the type of attitude involved: film communications had a significant effect on opinions related to straightforward interpretations of policies and events, but had little or no effect on more deeply intrenched attitudes and motivations. Further work on the nature of issues is represented in the study by Sherif, Harvey, and the writer (1957) which was discussed above. There we found a marked contrast between susceptibility to influence and the amount of ego-involvement in the issue. But the whole concept of ego-involvement is a fuzzy one, and here is an excellent area for further work seeking to determine the theoretical factors involved in different types of issues.

With this brief survey of possible ways to bridge the gap between experiment and survey I must close. I should like to stress in summary the mutual importance of the two approaches to the problem of communication effectiveness. Neither is a royal road to wisdom, but each represents an important emphasis. The challenge of future work is one of fruitfully combining their virtues so that we may develop a social psychology of communication with the conceptual breadth provided by correlational study of process and with the rigorous but more delimited methodology of the experiment.

REFERENCES

Berelson, B. R., Lazarsfeld, P. F., & McPhee, W. N. *Voting: A study of opinion formation in a presidential campaign.* Chicago: Univer. Chicago Press, 1954.

Cooper, Eunice, & Jahoda, Marie. The evasion of propaganda: How prejudiced people respond to anti-prejudice propaganda. *J. Psychol.*, 1947, 23, 15–25.

Doob, L. W. *Public opinion and propaganda.* New York: Holt, 1948.

French, J. R. P., Jr. A formal theory of social power. *Psychol. Rev.*, 1956, 63, 181–194.

Goldberg, S. C. Three situational determinants of conformity to social norms. *J. abnorm. soc. Psychol.*, 1954, 49, 325–329.

CARL I. HOVLAND: Results From Studies of Attitude Change

Gosnell, H. F. *Getting out the vote: An experiment in the stimulation of voting.* Chicago: Univer. Chicago Press, 1927.

Hovland, C. I. Effects of the mass media of communication. In G. Lindzey (Ed.), *Handbook of social psychology* Vol. II. *Special fields and applications.* Cambridge, Mass.: Addison-Wesley, 1954. Pp. 1062–1103.

Hovland, C. I., Harvey, O. J., & Sherif, M. Assimilation and contrast effects in reactions to communication and attitude change. *J. abnorm. soc. Psychol.,* 1957, 55, 244–252.

Hovland, C. I., Janis, I. L., & Kelley, H. H. *Communication and persuasion.* New Haven: Yale Univer. Press, 1953.

Hovland, C. I., Lumsdaine, A. A., & Sheffield, F. D. *Experiments on mass communication.* Princeton: Princeton Univer. Press, 1949.

Hovland, C. I., Mandell, W., Campbell, Enid H., Brock, T., Luchins, A. S., Cohen, A. R., McGuire, W. J., Janis, I. L., Feierabend, Rosalind L., & Anderson, N. H. *The order of presentation in persuasion.* New Haven: Yale Univer. Press, 1957.

Hovland, C. I., & Pritzker, H. A. Extent of opinion change as a function of amount of change advocated. *J. abnorm. soc. Psychol.,* 1957, 54, 257–261.

Hovland, C. I., & Weiss, W. The influence of source credibility on communication effectiveness. *Publ. opin. Quart.,* 1951, 15, 635–650.

Janis, I. L., Hovland, C. I., Field, P. B., Linton, Harriett, Graham, Elaine, Cohen, A. R., Rife, D., Abelson, R. P., Lesser, G. S., & King, B. T. *Personality and persuasibility.* New Haven: Yale Univer. Press, 1959.

Katz, E., & Lazarsfeld, P. F. *Personal influence.* Glencoe, Ill.: Free Press, 1955.

Kelman, H. C., & Hovland, C. I. "Reinstatement" of the communicator in delayed measurement of opinion change. *J. abnorm. soc. Psychol.,* 1953, 48, 327–335.

Kendall, Patricia L., & Lazarsfeld, P. F. Problems of survey analysis. In R. K. Merton & P. F. Lazarsfeld (Eds.), *Continuities in social research: Studies in the scope and method of "The American Soldier."* Glencoe, Ill.: Free Press, 1950. Pp. 133–196.

Klapper, J. T. *The effects of mass media.* New York: Columbia Univer. Bureau of Applied Social Research, 1949. (Mimeo.)

Lazarsfeld, P. F., Berelson, B., & Gaudet, Hazel. *The people's choice.* New York: Duell, Sloan and Pearce, 1944.

Lipset, S. M., Lazarsfeld, P. F., Barton, A. H., & Linz, J. The psychology of voting: An analysis of political behavior. In G. Lindzey (Ed.), *Handbook of social psychology.* Vol. II. *Special fields and applications.* Cambridge, Mass.: Addison-Wesley, 1954. Pp. 1124–1175.

Maccoby, Eleanor E. Pitfalls in the analysis of panel data: A research note on some technical aspects of voting. *Amer. J. Sociol.,* 1956, 59, 359–362.

Riecken, H. W. (Chairman) Narrowing the gap between field studies and laboratory experiments in social psychology: A statement by the summer seminar. *Items Soc. Sci. Res. Council,* 1954, 8, 37–42.

Sherif, M., & Sherif, Carolyn W. *Groups in harmony and tension: An integration of studies on intergroup relations.* New York: Harper, 1953.

Zimbardo, P. G. Involvement and communication discrepancy as determinants of opinion change. Unpublished doctoral dissertation, Yale University, 1959.

ARTHUR KORNHAUSER

The Problem of Bias
in Opinion Research

THE TERM "BIAS" is used to cover a multitude of opinion research sins. Considerable current attention is devoted to specific practical problems at the procedural level—biased questions, interviewer bias, sampling bias, respondents' bias; and beyond this, one encounters vague and general condemnations of biased research. But remarkably little discussion has been focused upon the problem of bias at high levels, the bias of those who control the studies.

As long as bias, like evil, remains an amorphous something to be "against" or, alternatively, as long as it is identified as a series of technical operating faults in the field, we who are responsible for the research conveniently evade the disturbing issue of our own biases and how they affect our research. At times, with unbecoming psychological naivete, we even hide behind indignant declarations about our personal honesty and professional integrity, as if that were an answer. By avoiding the problem, we fail to sensitize ourselves to the manifestations of our own biases and consequently neglect to set up safeguards and correctives. It is more comfortable to concentrate on improving our foot soldiers than our headquarters staff—that is, ourselves.

The purpose of this paper is to offer a sketchy analysis of the problem and to urge more lively attention to it. The objective is clarification, to the end that all of us in opinion research will face up to the issues and do what we can to find remedies. No one of us can be complacent on this score. Variegated beams and motes are pretty well distributed among our respective eyes. The problem constitutes a major challenge to the vigorous young profession of opinion surveying. For if opinion "facts" depend on

Reprinted from *The International Journal of Opinion and Attitude Research*, Vol. 1 (1947), pp. 1–13, by permission of the author and publisher.

670

the particular polling agency hired to gather them, the buyers and users of opinion research will soon raise most embarrassing questions. Opinion studies must guard against becoming competitive tools of salesmanship and propaganda instead of scientific research instruments.

If we are to deal with the central and distinctive questions of research bias, the first necessity is to cut through the confusion of accidental and secondary characteristics which cluster about the term. The core issue, stated most simply, is this. Do the inclinations or prepossessions of those responsible for an opinion survey lead to results and conclusions that are one-sided, untrue, or misleading in reference to what they purport to describe? If so, bias is present—and is to be further analyzed and, if possible, "cured." If the essential relationship specified is not present, that is if there are not subjective leanings which produce a corresponding twist of results, then the case is not one of "bias" even though other serious types of error may be in evidence.

The judgment that given research is or is not biased is always a difficult one; in most cases the evidence remains inconclusive. But the problem is no less important because the answer is not sharply black and white.

There is need for thorough detailing of criteria and procedures for judging bias but we shall make no attempt to perform that formidable task in this paper. Certain guiding considerations must suffice. Two elements are always involved: (1) the detection of flaws which mean that opinions under study are misrepresented and (2) interpretation which ascribes these errors to predispositions or desires of the researcher (whether or not he is aware of their biasing influence).

The judgment that material is one-sided, untrue, or misrepresentative contrasts it with an "authentic" picture that presents all that is relevant and important within the context of the particular purposes and uses of the results. The comparison is made partly by noting departures from other parallel information that stands up better under critical scrutiny; partly by testing audiences exposed to the results to see whether they do, in fact, draw erroneous conclusions; partly by rigorous logical analysis that exposes the weaknesses and one-sided implications of method, results, and manner of presentation.

If one has independent evidence about the research man's attitudes, tendencies, and research behavior, the inference as to bias may be more confidently made. Where many lines of evidence concerning the research and the researcher dovetail consistently, one's judgment is reenforced; he concludes that "everything points to bias." Even without confirmatory evidence regarding the subjective inclinations that went into the research, if enough signs in the procedure and report point cumulatively to "slanting" of the material in a constant direction, we can *assume* the subjective bias.

Where sufficient corroboration is lacking or where evidence is meager and conflicting, judgment must be suspended. It is important to emphasize that no *objective* technique can yield a final answer. All we can do is keep ourselves alert to whatever looks like biased procedure and results, in our own work and that of others, and take what steps we can to minimize such errors.

The foregoing general formulation of top-level bias may be clarified by contrasting it with several untenable conceptions that are frequently advanced.

In the first place, it will not do to view the problem in absolutist or perfectionist terms. This easily leads to the position that since our attitudes and desires are operating constantly in everything we do, bias is bound to exist in *all* observation and *all* interpretation. Everyone is biased. It can't be avoided.

The obvious answer is that the mere existence of personal inclinations does not mean their inevitable expression in any given research behavior. One has other conflicting and inhibiting values as well. We can set up checks and safeguards against letting our own partisan tendencies lead to differential results in favor of "our side." We can learn to "lean over backwards." Moreover, it is apparent that the operation of biases is not an "all or nothing" matter, as this argument suggests. The practical aim is to reduce the distorting influence to a minimum, not to attain perfection.

A special (and specious) case of this view that sees bias everywhere is the contention that in addressing a question to a person—any question about any topic—one is guiding the individual's thinking and response in a definite direction, that is *"biasing"* it. Asking him what magazines he reads, by this argument, reflects a bias against newspapers and radio since they are not brought to his attention. Clearly this is stretching the definition of "bias" beyond a point of possible usefulness. To be sure, asking about one of the media and not the others *may* indicate bias—but that must be judged with reference to the purposes and use of the inquiry. The essence of the problem lies in distinguishing between those instances in which the directiveness of the questioning does and does not lead to false conclusions. A study purporting to compare magazines can scarcely give misleading results through omitting mention of other media. However, if the problem is to tell an advertiser how he can best reach certain households with his message, obviously the cards are stacked by asking about certain media and not others. Our concern here is simply to warn against the confusion that calls *all* "directing of attention" a process of "biasing."

Another fallacy is contained in the argument that if the research director is *honest*, if he has high regard for professional standards, these motivations guarantee freedom from bias (identified with dishonesty) in his work. Unfortunately for this simple ethical dismissal of the problem, most of our biases sneak in unobserved and without declaring themselves. They are not acts of recognized dishonesty. They adopt many disguises and rely upon the convenient blind-spots and ready rationalizations that keep our moral sentries from detecting them.

According to another conception, research bias is made to cover a wide assortment of technical deficiencies more or less regardless of their source. Thus a "biased sample" usually means a faulty or unrepresentative sample, whether this is due to incompetence or to subjective preferences—and whether the errors are introduced in planning the sample, in instructing interviewers, or in the failure of the interviewers to follow orders.

Two important distinctions are called for here. The first is that between low quality research and biased research. Opinion studies (and the constituent procedures) may be admirably free from bias and yet be poor in quality and untrustworthy. Likewise they may be biased and yet manifest, otherwise, high technical proficiency. Problems of inadequate knowledge and skill and problems of conscious or unconscious slanting of procedures need to be perceived and tackled separately. To keep the distinction clear, it is suggested that we use the terms "sampling *error*," "interviewer *error*," etc., save where we definitely mean "bias" in the sense of *purposive* slanting (either intentionally or "unconsciously").

The second distinction is that between biases at lower levels and those at the top. A biased or dishonest interviewer or statistician constitutes no genuine problem of "research bias," as we are using the term. The errors he introduces are usually evidences rather of technical imperfections at higher levels in the selection, training, and supervision of personnel. However, these processes of selection, training, etc., may also express and implement top-level bias. In that case, the serious problem does have to do with the higher-ups. They are using their agents (again, wittingly or unwittingly) to slant results just as they might otherwise use loaded questions or deceptive samples.

Anyone in touch with opinion research activities over the years has inevitably encountered numerous examples of what we are calling "top-level bias." Most of us can readily testify, if we care to do so, even against our own past slips.

"Off the record," there is more than a little scepticism regarding each new set of research results published by partisan clients—whether cigarette and dentifrice manufacturers, magazines, radio networks, or political groups. It is remarkable how commonly the research conclusions support the sponsor's position and supply him with sales ammunition. Quite apart from partisan sponsorship, however, opinion inquiries are in constant danger of leaning one way or another under the influence of social valuations and predispositions of the research organization and the inescapable social pressures playing upon it. It never ceases to be astonishing how easily, in all good conscience, we adopt those procedures and overlook those errors which conspire to produce results congenial to our own beliefs and our clients' expectations.

It is worth considering the different forms these expressions of bias take, in order to note at what points the research director must be especially on guard against their intrusion.

It is scarcely necessary to state that different opinion research organizations differ enormously in the quality of their work, including prominently differences in the success with which they reduce the play of bias. This paper is in no sense an indictment of opinion research agencies, singly or collectively. A number of them are fully alive to the dangers discussed here and are doing their utmost to minimize bias in their work.

1. Bias in Choice of Subject Matter for Polls: In an earlier paper we summarized certain evidence on the one-sided leanings of polls dealing with labor issues.[1] An examination of 155 questions published by leading polling agencies from 1940 to 1945 revealed that only 8 dealt with favorable features of unionism while 81 were concerned with faults and proposed restrictions. Not a single question was aimed at such an important topic, for example, as whether labor disputes are fairly treated in newspaper and radio.

Similar bias in selection of issues tends to occur in other fields where strong sentiments prevail at "upper" levels. For example, how much attention, relatively, is given to fascism and the threat from the right as compared to that devoted to communism and the threat from the left? How commonly do polls on attitudes toward advertising go beyond the question whether the ads are noticed, whether they are annoying, how much they increase the price of a cake of soap if at all, whether advertised products are superior, etc., to dig into such unpalatable topics as whether the ads whip up desire beyond people's ability to satisfy them, whether they foster false values, and in general, what their larger effects on character are, considered within a broad social and human frame of reference instead of adhering to the businessman's viewpoint?

Opinion research in regard to minority groups seems rarely to focus questions on *economic* and *religious* influences supporting prejudice; such questions might well yield results embarrassing to powerful individuals and groups. Hence we do not ask questions, for example, to get at comparative feelings about seeing mass resentments and aggressions channeled against racial, religious, and nationality groups rather than against wealth and special privilege.

2. Bias in Study Design and Procedure: In selecting research methods, one is prone to accept procedures that promise acceptable results and to adopt rigorous standards leading to more ready rejection of techniques likely to produce unwelcome material. Suppose the research assignment is to compare the value of several magazines as advertising media. In one case the client is publisher of an outstandingly popular magazine; in another case he is owner of a magazine well down the list according to circulation figures. Will not the research man typically emphasize accurate readership counts in the first case and, with equally scientific arguments, turn to other measures for the second client—such as the high social status of readers, the trust they express in the publication, the amount of time the average reader devotes to it, and so on. Two different pictures are thus obtained, not *contradictory* but *partial*. Whether one approves of the differential procedure or not, it seems difficult to deny the presence of "bias."

Instances of sampling and interviewing bias should likewise be noted at this point. For example, a survey on infringements of civil rights conducted among white people only is certain to conceal the true gravity of the problem. A survey of social attitudes, limited to women at home during the day and without callbacks to reach those who are out, can be expected to secure an unduly traditional and uncritical picture since better educated, socially and professionally active women are likely to be underrepresented. Such errors are relevant to the present discussion insofar as they are consciously or unconsciously purposive.

Our procedures often serve to obtain "illustrative evidence" for conclusions held in advance rather than constituting fair *tests* of our tentative answers. If one has the conviction, for example, that anti-Semitism is an expression of over-aggressive, pathological personalities he readily designs a study based on interviews with known violent anti-Semites and the comparison of their personality patterns and attitudes with those of persons known to be passive, indifferent, or friendly toward Jews. The results are pretty well assured. An adequate test would demand the examination of additional groups consisting of persons aggressively and violently active in other directions—say Communists, passionate anti-Catholics, anti-alcohol crusaders, etc. Otherwise conclusions associating aggressive qualities with anti-Semitism are imposed by the design of the study.

3. *Bias in Question Wording and Sequence:* Unfair or loaded phrasing of questions is the most commonly noted manifestation of bias in opinion polling. The more extreme forms of question bias are now generally avoided. Less pronounced slanting, however, insinuates itself into many surveys.

A good illustration is furnished by two polls conducted in the United States a year or two ago on the topic of governmental health insurance and medical care. Different questions were asked in the two surveys and markedly different conclusions emerged, the one set indicating much greater popular approval of a federal health program than the other. The contrasting conclusions, it happened, coincided with the opposed positions of the two medical groups that sponsored the studies.

Not less interesting than this last fact is the observation that a research director for one of the surveying agencies, in a scientific article dealing with the discordant results, fails to mention the relationship of results to sponsor's views. The reader is given no hint that the results came out "right" for each of the propaganda groups.[2]

A few examples taken from recent published polls will illustrate other instances of questions in which it seems probable that bias is evidenced.

Which do you think is better Americanism: (a) every man should accept the responsibility for getting his own job and a living, or (b) the government should see to it that every man has a job and a living.

Several biasing elements can be noted here. The attractive moral quality of the expression "every man should accept the responsibility" is contrasted with the harsh words "government should see to it." This difference is accented by introducing the "Americanism" context. Moreover, asking the question in terms of Americanism may cause some respondents to express not their personal preference between (a) and (b) but a judgment as to which accords better with generally accepted views (but perhaps not the respondent's) of Americanism. Finally, the question imposes a fictitious choice by omitting a most important and realistic alternative to (a) and (b), namely: (c) every man should accept the responsibility for getting his own job *under conditions where the government sees that every one has the opportunity to work.* (As asked, the question showed 76% for "a" and 18% for "b"; even at the lowest income level, 58% said "a" against 32% "b." A comparable Fortune Survey question asked: "Do you think the government should provide for all people who have no other means of obtaining a living?" Working people voted 73% "yes," in contrast to the above 18% or 32%.)

Do you think that the manufacture of atomic bombs should be continued, or that it is necessary to prohibit it for all countries, by international agreement?

This question, recently used in a Mexican opinion poll, found 66% for prohibiting manufacture of bombs against 26% for continuing. It is a reasonably safe assumption that many of the majority group were expressing a general sentiment in favor of avoiding atomic war. Looked at afterward, however, their responses seem also to be votes to stop current manufacture of bombs—that is, to compel the *United States* to discontinue manufacturing bombs *now.* Therein lies the bias. The question must mislead certain respondents into a simple humanitarian reply while at the same time smuggling in an implication unrecognized and unexamined by most of these people. (Interesting in this connection is the fact that the 66% drops to 51% for professional people; presumably they are more aware of the hidden implications.) The result is obtained by omitting salient features of the issue—that only the U.S. is manufacturing bombs, that serious doubt exists whether completely effective international control can be instituted, and that *when* the manufacture is discontinued is of the essence of the problem. To avoid bias, it is necessary that these points be brought out in a series of questions.

Two further examples are these:

Would you describe Russia as a peace-loving nation, willing to fight only if she has to defend herself, or as an aggressive nation that would start a war to get something she wants?

Clearly this dichotomy does not exhaust the possibilities. By omitting intermediate and qualified alternatives and by wording the extremes as they are worded, the question naturally induces large numbers to choose the "aggressive" answer.

Here is a list of different systems of government operating in the world today. Which form of government do you think most of the people in Russia, Spain, Germany, France, would choose today if they could vote freely for what they wanted?

Form of government that would be chosen:

> Communistic
> Democratic
> Fascistic
> Socialistic
> Monarchistic
> Don't know

It is hardly necessary to point to the alarming bias involved in offering "democratic" and "socialistic" as alternative responses.

4. Bias in Interpretation and Reporting: An interesting recent illustration in the labor opinion field is an article reporting workers' responses to questions on the Taft-Hartley law.[3] A majority of the respondents expressed opposition to the law but a majority also voted *in favor* of each of ten leading provisions of the law when these were asked about separately. The conclusion is drawn that workers have been propagandized into being against the law without their understanding what they are against; they vote *for* the actual content of the law (the ten points) when the "bad" over-all label is removed. The bias in this presentation consists in its offering a simple one-sided interpretation and ignoring two important difficulties. The neglected considerations are these: (a) Single simple questions on separate parts of the law do not, and cannot, approach an adequate summary of the issues. The law is long and complicated. Its provisions would require detailed explanation before the respondent could understand what he is voting on. The ten questions that were asked are deceptively innocent. (b) The results are presented as if they prove that respondents are guilty of self-contradiction, by being *for* the parts of the law but *against* the whole. This overlooks the elementary logical point that different persons can be opposed to the law as a whole for different specific reasons—some being against provision "x," others against "y," "z," etc. The crucial question is how many persons are against the law and yet in favor of *all ten* points asked in the separate items. This could easily be determined and stated in one sentence. It seems fair to interpret its omission as an instance of bias.

Another type of bias in the analysis and reporting of results appears in the use of misleading cross-tabulations. This frequently takse the form of relating social-political opinions to respondents' *education* in a way that indicates, for example, that Republican views on an issue are approved by the better educated people—by implication, because they are better qualified thinkers. A "fair" presentation would have to show the relationship also to *economic* status. The imputed influence of education may disappear when the relation is analyzed within groups homogeneous in respect to economic position.

A similar illustration is that of a survey report that tabulates working people's responses indicative of dissatisfaction, hostility toward employers, etc., according to membership in A. F. of L. unions, CIO unions, independent unions, and no unions. The greater dissatisfaction and antagonism thus associated with the CIO is easily subject to misinterpretation which the report fails adequately to warn against. The correlation may stem in considerable part from differences between CIO members and others in respect to types of occupations, levels of skill, and perhaps age and other factors.

Another form of bias consists of failure to warn readers that the sample of respondents is specially selected or non-representative in a manner that pushes the findings in one direction. This fault occurs notably often in the case where only a fraction of the total sample answers a question, either because others are unable to respond or because replies to preceding questions make this question inappropriate for them. Percentages of those who do answer may be highly deceptive as a consequence, since they constitute a specially informed or specially oriented group. Omission of clear explanations regarding such partial samples easily leads to misinterpretation, whether caused deliberately or through "purposive inadvertence."

Bias may similarly manifest itself in the simple choice of one rather than another method of statistical presentation. If groups are compared by means of an attitude scale, for example, on which each person receives a total score based on a number of questions, the divergence or contrast between groups may be made to appear large by reporting only the difference in *average scores* for the groups. Contrariwise, if the report leans toward minimizing the differences, it neglects averages and instead stresses the percentage of overlapping among individuals in the groups. The same difference in emphasis characterizes alternative ways of reporting correlation figures and other statistical measures. In all such cases, the more adequately the statistical material is reported, the less the danger that it will be misleading. The different summary figures are not *alternatives;*

where misunderstanding may occur, *both* averages and percentage overlap (or measures of scatter) are needed.

The remedy for bias is certainly not to be found by denying its existence nor by each of us resolving to abandon his biases. The course of wisdom is rather to take note of the biasing tendencies and influences and to set up conditions and procedures calculated to offset and minimize them. Research bias consists not in *having* inclinations but in letting them affect our research results.

The biases that insinuate themselves into our research express the value systems and inclinations that are integral parts of our personalities. They reflect the cultural influences and conditioning pressures that constitute inescapable features of our lives. For convenience, we shall divide the biases into three classes: personal biases determined by relationship to the client, other personal biases, and "common" or group-membership biases.

Bias that grows out of the client-researcher relation ranges from direct inclination to serve the client's interests in proving a case or securing sales ammunition to subtle deviations in research planning, such as unwittingly accepting his viewpoint or "facts" without sufficient check. Pressures toward this type of bias are particularly marked in advertising and marketing research but they are likewise not too hard to locate in other branches of the opinion research industry. They need to be recognized and guarded against in university studies and in research for non-profit organizations as well as in commercial activities.

It should be noted that the research man who insists that his role is that of a "disinterested" technician and that as such he simply accepts the research assignment as it comes, is especially vulnerable. He easily accepts the client's values and frame of reference along with his problem—and his cash. What he likes to picture as his simple preoccupation with the "facts" turns out to be concern with *particular* facts, selectively viewed from a *particular* standpoint, and seen through *particular* glasses of peculiar and unexamined optical properties. In social research, to be "above" concern for biasing values is to succumb to them.

It must be emphasized that clients are by no means always special pleaders. Very often they want opinion studies to give them unvarnished, authentic knowledge. In this case, the chief danger of bias in the client relationship may arise from an urge to produce unjustifiably positive, definitive results that will impress the client—and lead to further assignments. At times, also, the aim is to come out with conclusions that will win the goodwill of *other* clients.

Quite apart from relations with clients, however, many additional biasing factors are bound to characterize the individual research man and his organization. Each of us has his peculiar, unanalyzed emotional preferences, aversions, blind-spots. For example, strong personal pride and ambitions can readily predispose one to accept or overemphasize questionable evidence that happens to support a view to which he has previously committed himself. Or the research man is swayed by his determination to make his research promote certain policy decisions that he personally favors. Or he over-reaches in efforts to obtain distinctive and spectacular findings. Or he consistently leans in a conservative or a radical direction in his research.

A third set of biases consists of those shared by large groups with which the researcher identifies. Probably the most prominent of these are "class" feelings and national loyalties. But radical and religious prejudices also play a part, as do political party affiliations, regional and occupational ties, and many other group membership influences. No one of us escapes his cultural background, the current climate of opinion, and his present associates. These factors inevitably influence the research we do—the issues we choose to inquire into, the kinds of evidence we consider important, the frames of reference within which we formulate our questions and interpret our results.

Certainly it must not be overlooked that we also have personal ideals, loyalties and group pressures that exert opposing influences to the free play of "biases." Our devotion to "fair play," untrammeled pursuit of scientific truth, maintenance of high professional standards, personal integrity—these contribute powerful forces to hold our biases in check.

The problem is to harness the positive impulses to effective measures of prevention. The constant threat imposed by our biases need not cause despair; the challenge is to achieve impartial results by successfully meeting the threat. In my opinion, this achievement will require much greater attention to the problem than it currently receives.

NOTES

1. "Are Public Opinion Polls Fair to Organized Labor?" *Public Opinion Quarterly*, Winter 1946–47, pp. 484–500. This article contains a number of illustrations of the different types of bias discussed in the next few pages.

2. Stanley L. Payne, "Some Opinion Research Principles Developed Through Studies of Social Medicine," *Public Opinion Quarterly*, Vol. 10, 1946–47, pp. 93–98.

3. Claude Robinson, "The Strange Case of the Taft-Hartley Law," *Look*, September 30, 1947, pp. 68–71.

PAUL F. LAZARSFELD

The Controversy
Over Detailed Interviews

IF TWO PEOPLE vigorously disagree on whether something is blue or green, the chances are that the object is composed of both colors and that for some reason the two contestants are either unable or unwilling to see more than the one. If in methodological discussions, competent workers assume vehemently opposite positions, it is generally a good time for someone to enter the scene and suggest that the parties are both right and wrong.

Two articles in the *Public Opinion Quarterly* (Summer, 1943) provide one of the many indications that such a situation has come about in the public opinion field. A representative of the Division of Program Surveys in the Department of Agriculture reports on large-scale research work, the core of which is an interviewing technique "intended to draw full intensive discussions" and using "various non-directive means of stimulating full discussion in the interviewing situation."[1] Preceding this report is an article by a well-known psychologist who dubs this technique "depth interview" and describes it in rather uncomplimentary terms. One of his conclusions is that "there is little or no evidence to support the tacit assumption that the so-called depth interview yields more valid responses from people than do other types."[2] For him, simple "yes-no" questions, used judiciously, are sufficient.

The matter is important from more than a scientific point of view. Applied social research is a new venture. Only yesterday did the government begin large-scale studies in public opinion. The market and consumer studies which are now finding acceptance in many industries are likewise

Reprinted with editorial adaptations from *The Public Opinion Quarterly*, Vol. 8 (Spring 1944), pp. 38–60, by permission of the author and publisher. (Copyright, 1944, by Princeton University Press.)

all of recent date. Managers in business as well as in public administration are faced with sharply contending factions among research professionals. Should they succumb to skepticism or discouragement and fail to give this new branch of the social sciences the opportunity to prove itself, then development might be seriously retarded. It therefore seems justified to present the problem to a larger public with an earnest effort toward impartiality.

Employing a neutral terminology, we shall allude to our subject as the "open-ended interview." The term serves to describe a crucial aspect of this type of interviewing—the fact that "open-ended interviews" do not set fixed answers in terms of which a respondent must reply. Eventually a more animated expression may be desirable. (To save space we shall abbreviate the term and refer to it hereafter as OI.) Rather than asking for a definition it would be better if the reader visualizes the situation in which an OI occurs. In the interview situation the interviewer by an appropriate introduction attempts to establish the best possible rapport between himself and the respondent because he is aware that he may have to interview the respondent an hour or longer. He then proceeds to ask one of the ten or fifteen questions which have been assigned to him by the central office. Sometimes the respondent himself immediately plunges into great detail, and the interviewer simply permits him to continue. If the first answer is brief, however, the interviewer is instructed to "probe." There are quite a number of devices for eliciting detailed, free response. Mere silence will sometimes induce the respondent to elaborate. Or, the interviewer may just repeat the respondent's own words with an appropriate inflection. Asking for examples will often prove helpful. Then again questions such as the following are used: "How did you happen to notice it? What makes you think so? How did you feel about it before? Do most of your friends have the same opinion?" The trained OI field worker has the goal of his inquiry clearly imprinted in his mind, but he adapts his inquiry to the concrete situation between the interviewee and himself.

If properly conducted, such an OI will result in a detailed document which covers the whole area under investigation, including the interviewer's observations of the respondent's reactions and background.

The OI is suggested by its proponents in opposition to what one might term the "straight poll question." The latter gives the respondent the occasion to answer only "Yes," "No," "Don't know," or to make a choice among a small number of listed possible answers. Between these two extremes there are, of course, several steps. Actually there is hardly a poll where there is not some freedom left for the respondent to express himself in his own way. It is not necessary here to discuss where the straight poll question ends and the OI begins. For all practical purposes the distinction is clear enough.

The Six Main Functions of the OI Technique

1. CLARIFYING THE MEANING OF
A RESPONDENT'S ANSWER

Before asking him whether war profits should be limited, we have to find out what the respondent thinks the word "profit" means. Some people talk of the total income of a company as profit, others believe it is the difference between wholesale and retail prices, still others are of the opinion that war profits are the difference between pre-war and war earnings. By discussing the general subject matter with him we are very likely to obtain a fairly clear picture of what would be equivalent to his *private definition* of these terms. One frequently underestimates the number of terms which seem obvious to the interviewer but which are ambiguous or even unknown to the lower educated section of the population.

In other cases it is not so much the meaning of words as the *implication of an opinion* which has to be clarified. If a respondent is in favor of reducing taxes, does he know that as a result many government services will have to be reduced? If he is in favor of free speech, does he realize that such freedom must also pertain to people who may express opinions that are very distasteful to him?

If respondents are asked to voice their thoughts on a course of action, it is important to know against what *alternative possibilities* they had weighed their choice. A respondent is for the continuation of the Dies Committee: has he weighed that against the possibility that the Department of Justice can adequately handle the problem of subversive activities, or did he feel that if the Dies Committee does not do so, no one else will? Another respondent is for government regulation of business: does he prefer this to completely free enterprise, or has he considered the different ways by which an individual business man be regulated through his own trade organizations?

Finally, the OI permits a respondent to clarify his opinion by introducing *qualifications*. He is in favor of rationing if it is administered fairly for everyone. He is in favor of married women getting defense jobs if it has been made sure that there are no unemployed men left. The respondent might not volunteer such qualifications if the interview is a too hurried one.

2. SINGLING OUT THE DECISIVE ASPECTS OF
AN OPINION

If we deal with attitudes toward rather complex objects, we often want to know the *decisive aspects* by which a respondent is guided. Take the opinion on *candidates* for public office. At this moment, for example, the Republicans in some mid-western states prefer Dewey to Willkie as Presidential nominee. What does Dewey stand for in the eyes of these people? Party Loyalty? Isolationism? Administrative ability? Gang-busting? Here again the OI would proceed in characteristic fashion. What has the respondent heard about the two candidates? What does he think would happen if Dewey were to become President? And so on. In the end we should be able to distinguish groups for which Dewey means quite different things, and fruitful statistical comparisons on a number of social characteristics could be carried through.

Similar possibilities can come up when people are called upon to judge *concrete situations*. They do or do not like the working conditions in their plants. If the answer is in the negative, what features do they especially dislike? In order to get a reasonable idea of people's complaints a rather detailed discussion is necessary; the OI is a good device for this purpose. Other examples of such procedure can easily be found: to what does the respondent attribute rising prices? Or the increase in juvenile delinquency?

Here belong also some recent efforts in the field of *communications* research. People like or dislike a film or a radio program. Through detailed discussions it is possible to bring out quite clearly which elements in the production make for the audience's reaction.[3]

The singling out of decisive aspects also pertains to *issues*. If respondents are against sending lend-lease supplies to Russia, it is important to know what about such a policy they dislike. Do they disapprove of Russian communism, or do they think that the Russians do not need the supplies, or do they feel that other parts of the world war panorama are more important? Here, again, the OI would not only ask for an opinion on the basic issues but would probe the respondents for further details.[4]

3. What Has Influenced an Opinion

If people approve of an issue or vote for a candidate (or buy a product), it is useful to divide the determining factors of such action into three main groups: the *decisive features* of the object in question, which account for its being chosen; the *predispositions* of the respondents, which make them act one way or another; and the *influences which are brought to bear upon them*, especially those which mediate between them and the object of their choice.[5] The use of the OI to investigate the first group has just been discussed. The quest for predispositions (attitude, motives) will be dealt with under points four and five. We now consider the use of the OI in the search for *influences*.

The typical research situation here is one wherein we try to assess the importance of a certain event. Let us turn, for example, to people who bought bonds after listening to Kate Smith or who started storing potatoes after a government campaign to this effect had been started or who improved their production records after a system of music-while-you-work had been introduced in a plant. A well-conducted OI should provide enough information so that the causal role of the exposure can be appraised. The rules for such interviews have been rather well worked out.[6]

4. DETERMINING COMPLEX ATTITUDE PATTERNS

A fourth group of applications comes into play when we turn to the *classification of rather complex attitude patterns.* If we want to ascertain how active people are in their war participation or how disturbed they are by current food shortages, the OI actually discusses such subject matters with the respondents, getting their recent experiences and reactions. The purpose is to make an adequate classification of the material so obtained. Further assumptions come easily to mind. People can be classified according to how satisfied they are with local handling of the draft situation, according to the ways they adjust to the lack of gasoline, according to their satisfaction or dissatisfaction with the amount of information they get on the war, etc. This procedure is singularly characteristic of Rensis Likert's work in the Department of Agriculture.[7]

If it is used to assess the extent to which respondents are concerned with a certain problem and how intensely they feel about it, this approach assumes special importance. Two respondents might give the same answer to a simple opinion poll question. For the one, however, it is an important issue on which he has spent much thought, whereas the other may have formed his opinion spontaneously as the poll investigator asked him about it. The possible perfunctory nature of replies to public opinion polls has been the object of much criticism. Those who feel strongly in favor of the OI emphasize that right at this point such a danger is obviated—the danger that poll results will be misleading because they do not take into account intensity of feeling or amount of concern.

This role of the OI does not necessarily terminate with a one-dimensional rating scale of, say, intensity of feeling. The OI is suitable for more complex ratings as well. In a study of people's reactions to changes in food habits, sponsored by the National Research Council, the interviewers were instructed to "watch carefully for all offhand comments to one of the following frames of reference: Money, Health, Taste, Status."[8] The procedure was to talk with people about current food shortages, the adjustments they had made, and the points at which they experienced difficulties. From their discussion it was possible to classify them into four groups according to which of the four contexts they spontaneously stressed. The study found, for example, that high-income groups refer to health twice as often as money, whereas in low-income groups money is the frame of reference three times more frequently than is health.

Finally we have what is known as the "gratification study." In an analysis of the gratification people get from the Professor Quiz programs, for example, a variety of appeals could be distinguished. Some listeners are very much intrigued by the competitive element of the contest; others like to test their own knowledge; still others hope to learn something from the questions posed on the program.[9] We could not expect the untrained respondent to explain clearly the psychological complexities of his interest or his reaction. It is not even likely that he would classify himself accurately if we let him choose among different possibilities. Again the OI is needed to provide the necessary information for the trained analyst. Its practical use lies in the following direction: If we know what attitudes are statistically dominant we can either strengthen the "appeal" elements in the program which are likely to get an enlarged audience; or we can try to change these attitudes if, for some ulterior reason, we consider the prevailing distribution unsatisfactory.

Such studies have also been made in the public opinion field; for example, in analyzing the gratification people get out of writing letters to senators.[10]

5. Motivational Interpretations

Ratings, attitude types, and gratification lists are only the beginning of a conceptual line which ends in studies based on *broad motivational interpretations*. We cannot hope here to present systematically the ways in which psychologists distinguish between the different kinds of "drives" according to their range, depth, or the specificity of their relations to the world of objects.[11] The picture would not be complete, nevertheless, if we were to omit a mention of the use of the OI technique for the purpose of understanding people's reactions in such conceptual contexts.

The OI collects a variety of impressions, experiences and sidelines which the respondent offers when he is asked to discuss a given topic. The man who does the study then makes a kind of psychological construction. He creates a picture of some basic motivation of which all these details are so to speak, manifestations.

Consider an example. In studying certain groups of unemployed one makes a variety of observations: they walk slowly, they lose interest in public affairs, do not keep track of their time, express opinions only with hesitation, stop looking for jobs—in short, they can best be understood as discouraged, resigned beings whose psychological living space has been severely contracted. On the basis of this conceptualization we would not expect them, e.g., to join revolutionary movements which require initiative. If, on the other hand, we are interested in retaining whatever morale they do have left, we would reject the idea of a straight dole in favor of work relief which would keep them psychologically "on the go."

There is only a rather short step from this example to the kind of OI studies which we want to discuss. For a number of reasons most of them have been done in the field of advertising.

People who talk about their shoe purchases often mention how embarrassing it is to expose one's feet in stockings, how one is virtually a prisoner in the hands of the salesman, etc. They are also likely to point out that such-and-such a salesman was friendly, or that they do like stores where the customers are not seated too near each other. The study director finally forms the hypothesis that the shoe-buying situation is one likely to evoke a feeling of inferiority. To alleviate this feeling and thus lead to a larger and more satisfied patronage, a number of obvious suggestions can be made for the training of salesmen and the arrangement of the store.

To discuss this use of OI's in a short space is impossible, especially since its logic has not yet been thought through very well. The social scientist who tries to clarify such analysis faces a conflict between two goals to which he is equally devoted. On the one hand, these interpretations serve to integrate a host of details as well as make us aware of new ones which we might otherwise overlook; often they are very brilliant. On the other hand, they violate our need for verification because by their very nature they can never be proved but only made plausible. It is no coincidence that in the two examples given above we have added to each interpretation some practical advice derived from it. What such motivational analysis does is to see past experiences as parts of some psychological drive which can be reactivated by related material, be it propaganda or institutional devices.[12]

6. CLARIFYING STATISTICAL RELATIONSHIPS

In the five areas outlined so far the OI was the point of departure for all subsequent analysis. Now finally we have to deal with studies where statistical results are available and where the OI serves to *interpret and refine statistical inter-relationships*. The procedure could be called the analysis of deviate cases.

When, for instance, the panic was studied which followed the famous broadcast on the "Invasion From Mars," it was found that people on a lower educational level were most likely to believe in the occurrence of the great catastrophe.[13] Yet some lower-educated people were not frightened at all. When these deviate cases were subject to an OI, many turned out to be mechanics or people who had mechanical hobbies; they were accustomed to checking up on things, a habit the "regular" people had acquired by a successful formal education. On the other hand, quite a number of well-educated people were frightened. When an OI was made with them, the following was sometimes found: During the broadcast they had been in special social situations where it was not clear who

687

should take the initiative of checking up; the lack of social structure impeded purposeful action, and everyone got panicky.

Another example can be taken from unemployment studies. In general it is found that the more amicable the relations in a family prior to the depression, the more firmly would the family stand the impact of unemployment. Again we can inspect deviate cases. A couple fights constantly before the depression, but after the husband becomes unemployed, they get along better. A detailed interview reveals the probability that here the husband wanted to be submissive and the wife dominant, but folkways prevented them from accepting this inverse role. Unemployment, then, enforces a social situation here which is psychologically adequate. Or, a good marriage breaks down surprisingly quickly as a result of the husband's unemployment. A specification of the case shows that the man's sexual habits are rather vulnerable and become disorganized under the blow of the loss of his job.[14]

The general pattern of these studies proceeds from an empirical correlation which is usually not very high. We take cases which do not follow the majority pattern and try to gain an impression or to account for their irregularity. The political scientist is used to such procedure.[15] He knows, for instance, that the more poor people and Catholics live in a given precinct of a big city, the more Democratic votes he can expect. But here is a precinct which qualifies on both scores, and still it went Republican. What accounts for this deviation? Is the Democratic machine inefficient? Has a special local grievance developed? Was there a recent influx of people with different political tradition? This is quite analogous to what we are trying to do when we are faced with individual cases which went statistically out of line. With the help of the OI we try to discover new factors which, if properly introduced, would improve our multiple correlation.

The Issue Becomes a Problem

The six areas just outlined could be looked at in two ways. For one, they represent desirable goals for public opinion research. We need more detailed knowledge as to what the answers of our respondents mean, on what specific points their opinions are based, in what larger motivational contexts they belong, etc. At the same time, the different applications of the OI also imply criticism to the effect that one straight poll question will hardly ever reach any of these goals successfully.

One can agree with this criticism without concluding that the OI technique is the only remedy. If this paper were written for a psychological journal, for instance, the course of our discussion from here on would be prescribed. We should have to compare results obtained by straight poll questions with those collected by OI's and decide which are preferable according to some adequate criteria. The present analysis, however, falls under the heading of "Research Policy." The research administrator has to make decisions as to the most desirable procedures long before we have provided all the necessary data on the comparative merits of different research methods.

What line of argument would one take in such a situation? No one can close his eyes to the shortcomings of many of the current opinion-poll practices. Having begun with the simple problem of predicting elections, they use, very often, a greatly oversimplified approach for the gauging of attitudes toward complex issues. We shall also agree that a well-conducted OI gives us a fascinating wealth of information on the attitude of a single respondent. When it comes to the statistical analysis of many OI's, the matter is already not so simple. It is in the nature of this technique that just the most valuable details of one OI become difficult to compare with the answers obtained in another interview. It can safely be said that the proponents of the OI technique have made much more progress in the conduct of the interviews than in their statistical analysis.

But even if the OI technique were not to have methodological troubles of its own, it would still be open to one very serious objection. It is necessarily an expensive and slow procedure and, as a result, studies which are made for practical purposes will always be based on a small number of cases. It is inconceivable at this moment that an agency would have the resources or the time to make many thousands of OI's on one subject. This is a decisive drawback. True, a surprisingly small number of cases is needed for a fairly correct estimate of how many Republicans there are in a community or how many people save their fat and grease. But do we want to stop here? Don't we want to know in which social groups some of those activities are more frequent than in others? Aren't we trying to account for the reasons why some people do a thing and others do not? And how can this be done except by careful cross-tabulation of one part of our data against other parts? And for this, a much larger number of cases is needed.

In other words, the OI technique, even if it were perfect in itself, places us in a dilemma. By laying all the stress on the detailed description of the single respondent's attitude, it forces us into relatively small numbers of interviews. This in turn handicaps another important progress in public opinion research: the progress which consists of comparing carefully the distribution of opinions in different sub-groups of the population and relating a given opinion to the personal characteristics and to other attitudes of the respondent.

From the standpoint of research policy, therefore, which is the standpoint taken in this paper, the whole problem comes to this. Is there not some way to use all the good ideas which the proponents of the OI technique have and still to develop methods which are more objective, more manageable on a mass basis—which, in short, give us sufficient material to do a thorough analysis of the factors which make for a given distribution of public opinion?

Under these aspects we shall go once more through the six areas discussed above. In each case we shall look for procedures which combine the administrative advantages of the straight poll question with the psychological advantages of the OI. Quite frankly we want to "eat our cake and have it, too." All folklore notwithstanding, research progress consists in the art of doing things which at first seem incompatible. As we proceed, it will turn out that these compromise techniques do not make the OI superfluous but give it a new and, as we feel, more valuable place in the whole scheme of public opinion research.

To bring out more clearly our trend of thought, we begin with a little scheme. To the left we have our six areas; to the right we have short names for the procedures which would overcome some of the shortcomings of the straight poll question and still be more formalized and manageable on a mass basis than the OI.

Current Applications of the OI Techniques	Possible Objective Alternatives for the OI
1. Clarifying the meaning of a respondent's answer	1. Interlocking system of poll questions
2. Singling out the decisive aspects of an opinion	2. Check lists
3. Discerning influences	3. None
4. Determining complex attitude patterns	4. Scales and typologies
5. Interpreting motivation	5. Projective tests
6. Clarifying statistical relationships	6. None

It is to the short description and evaluation of the right side of the scheme that we now turn.

1. Clarifying meaning by the use of interlocking poll questions: In the first area we dealt with the clarification of the respondent's opinion. Did he know the significance of what he was talking about? In the course of an OI, by making the respondent elaborate in more detail, we will find out. But after all, the number of possible variations is not so great; it is often possible to get by explicit questions all the material we can use for comparative analysis of many interview returns.

Consider the following two cases. Studenski has pointed out that when people are asked whether they want lower taxes, most of them will say "yes."[16] After having asked this general question, however, he then asked a series of specific questions on whether the government should discontinue relief, work projects, expenses for national defense, expenses for schools, police, etc. Respondents who wanted taxes reduced but services maintained had obviously, to say the least, an inconsistent attitude toward the problem.[17] In a different context, Kornhauser has pointed out the shortcomings of the question: Should Congress pass a law forbidding strikes in war industries or should war workers have the right to go on strike? Obviously there are other devices, such as an improved arbitration system or the endowment of union leaders with some semi-public power to keep their members from striking. By offering a whole set of such alternatives it is undoubtedly possible to get a much clearer picture of the respondent's real attitude.

In this and many similar examples the technique used consists of an *interlocking system of poll questions*, each of which is very simple but which through proper cross-tabulation permits the separation of respondents according to the extent to which they see the implications of their opinion.

Although we cannot go into details here, we have studied dozens of pertinent cases and are satisfied that for any given topic it is always possible to find an appropriate system of interlocking questions. The right procedure consists of beginning the study with a considerable number of very detailed OI's. These should come from different parts of the country and should serve to develop the structure of the problem. Experience shows that after one to three hundred such reports have been studied, very few new factors come up. At this point we can begin to develop a set of specific questions centering around the main attitude and bringing out its implications and qualifications. There is no reason why we should not ask specifically (by the use of ordinary poll questions) what knowledge and experience the respondent has in this field; what his opinions are in related fields; whether he does or does not expect certain things to happen; whether he has ever thought of the problem, or whether he cannot make up his mind about it, and so on.

Here we come across a very characteristic relationship between the OI and more formalized methods in opinion research. The OI serves as a source of observation and of ideas from which sets of precise poll questions can be derived which will be more manageable in the field and more susceptible to statistical analysis. On one occasion the useful suggestion was made that the special job of *converter* should be developed: that people should specialize in studying OI's and seeing how they could be converted into systems of interlocking questions.

2. *Using check lists to get at the decisive aspects of an opinion:* If we want to know what people like about a candidate or what bothers them about the present rationing system, we can make a list of the probable answers and ask the respondents which answer fits their case.

The advantages and disadvantages of *check lists* have been repeatedly discussed. *The minimum requirement* is that they contain an *exhaustive list of all the possibilities*, for it is known that items not mentioned in a check list are less likely to be mentioned by the respondents. But even a good check list has certain dangers. If people are asked what wish they would make if they had a magic ring, they seldom mention "being very bright," because they do not think of intelligence as something that can be wished for. If, however, they get a check list of possible wishes which includes "intelligence," they are more likely to pick it. *The less concrete the topic is, the more will the check list influence the answers.*

As long as all this is not better explored by comparing the results from large-scale check lists and from the classifications of free answers, it is not possible to make a valid decision. Yet with the help of a careful analysis of OI's it seems logical to assume that exhaustive check lists can be safely constructed—ones which would be as safe as the results of open-ended interviewing. For complex topics the cautious research student will, of course, be hesitant to rely too easily on check lists. When in doubt he will prefer to rely on OI's recorded by conscientious interviewers and classified by sensitive analysts for the study of decisive features.

Again the OI is indispensable in preliminary studies to give one an idea as to what aspects should be considered. If, however, a large number of interviews is to be collected, the interlocking system of questions might be preferable, especially if great effort is made to get an appropriate conversion of preliminary OI's into a system of more precise questions.

3. *Are there other ways of studying what has influenced opinion?:* Whether it is possible to discern influences which are exercised upon people is a controversial question. In more extreme cases such decisions are obviously possible or impossible. If a child goes down to the grocer's "because my mother sent me down," we should consider such a statement as equivalent to a controlled experiment. Putting it rather exaggeratedly: if we set up two groups of well-matched children and had the mothers of the children in one group tell them to go to the grocer's, we should certainly expect to find more children from the "experimental" than from the control group at the grocer's. On the other hand, if a person has committed a crime and we ask him whether that is due to the fact that his parents immigrated to this country, we shall consider whatever he says not very reliable. The command of the mother is much more "discernible" as an influence than the whole background of family life.[18]

Fortunately, in public opinion research we are mostly interested in rather "discernible" influences. Whether people began to salvage paper under the influence of a government campaign or whether a specific pamphlet made them contribute blood to the Red Cross can be discovered fairly well by direct interviewing. For such studies the OI appears to be an important research tool. Thus, it becomes even more urgent to make its use as expert as possible. Sometimes it is not used wisely. Studies of the following kind have been circulated. People who began to can fruit were asked why they did so. Sixty per cent said "because of the campaign,"

15% "because it is necessary for the war effort." Here is obviously a meaningless result—for OI or otherwise. Many of the 15% may have learned from the campaign that private canning was a patriotic duty. However, the interviewer was too easily satisfied with the first answer which came to the mind of the respondent instead of asking "Where did you learn that canning is important for the war effort?"[19]

4. *Scales and typologies for the analysis of attitude patterns:* When it comes to the objective correlates for the use of the OI in the classification of complex attitude patterns, we find ourselves in a peculiar situation. The topic has been a favorite one for social-research students; we have discussed "case studies" versus quantitative methods for a decade.[20] An appropriate instance comes from the study which this writer made during the presidential election of 1940. The task was to appraise how interested people were in the election. Had we used the OI technique, the interviewer would have talked with the respondent and by taking down what he said, by observing his participation in the discussion, he would have formed an opinion on his interest and then noted it in the form of a rating. Instead we asked the respondent three questions: whether he had tried to convince someone of his political ideas; whether he had done anything for the success of his candidate; and whether he was very anxious to see his candidate elected. Each respondent got a definite score according to how he answered the three questions.[21]

But how does such an objective scale compare with the impressionistic ratings obtained from an OI? The problems involved can best be explained by an example.

If in everyday life we call another person timid, we do so because of the way he walks or because of his hesitant speech and sometimes because of cues of which we are not precisely aware ourselves. In each case we use whatever cues the situation offers; they might be quite different from one case to the next. A "timidity rating," on the other hand, would provide us with a list of items on which an interviewer would have to get an observation for every case, if necessary by asking a direct question. The more timidity characteristics on this list applied to the respondents, the higher would be his timidity score. Using such a scale, the interviewer could not make use of incidental observations if they were not included in the list, even if in a special case he had a strong conviction that the respondent was much more timid than his scale value indicated.

All this can be directly applied to our problem. A good OI reproduces the full vividness of an actual observation; but if nothing characteristic happens in the interview situation or if the interviewer misses cues, then we have little on which to base our final classification. With the scale we can count on a definite amount of data, but some of them might be rather artificial and often we must forego valuable observations within our reach. *Thus, a scale because of its rigidity will hardly be as good as an OI under its best conditions but can hardly let us down as much as an OI sometimes does.*

5. Is there an easy way to get at motivation? When we discussed broad motivational interpretations, we stressed all the hazards involved in this method. Correspondingly, it is very difficult to find an objective or formalized method for such an approach. *Projective tests* come nearest to it. The general idea of these tests is that people are presented with un-structured material. Here is a crying girl; other children are asked to guess why she is crying. Or, an inkblot is shown to some people, as in the Rohrshach test, and they are asked to state what form it signifies to them. It is then assumed that the way people interpret such material, which has no definite meaning of its own, is indicative of what people themselves are concerned with.[22]

Applications to a public-opinion problem can only be invented be-cause, to our knowledge, such studies have never been tried. If one wants to test people's attitudes toward public administration, one might, for in-stance, tell a short story of a successful public official who was suddenly dismissed. What was the reason? Was he found to be corrupt? Or was he the victim of a political intrigue? Or didn't he agree with the govern-ment's policy?

After Pearl Harbor, when so many people were concerned about the weakness of the American Navy, it would not have been easy to ask di-rect questions on this subject; few people would have cared to give an unpatriotic answer. One might, however, have shown them a series of pictures of battleships varying in degree of technical perfection. Which, in the opinion of the respondent, is an American and which a Japanese battleship? The proportion of people picking out the poor ship as an American model might have been a good index of concern about Ameri-can armaments.

The psychological assumptions involved in a projective test have yet to be studied exhaustively. The answers are usually quite difficult to classify, and much depends upon the interpretation of the analyst. In the future such techniques may provide a very important tool for public opinion research. For the moment it can hardly be claimed that they are much better formalized than a good OI. If, therefore, one is interested in broad motivational interpretations, a well-conducted OI is probably still the best source for material.

6. The means of statistical relationships. Nothing has to be added to our discussion of the analysis of deviate cases in the preceding section. Here the OI is in its most legitimate place.

If we now summarize briefly this critical survey of the OI technique, we can make a number of points as to its position in the general scheme of public opinion research.

We saw that the problem is not new. Since the beginning of social research, students have tried to combine the detailed qualitative applications with the advantages of more formalized techniques which could be managed on a mass basis.

We saw, furthermore, that a line along which such an integration could come about emerges. The OI is indispensable at the beginning of any study where it classifies the structure of a problem in all its details. It is also invaluable at the end of a study for anyone who is not satisfied with the mere recording of the low correlations we usually obtain. Good research consists in weaving back and forth between OI's and the more cut-and-dried procedures.

NOTES

1. Hans E. Skott, "Attitude Research in the Department of Agriculture," *Public Opinion Quarterly*, 1943, 7, 280–292.
2. Henry C. Link, "An Experiment in Depth Interviewing," *Public Opinion Quarterly*, 1943, 7, 267–279.
3. P. F. Lazarsfeld and R. K. Merton, "Studies in Radio and Film Propaganda," *Transactions of the New York Academy of Sciences*, Series II, 1943, 6, No. 2, 58–79.
4. It should be emphasized that the question "why" is useful also for other purposes which will be discussed in the remaining four points. This is easily understood if one considers that the word has hardly any meaning in itself. It is about equivalent to saying that the respondent should talk some more. "Why" is a good start, but it seldom leads to a constructive end if it is not followed by specific questions directed toward what the interviewer really wants to know.
5. Paul Lazarsfeld, "The Art of Asking Why," *National Marketing Review*, 1, 1935, 32–43.
6. Paul Lazarsfeld, "Evaluating the Effectiveness of Advertising by Direct Interviews," *Journal of Consulting Psychology*, July–August, 1941.
7. Likert's work is mainly done for Government agencies and therefore cannot be quoted at the present time. The present paper owes much to discussions with him and some of his associates, especially Bill Gold. (Editor's note: Since the original publication of this article a number of articles on the methodology of this research group have been published, for example, see Maccoby, E. & Holt, R., "How Surveys Are Made," in this volume.)
8. Kurt Lewin, "Forces Behind Food Habits and Methods of Change," *The Problem of Changing Food Habits*, Bulletin of the National Research Council, Number 108, October 1943.
9. Herta Herzog, "On Borrowed Experience," *Studies in Philosophy and Social Science*, 1941.
10. R. Wyant and H. Herzog, "Voting Via the Senate Mailbag," this *Quarterly*, 1941, 5, 590–624.
11. Gordon W. Allport, "Attitudes," Handbook of Social Psychology (ed. C. Murchison), Worcester: Clark University Press, 1935, 798–844.
12. Rhoda Metraux, "Qualitative Attitude Analysis—A Technique for the Study of Verbal Behavior," *The Problem of Changing Food Habits*, Bulletin of the National Research Council, No. 108, October 1943.

13. Hadley Cantril, Herta Herzog, and Hazel Gaudet, *Invasion from Mars*. Princeton: Princeton University Press, 1939.

14. Mirra Komarovsky, *The Unemployed Man and His Family*. New York: Institute of Social Research, 1940.

15. Harold F. Gosnell, *Getting out the Vote*. Chicago: Chicago University Press, 1927.

16. Paul Studenski, "How Polls Can Mislead," *Harpers Magazine*, December 1939.

17. This is the technique which Henry Link used in a more recent study ("An Experiment in Depth Interviewing," this *Quarterly*, 1943, 7, 267–279). He first obtained a broad commitment on world participation for the post-war period from his respondents; then he asked a series of definite questions: for the sake of America's participation in world affairs, what would people be willing to accept? A standing army? Higher taxes? A lower standard of living? Etc. As a device to clarify the implications of people's opinions this is an appropriate procedure, but it is very confusing if it is suggested as a substitute for or even an improvement on the OI in all areas. It is precisely the purpose of the present paper to provide a general scheme, so that in discussing "depth interviews" *each participant can point to the specific sector of the entire field he has in mind.*

18. E. Smith and E. Suchman, "Do People Know Why They Buy?" *Journal of Applied Psychology*, 1940, 24, 673–684.

19. We find here a mistake which corresponds to the objection we voiced above against Henry Link's paper. Because he used interlocking questions in one area, he thought that he had shown the usefulness of the OI technique in all other areas. Many of the proponents of the OI, on the other hand, do careful interviewing for the description of attitudes; but when it comes to the discerning of influences, they do bad interviewing and subject their returns to poor classification.

20. Paul Wallin, *Case Study Methods in the Prediction of Personal Adjustment* (ed., Paul Horst). New York: Social Science Research Council, 1941.

21. If such an interest score was used, it was found that for men the correlation between interest and voting was .20, whereas for women it was .50. Women, if they are not interested, do not vote. Men vote even if they are not interested, probably because they are more subject to social pressure. For a general theory of this score procedure see P. Lazarsfeld and W. Robinson, "Quantification of Case Studies," *Journal of Applied Psychology*, 1940, 24, 831–837.

22. P. Symonds and W. Samuel, "Projective Methods in the Study of Personality" (Chap. VI of *Psychological Tests and Their Uses*), *Review of Educational Research*, 1941, 11, 80–93.

CHARLES E. OSGOOD

The Measurement of Meaning

SPEAKING IN MOST GENERAL TERMS, we have communication whenever one system, a *source*, influences the states or actions of another system, the *destination* or *receiver*, by selecting among the alternative signals that can be carried in the *channel* connecting them. In dealing with human communication systems we usually refer to signal sets as *messages*; and these are most often, though not necessarily, *language* messages. It is the job of the linguist to describe the structure or *code* according to which these messages are organized. Also, in dealing with human communication, it is necessary to further analyze both source and receiver into integrated subsystems. The individual human communicator is equipped both to receive and transmit messages more-or-less simultaneously—indeed, he is regularly the receiver of the messages he himself produces, via feedback mechanisms. But beyond such sensory reception skills and motor transmitting skills, the human communicator is equipped to learn symbolic, representational processes, or meanings. On the input side, certain patterns of signals in the channel, as *signs*, acquire association with certain representational mediators and hence have *significance*; on the output side, these mediators acquire selective association with certain motor skills (speaking, writing, etc.), which thereby express *intentions*. We refer to the process whereby signs in messages select among representational mediators as *decoding*; the process whereby representational mediators select among motor expressions in messages is referred to as *encoding*.

The types of human communication systems are many and varied. At one extreme we have the *one-to-many* system, e.g., when the President of the United States encodes a message which is amplified via the mass media of radio, TV, and the press into the receptive field of many millions of citizen receivers, each of whom decodes according to his own fashion. At another extreme we have the *many-to-one* system, e.g., the dependence of the meanings, attitudes, and beliefs of some particular individual upon the sum total of messages received from parents, from friends, from school, from magazines, from TV, and so on. At yet a different extreme we have the *one-to-himself* system, e.g., an individual solving a problem, working out a theory, ruminating, or even dreaming —being stimulated by the symbols he produces himself. Between these (and other) extremes there are all kinds of variations—the interactions in a small face-to-face group like a boys' gang, the communication of a relatively small group (institution like a newspaper staff) to a relatively large group (the readership), cross-culture and cross-language communication via the mediation of an interpreter, and so on.

Nor is it necessary that the communication channel be "linguistic" in the usual sense. The language channel is admittedly the most finely coded and important coupling between human communicators, but it is not the only channel. There is also, for example, the *visuo-gestural channel* of facial and postural expressions—one may study the efficiency of communication between intentions of "actors" and significances in "judges" via this medium (see Osgood, 1956). Similarly, *aesthetics* may be studied as a kind of communication: the source (artist, composer, writer, poet) encodes in the medium of his special talent, presumably expressing his own meanings or intentions by his selection among alternatives (colors, texture, tempo, harmonics, metaphor, word-choice, etc.); there is aesthetic communication to the extent to which receivers (the audience) experience corresponding meanings or significances upon decoding the signs produced by the source. If the artist skillfully employs rough-textured reds to convey aggression, for example, and those viewing his canvas (message) experience appropriate feelings and meanings, then to this extent, at least, there has been aesthetic communication. Bordering between aesthetics and "ordinary" communication are many of the communications in contemporary society—the use of color in advertising, application of captions to pictorial matter, the effects of political cartoons, and so forth.

Where does semantic measurement enter this communications picture? The semantic differential is proposed as an index of certain aspects of *meaning*, particularly connotative aspects. In human communication, be it via linguistic, aesthetic, or other channels, meaning is critically involved at both the initiation (the intentions being encoded by the source) and the termination (the significances being decoded by the receiver) of any communicative act. Most often the researcher will be interested in the significances derived from messages by receivers, i.e., *effect studies* (What effect does this pictorial display have upon the meaning of this advertised product? What effect upon changing attitudes toward this candidate does this particular cartoon have? What are the connotations of various technical devices in abstract art?), because, if our general model is correct, upon such semantic effects depend the overt behaviors and decisions of audiences. It was obviously the significance of Orson Welles' "Invasion of Mars" broadcast, uncritically accepted, that led some receivers to make a mad dash for the Jersey hills. Less often, perhaps, but equally important, the researcher in communications may be interested in the intentions of sources, the meanings behind the signs selected by the source for communication. How facile, for example, are various speakers at encoding words which accurately express their own meanings for objects and situations? Could the significance of a scene to a poet or artist be estimated with the differential and this profile compared with the meanings derived by the audience from his aesthetic product?

The applications of semantic measurement to human communications problems are potentially as broad and varied as the communication area itself. In this chapter we report a number of applications which have been made, but they by no means exhaust the possibilities and should be considered as illustrative samples. The chapter is organized quite arbitrarily in terms of subject matter rather than method: (1) *Psycholinguistic studies*—more-or-less "pure" research on the nature, development, and combination of signs in relation to the semantic states of language users; (2) *Studies in experimental aesthetics*—focusing on the dimensionality of the aesthetic meaning space for artists and non-artists and the effects of color in visual abstraction and in advertising; (3) *Communication effect studies*—attitude and meaning change in political, advertising, and other areas, as produced by messages carried in the mass media. . .

Application to Communications Effect Studies

The dividing line between aesthetic and communications effects is not always clear—certainly both the experiment on color in advertising and that on musical background for a play could have been included as studies in communication effects. In both of these experiments it was the greater dimensionality of judgment provided by the semantic differential that enriched the results obtained. From the point of view followed here, communication effects are changes in the meaning of concepts central to the message, changes in the location of these concepts in the (potentially) *n*-dimensional space provided by a semantic differential. Such changes may be measured *in toto* by applying the *D* measure between pre- and post-message scores on all factors, or they may be assayed on a unidimensional (or even single scale) basis. In either case, a greater wealth of information derives from such a multi-dimensional instrument.

However, many of the studies on communication effects to be reported here have been limited to the single evaluative dimension and hence are properly to be considered experiments on attitude change. The usual procedure in these cases has been to use a number of purely evaluative scales (as determined by factor analyses), sometimes imbedded among scales tapping other factors which merely serve a masking purpose, and to sum over these evaluative scales for an "attitude score." The analysis is then conducted as it would be with any other unidimensional measure. In this section are included studies ranging from the effects of TV coverage of a congressional hearing to the influence of verbal captions upon response to pictures, but all having in common the fact that they deal with the effects of messages in the mass media upon the meanings and attitudes of people receiving them.

EFFECTS OF TV COVERAGE OF A CONGRESSIONAL HEARING

In early May, 1954, a subcommittee of the House Committee on Un-American Activities convened in Lansing, Michigan, at a two-day public hearing. According to the subcommittee chairman, ex-Representative Kit Clardy, the hearings were held to "investigate Communist infiltration into local educational and labor institutions." About a dozen witnesses were called, most of whom invoked the fifth amendment at some point during their testimony.

A complete coverage of these hearings was carried by WKAR-TV, the Michigan State University television station, as "a public service." As conceived by the station personnel, the purpose of the telecast was "to present an objective study of this one phase of governmental activity—the proceedings of a congressional investigating sub-committee." Toward this end, two major ingredients were included in the telecast: (a) A straightforward camera-eye's view and microphone-ear's report of the proceedings. This reportorial function was restricted somewhat by the request of several witnesses that no telecast of them be made during their testimony—a right that is guaranteed by the procedural rules of the committee. This restriction applied only to the visual element of the coverage and not to the witnesses' oral testimony. (b) Background and interpretative commentary by two qualified political scientists before and after the hearings and during the periodic recesses. This commentary included discussions of the rights of witnesses, the fifth amendment, functions of congressional investigating committees, and so on, and was designed to provide a framework for following the hearings.

In order to investigate certain assumptions often made in connection

Table 1—Comparison between TV Group and Non-TV Group on Total Amount of Change on Semantic Differential Ratings

Concept	SUM OF RANKS		p
	TV Group	Non-TV Group	
Kit Clardy	1347.5	998.5	.05
Congressional			
Investigating Committees	1277.5	1068.5	.20
Communist Infiltration			
into Local Institutions	1214.0	1132.0	.60
Fifth Amendment	1356.0	990.0	.05
Televising of			
Committee Hearings	1369.0	977.0	.02

with such televised coverage of committee proceedings, a program of research was conducted in conjunction with the broadcast (Tannenbaum, 1955). Here we report only on that part of the research which utilized the semantic differential.

Procedure—Prior to the hearings, a panel of 68 persons was established. Each panel member was told the purpose of the study and was asked to keep a record of his communication exposure to the hearings over the two-day period. Among other things, he also rated five concepts (KIT CLARDY, CONGRESSIONAL INVESTIGATING COMMITTEES, COMMUNIST INFILTRATION INTO LOCAL INSTITUTIONS, THE FIFTH AMENDMENT, and TELEVISING OF COMMITEE HEARINGS—all believed on a priori grounds, to have relation to the hearings) against ten semantic differential scales. Four scales (*good-bad, valuable-worthless, fair-unfair,* and *pleasant-unpleasant*) were representative of the evaluative factor, three (*weak-strong, heavy-light,* and *large-small*) of the potency factor, and three (*active-passive, fast-slow,* and *calm-agitated*) of the activity factor. During the three days immediately following the hearings, panel members were again contacted and repeated the same ratings.

For purposes of analysis, the panel was divided into two groups according to the kinds of communications exposure experienced: The *TV Group* consisted of subjects who had at least one and one-half hours of exposure to the WKAR-TV telecast, including some exposure to the background commentary (most subjects here had considerably more than this minimum). The *Non-TV Group* was composed of those subjects who had seen little or none of the TV coverage (most subjects here had not seen it at all, while only a few had fleeting glimpses; but all had followed the hearings via the newspaper). There were 34 subjects in each group.

Table 2—Change from Pre-Test to Post-Test in Semantic Differential Judgments for TV Group

(The sign represents the direction of change and the value represents the significance of the change.)

Concept	Evaluation	CHANGE ON Potency	Activity
Kit Clardy	—(.20)	+(.10)	+(.30)
Congressional Investigating Committees	—(.20)	—(.20)	+(.50)
Communist Infiltration into Local Institutions	—(.90)	+(.05)	+(.20)
Fifth Amendment	—(.05)	—(.05)	+(.30)
Televising of Committee Hearings	—(.10)	—(.05)	—(.70)

Results—The analysis was directed at two main questions: First, did the TV Group change more in their over-all judgment for each concept than did the Non-TV Group? Second, what was the direction and magnitude of change for each concept on each of the three factors within the TV Group?

To answer the first question, D scores between the pre-test and post-test ratings across the ten scales were computed for each subject in each group, and separately for each concept. Thus, for any one concept, there were 68 D-scores—34 in each group. The two groups were then compared on each concept by means of the Wilcoxon Unpaired Replicates Test. The results, as summarized in Table 1, show significantly greater (at or beyond the 5 per cent level) changes in meaning for the TV Group on three concepts (CLARDY, FIFTH AMENDMENT, and TELEVISING COMMITTEE HEARINGS). On the other two concepts, the differences are in the same direction (i.e., a greater shift for the TV Group), but are not significant. Testing across all five concepts at once (by means of analysis of variance by ranks) indicates a significant over-all difference.

To answer the second question, separate factor scores were computed on each concept for each subject in the TV Group—an *evaluative* score by summing over the four evaluative scales (possible range of scores, 4-28); a *potency* score over the three potency scales (range, 3-21), and an *activity* score over the three activity scales (range, 3-21). This was done both for the pre-exposure ratings, and for the post-exposure ratings. Table 2 presents both the directions and levels of magnitude of the changes for each concept. The sign (+ or —) represents the direction of change, a plus (+) sign indicating the mean judgment of the post-rating to be more favorable, more powerful, or more active, respectively, than on the pre-ratings, and conversely for the minus (—)

sign. The approximate significance level (as determined by a Wilcoxon Paired Replicates Test) of the magnitude of change is indicated by the parenthetically enclosed value associated with each directional index— the lower the value, the more significant the change. Although only three of the changes reached the 5 per cent level of significance, some of the other changes were quite substantial, indicating that the TV coverage was not without its effects.

Some observations of these changes in meaning on each concept may be of interest:

1 KIT CLARDY

The changes on this concept were all quite substantial, although none reaches the 5 per cent level. Clardy was perceived as more powerful than before the hearings, but also less favorable. Some of the changes in evaluation were quite extensive, including complete reversals from originally favorable ratings to equally unfavorable ones. One may speculate whether this was a harbinger of things to follow six months later when Clardy, whose constituency included the television coverage area, was defeated in his bid for re-election.

2 CONGRESSIONAL INVESTIGATING COMMITTEES

Apparently, these particular hearings did not endear those exposed to them to the general notion of congressional investigating committees. This concept was judged less favorable and weaker than prior to the hearings, with no real change on the activity factor. It is possible, however, that these changes were as much a carry-over of other public hearings (particularly the "Army-McCarthy" hearings then still in the public eye) as they were a function of the Lansing hearings, with the latter serving to precipitate already existing predispositions. The design of the present research unfortunately did not include provisions for studying this and related factors systematically.

3 COMMUNIST INFILTRATION

This was the alleged main focus of the hearings, and the greatest single change noted on this concept was its being judged much more potent. One reason no real change was noted in evaluation may be that most of the initial, pre-exposure judgments were so extremely unfavorable that there was no room on the scale for further unfavorable shift.

4 FIFTH AMENDMENT

This concept showed the most change on the average, becoming much more unfavorable, less strong, and somewhat more active. No doubt, these changes were largely a reflection of the relatively high frequency of application of the fifth amendment during the current hearings. Equally probable, they were also a manifestation of latent dissatisfaction brought to the surface by the TV viewing. If the present hearings are any criterion, then, public exposure to such proceedings can apparently do as much to undermine judgment of the fifth amendment as it can encourage the perception of Communism as a menace.

5 TELEVISING COMMITTEE HEARINGS

When this concept was presented, it was emphasized that the general idea of televising this type of governmental activity, and not the Lansing hearings in particular, was to be judged. If these instructions were followed, the effect of the Lansing coverage was quite detrimental to the general notion. The lackluster nature of these particular hearings may have been a major factor influencing these changes; the television coverage, as such, appeared to be quite adequate.

Summary—From the practical communications point of view, this study has shown that televising a congressional hearing may have significant effects upon the attitudes and meanings of relevant concepts in the public mind. TV viewers were found to be changed more than those who got their information from other channels. The semantic changes engendered in TV viewers were in part those which may have been intended by the committee chairman, Kit Clardy (the concept of COMMUNIST INFILTRATION INTO LOCAL INSTITUTIONS became stronger and more active, and FIFTH AMENDMENT became less favorable and weaker), but in part they were certainly not those intended (KIT CLARDY, although becoming somewhat stronger, became less favorable also, and both CONGRESSIONAL INVESTIGATING COMMITTEES and TELEVISING OF COMMITTEE HEARINGS became less favorable and less potent in connotation). Although the urge to generalize these findings, e.g., to the Army-McCarthy hearings of not so long ago, is inviting, it would be open to serious question.

From the methodological point of view, this study gives some indication of the kind of information that can be obtained from the semantic differential when applied in a situation of this type. The instrument revealed many effects that might otherwise have been completely overlooked in straight polling-type questions or ordinary attitude scales. Indeed, many of the critical changes revealed were not in attitude per se (the evaluative factor) but along other dimensions of meaning—the dimension showing the largest changes over all five concepts was the potency dimension. The greater the dimensionality of judgment sampled, the more likely is the investigator to detect the effects of communications and the more readily interpretable are these effects. It follows, too, that the development of a theory of communication effects will be considerably enhanced by determining the full dimensionality that such effects assume in given situations.

EXPERIMENTAL STUDIES IN ATTITUDE CHANGE

In this area, except for one study which measured attitude change resulting from a bona fide communication message, the main focus has been on investigating the effect of different variables on the direction and amount of attitude change produced by deliberately prepared communication messages. As such, they are very much along the lines of the work of Hovland and his group at Yale (see Hovland, Janis, and Kelley, 1953), differing principally in the measure of attitude employed. We will first report on the study dealing with the straightforward effects analysis, and then proceed to reports of several investigations of a more experimental nature. It might be mentioned in passing that at least two investigations already reported—those of Tannenbaum (1953) and Kerrick (1954)—also may be included within this latter category.

Attitude Change from a Radio Satire—When the program "The Investigator," a biting radio satire on Senator Joseph McCarthy and McCarthyism, was performed by the Canadian Broadcasting Corporation some years back, it aroused considerable comment on both sides of the border. The program was in the form of an allegorical satire in which no specific verbal identification was made of the two main issues—McCarthy and Congressional investigations—but only to the most naïve listener would these not be apparent. Like most such satires, it had its humorous moments, but it also carried a message of some importance.

Berlo and Kumata (1956) had 45 subjects (undergraduates) rate each of eight concepts against nine evaluative semantic differential scales before and after exposure to a recording of "The Investigator." A control group ($N = 37$) did both sets of ratings but was not exposed to the recording. The concepts rated included: SOCRATES, JEFFERSON, MILTON, and MACKENZIE (persons who were "deported" from Heaven by the investigating committee); SENATOR MCCARTHY (the Investigator); CANADIAN BROADCASTING CORPORATION (the source of the message); CONGRESSIONAL INVESTIGATIONS and SECURITY CLEARANCES (two concepts felt to be related to the general tenor of the program). Subjects also answered selected items from the F-scale, but no correlation was noted between F-scores and ratings of any single concept.

After exposure, the experimental group showed only two significant changes in attitude—on the concept CONGRESSIONAL INVESTIGATIONS, which became much less favorable, and on MACKENZIE, who changed in a favorable direction. Near significant changes ($.10 > p > .05$) were obtained for CBC and SECURITY CLEARANCES, both in a negative direction. No other concepts changed significantly, although there was a substantial shift on MCCARTHY toward a more *favorable* attitude ($p = .10$). The congruity hypothesis was also applied to these data, using CBC as the source and MCCARTHY and CONGRESSIONAL INVESTIGATIONS as the respective concepts. For the CBC-MCCARTHY combination, the results indicated a "boomerang" effect as hinted at in the attitude change above—CBC became less favorable and MCCARTHY more favorable, instead of the reverse as predicted. For the CBC-CONGRESSIONAL INVESTIGATIONS combination, however, the direction of attitude change was significant and as predicted. To interpret these results, it appears that the subjects felt the satire was unfair to MCCARTHY (already something of an underdog by the time of the experiment), but were affected in the intended way toward CONGRESSIONAL HEARINGS. MACKENZIE—an unknown to most of these subjects—became definitely more favorable by virtue of his association with MILTON, JEFFERSON, *et al.*, and his dissociation from MCCARTHY and inquisitions in general.

"One-sided" vs. "Two-sided" Communication—The comparative effectiveness of one-sided messages (i.e., where the source directly favors one side of a controversial issue) vs. two-sided messages (where the source favors the same side, but also outlines the arguments of the other side) was investigated by Hovland, Lumsdaine, and Sheffield (1949), with the focus on change in opinion toward the issue of the message. A recent study by Wolfinger (1955) measured attitude change toward both the issue (or concept) and the perceived source of the message, as a function of the same presentation variable.

College freshmen rated the concepts FIFTH AMENDMENT and an imaginary GEORGE HASTINGS against a semantic differential form including five evaluative scales. Immediately following this pretest, one group of subjects ($N = 125$) was exposed to the two-sided version of a tape-recorded speech, by one GEORGE HASTINGS, on the FIFTH AMENDMENT, with this source indicating his favoring of the concept. A second group ($N = 124$) received the one-sided version, which was identical with the two-sided one except that all opposing arguments had been deleted from the tape. A control group ($N = 56$) heard another speech unrelated to the experimental topic. After exposure, all subjects again rated the source and concept.

Both experimental versions produced attitude changes toward both the concept and the source which was significantly greater ($p < .01$ in each case) than the change in the control group. Regarding attitude change toward FIFTH AMENDMENT, subjects originally favorable to the concept were affected more by the two-sided presentation than by the one-sided one; subjects originally unfavorable to the concept were more affected by the one-sided message. These findings are contrary to predictions arising from the Hovland *et al.*, work, but they do not reach satisfactory statistical significance. It may be, also, that differences in intelligence were operating here. With respect to attitude change toward the source (which, being more-or-less hypothetical, was initially judged neutral by almost every subject), the following results were obtained: Subjects originally favoring the position advocated by the source were more favorably affected by the one-sided message than by the two-sided one; the difference here was significant at the .10 level. However, the hypothesis that subjects originally unfavorable to the source's position would become relatively more favorable toward the source as a result of the two-sided message was not upheld by the data, the difference between the two groups being well within chance limits. Considering change in attitude toward both source and concept simultaneously, the one-sided presentation produced significantly more favorable changes than did the two-sided version.

Effects of Message Order and Structure—One experimental study[1] was directed at the problem of the serial order of arguments in an oral message in terms of producing the desired attitude change. Two variables were investigated: one consisted of three orders of argumentation—*climactic* (from weakest to strongest); *anticlimactic* (strongest to weakest); and *pyramidal* (strongest assertion at the middle of the message, weakest at both beginning and end); the other variable referred to the position of the assertion in relation to its supporting evidence—*deductive structure*, where the assertion precedes the evidence, and *inductive structure*, where the assertion follows the evidence. This led to a two-variable, three-by-two factorial design, with six separate groups of experimental subjects ($N = 29$ in each group). A control group ($N = 27$) was also used.

Each experimental group was exposed to its respective version of a tape recording on the merits of general education courses in the college curriculum, with the various assertions selected from relevant literature. Pre- and post-exposure attitudes toward the concepts GENERAL EDUCATION COURSES and RESEARCH PROFESSOR (the ostensible message source) were obtained. Each experimental group showed a significant shift in attitude toward the proposition when compared with the control group. An analysis of variance between the six groups, however, showed no significant differences for either the orders or argumentation or the deductive vs. inductive structures, nor was the interaction significant. When the data were analyzed in terms of prediction from the congruity model, it was found that approximately 70 per cent of the changes were in the predicted direction—a significantly greater than chance prediction. In terms of magnitude of change, the Pearson product-moment correlations between predicted (via congruity) and obtained results were .63 on the source, and .71 for the concept—both highly significant.

Being essentially unrelated studies, these experiments permit no substantive summary. Methodologically, they further extend the types of research problems to which the semantic differential may be applied;[2] theoretically, they include some additional tests of the congruity principle.

INFLUENCE OF VERBAL CAPTIONS ON PICTURE IDENTIFICATION

Another study which can be considered within the general realm of communications research with the semantic differential has been contributed by Kerrick (1955). It was designed to test the effect of different captions on the significance of pictures. It has often been claimed that the meaning of a particular photograph can be entirely altered by ingenious choice of words in the caption accompanying it—the expression on a face can be made to seem calm or irritated, a street scene can be made shabby or neat, a charge may be turned into a retreat, and so on.

Kerrick selected five pictures from the Thematic Apperception Test for their somewhat ambiguous qualities. She had different groups of subjects rate each picture (1) without a caption, (2) with a caption loading the meaning in one direction, and (3) with a caption loading the meaning in the opposite direction. The results showed a significant effect of the caption in altering the judgment on the intended scales (e.g., toward *happy* in the case of a picture captioned *At the Station: Reunion*, and toward *sad* when the same picture was captioned *At the Station: Parting*). Moreover, the effect of the caption generalized to other scales *within the same factor*, so that the total interpretation was congruent with that aspect made explicit in the caption. Although, generally, a caption that was quite opposite to the basic pictorial content failed to shift judgment, there were several instances where this caption effect was sufficient to cause a complete reversal in meaning on certain scales. Unfortunately, independent judgments for the captions alone were not obtained, so no check on the possible operation of congruity can be made with these data.

STUDIES ON ADVERTISING EFFECTS

The semantic differential technique has had considerable application to advertising research. Most of the applications to date have been restricted to the use of the evaluative factor, but this is not a necessary limitation. Indeed, it seems likely, on an intuitive basis, that many of the significant changes that result from advertising campaigns would be reflected on semantic dimensions other than the evaluative one. One instance of the use of the semantic differential in this field—on the effects of color on product meanings—has already been reported in some detail (see pp. 299–301). In this section we report on several studies that have been conducted in or through our own research center.[3]

The Comparative Effectiveness of Five Advertising Appeals—Mindak (1955) used eight evaluative scales of the semantic differential to compare the effectiveness of five different types of radio appeals dealing with a new hand lotion that was being readied for marketing. Five one-minute radio commercials were written, emphasizing each of these five appeals: *negative appeal* (emphasis on symptoms of cracked skin, calloused hands, etc.); *testimonial appeal* (Marilyn Monroe suggests use of product because of her own personal success with it); *scientific appeal* (emphasis on the scientific newness of product, using several pseudo-scientific terms); *"romance despite work" appeal* (emphasis on maintaining lovely hands despite their use in household tasks); and the *"zany" appeal* (whimsical appeal with considerable use of puns). Each of these five versions was imbedded at the opening and closing of a 15-minute, musical comedy highlight radio program, especially produced for the experiment. These five versions were presented to different groups of subjects (female undergraduates) who rated a number of concepts associated with the content of the commercials (e.g., IDEAL HAND LOTION, MARILYN MONROE, ROMANCE, etc.) against the eight-scale differential, both before and after the program.

The results showed that each of the five appeals produced significant change in attitude toward the product (when tested by Wilcoxon's Paired Replicates Test), but on only one version—the scientific one—was the change in a favorable direction. All other appeals produced unfavorable changes, with the testimonial appeal producing the largest negative change (of course the fact that the subjects were female undergraduates and the testimonial source was Miss Monroe is probably the reason for this).

Believability of Beer Advertising—In another study reported by Mindak (1955), a selected sample of 100 male beer drinkers rated the slogans used by four different brands of beer, including one being pretested for marketing purposes, and the concepts BEER ADVERTISING and ADVERTISING IN GENERAL on a series of semantic differential-type scales especially constructed to measure the believability of the advertising. Among the findings were the following: (1) The slogans used were generally rated more favorable than the concept BEER ADVERTISING. (2) The slogans for the "new" beer were judged significantly more favorable than the others. (3) BEER ADVERTISING was judged generally more *exaggerated*, more *dishonest*, and more *untrue* than ADVERTISING IN GENERAL. All of these findings, and several specific ones of less importance for our purposes here, were then used in constructing the advertising campaign for the new beer when it was placed on the market.

Effect of Slogans on Attitude Toward Products—Another problem in the advertising field concerns the effects of slogans upon attitudes toward the products they represent—entirely apart from the sheer frequency effect upon recall and association. This problem was investigated in a study[4] which had subjects in an introductory course in advertising first try to recall the product names associated with a number of slogans—e.g., "Man of Distinction" with Calvert's Whiskey. The subjects then rated both the products and the slogans against the same form of the semantic differential which included 12 evaluative scales, mostly selected on the basis of available factor loadings, but also including several that were thought to have direct bearing on advertising. The most significant finding was that while most products were more favorably rated by those subjects who recognized their slogans, for others just the reverse was true. For Calvert's Whiskey, for example, subjects who did *not* associate the slogan "Man of Distinction" with the product gave significantly *more* favorable mean ratings of the product than subjects who did make the association—evidence that for this college population, at least, the slogan was working against acceptance of the product.

Evaluation of the Components of an Ad—In another study,[5] subjects rated the different components (copy, illustration, headline, trade-mark, and signature) of four different and diverse advertisements against nine scales selected (on a subjective basis) to represent three supposed subfactors of general evaluation—utility, pleasurableness, and morality. However, subsequent factor analysis failed to reveal anything but a single, general evaluative factor. In addition subjects also rated the advertisements as wholes, the products being advertised, and the specific product brands advertised.

Among other things, Richmond found that in each of the four cases, the illustration was judged significantly more favorable than the copy, when each was judged separately. Another interesting result was that the evaluation of the *product itself*—whether presented in terms of the generic product class (e.g., AUTOMOBILES) or in terms of a specific brand of that product (e.g., OLDSMOBILE)—was consistently more favorable than the evaluation of the respective *advertisements* for these products. Richmond also applied the congruity principle to predict the evaluative judgment of the total advertisement from knowledge of the judgment of the several components. Although this situation was admittedly a crude approximation to an ideal one (for purposes of prediction), he found that the predicted results correlated significantly with the obtained ones (when the subjects judged the advertisement per se).

SUMMARY

The above examples help point out one of the values of the semantic differential for advertising research. Here the need very often is for some instrument that allows for *comparability*, and the generality of the technique lends itself to such purposes. The same set of scales—whether selected on the basis of the factor analysis or developed for a particular study—can be used to get judgments of different products, different brands of a single product, different ads on a single brand, or even different segments of a single ad. For example, the instrument may be used to determine which of a number of alternate ads, as a unit, best gets across the intended message, and which does best on a certain dimension of judgment, or, if desired, on a certain single scale. Analysis of such data may indicate, for example, that a revamping may be in order wherein a completely new ad would be constructed incorporating the best features of each of the test ads. In much the same manner variations of the components of an ad may be pretested individually and in combination, to determine the best single aggregate.

Another feature of the technique that might be important for advertising research is its ability to get at connotative judgments so difficult to obtain otherwise. For example, the instrument may be used to determine how close the profile of judgment for a particular brand of beer, say, approximates that for the concept IDEAL BEER in comparison with other competing brands. As one pilot study showed, the instrument was able to differentiate between different brands of beer tasted blindly by subjects, according to their smoothness, mellowness, and so on—all richly connotative terms which may be useful in constructing an advertising campaign.

So far, the research has been concentrated on the use of the semantic differential in judging specific brands or products. There is another kind of advertising to which it might be fruitfully applied—so-called *institutional advertising*. A study that has been proposed in this area would deal with the meanings of various *corporate personalities*—e.g., GENERAL MOTORS, SEARS ROEBUCK, U.S. STEEL, etc. As lawyers who represent such corporations know, the subtle connotations of such terms as "bigness," "power," "fairness," and "honesty" associated with these stereotypes can have substantial effects on public relations and even courtroom decisions. The differential may also be applied in this respect to compare judgments of such concepts across different population groups, and to index the effectiveness of advertising designed to alter these stereotypes.

NOTES

1. Conducted by Dr. H. E. Gulley and Mr. David K. Berlo at the University of Illinois in 1955.
2. Walter B. Essman (University of North Dakota) has reported to us a study in which the degree of self-confidence (indexed by self-ratings on a *stable-unstable* scale) was found to be inversely related to the amount of attitude change toward ESP induced by a lecture on that topic. Helen Peak (University of Michigan) is presently using the semantic differential in an investigation of the structure of attitudes.
3. Applications of the semantic differential to advertising research being made elsewhere include studies by Mary Jane Grunsfeld (Weiss and Geller, Inc., Chicago, Illinois) on brand comparisons, appeal comparisons, blind product testing, etc. Miss Grunsfeld has prepared a "manual" for the use of semantic measurement in advertising.
4. Conducted by Dr. W. A. Mindak at the University of Illinois in 1953.
5. Conducted by Mr. D. Richmond at the University of Illinois in 1953.

WILBUR SCHRAMM

Information Theory
and Mass Communication

FOR MOST OF US, information theory dates back to Claude Shannon's notable article in the *Bell System Technical Journal*, in 1948, but its roots are far older. They reach back at least as far as the statistical mechanics of Boltsmann and Gibbs, Szilard's and von Neumann's treatments of information in physics, Nyquist's and Hartley's work with communication circuits, Wiener's development of cybernetics and Shannon's own earlier work on switching and mathematical logic. But since 1948 the theory has been responsible for significant advances in the design of electronic "brains" and governors, and for deeper understanding of electronic communication generally. It has been applied to the study of biological processes (Quastler and others), human mental processes (Wiener, McCulloch and others), mental tests (Cronbach and others), psycholinguistics (Miller, Osgood, Wilson and others) and the problem of readability (Taylor). Application has, so far, stopped short of mass communication. There has been a feeling that information theory might help us understand what goes on in a newspaper or a broadcast, but we have never been able to say just how.

It is proposed in this paper to take a brief overview of information theory itself, then to examine broadly its applicability to mass communication, and finally to look in more detail at some of the areas of mass communication in which it promises to be most helpful.

Reprinted from *Journalism Quarterly*, Vol. XXXII, (Spring 1955), pp. 131–146, by permission of the author and the publisher. (Copyright, 1955, *Journalism Quarterly*.)

The Nature of Information Theory

Let us be clear at the outset that information theory is not a theory of information in the same sense in which that term is ordinarily used by social scientists. In fact, as Kellogg Wilson has cogently remarked (10), it might well be called a *theory of signal transmission*. Its highly ingenious mathematics are concerned chiefly with the entropy or uncertainty of sequences of events in a system or related systems. Therefore, let us begin by saying what information theory means by "system."

A system is any part of an information chain which is capable of existing in one or more states, or in which one or more events can occur. The vibrating metal diaphragm of a telephone or a microphone is a system. So is the radio frequency amplifier circuit of a radio receiver. So is a telegraph wire. So is the air which carries the pulsations of sound waves. So is the basiliar membrance of the ear. So is the optic nerve. So, in a little different sense, is the semantic system of an individual. Each of these is capable of assuming different states or playing host to different events, and each can be coupled to other systems to make a communication chain.

If information is to be transferred, systems must obviously be *coupled*. We say systems are coupled when the state of one system depends to some degree on the state of the system that adjoins it. Thus when a microphone diaphragm is depressed so as to cause a coil to cut magnetic lines of force and generate a current in a wire, those systems are coupled. When light frequencies strike the eye and cause discharges in the optic nerve, those systems are coupled. A break in the coupling will obviously prevent any information from being transferred. That is what happens when a microwave link goes out during a television broadcast, or when a student's attention wanders in class.

Most human communication chains contain a large number of coupled systems, and they contain one kind of system which Dr. Shannon has not primarily dealt with: the *functional*, as opposed to the *structural*, system. A functional system is one that *learns;* its states depend on its own past operation. The air that carries sound waves or the metal diaphragm of the microphone is a structural system. So is the sensory system of a human being. But the central nervous system, and especially the aspect of it to which we refer as the semantic system, is a functional system. It is capable of learning. It codes and decodes information on the basis of past experience. Incidentally, this is one of the pitfalls in the way of applying information theory mathematics to human communication. These are probability formulas, and if the probabilities are altered—i.e., if any learning takes place—during the experiment, the events can no longer be regarded as a stochastic process and the formula will not apply. It is therefore necessary rigidly to control the learning factor.[1]

Systems may be either *corresponding* or *non-corresponding*. Corresponding systems are capable of existing in identical states. Thus, the sound input of the microphone and the sound output of the loudspeaker are capable of existing in identical states—therefore, corresponding. But the air and the diaphragm are not corresponding. Neither are the diaphragm and the current, or the light signal and the central nervous system.

We can now say what information theory means by *communication*. Communication occurs when two corresponding systems, coupled together through one or more non-corresponding systems, assume identical states as a result of signal transfer along the chain. Unless the sound that goes into the telephone is reproduced by the sound that comes out of the telephone at the other end of the line, we do not have communication. Unless the concept in the semantic system of Mr. A is reproduced in the semantic system of Mr. B., communication has not taken place. Begging the question of whether a meaning as seen by one individual can ever be reproduced exactly by another individual—or whether we can test it accurately enough to be sure—we have no great difficulty in adapting this definition to our common understanding of the term communication.

But when we define *information* in terms of information theory, then we have to get used to a somewhat different approach. We can, of course, measure the "information" transmitted along a communication chain in terms of many kinds of units—letters, morphemes, phonemes, facts (if we can satisfactorily define a fact). But none of these is satisfactory for the precise needs of information theory. Information is there defined in terms of its ability to reduce the uncertainty or disorganization of a situation at the receiving end.

Let us take an example. Suppose I tell you one "fact" about a coin toss and one "fact" about typewriter keys. I tell you that tails will not come up when the coin is next tossed, and that the letter G will not be struck when the next key is depressed on the typewriter. Now it is obvious that the information about the coin is more useful to you than the information about the typewriter in predicting what will happen. You will have no remaining doubt as to which side of the coin will come up, whereas you will still be uncertain which of the remaining 41 keys of the typewriter will be struck. In terms of information theory, *more information* has been transferred about the coin than about the typewriter. When a transmitted signal succeeds in reducing the number of equally probable outcomes at the receiving end by one-half, one *bit* of information is said to have been transferred. (*Bit* comes from *binary digit*.) Thus, when you reduce the two equally probable outcomes of a coin toss to one, you are using one *bit* of information. You can see that the computing of this information readily lends itself to using logarithms to the base 2, rather than our common base 10. In the case of the coin toss, $\log_2 2 = 1$ bit. But it would take

$\log_2 42$ or about 5.4 bits of information to predict which typewriter key would be struck at random, or $\log_2 26$ (4.7 bits) to predict which letter of the alphabet will come up, if one is chosen at random.

This brings us to the basic terms of information theory, *entropy* and *redundancy*. Entropy simply means the uncertainty or disorganization of a system; redundancy is the opposite. Entropy is, of course, a famous term derived from mathematical physics, where it has been used to talk about Newton's second law of thermodynamics. The law that "entropy always increases," said Eddington, "holds, I think, the supreme position among the laws of Nature." It is this law, he also said—the tendency of physical systems to become always more shuffled, less organized—which is the only way we could tell whether a movie of the physical world were being run backward or forward. It is not surprising that Shannon, trying to describe information in terms of the reduction of uncertainty, should use the term entropy and the traditional mathematical symbol for that term, H.

Entropy is measured in terms of the information required to eliminate the uncertainty of randomness from a situation within a system or involving two systems. Entropy will obviously be at its maximum when all states of the system are equally probable—that is, when they occur completely at random, as when a coin is tossed. The formula for maximum entropy is therefore the same as the formula for information,

$$H_{max} = \log_2 n$$

where n is the number of equally probable outcomes.

Most situations with which we deal in human communication do not have equally probable outcomes. For example, the letters of a language do not occur completely at random. If they did, the language would be complete chaos. Because we know that *e* in the English language occurs oftener than any other letter, we give it the simplest symbol in the radio-telegraph code—one dit, or short. Because there are certain combinations of letters and sounds more likely than others to occur together, we find it possible to learn to spell and understand speech. Therefore, in most communication situations, we use entropy formulas which measure the *degree* of predictability and randomness.

In order not to clutter up the path at this point, the principal formulas of information theory have been put in a brief appendix to this paper. The non-mathematical reader need remember only that mathematical tools are available to measure, among other things, the amount of uncertainty in a system (observed entropy), the degree of certainty or predictability in a system (redundancy), the degree of uncertainty in a system (relative entropy), the uncertainty of occurrence of pairs of events (joint entropy), the uncertainty of occurrence of events in sequence (conditional en-

715

tropy), the amount of information transmitted under various conditions, and the capacity of a channel to transmit information.

How Applicable is the Theory?

The concepts of information theory have an insightful quality, an intuitive sort of fit, when they are applied freely to mass communication situations.

For one thing, it is obvious that human communications, like any other kind of communication, is merely a chain of coupled systems, thus,

In mass communication, these chains take on certain remarkable characteristics. They are often very *long*. The account of a news event in India must pass through very many coupled systems before it reaches a reader in Indiana. Again, some of the systems have phenomenally high rates of output compared to their input. Shannon would call them high-gain *amplifiers*. These are the mass media, which have the power to produce many simultaneous and identical messages. Also, in this kind of chain, we have certain networks of systems within systems. Two of these are very important. The mass media themselves are networks of systems coupled in a complicated way so as to do the job of decoding, interpreting, storage and encoding which we associate with all communicators. Likewise, the individual who receives a mass media message is a part of a network of group relationships, and the workings of this network help to determine how he responds to the message.

But each system in the mass communication chain, whatever the kind of system, is host to a series of events which are constrained by their environments and by each other, and therefore to a certain degree predictable and subject to information theory measurements. Much of the scholarly study of mass communication consists of an examination of the constraints on these events, and discovering the dependency of events in one of these systems on events in another system.

For example, a large part of what we call "effects" study is the comparison of events in one system with events in another. A readership study compares the events in a newspaper with the events in an individual's reading behavior. A retention study compares the events in a medium with the events in an individual's recall. And so forth. We have every reason to suspect, therefore, that a mathematical theory for studying electronic communication systems ought to have some carry-over to human communication systems.

Entropy and Redundancy

The term *entropy* is still strange to students of social communication, but *redundancy* is an old and familiar idea. The redundancy concept of information theory gives us no great trouble. Redundancy is a measure of certainty or predictability. In information theory, as in social communication, the more redundant a system is, the less information it is carrying in a given time. On the other hand, any language or any code without redundancy would be chaos. In many cases, increasing the redundancy will make for more efficient communication.

For example, on a noisy teletype line, it helps considerably to have certain probabilities controlling what letters follow others. If a q (in English) occurs followed by two obvious errors, the operator at the receiving end can be quite sure that the q is followed by a u and that the next letter will be another vowel. When a circuit is bad, operators arbitrarily repeat key words twice. Remember the familiar cable language—THIS IS NOT —REPEAT, NOT . . .

The amount of redundancy—using that term freely—is therefore one of the great strategy questions confronting mass communication. The most economical writing is not always the most effective writing. We could write this entire paper in the terse, economical language of mathematics, but that would not necessarily communicate most to the people who will read this paper. A newspaper reporter may choose to explain the term *photosynthesis* in twenty words, which is redundancy unnecessary to a scientist but highly necessary to a layman. There is a kind of rule of thumb, in preparing technical training materials, that two or more examples or illustrations should be given for each important rule or term. There is another rule of thumb, in broadcast commercials, that product names should be repeated three times. All these are strategy decisions, aimed at using the optimum of redundancy. And indeed, finding the optimum degree of redundancy for any given communication purpose is one of the chief problems of encoding.

Relative entropy, as we have pointed out, is merely the other side of the coin from redundancy. The lower the redundancy, the higher the relative entropy.

One of the aspects of human communication where entropy and redundancy measures have already proved their usefulness is in the study of language. Morphemes, phonemes, letters and other linguistic units obviously do not occur in a language completely at random; they are bound by certain sequential relationships, and therefore subject to measures of entropy and redundancy. We know, among other things, that the relative entropy of English is slightly less than 50%.[2] Shannon has estimated, incidentally, that if the relative entropy of the language was only 20%—if the next letter in a sequence were, on the average, 80% predictable—then it would be impossible to construct interesting cross-word puzzles. But if the relative entropy were 70%—if the structure were only 30% redundant—then it would be easily possible to construct *three-dimensional* crossword puzzles (1). This information about crossword puzzles, of course, is not intended to represent the results of modern linguistic scholarship. For a more representative example, see Jacobson, Halle and Cherry on the entropy of Russian phonemes (9).

Wilson Taylor's "Cloze" procedure[3] is one of the interesting ways we have available for use in estimating the entropy or redundancy of prose. Taylor deletes every *n*th word in a passage, and asks readers to supply the missing words. The scatter of different words suggested for each of the missing terms provides a measure of the predictability of the passage to that particular audience. For example, if we present two paragraphs to the same group of 20 readers, and on the average this is the score they make:

Paragraph A

16	specify	word A (correct)
2		B
2		C

Paragraph B

6	specify	word A (correct)
4		B
4		C
3		D
1		E
1		F
1		G

—if we get this result, it is clear that the uncertainty or relative entropy of Paragraph B is considerably greater for this audience than is that of Paragraph A. Paragraph A is apparently more redundant than B. Taylor has gone into this use of information theory in his doctoral dissertation, and it is clear that the redundancy or relative entropy of a passage is closely related to its readability.

If we consider an entire mass medium as a system, then it is evident that the maximum entropy of a newspaper or a broadcasting station is immensely greater than that of a semaphore, a calling card, a personal letter or a sermon. The paper or the station has a very great freedom to do different things and produce strikingly different products. A large newspaper, like the New York *Times*, has higher maximum entropy than a smaller newspaper. If we could devise any way to make a valid comparison, I think we should find that the relative entropy of radio and television would be less than that of newspapers. If this is indeed the case, it may be that the tremendous wordage of broadcasting puts a burden on originality, and the scant feedback to a broadcasting station puts a premium on any formula which has proved popular. A popular program promptly spawns a whole family that look like it. A joke passes quickly from comedian to comedian. We might say that for comedians, joint and conditional entropy are quite low. For comic strips, relative entropy is obviously very low, and redundancy very high.

But it is also evident that no medium uses as much of the available

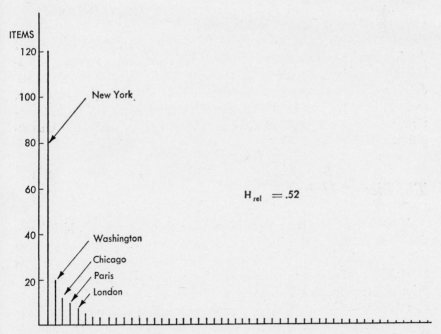

Figure 1—Sources of news by cities.

New York Times, 11/8/54.

freedom as it could. Complete freedom would mean random content. The art of being an editor or a program manager consists in no small degree of striking the right balance between predictability and uncertainty—right balance being defined as the best combination of satisfied anticipation and surprise. From time to time we have tried to quantify this amount of organization or predictability in a mass medium. One of the simpler ways to approach it is to tabulate the news sources in a paper.

For example, Figure 1 is a typical distribution of news items by source in a metropolitan newspaper for one day.

The usual way we handle figures like this is by means of the statistics of central tendency—mean, standard deviation, etc. Suppose we were to handle it by information theory mathematics. If relative entropy were at a maximum, each of these news sources would be represented equally. Actually, the relative entropy of news sources in the *Times* for that day was about 52%. Throughout that week it hung around 50%, minus or plus 5. This seems quite typical of large newspapers. Four Chicago papers, two other New York papers, and the Washington *Post and Times Herald*, all were between 41 and 57% for the same period. The London *Times* and Paris *Figaro* were a little over 40%. During the same period, a radio news wire averaged about 45% relative entropy.

This rather remarkable order of agreement represents a pattern of constraint which, if we understood it completely, would tell us a great deal about mass media. Why do large papers, on the average, use about half the freedom open to them to represent different news sources? Availability is one reason, but the chief reason is simply that this is the editors' definition of what their clientele want, and can absorb, and *should* have, and can be given within the bounds of physical limits and custom. Information theory appears to offer us a new way to study this characteristic of the media.

The Idea of Noise

The idea of noise is another information theory concept which intuitively makes sense in the study of mass communication. Noise, as we have said, is anything in the channel other than what the communicator puts there. Noise may be competing stimuli from inside—AC hum in the radio, print visible through a thin page in a magazine, day-dreaming during a class lecture—or from outside—competing headline cues on a newspaper page, reading a book while listening to a newscast, the buzz of conversation in the library. In general, the strategy of a mass communicator is to reduce noise as much as possible in his own transmission, and to allow for expected noise in the reception. An increase in redundancy, as we have already suggested, may combat noise; a radio announcer may be well advised to repeat a highly important announcement.

The information theory formula for maximum transmission capacity in the face of noise also furnishes some guides as to what can be done.

$$W \log_2 \left(\frac{P + N}{N} \right)$$

This formula is in which W is band width, P is power of transmission, N is noise. In other words, you can approach maximum efficiency by reducing noise, increasing band width or increasing power. Two of the great problems of mass communication, of course, are to understand exactly what is meant by band width and power, for any given situation. Is the band width of a talking picture or television greater than that of a silent picture or radio?[4] Is the band width of a sight-sound medium like television greater than that of print? You can certainly increase band width by using a high fidelity phonograph, but can you also increase it by buying time on more radio stations? Similarly, what constitutes power, in this sense, within persuasive communication? Supposedly, the nature of the arguments and the source will contribute to it. Will talking louder contribute to power, so defined? Will buying bigger ads?

To basic questions like these, information theory is unlikely to contribute except by stimulating insights, but it should be pointed out that there are formulas for calculating noise which may well prove to be useful in tests of learning and retention from mass communication, and in rumor analysis and other functions of communication chains.

Coupling

That brings us to talk of coupling, which is another point at which information theory comes very close to our usual way of thinking about human communication. We are accustomed to think of "gatekeepers." Strictly speaking, every system that couples two other systems is a gatekeeper. But there are certain especially important gatekeepers in mass communication: the reporter walking his beat, the telegraph editor deciding on what to select from the wire, the press association wire filer deciding what stories to pass on, the commentator deciding what aspect of current life to focus on, the magazine editor deciding what parts of the environment to represent, and others. All these are subject to the stability and fidelity measures of information theory: how likely are they to pass on the information that comes to them? How faithfully are they likely to reproduce it?

Even the terms used to talk about fidelity in electronic systems sound familiar to us in light of our experience with mass communication. How much of the information do the gatekeepers *filter out?* How much *fading* and *booming* do they introduce (by changing the emphasis of the message)? How much *systematic distortion* are they reponsible for (through bias)? How much *random distortion* (through carelessness or ignorance)?

The newspaper itself—if we want to consider it as a system—is a gatekeeper of the greatest importance. The daily life of a city presents itself to the paper's input. Selected bits of the daily life of the rest of the world enter the input through the telegraph desk. What comes out? What is the stability of the paper for reproducing local news as compared with national news, civic news as compared with crime news, news of one presidential candidate as compared with news of another? And what about fidelity? To what extent does the paper change its input by cutting, by rewriting, by choosing a headline which affects the meaning, by giving one story better position than another?

Think of the reporter walking his beat. Everything he sees and hears is news for someone, but he must make a selection in term of what his editors and—supposedly—his readers want. His stability is necessarily low. But how is his fidelity? Does he get the quotes from a speech right? Does he report an accident accurately?

Or think of the receiver at the end of the mass communication chain. What stories from the *Reader's Digest*, what items from the newspaper, does he pass on to his friends? And how accurately does he represent the content? Does he reproduce the part of the content which reinforces his previous attitudes? Does he get the point of an article?

Rumor analysis is a fascinating use for the coupling concepts of information theory. What kinds of rumors encourage the stability of the chain—that is, what kinds of rumors will tend to be passed on? And what factors govern how faithfully a rumor is passed on?

Content analysis codes are subject to study for stability and fidelity. How much of the information in the measured content do they respond to? How faithfully do they reproduce it? As a matter of fact, many of the concepts of information theory are stimulating to content study. For example, the heavy redundancy of Communist propaganda shows up from almost any content study, as does the relatively low entropy of the semantic systems within which the Communist propagandist works. The close coupling of units in the Communist propaganda chain is striking. And the stability and fidelity of the Communist gatekeepers, transmitting the official line, are very high. If they are not, the Party gets a new gatekeeper.

Measures of stability and fidelity are available, in information theory, and relatively easy to use. When they are applied to a long chain—such as the one, previously referred to, which carries news from "India to Indiana" and back—it becomes apparent that the stability of the main points along the chain is quite high: that is, a bureau like London is quite likely to pass along a story that comes from New Delhi. The closer one gets to the source of news, the lower the stability, because the input is large, the output capacity relatively small. Bloomington, for example, regularly publishes about 65 local stories, but can only put two or three on the wire. Delhi, likewise, can send London only a small part of the Indian news. Chicago, on the other hand, can send out more than half the stories available. The problem in measuring the fidelity of this kind of chain is to define measurable units. Using length as one criterion, it becomes apparent that the greatest loss is near the source of news. Using rewriting as a criterion, it seems that the chief rewriting is done at the first wire points and the chief national bureaus.

Channel Capacity

Channel capacity is another important concept which is common both to information theory and to mass communication. All channels, human, electronic or mechanical, have an upper limit on their ability to assume different states or carry different events. We can estimate, for example, the amount of information the eye is capable of transmitting to the optic nerve, and it is less than the information available to the eye, although apparently more than the semantic system can handle. We can estimate the capacity of a telephone line or a microphone, and have very good formulas for doing so. But when we consider the characteristics of a chain and recall that the chain is no stronger than its weakest link, then our chief interest turns to the channel capacity of man, who is the weakest link in most communication chains.

Perceptual experiments have told us a great deal about the ability of man to transmit information through some of his systems. In general, we can say that man's ability to handle information is faster than most mechanical systems (such as smoke signals and flags), but far slower than that of most electronic devices (e.g., the electronic computers). We still have a great deal to find out about man's capacity for handling language and pictorial information.

Many of the capacity problems of mass communications, of course, find man at the mercy of his works. The reporter who has only 30 minutes to write his story before deadline, the editor who is permitted to file only 200 words on the wire, the radio news bureau desk which has room for only 13 minutes of copy and must select from 300 stories, the editor who finds a big advertising day crowding out his news—all these are communicators suffering from capacity problems they have helped to make. It is also obvious that the channel capacity of the New York *Times* is greater than that of a small daily. But for the *Times* and its smaller brothers there is an even greater channel restriction: the reader. The reader of a daily can spend, on the average, about 40 minutes on his paper. And he reads rather slowly. Even so, he can read faster than he can listen, so to speak. A radio speaker usually stays under 150 words a minute, not because he cannot talk faster, but because he fears he will crowd the channel capacity of his listeners.

Shannon has developed a theorem for a channel with noise which is both remarkable in itself and highly meaningful for persons concerned with mass communication (1). His theorem says, in effect, that for rates of transmission less than the capacity of a channel it is possible to reduce noise to any desired level by improving the coding of the information to be transmitted; but that for rates of transmission greater than channel capacity it is never possible to reduce noise below the amount by which the rate of transmission exceeds channel capacity. In other words, as Wilson notes, error can be reduced as much as desired if only the rate of transmission is kept below the total capacity of the channel; but if we overload the channel, then error increases very swiftly.

Information theory thus promises us real assistance in studying the capacity of channels. For example, in a recent publication (10) an information theory model is proposed to measure an individual's channel capacity for semantic decoding. Verbal information is to be fed the individual at increasing rates. This information consists of a group of adjectives describing an object. The receiver is asked to respond in each case by touching the corresponding object, in a group of objects, in front of him. (He has already over-learned this response, so supposedly no learning takes place during the experiment.) The time from the stimulus until the subject touches an object is taken as the total time for decoding and encoding. It is hypothesized that as the rate increases this total time will decrease until it becomes stable. As the rate increases further, the number of errors will

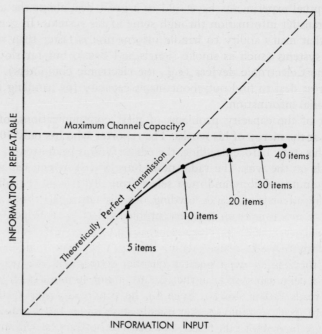

Figure 2—Ability to repeat information from newscasts.

begin to increase, until at a certain rate the time will become highly variable and the process will break down. The rate at which the total time becomes stable is taken as the optimum channel capacity, because it is there that the largest amount of accurate information is being transmitted.

This experiment has not yet been done with the accurate controls which would be required, but some striking confirmation of it comes out of experiments with retention of newscasts. Subjects were presented newscasts of increasing density but constant length—5, 10, 20, 30, 40, 50 items. The average subject's ability to recall the subject of these items leveled off very sharply between 10 and 20. There was practically no additional learning between 20 and 30. After 20, the number of errors began to increase rather sharply. In other words, the amount of information transmitted behaved about as hypothesized above, and the resulting curve was strikingly like those typically resulting from experiments on the capacity of subjects to discriminate among stimuli—as shown in Figure 2.

Networks

Of all the potential contributions of information theory to mass communication, perhaps the most promising is in the study of communication networks. Networks are as important in mass communication as in electronic communication. Every functional group is a communication network. The staff of a newspaper or a broadcasting station, a film production crew, the group with which a member of the mass communication audience talks over what he reads, hears and sees—all these are communication networks. The inter-communication within the network is measurable, whether it consists of conversation, print, gestures or electronic currents.

Osgood and Wilson, in a mimeographed publication,[5] have suggested a series of measures derived from information theory, for dealing with groups. In addition to the common entrophy, redundancy, noise, fidelity and capacity measures, they suggest *traffic* (what members do the most talking, and how much talking is done?), *closure* (to what extent is the group a closed corporation?), and *congruence* (to what extent do members participate equally in the communication of the group, or to what extent are there members who are chiefly talkers and others who are chiefly listeners?). All these formulations can be dealt with mathematically. Measures like these suggest a quite different and stimulating way of studying small groups, and in particular they commend themselves for use in studying the important groups within mass communication.

Suppose, for example, we want to study some part of the world news network. Suppose that we take the chief newspapers of the leading cities in half a dozen countries—for example, the United States, Great Britain,

France, Germany, Italy and the Soviet Union—and tabulate for one week the stories which the papers in each city carry from the other cities in the network. This has been done in a small way, with interesting results. Washington has the greatest output traffic, New York the greatest input traffic. Moscow has the greatest degree of individual closure: that is, it is most likely to talk, if at all, to itself. Within a country, there are startling differences in the amount and distribution of input. In general there appears to be a little more organization (redundancy) in the pattern of input than in the pattern of output: that is, source entropy is higher than destination entropy. And the congruence (the correlation between source and destination frequencies of points in the network) varies markedly with political conditions and cultural relationships at a particular time.

Let us take a simpler example of group communication. Here is a record of telephone calls amongst four boys (who telephoned incessantly). The calls were tabulated at periods two months apart—20 calls while the boys were organizing a school newspaper, and 20 calls two months later after the paper was well launched.

Twenty Telephone Calls by Four Boys

A. In process of organizing a school newspaper:

	Mike	Bud	Mike T.	John	
Mike		4	4	2	10
Bud	3		1	2	6
Mike T.	1	1		0	2
John	1	1	0		2
	5	6	5	4	

B. After school newspaper had been published 2 months:

	Mike	Bud	Mike T.	John	
Mike		3	1	1	5
Bud	7		1	0	8
Mike T.	5	1		0	6
John	1	0	0		1
	13	4	2	1	

It is clear that the relative transitional entropy of this group became less in the two months—that is, it became better organized—and also that the congruence had changed so that increasingly one pattern could be predicted: i.e., the boys would call Mike. It seems that whereas Mike must have been the organizer at first, he became the leader later, and the other boys turned to him for advice or instructions.

This kind of result suggests the hypothesis that the entropy of communication within a functional group decreases as the group becomes more fully organized into work roles and better perceives the existence of leadership. By way of testing this and preparing the way for studying actual media staffs, some experiments have been done with groups of five journalism students who were given assignments that simulated the work of an actual newspaper staff, including reporting, reference, editing, copyreading and setting in type. All their intercommunications were recorded.

Not enough groups have yet been put through the procedure to reveal all the variables, but the pattern so far is very clear and interesting. Some of the groups were started on their assignments entirely unstructured—that is, no roles were assigned. In others a leader was appointed. In still others, every person was assigned a job. Inasmuch as some measure of leadership almost always appeared, regardless of assignment, participants were asked at the end whether they perceived a leader or leaders, and if so, whom? This, in general, seems to be the pattern:

(*1*) As the perception of leadership increases, the relative transitional entropy of communication in the group decreases—that is, it becomes easier to predict who will talk to whom.

(*2*) As the degree of initial organization is increased, the total amount of communication decreases and the total time required to do the job decreases.

(*3*) However, between the group in which a leader is appointed and the group in which all members are assigned roles, these measures change much less than between the other groups and the unstructured group. In some cases, the group in which a leader only was appointed actually finished the job more quickly than the group in which all roles were assigned. This suggests that there may be a stage in which increasing organization does not contribute to efficiency; and also, that it must make a difference who is appointed leader, even in these previously unacquainted groups.

These results are presented only to suggest that the approach is a promising one for group study, and especially for the study of the kind of functional groups that play such an important part in mass communication.

Finally

How can we sum up the import of all this for the study of mass communication?

Even such a brief overview as this must make it clear that information theory is suggestive and stimulating for students of human communication. It must be equally clear that the power of the theory and its stimulating analogic quality are greatly at variance with the puny quality of the mathematical examples I have been able to cite—that is, examples of the use so far made of information theory mathematics in studying mass communication. Why should this be?

The theory is now—1948, as I have said, for most of us. Its application is fringed with dangers. One of these has been indicated—the danger of working with stochastic processes in functional systems which may learn and thereby change the probabilities. It should also be said that we do not as yet know much about the sampling distributions of these entropy formulas, and it is therefore not always wise to use them for hypothesis testing and statistical inference. Finally, we must admit frankly the difficulty of bridging the gap between the formula's concept of information (which is concerned only with the number of binary choices necessary to specify an event in a system) and our concept of information in human communication (which is concerned with the relation of a fact to outside events—e.g., how "informative" is it?).

This is not to say that the transfer cannot be made. Certainly I have no intention of saying that the theory has only analogic value, and that the contribution of its mathematical tools is necessarily small. These tools seem to me to be extremely promising in the study of language, channel capacities, couplings, and network groups, if nowhere else. It will be to our advantage to explore these uses and others.

Appendix

THE BASIC FORMULAS

It may be helpful to explain the basic entropy formula here in order to give a better idea of what information theory has to offer mathematically.

Let us begin with an event which we call i within a system which we can call I.[6] (For example i may be the yellow light on a traffic light I.) Then let us call $p(i)$ the probability of event i occurring within the system. This is equivalent to saying that $p(i)$ equals $1/a$, in which a is a certain number of equally probable classes. (For example, the yellow light in a traffic light occurs two times in four events, so that its probability is $1/2$.) The information we need to predict the occurrence of event i is therefore $\log_2 a$. By algebraic transformation, we can say that, since $p(i)$ equals $1/a$, a equals $1/p(i)$. Therefore the information necessary to specify the one event i is $\log_2(1/p(i))$. Since the logarithm of x/y always equals $\log x - \log y$, we have the information necessary to specify event i equals to $\log_2 1 - \log_2 p(i)$. The log of 1 is always zero, and therefore we arrive at an equation which states the amount of information necessary to specify one event in a system (let us call this information $h(i)$),

$$h(i) = -\log_2 p(i)$$

Now what we need is an estimate of the average amount of entropy associated with all the states of a system. The average of a sample of numbers can be expressed as

$$\sum_i \frac{i \, f(i)}{n}$$

where i is the numerical value of any class of numbers, f(i) is the frequency of occurrence of that class, n is the sample size, and Σ is the term

$$i$$

for sum of all the i's. But f(i)/n is the same as an estimate of probability, which we called p (i), and which we can here substitute in the term for an average as follows:

$$\Sigma\ i\ p(i)$$
$$i$$

Therefore, if we want the average amount of information needed to predict the occurrence of the states of a system I, we can use this term and substitute the information symbol for the numerical value, thus,

$$H(I) = \Sigma\ h(i)\ p(i),\ or$$
$$i$$
$$H(I) = -\ \Sigma\ p_i \log_2 p(i)$$
$$i$$

This last expression is the basic formula for observed entropy.

It is clear that this formula will equal zero when the probability of one event is unity and the probability of all other events is zero: in other words, when there is no uncertainty in the system. It is also clear that the formula will approach H_{max} (which, you will remember, is $\log_2 n$) as the events in the system become more nearly equally probable, so that there is maximum uncertainty in the system. In a coin toss, for example, observed entropy is the same as maximum entropy ($\log_2 2$, or 1) because the events are equally probable. However, the more events in a system, the higher the observed entropy is likely to grow. Therefore, it becomes useful to have a measure by which to compare systems which have different numbers of states. This is the formula for *relative entropy*, which is simply the observed entropy of a system divided by its maximum entropy—

$$H_{rel}(I) = \frac{H(I)}{H_{max}}$$

From the basic formula, we get the formula for *joint entropy*, which is simply the entropy for the occurrence of pairs of events (for example, q and u together in a sample of English words) and which is written,

$$H(I,J) = -\ \Sigma\ p(i,j)\log_2 p(i,j)$$
$$i,j$$

This is read exactly like the basic entropy formula except that (i,j) stands for the occurrence of events n and j together. We also get a formula for *conditional entropy*, which deals with the occurrence of two events in se-

729

quence (for example, the occurrence of u after q in a sample of English words). This is written,

$$H_iJ = \sum_{i,j} p(i,j)\log_2 p_1(j)$$

in which p_{ij} represents the probability of the occurrence of j after i has occurred.

Among the other formulas available are those for redundancy (basically, $1 - H_{tel}$), amount of information transmitted, channel capacity, noise and maximum effective coding in the face of noise. It is not believed necessary to speak in any greater detail of these measures at this point, inasmuch as the purpose of these pages is to give a general idea of the theory rather than a complete description of it.

Computing the Commoner Measures

Maximum entropy, of course, may be computed simply by taking the log (to the base 2) of the total number of events in the system.

In computing the other entropy measures from social data, it will be necessary to estimate the probabilities of events within systems by counting frequencies of occurrence over some uniform time period. For example, if a traffic light were a new phenomenon to us, we might count the occurrence of red, yellow and green events for a certain length of time and get, say, 10 each for red and green, 20 for yellow, out of 40 events. From these we should estimate the probability of red and green as $\frac{1}{4}$ each, of yellow as $\frac{1}{2}$. To estimate the probabilities of events in two systems or of sequential events in one system, it is helpful to use a table like this one:

Having computed the values of $H(I)$, $H(J)$, $H(I,J)$ from this kind of table, the values of the conditional entropies may be obtained, if desired, by the following relationships:

$$H_I(J) = H(I,J) - H(I)$$
$$H_J(I) = H(I,J) - H(J)$$

It is not necessary to do all the calculation which would seem to be required to turn the probabilities into entropy scores, if one uses such a table as that of Dolansky and Dolansky (see bibliography) which is recommended to anyone making extensive use of these formulas.

A Short List of Readings on Information Theory

The basic theory:

Shannon, C. E., and Weaver, Warren, *The Mathematical Theory of Communication.* Urbana, 1949. (Contains the classical article by Shannon, with comments by Weaver. For readers without a good mathematical background, Weaver is a better beginning article than Shannon.)

Wiener, Norbert, *Cybernetics.* New York, 1948. (Stimulating in that it contains much of the viewpoint for Shannon's later development.)

Fano, R. M., *The Transmission of Information.* MIT Technical Reports 65 and 149. Cambridge, 1949–50. (Highly mathematical.)

Goldman, Stanford, *Information Theory.* New York, 1953. (Textbook for graduate students in electrical engineering.)

Miller, G. A., "What Is Information Measurement?", *American Psychologist,* 8:3–11 (1953). (Non-technical, and a good beginning point for non-mathematicians.)

Tables for Computing Information Theory Measures:

Dolansky, L., and Dolansky, M. P., *Table of $\log_2 1/p$, $p \log_2 1/p$, $p \log_2 +$ $(1-p) \log_2 (1-p)$.* MIT Technical Report 277. Cambridge, 1952. (The most complete tables.)

Newman, E. B., "Computational Methods Useful in Analyzing Series of Binary Data," *American Journal of Psychology,* 64:252–62 (1951).

Examples of Applications:

Garner, W. H., and Hake, H. W., "The Amount of Information in Absolute Judgments," *Psychological Review,* 58:446–59 (1951). (Joint and conditional entropy used to measure stimulus-response relationships.)

Jakobson, R., Halle, H., and Cherry, E. C., "Towards the Logical Description of Languages in Their Phonemic Aspect," *Language,* 29:34–46 (1953).

Osgood, C. E., editor, Sebock, T. A., and others, *Psycholinguistics: A Survey of Theory and Research Problems.* Supplement to *International Journal of American Linguistics,* 20:4 (1954). (Sections on information theory are stimulating and easy to read; they are written mostly by K. Wilson.)

NOTES

1. Which may be accomplished either by keeping the periods of experimentation very short, or by using a response already over-learned.

2. This is calculated as follows: The maximum entropy of 26 English

letters is $\log_2 26$ or about 4.7 bits per letter. The sequential entropy of groups of eight letters as they occur in English usage is about 2.35 bits per letter. Therefore, the relative entropy is 2.35/4.7 or about .5. This would be lower if we figured sequential entropy for sequences longer than eight letters.

3. See Wilson L. Taylor, "Cloze Procedure: A New Tool for Measuring Readability," JOURNALISM QUARTERLY, 30:415–33 (Fall 1953).

4. Putting simultaneous and reinforcing cues in a single band of communication supposedly adds to the "power" of a message. For example, a speaker may emphasize a point by speaking louder, by pausing just before the key word, by gestures, by facial expression, etc. But suppose one of these cues is not congruent with the others. For example, suppose the speaker winks in the midst of all this seriousness. Or suppose his voice trails up when it should go down. This seems to be the way we use simultaneous cues in a wide band to represent satire or humor or irony.

5. "A Vocabulary for Talking about Communication," colloquium paper, Institute of Communications Research, University of Illinois.

6. This explanation of the formula for observed entropy in general follows the approach of Wilson in bibliography item (10). Wilson's treatment of the subject is easy to read and still both solid and stimulating, and is recommended to beginners in this field.

WILLIAM MCPHEE

Note on a Campaign Simulator

THIS IS A PRELIMINARY REPORT on experiments conducted during 1960 with a working model of the formation of opinion in response to election campaign appeals. The model is of the computer simulation type.[1] It does the following:

1. Accepts as initial input a miniature electorate consisting of a 1:1 representation of each respondent in a sample survey

2. Then sets this replica of the electorate "in motion" toward conceivable future states of affairs, with opinions changing or not as a function of:

    a. Internal processes of the model such as discussion and learning

    b. External inputs of new stimuli representing subsequent campaign appeals

3. Until finally the survey population is reported back, along with analytic information, as it would stand on "election day."

4. Such outcomes depend on assumptions (2b), which are next varied, the trial campaign repeated, and so on, thus analyzing the original situation by "realizing" its different dynamic possibilities.[2]

Needless to say, all this is highly experimental. The 1960 tests were made possible by data kindly supplied by Elmo Roper, Inc., who to assist this purpose modified some of its customary procedures in a survey for Columbia Broadcasting System of the Wisconsin Presidential primary between Humphrey, Kennedy, and Nixon.[3] The model has not and will not be used for a party or candidate.

Reprinted from *Mass Behavior*, (1963), pp. 169–183, by permission of the author and the publisher. (Copyright, 1963, The Free Press, New York.)

1. Technique

We choose for illustration of the technique one major problem on which the 1960 tests with practical data made progress beyond previous academic work on the theory, reported in detail elsewhere.[4] The problem is how an "appeal" or similar event in the external campaign can be represented realistically. That is, how can live content from actual situations be used to characterize the input that, in turn, affects internal processes? About the latter processes, one needs to know only the general idea in Figure 1 for present purposes.

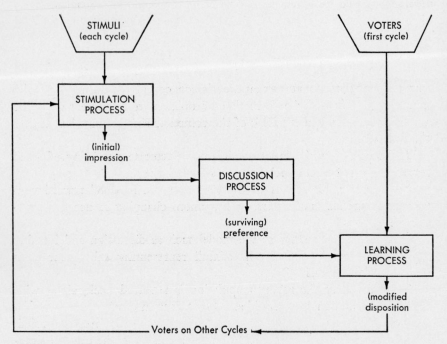

Figure 1—Flow chart of the model.

As Figure 1 suggests, the scheme works so that:

1. "Voters" representing prior survey respondents proceed around an endless loop of response to, discussion of, and further learning from *samples* of new stimuli

2. Which they pick up from a now-developing "campaign," whose new events are represented by changing *distributions* of stimuli that are available for sampling by voters of different groups.

The second point is the problem here and seems not intuitive. The idea is that an appeal or issue or news event is a *distribution* of stimuli.

Actually, this is a familiar fact of life in other guises. As one example, suppose we wish to test in a survey the strength of appeal of a given argument for a given cause. Most persons would agree that this requires, if we want to reflect the full variation of appeal that such an argument has for

Figure 2a—Scale for rating the appeal of an argument for (candidate).

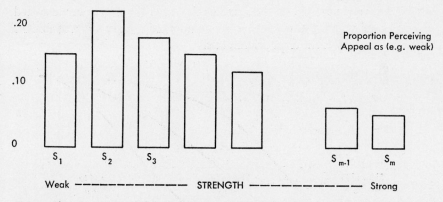

Figure 2b—Proportion of people perceiving each such strength of its appeal.

different people, some kind of scale of gradation as across Figure 2a. Then a person indicates on the scale how compelling he perceives this argument to be in behalf of cause X.

Over many people, answers are dispersed, as in distribution like Figure 2b. Thus, the notion of "the" appeal of an argument is actually *many* appeals, a distribution. For reasons made evident below, call this a "perceptual distribution."

Next, while the connection between the two is ordinarily not drawn, there is another idea familiar in survey analysis that illustrates what is meant by the *effect* of such an appeal. As one example, consider how poll analysts predict "turnout" in response to the election attraction. They make an index locating people along a general scale of disposition to vote. Then they establish a cutting point, above which the sample is treated as representative of voters, below nonvoters. For our purposes this is the same as giving the former probability 1 and the latter 0 of responding. Pollers know this is a simplification and that there is actually a sequence of increasing probabilities of voting as one proceeds up the scale.[5] Call this sequence, some function of the basic disposition, a "response curve."

The *form* of this function, while it probably always increases monotonically with increasing disposition, is obviously conditional on the stimulus situation. If the appeal is great, for example, a Roosevelt or Eisenhower on the ticket, then "fair weather friends" of the party come out in unusual numbers. That is, the response curve bulges up at low and intermediate disposition levels, where it is ordinarily undependable. Whereas on a rainy day with a dull content, the curve is concave. "Only the diehards" at high disposition levels respond with high probability. Lazarsfeld calls these different functions evoked by different stimulus items "trace lines," but for present purposes they are best referred to as *conditional* response functions; that is, functions of the disposition but in a way that is conditional on the stimulus situation. Figure 3 gives idealized examples, of which the vertical is the (smoothed) curve of probabilities of response at different disposition levels.

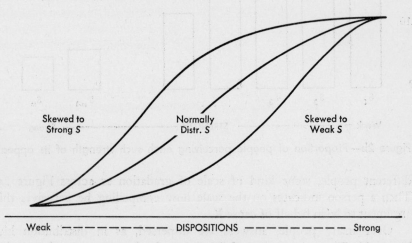

Weak ——————————— DISPOSITIONS ——————————— Strong

Figure 3—Response functions from *s* distributions.

Now, what one of the three processes of the model, the stimulation process, accomplishes as its contribution to the total is to *connect* the two problems above. It takes as input "appeals" that are actually distributions of stimuli that vary in their perceived cogency. Then the "impressions" that voters gain from sampling these stimuli are, when aggregated, varying forms of a function of the basic disposition, for example, of general party tendency. This basic disposition is always controlling. (All variants are some monotonic function of it.) But the idea of the effect of a stimulus situation is to change the *form* of the response curve in favorable or unfavorable ways.

The mechanism that elicits a single response for each individual voter was designed without such any explicit statistical connection in mind. Its assumption is like that revealed in Guttman scales.[6] The weaker the person's disposition, the stronger the attraction needed to elicit a "yes" impression. The stronger the disposition, the weaker the attraction needed and thus the *more* stimulus items that would be acceptable (or more likely a single random stimulus encountered will be acceptable, since in the model they are only sampled, one at a time).

An aggregate statistical version of these individual assumptions, however, better reveals the remarkably simple connection between dispersion of appeal and form of response. Assume that a broad appeal is presented to various people, for example, Senator Humphrey stressed the "farm" issue as an appeal in his behalf to Wisconsin people in 1960. Assume that this is not the same stimulus for each person, but different stimuli of different cogency as arguments for the given cause. Let this appeal be a random variable, s, that could take values between 0 and 1, the values being grades of attractiveness or cogency as an argument for the cause. The sample space might be thought of as continuous, if one wishes, but empirical cases would tend to cluster in discrete gradations, m in number, $s = 0 \leq s = s_1 < s = s_2 = \ldots < s = s_m \leq 1.0$, in order of attractiveness or acceptability.

Table 1—Rule for Accepting Perceived Appeal

			Appeal				
			WEAK			STRONG	
		s_0	s_1	s_2	$\ldots$	s_{m-1}	s_m
Strong	P_m		OK	OK		OK	OK
	P_{m-1}			OK		OK	OK
	.						
Disposition	.						
	.						
	P_2					OK	OK
Weak	P_1						OK
	P_0						

In many applications, this variation would be due to the variable attractiveness of different *interpretations* that can be placed on the stimulus content, as different people see it in their sampling of the news. For example, in social distance scales and perhaps in an actual civil rights issue in the South, the idea of "Negroes and whites eating together" could strike some people as an argument about eating together in restaurants, others about eating together at home. Persons with little disposition to be friendly to the opposite race would accept only the former, while those of friendlier disposition would accept either.

The higher the disposition, the more grades of interpretation would be acceptable. Therefore, define these gradations in conjunction with a corresponding classification of people's disposition levels, p, also between 0 and 1. Since the higher p is, the more stimuli would be acceptable, define the top gradation, where *all* m stimuli would be, as $p = p_m$ (with $p_m \leqq 1.0$). Define the next lower disposition as one where all but the weakest stimulus, $s = s_1$, should be acceptable, and call it $p = p_{m-1}$. And so on down by decreasing disposition, $p = p_{m-2} > p = p_{m-3} > \ldots > p = p_{m-m} \geqq 0$, where no stimulus would be acceptable.

Then, if persons of different dispositions are exposed to stimuli or interpretations of different strength, the rule is the same as in Guttman scales. This is made intuitive in Table 1. For the record, a (rather non-intuitive) formal version of Table 1 is:

If $s = s_i$ and $p = _j$, then
$i > j$ implies: yes, acceptable
$i \leqq j$ implies: no, not acceptable (1)

We account for the observed error in real scales and for probabilistic answers generally, for example, in latent-structure analysis, by noting that in the empirical world those methods must try to measure response to one "whole" appeal. Whereas that appeal is here visualized as a set of sub-stimuli, and we postulate that people only *sample* from all such possible subinterpretations.[7]

When a homogenous social group samples from the same array of such substimuli, let $s = s_i$ occur with probability x_i. For example, in sampling the news, x_i might be the frequency of "exposure" of people to interpretations at this ith level of attractiveness. Then an over-all appeal is a set of such frequencies, $F(s)$, where $F(s) = x_1, x_2, x_3, \ldots, x_m$. For example, $F(s)$ might be a normal dispersion around some mean s value.

By the assumptions above, the probability of "yes," or acceptable answers, $Pr\ (yes|p_j)$ at each level of disposition, p_j would be a simple sequence:

$$Pr\ (yes|p_1) = x_m$$
$$Pr\ (yes|p_2) = x_m + x_{m-1}$$
$$Pr\ (yes|p_3) = x_m + x_{m-1} + x_{m-2}$$

$$\cdot$$
$$\cdot$$
$$\cdot$$

$$Pr\ (yes|p_m) = x_m + x_{m-1} + \ldots x_2 + x_1$$

This function is the abstraction in the model corresponding to a "response curve" in real data. We see the simple way it depends on the abstraction, $F(s)$, a concept very close to the distributions earlier called "perceptual distributions" in real data. The former is simply a *cumulative* version of the frequencies, or probabilities, of the latter.[8] But it is accumulated backwards, starting with the probabilities of high stimuli that are the only ones cogent to persons at the low end of the disposition scale. For example, Figure 3 showed how skewed distributions of many *high* or compelling *s* bring out the "fair weather friends" at *lower* dispositions. In contrast, "only the diehard" very high on the basic disposition still responds well when $F(s)$ is such that lower or weaker *s* are most common.

Both the p_i and the s_i are technically unobservables; but a fair approximation to the former, the location of people relative to one another along a disposition scale, is provided by scaling methods. Latent structure was used.[9] Table 2 illustrates how it converts a person's answers to five or more qualitative questions (with + yes, − no, in the table) into a relative location along the disposition scale.

The stimulus distributions $F(s)$ are the problem. One each is needed for each appeal as it bears on each candidate, within each homogenous

Table 2—How Patterns of Answers Locate People Along a Disposition Scale

	ANSWERS OF PERSONS		
Question	i	j	k
1	+	+	+
2	+	−	+
3	−	+	+
4	−	−	−
5	−	−	+
	.	.	.
	.	.	.
	.	.	.
$P_\bullet$	P_i	P_j	P_k P_m

demographic group, of which 20 groups were used in stratifying Wisconsin. The mechanically best raw data from which to postulate the form of such a stimulus distribution, to use as input to a given group in the model, are the dispersions of answers obtained when *real* members of the corresponding group in a prior survey were asked to rate how the given appeal struck them as an argument for the given cause (on scales like that shown in Figure 2 earlier).[10]

Answers cannot be used in the raw, of course. All such distributions of answers are averaged. This average is then equated with a *standard* distribution of $F(s)$ that is known to bring out the best possible response function we can postulate in the absence of other information (the expected values when the p_i are used as if probabilities.).[11] Then every particular distribution of perceptions, of each argument for each cause rated by every group separately, is expressed as a set of deviations from the empirical average. These deviations are then transformed into a corresponding set of deviations from the standard $F(s)$. Absolute scale connecting p's and s's is unknown.[12] But since the set of p's is the same for all appeals, the variation in each's effect is almost wholly due to how the survey respondents in each and every group perceived it to differ from other test appeals. Thus, *relative* effect of different appeals is here an issue not substantially different from survey validity generally.[13]

2. An Illustrative Problem

Figures 4 and 5 give a very brief illustration of some results. The purpose is to study dynamics, in the model but reflecting what official returns in Wisconsin indicated was necessary to get from the original survey situation, almost a month before, to the final vote.

Since it was legal to cross over into either primary, without registration, we treat it as a three-way race. The chief change was a disap-

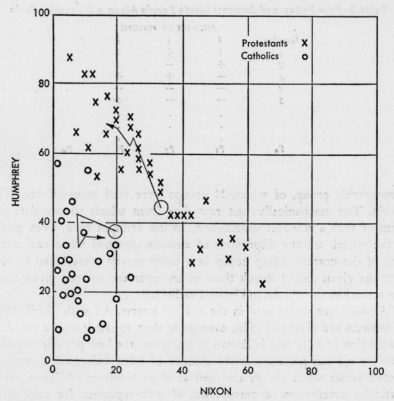

Figure 4—Humphrey farm issue among farmers in northwestern Wisconsin.

pearance of 25–30 per cent of the intended vote in the Republican column where Nixon was uncontested, a drop from about 40 per cent to under 30 per cent of the total.[14] In each figure along the bottom is shown this Nixon percentage of the three-way vote. The vertical here happens to be the Humphrey percentage. Thus, a point defines these two votes at any time, and their difference from 100 per cent is the Kennedy vote. (Since Kennedy opposed Humphrey, his direction is down.) Movements across the plane represented by the arrows are the *changes* in the vote division, reported by the model. For instance, the start of each arrow is the model's best estimate as of the original survey (although N's are only 20 to 50 cases in any one such homogeneous group).

The test problem shown is one which, in principle, could have been fully analyzed before the election, because it was plainly impending. It is the question:

What would happen if the Democratic contest were "heated up" by using Humphrey's and Kennedy's strongest appeals, while simultaneously *weakening Nixon* as an attraction? That is, if we relax one of the three forces in a previously "taut" situation (most votes committed), which of the other two would now benefit?

This was simulated for all candidates in all 20 population groups simultaneously, but we illustrate the best situation for the underdog, Humphrey. Figure 4 shows Humphrey's strongest group, farmers in his bastion of the northwest half of the state. And the issue that Kennedy and Humphrey are stressing in this illustrative model run is also Humphrey's best—"farm" appeal. Given ideal circumstances, he runs away with the vote. (The upper arrow moves dramatically to the upper left, which is high for Humphrey and low for Kennedy and Nixon.)

And these ideal circumstances were realized by Humphrey in this group, in part, in the actual election. This is shown by the asterisks or X's on Figure 4. Each is a precinct vote in the official election.[15] The precincts contained comparable types of people (farmers) in the same part of the state. The X precincts suggest a response much like the model's: where Nixon's hold on certain normally Republican groups was relaxed, paradoxically it was Humphrey who benefited. Why didn't he forge ahead, then, when the Nixon vote relaxed, as it did in the real campaign as well?

As Humphrey's first problem, note that the upper arrows in each chart and the related X precincts concern Protestants only. The lower arrow (model) and the open circles (precincts) are Catholics. The latter went to Kennedy even under the ideal circumstances we set in motion here for Humphrey. And in virtually all groups over the state, the model and the official precincts showed much the same. Next, as a sec-

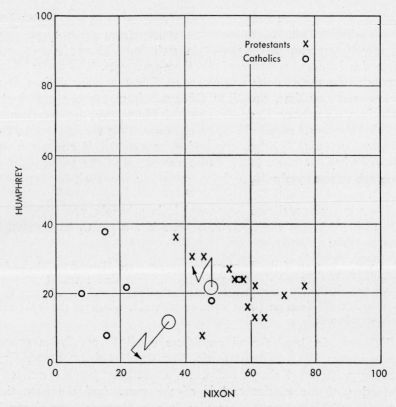

Figure 5—Humphrey farm issue among town middle class in northwestern Wisconsin.

ond and more serious problem for Humphrey, now consider Figure 5. It is selected exactly to match the groups in the first. The one difference is that these are now middle-class rural townspeople. They are similar to farmers except that, unlike farmers but like most other Republican groups in the state, they did not have such an immediate stake in the "farm" problem of 1960 that was Humphrey's strongest appeal and that he stressed in the real campaign (and in this model run). Among such people, the farm issue, and indeed most Humphrey appeals, tended not to "go anywhere." For, other than what Humphrey already had, the remaining Protestants were mostly traditional Republican types. They held, weak appeal or not, for *Nixon*. (Both model arrow and precincts stayed to the low right center.)[16]

In a greater or a usually somewhat lesser degree all over the state, this same situation was revealed: Humphrey was in a "squeeze" between Kennedy and Nixon. With Kennedy holding much of the Catholic vote and getting more with each move, Humphrey's potential was in the remaining Protestant vote. But most of that is normally *Republican,* and thus the presence of Nixon on the ballot tied down the other main bloc of votes, the only major exception being farmers[17] like those shown in Figure 4 and to a lesser degree urban lower-income Protestants. Humphrey fell, then, between two blocs.

As a result, the net outcome of the test problem above was that the weakening of the Nixon appeal released a (high) proportion of Republican Catholics for Kennedy that almost exactly matched a (lower) proportion of the more numerous Protestant groups who were less willing to leave Nixon for Humphrey. Thus, even though the total cross over party lines in the final weeks was perhaps 25–30 per cent of the original Nixon vote—at least 10–12 per cent of the total—it left the statewide ratio between Kennedy and Humphrey almost exactly the same![18]

Judging from the vote versus the survey, there was also little net trend in that two-way ratio in Wisconsin either. Therefore, a lot of "dynamics" went nowhere, in the net trend, a result that is, if disappointing, realistic.

NOTES

1. This academic theory of processes is unrelated to an interesting model of the actual U.S. electorate built by Ithiel Pool and Robert Abelson for the 1960 campaign. Data are acknowledged in the text and, among other collaborators, Charles Higby of the University of Wisconsin was helpful in these tests.

2. The original model was designed for the study of whole electoral systems over long periods. It defines the time period as different elections, for example, every four years instead of, say, every week or two in this case. Extensive reinterpretation of variables is necessary in the shortened time version, but the abstract structure proved retainable.

3. Tests not reported here were also made with 1956 data from the files of the Roper Opinion Research Center, Williams College.

4. In W. McPhee and W. Glaser, eds., *Public Opinion and Congressional Elections* (New York: The Free Press of Glencoe, 1962).

5. See the papers by H. Freeman and W. Glaser in *Public Opinion and Congressional Elections, op. cit.*

6. See, as a widely available reference, Guttman's contribution in *Measurement and Prediction,* Vol. IV of the series, "Studies in Social Psychology in World War II," Samuel A. Stouffer, ed. (Princeton, N.J.: Princeton University Press, 1950).

7. This implies that if we really knew what people were responding to, e.g., as Asch used to question experimental subjects about what they perceived the stimulus content to mean that response would *not* be stochastic. People answer "as they see it" (to what they see).

8. Technically the *distribution* (cumulative) *function,* reversed to start at the high levels, if the expected frequencies $x_1, x_2, \ldots$ were approximated by some function of s, as we imply they could be by the notation $F(s)$.

9. With $p_i =$ "probability of being in class I" assigned to people respond-

743

ing in a given pattern, in Lazarsfeld's two-class model described in *Measurement and Prediction, op. cit.* Different but comparable scales are made for *each* candidate or party. For example, disposition to party *B* is not just the complement of that to party *A*, although empirically that tends to be so.

10. This mechanically ideal form of data is being approached in recent work since Wisconsin. In that case, to cover a wider range of issues compactly, questions of the kind "Which candidate is best for (farm, etc.)?" were used. The answers can be transformed only into linear $F(s)$.

11. This obviously has to be kept in mind in choice of scale. The p_i used, "probabilities of being in Class I" in Lazarsfeld's two-class model, were tested by Murray Gendell as to their correspondence to subsequent turnout probabilities in a panel study of the 1950 election. The correspondence is not systematically bad. In practice, the results in 1956 and 1960 tests were not significantly different from poll predictions based on the same data.

12. One can change it to make response to all appeals "livelier" or "stickier," but cannot influence the relative response to different issues differently, which is determined empirically as above.

13. For example, in tests with both 1956 and 1960 data the model drew no conclusions about the relative effect of different issues not plainly evident in the original surveys used. The model adds something only where there are further complications, as in the differential response of 20 different groups to a three-way contest in the Nixon-Humphrey example below.

14. Roper made the survey prior to the main campaigning and, of course, did not attempt to say what would happen to the uncontested Nixon vote. (Nixon did not campaign.)

15. All relevant precincts from an analysis carried out with detailed demographic data by historian Lee Benson for other purposes.

16. No pretense at "fit" is made, and these illustrations chosen for other reasons are a little *better* than the average. A crude test of portraying dynamics would be for the model to move closer to the precincts in the 20 subgroups than the survey a month before. The model would "pass" this test well, but *only* by choosing its stimuli in the light of the outcome (weak Nixon and selected strong Humphrey appeals to go with the generally strong Kennedy appeals).

17. A model that shows "what could be" also suggests "what might have been." The chief potential of the latter kind was, by every indication, an impending farm revolt against the Republicans in 1960, muted later by the nomination of Kennedy. Usually Protestant farmers were the most volatile in leaving the Republicans, but least went to Kennedy. So any Republican feeling that Kennedy's eastern vote later in 1960 was fortuitous might equally subtract some of the GOP's compensating farm states.

18. The only dramatic potentials for net change were, with choice of appeals unfavorable to Humphrey, for him to take a bad beating as he subsequently did in West Virginia. The model, incidentally, is mechanically able to generate a West Virginia or any other known population's vote from responses of corresponding persons in Wisconsin. If it had, however, many runs would have been wrong. (Protestants in West Virginia voted much more for Kennedy.)

LLOYD RUDOLPH AND SUSANNE H. RUDOLPH

Opinion Surveys in India

THE SCHOLAR engaged in survey research who presents himself to the American houswife can do so with considerable confidence of a friendly and understanding reception. There is a very good chance that she has seen or heard of someone like him before. But the interviewer who faces an illiterate *Harijan* woman in village India is not likely to rouse any familiar images or ideas. Indeed, he will probably be seen as a threatening figure. That many expectations on which social science, particularly the opinion survey, has flourished in the United States do not hold for a country like India is not startling; but this fact warrants careful examination in terms of its consequences for further research.

The responses of both sophisticated and unsophisticated Indians to the opinion survey reveal that certain familiar assumptions may not be operative in an underdeveloped country. That these assumptions are not met fully does not mean that survey work can not be carried out in such areas, but it does mean that the researcher must demonstrate imagination and flexibility in his work.

We propose to examine six such assumptions in the light of our field experience: (1) that most people hold opinions on a broad range of issues and are capable of articulating them; (2) that the unit or source of opinion is the individual; (3) that for purposes of a sample survey, all opinions are equal; (4) that a clinical or neutral stance on matters of concern to social science is possible or legitimate; (5) that private research carried out by *bona fide* scholars is entitled to respect and cooperation from the general public, including public officials; and (6) that a climate of commitment to and understanding of professional standards in the social sciences exists in some measure.

Reprinted from *Public Opinion Quarterly*, Vol. XXII, (Fall 1958), pp. 235–244, by permission of the authors and the publisher. (Copyright, 1958, Princeton University Press.)

745

The Sample

Our observations are drawn from a sample survey of 600 persons in Madras State during April 1957, while were were in India under a Ford Foundation grant. The survey had the financial support of the Bureau of Social Science Research and was conducted under the auspices of the Indian Institute of Public Opinion. Professor S. Chandrasekhar recruited the team of ten interviewers from among his M.A. students in economics at Madras Christian College and accompanied us during the three weeks in which the survey was carried out. Training of the team included familiarization with survey theory and method, close study of the objectives of the questionnaire as a whole and of each question, and practice interviews. The sample of 600 was divided evenly between urban and rural populations. Rural results were multiplied by four when used in state-wide calculations, to match the 80 per cent rural-20 per cent urban distribution reported by the 1951 cenus. The urban population was defined as the five largest cities in the State while the rural sample was drawn from five villages lying at a radius of fifteen miles from each of the five cities, twenty-five villages in all. The particular villages around each of the cities were selected systematically from the list of villages lying on the fifteen-mile circumference. The virtue of this method of selection was its practicality. With a team of ten interviewers distributed two to a village, it was possible to carry out the rural interviews around each of the cities in one day. Public means of transport went to or near many of the villages. Where no public transport was available, we took interviewers in and out in our four-wheel drive station wagon.

In choosing the urban sample, we first made a systematic selection of areas by choosing ten polling stations from the hundreds into which all cities are divided. Each polling station carries approximately 1,000 voters. From the numerical listing, we systematically selected the names and addresses of the actual interviewees. Sixty urban and sixty rural interviews—twelve in each of the five villages—were carried out in or around each of the five city centers.

Self-awareness

The flaws in the assumption that most people hold opinions on a broad range of issues and are capable of articulating them became apparent as soon as field work began. To have an "opinion," for the purposes of the public opinion survey, is to be capable of articulating it. But articulation involves at least some degree of self-consciousness, sufficient to see that the dictates of custom are not the only source of beliefs and attitudes. Even if he clings to his customs and tradition, the person who has developed some self-awareness realizes, however dimly, that other ways of seeing the world exist. Only when this perception of alternatives arises does the individual appreciate that his views are in some sense peculiar to himself, that he *has* opinions. In the area of the political culture—political self-consciousness, information, literacy—this transformation had not as yet taken place among many of our interviewees.

The anthropologist is obviously in a better position with respect to this problem. He does not "ask" an individual about his opinions nor does he have to rely upon the coming to self-awareness of his subjects. He formulates his findings concerning "opinions" by observing rules and patterns of behavior. Thus, while the subject's awareness that he "has" views does not necessarily pose difficulties for the anthropologist, it does for those engaged in opinion surveys; they are likely to find themselves faced with an extremely large "don't know" category.

The Unit of Opinion

The second assumption, that the unit or source of opinion is the individual, is equally difficult to sustain *in toto*. Where life is lived more communally, opinions are likely to have a communal base. The unit of opinion is more likely to be the extended family, the sub-caste, the village, etc., than the individual. Opinion on many subjects is often the product of group traditions or deliberations. To the extent that it is, it is not easily accessible to the random sample survey technique. Especially on matters concerned with the political culture, many respondents did not know what their opinion was until they had spoken to the individuals who ordinarily participated in or led the process of finding or making opinion.

This is not to deny that individual opinion in the United States is not also often a function of group opinion, of a process which is social, not merely individual. But the groups which play a key role in the formation of opinion are more likely to be voluntary associations which the individual has joined because he already possessed the interests, attitudes, or beliefs shared in some measure by the group. Further, the individual in the United States is likely to play a much larger number of social roles than is normally the case for the individual in India. This complexity, this experiencing of the self in many contexts, has the result, on the one hand, of making another contribution to the social basis of individual opinion but, on the other, of sharpening and deepen-

747

ing the awareness of having and holding *individual* opinions. And while individual opinion in the United States is also the result of a social process in the sense that the mass media play an important part in its formation, the fact that the degree of exposure in India is *much* lower merely places an even greater emphasis on the non-voluntary or "natural" associations, i.e., the extended family, the sub-caste, the village. Thus, while in both the United States and India opinion is largely a product of a social process, the differences between the kinds or degrees of social processes have important implications for survey research. A crucial one is that the assumption of the opinion survey that the individual is the meaningful unit or source of opinion accords more closely with reality in the United States than it does in India.

This problem was posed directly for our interviewers by the groups which formed around them and their subjects, especially in villages, helpfully answering questions, sometimes individually, sometimes after some discussion. From the point of view of eliciting the most "valid" answer, the strategy to pursue was by no means obvious: *should* the researcher ask the others to disperse, or be quiet, or would the opinion emerging from the group process really be the most reliable statement of what the individual thought?

We resolved the matter on the side of individual interviewing for several reasons. We could not expect candid answers on certain questions, for example those concerning village leaders, unless interviewers spoke to people individually. Since we were also interested in the amount of information subjects had on public affairs, the individual was again the appropriate unit. But the *decisive* factor was that only individual interviewing could indicate which and how many individuals had passed through the process of differentiation that would make it possible to view them as the unit or source of opinion, a question which was a central concern of our survey.

Our interviewers were therefore instructed to get the subject alone whenever it was possible to do so without frightening him or offending his neighbors and family. Some of our interviewers succeeded in doing this by returning to the subject later and, on the whole, they had less difficulty than we had anticipated. Their tact was put to the most severe test when husbands insisted on helping their wives.

Equal Weight of Opinions

The egalitarian premises of the random sample, that all opinions have equal weight and importance, were frequently challenged. To assure themselves a hospitable reception in the villages, our interviewers were instructed to search out, wherever possible, a leading village official or headman to whom they could explain their mission and from whom they might get help in locating the persons selected for the sample.[1] The usual response of such a leader, upon seeing the chosen names, was one of great consternation: "Why do you want to ask this poor *Harijan* woman any questions? I can tell you more than she can!" Or, from the point of view of the woman: "Why ask me? I am only an ignorant woman! Ask my husband!"

Both were immediately struck by the anomaly of considering a poor, ignorant woman's remarks as interesting as those of a well-informed man, or at least of one accustomed to leadership. Even our interviewers, whom we had instructed in the theory of the random sample, returned occasionally with an extra questionnaire so that they could call our attention the views of some particularly interesting or important person. We never discouraged this, as long as the questionnaires were in addition to and separate from the regular questionnaires. The device of questioning the headman both improved our interviewers' reception in the villages and gave them a stronger position from which to discourage the headman's desire to follow them around in the interviews.

In some cases, the view that a "poor backward woman's" opinion counted for nothing was so strong both on her part and that of her neighbors, that they could only suspect the most mysterious and fearful reasons why an educated man from the city would wish to talk to her. "Police?," was a question the interviewers encountered more than once, and one woman was so persuaded that the questions were a preliminary to a criminal proceeding that she answered while weeping bitter tears. The interviewer decided neither science nor happiness was being promoted by the questions, and gave up.

On the first day, one of the interviewers came up with a formula which explained the equal weighting of opinions which so troubled some of our respondents. A well-known Tamil proverb advises, "If you wish to know whether the rice is done, pick out a grain and taste it." The simplicity of the explanation was its virtue—many subjects were content to know that they were so homely a thing as a kernel out of the Madras rice pot.

Neutral Opinion Research

If some of the assumptions underlying a polling survey have difficulty surviving in a traditional or transitional society, so do the assumptions underlying the broader and more basic notion of an "objective" or neutral social science. The basic issue turns on the question, why is the research being done? Is it to gain a deeper and broader understanding of reality or is it to realize certain social values? To answer these questions unequivocally is rarely possible, but the emphasis can be made clear. If values other than social science theory dominate the exploration of reality, there is a danger of obscuring the clarity with which the reality at issue is understood. This, in turn, may jeopardize the realization of the values. It is in this sense that we are using the term "neutral." While American social scientists have by no means achieved unanimity on the degree to which such neutral social science is possible or desirable, there is greater agreement than in some underdeveloped areas. For a number of reasons, many Indian social scientists quite explicitly believe that social science should not be value-neutral, but should serve a moral purpose. As a result, social science research in India tends to have strong normative overtones. The tendency is the result of complex and often contradictory forces.

It may be that the failure of large segments of the indigenous intellectual heritage to separate normative from descriptive or analytic writing is a fundamental influence. Certainly descriptive social science—as old as Aristole in the West—has played an insignificant role in Indian thought. But this influence could be expected to operate most decisively among traditionally trained scholars concerned with traditional learning. How to account for the very strong feeling among Indian scholars trained in a heavily Western-influenced educational system that neutral social science is suspect? In the field of social science, knowledge for knowledge's sake or knowledge for the sake of greater realism, understanding, and effectiveness gains scant support or appreciation in India today.

This attitude seems to derive, at least in part, from the transformation in values and institutions that is taking place. The effort to break down old norms and methods and create new ones in politics, society, and economics has been accompanied by an effort to create a moral climate favorable for the new values and techniques. The resulting conflict between reformers and traditionalists is often phrased in polemic terms, and objective research and discussion concerning the factual setting of change is sometimes difficult.

In this situation of transition, the very individuals from whom one might most readily expect a capacity for the clinical stance—the Indian social scientists trained in a Western tradition—are also the vanguard of those who want changed values and institutions. They are anxious to harness social science in their service. To them, a neutral social science becomes at best a luxury which they can not afford, and at worst a species of immorality, deception, or hypocrisy. The clinical stance, in their view, favors the status quo. That a clinical stance and a moral commitment may be compatible, that science may help the reformer by exploring the boundaries of the possible and indicating the range of alternatives, is not altogether accepted.

This climate in which social science is received is likely to have some very specific implications for those engaged in survey work, as well as for other researchers. That moral responsibility and the clinical stance were viewed in some conflict was made apparent to us by our interviewers. Though city boys, most of them were by no means unfamiliar with village life. Their families often maintained a home in the native village in addition to the town residence. But the first days of village interviewing, which forced them to talk for hours on end to villagers who often lived on the slimmest of margins, ("Are you *sure* your sample is random? I think I have talked to nothing but untouchables for days!") had a powerful impact. We had ten troubled consciences on our hands.

For example, the response to the question, "Do you have any problems? What is the most important one?" loosed all the woes of India on the heads of our interviewers. "How can we ask these people all these questions if we're not going to do anything about what we're finding out? They have so many problems, and they think that because we ask, we'll do something for them."

Our interviewers knew that we were using the survey tour around Madras to speak with District Collectors and familiarize ourselves with administration problems. They began to bring us requests from their villages for tubewells, road improvements, and clinics. Would we please convey these to the Collector? We did, with some diffidence. Our interviewers would have been happier if the survey had resulted in a ten-point report recommending improvements. Journal articles appeared to them a slim contribution to social reform.

The more painful way in which the suspicion of a neutral social science hit us was as foreigners. Because of the value-laden aspect of much of Indian social science, there is a tendency to look for everybody's hidden premises. In the present not always cordial climate of Indo-American relations, what more promising premise offers itself than that some nefarious Western purpose is at work? The Indian experience with English social scientists has given their suspicions some historical foundation. While most Englishmen wrote scholarly and dispassionate studies of Indian castes and religions, some used analyses of social divisions in India primarily to justify the continuation of British rule. The suspicion remains that the foreign scholar may "want to understand us the better to manipulate us."

In the middle of our survey trip, when the temperature had been over 100 for a week, when the villages had become dustier and more difficult of access, when the morale of our interviewers was, in short, at a low point, somebody in the group suddenly decided to question

751

our *bona fides*. A series of critical remarks by interviewees plus an allegation in the press that an American professor in Ceylon was engaged in intelligence work[2] culminated in an interrogation, led by one of our interviewers, concerning the *real* objectives of our own research. Since there is no way of proving that one is not working for foreign intelligence, we had to rely on (1) the interviewers' capacity to understand that people may pursue social science research for its own sake; (2) the personal trust which we had been able to inspire; (3) the support we received from the Indian professor in charge of the team, who did understand that scholars pursue research for purely academic reasons. The first reason by itself would not have seen us through.

The Researcher's Status

The assumption that private research carried out by bona fide scholars is entitled to respect and cooperation from the general public, including public officials, is one which is open to serious challenge in India today. Beyond the problem of "neutral" social science lies another, the problem of the status of the academic or scholarly role in India. Despite the laments that are voiced over the relatively low status of the academician in American society, his position vis à vis the government servant or the politician is quite strong, partly because their positions are not rated very high either. But with the possible exception of a very few economists, Indian social scientists do not enjoy a similar relationship. They usually find themselves at a status disadvantage. The bureaucrat, who is as highly placed as anyone in India today, is less likely to think of the academician as his peer, a supposition which is to some extent *shared* by the academician who may regret that he didn't "make it" when he took the IAS examinations.

The consequences of this situation for social science research are serious. While a tradition of bureaucratic secrecy like that of England and unlike that of America already raises a barrier to private research in public affairs, the status of the academician raises a second one. The scholar, therefore, has to assume the burden of proof when the issue of whether or not he should be allowed to inquire about something arises. Certainly there is no presumption in his favor.

Here the foreign scholar has an advantage. Believing himself to be a peer of the bureaucrat and backed by the prestige derived from the fact that he is a foreigner (and Western) who is sufficiently important somewhere to be sent thousands of miles to do something, he is more likely to gain the respect and cooperation of the civil servant than his Indian counterpart.

Survey work requires the scholar to deal with a large number of major and minor functionaries. Our sample was based on the electoral rolls,[3] and these are scattered throughout Madras State, sometimes at District Headquarters, sometimes at Tehsil Headquarters.

Our Indian colleague, aware of the fact that scholarly research would not necessarily be an adequate justification to gain access to what were presumably public electoral rolls, took the precaution of establishing his identity and *bona fides* with the Madras Election Commissioner and having him write to the five Collectors of the Districts we were to visit, alerting them to our arrival and stating that we could use the rolls. While this was certainly a useful measure, it did not solve all our problems. In one case, a new Collector was on the job and had no knowledge of the letter. In another, the Collector was on tour. In several instances, the relevant rolls were in Tehsil rather than district headquarters and the logic of our work dictated gaining access to them before contacting the Collector. It was under these circumstances— without *official* identification and authority—that difficulties which might have proved insurmountable arose. But through the use of a variety of strategems and symbols of authority and legitimacy we were able to muddle through.

Sometimes the presence of a Professor from Madras University helped; sometimes the fact that the Professor was *personally* known (by reputation, by family connections, by mutual friends or acquaintances) saved the situation; sometimes the fact that we were operating under the auspices of the Delhi-centered Indian Institute of Public Opinion turned the trick; and sometimes the fact that we were foreign scholars from a well-known Western university helped. It was the application of a combination of these various elements—plus patience and persistence— that served eventually to carry us through in an environment which presumed that scholarly research, particularly by foreigners, was suspect until and unless proved otherwise.

Professional Standards

The last assumption, understanding and commitment concerning professional standards in the social sciences, opens a fairly broad field for discussion. In survey work, the problem is perhaps more acute than in other types of social science research. At its simplest, the fact that there are *very few* people with any kind of professional training in this field immediately poses the most serious problems. That survey research of various kinds has been carried on in India for a number of years does not mean that sufficient trained personnel are actually available. One survey that needs to be made with an eye to action is of the number, kind, and caliber of training centers in survey theory and methods, as well as some assessment of the number of persons with the various levels of knowledge and skills required.

A deeper and more baffling aspect of the problem concerns the inner meaning of such commitment to and understanding of social science, including survey research, as does exist. It is our impression that while there is a widespread belief among educated opinion in India that social science is desirable and "scientific," the kind of "good thing" that modern India needs, there is little awareness that a long intellectual tradition lies behind social science theory and method, that it takes considerable effort and study to master it, and that the validity of the results obtained depends not only on understanding the concepts but also on the care and diligence with which research is actually carried out. In practice there is not always a commitment to the whole range of instrumental details that follow from belief in the value of social science. The appreciation of the end is not always supported by appreciation of the necessary means.

Appreciation of means requires an internalization of professional standards which can provide the individual discipline and effort so necessary for sound research. Absence of this internalization process leads to a kind of ritualistic simulation of research symbols and ceremonials which is designed to gain for the practioner the fruits of being scientific and modern. But these fruits prove illusory when an inadequate appreciation of means takes its toll in the form of misleading, false, or superficial findings.

Our approach to this problem was to take considerable care in the recruitment, training, and supervision of our team of ten interviewers. Instead of the usual practice in Indian survey work of decentralizing the responsibility for these three key tasks to persons located in the areas where the actual interviewing is to be carried out, we, along with our Indian colleague from Madras Christian College, accompanied our team on a thousand mile, three week swing around Madras State, checking their work, meeting problems as they arose, and keeping up morale by stressing the interest and importance of the work. Without centralized recruitment, training, and supervision in sample survey work, we believe it is doubtful that reliable results can be obtained at this time.

Conclusions and Objectives

What does all this mean for opinion survey research in India and other underdeveloped countries? The *caveats* discussed above suggest that methods and, to some extent, objectives, should be re-oriented in such a way as to take them into account. In the area of methods, the discussion has highlighted what seem to be the key problems to be faced and has suggested some of the means available for coping with these problems in the planning and administration of research.

In the area of objectives, our experience indicates that *some* of the questions which the opinion survey can answer in the West can be better answered, at least for the present, by the anthropologist using methods of clinical observation. As political scientists concerned with survey research, we subscribe to Professor Richard Park's suggestion that there is a need for more *political* anthropology if social science as a whole is to grapple successfully with the problems raised by the study of underdeveloped areas.[4]

But while admitting that certain questions which fall within the purview of survey research in the West can be better answered by the methods of the anthropologists in underdeveloped areas, we would continue to hold that there are broad and important areas of research which can be suitably and perhaps best handled by survey methods. One important focus for survey research is the *growth* of public opinion in underdeveloped areas. This broad objective would include concern for the conditions and reasons for growth as well as evaluation and measurement of its content over time. Such an objective should include the specific tasks of identifying *who, how many, to what degree,* and *why* individuals have opinions.[5]

NOTES

1. We instructed them to content themsleves with finding one such person. Our time schedule did not permit locating all possible leaders in villages which had a complex leadership structure.

2. This charge was subsequently denied by Prime Minister Banderanaike himself.

3. India has compulsory registration of all voters. The rolls are compiled at official initiative with official personnel.

4. Made in a paper delivered at the Association for Asian Studies meeting in New York, April 2, 1958.

5. For a research effort along these lines see Rudolph, Lloyd and Susanne H. "Communications and the Study of Political Development," *Public Opinion Surveys,* Vol. III, Nos. 1–3, 1957.

Bibliography

General Titles

The Annals of the American Academy of Political and Social Science, *Communication and Social Action*, 250, March 1947.

Eleanor Blum. *Reference Books in the Mass Media.* Urbana: University of Illinois, 1963.

Lyman Bryson, editor. *The Communication of Ideas.* New York: Harper, 1948.

Morris Janowitz. *The Community Press in an Urban Setting.* Glencoe: The Free Press of Glencoe, 1952.

Daniel Katz and others, editors. *Public Opinion and Propaganda.* New York: Holt, Rinehart and Winston, 1954.

Paul F. Lazarsfeld and Frank Stanton, editors. *Communications Research, 1948-49.* New York: Harper, 1949.

Warren C. Price, comp., *The Literature of Journalism: An Annotated Bibliography.* Minneapolis: University of Minnesota Press, 1959.

Wilbur Schramm, editor. *The Process and Effects of Mass Communication.* Urbana: University of Illinois Press, 1954.

756

Wilbur Schramm, editor, *Mass Communications* (2nd edition). Urbana: University of Illinois Press, 1960.

Wilbur Schramm, editor. *Communications in Modern Society*. Urbana: University of Illinois Press, 1948.

Bruce L. Smith, Harold D. Lasswell and Ralph D. Casey. *Propaganda, Communication, and Public Opinion*. Princeton: Princeton University Press, 1946.

Propaganda and Promotional Activities. Minneapolis: University of Minnesota Press, 1935.

Bruce L. Smith and C. Smith. *International Communication and Political Opinion: A Guide to the Literature*. Princeton: Princeton University Press, 1956.

United Nations Educational, Scientific and Cultural Organization. *Reports and Papers in Mass Communications*.

Douglas Waples, editor. *Print, Radio and Film in a Democracy*. Chicago: University of Chicago Press, 1942.

Charles R. Wright. *Mass Communication: A Sociological Perspective*. New York: Random House, 1959.

1 Theory of Public Opinion

Floyd H. Allport. "Toward a Science of Public Opinion," *Public Opinion Quarterly*, 1, January 1937, pp. 7–23.

Norman Angell. *The Public Mind: Its Disorders and Its Exploitation*. London: Douglas, 1926.

Wilhelm Bauer. *Die Offentliche Meinung in der Weltgeschichte*. Wildpark-Potsdam: Athenaion, 1930.

Wilhelm Bauer. "Public Opinion," *Encyclopedia of the Social Sciences*, 12, pp. 669–674.

James Bryce. *The American Commonwealth*. New York: Macmillan, 1899, pp. 247–254.

Karl W. Deutsch. *Nationalism and Social Communication: An Inquiry into the Foundation of Nationality*. The Technology Press of M.I.T. and Wiley (New York), 1953.

Leonard W. Doob. *Public Opinion and Propaganda*. New York: Holt, 1948.

Leon A. Festinger. *A Theory of Cognitive Dissonance*. Evanston, Ill.: Row, Peterson, 1957.

Sigmund Freud. *Group Psychology and the Analysis of the Ego*. London: Hogath Press, 1922.

Daniel Katz. "Three Criteria: Knowledge, Conviction and Significance," *Public Opinion Quarterly*, 4, June 1940, pp. 277–284.

Robert E. Lane and David O. Sears. *Public Opinion*. Englewood Cliffs, N.J.: Prentice-Hall, 1964.

Kurt Lang and Gladys E. Lang. *Collective Dynamics*. New York: Crowell, 1961.

Karl Mannheim. *Ideology and Utopia: An Introduction to the Sociology of Knowledge*. New York: Harcourt, Brace, 1936.

Peter Odegard. *The American Public Mind*. New York: Columbia University Press, 1930.

Paul A. Palmer. "The Concept of Public Opinion in Political Theory," in *Essays in History and Political Theory in Honor of Charles Howard McIlwain*. Cambridge: Harvard University Press, 1936.

Kurt Riezler. "What Is Public Opinion," *Social Research*, 11, 1944, pp. 397–427.

Mortimer B. Smith, Jerome S. Bruner and Robert W. White. *Opinions and Personality*. New York: Wiley, 1956.

Hans Speier. "Historical Development of Public Opinion," *American Journal of Sociology*, 55, January 1950, pp. 376–388.

Jean Stoetzel. *Theories des Opinions*. Paris: Presses Universitaires de France 1943.

William Graham Sumner. *Folkways: A Study of the Sociological Importance of Usages, Manners, Customs, Mores and Morals*. Boston: Ginn, 1906.

Alexis de Tocqueville. *Democracy in America*. New York: Oxford University Press, 1947. Chapters 9–17, Part I.

Ferdinand Tönnies. Kritik der Öffentlichen Meinung. Berlin: J. Springer, 1922.

Ralph H. Turner and Lewis M. Killian. *Collective Behavior*. Englewood Cliffs, N.J.: Prentice-Hall, 1957.

Graham Wallas. *The Great Society*. New York: Macmillan, 1914.

Francis G. Wilson. "Concepts of Public Opinion," *American Political Science Review*, 27, 1933, pp. 371–392.

II Formation of Public Opinion

Herbert I. Abelson. *Persuasion: How Opinions and Attitudes Are Changed*. New York: Springer Publishing Co., 1959.

Theodore W. Adorno, Else Frenkel-Brunswick, Daniel J. Levinson, and R. Nevitt Sanford. *The Authoritarian Personality*. New York: Harper, 1950.

William Albig. *Modern Public Opinion*. New York: McGraw-Hill Book Co., 1956.

Gabriel Almond. "The Political Attitudes of Wealth," *Journal of Politics*, 8, August 1945, pp. 213–255.

Louis Bean. *Ballot Behavior: A Study of Presidential Elections*. Washington, D.C.: American Council on Public Affairs, 1940.

Louis Bean. *How to Predict Elections*. New York: Knopf, 1948.

Robert T. Bower. "Opinion Research and Historical Interpretation of Elections," *Public Opinion Quarterly*, 12, Fall 1948, pp. 455–469.

Angus Campbell, P. E. Converse, W. E. Miller and D. E. Stokes. *The American Voter*. New York: Wiley, 1960.

Hadley Cantril. "Trends of Opinion During World War II: Some Guides to Interpretation," *Public Opinion Quarterly*, 12, Spring 1948, pp. 30–44.

Frank V. Cantwell. "Public Opinion and the Legislative Process," *American Political Science Review*, 60, 1946, pp. 924–935.

Bjorn Christiansen. *Attitudes Towards Foreign Affairs as a Function of Personality*. Oslo: Oslo University Press, 1959.

Helen Dinerman. "1948 Votes in the Making," *Public Opinion Quarterly*, 12, Winter 1948–49, p. 586–598.

Leon Festinger. "The Role of Group-belongingness in a Voting Situation," *Human Relations*, 1, 1947, pp. 154–180.

Leon Festinger, Henry W. Riecken, Jr., Stanley Schachter. *When Prophecy Fails*. Minneapolis: University of Minnesota Press, 1956.

Herbert Goldhamer. "Public Opinion and Personality," *American Journal of Sociology*, 55, January 1950, pp. 346–354.

Alfred W. Jones. *Life, Liberty and Property*. Philadelphia: Lippincott, 1941.

Arthur W. Kornhauser. "Analysis of 'Class' Structure of Contemporary American Society: Psychological Bases of Class Divisions," in *Industrial Conflict: A Psychological Interpretation*. New York: Society for the Psychological Study of Social Issues, 1939.

Arthur W. Kornhauser. "Public Opinion and Social Class," *American Journal of Sociology*, 55, January 1950, pp. 333–345.

Robert E. Lane. *Political Ideology: Why the American Common Man Believes What He Does*. New York: The Free Press of Glencoe, 1962.

Paul F. Lazarsfeld. *The Academic Mind: Social Scientists in a Time of Crisis*. Glencoe: The Free Press of Glencoe, 1958.

Seymour M. Lipset, Paul F. Lazarsfeld, A. H. Barton and J. Linz. "The Psychology of Voting: An Analysis of Political Behavior," in *Handbook of Social Psychology*, II, edited by Gardner Lindzey. Cambridge, Mass.: Addison-Wesley Press, 1954, pp. 1144–1148.

Gardner Murphy and Rensis Likert. *Public Opinion and the Individual*. New York: Harper, 1938.

Theodore Newcomb. *Personality and Social Change*. New York: Dryden, 1943.

Milton J. Rosenberg and others. *Attitude Organization and Change: An Analysis of Consistency Among Attitude Components*. Vol. III of the Yale Studies in Attitude and Communication. New Haven: Yale University Press, 1960.

Morris Rosenberg. "Some Determinants of Political Apathy," *Public Opinion Quarterly*, 18, Winter 1954, pp. 349–366.

William A. Scott and Stephen B. Withey. *The United States and the United Nations: The Public View 1945–1955*. New York: Manhattan Publishing Co., 1958.

Muzafer Sherif and Hadley Cantril. *The Psychology of Ego-Involvements, Social Attitudes, and Identifications*. New York: Wiley, 1947.

Samuel A. Stouffer. *Communism, Conformity and Civil Liberties: A Cross-Section of the Nation Speaks Its Mind*. New York: Doubleday, 1955.

Samuel Stouffer and others. *The American Soldier: Vol. 1, Adjustment During Army Life: Vol. II, Combat and Its Aftermath*. Princeton: Princeton University Press, 1949.

759

U.S. Strategic Bombing Survey. *The Effects of Strategic Bombing on German Morale*. Washington: Government Printing Office, 1947.
U.S. Strategic Bombing Survey. *The Effects of Strategic Bombing on Japanese Morale*. Washington: Government Printing Office, 1947.

III Impact of Public Opinion on Public Policy

Gabriel A. Almond. *The American People and Foreign Policy*. New York: Harcourt, Brace, 1950.
Jerome S. Bruner. *Mandate from the People*. New York: Duell, Sloan and Pearce, 1944.
Lewis E. Gleek. "96 Congressmen Make Up Their Minds," *Public Opinion Quarterly*, 4, March 1940, pp. 3–24.
Morton Grodzins. *Americans Betrayed*. Chicago: University of Chicago Press, 1949. Chapters 2–7, Appendices I and II.
S. Kelley, Jr. *Professional Public Relations and Political Power*. Baltimore: Johns Hopkins University Press, 1956.
Avery Leiserson. "Opinion Research and the Political Process," *Public Opinion Quarterly*, 13, Spring 1949, pp. 31–38.
Lester Markel, editor. *Public Opinion and Foreign Policy*. New York: Harper, 1949.
William N. McPhee. *Public Opinion and Congressional Elections*. New York: The Free Press of Glencoe, 1962.
"The Parliamentary Profession" (Issue title). *International Social Science Journal*, 13, 4, 1961.
"The Public Opinion Polls: Dr. Jekyll or Mr. Hyde," *Public Opinion Quarterly*, 4, June 1940, pp. 212–284.
Lindsay Rogers. *The Pollsters: Public Opinion, Politics and Democratic Leadership*. New York: Knopf, 1949.
David Truman. "Public Opinion Research as a Tool of Public Administration," *Public Administration Review*, 5, 1945, pp. 62–72.

IV Theory of Communication

Gordon W. Allport and Leo Postman. *Psychology of Rumor*. New York: Holt, 1947.
Frederick Charles Bartlett. *Political Propaganda*. New York: Macmillan, 1940.
Daniel Bell. *The End of Ideology: On the Exhaustion of Political Ideas in the Fifties*. New York: The Free Press of Glencoe, 1960.
Edmund S. Carpenter and Marshall McLuhan, editors. *Explorations in Communication*. Boston: Beacon Press, 1960.
Hugh D. Duncan. *Communication and the Social Order*. New York: Bedminster Press, 1962.
S. N. Eisenstadt. "Conditions of Communicative Receptivity," *Public Opinion Quarterly*, 17, Fall 1953, pp. 363–374.

Eliot Freidson. "Communications Research and the Concept of the Mass," *American Sociological Review*, 18, June 1953, pp. 313–317.

Carl I. Hovland. "Social Communication," *Proceedings of the American Philosophical Society*, 92, 5, 1948, pp. 371–375.

Paul Kecskemeti. Meaning, *Communication and Value*. Chicago: University of Chicago Press, 1952.

Ernst Kris. "Danger of Propaganda," *American Imago*, 2, 1941, pp. 3–42.

Harold D. Lasswell. "The Theory of Political Propaganda," *American Political Science Review*, 21, 1927, pp. 627–630.

Harold D. Lasswell. "Propaganda," *Encyclopedia of the Social Sciences*, 12, pp. 521–527.

Harold D. Lasswell. "The Triple-Appeal Principle," *American Journal of Sociology*, 37, May 1932, pp. 523–538.

Harold D. Lasswell. "The Strategy of Revolutionary and War Propaganda," in *Public Opinion and World Politics*, edited by Quincy Wright. Chicago: University of Chicago Press, 1933.

Robert K. Merton. "Introduction to Part III, The Sociology of Knowledge and Mass Communication" in *Social Theory and Social Structure*. Glencoe: The Free Press of Glencoe, 1949, pp. 199–216.

Charles Morris. *Signs, Language and Behavior*. New York: Prentice-Hall, 1946.

Charles K. Ogden and Ivan A. Richards. *The Meaning of Meaning: A Study of the Influence of Language upon Thought and of the Science of Symbolism*. New York: Harcourt, Brace, 1936.

Robert E. Park. "The Natural History of the Newspaper," *American Journal of Sociology*, 22, November 1923, pp. 273–289.

Robert E. Park. "News as a Source of Knowledge," *American Journal of Sociology*, 45, 1940, pp. 669–689.

Claude E. Shannon and Warren Weaver. *A Mathematical Theory of Communication*. Urbana: University of Illinois Press, 1949.

William Issac Thomas and Florian Znaniecki. "The Wider Community and the Role of the Press," in *The Polish Peasant in Europe and America*. Boston: Gorham Press, 1920, Vol. IV, pp. 241–271.

Norbert Weiner. *Cybernetics, or Control and Communication in the Animal and Machine*. New York: Wiley, 1948. Chapter 8: "Information, Language and Society."

V Communication Media: Structure and Control

W. C. Ackerman. "The Dimensions of American Broadcasting," *Public Opinion Quarterly*, 9, Spring 1945, pp. 1–18.

H. M. Belville, Jr. "The Challenge of the New Media," in *Communication in Modern Society*, edited by Wilbur Schramm. Urbana: University of Illinois Press, 1948, pp. 126–141.

Donald Blaisdell. *Economic Power and Political Pressure*. (Temporary National Economic Committee Monograph No. 26). Washington: Government Printing Office, 1941.

Neil H. Borden. *The Economic Effects of Advertising*. Chicago: Richard D. Irvin, 1942.

Roy F. Carter, Jr. "Newspaper 'Gatekeepers' and the Sources of News," *Public Opinion Quarterly*, 22, Summer 1958, pp. 133–144.

Ralph D. Casey. "Pressure Groups and the Press," in *The Polls and Public Opinion*, edited by Norman C. Meier and Harold W. Saunders. New York: Holt, 1949, pp. 124–140.

James T. Farrell. *The Fate of Writing in America*. New York: New Directions, 1946.

Federal Communications Commission. *Report on Chain Broadcasting*. Washington: Government Printing Office, 1941.

Federal Communications Commission. Office of Network Study. *Network Broadcasting: Report of the Network Study Staff* . . . (2 vols.), 1957; and *Interim Report of the Office of Network Study: Responsibility for Broadcast Matter* (Docket No. 12782), 1960; and *Digest of Record* (Docket No. 12782), 1960. Washington: F.C.C.

Marjorie Fiske. *Book Selection and Censorship: A Study of School and Public Libraries in California*. Berkeley: University of California Press, 1959.

Carl Friedrich and Evelyn Sternberg. "Congress and the Control of Radio Broadcasting," *American Political Science Review*, October and December, 1943, pp. 797–818; 1014–1026.

James Edward Gerald. *The Press and the Constitution, 1931–1947*. Minneapolis: University of Minnesota Press, 1948.

William Ernest Hocking. *Freedom of the Press*. Chicago: University of Chicago Press, 1947.

Lancelot Hogben. *From Cave Painting to Comic Strip: A Kaleidoscope of Human Communication*. New York: Chanticleer Press, 1949.

Mae Huettig. *Economic Control of the Motion Picture Industry*. Philadelphia: University of Pennsylvania, 1944.

Ruth Inglis. *Freedom of the Movies*. Chicago: University of Chicago Press, 1946.

International Press Institute. *La Presse Dans Les Etats Autoritaires*. Zurich: IPI, 1959.

John A. Irving, editor. *Mass Media in Canada*. Toronto: Ryerson Press, 1962.

Lewis Jacobs. *The Rise of the American Film: A Critical History*. New York: Harcourt, Brace, 1939.

V. O. Key. "The Role and Technique of Pressure Groups," in *Politics, Parties and Pressure Groups*. New York: Crowell, 1942.

Ernst Kris. "Mass Communications Under Totalitarian Governments," *Print, Radio, and Film in a Democracy*, edited by Douglas Waples. Chicago: University of Chicago Press, 1942, pp. 14–38.

PERSONNEL

Theodore Adorno. "Anti-Semitism and Fascist Propaganda," in *Anti-Semitism: A Social Disease*, edited by Ernst Simmel. New York: International Universities Press, 1946, pp. 125–137.

762

Wendell Bell, Richard J. Hill and Charles Wright. *Public Leadership: A Critical Review with Special Reference to Adult Education.* San Francisco: Chandler Publishing Co., 1961.

George B. de Huszar. *The Intellectuals.* New York: The Free Press of Glencoe, 1960.

R. L. Jones and G. E. Swanson. "Small-City Daily Newspaperman: Their Abilities and Interests," *Journalism Quarterly,* 31, 1954, pp. 38–55.

Harold D. Lasswell. "The Person: Subject and Object of Propaganda," *Annals,* 1935, pp. 187–193.

Harold D. Lasswell. *Psychopathology and Politics.* Chicago: University of Chicago Press, 1930.

Karl Mannheim. "The Problem of the Intelligentsia: An Inquiry into Its Past and Present Role," in *Essays on the Sociology of Culture.* New York: Oxford University Press, 1956.

Lester W. Milbrath. *The Washington Lobbyists.* Chicago: Rand McNally Co., 1963.

Leo C. Rosten. *Hollywood.* New York: Harcourt, Brace, 1941. Part II.

Leo C. Rosten. *The Washington Correspondents.* New York: Harcourt, Brace, 1937. Chapters I, V, VI, VIII, IX.

Guy Swanson. "Agitation Through the Press: A Study of the Personalities of Publicists," *Public Opinion Quarterly,* 20, Summer 1956, pp. 441–456.

United Nations Educational, Scientific and Cultural Organization, Division of Free Flow of Information. *Professional Associations in the Mass Media.* Paris: UNESCO, 1959.

Alfred McClung Lee. *The Daily Newspaper in America: The Evolution of a Social Instrument.* New York: Macmillan, 1937.

Harvey J. Levin. *Broadcast Regulation and Joint Ownership of Media.* New York: New York University Press, 1960.

James L. McCamy. *Government Publications for the Citizen.* New York: Columbia University Press, 1949.

James L. McCamy. *Government Publicity: Its Practice in Federal Administration.* Chicago: University of Chicago, 1939, Ch. VIII.

Duncan MacDougald, Jr. "The Popular Music Industry," in *Radio Research 1941,* edited by Paul F. Lazarsfeld and Frank Stanton. New York: Duell Sloane and Pearce, 1941, pp. 65–109.

William Miller. *The Book Industry.* New York: Columbia University Press, 1950.

Frank Luther Mott. *American Journalism: A History of Newspapers in the United States Through 250 Years: 1690–1940.* New York: Macmillan, 1941.

Gunnar Myrdal. *An American Dilemma.* New York: Harper, 1944. Vol. II, Ch. XLII. The Negro Press.

Peter H. Odegard. *Pressure Politics: The Story of the Anti-Saloon League.* New York: Columbia University Press, 1928.

Robert E. Park. *The Immigrant Press and Its Control.* New York: Harper, 1922, Chapters XV, XVIII.

Burton Paulu. *British Broadcasting in Transition.* Minneapolis: University of Minnesota Press, 1961.

Ernest M. Pittaro. *TV and Film Production Data Book.* New York: Morgan & Morgan, 1959.

Political and Economic Planning Group. *Report on the British Press.* London:

David Riesman. "Civil Liberties in a Period of Transition," in *Public Policy: Yearbook of Harvard Graduate School of Public Administration,* 3, 1942, pp. 33–96.

Thomas P. Robinson. *Radio Networks and the Federal Government.* New York: Columbia University Press, 1943, Chs. I–V.

Temporary National Economic Committee. *The Motion Picture Industry— A Pattern of Control* (Monograph No. 43). Washington: Government Printing Office, 1941.

Strother H. Walker and Paul Sklar. *Business Finds Its Voice.* New York: Harper, 1938.

Llewellyn White. "The American Radio: Toward Self-Regulation," *The American Radio,* Chicago: University of Chicago Press, 1947.

Malcolm Willey and Stuart A. Rice. *Communication Agencies and Social Life.* New York and London: McGraw-Hill, 1933, Part III. The Agencies of Mass Impression. Extended in Douglas Waples, "Communications," in *American Journal of Sociology,* 47, May 1942, pp. 907–917.

Raymond Williams. *Britain in the Sixties: Communications.* Baltimore: Penguin Books, 1962.

VI *Communication Content*

ANALYSIS OF MEDIA CONTENT

Milton C. Albrecht. "Does Literature Reflect Common Values?" *American Sociological Review,* 21, 1956, pp. 722–729.

Gordon Allport and Janet M. Faden. "The Psychology of Newspapers: Five Tentative Laws," *Public Opinion Quarterly,* 4, December 1940, pp. 687–703.

Lester Asheim. *From Book to Film,* unpublished PhD dissertation, Graduate Library School, University of Chicago, 1949.

James H. Barnett and Rhoda Gruen. "Recent American Divorce Novels, 1938–1945: A Study in the Sociology of Literature," *Social Forces,* 26, 1948, pp. 322–327.

Bernard Berelson and Paul Lazarsfeld. *The Analysis of Communication Content.* University of Chicago, Mimeographed, 1948.

Bernard Berelson and Patricia Salter. "Majority-Minority Americans: An Analysis of Magazine Fiction," *Public Opinion Quarterly,* 10, Summer 1946, pp. 168–190.

Maxwell R. Brooks. *The Negro Press Re-Examined: Political Content of Leading Negro Newspapers.* Boston: Christopher Publishing House, 1959.

Alexander L. George. *Propaganda Analysis: A Study of Inferences Made from Nazi Propaganda in World War II.* Evanston: Row, Peterson and Co., 1959.

Hornell Hart. "Changing Social Attitudes and Interests," in *Recent Social Trends in the U.S.* New York: McGraw-Hill, 1934, pp. 382–443.

Susan Kingsbury, Hornell Hart and others. *Newspapers and the News: An Objective Measurement of Ethical and Unethical Behavior by Representative Newspapers.* New York: Putnam's Sons, 1937, Ch. I, II, III.

Siegfried Kracauer. *Theory of Films, the Redemption of Physical Reality.* New York: Oxford University Press, 1960.

Siegfried Kracauer. *From Caligari to Hitler.* Princeton: Princeton University Press, 1947.

Siegfried Kracauer. "National Types as Hollywood Presents Them," *Public Opinion Quarterly*, 13, 1949, pp. 53–72.

Ernst Kris and Hans Speier. *German Radio Propaganda.* New York: Oxford University Press, 1944.

Harold D. Lasswell. *Propaganda Technique in the World War.* New York: Knopf, 1927.

Harold D. Lasswell, Nathan Leites and others. *Language of Politics: Studies in Quantitative Semantics.* New York: Stewart, 1949.

Leo Lowenthal. "Biographies in Popular Magazines," in *Radio Research, 1942–43*, Paul F. Lazarsfeld and Frank Stanton, editors. Fairlawn, N.J.: Essential Books, 1943.

Leo Lowenthal. *Literature, Popular Culture and Society.* Englewood Cliffs, N.J.: Prentice-Hall, 1961.

Raymond Nixon. "The Content of Non-Competitive Versus Competitive Newspapers," *Journalism Quarterly*, 33, Summer 1956, pp. 299–314.

Ithiel de Sola Pool, editor. *Trends in Content Analysis.* Urbana: University of Illinois Press, 1959.

Jorgen Westerstahl and Carl-Gunnar Janson. *The Political Press: Studies Illustrating the Political Role of the Daily Press in Sweden* (with table headings in English and a comprehensive English summary). Gothenburg: Political Science Institute, University of Gothenburg, 1958.

Martha Wolfenstein and Nathan Leites. *Movies: A Psychological Study.* Glencoe: The Free Press of Glencoe, 1950.

POPULAR CULTURE

Mortimer Adler. *Art and Prudence.* New York: Longmans, Green, 1937.

Theodore W. Adorno. "A Social Critique of Radio Music," *The Kenyon Review*, 7, 1945, pp. 208–217.

Theodore W. Adorno. "The Radio Symphony: An Experiment in Theory," in *Radio Research, 1941*, pp. 110–139.

Rudolph Arnheim. "The World of the Daytime Serial," in *Radio Research, 1942–43*, edited by Paul F. Lazarsfeld and Frank Stanton. New York: Duell, Sloan and Pearce, 1943, pp. 507–548.

Bernard Berelson and Patricia J. Salter. "Majority and Minority Americans: An Analysis of Magazine Fiction," *Public Opinion Quarterly*, 10, Summer 1946, pp. 168–190.

Herbert Gans. "The Rise of the Problem Film," *Social Problems*, Spring 1964, pp. 327–336.

Lennox Gray. "Communication and the Arts," in *The Communication of Ideas*, edited by Lyman Bryson. New York: Harper, 1948, pp. 119–142.

William E. Henry. "Art and Culture Symbolism: A Psychological Study of Greeting Cards," *Journal of Aesthetics and Art Criticism*, 6, September 1947, pp. 36–44.

Richard Hoggart. *The Uses of Literacy: Changing Patterns in English Mass Culture*. Fair Lawn, N.J.: Essential Books, 1957.

Helen MacGill Hughes. "Human Interest Stories and Democracy," *Public Opinion Quarterly*, 1, April 1937, pp. 73–83.

Patrick Johns-Heine and Hans H. Gerth. "Values in Mass Periodical Fiction, 1921–40," *Public Opinion Quarterly*, 13, Spring 1949, pp. 95–118.

Paul F. Lazarsfeld and Robert K. Merton. "Mass Communication, Popular Taste and Organized Social Action," in *The Communication of Ideas*, pp. 95–118.

Leo Lowenthal. "Historical Perspectives of Popular Culture," *American Journal of Sociology*, 55, January 1950, pp. 323–332.

Dwight MacDonald. "A Theory of 'Popular Culture,'" *Politics* I, February 1944, pp. 20–23.

"Mass Culture and Mass Media" (Issue title). *Daedalus*, 89, Spring 1960.

J. P. Mayer. *British Cinemas and Their Audiences: Sociological Studies*. London: Dennis Dobson, 1948.

George Orwell. *Dickens, Dali and Others: Studies in Popular Culture*. New York: Reynal and Hitchcock, 1946.

Bernard Rosenberg and David Manning White. *Mass Culture: The Popular Arts in America*. Glencoe: The Free Press of Glencoe, 1957.

Edward A. Suchman. "Invitation to Music," in *Radio Research, 1941*, pp. 140–188.

Katherine M. Wolf and Marjorie Fiske. "The Children Talk About Comics," in *Communications Research*, 1948–49, edited by Paul F. Lazarsfeld and Frank Stanton. New York: Harper, 1949, pp. 3–50.

VII Communication Audiences

THE AMERICAN AUDIENCE

Bernard Berelson. *The Library's Public*. New York: Columbia University Press, 1949.

Bernard Berelson. "The Public Library, Book Reading, and Political Behavior," *Library Quarterly*, 15, October 1945, pp. 281–299.

H. M. Beville, Jr., "The ABCD's of Radio Audiences," *Public Opinion Quarterly*, 4, June 1940, pp. 195–206.

Leo A. Handel. *Hollywood Looks at Its Audience*. Urbana: University of Illinois Press, 1950.

Herta Herzog. "What Do We Really Know About Day-Time Serial Listeners?" in *Radio Research, 1942–43*, Paul F. Lazarsfeld and Frank Stanton, editors. Fairlawn, N.J.: Essential Books, 1943.

Paul F. Lazarsfeld and Harry Field. *The People Look at Radio*. Chapel Hill: University of North Carolina Press, 1948.

Paul F. Lazarsfeld and Patricia Kendall. *Radio Listening in America*. New York: Prentice-Hall, 1948.

Robert S. Lynd and Helen M. Lynd. *Middletown in Transition*. New York: Harcourt, Brace, 1937. Chapter X.

W. S. Robinson. "Radio Audience Measurement and its Limitations," *Journal of Social Issues*, 3, Summer 1947, pp. 42–60.

Wilbur Schramm, Jack Lyle and Ithiel de Sola Pool. *The People Look at Educational Television*. Stanford: Stanford University Press, 1963.

Wilbur Schramm and David M. White. "Age, Education, and Economic Status as Factors in Newspaper Reading," *Journalism Quarterly*, Vol. 26, June 1949, pp. 149–59.

Gary A. Steiner. *The People Look at Television: A Study of Audience Attitudes*. New York: Knopf, 1963.

Douglas Waples. *People and Print: Social Aspects of Reading in a Depression*. Chicago: University of Chicago Press, 1937.

W. Lloyd Warner and Paul S. Lunt. *The Social Life of a Modern Community*. New Haven: Yale University Press, 1941. Chapter XIX.

Louis R. Wilson. *The Geography of Reading*. Chicago: University of Chicago Press, 1938.

INTERNATIONAL COMMUNICATIONS

Robert C. Angell. "International Communication and the World Society," in *The World Community*, edited by Quincy Wright. Chicago: University of Chicago Press, 1948.

Frederick C. Barghoorn. *The Soviet Cultural Offensive: The Role of Cultural Diplomacy in Soviet Foreign Policy*. Princeton: Princeton University Press, 1960.

George G. Bruntz. *Allied Propaganda and the Collapse of the German Empire in 1918*. Stanford: Stanford University Press, 1938.

Harwood Childs and John B. Whitton. *Propaganda by Short Wave*. Princeton: Princeton University Press, 1942.

George A. Codding, Jr. *Broadcasting Without Barriers*. Paris: UNESCO, 1959.

William E. Daugherty and Morris Janowitz. *A Psychological Warfare Casebook*. Baltimore: Johns Hopkins University Press, 1958.

Murray Dyer. *The Weapon on the Wall: Rethinking Psychological Warfare*. Baltimore: The Johns Hopkins University Press, 1959.

Alfred O. Hero. *Mass Media and World Affairs*. Boston: World Peace Foundation, 1959. (Studies in Citizen Preparation in International Relations, Vol. 4).

Robert T. Holt. *Radio Free Europe*. Minneapolis: University of Minnesota Press, 1958.

Robert T. Holt and Robert W. van de Velde. *Strategic Psychological Operations and American Foreign Policy*. Chicago: University of Chicago Press, 1960.

Alex Inkeles. "Domestic Broadcasting in the U.S.S.R.," in *Communications Research, 1948–49*, pp. 223–296.

International Press Institute. *The Flow of News: A Study by the International Press Institute.* Zurich: IPI, 1953.

Martin Kriesberg. "Soviet News in the *New York Times*," *Public Opinion Quarterly*, 10, Winter 1946–47, pp. 540–564.

Paul F. Lazarsfeld and Genevieve Knupfer. "Communications Research and International Cooperation," in *The Science of Man in the World Crisis*, edited by R. Linton. New York: Columbia University Press, 1945.

Daniel Lerner. *Propaganda in War and Crisis.* New York: G. W. Stewart, 1951.

Daniel Lerner. *Sykewar: Psychological Warfare Against Germany.* New York: G. W. Stewart, 1949.

L. John Martin. *International Propaganda: Its Legal and Diplomatic Control.* Minneapolis: University of Minnesota, 1958.

Louis Nemzer. "Soviet Friendship Societies," *Public Opinion Quarterly*, 13, Summer 1949, pp. 265–284.

Ithiel de Sola Pool. *Communication and Values in Relation to War and Peace.* New York: Institute for International Order, no date.

Charles Thompson. *Overseas Information Service of the United States.* Washington: Brookings Institution, 1948.

United Nations Educational, Scientific and Cultural Organizations. *Report of the Commission on Technical Needs in Press, Film, Radio.* Paris: 1948.

Douglas Waples and Harold Lasswell. *National Libraries and Foreign Scholarship.* Chicago: University of Chicago Press, 1936.

L. W. White and Robert D. Leigh. *Peoples Speaking to Peoples.* Chicago: University of Chicago Press, 1946. Ch. I, II, VI.

Ralph K. White. "The New Resistance to International Propaganda," *Public Opinion Quarterly*, 16, Winter 1952, pp. 539–551.

VIII Communication Effects

Gordon Allport and Hadley Cantril. *The Psychology of Radio.* New York: Harper, 1935.

Bernard Berelson. "Communications and Public Opinion," in *Communications in Modern Society*, edited by Wilbur Schramm. Urbana: University of Illinois Press, 1948.

Bernard Berelson. "What Missing the Newspaper Means," in *Communications Research, 1948–49*, edited by Paul F. Lazarsfeld and Frank Stanton. New York: Harper, 1949.

Leonard Berkowitz, Ronald Corwin, and Mark Heironimus. "Film Violence and Subsequent Aggressive Tendencies," *Public Opinion Quarterly*, 27, Summer 1963, pp. 217–229.

Leo Bogart. *The Age of Television.* New York: Frederick Ungar Publishing Co., 1958.

Hadley Cantril, Hazel Gaudet and Herta Herzog. *Invasion from Mars.* Princeton: Princeton University Press, 1940.

Melvin L. DeFleur and Otto N. Larsen. *The Flow of Information.* New York: Harper, 1958.

S. N. Eisenstadt. "The Place of Elites and Primary Groups in the Absorption of New Immigrants in Israel," *American Journal of Sociology,* 57, November 1951, pp. 222–231.

Frederick E. Emery and O. A. Oeser. *Information, Decision and Action: A Study of the Psychological Determinants of Changes in Farming Techniques.* Melbourne: Melbourne University Press, 1958.

Ira O. Glick and Sidney J. Levy. *Living with Television.* Chicago: Aldine Publishing Co., 1962.

H. F. Gosnell. *Machine Politics: Chicago Model.* Chicago: University of Chicago Press, 1937.

Carl I. Hovland. "Effects of the Mass Media of Communication," in Gardner Lindzey, editor. *Handbook of Social Psychology,* II. Cambridge, Mass.: Addison-Wesley, 1954, pp. 1062–1103.

Carl I. Hovland, Irving L. Janis and Harold H. Kelley. *Communication and Persuasion.* New Haven: Yale University Press, 1953.

Carl I. Hovland, Irving L. Janis and others. *Personality and Persuasibility.* New Haven: Yale University Press, 1959.

Carl I. Hovland and others. *The Order of Presentation in Persuasion.* New Haven: Yale University Press, 1957.

Carl I. Hovland and others. *Experiments on Mass Communications.* Princeton: Princeton University Press, 1949.

Marie Jahoda and Eunice Cooper. "The Evasion of Propaganda: How Prejudiced People Respond to Anti-Prejudice Propaganda," *Journal of Psychology,* 23, 1947, pp. 15–25.

Daniel Katz. "Psychological Barriers to Communication," *The Annals,* 250, March 1947, pp. 17–25.

Elihu Katz and Jacob J. Feldman. "The Debates in the Light of Research: A Survey of Surveys," pp. 173–223 in *The Great Debates: Background-Perspective-Effects,* Sidney Kraus, editor. Bloomington, Ind.: Indiana University Press, 1962.

Joseph T. Klapper. *The Effects of Mass Media: A Report to the Director of the Public Library Inquiry.* New York: Bureau of Applied Social Research, Columbia University, 1949.

Harold D. Lasswell. "Radio as an Instrument of Reducing Personal Insecurity," *Studies in Philosophy and Social Sciences,* 9, 1941.

Harold D. Lasswell and Dorothy Blumenstock. *World Revolutionary Propaganda.* New York: Knopf, 1939.

Paul F. Lazarsfeld, editor, *Radio and the Printed Page.* New York: Duell, Sloan and Pearce, 1940.

Paul F. Lazarsfeld and Frank Stanton, editors. *Radio Research, 1941, Radio Research, 1942–43.* New York: Duell, Sloan and Pearce, 1941, 1944.

Eleanor Maccoby. "Why Do Children Watch TV?" *Public Opinion Quarterly,* 18, Summer 1954, pp. 239–244.

Gerhard Maletzke. *Fernsehen im Leben der Jugend.* Hamburg: Hans Bredow-Institut, 1959.

Herbert Menzel and Elihu Katz. "Social Relations and Innovation in the Medical Profession," *Public Opinion Quarterly*, 19, Winter 1955, pp. 337–353.

Frank L. Mott. "Newspapers in Presidential Campaigns," *Public Opinion Quarterly*, 8, Fall 1944, pp. 348–367.

Ruth C. Peterson and L. L. Thurstone. *Motion Pictures and the Social Attitude of Children.* New York: Macmillan, 1933.

J. W. Riley, Jr. and M. W. Riley. "Mass Communication and the Social System," in R. K. Merton, L. Broom and L. S. Cottrell, Jr., editors. *Sociology Today: Problems and Prospects.* New York: Basic Books, 1959. pp. 537–578.

William S. Robinson. "Radio Comes to the Farmer," in *Radio Research, 1941,* pp. 224–294.

Everett M. Rogers. *Diffusion of Innovations.* New York: The Free Press of Glencoe, 1962.

Wilbur Schramm. *The Impact of Educational Television:* Selected Studies from Research Sponsored by the National Educational Television and Radio Center. Urbana: University of Illinois Press, 1960.

Wilbur Schramm, Jack Lyle and Edwin B. Parker. *Television in the Lives of Our Children.* Stanford: Stanford University Press, 1961.

Herbert A. Simon and Frederick Stern. "The Effect of Television Upon Voting Behavior in Iowa in the 1952 Presidential Elections," *American Political Science Review*, Vol. 49, June 1955, pp. 470–477.

Richard F. Sterba. "Some Psychological Factors in Pictorial Advertising," *Public Opinion Quarterly*, 14, Fall 1950, pp. 475–483.

Douglas Waples, Bernard Berelson and Franklyn Bradshaw. *What Reading Does to People.* Chicago: University of Chicago Press, 1940.

W. Lloyd Warner and William E. Henry. "The Radio Day-time Serial: A Symbolic Analysis," *Genetic Psychology Monographs*, 37, 1948, pp. 7–13, 55–64.

IX Public Opinion, Communication, and Democratic Objectives

Raymond Bauer and Alice Bauer. "American Mass Society and Mass Media," *Journal of Social Issues*, 16, 1960, pp. 3–66.

Bernard Berelson, Paul F. Lazarsfeld and William McPhee. *Voting: A Study of Opinion Formation in a Presidential Campaign.* Chicago: University of Chicago Press, 1954.

Robert J. Blakely. "The Responsibilities of an Editor," in *Communications in Modern Society*, pp. 220–238.

John Dewey. *The Public and Its Problems.* New York: Holt, 1927.

Manuel R. Garcia-Mora. "International Responsibility for Subversive Activities and Hostile Propaganda by Private Persons Against Foreign States," *Indiana Law Journal*, 35, Spring 1950.

James Edward Gerald. "The British Press Council: A Summary and an Evaluation," *Journalism Quarterly*, 23, Summer 1959, pp. 295–306.

Ralph Harris and Arthur Sheldon. *Advertising in a Free Society*. London: Institute of Economic Affairs, 1959.

William E. Hocking. *Freedom of the Press: A Framework of Principle*. Chicago: University of Chicago Press, 1947.

Joseph T. Klapper. "Mass Media and the Engineering of Consent," *American Scholar*, 17, October 1948, pp. 419–429.

Eberhard Kronhausen and Phyllis Kronhausen. *Pornography and the Law*. New York: Ballantine Books, 1959.

Harold D. Lasswell. *Democracy Through Public Opinion*. Menasha, Wis.: George Banta Publishing Co., 1941.

Harold D. Lasswell. "Policy and the Intelligence Function: Ideological Intelligence," in *The Analysis of Political Behavior*. New York: Oxford University Press, 1947, pp. 120–132.

Robert K. Merton. "Mass Persuasion: The Moral Dimension," in *Mass Persuasion*. New York: Harper, 1947.

Talcott Parsons. "Propaganda and Social Control," *Psychiatry*, 4, November 1942, pp. 551–572.

James N. Rosenau. *Public Opinion and Foreign Policy: An Operational Formulation*. New York: Random House, 1961.

Charles Siepmann. *Radio, Television and Society*. New York: Oxford University Press, 1950.

Charles Siepmann. *Radio's Second Chance*. Boston: Little, Brown, 1946.

Charles A. H. Thomson. *Television and Presidential Politics: The Experience in 1952 and the Problems Ahead*. Washington, D.C.: Brookings Institution, 1956.

Winston White. *Beyond Conformity*. New York: The Free Press of Glencoe, 1961.

Louis Wirth. "Consensus and Mass Communication," *American Sociological Review*, 13, February 1948, pp. 1–14.

X *Toward Comparative Analysis*

Robert R. Alford. *Party and Society: The Anglo-American Democracies*. Chicago: Rand McNally, 1963.

Gabriel A. Almond. *The Appeals of Communism*. Princeton: Princeton University Press, 1954.

Theodore H. E. Chen. *Thought Reform of the Chinese Intellectuals*. New York: Oxford University Press, 1960. (For the Hong Kong University Press.)

Leonard W. Doob. *Becoming More Civilized: A Psychological Exploration*. New Haven: Yale University Press, 1960.

Leonard W. Doob. *Communications in Africa: A Search for Boundaries*. New Haven: Yale University Press, 1961.

S. N. Eisenstadt. "Communications Systems and Social Structure: An Exploratory Comparative Study," *Public Opinion Quarterly*, 19, Summer 1955, pp. 153–167.

Franklin W. Houn. *To Change a Nation: Propaganda and Indoctrination in Communist China.* The Free Press of Glencoe (New York), and The Bureau of Social and Political Research (East Lansing, Michigan), 1961.

Alex Inkeles. *Public Opinion in the Soviet Union: A Study in Mass Persuasion.* Cambridge: Harvard University Press, 1950.

Harold R. Issacs. *Scratches on Our Minds: American Images of China and India.* New York: J. Day Co., 1958.

Hidetoshi Kato, editor and translator, Tokyo. *Japanese Popular Culture: Studies on Mass Communication and Cultural Change.* [Made at the Institute of Science of Thought, Japan]. Rutland, Vt.: Charles E. Tuttle Co., 1959.

Harold D. Lasswell. "Propaganda and Mass Insecurity," *Psychiatry*, August 1950, pp. 283–300.

Daniel Lerner. *The Passing of Traditional Society.* Glencoe: The Free Press of Glencoe, 1958.

Robert J. Lifton. *Thought Reform and the Psychology of Totalism.* New York: Norton, 1963.

Leo Lowenthal, editor. "International Communications Research" (Special Issue), *Public Opinion Quarterly*, 16, Winter 1952.

Lucian Pye, editor. *Communications and Political Development.* Princeton: Princeton University Press, 1963.

Wilbur Schramm. *Mass Media and National Development: The Role of Information in the Developing Countries.* Stanford: Stanford University Press, 1964.

Wilbur Schramm and J. W. Riley, Jr. "Communication in the Sovietized State as Demonstrated in Korea," *American Sociological Review*, 16, 1951, pp. 757–766.

Edward A. Shils. *The Intellectual Between Tradition and Modernity: The Indian Situation.* The Hague: Mouton, 1961.

Edward A. Shils. "Intellectuals, Public Opinion and Economic Development," *World Politics*, 10, January 1958, pp. 232–255.

XI Research Methods

Leon Arons and Mark A. May. *Television and Human Behavior: Tomorrow's Research in Mass Communication.* New York: Appleton-Century Crofts, 1963.

Albert Blankenship. *How to Conduct Consumer and Opinion Research.* New York: Harper, 1946.

Hadley Cantril. *Gauging Public Opinion.* Princeton: Princeton University Press, 1947.

John Dollard. "Under What Conditions Do Opinions Predict Behavior?" *Public Opinion Quarterly*, 12, Winter 1948–49, pp. 623–632.

J. G. Ferraby. "Planning a Mass-Observation Investigation," *American Journal of Sociology*, 51, July 1945, pp. 1–6.

Morris H. Hansen and Philip M. Hauser. "Area Sampling-Some Principles of Sampling Design," *Public Opinion Quarterly*, 9, Summer 1945, pp. 183–193.

Hearings Before the Committee to Investigate Campaign Expenditures. House of Representatives, 78th Congress, 2nd Session, on H. Res. 551, Pt. 12, Washington: Government Printing Office, 1945.

Harry Henry. *Motivation Research: Its Practice and Uses for Advertising, Marketing and Other Business Purposes.* New York: Frederick Ungar Pub. Co., 1958 and London: Cosby Lockwood and Sons, 1958.

Herbert Hyman. "Problems in the Collection of Opinion-Research Data," *American Journal of Sociology*, 55, January 1950, pp. 362–370.

Herbert Hyman and others. *Interviewing in Social Research.* Chicago: University of Chicago Press, 1954.

Daniel Katz. "Do Interviewers Bias Polls?" *Public Opinion Quarterly*, 6, Summer 1942, pp. 248–268.

Daniel Katz. "The Interpretation of Survey Findings," *Journal of Social Issues*, 2, 1946, pp. 32–43.

Patricia Kendall. *Conflict and Mood: Factors Affecting Stability of Response.* New York: The Free Press of Glencoe, 1954.

Arthur Kornhauser. "The Problems of Bias in Opinion Research," *International Journal of Opinion and Attitude Research*, 1, December 1947, pp. 1–16.

Arthur Kornhauser. "Are Public Opinion Polls Fair to Organized Labor?" *Public Opinion Quarterly*, 11, Winter 1946–47, pp. 484–500.

Paul F. Lazarsfeld. "The Controversy Over Detailed Interviews—An offer for Negotiation," *Public Opinion Quarterly*, 8, Spring 1944, pp. 38–60.

Daniel Lerner, editor. "Attitude Research in Modernizing Areas," Special Issue of *Public Opinion Quarterly*, 22, Fall 1958.

E. E. Maccoby and R. R. Holt. "How Surveys Are Made," *Journal of Social Issues*, 2, 1946, pp. 45–57.

Quinn McNemar. "Opinion-Attitude Methodology," *Psychological Bulletin*, 43, July 1946, pp. 289–374.

Norman Meier and Harold W. Saunders, editors. *The Polls and Public Opinion.* New York: Holt, 1949.

Frederick Mosteller and others. *The Pre-Election Polls of 1948.* New York: Social Science Research Council, 1949.

Ralph O. Nafziger and David M. White, editors. *Introduction to Mass Communications Research.* Revised edition. Baton Rouge: Louisiana State University Press, 1963.

National Opinion Research Center. *Interviewing for N.O.R.C.*, Denver, 1945.

"Opinion Surveys in Developing Countries" (Issue title). *International Social Sciences Journal*, 15, 1, 1963.

Arnold M. Rose. "Attitude Measurement and the Questionnaire Survey," *The Scientific Monthly*, 68, 1949, pp. 92–101.

William Schutz. "On Categorizing Qualitative Data in Content Analysis," *Public Opinion Quarterly*, 22, Winter 1958, pp. 503–515.

George H. Smith. *Motivation Research in Advertising and Marketing.* New York: McGraw-Hill Book Co., 1954.

Frederick F. Stephan. "History of the Uses of Modern Sampling Procedures," *Journal of the American Statistical Ass'n.*, 43, March 1948, pp. 12–39.

Frederick F. Stephan. "Sampling," *American Journal of Sociology*, 55, January 1950, pp. 371–375.

Frederick F. Stephan. "Sampling in Studies of Opinions, Attitudes and Consumer Wants," *Proceedings of the American Philosophical Society*, 92, November 1948, pp. 387–398.

Samuel A. Stouffer. "Some Observations on Study Design," *American Journal of Sociology*, 55, January 1950, pp. 355–361.

Samuel A. Stouffer and others. *Measurement and Prediction.* Princeton: Princeton University Press, 1950.

L. L. Thurstone. "The Measurement of Opinion," *Journal of Abnormal and Social Psychology*, 22, 1928, pp. 415–430.

Ralph K. White. *Value-Analysis: The Nature and Use of the Method.* Society for the Psychological Study of Social Issues, 1951.

Index

775